Cloud Computing: A Futuristic Approach

Cloud Computing:
A Futuristic Approach

Edited by Amanda Wegener

MURPHY & MOORE
www.murphy-moorepublishing.com

Murphy & Moore Publishing,
1 Rockefeller Plaza,
New York City, NY 10020, USA

ISBN: 978-1-63987-115-5

Cataloging-in-Publication Data

Cloud computing : a futuristic approach / edited by Amanda Wegener.
    p. cm.
Includes bibliographical references and index.
ISBN 978-1-63987-115-5
1. Cloud computing. 2. Electronic data processing--Distributed processing.
3. Web services. I. Wegener, Amanda.
QA76.585 .C56 2022
004.678 2--dc23

For information on all Murphy & Moore Publications
visit our website at www.murphy-moorepublishing.com

 **MURPHY & MOORE**

Contents

Preface

The main aim of this book is to educate learners and enhance their research focus by presenting diverse topics covering this vast field. This is an advanced book which compiles significant studies by distinguished experts in the area of analysis. This book addresses successive solutions to the challenges arising in the area of application, along with it; the book provides scope for future developments.

Cloud computing is the on demand availability of computing services such as servers, storage, databases, networking, software, analytics, and intelligence over the internet. It not only facilitates faster innovation and flexible resources but also offers economies of scale. It is cheaper, faster, more secure, reliable, efficient, and accessible compared to the traditional way of availing IT resources. Public cloud, private cloud, and hybrid cloud are the three ways to deploy cloud services. Public clouds are owned and handled by third-party cloud service providers whereas a private cloud is used exclusively by a single entity. Hybrid clouds are a mix of both public and private clouds. This book is compiled in such a manner, that it will provide in-depth knowledge about the theory and practice of cloud computing. There has been rapid progress in this field and its applications are finding their way across multiple industries. This book is a resource guide for experts as well as students.

It was a great honour to edit this book, though there were challenges, as it involved a lot of communication and networking between me and the editorial team. However, the end result was this all-inclusive book covering diverse themes in the field.

Finally, it is important to acknowledge the efforts of the contributors for their excellent chapters, through which a wide variety of issues have been addressed. I would also like to thank my colleagues for their valuable feedback during the making of this book.

Editor

Scheduling Multilevel Deadline-Constrained Scientific Workflows on Clouds Based on Cost Optimization

Maciej Malawski,[1] Kamil Figiela,[1] Marian Bubak,[1,2] Ewa Deelman,[3] and Jarek Nabrzyski[4]

[1]*Department of Computer Science, AGH University of Science and Technology, Aleja Mickiewicza 30, 30-059 Kraków, Poland*
[2]*ACC CYFRONET AGH, Ulica Nawojki 11, 30-950 Kraków, Poland*
[3]*USC Information Sciences Institute, 4676 Admiralty Way, Marina del Rey, CA 90292, USA*
[4]*Center for Research Computing, University of Notre Dame, Notre Dame, IN 46556, USA*

Correspondence should be addressed to Kamil Figiela; kfigiela@agh.edu.pl

Academic Editor: Roman Wyrzykowski

This paper presents a cost optimization model for scheduling scientific workflows on IaaS clouds such as Amazon EC2 or RackSpace. We assume multiple IaaS clouds with heterogeneous virtual machine instances, with limited number of instances per cloud and hourly billing. Input and output data are stored on a cloud object store such as Amazon S3. Applications are scientific workflows modeled as DAGs as in the Pegasus Workflow Management System. We assume that tasks in the workflows are grouped into levels of identical tasks. Our model is specified using mathematical programming languages (AMPL and CMPL) and allows us to minimize the cost of workflow execution under deadline constraints. We present results obtained using our model and the benchmark workflows representing real scientific applications in a variety of domains. The data used for evaluation come from the synthetic workflows and from general purpose cloud benchmarks, as well as from the data measured in our own experiments with Montage, an astronomical application, executed on Amazon EC2 cloud. We indicate how this model can be used for scenarios that require resource planning for scientific workflows and their ensembles.

1. Introduction

Today, science requires processing of large amounts of data and use of hosted services for compute-intensive tasks [1]. Cloud services are used not only to provide resources, but also for hosting scientific datasets, as in the case of AWS public datasets [2]. Scientific applications that run on these clouds often have the structure of workflows or workflow ensembles that are groups of interrelated workflows [3]. Infrastructure as a service (IaaS) cloud providers offer services where virtual machine instances differ in performance and price [4]. Planning computational experiments requires optimization decisions that take into account both execution time and resource cost.

Research presented in this paper can be seen as a step towards developing a "cloud resource calculator" for scientific applications in the hosted science model [1]. Specifically, we address the cost optimization problem of large-scale scientific workflows running on multiple heterogeneous clouds, using mathematical modeling with AMPL [5] and CMPL [6], and mixed integer programming. This approach allows us to describe the model mathematically and use a set of available optimization solvers. On the other hand, an attempt to apply this method to the general problem of scheduling large-scale workflows on heterogeneous cloud resources would be impractical due to the problem complexity and therefore simplified models need to be analyzed. In our previous work [7], we used a similar technique to solve the problem where the application consists of tasks that either are identical or vary in size within a small range. As observed in [8, 9], large-scale scientific workflows often consist of multiple parallel stages or levels, each of which has a structure of set of tasks; that is, the tasks in each level are similar and independent of each other. In the case of large workflows, when the number of tasks in the level is high, it becomes more practical to optimize the execution of the whole level instead of looking at each task individually, as many scheduling algorithms do [10]. Therefore, in this paper, we extend our model to deal with applications that are workflows represented as DAGs consisting of levels of uniform tasks.

The main contributions of this paper are summarized as follows.

(i) We define the problem of workflow scheduling on clouds as a cost optimization problem of assigning levels of tasks to virtual machine instances, under a deadline constraint.

(ii) We specify the application model, infrastructure model, and the scheduling model as mixed integer programming (MIP) problems using AMPL and CMPL modeling languages.

(iii) We discuss the alternative scheduling models for coarse-grained and fine-grained tasks.

(iv) We evaluate the models using infrastructure performance data: one obtained from CloudHarmony benchmarks, and the one based on our own experiments with Montage workflows on Amazon EC2 cloud.

This paper is an extension of our earlier conference publication [11]. The most important extension is a new scheduling model dedicated to fine-grained workflows with short deadlines. Moreover, for evaluation, we use more detailed cloud benchmark dataset, based on our recent experiments with Montage workflow on Amazon EC2.

After outlining the related work in Section 2, we introduce our methodology in Section 3. We describe the application and infrastructure model in Section 4. In Section 5, we provide the mathematical formulation of the problem, including the application model, the infrastructure model, and the scheduling models for coarse-grained and fine-grained workflows. Section 6 describes the datasets used for evaluation of our models. Finally, Section 7 describes the evaluation of our models on a set of benchmark workflows, while Section 8 gives conclusions and future work.

2. Related Work in Cloud Workflow Scheduling

Our work is related to heuristic algorithms for workflow scheduling on IaaS clouds. In [12], the model assumes that infrastructure is provided by only one provider. The cloud-targeted autoscaling solution [10] considers dynamic and unpredictable workloads containing workflows. In [13], a multiobjective list-based method for workflow scheduling (MOHEFT) is proposed and evaluated. The solution presented in [14] focuses on cloud bursting scenario, where a private cloud is combined with a public one, and the goal is to minimize the cost while maintaining the workflow deadline. Our work is different from these approaches in two aspects. First, in our infrastructure model we assume multiple heterogeneous clouds with object storage attached to them, instead of individual machines with peer-to-peer data transfers between them. Moreover, rather than scheduling each

task individually, our method proposes a global optimization of placement of workflow tasks and data.

The deadline-constrained cost optimization of scientific workloads on heterogeneous IaaS described in [15] addresses multiple providers and data transfers between them, where the application is a set of tasks. The global cost minimization problem on clouds addressed in [16] focuses on data transfer costs and does not address workflows. Other approaches presented in [17, 18] consider unpredictable dynamic workloads on IaaS clouds and optimize the objectives, such as cost, runtime, or utility function, by autoscaling the resource pool at runtime.

Pipelined workflows consisting of stages are addressed in [19]. The processing model is a data flow and multiple instances of the same workflow are executed on the same set of cloud resources, whereas in our approach we focus on cost optimization instead of meeting the QoS constraints.

Integer linear programming (ILP) method is applied to scheduling workflows on hybrid clouds in [20]. The objective is to minimize monetary cost under a deadline constraint. The scheduler uses varying discretization of the schedule timeline to reduce the complexity of the problem so that the employed CPLEX solver can find acceptable solutions within a 10-minute limit. The evaluation, however, is performed on the Montage and random fork-join workflows of 30 tasks with randomly chosen runtimes, while we focus on larger scale workflows and we address the complexity by grouping tasks into levels.

3. Methodology Based on Mathematical Optimization

The core of our methodology (see Figure 1) is to use mathematical modeling languages that can be coupled with a set of solvers dedicated to linear, nonlinear, or mixed integer programming problems. As modeling languages we use AMPL [5], as it is one of the most advanced modeling languages, and CMPL [6], as its open source alternative. These languages provide interfaces to a wide set of solvers, both commercial, such as CPLEX [21], and open source, such as CBC [22].

The mathematical programming approach enables us to formally define optimization problem. AMPL (a mathematical programming language) and CMPL (COIN mathematical programming language) are algebraic mathematical modeling languages that resemble traditional mathematical notation to describe variables, objectives, and constraints. Algebraic modeling languages allow expressing a wide range of optimization problems: linear, nonlinear, and integer. The advantage of AMPL is that it is one of the most advanced mathematical programming languages, while CMPL is easier to use in open source projects. AMPL or CMPL enables us to separate model definition and instance specific data, usually into three files: model, data, and calling script. The model file defines abstract optimization model: sets and parameters, objective and constraints. The data file populates the sets and parameters with the numbers for the particular instance of the problem. Both model and data files are loaded from

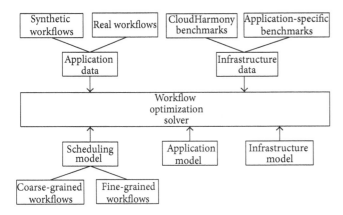

FIGURE 1: An overview of our approach to workflow scheduling. Mathematical models are input to the solver: application, infrastructure, and scheduling models, together with corresponding datasets.

calling script that may do some pre- or postprocessing. In addition, it is possible to import and export data and results into some external format such as YAML for analysis or integration with external programs.

The input to the solver has to be prepared in the form of a problem description. We separate the problem into an application model (in this case the leveled workflows) and infrastructure model (cloud consisting of compute sites running virtual machines and object storage such as Amazon S3). In addition, a scheduling model has to be defined, specifying how to calculate the objective and constraints using the application and infrastructure models. The challenge in the scheduling model is that it has to be developed to allow the solver to find a solution in a reasonable amount of time, so it must incorporate appropriate assumptions, constraints, and approximations. We discuss these assumptions in detail in Section 5.

The scheduling problems that we deal with in this paper are formulated as mixed integer programming (MIP) problems. This class of optimization problems has linear objective and constraints, while some or all of variables are integer-valued. Such problems are solved by using branch-and-bound approach that uses a linear solver to solve subproblems. Moreover, the solvers can relax the integrality of the variables in order to estimate the solution, since no integer solution can be better than the solution of the same problem in continuous domain. The difference between the best integer solution found and the noninteger bound can be used to estimate the accuracy of solution and to reduce the search time (see Section 7.1).

In this paper, we describe two alternative scheduling models: for workflows with fine-grained and coarse-grained tasks. This is motivated by the observation [11] that the granularity of the tasks in the workflows has significant influence on the results of the optimization. The best results can be obtained when the average runtime of the tasks is similar to the billing cycle of the cloud provider, such as 1 hour on Amazon EC2. To address this issue, we developed

another scheduling model for fine-grained tasks and deadlines shorter than one hour, which corresponds to the real characteristics of the Montage workflow.

The scheduling models have to be provided with the actual values of parameters, consisting of the application data and infrastructure data. To evaluate our models, we use two sources of application data: synthetic workflows obtained from the workflow generator gallery [23] and real data obtained from our recent benchmarks performed on Amazon EC2. As infrastructure parameters, we use two sources: CloudHarmony benchmarks [24] that publish CPU performance of selected cloud providers and our own application-specific benchmark results. For research presented in this paper, we selected the Montage workflow and EC2 cloud as an example of a real workflow and infrastructure.

In the following sections, we describe the models and datasets used in more detail.

4. Application and Infrastructure Models

In this paper we focus on large-scale scientific workflows [23]. Examples of such workflows come from a wide variety of domains including bioinformatics (Epigenomics [25], SIPHT [26]), astronomy (Montage [27]), earthquake science (CyberShake [28]), and physics (LIGO [29]). Such workflows typically consist of a large number of computationally intensive tasks, processing large amounts of data.

We assume that each workflow may be represented with a directed acyclic graph (DAG) where nodes in the graph represent computational tasks, and the edges represent data- or control-flow dependencies between the tasks. Each task has a set of input and output files. We assume that the task and file sizes are known in advance.

Based on the characteristics of large-scale workflows, we assume that a workflow is divided into several levels that can be executed sequentially and tasks within one level not do depend on each other (see Figure 2). Each level represents a set of tasks that can be partitioned in several groups (A, B, etc.) that share computational cost and input/output size. We assume that only one task group is executed on a specific cloud instance. This forbids instance sharing between multiple levels, which means that each application may need its own specific VM template.

Similar to what is in [7], we assume multiple heterogeneous cloud IaaS infrastructures such as Amazon EC2, RackSpace, or ElasticHosts. Clouds have heterogeneous virtual machine instance types, with limits on the number of instances per cloud, for example, 20 for EC2 and 15 for RackSpace. Input and output data are stored on a cloud object store such as Amazon S3 or RackSpace CloudFiles. In our model, all virtual machine instances are billed per hour of usage, and there are fees associated with data transfer in/out of the cloud. In the application model, we also assume that there is a small constant cost of execution of a single task, which can correspond, for example, to the cost of a request to the queuing system such as Amazon SQS. The model allows us to include a private cloud where costs are set to 0.

For evaluation, we use synthetic workflows that were generated using historical data from real applications [23], as

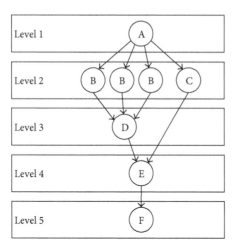

FIGURE 2: Example application structure.

well as the data from our own measurements. The synthetic workflows were generated using code developed in [30], with task runtimes based on distributions gathered from running real workflows. The experimental data come from execution of Montage workflow on Amazon EC2 using the HyperFlow workflow management system [31].

5. Formulation of the Scheduling Problem

In this section we give the mathematical formulation of the models, beginning with application and infrastructure models, and then describe the scheduling models for coarse-grained and fine-grained workflows. We have intentionally decided to present the problem in a form which is different from the routine statement of mathematical progrramming way. The main reason was to make it easily understood for reasearchers engaged in workflow execution optimization.

To perform optimization of the total cost of the workflow execution, mixed integer problem (MIP) is formulated and implemented using a mathematical programming language. First, we have implemented the optimization model using AMPL [5] and solved it with CPLEX solver, then we ported it to open source CMPL [6] and solved it with CBC solver. Both systems require to specify input datasets and variables to define the search space, as well as constraints and an objective function to be optimized.

5.1. Application and Infrastructure Model

Input Data. The formulation requires a number of input sets to represent the infrastructure model. This is a similar way to an approach presented in [7]. The infrasructure is described with the following sets:

    (i) S = {s3, cloudfiles}: set of available cloud storage sites,

    (ii) P = {amazon, rackspace, ...}: set of possible computing cloud providers,

    (iii) I = {m1.small, ..., gg.1gb, ...}: set of instance types,

    (iv) $PI_p \subset I$: set of instances that belong to provider $p \in P$,

    (v) $LS_s \subset P$: set of compute cloud providers that are local to the storage platform $s \in S$,

    (vi) $n_p^{P\,max}$: upper limit of number of instances allowed by a cloud provider $p \in P$.

Introducing PI_p and LS_s enables one to describe the locality between compute and storage resources. This is an important aspect, since the cloud providers typically charge for the cost of data transfer out of a cloud site, while the transfers within the site are free.

Each instance type $i \in I$ is described with the following parameters:

    (i) p_i^I: a fee (in US dollars) for running the instance of type i for one hour,

    (ii) ccu_i^I: performance of instance of type i in CloudHarmony Compute Units (CCU),

    (iii) cpu_i^I: number of virtual CPU cores assigned to an instance of type i,

    (iv) p_i^{Iout}, p_i^{Iin}: price for nonlocal data transfer to and from an instance of type i in US dollars per MiB (1 MiB = $1024 \cdot 1024$ bytes),

    (v) $n_i^{I\,max}$: upper limit of the number of instances of type i, equal to $n_p^{P\,max}$, where p is the provider of instance type i.

This instance model assumes the hourly billing cycle, which is the case for most of the cloud providers, notably for Amazon EC2.

Storage site $s \in S$ is characterized by

    (i) p_s^{Sout} and p_s^{Sin}: price in dollars per MiB for nonlocal data transfers.

Additionally, we need to provide data transfer rates $r_{i,s}$ between a given storage site s and instance i in MiB per second.

Our application model is different from that in [7] because it is designed for workflow scheduling where tasks are grouped into levels. This fact is described with the following characteristics:

    (i) L: a set of levels the workflow is divided into,

    (ii) G: a set of task groups (A, B, etc., in Figure 2); tasks in groups have the same computational cost and input/output size,

    (iii) $G_l \subset G$: a set of task groups belonging to a level $l \in L$,

    (iv) A_g^{tot}: number of tasks in a group $g \in G$,

    (v) t_g^x: execution time in hours of a single task in a group g on a machine with the processor performance of 1 CloudHarmony Compute Unit (CCU) [32],

    (vi) d_g^{in}, d_g^{out}: data size for input and output of a task in group g in MiB,

(vii) p^R: price per task for a queuing service, such as Amazon SQS,

(viii) t^D: total time allowed for completing workflow (deadline).

The application model assumes that the estimated execution time t_g^x is known in advance; that is, it is obtained using benchmarks or other estimation methods [33], such as regression or performance modelling. When using general purpose cloud benchmarks, such as CloudHarmony [24], which provide processor performance measured in CCU, the t_g^x depends only on a task in group g since we assume that the actual task execution time on a specific instance is inversely proportional to the processing speed of the instance expressed in the number of CCU. As it is not always the case, since different tasks may have different processing speeds on different instances, it is also possible to provide execution time predictions at instance level: $t_{g,i}^x$. The scheduling model can use such data if it is available. In Section 6.2 we provide an example of such a dataset for the Montage workflow on Amazon EC2.

5.2. Scheduling Model for Coarse-Grained Workflows. In this model, we schedule groups of tasks of the same type divided into levels. We do not schedule individual tasks as in [34] to keep MIP problem small, as one of the requirements is that optimization time is shorter than the workflow execution time. The coarse-grained workflows are such workflows where task execution times are in the order of one hour. This is important, as we assume the hourly billing cycle of the cloud, so the model has to optimize the task assignment in such a way that the hourly slots of allocated resources (VM instances) are as fully utilized as possible.

To keep this model in the MIP class, we had to take a different approach than in [7] and schedule each virtual machine instance separately. A drawback of this approach is that we need to increase the number of decision variables. We have also divided the search space by storage providers, solving the problem separately for each storage and selecting the best result. Additionally, the deadline becomes a variable with an upper bound, as it may happen that a shorter deadline may actually give a cheaper solution (see Figure 5 and its discussion).

Auxiliary Parameters. Based on the input parameters, in the scheduling model we derive a set of precomputed parameters that are used for expressing objectives and constraints. The transfer time is computed based on the input and output data size and the transfer rate between an instance and the storage. The time for processing a task is a sum of computing and data transfer time. The cost of data transfer is a sum of cost of input and output data, both including the transfer fees at the source and destination cloud site. The indexing of instances is introduced; for example, all m1.small instances are numbered $0, 1, 2, \ldots$, to distinguish between individual instances of a given type:

(i) $s \in S$: a selected storage site,

(ii) $t_{g,i,s}^{net} = (d_g^{in} + d_g^{out})/(r_{i,s} \cdot 3600)$: transfer time in hours, that is, time for data transfer between instances of type i and storage site s for a task in task group g,

(iii) $t_{g,i,s}^u = t_g^x/ccu_i^I + t_{g,i,s}^{net}$: time in hours for processing a task in group g on instance of type i using storage site s,

(iv) $c_{g,i,s}^T = (d_g^{out} \cdot (p_i^{Iout} + p_s^{Sin}) + d_g^{in} \cdot (p_s^{Sout} + p_i^{Iin}))$: a cost of data transfer between an instance of type i and a storage site s when processing task in group g,

(v) I_i^{idx}: a set of possible indices for instances of type i (from 0 to $n_i^{I\,max} - 1$).

Variables. Variables of the optimization problem are

(i) $N_{g,i,k}$: 1 iff (if and only if) instance of type i with index $k \in I_i^{idx}$ is launched to process task group g, otherwise, 0 (binary);

(ii) $H_{g,i,k}$: for how many hours the instance of index k is launched (integer);

(iii) $T_{g,i,k}$: how many tasks of g are processed on that instance (integer);

(iv) D_l^t: actual computation time for level l (real);

(v) D_l: maximal number of hours (deadline) that instances are allowed to run at level l (integer).

The variables defined in this way allow the solver to search over the space of possible assignments of instances to task groups ($N_{g,i,k}$) with a varying number $H_{g,i,k}$ of hours each instance is launched and number $T_{g,i,k}$ of tasks processed on these instances. The deadline is divided into subdeadlines for each workflow level l, while the actual computation time D_l^t can be shorter than the deadline D_l.

Objective. The scheduling problem is represented as a cost minimization problem. The cost of running a single task is defined as follows:

$$\left(t_g^{net} + t_g^u\right) \cdot p_i^I + \tag{1}$$

$$d_g^{in} \cdot \left(p_s^{Sout} + p_i^{Iin}\right) + \tag{2}$$

$$d_g^{out} \cdot \left(p_i^{Iout} + p_s^{Sin}\right) + \tag{3}$$

$$p^R, \tag{4}$$

and it includes the cost of the computing time of instance (1), the cost of transfer of input data (2), that of output data (3), and request price (4).

The objective function C_{tot} represents the total cost which is a sum of task costs computed over all the task groups, all the instance types, and the individual instances. It is defined as

$$C_{tot} = \sum_{g \in G, i \in I, k \in I_i^{idx}} \left(p_i^I \cdot H_{g,i,k} + p^R + c_{g,i,s}^T\right) \cdot T_{g,i,k}. \tag{5}$$

To properly implement the assumptions we impose on the application, infrastructure, and scheduling models, the following *constraints* have to be introduced.

(1) $\sum_{l\in L} D_l \leq t^D$ ensures that the sum of subdeadlines of all levels is not greater than the workflow deadline, that is, that the workflow finishes in the given deadline.

(2) To fix that the actual execution time of a level, rounded up to a full hour, gives us the level subdeadline ($D_l = \lceil D_l^t \rceil$), we require that $\forall_{l\in L} D_l^t \leq D_l \leq D_l^t + 1$.

(3) $\forall_{g\in G, i\in I, x\in I_i^{idx}} N_{g,i,k} \leq H_{g,i,k} \leq N_{g,i,k} \cdot \lceil t^D \rceil$ ensures that the number of computing hours of an instance $H_{g,i,k}$ may be nonzero only if instance is active ($N_{g,i,k}$ is 1), and it cannot exceed the deadline.

(4) $\forall_{g\in G, i\in I, k\in I_i^{idx}} N_{g,i,k} \leq T_{g,i,k} \cdot N_{g,i,k} \cdot A_g^{tot}$ ensures that the computing tasks $T_{g,i,k}$ may be allocated to an instance only if the instance is active and that their number does not exceed the total number of tasks in group t.

(5) $\forall_{l\in L, g\in G_l, i\in I, k\in I_i^{idx}} H_{g,i,k} \leq D_l$ enforces the level deadline on the actual runtimes of each instance.

(6) $\forall_{l\in L, g\in G_l, i\in I, k\in I_i^{idx}} T_{g,i,k} \cdot t_{g,i,s}^u \leq D_l^t$ enforces that all the tasks allocated to the instance complete their work within the computing time of their level D_l^t.

(7) To make sure that all the instances run for enough time to process all tasks allocated to them we adjust $H_{g,i,k}$, respectively, to $T_{g,i,k}$: $\forall_{g\in G, i\in I, k\in I_i^{idx}} T_{g,i,k} \cdot t_{g,i,s}^u \leq H_{g,i,k} \cdot T_{g,i,k} \cdot t_{g,i,s}^u + 1$.

(8) $\forall_{g\in G} \sum_{i\in I, k\in I_i^{idx}} T_{g,i,k} = A_g^{tot}$ ensures that all the tasks are processed.

(9) To reject symmetric solutions and thus to reduce the search space, we add three constraints:

   (a) $\forall_{g\in G, i\in I, k\in\{1\cdots(n_i^{I\,max}-1)\}} H_{g,i,k} \leq H_{g,i,k-1}$,
   (b) $\forall_{g\in G, i\in I, k\in\{1\cdots(n_i^{I\,max}-1)\}} N_{g,i,k} \leq N_{g,i,k-1}$,
   (c) $\forall_{g\in G, i\in I, k\in\{1\cdots(n_i^{I\,max}-1)\}} T_{g,i,k} \leq T_{g,i,k-1}$.

(10) Finally, the constraint $\forall_{l\in L, p\in P} \sum_{i\in PI_p, g\in G_l, k\in I_i^{idx}} N_{g,i,k} \leq n_p^{P\,max}$ enforces instance limits per cloud.

The scheduling model presented above shows its advantages if the workflow tasks are about one hour long or larger, and the deadline exceeds one hour. For fine-grained workflows, such as Montage where most task execution times are in order of seconds and the whole workflow may be finished within an hour, a model can be simplified.

5.3. Scheduling Model for Fine-Grained Workflows. When scheduling workflows with many short tasks and with deadlines shorter than the cloud billing cycle (one hour), we do not need to use the $H_{g,i,k}$ variable that counts the number of hours the instance is running. Thus we can assume that each level completes its work in one hour. This assumption reduces the number of decision variables making the MIP problem faster to solve. We also add an assumption that only one instance type may be used for each task type, which also reduces the search space.

In addition to these assumptions, we changed the way how the data transfer time is computed. Since for short tasks the data access latency is important, in addition to transfer rate $r_{i,s}$ we also provide the latency parameter $r_{i,s}^{lat}$. The actual values come from linear regression of experimental data, where we run Montage workflow on Amazon S3. In the fine-grained scheduling model, we also use execution time predictions at instance level: $t_{g,i}^x$. The t^u is normalized by the number of CPU cores present on the VM if there are enough tasks to be processed in parallel. The modifications mentioned in this paragraph may also be applied to the coarse-grained model if needed.

Based on these modifications, the auxiliary parameters transfer time $t_{g,i,s}^{net}$ and unit time $t_{g,i,s}^u$ are computed as follows:

   (i) $t_{g,i,s}^{net} = (d_g^{in} + d_g^{out})/(r_{i,s} \cdot 3600) + r_{i,s}^{lat}$;

   (ii) $t_{g,i,s}^u = (t_{g,i}^x + t_{i,s}^{net})/\min(cpu_i^I, A_g^{tot})$.

The remaining part of the model has the following form.

Variables. Variables are similar to the ones in the coarse-grained model, but the problem has less dimensions, since there is no need to use $H_{g,i,k}$ and to distinguish instances by index x:

   (i) $A_{g,i}$ tells if instances of type i are used to process task group t (binary);

   (ii) $N_{g,i}$ tells how many instances of type i are launched to process task group g (integer);

   (iii) $T_{g,i}$ tells how many tasks in group g are processed on instances of type i (integer);

   (iv) D_l^t tells actual computation time for level l (real).

Objective. The cost function C_{tot} is computed in a similar way, by summing the costs of all the task groups over all of the instances, taking into account the task assignment $T_{g,i}$:

$$C_{tot} = \sum_{g\in G, i\in I} \left(p_i^I \cdot N_{g,i} + p^R + c_{g,i,s}^T\right) \cdot T_{g,i}. \tag{6}$$

Constraints. The constraints are as following:

(1) $\sum_{l\in L} D_l \leq t^D$ ensures that workflow finishes before the given deadline;

(2) $\forall_{g\in G, i\in I} A_{g,i} \leq N_{g,i} \leq A_{g,i} \cdot n_i^{I\,max}$ ensures that the number of active instances $N_{g,i}$ is consistent with the binary variable $A_{g,i}$ and does not exceed the instance limit;

(3) $\forall_{g\in G, i\in I} N_{g,i} \leq T_{g,i} \leq N_{g,i} \cdot A_g^{tot}$ ensures that there are no empty instances and that the number of assigned tasks does not exceed the total number of tasks;

(4) $\forall_{l \in L, g \in G_l, i \in I} T_{g,i} \cdot t_{g,i,s}^u \leq D_l^t \cdot N_{g,i}$ enforces that a level finishes work in D_l^t;

(5) $\forall_{g \in G} \sum_{i \in I} T_{g,i} = A_g^{\text{tot}}$ ensures that all tasks are processed;

(6) $\forall_{g \in G} \sum_{i \in I} A_{g,i} = 1$ ensures that only one instance type is used for a given task;

(7) $\forall_{g \in L, p \in P} \sum_{i \in PI_p, g \in G_l} N_{g,i} \leq n_p^{P\max}$ enforces instance limits per cloud, for each task group and instance type.

This scheduling model yields reasonable results only for the cases when it is actually possible to complete all the workflow tasks before the deadline. If not, the solver will not find any solution.

The optimization models introduced in this section were implemented using CMPL and AMPL effectively being workflow schedulers. The source code of the schedulers is available as an online supplement (https://github.com/kfigiela/optimization-models/tree/ppam-extended/workflows). The public repository on GitHub includes the model files, the data, and the scripts we used to run the solvers.

6. Application and Infrastructure Data Used for Evaluation

To perform optimization we need to provide optimization models defined in the previous section with data describing an application and an infrastructure. First, we used the generic infrastructure benchmarks obtained from CloudHarmony and the application data from the workflow generator gallery. Next, we performed our own experiments using the Montage workflows on Amazon EC2, which provided the application-specific performance benchmark of cloud resources together to obtain the real application data. The data gathered during experiments are inputs for the scheduler.

6.1. Data for Coarse-Grained Scheduler. To evaluate the coarse-grained scheduler on realistic data, we used CloudHarmony [24] benchmarks to parameterize the infrastructure model, and we used the workflow generator gallery workflows [23] as test applications. In the infrastructure model we assumed that we had 4 public cloud providers (Amazon EC2, RackSpace, GoGrid, and ElasticHosts) and a private cloud with 0 costs. The infrastructure had two storage sites: S3 which is local to EC2, and CloudFiles which is local to RackSpace, so data transfers between local virtual machines and storage sites are free.

We used the first generation of CloudHarmony CPU benchmarks described in [24]. CloudHarmony CPU benchmarks use CloudHarmony Compute Unit (CCU) as a unit for measuring CPU performance. It is calculated based on a set of general-purpose CPU benchmarks [32]. First generation benchmarks were calibrated relative to Amazon's `m1.small` instance and are now deprecated in favor of new benchmarks that are calibrated to nonvirtualized hardware. The new benchmark is compared to

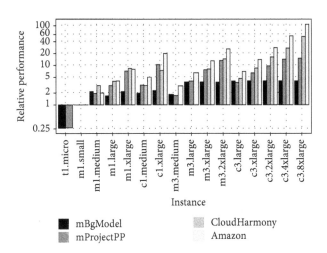

FIGURE 3: Amazon instance benchmarks for different tasks compared to the generic CloudHarmony benchmark and Amazon ECU. Data was normalized to `m1.small` instance type having relative performance of 1.0.

our benchmark data in Figure 3. Actual datasets are provided as an online supplement (https://github.com/kfigiela/optimization-models/tree/ppam-extended/workflows).

We tested the coarse-grained scheduler with all of the applications from the gallery: Montage, CyberShake, Epigenomics, LIGO, and SIPHT for all available workflow sizes (from 50 to 1000 tasks per workflow up to 5000 tasks in the case of SIPHT workflow). We varied the deadline from 1 to 30 hours with 1-hour increments. We solved the problem for two cases, depending on whether the data are stored on S3 or on CloudFiles.

6.2. Data for Fine-Grained Scheduler. Cloud benchmarks, such as CloudHarmony [24], are based on set of general-purpose benchmarks that do not necessarily represent scientific applications that are to be scheduled. In order to find out how it may differ, we run Montage workflow on several Amazon EC2 instance types. The workflow of 12700 tasks processing 8.5 GiB of photos rendered a mosaic of an 8×8 degree region at Orion Nebula from 2MASS survey.

Usually, benchmarks take into account the fact that instances provide multiple virtual cores that speed up multithreaded applications, but it has no impact on single threaded ones. Montage workflow tasks are single threaded and therefore in our experiment the number of execution threads running in parallel was equal to the number of virtual cores. We used the HyperFlow workflow engine [31] to drive workflow execution. In the experiment, we used EBS (elastic block storage) volume for data storage instead of S3 (simple storage service); however we measured the transfer times to and from S3 separately. EBS is different from S3 as it provides block level access (i.e., filesystem) to the data volume, while S3 is object store available as a service by REST API.

The data we gathered in experiments may be used to calculate application-specific performance metric of the instance (ECU-like). In Figure 3 we compare our results with CloudHarmony benchmarks. It shows that, for the

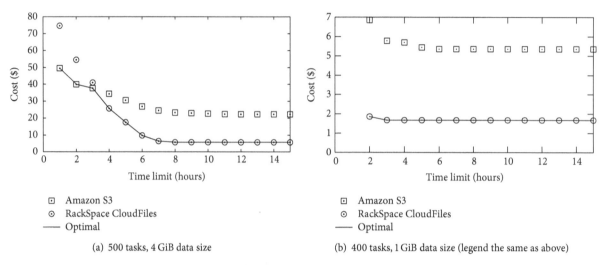

(a) 500 tasks, 4 GiB data size   (b) 400 tasks, 1 GiB data size (legend the same as above)

FIGURE 4: Result of coarse-grained scheduling for the Epigenomics application.

tasks forming the parallel levels of Montage workflow (such as mProjectPP [27]), the performance of the instances is proportional to the generic CPU benchmark. On the other hand, for the levels that are not parallel (e.g., mBgModel), there is no difference between cheaper m3.large and more expensive instance types (e.g., c3.8xlarge). Those instance types are deployed on the same generation of hardware, so their performance for single threaded applications is very similar. Additionally, as a reference we show the instance performance provided by Amazon in ECU (EC2 Compute Units).

The observation from this evaluation is that the benchmarks from CloudHarmony give better approximation to the task performance than the generic ECU value. Moreover, it is important to distinguish between parallel and sequential workflow levels when selecting the virtual machine instance type. The dataset obtained in this experiment was used for evaluation of fine-grained scheduling model in Section 7.2.

7. Evaluation of Optimization Models

In this section, we present the results of optimization, obtained by applying our schedulers to the application and infrastructure data. First, we show the results of using the coarse-grained scheduler applied to the generic CloudHarmony datasets. Next, we present the results of the fine-grained scheduler applied to the dataset obtained from our experiments with the Montage workflow on EC2.

7.1. Results for Coarse-Grained Scheduling. Figure 4 shows the cost of execution of the Epigenomics application with two workflows of sizes 400 and 500 tasks as a function of deadline. For longer deadlines (over 6 hours), the private cloud instances and the cheapest RackSpace instances are used so the cost is low when using CloudFiles. For shorter deadlines, the cost grows rapidly, since we reach the limit of instances per cloud and additional instances must be spawned on a different provider, thus making the transfer

costs higher. This effect is amplified in Figure 4(a), which differs from Figure 4(b) not only by the number of tasks, but also by the data size of the most data-intensive level. This means that the transfer costs are growing more rapidly, so it becomes more economical to store the data on Amazon EC2 that provides more powerful instances required for short deadlines.

One interesting feature of our scheduler is that for longer deadlines it enables finding the cost-optimal solutions that have shorter workflow completion time than the requested deadline. This effect can be observed in Figure 5 and is caused by the fact that for long deadlines the simple solution is to run the application on a set of the least expensive machines.

Figures 6(a) to 7(b) show results obtained for Cybershake, LIGO, Montage, and SIPHT workflows. These workflows have relatively small execution time, so even for short deadlines the scheduler is able to schedule tasks on the cheapest instances on a single cloud, thus resulting in flat characteristics.

To investigate how the scheduler behaves for workflows with the same structure, but with much longer runtimes of tasks, we run the optimization for Montage workflow with tasks 1000x longer. This corresponds to the scenario where tasks are in the order of hours instead of seconds. The results in Figure 8 show how the cost increases very steeply with shorter deadlines, illustrating the trade-off between time and cost. The difference between Figures 7(a) and 8 illustrates that the scheduler is more useful for workflows when tasks are of granularity that is similar to the granularity of the (hourly) billing cycle of cloud providers. Additionally, Figure 8 shows how the optimal cost depends on available clouds.

The runtime of the optimization algorithm for workflows with up to 1000 tasks ranges from a few seconds up to 4 minutes using the CPLEX [21] solver running on a server with 4 16-core 2.3 GHz AMD Opteron processors (model 6276), with CPLEX limited artificially to use only 32 cores. Figure 9(a) shows that the time becomes much higher for shorter deadlines and increases slowly for very long deadlines. This is correlated with the size of search space: the

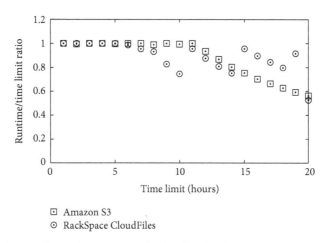

FIGURE 5: Ratio of the actual completion time to the deadline for the Epigenomics workflow with 500 tasks.

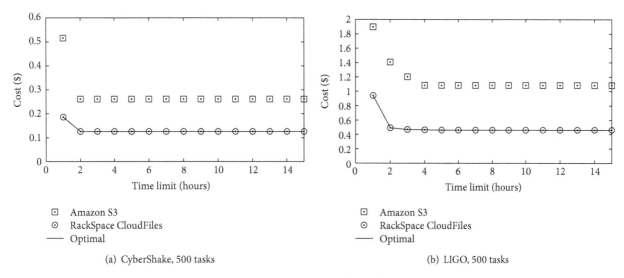

FIGURE 6: Optimal cost found with the coarse-grained scheduling for CyberShake and LIGO applications.

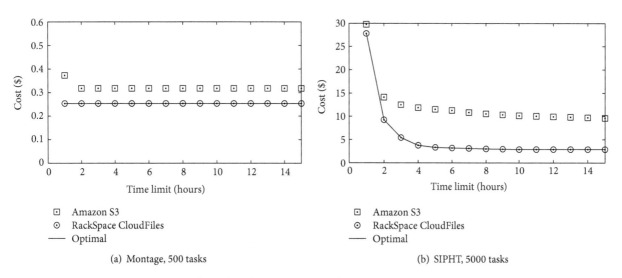

FIGURE 7: Optimal cost found by the scheduler for Montage and SIPHT applications.

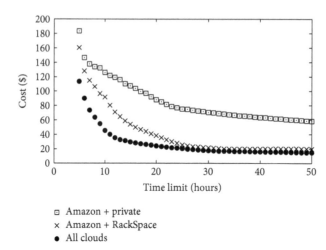

FIGURE 8: Optimal cost found by the coarse-grained scheduler for Montage workflow of 500 tasks with runtimes artificially multiplied by 1000 for different cloud infrastructures.

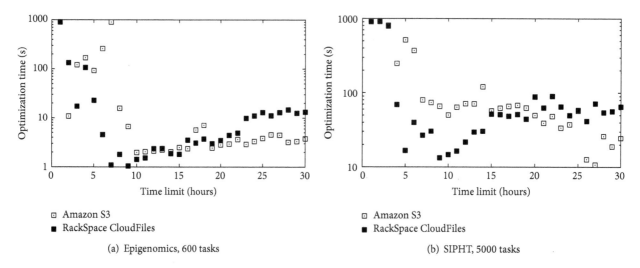

FIGURE 9: Optimization time of the solver.

longer the deadline, the larger the search space, while for shorter deadlines the problem has a very small set of acceptable solutions. The problem becomes more severe for bigger and more complex workflows like SIPHT as optimization time becomes very high (Figure 9(b)).

Figure 10 illustrates how the optimization time depends on MIP gap solver setting. The relative MIP gap is a relative diference between the best integer solution found by the solver and the possible optimal noninteger solution. The MIP gap value indicates to solver to stop when an integer feasible solution has been proved to be within a given percent of optimality [21]. Applying a relative MIP gap of 1% or 5% instead of default 0.01% shortens optimization time in orders of magnitude. Increasing the MIP gap to 5% did not decrease the quality of the result noticeably: the minimum cost obtained for the gap of 5% was higher only by 3.63% in the worst case.

7.2. Results for Fine-Grained Workflows and Short Deadlines. We performed optimization for deadlines ranging from 13 to 60 minutes, using the Amazon EC2 cloud, with S3 or local storage. When assuming that the storage is local, we set the $t_{g,i,s}^{net}$ fixed to 0, which may represent, for example, a very fast NFS storage when transfer times are negligible.

The results shown in Figure 11 have similar character to those we got in [7] and to the ones obtained using the coarse-grained scheduler and task runtimes artificially expanded (Figure 8). This observation leads to the conclusion that the granularity of the workflow tasks versus the granularity of the billing cycle of the cloud provider plays an important role in scheduling. In our case, we had to define two separate schedulers to address this issue. The problem, however, may be more complex when we assume more cloud providers with different billing cycles, such as hourly, 5-minute, or per-minute billing. This may be an interesting subject for further research.

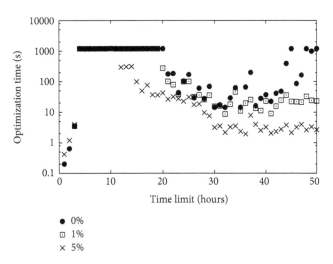

FIGURE 10: Solver runtime with different relative MIP gap (in percent), showing the relation between accuracy and runtime of the solver for the coarse-grained scheduler for Montage workflow of 500 tasks with runtimes artificially multiplied by 1000 for different cloud infrastructures.

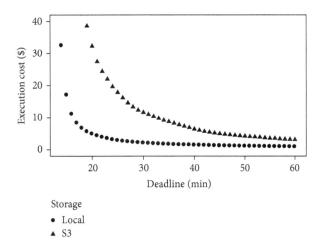

FIGURE 11: Montage workflow execution cost (8×8 degrees at M42) with S3 storage and local storage (i.e., very fast NFS).

8. Conclusions and Future Work

In this paper, we presented the schedulers using cost optimization for scientific workflows executing on multiple heterogeneous clouds. The models, formulated in AMPL and CMPL, allow us to find the optimal assignment of workflow tasks, grouped into levels, to cloud instances. We validated our models with a set of synthetic benchmark workflows as well as with the data of real astronomy workflow, and we observed that they gave useful solutions in a reasonable amount of computing time.

Based on our experiments with execution of Montage workflow on Amazon EC2 cloud and its characteristics, we developed separate scheduling models dedicated to coarse-grained workflows and to fine-grained workflows with short deadlines. We also compared the general-purpose cloud benchmarks, such as CloudHarmony, with our own measurements. The results underline the importance of application-specific cloud benchmarking, since the general purpose benchmarks can serve only as the rough approximation of

the actual application performance. The observed relations between the granularity of the tasks and the performance of optimization models shows the influence of the cloud billing cycle on the cost optimizing workflow scheduling.

By solving the models for multiple deadlines, we can produce trade-off plots, showing how the cost depends on the deadline. We believe that such plots are a step towards a scientific cloud workflow calculator, supporting resource management decisions for both end-users and workflow-as-a-service providers.

In the future, we plan to apply this model to the problem of provisioning cloud resources for workflow ensembles [3], where the optimization of cost can drive the workflow admission decisions. We also plan to refine the models to better support smaller workflows by reusing instances between levels, to fine-tune the model, and to test different solver configurations to reduce the computing time, as well as to apply the optimization models to the problem of dynamic workflow scheduling in order to better handle the uncertainties in the infrastructure and the application.

Conflict of Interests

The authors declare that there is no conflict of interests regarding the publication of this paper.

Acknowledgments

This research was partially supported by the EC ICT VPH-Share Project (Contract 269978) and the KI AGH Grant 11.11.230.124. The work of K. Figiela was supported by the AGH Dean's Grant. E. Deelman acknowledges support of the National Science Foundation (Grant 1148515) and the Department of Energy (Grant ER26110). Access to Amazon EC2 was provided via the AWS in Education Grant. The authors would like to express their thanks to the reviewers for their constructive recommendations that helped them improve the paper.

References

[1] E. Deelman, G. Juve, M. Malawski, and J. Nabrzyski, "Hosted science: managing computational workflows in the cloud," *Parallel Processing Letters*, vol. 23, no. 2, Article ID 1340004, 2013.

[2] AWS, "AWS public datasets," 2013, http://aws.amazon.com/publicdatasets/.

[3] M. Malawski, G. Juve, E. Deelman, and J. Nabrzyski, "Cost- and deadline-constrained provisioning for scientific workflow ensembles in IaaS clouds," in *Proceedings of the 24th International Conference for High Performance Computing, Networking, Storage and Analysis (SC '12)*, IEEE, November 2012.

[4] M. Bubak, M. Kasztelnik, M. Malawski, J. Meizner, P. Nowakowski, and S. Varma, "Evaluation of cloud providers for VPH applications," in *Proceedings of the 13th IEEE/ACM International Symposium on Cluster, Cloud and Grid Computing (CC-Grid '13)*, May 2013.

[5] R. Fourer, D. M. Gay, and B. W. Kernighan, *AMPL: A Modeling Language for Mathematical Programming*, Duxbury Press, 2002.

[6] M. Steglich, "CMPL (Coin mathematical programming language)," 2014, https://projects.coin-or.org/Cmpl.

[7] M. Malawski, K. Figiela, and J. Nabrzyski, "Cost minimization for computational applications on hybrid cloud infrastructures," *Future Generation Computer Systems*, vol. 29, no. 7, pp. 1786–1794, 2013.

[8] S. Bharathi, A. Chervenak, E. Deelman, G. Mehta, M.-H. Su, and K. Vahi, "Characterization of scientific workflows," in *Proceedings of the 3rd Workshop on Workflows in Support of Large-Scale Science (WORKS '08)*, pp. 1–10, IEEE, November 2008.

[9] R. Duan, R. Prodan, and X. Li, "A sequential cooperative game theoretic approach to storage-aware scheduling of multiple large-scale workflow applications in grids," in *Proceedings of the 13th ACM/IEEE International Conference on Grid Computing (Grid '12)*, pp. 31–39, IEEE, September 2012.

[10] M. Mao and M. Humphrey, "Auto-scaling to minimize cost and meet application deadlines in cloud workflows," in *Proceedings of the International Conference for High Performance Computing, Networking, Storage and Analysis (SC '11)*, ACM, New York, NY, USA, November 2011.

[11] M. Malawski, K. Figiela, M. Bubak, E. Deelman, and J. Nabrzyski, "Cost optimization of execution of multi-level deadline-constrained scientific workflows on clouds," in *Parallel Processing and Applied Mathematics—10th International Conference, PPAM 2013, Warsaw, Poland, September 8–11, 2013, Revised Selected Papers, Part I*, vol. 8384 of *Lecture Notes in Computer Science*, pp. 251–260, Springer, Berlin, Germany, 2014.

[12] S. Abrishami, M. Naghibzadeh, and D. H. J. Epema, "Deadline-constrained workflow scheduling algorithms for infrastructure as a service clouds," *Future Generation Computer Systems*, vol. 29, no. 1, pp. 158–169, 2013.

[13] J. J. Durillo, H. M. Fard, and R. Prodan, "MOHEFT: a multi-objective list-based method for workflow scheduling," in *Proceedings of the 4th IEEE International Conference on Cloud Computing Technology and Science (CloudCom '12)*, pp. 185–192, Taipei, Taiwan, December 2012.

[14] L. F. Bittencourt and E. R. M. Madeira, "HCOC: a cost optimization algorithm for workflow scheduling in hybrid clouds," *Journal of Internet Services and Applications*, vol. 2, no. 3, pp. 207–227, 2011.

[15] R. van den Bossche, K. Vanmechelen, and J. Broeckhove, "Online cost-efficient scheduling of deadline-constrained workloads on hybrid clouds," *Future Generation Computer Systems*, vol. 29, no. 4, pp. 973–985, 2013.

[16] S. Pandey, A. Barker, K. K. Gupta, and R. Buyya, "Minimizing execution costs when using globally distributed Cloud services," in *Proceedings of the 24th IEEE International Conference on Advanced Information Networking and Applications*, pp. 222–229, April 2010.

[17] J. Chen, C. Wang, B. B. Zhou, L. Sun, Y. C. Lee, and A. Y. Zomaya, "Tradeoffs between profit and customer satisfaction for service provisioning in the cloud," in *Proceedings of the 20th International Symposium on High Performance Distributed Computing (HPDC '11)*, pp. 229–238, ACM, San Jose, Calif, USA, 2011.

[18] H. Kim, Y. El-Khamra, I. Rodero, S. Jha, and M. Parashar, "Autonomic management of application workflows on hybrid computing infrastructure," *Scientific Programming*, vol. 19, no. 2-3, pp. 75–89, 2011.

[19] R. Tolosana-Calasanz, J. Á. Bañares, C. Pham, and O. F. Rana, "Enforcing QoS in scientific workflow systems enacted over Cloud infrastructures," *Journal of Computer and System Sciences*, vol. 78, no. 5, pp. 1300–1315, 2012.

[20] T. A. L. Genez, L. F. Bittencourt, and E. R. M. Madeira, "Using time discretization to schedule scientific workflows in multiple cloud providers," in *Proceedings of the IEEE 6th International Conference on Cloud Computing (CLOUD '13)*, pp. 123–130, Santa Clara, Calif, USA, July 2013.

[21] IBM, "IBM ILOG CPLEX Optimization Studio CPLEX User's Manual," 2013, http://pic.dhe.ibm.com/infocenter/cosinfoc/v12r5/topic/ilog.odms.studio.help/pdf/usrcplex.pdf.

[22] J. Forrest, "Cbc (coin-or branch and cut) open-source mixed integer programming solver," 2012, https://projects.coin-or.org/Cbc.

[23] G. Juve, A. Chervenak, E. Deelman, S. Bharathi, G. Mehta, and K. Vahi, "Characterizing and profiling scientific workflows," *Future Generation Computer Systems*, vol. 29, no. 3, pp. 682–692, 2013.

[24] CloudHarmony, "Benchmarks," 2014, http://cloudharmony.com/benchmarks.

[25] USC epigenome center, http://epigenome.usc.edu.

[26] J. Livny, H. Teonadi, M. Livny, and M. K. Waldor, "High-throughput, kingdom-wide prediction and annotation of bacterial non-coding RNAs," *PLoS ONE*, vol. 3, no. 9, Article ID e3197, 2008.

[27] G. B. Berriman, E. Deelman, J. C. Good et al., "Montage: a grid enabled engine for delivering custom science-grade mosaics on demand," in *Optimizing Scientific Return for Astronomy through Information Technologies*, vol. 5493 of *Proceedings of SPIE*, pp. 221–232, June 2004.

[28] P. Maechling, E. Deelman, L. Zhao et al., "SCEC cyber-shake workows—automating probabilistic seismic hazard analysis calculations," in *Workows for e-Science*, I. Taylor, E. Deelman, D. Gannon, and M. Shields, Eds., pp. 143–163, Springer, London, UK, 2007.

[29] A. Abramovici, W. E. Althouse, R. W. P. Drever et al., "LIGO: the laser interferometer gravitational-wave observatory," *Science*, vol. 256, no. 5055, pp. 325–333, 1992.

[30] Workflow Generator, 2014, https://confluence.pegasus.isi.edu/display/pegasus/WorkflowGenerator.

[31] B. Balis, "Hypermedia workflow: a new approach to Data-Driven scientific workflows," in *Proceedings of the SC Companion: High Performance Computing, Networking Storage and Analysis (SCC '12)*, pp. 100–107, November 2012.

[32] Cloud Harmony, "What is ECU? CPU benchmarking in Cloud," 2010, http://blog.cloudharmony.com/2010/05/what-is-ecu-cpu-benchmarking-in-cloud.html.

[33] R. F. da Silva, G. Juve, E. Deelman et al., "Toward fine-grained online task characteristics estimation in scientific workflows," in *Proceedings of the 8th Workshop on Workows in Support of Large-Scale Science (WORKS '13)*, pp. 58–67, ACM, Denver, Colo, USA, November 2013.

[34] R. Van Den Bossche, K. Vanmechelen, and J. Broeckhove, "Cost-optimal scheduling in hybrid IaaS clouds for deadline constrained workloads," in *Proceedings of the 3rd IEEE International Conference on Cloud Computing (CLOUD '10)*, pp. 228–235, Miami, Fla, USA, July 2010.

RVLBPNN: A Workload Forecasting Model for Smart Cloud Computing

Yao Lu,[1] John Panneerselvam,[2] Lu Liu,[1,2] and Yan Wu[1,3]

[1]*School of Computer Science and Telecommunication Engineering Jiangsu University, Jiangsu, China*
[2]*Department of Computing and Mathematics, University of Derby, Derby, UK*
[3]*Department of Computer Science, Boise State University, Boise, USA*

Correspondence should be addressed to Lu Liu; l.liu@derby.ac.uk

Academic Editor: Wenbing Zhao

Given the increasing deployments of Cloud datacentres and the excessive usage of server resources, their associated energy and environmental implications are also increasing at an alarming rate. Cloud service providers are under immense pressure to significantly reduce both such implications for promoting green computing. Maintaining the desired level of Quality of Service (QoS) without violating the Service Level Agreement (SLA), whilst attempting to reduce the usage of the datacentre resources is an obvious challenge for the Cloud service providers. Scaling the level of active server resources in accordance with the predicted incoming workloads is one possible way of reducing the undesirable energy consumption of the active resources without affecting the performance quality. To this end, this paper analyzes the dynamic characteristics of the Cloud workloads and defines a hierarchy for the latency sensitivity levels of the Cloud workloads. Further, a novel workload prediction model for energy efficient Cloud Computing is proposed, named RVLBPNN (Rand Variable Learning Rate Backpropagation Neural Network) based on BPNN (Backpropagation Neural Network) algorithm. Experiments evaluating the prediction accuracy of the proposed prediction model demonstrate that RVLBPNN achieves an improved prediction accuracy compared to the HMM and Naïve Bayes Classifier models by a considerable margin.

1. Introduction

Cloud Computing is emerging as a prominent computing paradigm for various business needs, as it is known to be a low-cost any-time computing solution. The on-demand service access features of the Cloud Computing help the Cloud clients to adopt or transform their business model to Cloud datacentres for computing and storage resources [1]. This increasing number of Cloud adoptions by various business domains over the recent years is also reflected in the increase in the number of Cloud service providers. An immediate impact of this is that Cloud datacentres are addressed to be one of the major sources of energy consumers [2] and environmental pollutants. To this end, Cloud datacentres are addressed to be causing energy, economic, and environmental impacts to an irresistible margin. It has been reported [3] that ICT (Information Communication Technology) energy consumption will contribute up to 50% of the total energy expenditures in the United States in the next decade, which was just 8% in the last decade. Energy efficient computing has been promoted and researched under various dimensions for the purpose of reducing the energy consumption levels of the datacentre whilst processing workloads and cooling the server resources. It is worthy of note that cooling system in a typical Cloud datacentre would incur considerable amount of energy cost of those spent towards the actual task execution [4]. Thus it is apparent that energy efficient Cloud Computing is one of demanding characteristics of Cloud Computing.

Resource management driven by forecasting the future workloads is one of the possible ways of achieving energy efficiency in Cloud Computing. In general, the intrinsic dynamic [5] nature of the Cloud workloads imposes complexities in scheduling, resource allocation, and executing workloads in the datacentres. Predicting the nature of the future workloads can help reduce the energy consumption levels of the server resources by the way of effectively scheduling the incoming workloads with the most appropriate level of resource allocation. Alongside energy efficient computing, predictive analytics in Cloud Computing also benefits [5] effective resource utilization, optimum scalability of resources, avoiding process failures, capacity planning, network allocation, task scheduling, load balancing, performance optimization and maintaining the predetermined QoS (Quality of Service) and SLAs (Service Level Agreements), and so forth.

Owing to the extravagant dynamicity of Cloud workloads, understanding the characteristic behaviors of the Cloud workloads at the datacentre environment is often a complex process. Mostly, Cloud workloads are of shorter duration and arrive more frequently at the datacentres and are generally not computationally more intensive unlike scientific workloads. Furthermore, every submitted workloads are bound to a certain level of latency sensitiveness [6] which decides the time within which the workload has to be processed. Workloads with increased latency sensitivity levels usually demand quicker scheduling from the providers. This implies that an effective prediction model should possess the qualities of understanding the inherent characteristics and nature of the Cloud workloads and their corresponding behaviors at the datacentres.

Despite the existing and ongoing researches, Cloud Computing still demands extensive analyses of the Cloud entities for the purpose of modelling the relationship between the users and their workload submissions and the associated resource requirements. An effective prediction model should necessarily incorporate the knowledge of three important characteristic events in a datacentre environment in order to achieve reliable level of prediction accuracy. Firstly, the volume and the nature of the workloads submitted are driven by the users based on their requirements and resource demands. Increased amounts of jobs submissions obviously demand increased amounts of resource allocation and thus causes increased energy expenditures. Secondly, the actual execution of the workloads would not necessarily consume all the allocated resources. The immediate implication is that increased proportions of allocated resources remain idle during task execution and incur undesirable energy consumptions. Finally, the user behavioral pattern of job submission and associated resource consumption are subjected to change over time.

The intrinsic dynamism of both the Cloud workloads and the server resources should be effectively captured [7] by the prediction model over a prolonged observation period. Existing works in analyzing the intrinsic characteristics of the Cloud entities have not contributed suffice inferences [5, 8, 9] required for an effective prediction model. Imprecise knowledge of such aforementioned parameters of the Cloud entities would increase the prediction error margin, which would directly affect the Quality of Service (QoS) by violating the Service Level Agreement (SLA). With this in mind, this paper proposes a novel forecast model named RVLBPNN (Rand Variable Learning Rate Backpropagation Neural Network), based on an improved BPNN (BP Neural Network) for accurately predicting the user requests. Exploiting the latency

sensitivity levels of the Cloud workloads, our proposed model predicts the user requests anticipated in the near future in a large-scale datacentre environment.

The rest of this paper is organized as follows: Section 2 introduces the previous works in Cloud workload prediction modelling. Section 3 presents a background study on Cloud workloads, exhibiting the dynamic nature of the Cloud workloads. The computational latencies affecting the Cloud workloads are defined in Section 4 and Section 5 proposes our prediction model based on the modified BP Neural Network. Our experiments are presented in Section 6 and Section 7 concludes this paper along with our future research directions.

2. Related Works

A number of researches are being conducted with the motivation of promoting green computing in the recent past. For instance, the approach of capacity management and VM (Virtual Machine) placement have been the strategies of [10, 11]. A workload placement scheme, called BADP, combines task's behavior to place data for improving locality at the cache line level. Further, [11] proposes a remaining utilization-aware (RUA) algorithm for VM placement. In general, workload placement and task allocation can be more effective when driven by a proactive prediction of the incoming workloads. Time series [12] approach incorporates the repeatable behaviors such as periodicity and timely effects of the various Cloud entities such as VMs and users and explores the temporal and spatial correlations in order to provide the prediction results. However, such technique usually explores the entities individually and often leads to inaccurate results resulting from the random behaviors of the individual entities.

A multiple time series approach [13] has been proposed to improve the prediction accuracy, by the way of analyzing the Cloud entities at the group level rather individually. Nonlinear time series approach works with the assumption that the observations are real valued and such techniques often require special emphasis on extracting the chaotic invariants for prediction analysis. Autoregression (AR) is a prediction technique [14] which usually predicts the next state transition by recursively acting on the prediction values. However, AR method has a conspicuous shortcoming that the prediction errors will be accumulated for long term prediction analysis because of the recursive effect. Another drawback of AR methods is that they only deliver accurate forecasts for datasets characterized with reasonable periodicity, which is shown in [15], where a number of different linear prediction models based on AR have been deeply analyzed. Poisson process [16] models the incoming workload arrival pattern for prediction analysis and has the capability of capturing complex nonexponential time varying workload features. Moving average approaches [14, 16] such as first-order and second-order moving average techniques used for prediction analysis cannot capture important features required to adapt to the load dynamics.

Recently, Bayes and Hidden Markov Modelling (HMM) [5] approaches were analyzed in our earlier works for evaluating their prediction efficiency in Cloud environments.

Byes technology predicts the future samples based on a predefined evidence window. The adjacent samples contained in the evidence window should be mutually correlated for delivering a reliable prediction output. Thus Bayes model will lose efficiency in a dynamic Cloud environment. However, Bayes model could still be deployed in situations where there are less fluctuations among the workload behavior. HMM is a probabilistic approach which is used to predict the future sate transition from the current state. In spite of the dynamic nature of the Cloud workloads, probabilistic approach may not scale well for predicting the future workloads with a reliable level of prediction accuracy. Despite the existing works, Cloud Computing still demands a smart prediction model with the qualities of relative high precision and the capacity of delivering a reliable level of prediction accuracy. With this in mind, this paper proposes a novel prediction model named RVLBPNN. Exploiting the workload characteristics, our proposed model achieves a reliable level of prediction accuracy. Our proposed model has been sampled and tested for accuracy based on a real life Cloud workload behaviors.

3. Background

3.1. Cloud Workloads. Cloud workloads arrive at Cloud datacentres in the form of jobs [15] submitted by the users. Every job includes certain self-defining attributes such as the submission time, user identity, and its corresponding resource requirements in terms of CPU and memory. A single job may contain one or more tasks, which are scheduled for processing at the Cloud servers. A single task may have one or more process requirements. Tasks belonging to a single job may also be scheduled to different machines but it is desirable to run multiple processes of a single task in a single machine. Tasks are also bound to have varied service requirements such as throughput, latency, and jitter, though they belong to the same job. The tasks belonging to the same job not necessarily exhibit higher correlating properties among them. Thus, tasks within the same job might exhibit greater variation in their resource requirements. Tasks might also interact among each other during their execution. Furthermore, two jobs with the same resource requirements may not be similar in their actual resource utilization levels because of the variation found among the tasks contained within the jobs. Based on the resource requirements, tasks are scheduled either within the same or across different servers. Usually, the provider records the resource utilization levels of every scheduled task and maintains the user profiles.

The attributes encompassed by the Cloud workloads, such as type, resource requirements, security requirements, hardware, and network constraints, can be exploited to derive the behaviors the Cloud workloads. Interestingly, Cloud workloads behave distinctively with different server architectures. Such distinctive workload behaviors with different server architectures strongly influence the CPU utilization, with the memory utilization generally remaining stable across most of the server architectures. Thus the resource utilization highly varies across the CPU cores compared to the memory or disc, as the disc utilization mostly shows similar utilization patterns across different server architectures. Thus the behaviors

of workloads at the Cloud processing environment are strongly correlated with the CPU cores compared to RAM capacity of the machines at the server level. The capacity levels of CPU and memory in a physical server usually remain static. Resource utilization levels are more dynamic and vary abruptly under different workloads. Such dynamic parameters of the server architectures are usually calculated as the measure of the number of cycles per instruction for CPU and memory access per instruction for memory utilizations, respectively. Thus the task resource usage is usually expressed as a multidimensional representation [5] encompassing task duration in seconds, CPU usage in cores, and memory usage in gigabytes. It is commonly witnessed that most of the allocated CPU and memory resource are left unutilized during task execution.

3.2. Characterizing Workloads. User demand often changes over time which reflects the timely variations of the resource consumption levels of the workloads generated as they are driven by the users. User demands are generally influenced by the time-of-the-day effects, showing a repeating pattern [13] in accordance to the changing business behaviors of the day and by the popular weekend effects showing weekend declines and weekday increase trend in the arrival of the workloads. The relationships [17] between the workloads and user behaviors are primarily the integral component in the understanding of the Cloud-based workloads and their associated energy consumptions.

Different workloads will have different processing requirements such as CPU, memory, throughput, and execution time, and this variation results from the characteristic behaviors of different users. Nowadays, Cloud environments are more heterogeneous composing different servers with different processing capacities. In order to satisfy the diverse operational requirements of the Cloud user demands, normalization of this machine heterogeneity is now becoming an integral requirement of the Cloud providers, by which virtually homogenizing the heterogeneous server architectures and thereby eliminating the differentiation found in both the hardware and the software resources. In general, the different forms of workloads from the provider's perspectives include computation intensive with larger processing and smaller storage, memory intensive with larger storage and smaller processing, workloads requiring both larger processing and larger storage, and communication intensive with more bandwidth requirements. Workloads are usually measured in terms of the user demands, computational load on the servers, bandwidth consumption (communication jobs), and the amount of storage data (memory jobs). User demand prediction modelling requires an in depth quantitative and qualitative analysis of the statistical properties and behavioral characteristics of the workloads including job length, job submission frequency, and resource consumption of the jobs, which insists that the initial characterization of the workloads is more crucial in developing an efficient prediction model. Rather than the stand-alone analysis of the above stated workload metrics, modelling the relationships between them across a set of workloads is more significant in order to achieve more reliable prediction results. Statistical properties [18] of the workloads are more significant for the prediction accuracy since they remain consistent in longer time frames. Some of the important characteristics of Cloud workloads affecting prediction accuracy include job length, job submission frequency, resource request levels, job resource utilization, and self-similarity.

3.3. Categorizing Workloads. In the Cloud Computing service concept, the workload pattern, the Cloud deployment types (public, private, hybrid, and community), and the Cloud service offering models (SaaS, PaaS, and IaaS) are closely interconnected with each other. From the perspectives of the Cloud service providers, the incoming Cloud workloads can be categorized into five major types [9] as static, periodic, unpredictable, continuously changing, and once-in-a-lifetime workloads. Static and periodic workloads usually follow a predictable pattern in their arrival frequency. Continuously changing workloads exhibit a pattern of definite variations characterized by regular increasing and declining trend in their arrival frequencies. Unpredictable workloads exhibit a random behavior in their arrival frequency and are the most challenging type of workloads for prediction analysis. Once-in-a-lifetime workloads are the rarely arriving workloads and their submissions are mostly notified by the clients.

4. Workload Latency

Latency plays an important role at various levels of processing the workloads in a Cloud processing infrastructure. This paper mainly focuses the influence of the workload latency sensitivity upon prediction accuracy. The most dominating types of latencies are the network latency and the dispatching latency, both of which actually result from the geographical distribution of the users and the Cloud datacentres. Both of these latencies depend on the Round Trip Time (RTT) [19], which defines the time interval between the user requests and the arrival of the corresponding response. Another type of latency existing in the process architecture is the computational latency which is the intracloud latency [20] found among the processing VMs located within a single datacentre. This latency depends on both the software and the hardware components [6, 21] such as CPU architecture, runtime environment, and memory, guests and host operating system, instruction set, and hypervisor used. CPU architecture, Operating System, and the scheduling mechanisms are the most dominating factors of this type of in-house computing latency, and efficient handling of such resources helps reducing the impacts of the computational latencies.

Jobs submitted at the Cloud datacentre undergo various levels of latencies depending on the nature of their process requirements and the end-user QoS expectations. Since a single job might contain a number of tasks, the latency sensitivity of every single tasks has to be treated uniquely. A single definition of the computing latency cannot fit all types of jobs or tasks, since every job is uniquely viewed at the datacentre. For instance, processing a massive scientific workload may span across several days or months, in which latencies of a few seconds are usually acceptable. Common example of

the latency sensitive workloads is the World Wide Web, among which different applications have different latency levels. The acceptable level of latencies is usually the measure of the end-user tolerances. Workloads resulting from users surfing the internet are generally latency-insensitive. Jobs including online gaming and stock exchange data are the commonly witnessed latency sensitive applications. The level of sensitivity is determined by the allowed time-scale for the providers to provide an undisrupted execution of the workloads for delivering the desired levels of QoS, ranging from a few microseconds to a few tens of microsecond end-to-end latencies.

The taxonomy of the latency levels of the Cloud workloads studied in this paper are attributed from level 0 representing the least latency sensitive tasks to level 3 representing the most latency sensitive tasks. Least latency sensitive tasks (level 0) are nonproduction tasks [22] such as development and nonbusiness critical analyses, which do not have a significant impact on the QoS even if these jobs are queued at the back end servers. Level 1 tasks are the next level of latency sensitive tasks and are generally the machine interactive workloads. Level 2 tasks are the real time machine interactive workloads and the latency tolerance levels of these tasks stay at tens of milliseconds. Level 3 tasks are the most latency sensitive tasks with latency tolerance levels at the range of submilliseconds, and are generally the revenue generating user requests such as stock and financial analysis. Workloads characterizing an increased level of latency sensitivity are usually treated with higher scheduling priorities at the datacentres. Latency analysis has a prime importance in greening the datacentre, since every job or task submitted to the Cloud has its own level of latency tolerances, directly affecting not only the various workload behaviors at the datacentres but also the end-user QoS satisfaction.

Based on our earlier analysis conducted on a Cloud dataset [23], we perform a latency aware quantification of the jobs submitted to the datacentre comprising a total of 46093201 tasks in our recent work [24]. Figure 1 illustrates a day-wise submission of tasks across the observed 28 days. Figure 2 quantifies the total number of task submissions in terms of their latency sensitivity levels. It can be observed that most of the task submissions are least latency sensitive accounting for 79.52% of the total task submissions, followed by level 1, level 2, and level 3 with 12.46%, 7.54%, and 0.47%, respectively.

5. Proposed Prediction Model

This section describes our novel prediction model aimed at predicting the anticipated workloads in a large-scale datacentre environment.

5.1. BP Neural Network Method. BP Neural Network is a multilayer hierarchical network composed of upper neurons and fully associated lower neurons. Upon training the input samples into this multilayer network structure, the transformed input values are propagated from the input layer through the middle layer, and the values are outputted by the neurons in the output layer. The error margins

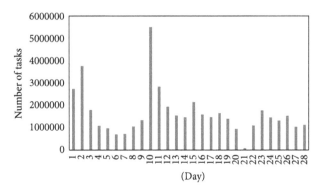

FIGURE 1: Total number of task submissions.

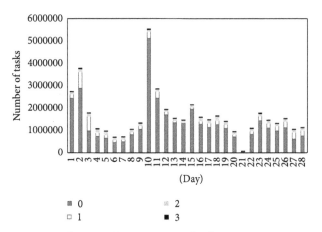

FIGURE 2: Latency-wise task submission.

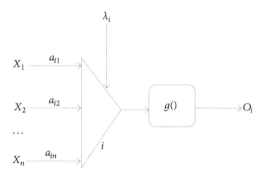

FIGURE 3: Neuron model.

5.3. An Improved BP Neural Network Algorithm for Prediction. BPNN can effectively extract the hidden nonlinear relationships among the Cloud workloads. However, BPNN with a fixed learning rate cannot extract this nonlinear relationships among the samples of large datasets, since BPNN has a slow convergence rate for large-scale datasets in the range of Big Data. A modified BP algorithm named VLBP (variable learning rate backpropagation) has been proposed to enhance this convergence rate [29]. In comparison with the BP algorithm, VLBP has a characteristic enhancement in both the computation speed and precision of the output. But the VLBP algorithm can be susceptible to several numbers of local minima resulting from the irregular shake surface error. This slows down the update process of Mean Square Error (MSE) and increases the presence of local minimum points. This results in a higher approximation precision despite the improvement in the convergence rate. VLBP exhibits a fluctuating and slower learning process and increases the length of the computation.

This necessitates further improvements in the BP Neural Networks for the purpose of enhancing its prediction efficiency whilst training large datasets. This paper proposes a novel prediction method using a modified BP algorithm by incorporating variant conceptions of a genetic algorithm. Our proposed prediction method effectively adjusts the learning rate of the neurons to a certain probability in accordance with the trend of the MSE during the execution of the VLBP algorithm. The learning rate may not be changed or multiplied by the factor ρ greater than 1 when MSE increases beyond the set threshold ζ.

Our proposed prediction algorithm is described as follows:

(1) Generate a random number rand(u) (0 < rand(u) < 1).

(2) If rand(u) is less than a defined value (set as 0.8 in experiments), then execute VLBP algorithm.

(3) If rand(u) is greater than the defined value, else if MSE has increased, then the learning rate is multiplied by a factor greater than 1 despite MSE exceeding ζ or not; if MSE decreases after updating the connection weight, then the learning rate is multiplied by a factor between 0 and 1.

We named our proposed algorithm as RVLBPNN (Rand Variable Learning Rate Backpropagation Neural Network).

between the actual and the expected output are normalized by the way of the output neurons adjusting the connection weights of the neurons in both the middle layer and the input layer. This back propagation mechanism of connection weight adjustment enhances the correctness of the network responses of the neurons to the input values. As the BP algorithm implements a middle hidden layer with associated learning rules, the network neurons can effectively identify the hidden nonlinear pattern among the input samples.

5.2. BP Neural Network Architecture. A typical neuron model can be derived according to characteristics of the neurons [25–28], which is shown in Figure 3. In this figure, $X_1, X_2, \ldots, X_n$ are n input data to the neurons; $a_{i1}, a_{i2}, \ldots, a_{in}$ are the weight factor of $X_1, X_2, \ldots, X_n$, respectively; $g()$ is a nonlinear function; O_i is the output result; and λ_i is the threshold.

Based on the above neuron structure, we make $O_i = g(P_i)$, where, $P_i = \sum_{j=1}^{n} a_{ij} X_j - \lambda_i$. In the formula, X represents the input vector, a_i represents the connection weight vector for neuron i, and P_i is the input of the neurons. In most cases, λ_i is considered to be the 0th input of the neuron. Thus, we can get a simplified equation of the above expression, which is shown in formula (1). In this equation, value $X_0 = -1$, and $a_{i0} = \lambda_i$.

$$P_i = \sum_{j=0}^{n} a_{ij} X_j. \tag{1}$$

Through this method, the learning rate of the neurons will not be decreased at any time resulting from the slow renewal of MSE near the local minimum point. But, there is also a certain probability of increasing the learning rate of the neurons. RVLBP algorithm can identify the global minimum point by effectively avoiding the local minimum points. Thus our proposed algorithm reduces the presence of local minimum points during the learning process, thereby improving the learning efficiencies of the network neurons.

6. Performance Evaluation

6.1. Experiment Sample. This section demonstrates the efficiency of our proposed prediction model based on RVBLPNN. We train the input data sample to predict the anticipated values in the near future representing the future workloads expected to arrive at the datacentre. The experiment samples are trained in MATLAB 7.14 and the test datasets used are the publically available Google workload traces [23]. The datasets are a collection of 28 days of Google usage data workloads consisting of 46093201 tasks comprising CPU intensive workloads, memory-intensive workloads, and both CPU and memory-intensive workloads. The dataset parameters include time, job id, parent id, number of cores (CPU workloads), and memory tasks (memory workloads), respectively, to define the sample attributes. We compare the prediction efficiencies of our proposed prediction model against the efficiencies of Hidden Markov Model (HMM) and Naïve Bayes Classifier (NBC); both of them were evaluated in our earlier works [5]. All the three models are evaluated for their efficiencies in predicting memory and CPU intensive workloads accordingly. We train the prediction model with a set of 10 samples and contrast the prediction output with the actual set of successive 10 samples.

MATLAB simulation environment provides a built-in model for RVLBPNN technique, modelling RVLBPNN as a supervised learning. The Neural Network is comprised of a three-layer network structure. This three-layer Neural Network can approximate any type of nonlinear continuous function in theory. We ultimately use 10 input nodes, 12 hidden nodes, and 10 output nodes through a number of iterations for enhancing the prediction accuracy. The data samples are normalized and imploded in the interval (0, 1). "logsig" function is selected as the activation function of input layer, hidden layer, and the output layer, so that the algorithm exhibits a good convergence rate. Further, variable learning rate and random variable learning rate are adopted, respectively. This experiment uses 100,000 workload data samples as the training data and another 100000 data samples as the reference data. The prediction accuracy is the measure of correlations between the predicted and actual set of sample values.

6.2. Result Analysis and Performance Evaluation

6.2.1. Memory Workloads Estimation. Figure 4 depicts the estimation results of RVLBPNN, HMM, and NBC model, respectively, in terms of their prediction accuracy whilst predicting the memory-intensive workloads. The number of test

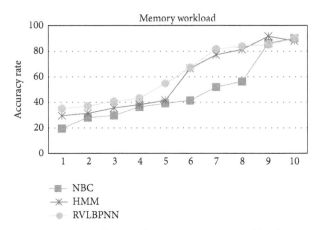

FIGURE 4: Prediction of memory-intensive workloads.

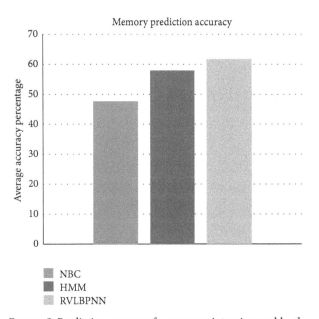

FIGURE 5: Prediction accuracy for memory-intensive workloads.

samples (*x*-axis) are plotted against the prediction accuracy (*y*-axis) for the three models; every set of sample consists of 10000 workload samples. For presenting the test results with a better interpretation, the sample results are sorted ascendingly from 1 to 10 based on the prediction results. The average accuracy percentage in estimating the memory-intensive workloads without considering the latency levels of individual workloads for NBC, HMM, and RVLBPNN are 47.69%, 57.77%, and 61.71%, respectively, as shown in Figures 4 and 5. It is evident from Figures 4 and 5 that the RVLBPNN exhibits a better prediction accuracy than both HMM and NBC techniques. It can be depicted from the estimation results that our proposed RVLBPNN model is demonstrating a minimum of 3% prediction accuracy better than HMM and 13% better than NBC, respectively.

This improved prediction accuracy of the RVLBPNN model is attributed to its ability of capturing the intrinsic relationship features among the arriving Cloud workloads. We further evaluate the efficiency of our proposed model in

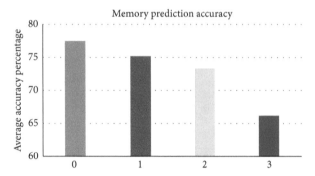

FIGURE 6: Latency-wise prediction accuracy for memory workloads.

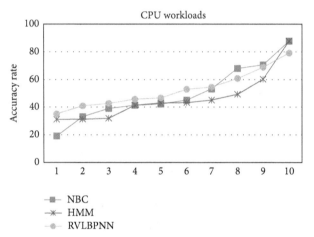

FIGURE 7: Prediction of CPU intensive workloads.

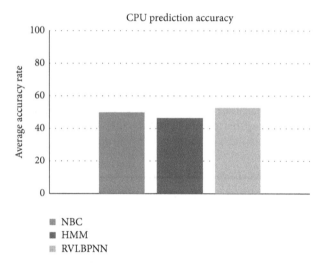

FIGURE 8: Prediction accuracy for CPU intensive workloads.

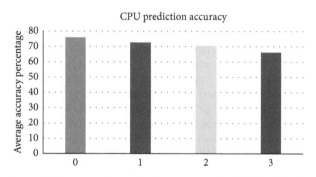

FIGURE 9: Latency-wise prediction accuracy for CPU workloads.

forecasting memory-intensive workloads of different latency sensitivity levels. Figure 6 depicts the estimation results of our proposed RVLBPNN model in terms of their prediction accuracy whilst predicting memory-intensive workloads of different latency sensitivity levels as described earlier in Section 4. It can be observed from Figure 6 that less latency sensitive memory workloads exhibit better predictability, with the prediction accuracy being 66.17% for level 3 workloads and 77.48% for level 0 workloads, respectively.

6.2.2. CPU Workloads Prediction. Similar to the memory-intensive workloads, the experiments are repeated for the CPU intensive workloads from the dataset. Figure 7 depicts the estimation results of RVLBPNN, HMM, and NBC whilst predicting the CPU intensive workloads. The average prediction accuracy of NBC, HMM, and RVLBPNN models is 49.87%, 46.36%, and 52.70%, respectively, whilst predicting CPU intensive workloads, as shown in Figure 8. It can be observed that RVLBPNN exhibits better prediction accuracy than both HMM and NBC models by a margin of around 3% and 6%, respectively.

We further evaluated the efficiency of our proposed prediction model in predicting the CPU intensive workloads of different latency levels. Figure 9 depicts the estimation results of our proposed RVLBPNN model whilst predicting the CPU intensive workloads of different latency sensitivity levels. We observe a similar trend of prediction accuracy

between both memory and CPU workloads of different latency sensitivity levels. Again CPU intensive workloads of less latency levels are exhibiting better predictability, with the accuracy being 66.08% for level 3 workloads and 75.90% for level 0 workloads. This leads us to infer that least latency sensitivity level workloads exhibit a better rate of prediction accuracy for both CPU and memory-intensive workloads.

6.2.3. Interpretation and Discussion. From the experiment results, it is clearly evident that our proposed RVLBPNN model demonstrates better prediction accuracy than both HMM and NBC models by a considerable margin. Our proposed model outperforms the other two models whilst predicting both the CPU intensive and memory-intensive workloads. Meanwhile, we also observe that increasing levels of latency sensitivity of both CPU and memory-intensive workloads impose increasing error margin in the prediction results. Lower level of latency sensitivity exhibits better predictability. Since the majority of the Cloud workloads are of lower latency sensitivity levels, our proposed prediction model can accurately predict the trend of most of the arriving workloads. An increased level of intrinsic similarity among the arriving workloads facilitates a better learning rate of the neurons in the RVLBPNN model, which results in an increased prediction accuracy. From the experiments, we postulate that workloads should be treaded uniquely with respect to their computational demand latency sensitivity and user requirements for achieving a reliable level of prediction accuracy. Furthermore, workload prediction analytics can be benefitted with better accuracy when the workloads are analyzed at the task level rather than at the job level.

7. Conclusion

Green computing has turned out to be one of the important characteristics for achieving sustainable smart world in the future. Resource management by the way of predicting the expected workloads facilitates optimum scaling of the server resources, reducing the presence of idle resources and allocating appropriate levels of server resources to execute the user requests. The reliability and accuracy levels of such prediction techniques directly impacts important decision making in large-scale Cloud datacentre environments. In this paper, we propose a novel workload prediction model for the purpose of predicting the future workloads in Cloud datacentres. Our proposed novel workload prediction model, called RVLBPNN, is based on BP Neural Network algorithm and predicts the future workloads by the way of exploiting the intrinsic relationships among the arriving workloads. The experimental results indicate that the proposed RVLBPNN model achieves better precision and efficiency than the HMM-based and NBC-based prediction techniques. As a future work, we plan to explore the possibilities of further improving the prediction accuracy of our proposed approach. For instance, incorporating the periodicity effects of the workload behavior into RVLBPNN can further enhance the prediction accuracy. Meanwhile, investigating the efficiencies of our novel prediction method in predicting the anticipated workloads in similar distributed environments will be one of our future research directions.

Competing Interests

The authors declare that there is no conflict of interests.

Acknowledgments

This work was partially supported by the National Natural Science Foundation of China under Grants nos. 61502209 and 61502207 and the Natural Science Foundation of Jiangsu Province under Grant no. BK20130528.

References

[1] H. Al-Aqrabi, L. Liu, R. Hill, and N. Antonopoulos, "Cloud BI: future of business intelligence in the cloud," *Journal of Computer and System Sciences*, vol. 81, no. 1, pp. 85–96, 2015.

[2] T. V. T. Duy, Y. Sato, and Y. Inoguchi, "Performance evaluation of a green scheduling algorithm for energy savings in cloud computing," in *Proceedings of the IEEE International Symposium on Parallel & Distributed Processing, Workshops and Phd Forum (IPDPSW '10)*, pp. 1–8, Atlanta, Ga, USA, April 2010.

[3] L. Ceuppens, A. Sardella, and D. Kharitonov, "Power saving strategies and technologies in network equipment opportunities and challenges, risk and rewards," in *Proceedings of the International Symposium on Applications and the Internet (SAINT '08)*, pp. 381–384, August 2008.

[4] J. Li, B. Li, T. Wo et al., "CyberGuarder: a virtualization security assurance architecture for green cloud computing," *Future Generation Computer Systems*, vol. 28, no. 2, pp. 379–390, 2012.

[5] J. Panneerselvam, L. Liu, N. Antonopoulos, and Y. Bo, "Workload analysis for the scope of user demand prediction model evaluations in cloud environments," in *Proceedings of the 7th IEEE/ACM International Conference on Utility and Cloud Computing (UCC '14)*, pp. 883–889, December 2014.

[6] Z. Wan, "Sub-millisecond level latency sensitive cloud computing infrastructure," in *Proceedings of the 2010 International Congress on Ultra Modern Telecommunications and Control Systems and Workshops (ICUMT '10)*, pp. 1194–1197, Moscow, Russia, October 2010.

[7] H. Zhang, G. Jiang, K. Yoshihira, H. Chen, and A. Saxena, "Intelligent workload factoring for a hybrid cloud computing model," in *Proceedings of the Congress on Services—I (SERVICES '09)*, pp. 701–708, 2009.

[8] C. Glasner and J. Volkert, "Adaps—a three-phase adaptive prediction system for the run-time of jobs based on user behaviour," *Journal of Computer and System Sciences*, vol. 77, no. 2, pp. 244–261, 2011.

[9] C. A. L. Fehling, Frank, Retter et al., "CloudComputingPatterns2014," 2014.

[10] J. Wang, G. Jia, A. Li, G. Han, and L. Shu, "Behavior aware data placement for improving cache line level locality in cloud computing," *Journal of Internet Technology*, vol. 16, no. 4, pp. 705–716, 2015.

[11] G. Han, W. Que, G. Jia, and L. Shu, "An efficient virtual machine consolidation scheme for multimedia cloud computing," *Sensors*, vol. 16, no. 2, article 246, 2016.

[12] S. Mahambre, P. Kulkarni, U. Bellur, G. Chafle, and D. Deshpande, "Workload characterization for capacity planning and performance management in IaaS cloud," in *Proceedings of the 1st IEEE International Conference on Cloud Computing for Emerging Markets (CCEM '12)*, pp. 1–7, Bangalore, India, October 2012.

[13] A. Khan, X. Yan, S. Tao, and N. Anerousis, "Workload characterization and prediction in the cloud: a multiple time series approach," in *Proceedings of the IEEE Network Operations and Management Symposium (NOMS '12)*, pp. 1287–1294, IEEE, Maui, Hawaii, USA, April 2012.

[14] A. K. Mishra, J. L. Hellerstein, W. Cirne, and C. R. Das, "Towards characterizing cloud backend workloads: insights from Google compute clusters," *ACM SIGMETRICS Performance Evaluation Review*, vol. 37, no. 4, pp. 34–41, 2010.

[15] P. A. Dinda and D. R. O'Hallaron, "Host load prediction using linear models," *Cluster Computing*, vol. 3, no. 4, pp. 265–280, 2000.

[16] S. Di, D. Kondo, and W. Cirne, "Google hostload prediction based on Bayesian model with optimized feature combination," *Journal of Parallel and Distributed Computing*, vol. 74, no. 1, pp. 1820–1832, 2014.

[17] I. S. Moreno, P. Garraghan, P. Townend, and J. Xu, "An approach for characterizing workloads in google cloud to derive realistic resource utilization models," in *Proceedings of the IEEE 7th International Symposium on Service-Oriented System Engineering (SOSE '13)*, pp. 49–60, IEEE, Redwood City, Calif, USA, March 2013.

[18] N. Roy, A. Dubey, and A. Gokhale, "Efficient autoscaling in the cloud using predictive models for workload forecasting," in

Proceedings of the IEEE 4th International Conference on Cloud Computing (CLOUD '11), pp. 500–507, Washington, DC, USA, July 2011.

[19] Z. Wan, "Cloud Computing infrastructure for latency sensitive applications," in *Proceedings of the IEEE 12th International Conference on Communication Technology (ICCT '10)*, pp. 1399–1402, November 2010.

[20] M. S. Bali and S. Khurana, "Effect of latency on network and end user domains in cloud computing," in *Proceedings of the 2013 International Conference on Green Computing, Communication and Conservation of Energy (ICGCE '13)*, pp. 777–782, Chennai, India, December 2013.

[21] Z. Wan, P. Wang, J. Liu, and W. Tang, "Power-aware cloud computing infrastructure for latency-sensitive internet-of-things services," in *Proceedings of the UKSim 15th International Conference on Computer Modelling and Simulation (UKSim '13)*, pp. 617–621, April 2013.

[22] C. Reiss, J. Wilkes, and J. L. Hellerstein, "Google cluster-usage traces: format + schema," Tech. Rep., Google Inc., Mountain View, Calif, USA, 2011.

[23] Google, "Google Cluster Data V1," 2011, https://github.com/google/cluster-data/blob/master/ClusterData2011_2.md.

[24] J. Panneerselvam, L. Liu, N. Antonopoulos, and M. Trovati, "Latency-aware empirical analysis of the workloads for reducing excess energy consumptions at cloud datacentres," in *Proceedings of the IEEE 11th Symposium on Service-Oriented System Engineering (SOSE '16)*, pp. 62–70, Oxford, UK, March 2016.

[25] Z. Uykan, C. Güzeliş, and H. N. Koivo, "Analysis of input-output clustering for determining centers of RBFN," *IEEE Transactions on Neural Networks*, vol. 11, no. 4, pp. 851–858, 2000.

[26] X. Sun, Z. Yang, and Z. Wang, "The application of BP neutral network optimized by genetic algorithm in transportation data fusion," in *Proceedings of the IEEE 2nd International Conference on Advanced Computer Control (ICACC '10)*, pp. 560–563, Shenyang, China, March 2010.

[27] W. C. Wang, *BP Neural Network and Application in Automobile Engineering*, BeiJing Institute of Technology University, 1998.

[28] Z. Li, Q. Lei, X. Kouying, and Z. Xinyan, "A novel BP neural network model for traffic prediction of next generation network," in *Proceedings of the 5th International Conference on Natural Computation (ICNC '09)*, pp. 32–38, Tianjin, China, August 2009.

[29] M. T. Hagan, H. B. Demuth, and M. Beale, *Neural Network Design*, PWS Publishing, Boston, Mass, USA, 1996.

3

Applying Data Mining Techniques to Improve Information Security in the Cloud: A Single Cache System Approach

Amany AlShawi

King Abdulaziz City for Science and Technology, P.O. Box 6086, Riyadh 11442, Saudi Arabia

Correspondence should be addressed to Amany AlShawi; aalshawi@kacst.edu.sa

Academic Editor: José L. Vázquez-Poletti

Presently, the popularity of cloud computing is gradually increasing day by day. The purpose of this research was to enhance the security of the cloud using techniques such as data mining with specific reference to the single cache system. From the findings of the research, it was observed that the security in the cloud could be enhanced with the single cache system. For future purposes, an Apriori algorithm can be applied to the single cache system. This can be applied by all cloud providers, vendors, data distributors, and others. Further, data objects entered into the single cache system can be extended into 12 components. Database and SPSS modelers can be used to implement the same.

1. Introduction

The cloud is a combination of networks, management solutions, computing resources, business applications, and data storage. It supports a new era of information technology and customer service. Cloud computing is a technology that provides various services at minimal cost. It facilitates data storage and provides multiple levels of information security. By adopting cloud services, a user forgoes the additional cost of buying unnecessary computational resources. Cloud providers, such as Google and Microsoft, might adopt various data analysis techniques to extract valuable information from huge volumes of user data. They use these techniques to identify users' behaviors based on their search history analysis [1, 2].

Clouds offer three types of services: platform as a service (PaaS), infrastructure as a service (IaaS), and software as a service (SaaS). Most of the major technology firms, like Microsoft, Google, and Amazon, are now providing cloud facilities to different organizations. The cloud involves computing resources, namely, software and hardware. These are delivered as a service through the Internet. Organizations avoid constructing their own information technology infrastructures. Rather, they are provided with a substitute for hosting their data on the third-party system [3].

According to Wang et al. [4] and Van Wel and Royakkers [5], data mining is the process of examining data from various perspectives and converting it into useful information. It is widely used in economics and business applications. In addition, data mining is an essential component for knowledge discovery. It is usually applied to extract information and patterns understood by humans. Cloud computing providers use data mining to offer users cost-effective services.

If clients are unaware of the data being gathered, then ethical issues such as individuality and privacy are violated. If cloud providers misuse the data, such things could become a serious threat to the privacy of data. An attacker who rests outside the cloud network does not have authorized access to the cloud. Simultaneously, he does not have the chance to mine the data of the cloud. In both cases, attackers could adapt raw and cheap computing power given by cloud computing to mine data and obtain required information from the data [6, 7].

2. Problem

Cloud computing is gaining popularity because of its features, including multitenancy, scalability, minimized maintenance, and hardware cost. Cloud technology gives the client multifold facilities, but it also brings additional privacy and security issues. Cloud computing poses new, complicated security issues for numerous reasons. Conventional cryptographic primitives used for ensuring data security cannot be used directly. Assured correctness of storage under an update of dynamic data could be provided by the modification, insertion, and deletion of stored data [8]. Therefore, this study intended to focus on enhancing the security of the cloud. This was achieved through techniques of data mining, with specific reference to a single cache system.

3. Objectives

The objectives are as follows:

(i) Identify various security threats in cloud computing.

(ii) Enhance the security of the cloud through data mining techniques by making use of a single cache system.

(iii) Provide valuable suggestions to enhance the security of the cloud through data mining techniques.

4. Background

Dev et al. [3] developed an approach to safeguard cloud data privacy from the mining of database attacks. In their approach, it was stated that assuring the security of data in the cloud is a challenging issue. Cloud service providers and other third parties make use of these unique data mining techniques to obtain valuable information from users about the data stored on the cloud. The research focused on the effect of mining data on the cloud. Authors developed a distributed structure for eliminating mining-based privacy issues related to data in the cloud. The study approach integrated fragmentation, categorization, and distribution. Thereby, it safeguarded mining of the data by maintaining levels of privacy, separating chunks of data, and storing such data chunks for needed cloud providers. Apart from these functions, it was noted that the developed system provides an efficient way to protect privacy from mining-oriented attacks. However, this resulted in performance overhead when users require access to all data frequently. For example, some users might require carrying out a global analysis of data. Such analysis would require data to be obtained from various locations, which will result in degraded performance. It can be concluded that the developed system provided an efficient way to protect privacy from mining-oriented attacks. But it incorporated overhead performance when users require access to the entire data.

Sharma et al. [8] carried out research to enhance data security in cloud storage. This research focused on architectural components to provide data security for administrators and users. For ensuring the correctness of a client's information in the storage of cloud data, this study developed a flexible and effective distributed scheme. The scheme was an explicit support from dynamic data, encompassing block delete, update, and append operations. The study used the data encryption standard (DES) algorithm for information security. This algorithm allows information stored in the database to be seen in the required format. The database may be in the form of cipher text and, at the same time, can be accessed when the data are requested. This phenomenon is dependent on the erasure-correcting code distributing the file. The file is prepared to give vectors in redundancy parity and guarantee the dependability of data. By adopting tokens of homomorphism with erasure code and data distributed verification, the scheme achieved correct storage insurance integration and localization of data errors. That is, whenever corrupt data is tracked during the verification of storage correctness across the distributed servers, the misbehaving server's identification is guaranteed. Thus, it can be understood through the analysis that a distributed scheme was developed for assuring the accuracy of client information.

Aggarwal and Chaturvedi [9] reviewed how data mining techniques and relevant algorithms could play a significant role in ensuring data security in the cloud. The authors stated that, with the increase in humans' dependence on machines, developing a better and more effective framework for providing a secure electronic infrastructure is required. Clouds provide on-demand services at a much more minimal rate with fewer overheads. This practice maximizes the popularity of the cloud among different entities. However, the authors noted that problems with data security became crucial. This includes users' authentication services and data encryption and protection. In addition, they stated that it is essential to deploy data security in such a way that authorized users can obtain the maximum number of services. At the same time, it is important to enable the detection of unauthorized users in order to stop them from disrupting and misusing the cloud services. Data mining algorithms offer solutions for identifying and isolating data security attacks. Such attacks may range from information leakage to fraud and infringement.

Aishwarya S. Patil and Ankita S. Patil [10] reviewed data mining on the basis of cloud computing, which is a significant characteristic of infrastructure. It aids in making better and more efficient knowledge-driven decisions. It was noted that mining the data in cloud computing permits organizations to centralize software management and the storage of data. This resulted in the assurance of secure, reliable, and efficient client servicers.

Singh and Sapra [11] discussed the management of secure replication for storage in the cloud. They discussed general principles of a new approach to carry out secure replication, especially for stored data. The approach was a dominant technique that provides better outcomes for the availability and security of information. This research made use of the technique of secure replication for building a reliable and secure distributed storage. The enhancement carried out in this technique maximizes the quality by using unique data mart hosting with a cloud provider and this technique stores data based on its sensitivity. This technique is useful for financial organizations and cloud provider firms.

Thippa Reddy et al. [12] developed a novel framework for security management by deploying data for detecting, containing, and preventing attacks on cloud computing systems. The outcomes of the study were estimated and the

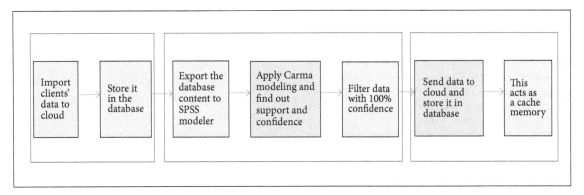

FIGURE 1: System architecture for a cloud provider.

architecture and its simulation outcomes were ratified by information security experts.

Sharma and Mehta [13] developed an effective distributed architecture to reduce the risks and enhance the security of the cloud using data mining. Authors sated that every day new attacks are discovered and new countermeasures are developed for keeping data secure. Providers and attackers utilize effective data mining techniques to obtain information regarding a client's data stored in the cloud. However, a distributed architecture was developed for eliminating such threats found in cloud computing. At the same time, the authors noted that overheads were seen in the system. Therefore, the concept of cache memory was deployed by creating frequent item sets with the help of tools related to data mining. Thus, it can be concluded that the cache memory concept was implemented to eliminate the threats identified in the cloud computing environment.

Zissis and Lekkas [14] developed unique cloud principles for controlling security threats. They adopted software engineering and information system design approaches. The study illustrated that security in a cloud environment requires a systemic point of view, from which security will be constructed based on trust, mitigating protection to a trusted third party. Kumar et al. [15] discussed encryption techniques. They applied data compression to utilize secret keys, especially at the main server level when uploading information to the clouds. Khorshed et al. [16] focused on types of attacks that are found in the cloud using a support vector machine.

Bhadauria et al. [17] discussed security at various levels through application, network, and virtualization in the cloud computing environment. Their study developed security frameworks on the basis of the mechanism of a one-time pass key. Apart from this, the authors found that the uniqueness of developed security protocols lies in their concept, and this gives security to users and service providers in a highly conflicting cloud computing environment.

Research by Sasireka and Raja [18] developed an approach to enhance the privacy of cloud data by safeguarding it from data mining-oriented attacks. It was observed that the developed approach adopts multiple cloud data distributors and providers. These distributors and providers perform data categorization, fragmentation, and distribution. In such a system, cloud providers are not aware of the identity of the user. However, date restoration from the clouds was a very complicated task.

5. Implementation

Cloud providers and distributors of data are two main system components. Distributors of cloud data acquire data in file form from the users. These files are separated into chunks, and then they are distributed across different providers in the cloud. In addition to this, the chunked data are stored by the cloud provider and are often accessed by a client after they are examined. The client stores such information separately in another file, which performs like a cache. The cloud provider responds to the queries of the distributor by providing data from the cache instead of searching through the whole chunk of data, which is a more time-intensive process. Therefore, the file is mostly accessed data that performs as cache memory, thereby maximizing the distributed architecture efficiency, as depicted in Figure 1. Users do not interact with providers in the cloud directly, rather doing so through a cloud data distributor.

This study deployed the single cache memory concept in the distributed architecture. Such architecture offers users better security for all of their cloud data. Whenever a client supplies information to a cloud, data chucks are created and stored by various cloud providers. If the user needs to perform global operations involving all data chunks frequently, this will result in performance overhead. This is due to the fact that the system must access information from different cloud providers resulting in degraded performance. In order to minimize the encountered overhead, the proposed system model examines the data chunks. The information is transmitted to a data mining tool to develop association rules that assist in determining frequent sets of items that have 100 percent confidence. This is achieved using a Carma model, an Apriori algorithm, and other methods. These are referred to as association rules in the mining in relational databases and large transactions [19, 20].

Input or target fields are not required in the Carma model. This is useful to make the algorithm work in a similar way to the construction of an Apriori model. You have the freedom to constrain or to select the items which should be listed as antecedents or consequents by refining the model after it has been created, for example, by the use of model browser which helps to locate either the list of products or the services (antecedents) whose subsequent is the item that you want to popularize.

SPSS modeler is a data mining workbench used for the analysis of organized numerical data to create outcomes and make future predictions that lend predictive intelligence to business decision-making. Use of predictive intelligence creates effective strategies as it permits the organization to analyze its trends and provide insight to future interpretation. For example, public sector organizations utilize SPSS modeler tools to predict their workforce capacity and take measures to maintain public safety issues. Additionally, the tools can quickly extract and determine personal opinions from text in more than 30 languages and help build more detailed outcomes.

Item sets that appear in most of the baskets are assumed to be frequent. To have a formal definition, assume that there is a number T support threshold. If S is an item set, support for S is the basket number for which S is a subset. Assume S is frequent, which means its support is T or greater. Frequent item data sets are denoted as an "if-then" collection of rules. Association rules form $S \rightarrow R$, where S is the items set and R is an item. An association rule's implication is that if all the S items are in some basket, then R is likely to be seen in the same basket. Moreover, a notion of what is likely could be formalized by explaining rule confidence $S \rightarrow R$ to be the support ratio for $S \cup \{R\}$. Rule confidence is the basket's fraction with all of S that involves R.

To deploy the cache memory, the following steps were implemented:

(1) User information was stored in a cloud database.

(2) A file was imported by a data mining tool (SPSS modeler) in an Excel format.

(3) Carma modeling was selected to develop the frequent set of items and association rules.

(4) Data were filtered for acquiring the values that have 100 percent confidence.

(5) Information with 100 percent confidence was then posted in the cloud environment.

6. Discussion

No one can claim that it is possible to develop a hundred percent secure network that is immune to all types of attacks. As new threats and compromises are being initiated every day, system developers must improve their countermeasures to keep data private and secure. In light of the tremendous benefits offered by cloud computing, more and more organizations chose to utilize their services to improve performance and decrease cost. However, cloud providers are susceptible to attacks and security threats from insiders and outsiders [1, 3, 4].

Attackers could use multiple computing techniques to extract information about the user from the data stored in

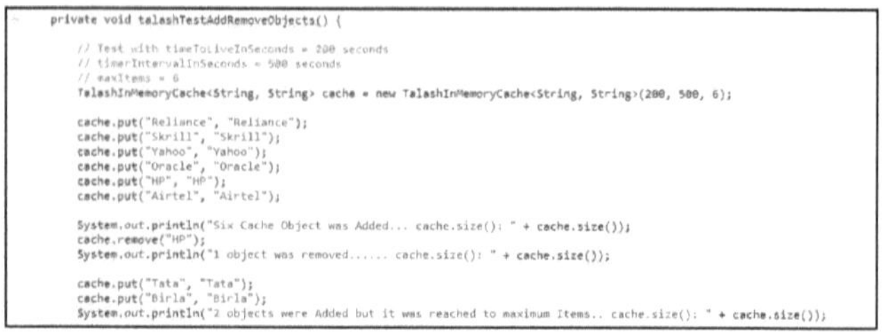

```
private void talashTestAddRemoveObjects() {

    // Test with timeToLiveInSeconds = 200 seconds
    // timerIntervalInSeconds = 500 seconds
    // maxItems = 6
    TalashInMemoryCache<String, String> cache = new TalashInMemoryCache<String, String>(200, 500, 6);

    cache.put("Reliance", "Reliance");
    cache.put("Skrill", "Skrill");
    cache.put("Yahoo", "Yahoo");
    cache.put("Oracle", "Oracle");
    cache.put("HP", "HP");
    cache.put("Airtel", "Airtel");

    System.out.println("Six Cache Object was Added... cache.size(): " + cache.size());
    cache.remove("HP");
    System.out.println("1 object was removed...... cache.size(): " + cache.size());

    cache.put("Tata", "Tata");
    cache.put("Birla", "Birla");
    System.out.println("2 objects were Added but it was reached to maximum Items.. cache.size(): " + cache.size());
```

FIGURE 2: Adding objects to the cloud.

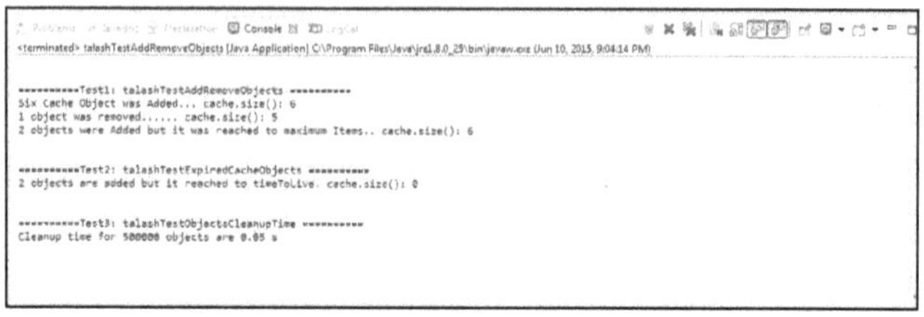

```
<terminated> talashTestAddRemoveObjects [Java Application] C:\Program Files\Java\jre1.8.0_25\bin\javaw.exe (Jun 10, 2015, 9:04:14 PM)

==========Test1: talashTestAddRemoveObjects ==========
Six Cache Object was Added... cache.size(): 6
1 object was removed...... cache.size(): 5
2 objects were Added but it was reached to maximum Items.. cache.size(): 6

==========Test2: talashTestExpiredCacheObjects ==========
2 objects are added but it reached to timeToLive. cache.size(): 0

==========Test3: talashTestObjectsCleanupTime ==========
Cleanup time for 500000 objects are 0.05 s
```

FIGURE 3: Removing objects from the cloud.

the cloud. This research proposes a distributed cloud architecture to increase security and minimize the effect of such malicious attacks. However, this will result in overheads since users might require to access certain data components very frequently. Hence cache memory concept was implemented in the proposed system by generating frequent item sets using data mining tools. Even if an attacker gains access to the cloud provider's storage space, only one chunk of data will be exposed. Even though this architecture increases data security, it involves a considerable amount of overhead if the user decides to access the whole data set frequently. To overcome this drawback, data mining tools are used to determine the most frequently used data chunks, which would then be stored in a temporary cache memory [2, 9].

The proposed distributed architecture provides better data privacy and security. This is achieved through having multiple attack targets, or cloud providers, instead of just one. This will surely require attackers to invest more time and effort to be able to gain access. Additionally, the system decreases the amount of data available at each target. So even if one cloud provider's system is compromised, attackers will gain access to incomplete data. Adding the concept of a single cache will ensure greater data availability.

Figure 2 is a snapshot of the code showing the objects added to the cloud. Six cloud provider items were utilized including Yahoo, Reliance, Aircel, Oracle, Skrill, and HP to store multiple data chunks. The six items would be stored in the temporary cache memory to be available for frequent access requests and after a specific amount of time the stored objects would be deleted from the cache.

Figure 3 is a snapshot of the code showing the removal of objects. When the six objects were added in the cache, they were not stored in any database. Storing them in the cache memory was a temporary operation to perform necessary analysis or any other computational operation. A time limit was generated for the purpose of testing to delete those data chunks. The data would be automatically deleted after a specific time limit. So objects were added in the cache and removed when each reached its maximum item time limit.

For example, if a big online e-commerce site adopting a cloud server needs to frequently store client-visiting data, it could combine the proposed tool and all of its related information with its Web application. That would be achieved through a direct connection with the function "cache.put" as shown in Figure 2. When entering information into the cache, there is a different procedure for each vendor. Vendors have to adopt their own functional application programming interfaces to connect with the cache system.

7. Conclusion and Future Work

The purpose of this research is to enhance the security of the cloud through data mining techniques with specific reference to a single cache system. This study is limited to specific cloud computing applications and the research findings make use of a single cache system. The proposed technique focuses on maintaining security of the cloud through data mining techniques.

As illustrated in the research, e-commerce websites adopt a cloud server and store multiple frequent data sets related to the clients who visit their websites. They combine their Web applications with the cloud services. In addition, they import users' data to the cloud and store them in the cloud database. Thereafter, the cloud exports the contents of the database to the SPSS modeler, applies Carma modeling, identifies support and confidence, and filters data or information with 100 percent confidence. It was observed that, with the single cache system, the security of the cloud application could be enhanced. For future work, an Apriori algorithm can be applied to the single cache system for all cloud providers, vendors, and data distributors. Further, the single cache system can be extended to include 12 objects, which could then be used to implement the database-to-SPSS modeler.

Competing Interests

The author declares no competing interests regarding the publication of this paper.

References

[1] L. Hao and D. Han, "The study and design on secure-cloud storage system," in *Proceedings of the International Conference on Electrical and Control Engineering (ICECE '11)*, pp. 5126–5129, Yichang, China, September 2011.

[2] S. Gupta, S. R. Satapathy, P. Mehta, and A. Tripathy, "A secure and searchable data storage in cloud computing," in *Proceedings of the 3rd IEEE International Advance Computing Conference (IACC '13)*, pp. 106–109, IEEE, Ghaziabad, India, February 2013.

[3] H. Dev, T. Sen, M. Basak, and M. Eunus Ali, "An approach to protect the privacy of cloud data from data mining based attacks," in *Proceedings of the 2012 SC Companion: High Performance Computing, Networking Storage and Analysis (SCC '12)*, pp. 1106–1115, 2012.

[4] J. Wang, J. Wan, Z. Liu, and P. Wang, "Data mining of mass storage based on cloud computing," in *Proceedings of the 9th International Conference on Grid and Cloud Computing (GCC '10)*, pp. 426–431, Shanghai, China, November 2010.

[5] L. Van Wel and L. Royakkers, "Ethical issues in web data mining," *Ethics and Information Technology*, vol. 6, no. 2, pp. 129–140, 2004.

[6] Q. Yang and X. Wu, "10 Challenging problems in data mining research," *International Journal of Information Technology and Decision Making*, vol. 5, no. 4, pp. 597–604, 2006.

[7] L. Torgo, *Data Mining with R: Learning with Case Studies*, Chapman & Hall/CRC, New York, NY, USA, 2010.

[8] S. Sharma, A. Chugh, and A. Kumar, "Enhancing data security in cloud storage," *International Journal of Advanced Research in Computer and Communication Engineering*, vol. 2, no. 5, pp. 2132–2134, 2013.

[9] P. Aggarwal and M. M. Chaturvedi, "Application of data mining techniques for information security in a cloud: a survey," *International Journal of Computer Applications*, vol. 80, no. 13, pp. 11–17, 2013.

[10] A. S. Patil, "A review on data mining based cloud computing," *International Journal of Research in Science and Engineering*, vol. 1, no. 1, pp. 1–14, 2014.

[11] S. Singh and R. Sapra, "Secure replication management in cloud storage," *International Journal of Emerging Trends and Technology in Computer Science*, vol. 3, no. 2, pp. 251–254, 2014.

[12] G. Thippa Reddy, K. Sudheer, K. Rajesh, and K. Lakshmanna, "Employing data mining on highly secured private clouds for implementing a security-asa- service framework," *Journal of Theoretical and Applied Information Technology*, vol. 59, no. 2, pp. 317–326, 2014.

[13] S. Sharma and H. Mehta, "Improving Cloud Security Using Data Mining," *IOSR Journal of Computer Engineering*, vol. 16, no. 1, pp. 66–69, 2014.

[14] D. Zissis and D. Lekkas, "Addressing cloud computing security issues," *Future Generation Computer Systems*, vol. 28, no. 3, pp. 583–592, 2012.

[15] A. Kumar, H. Lee, and R. P. Singh, "Efficient and secure cloud storage for handling big data," in *Proceedings of the 6th International Conference on New Trends in Information Science and Service Science and Data Mining (ISSDM '12)*, pp. 162–166, Taipei, Taiwan, October 2012.

[16] M. T. Khorshed, A. B. M. S. Ali, and S. A. Wasimi, "A survey on gaps, threat remediation challenges and some thoughts for proactive attack detection in cloud computing," *Future Generation Computer Systems*, vol. 28, no. 6, pp. 833–851, 2012.

[17] R. Bhadauria, R. Borgohain, A. Biswas, and S. Sanyal, "Secure authentication of cloud data mining API," *Acta Technica Corviniensis-Bulletin of Engineering*, vol. 3, no. 1, 2014.

[18] K. Sasireka and K. Raja, "An approach to improve cloud data privacy by preventing from data mining based attacks," *International Journal of Scientific and Research Publications*, vol. 4, no. 2, pp. 1–4, 2014.

[19] J. Han and M. Kamber, *Data Mining: Concepts and Techniques*, Morgan Kaufmann Publishers, San Francisco, Calif, USA, 2006.

[20] J. Han, "Data mining techniques," in *Proceedings of the ACM SIGMOD International Conference on Management of Data (SIGMOD '96)*, p. 545, Montreal, Canada, June 1996.

4

A Two-Tier Energy-Aware Resource Management for Virtualized Cloud Computing System

Wei Huang,[1] **Zhen Wang,**[2] **Mianxiong Dong,**[3] **and Zhuzhong Qian**[2]

[1]*School of Computer Engineering, Nanjing Institute of Technology, Nanjing 211167, China*
[2]*State Key Lab. for Novel Software Technology, Nanjing University, Nanjing 210023, China*
[3]*Department of Information and Electronic Engineering, Muroran Institute of Technology, Muroran 050-8585, Japan*

Correspondence should be addressed to Zhuzhong Qian; qzz@nju.edu.cn

Academic Editor: Tomàs Margalef

The economic costs caused by electric power take the most significant part in total cost of data center; thus energy conservation is an important issue in cloud computing system. One well-known technique to reduce the energy consumption is the consolidation of Virtual Machines (VMs). However, it may lose some performance points on energy saving and the Quality of Service (QoS) for dynamic workloads. Fortunately, Dynamic Frequency and Voltage Scaling (DVFS) is an efficient technique to save energy in dynamic environment. In this paper, combined with the DVFS technology, we propose a cooperative two-tier energy-aware management method including local DVFS control and global VM deployment. The DVFS controller adjusts the frequencies of homogenous processors in each server at run-time based on the practical energy prediction. On the other hand, Global Scheduler assigns VMs onto the designate servers based on the cooperation with the local DVFS controller. The final evaluation results demonstrate the effectiveness of our two-tier method in energy saving.

1. Introduction

Cloud computing provides elastic computing resources on a pay-as-you-go basis for most conceivable forms of applications but it also causes huge amounts of electric energy consumption. Almost 0.5% of world's total power usage is consumed by the servers in data centers [1]. Among them, processors (CPUs) account for the most significant part of power and have the most dynamical power that can be adjusted, while other components can only be completely or partially turned off [2]. Owing to these reasons, reducing energy consumption of processors using the dynamic nature of CPUs' power has become a hot research topic in cloud computing system.

To service more users for more income, service providers prefer to share cluster resources among users. In cloud environments, the virtualization technique is widely adopted to allow users to share the physical resources. Making the working servers for Virtual Machines (VMs) as less as possible and letting the idle servers be in a low-power mode will improve the utilization of resources and reduce energy consumption, which is known as VM consolidation. In each server, by applying Dynamic Voltage and Frequency Scaling (DVFS), which enables dynamic adjustment of execution frequency on demand, more energy can be saved. The dynamic power consumption of CPU is proportional to the frequency and to the square of voltage. Scaling down the execution frequency will reduce the power while it may also reduce the performance and increase the execution time, which may instead cause more energy consumption (energy is equal to the line integral of power P to time t, $E = \int_0^t P \, dt$). On the other hand, real-time tasks in the cloud computing system usually have requirements on execution speed; the extension of execution time may violate QoS requirements. Thus, it is nontrivial to reduce energy consumption by scaling the execution frequencies of tasks [3].

VM consideration could improve the resource indeed and many previous works [4–6] achieve significant result on energy saving in virtualized cloud system. However, most of them do not take the advantage of DVFS strategy. Some others only apply the DVFS after allocation while not considering the influence of DVFS before allocation. However, if taking impacts of DVFS technique on energy into consideration before allocation, much more energy can be reduced. But it is not trivial to minimize the total energy consumption by VM allocation algorithm and DVFS strategies in this way. Several problems need to be solved: (1) how to define Quality of Service (QoS) requirements; (2) which servers can load arrival VMs with requirements; (3) which server brings minimum energy consumption by DVFS for arrival VMs and ensures QoS requirements.

In this paper, we propose a cooperative two-tier energy-aware management by taking the DVFS into consideration, which offload real-time tasks to VMs on clusters and scaling frequencies. On the local tier, we propose a novel way to find the best combinations of frequencies of different CPUs that consume the least energy based on the practical energy prediction. We take both the frequency-power and utilization-power relationship into consideration when forecasting energy consumption. On the global tier, by cooperating with local DVFS controller, the Global Scheduler assigns a VM to its favourite processor in a cluster that brings minimum energy change. The frequency to execute the arrival workload has been decided before allocation instead of after allocation. The framework proposed in this paper takes both the energy consumption and performance into consideration and achieves good tradeoff between energy and consumption. The status of each hosts is controlled by the global master by regular communication, so the master can control the energy consumption and performance. Meanwhile, the computing can be done in parallel in each candidate for allocation to improve the effectiveness of computation. In summary, the main contributions of this paper are as follows:

(i) We propose the multiprocessor power model, which is shown to be close to the real power consumption of a server according to the evaluation of the model. The multiprocessor power model helps us to precisely estimate the energy consumption.

(ii) We transform the energy minimization problem of frequency scaling to a node searching problem in directed graphs. We also prove that the optimal state which consumes the least energy can be found from an initial state in which all processors' frequencies are maximum.

(iii) We provide a novel scheduling algorithm, which can work in parallel and efficiently cooperates with local DVFS controller, for the problem of energy-aware scheduling. The experiments justify the effectiveness of our strategy on energy saving.

The rest of this paper is organized as follows. Section 2 introduces some related works. Section 3 introduces the framework of our solution and Section 4 introduces the task model and the analysis of the request of a VM. In Section 5, we introduce the energy prediction method and energy minimizing algorithm of local DVFS controller. The global VM allocation algorithm is presented in Section 6. In Section 7, we evaluate our solution through some experiments. Finally, we conclude this paper in Section 8.

2. Related Work

Reducing energy consumption has already been a critical issue of data center in recent years. Many works study the energy saving strategies in virtualized environment. Kusic et al. [7] defined a dynamic resource management as a sequential optimization in virtualized environment. The sequential optimization whose objective is maximizing the profit of provider is solved using Limited Lookahead Control (LLC) by minimizing both energy cost and SLA. But the framework captures the behavior of each application by simulation-based learning and the complexity of the model makes the approach not suitable for large scale data center.

In [8], the authors have developed dynamic resource provisioning and allocation problem with virtualized technique for energy-efficient cloud computing. They propose self-manage and energy-aware mechanisms to allocate the Virtual Machines (VMs) and migrate VMs according to CPU utilizations and energy consumption. The placing problem of allocation which can be seen as a bin packing problem is solved by Modification Best Fit Decreasing (MBFD). For the migration problem, three policies are proposed to choose VMs to migrate in order to reduce energy consumption.

Cardosa et al. [9] have presented a novel approach for power-efficient VM placement for the heterogeneous data centers by leveraging min-max and share features of the VMs based on the DVFS and soft scaling technique. The power consumption and utilization obtained from the running time of a VM are optimized by being set a priori. However, their approach does not strictly support SLAs and the information of applications' priorities is needed. Cao and Dong [10] propose an energy-aware heuristic framework for VM consolidation which can obtain a better tradeoff between energy saving and performance. A SLA violation decision algorithm is proposed to determine hosts' status for SLA violation. Based on the hosts' status, the minimum power and maximum utilization policy for VM migration are used to achieve the energy saving.

Reference [11] maximizes the utilization at virtual machine level in the environment of container. The objective of the paper is to dynamically set the sizes of virtual machines in order to improve the utilization of VMs, which saves overall energy consumption. Experiments show that their method can achieve 7.55% of energy consumption compared to scenarios where the virtual machine sizes are fixed. Reference [12] proposes a VM allocation algorithm to reduce energy consumption and SLA violation, which uses the historical record of VMs' usage.

Some other works mainly focus on the DVFS strategy to decrease processors' power consumption in hosts. Some of them periodically adjust the frequency according to the performance of server. Reference [13] monitors the utilization of processors periodically and the frequency is decreased very carefully when there are observable impacts on execution time of tasks. Hsu and Feng [14] proposed a β-adaption algorithm that periodically evaluates the performance and automatically adapts the frequency and voltage at run-time. Reference [15] also developed the periodic DVFS controller for multicore processor without using any performance model.

However, the length of period has a great impact on the performance of algorithms, it should be evaluated very carefully.

Scaling the frequency according to the types of workloads is another efficient way to carry out DVFS control. They achieve the goal of energy saving with a little or limited performance loss by decreasing the frequency during the communication, data access, memory access, or idle phases. Lim et al. [16] proposed a run-time scheduler that applies DVFS control during the communication phases which is identified by intercepting the MPI calls. In [17], the authors presented a novel algorithm that utilizes the opportunities in execution of hybrid MPI/OpenMP application to scale the frequency and reduce energy consumption. Tan et al. implement the DVFS scheduling strategy for data intensive application in [18] and achieved the energy saving. Their strategy adaptively sets the suitable frequency according to the percentage of CPU-bound time in the total execution time of workloads and is implemented in source code level.

The DVFS is able to reduce the energy consumption, but it is limited on a single server. A lot of work developed the DVFS-based task scheduling among servers because the distribution of workloads influences the overall energy. References [19, 20] propose similar energy-aware strategies that schedule a set of tasks onto physical machine. They adjust supply voltage by utilizing slack time of noncritical jobs. Reference [19] also discussed the tradeoff between energy consumption and scheduling length. Khan and Ahmad [21] studied the problem of task allocation in grid and they utilized the cooperative game theory to minimize the energy consumption and makespan of tasks for DVFS-based clusters. Similar to [21], Mezmaz et al. studied the problem for the dependent precedence-constrained parallel applications [22]. Different to these works, we study the independent real-time services with deadline constraints in multiprocessor system.

References [23–27] researched energy-efficient task scheduling for real-time system. Luo and Jha studied the scheduling of periodic tasks in heterogeneous system and gave a power-efficient solution [27]. In [24], authors proposed an energy-aware task partitioning algorithm with polynomial time complexity for DVFS-based heterogeneous system. Awan and Petters proposed an energy-aware partitioning of tasks method which consists of two phases and they use a realistic power model to estimate power consumption [23]. Our task allocating algorithm cooperates with the local DVFS controller to predict the energy consumption in different situations; the influence of frequency scaling to energy consumption is taken into account before allocation for saving more energy.

3. Overview

Our framework can accept and analyze the arrival workloads and package them by Virtual Machines (VMs) and allocate them to the suitable server to reduce energy consumption. We first describe the architecture of our solution in Figure 1 and subsequently introduce the real-time analysis in this section [3]. In our solution, the *Global Scheduler* assigns a task to a VM to execute it and guarantees its QoS requirement. This VM will be allocated to a host which can offload it without

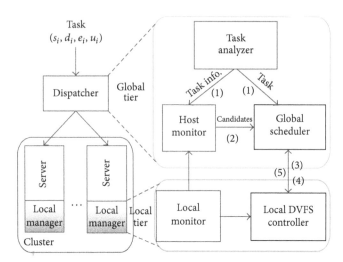

FIGURE 1: System architecture of our solution to the energy-aware resource management.

causing any violation of QoS requirement and brings minimum energy consumption. Our objective is to find the allocation method for VMs and frequencies scaling method for tasks to reduce the energy consumption.

Definition 1 (host model). Let $host_j = (U_j, F_j)$ be denoted as resources of jth host, where U_j and F_j are vectors that record the utilizations and frequencies of each processor.

The *Task Analyzer* in Dispatcher receives and analyzes the information of incoming task and sends it to other components when necessary. The *Host Monitor* is an assistant component which connects to each server and gathers the basic information of servers. The *Local Monitor* monitors the resources of a server and sends the basic information to *Host Monitor* when necessary. The basic information of servers is recorded in the *Host Model* (Definition 1). We mainly focus on the resource of processor, so we only record the states of processors in the *Host Model*. The main work mechanism of our solution to schedule a new task request $task_n$ is described as follows:

(1) When $task_n$ comes, the *Task Analyzer* analyzes the basic information of $task_n$ and sends it to the *Host Monitor* and *Global Scheduler* (Section 6).

(2) When the *Host Monitor* receives the information of $task_n$, it selects a set of candidates who can load $task_n$ according to the basic information of servers and sends the set to the *Global Scheduler*. In the large datacenter, the number of candidates can be carefully selected to improve the effectiveness of allocation.

(3) When the *Global Scheduler* receives the candidates and the basic information of $task_n$, it sends the task information to the servers who are in the candidate set.

(4) When a candidate receives the task information, the *local DVFS controller* (Section 5) will run to estimate the minimum energy change if $task_n$ is allocated to

one of its VM according to the monitored information. Then the controller returns the result to the *Global Scheduler*.

(5) When the *Global Scheduler* receives responses from all the candidates, it allocates $task_n$ to the best server using our allocation algorithm. There may be some network error in communications like packet error or loss or high network delay. We can set some threshold for the *Global Scheduler*, for example, time threshold for response time or retry times. When response time or retry times of a candidate are larger than the thresholds, the *Global Scheduler* can discard this candidate.

This is the simple architecture for energy-aware task scheduling and some project implemented details or optimizations are not discussed in this paper. We mainly focus on the energy-aware scheduling for tasks and provide a solution to this problem. Some problems like single point of failure and network error are also important for the distributed cloud system. We consider that these problems have the maturing solutions in today's cloud system and these aspects may not be a problem to our solution.

4. Task Model

The request of service in the cloud computing system usually has deadline constraints which is the major aspect of Service Level Agreements (SLAs). We explore energy saving method for the cluster that accepts request for tasks. We define the *task model* (Definition 2) to describe the request for a task. The task model records some important information that users provide. s_i and d_i describe the requirements of tasks and e_i and u_i describe the execution characters of tasks.

Definition 2 (task model). Let $task_i = (s_i, d_i, e_i, u_i)$ describe ith task, where s_i, d_i, e_i, u_i represent the start time, relative deadline, predicted execution time, and the average utilization, respectively.

For the isolation, scalability, and stability of system, tasks are usually run in the VMs independently in the cloud computing system. We can regard each task as a VM, so the allocation of the tasks is equivalent to the allocation of VMs in some degree. In our model, we assign a task to a VM to run and the VM will be allocated to appropriate host. When a task finishes, the VM loading this task will be shut off or turned into sleep. The living time for a VM to run a task is equal to the execution time of this task. Therefore, the living time for the VM should not exceed the deadline of the tasks. Let VM_i represent the virtual machine load $task_i$.

We designed the *Task Analyzer* to accept and analyze the incoming request of tasks. It sends the basic information of tasks to other components after preprocessing. The living time of a task (i.e., VM) usually includes computing time and CPU idle time. The CPU idle time may consist of communication, memory, or disk access. The real-time analysis we designed is to distinguish the computing time and CPU idle time. The average utilization of a VM can reflect

the computation and CPU idle time in some degree. Let $T_c(f)$ and T_i represent computing time at frequency f and idle time of a VM, respectively. We estimate the computing time $T_c(f_{max}) = e_i \cdot u_i$ and idle time $T_i = e_i \cdot (1 - u_i)$ for ith task. The *Task Analyzer* calculates $T_c(f_{max})$ and T_i and sends these information to other modules.

The computing time has a tight relation to the CPU frequency which shows a linear extension to the reduction in frequency [28, 29], while the idle time of a task will barely change due to frequency scaling. Therefore, the living time of the VM of ith task frequency f can be expressed as

$$T^i(f) = T_c(f_{max}) \frac{f_{max}}{f} + T_i. \tag{1}$$

When the *local DVFS controller* predicts the energy consumption in different frequency, the living time of VMs can be calculated by (1) according to the task information provided by Task Analyzer. Although the running time can be predicted under different frequency, the energy prediction and DVFS controller are not a easy task. We will introduce details of our method to solve them in next sections.

5. Local DVFS Controller

The *DVFS Controller* plays an important role in our framework and it has two main functions. On the one hand, it predicts the energy consumption of a multiprocessor server according to the processors' utilizations, frequencies, and the living time of VMs. On the other hand, based on the energy prediction, it runs the *k-Phase energy Prediction (kPP)* algorithm to find the best frequencies combinations that bring minimum energy consumption.

5.1. Energy Prediction for Multiprocessor Servers. The electric energy consumption is the integral of the active power with respect to time. Therefore, the power prediction of server is crucial. Previous works like [30–34] provided serval methods to estimate the power of a server. However, they only focused on the frequency-power or utilization-power relationship and the detailed power prediction for multiprocessor platform is also ignored. In this paper, we provide a practical power prediction for multiprocessor servers based on the frequency-power and utilization-power relationship. We utilize the fact that the homogenous processors will consume the same power when they are under the same condition to predict the power consumption.

The power consumption of a server consists of two parts: static and dynamic power consumption. The static parts include the power consumption of main board, hard disk, fan, and so forth. CPU accounts for the largest part of dynamic power. According to the previous studies, the dynamic power consumption of CPU is proportional to the frequency and to the square of voltage [34], which can be express as

$$P_{dynamic} \simeq A \times C \times V^2 \times f, \tag{2}$$

where A is the percentage of active gates, C is total capacitance, V is supply voltage, and f is the operating frequency. According to [31], the voltage has a linear relationship to

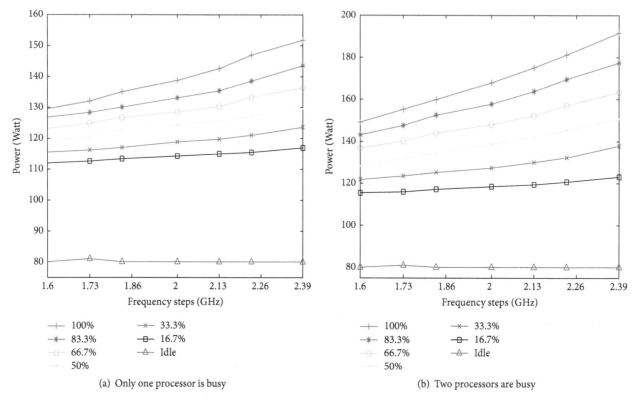

(a) Only one processor is busy

(b) Two processors are busy

FIGURE 2: Real power consumption of Dell R710 whose configurations are introduced in Table 1 and the legend represents the different utilizations.

frequency, so the dynamic power of a processor can be reduced as a function of frequency: $P_{\text{dynamic}} = \alpha \times f^3$, where α is a proportional coefficient. Processors also have static power when they are active. Let P_s represent the static power of a server and P_{CPU_s} represent the static power of processor. The power of a host in which all homogenous processors work in the same frequency f with full utilization can be expressed as follows:

$$P(f) = P_s + N_c \left(P_{\text{CPU}_s} + \alpha f^3 \right), \qquad (3)$$

where N_c is the number of CPUs. We want to eliminate the static power of processors, which is not easy to measure. For a given host, we can easily measure its maximum power which is $P_{\text{max}} = P_s + N_c(P_{\text{CPU}_s} + \alpha f_{\text{max}}^3)$. Therefore, we can estimate the power consumption of a host in which all processors work in the same frequency f:

$$P(f) = P_{\text{max}} - \alpha N_c \left(f_{\text{max}}^3 - f^3 \right). \qquad (4)$$

The power consumption is also related to utilizations. Figure 2(a) shows the power consumption with only one processor running and Figure 2(b) shows the power of two processors that work in same utilization and frequency. As we can see, the power with different utilization under same frequency is different. The power and the utilization present a linear relationship which is with one voice to [30, 32, 33].

Therefore, the power consumption of one homogenous CPU with frequency f and utilization u can be denoted as

$$P_{\text{CPU}}(u, f) = \frac{1}{N_c} \left[P_{\text{max}} - P_s - \alpha N_c \left(f_{\text{max}}^3 - f^3 \right) \right] u. \qquad (5)$$

Finally, the power of prediction of a homogenous multiprocessor server can be expressed as

$$
\begin{aligned}
P_{\text{host}} &= P_s + \sum_{c=1}^{N_c} P_{\text{CPU}}^c \\
&= P_s \\
&\quad + \frac{1}{N_c} \sum_{c=1}^{N_c} \left[P_{\text{max}} - P_s - \alpha N_c \left(f_{\text{max}}^3 - F_{j,c}^3 \right) \right] U_{j,c}.
\end{aligned} \qquad (6)
$$

We can view the power of jth host as a function of utilizations and frequencies, which is presented as $P_{\text{host}}(F_j, U_j)$, where U_j and F_j are defined in *Host Model*.

Definition 3 (Frequency Scaling Unit). A time interval $[t_1, t_2]$ is a Frequency Scaling Unit (FSU) if (1) $\forall t \in [t_1, t_2)$, $NT(t) = NT(t_1)$ and (2) $NT(\cdot)$ changes at t_1 and t_2, where $NT(t)$ represents the number of VMs at time t in a server.

The energy consumption depends on both the execution time and the power. We define the concept of *Frequency Scaling Unit* (FSU, Definition 3) to estimate the living time

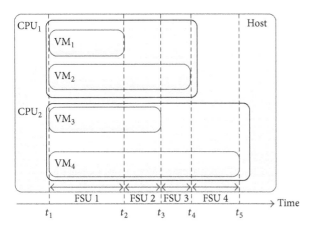

FIGURE 3: An example of FSU.

of VMs. The FSU represents a period of time that the number of VMs does not change. Once the number of VMs changes, that is, a VM coming or leaving, it enters the next FSU. An example of FSU is shown in Figure 3, which includes four FSUs. Assuming a VM is stopped at time t_2 and next VM is ended at time t_3, then $T = t_3 - t_2$ is an FSU. If a VM is allocated to the server at t_1 and the VM finished at t_2, $T = t_2 - t_1$ is said to the *first FSU* from current time. It is obvious that the number of VMs in the host is equal to the number of FSUs if all VMs finish at the different time, and we suppose that VMs are ended at the different time in a host in the rest of this paper.

If we set consistent frequencies for all processors in an FSU, the power state in this FSU is relatively stable because the workloads in this FSU are fixed. We know the length of this FSU, so the energy consumption in an FSU can be predicted conveniently and precisely by the following equation: $E = P \times T$, where P and T represent power and time, respectively. Based on the definition of FSU, power function, and related notations in Notations, the energy consumption of jth host to finish all the VMs can be predicted as follows:

$$E_j = \sum_{k=1}^{N_{j,p}} P_{j,k}\left(U_{j,k}, F_{j,k}\right) T_{j,k}, \tag{7}$$

where the power of host $P_{j,k}$ can be calculated by (6) in different situations. The length of FSU can also be estimated under different frequencies by (1).

5.2. kPP Algorithm for Energy Minimization. According to the analysis of energy prediction, if we set consistent frequencies in an FSU, then we can predict the energy consumption in an FSU conveniently. If we set FSUs with different frequencies, the living time of VMs and power state of server will be different, which brings different energy consumption. There is an optimal solution that consumes minimum energy when all VMs end in this server. We want to find the frequencies combinations for all FSUs that bring minimum energy on the promise of ensuring the requirements of VMs. Based on the energy prediction, the energy minimization problem of

frequency scaling in homogenous multiprocessor platforms can be formalized as follows:

$$\min_{F_{j,k} \in F_j} \sum_{k=1}^{N_{j,p}} P_{j,k}\left(U_{j,k}, F_{j,k}\right) T_{j,k}$$

$$\text{s.t.} \quad \forall j \in H, \ \text{VM}_i \in J_j, \ s_i + \sum_{m=1}^{N_p^i} t_{j,m}^i < d_i. \tag{8}$$

For clearly describing the problem, we define $(F_{j,1}, F_{j,2}, \ldots, F_{j,|J_j|})$ as a *state* of possible frequencies combinations for FSU 1 to $|J_j|$ using the notations in Notations. If there is only one frequencies combination that is different between two states, we say they are neighbors. For example, if there are two states $s_1 : (F_{j,1}, F_{j,2}, \ldots, F_{j,|J_j|})$ and $s_2 : (F_{j,1}, F_{j,2}, \ldots, F'_{j,|J_j|})$ and the frequencies combinations of FSU $|J_j|$ in s_1 and s_2 are different while others are the same, then s_1 and s_2 are neighbors. In addition, we define $E(s)$ as the cost function of total energy consumption of s according to (7) if we scale the frequencies like s in each FSU. Let a node present a state and an edge (u, v) between two nodes presents neighborhood between u and v. The minimization problem is to find the "optimal" node that brings minimum energy without any violation of SLAs from the initial node in the graph.

Lemma 4. *Let the initial node represent the state in which all processors' frequencies are highest in all FSUs. If the initial state ensures SLAs for all VMs, there is a path from initial node to the optimal node with minimum energy consumption without any violation of SLAs.*

Proof. Let $s_m = (F_{j,1}, F_{j,2}, \ldots, F_{j,|J_j|})$ represent the optimal state with minimum energy consumption without any violation of SLAs. If all processors' frequencies are highest in all FSU of s_m, the initial state is the optimal state. Otherwise, we select the FSU r in which the frequencies are not highest for all CPUs. If we scale the frequencies to highest in r, the new state s_n will also ensure the SLAs for all VMs because processors are working at higher frequencies which leads to shorter execution time. s_n is one of the neighbors of the optimal state, which means that s_n can also move to s_m. Repeating the process above, we can find a path from s_m to initial state s_i, which represents that there is a path from s_i to s_m. □

5.2.1. k-Phase Energy Prediction (kPP) Algorithm. By energy prediction of k FSUs, the best frequencies combinations can be found moving from the initial state according to Lemma 4. There are $|F_j|$ possible frequencies combinations in each FSU, so there may be $|F_j|^{|J_j|}$ possible states of all FSU with different energy consumption. Let FL_j represent the frequency levels of jth host; we have $|F_j| = |FL_j|^{|C_j|}$. We want to find the optimal solution with minimum energy consumption in these $|F_j|^{|J_j|}$ possible states while still ensuring SLAs. However, the searching space may be $|FL_j|^{|C_j||J_j|}$ which is too huge if there are many VMs. Therefore, we provide two heuristic algorithms to search the "optimal" solutions which are based on simulated annealing (SA) [35] and variable depth search (VDS) [36], respectively.

```
Input:
    The state of host_j;
Output:
    The possible state s;
(1)  J_j = host_j.getVM(),  F_j = host_j.getFreqSpace()
(2)  set s_0 be the state that the frequency is max for each CPU in all FSU
(3)  s = s_0,  e = e_max = E(s_0),  t = 0,  k = |J_j|
(4)  while t < t_max or s doesn't change in l rounds do
(5)      st = s, r = random(k)
(6)      F_{j,r} = random(F_j − s.get(r)) /*Select a neighbor*/
(7)      st.set(r, F_{j,r}) /*Change frequencies combination of FSU r to F_{j,r}*/
(8)      for i = 1 to k do
(9)          if VM_i violates SLAs according to st then
(10)             go to (17)
(11)         end if
(12)     end for
(13)     et = E(st)
(14)     if et ≤ e_max or random() < exp(−(et − e)t/pT) then
(15)         s = st,  e = et /*Change states*/
(16)     end if
(17)     t = t + 1
(18) end while
(19) return s
```

ALGORITHM 1: SA based kPP algorithm.

(1) Simulated Annealing Based Heuristic Algorithm. By comparing energy consumption of a random neighbor, we can find a better state that brings less energy. If we repeat the process many times, we may find the optimal state. Let s_0 represent the initial state in Lemma 4. In fact, since the simulated annealing (SA) algorithm has been proved to converge to the optimum with probability 1, it can be expected that our algorithm will output nice results by enough iterations. If we know the frequency steps and tasks' information, the living time of VMs is determined. Therefore, we can estimate the total energy of the situation of state s_0 (line 3) using the energy cost function $E(\cdot)$. The algorithm runs t_{max} iterations to find the state where less energy is consumed compared to the initial state. In each iteration, the algorithm randomly selects an FSU r to change the frequencies of processors and generates a new state st. This step takes $O(1)$ time. If the random neighbor st violates SLAs for any one of VMs, the state is discarded and our algorithm enters into the next iteration. This step takes $O(N_{j,p})$ time, where $N_{j,p}$ is the number of tasks. Otherwise, if predicted energy et is less than e, st is selected as compared state for next iteration due to less energy consumption. The energy prediction takes $O(N_{j,p} \cdot N_c)$ time according to (7), where N_c is the number of processors. Besides, the algorithm also changes the state from s to st with the probability $\exp(−(et − e)/pT)$ suggested by Metropolis et al. [37] to give the possible to find optimal solution. The details of the simulated annealing based kPP algorithm are presented in Algorithm 1. Obviously, the time complexity of SA-based kPP algorithm is $O(N_{j,p} \cdot N_c \cdot t_{max})$.

(2) Variable Depth Search Based Heuristic Algorithm. The VDS-based kPP algorithm selects the state that brings minimum energy in a subset of neighbors and compares it to the current state. If the selected state consumes less energy on the promise of ensuring the SLAs of VMs, we will change the state to it. The initialized state of VDS-based algorithm is the same as the initialization of SA-based algorithm. The algorithm selects a subset of neighbors whose frequencies combination of FSU r are different (lines 5-6). The frequencies combination of FSU r with minimum energy will be selected (line 7) and generates a new state. The energy prediction takes $O(N_{j,p} \cdot N_c)$ time, so the selection of state with minimum energy takes $O(|X| \cdot N_{j,p} \cdot N_c)$ time, where $|X|$ is the size of subset. The algorithm checks the violations of SLAs of new state (lines 9–13). The process repeats for t_{max} times or until the state s does not change in l iterations. Therefore, the time complexity of this algorithm is $O(|X| \cdot N_{j,p} \cdot N_c \cdot t_{max})$. The effectiveness of the variable depth search is proved in [36]. The details of VDS-based kPP algorithm are shown in Algorithm 2.

The *local DVFS controller* runs the kPP algorithm when the *Global Scheduler* asks it to predict the minimum energy consumption and return it to *Global Scheduler*. This is one of the opportunities to run kPP algorithm. When the workload changes, the power state will change. In addition, the execution time of VMs may have some errors which may lead to the error of energy prediction. Therefore, we apply the frequencies scaling when a VM finishes and scale the frequency for first FSU, which means that the algorithm only scales the CPUs' frequencies just for the first FSU while predicting the frequencies combinations for k FSUs. As the example shown in Figure 3, if the VM_4 comes at the time t_1 and is allocated to the host, this host applies the kPP algorithm at that time and sets the CPUs' frequencies like FSU 1 of the result. When

---

Input:
  The state of host$_j$;
Output:
  The possible state s;
(1) $J_j = \text{host}_j.\text{getVM}()$, $F_j = \text{host}_j.\text{getFreqSpace}()$
(2) set s_0 be the state that the frequency is max for each CPU in all FSU
(3) $s = s_0$, $t = 0$, $k = |J_j|$
(4) **while** $t < t_{\max}$ or s doesn't change in l rounds **do**
(5) $st = s$, $r = \text{random}(k)$
(6)   randomly select a subset $X \subseteq F_j$
(7) $x = \text{argmin}(E(st.\text{set}(r, x)))$, for all $x \in X$ /*Select the state form subset with minimum energy consumption*/
(8) $st.\text{set}(r, x)$ /*Change frequencies combination of FSU r to x*/
(9)   **for** $i = 1$ to k **do**
(10)   **if** VM$_i$ violates SLAs according to st **then**
(11)   go to (15)
(12)   **end if**
(13)   **end for**
(14) $s = st$ /*Change states*/
(15) $t = t + 1$
(16) **end while**
(17) **return** s

ALGORITHM 2: VDS-based kPP algorithm.

VM$_1$ finishes at the t_2, the kPP algorithm also runs to obtain the "optimal" state s and scales frequencies according to the result. Due to the specialities of kPP algorithm at running time, the iteration should be completed in a short time so that the local stage can scale the frequencies in time.

6. Global Scheduler

Different allocations of a new VM may affect the overall energy consumption, because the new VM executed on different servers will bring different energy consumption. We want to find the appropriate scheduling to minimize the energy consumption to finish all the VMs. We can obtain the different energy consumption with different allocation if we ask each host to predict the minimum energy consumption. Using the results of different allocations, we can select a better allocating scheme to reduce the energy consumption. Our goal is to minimize the overall energy cost of the whole cluster for finishing all VMs including the new VM VM$_n$. To solve the energy minimization problem of VM scheduling, we first formalize the problem. Let decision parameter $a_{j,c}^i$ be 1 if the ith VM is allocated to cth CPU of jth host, otherwise 0. The energy-efficient VM allocation problem can be expressed as

$$\min \quad \sum_{j \in H} \left\{ \min_{F_{j,k} \in F_j} \sum_{k=1}^{N_{j,p}} P_{j,k} \left(U_{j,k}, F_{j,k} \right) T_{j,k} \right\}$$

$$\text{s.t.} \quad \sum_{j \in H, c \in C_j} a_{j,c}^n \leq 1;$$

$$J_j = J_j \cup \{\text{VM}_n\}, \quad \text{if } a_{j,c}^n = 1;$$

$$\forall j \in H, \text{ VM}_i \in J_j, \ s_i + \sum_{m=1}^{N_p^i} t_{j,m}^i < d_i;$$

$$\forall k \in N_{j,p}, \ j \in H, \ \sum_{c \in C_j} U_{j,k}^c < UT_j.$$

(9)

The energy minimization problem of VM scheduling is to find the server which brings minimum energy of whole cluster if VM$_n$ is allocated to it. The minimum energy consumption of each server can be predicted by kPP algorithm, represented by EMIN$_j$ for jth host. If an incoming VM is allocated to jth host, the value of EMIN$_j$ changes while the minimum energy consumption of other hosts does not change. When VM$_n$ is allocated to the yth host, the energy consumption becomes EMIN$_y'$ + $\sum_{j \in H-\{y\}}$ EMIN$_j$, where EMIN$_y'$ is the minimum energy cost if VM$_n$ is allocated to yth host. We have

$$
\begin{aligned}
E_{\min} &= \text{EMIN}_y' + \sum_{j \in H-\{y\}} \text{EMIN}_j \\
&= \Delta\text{EMIN}_y + \text{EMIN}_y + \sum_{j \in H-\{y\}} \text{EMIN}_j \\
&= \Delta\text{EMIN}_y + \sum_{j \in H} \text{EMIN}_j.
\end{aligned}
$$

(10)

So we can select the host that brings minimum energy change ΔEMIN_y to run the incoming VM. We call the scheduling algorithm *Minimum energy Change* (MC), shown in Algorithm 3. The *Global Scheduler* sends the information of a VM after analyzing to a subset of host (line 1) and each host returns the predicted minimum energy change on it. Therefore, we can run the energy-efficient algorithm in parallel to

Input:
    A new VM VM_n;
Output:
    Designate host and processor for loading VM_n;
    (1) *Host Monitor* selects a subset of active hosts that can load the VM
    (2) notify the information of VM_n to all candidates
    (3) each host estimates the minimum energy change $\Delta EMIN_j$ if VM is allocated to processor c of $host_j$
    (4) $host_j = \text{argmin}_{j \in H}(\Delta EMIN_j)$
    (5) **return** $host_j$

ALGORITHM 3: Minimum energy change allocation.

obtain the minimum energy consumption for each host when a VM arrives. After the *local DVFS controller* predicts the minimum energy change, it also records the best processor to hold this VM. When this VM is really allocated to it, the VM will be scheduled onto this best processor. Once deciding the host, the selected host will start a VM to run the VM working under the selected frequencies. It is obvious that the time complexity is $O(|H|+L+T)$, where L and T represent the time complexity of local predicting algorithm and communication time, respectively.

The number of candidate hosts will affect the total cost of a cluster, we evaluate the influence of kPP strategy on the total energy cost. Assume the total VM number is N_t; the size of subset for candidate hosts is N_h and the average run-time of local DVFS algorithm is 0.5 seconds. Let the mean power consumed by a VM be $\overline{P}$ Watt and the average length of VMs be $\overline{t}$ seconds. The kPP algorithm runs when the MC algorithm asks candidate hosts to estimate energy consumption; the energy consumption of kPP algorithm in this part is $N_h \cdot \overline{P} \cdot N_t \cdot 0.5$. The kPP algorithm also runs when a VM is allocated and finished, so the energy for this part is $2 \cdot N_t \cdot \overline{P} \cdot 0.5$, and the total energy produced by all VMs is $N_t \cdot \overline{P} \cdot \overline{t}$. Therefore, the *energy consumption ratio* (ECR) of kPP algorithm compared to the total energy cost is

$$\text{ECR} = \frac{0.5 \cdot N_h + 1}{\overline{t}}. \tag{11}$$

In a large scale data center, the mean VM length can be acquired according to the historical data, and we can carefully select the size of candidate host estimating the energy change of offloading a new VM to increase the energy consumption of kPP algorithm as less as possible.

7. Experimental Evaluation

7.1. Evaluating Power Prediction. The energy prediction of server depends on the accuracy of power prediction under different utilizations and frequencies. We have evaluated the multiprocessor power prediction method by comparing the real power consumption to the estimation of power model in different status for a specific host. The real experimental environment is shown in Figure 4. The details of server R710 used in our paper are shown in Table 1. We explore the real power consumption R710 and use the first seven steps when

TABLE 1: Details of servers.

Name	Dell PowerEdge R710	Dell PowerEdge R720
CPUs	Two Intel Xeon processors E5645 @2.4 GHz	Two Intel Xeon processors E5-2620 @2.1 GHz
Frequency steps (GHz)	1.60, 1.73, 1.86, 2.00, 2.13, 2.26, 2.39, 2.40	1.20, 1.30, 1.40, 1.50, 1.60, 1.70, 1.80, 1.90, 2.00, 2.10
Memory	24 G 1333 Mhz DDR3	64 G ECC DDR3
Disk	Two 10 k SAS, 250 GB	One 10 k SAS, 300 GB
Operation system	CentOS 6.5	CentOS 6.5

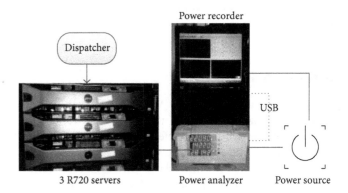

FIGURE 4: Real system architecture.

we evaluate the power model because the last frequency is very close to the frequency 2.39 GHz. The power consumption of the host when both processors are fully utilized at frequency level 2.39 GHz is 192 Watt and the static power when the system is not idle is 110 Watt. The proportional coefficient $\alpha = 2.33135$ is obtained and calibrated by offline experiments.

For evaluating the multiprocessor power prediction, we randomly select some frequencies and utilizations of two processors and use power model to estimate the power consumption. At the same time, we measure the real power consumption of R710 server with the same frequencies and utilizations of processors and results are shown in Table 2. We use the Aitek AWE 2101 power analyzer to measure power. Table 2 shows that the estimated power is very close to the real

TABLE 2: Power comparison.

Frequencies (GHz)		Utilizations		Power (Watt)		Error
CPU$_1$	CPU$_2$	CPU$_1$	CPU$_2$	Estimation	Real	
1.60	2.00	61%	87%	145.33	147.01	−1.14%
1.73	2.13	95%	84%	156.45	157.81	−0.86%
1.86	1.73	19%	14%	117.50	117.03	+0.40%
2.00	1.60	59%	9%	127.96	128.32	−0.28%
2.13	2.13	61%	84%	155.67	155.68	+0.00%
2.13	1.86	58%	57%	141.94	142.68	−0.52%
2.26	2.00	58%	30%	139.10	137.89	+0.87%
2.26	2.39	98%	81%	178.21	181.69	+1.91%
2.39	1.60	92%	18%	150.87	149.79	+0.72%
2.39	2.13	12%	59%	133.48	133.15	+0.25%

TABLE 3: Run-time versus SA iterations.

SA iterations	2 CPUs with 12 VMs		4 CPUs with 24 VMs	
	RT (ms)	EC (J)	RT (ms)	EC (J)
0	0	2466027	0	3210277
10	1	2397905	1	3195957
100	3	2385065	7	3117021
1000	20	2323755	50	3004518
10000	170	2301687	486	2952581
100000	1676	2293194	4895	2923625
1000000	16645	2289410	46070	2851156

TABLE 4: Run-time versus VDS iterations.

VDS iterations	2 CPUs with 12 VMs		4 CPUs with 24 VMs	
	RT (ms)	EC (J)	RT (ms)	EC (J)
0	0	2466027	0	3210277
10	5	2379716	12	3080983
100	38	2302226	118	2926700
1000	361	2293796	1145	2859979
10000	3519	2289368	11682	2855693
100000	35245	2289438	115659	2843434
1000000	349465	2289410	1140554	2848026

power consumption of the server with the same utilizations and frequencies of different processors.

7.2. Convergence Speed. In this subsection, we compare the convergence speeds of the two algorithms and present them in Tables 3 and 4. The reported run-times and iteration times are for running the two algorithms of a synthetic 2-processor and 4-processor with 7 frequency levels machine where 12 and 24 VMs are executed in parallel. The RT and EC in Tables 3 and 4 represent running time and energy consumption, respectively. We can draw three obvious conclusions: (1) the SA-based algorithm iterates significantly faster than the VDS-based algorithm which means that more iterations can be executed during the same period; (2) the VDS-based algorithm outperforms the SA-based algorithm while it leads to the same iteration times if the host is equipped with serval processors; (3) when the processor number and frequency levels are relatively small, both the two algorithms converge rapidly and obtain the close results. And the VDS-based algorithm perform better than SA-based algorithm when the number of processors is small. This conclusion suggests that the service provider may prefer the SA-based algorithm if they persist in finding the best frequency configurations.

Notice that, in this experiment, we use a very extreme set-up where a 4-processor host is enforced to run as much as 24 VMs at the same time, which means a processor must be responsible for 6 VMs on average. In fact, in the real data-centers, it can be expected that the average VM number on

a single processor is far less than 6. Thus our algorithm can run efficiently enough to serve for our online VM scheduling algorithm and obtain an accepted result within 1 second which is close to results of more iterations.

7.3. Experiments in Real Environment. Our real experimental environment has three servers and a controller on a virtual machine. The power is measured by Aitek Power Analyzer AWE2101. Each R720 server whose details are shown in Table 1 runs the kPP algorithm to predict energy and control processors' speed. We combine the kPP algorithm with the random (Ran) and first-fit (FF) VM scheduling. The *random* scheme allocates the coming task to the processor randomly from the subset of processors which can offload the new task without causing any violations of QoS requirements. The *first-fit* scheme gives each processor an index and allocates the coming task to the processor with smallest index who can offload the new task without causing any violations of QoS requirements. Meanwhile, the proposed global assignment (MC) is also combined with the default DVFS controller Ondemand [38] (DEF) in Linux. The two-tier energy-aware resource management proposed in this paper is represented by *MC-kPP*. We compare these six strategies to evaluate the performance of our solution on energy savings. For each VM, its execution time is generated uniformly at random between a *minimum* and *maximum* living time represented by ET_{min} and ET_{max}, respectively. The deadline of a VM is set from 1 to 1.5 times longer to its execution time randomly. Moreover,

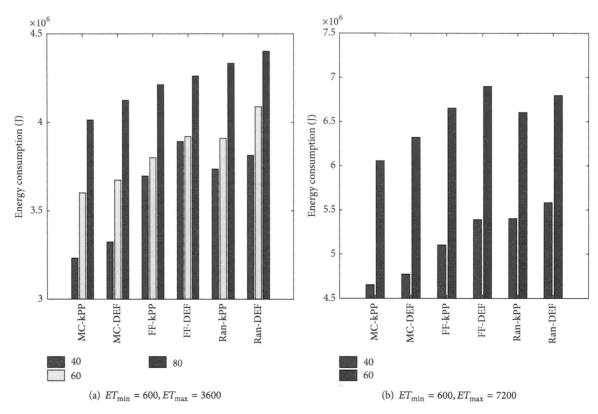

(a) $ET_{min} = 600, ET_{max} = 3600$ (b) $ET_{min} = 600, ET_{max} = 7200$

FIGURE 5: Energy consumption of real system. The legend in (a) and (b) means that the number of VMs needs to be allocated.

their utilizations requirements follow the normal distribution with $\mu = 0.75$ and $\sigma = 1$. In addition, the arriving times of VMs follow a Poisson distribution with different average rates.

In these experiments, the iteration times are 10000 for SA-based kPP and 1000 for VDS-based kPP and the number of neighbors in VDS-based kPP algorithm is 20. The results of SA-based and VDS-based algorithms are very close, so we show the results of VDS-based kPP algorithm in Figure 5 whose legend represents different numbers of VMs. Meanwhile, the size of candidates in MC algorithm is equal to the number of servers. As we can see in Figure 5, the energy savings of our solution can reach from 8% to 17% in the real environment with 3 servers.

7.4. Simulation Results. Due to the inaccessibility of a large scale datacenter, we conduct the simulations to evaluate MC-kPP solution in a larger cluster. We model Dell R710 servers to service the dynamically arriving VMs. Meanwhile, the attributes of generated VMs are the same as the attributes introduced in Section 7.3.

As we can see in Figure 6(a), the local kPP algorithm can reduce energy consumption of a specific server compared to Ondemand strategy. In addition, the influences of global scheduling algorithm are greater than the influences of local DVFS controller on energy savings when different scheduling algorithms are applied. The lengths of VMs in Figure 6(b) are generated uniformly and randomly between 600 and 7200 seconds. The legend in Figure 6(b) represents the arriving

ratio of VMs in one minute. The results show an increasing tendency of the energy saving ratio with the increments of VM numbers and the best result can reach about 28%. In Figure 6(c), we investigate the influence of lengths of VMs; VMs are generated in different lengths which are shown in the legend. As shown in Figure 6(c), MC-kPP can also save more energy when the VMs become more. At the same time, MC-kPP performs better when the average execution time of VMs becomes longer, because the influence of local kPP algorithm itself becomes smaller and the effectiveness of frequencies scaling becomes more obvious. In addition, the size of subset in MC algorithm is also investigated in Figure 6(d); the energy consumption of kPP algorithm in local machine is below 0.5% of total energy consumption when the average execution time is long. With the increment of subset size, the performance of MC-kPP is improved because a better server can be found in a larger scale. We also evaluate the effectiveness of MC-kPP in different scales of data centers ranging from 50 to 5000 servers with different features of arriving VMs. According to the results of Figure 7, the MC-kPP outperforms other strategies in different scales of datacenters, which can reach about 25% energy savings. With the increasement of host numbers and VM numbers, MC-kPP performs stably in different scenarios.

8. Conclusions

In this paper, we propose a cooperative two-tier energy-efficient strategy to manage the VM allocations and adapt

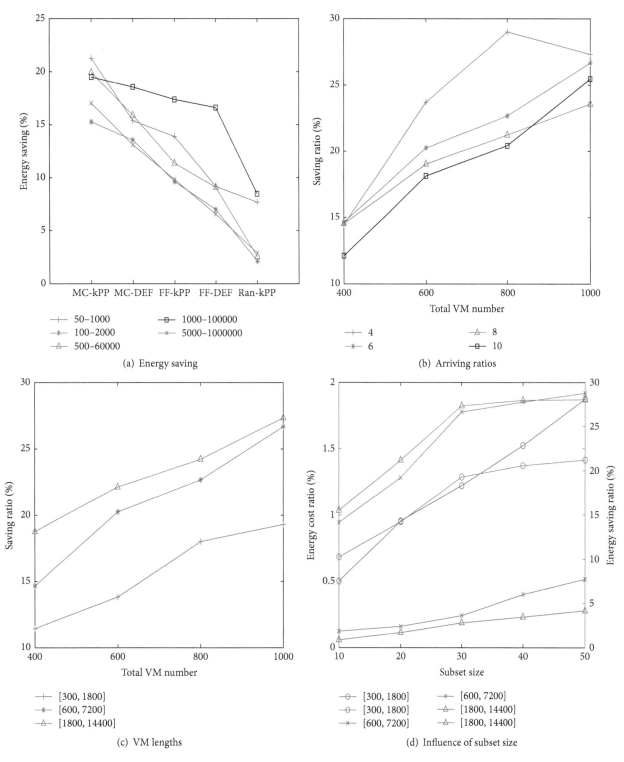

FIGURE 6: Performance evaluation on different aspects. The legend in (a) represents the "server numbers-total VM number." The legend in (b) represents the "VM request number arriving in a minute." The legend in (c) and (d) represents the "(minimum living time, maximum living time)."

frequencies scaling for saving energy. A frequency scaling algorithm is proposed based on the practical power and energy prediction. The Global Scheduler collaborates with local DVFS controller to assign VMs and save overall energy.

In addition, two heuristic algorithms are provided for searching the optimal solutions which predict minimum energy consumption. The time complexities of both the algorithms are acceptable with satisfactory results according to the

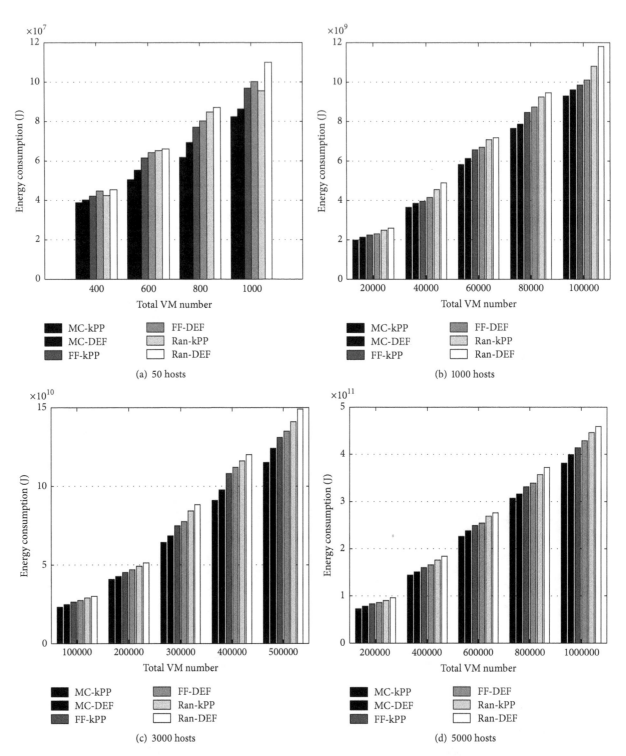

FIGURE 7: Energy consumption of different scale of datacenters with different number of VMs.

experiments. Finally, the real experiment results justify the effectiveness of MC-kPP.

Notations

J_j: The set of jobs (VMs) in jth host

C_j: CPU set of jth host

F_j: All possible combinations of frequencies for CPUs on jth host

$F_{j,k}$: Combinations of frequencies for CPUs on jth host in kth

$U_{j,k}$: Utilizations of CPUs of jth host in kth FSU

$U_{j,k}^c$: Utilization of cth CPU of jth host in kth FSU

$T_{j,k}$: Time length of kth FSU of jth host

$N_{j,p}$: The number of FSUs from the current time of jth host

$P_{j,k}(\cdot)$: The power function of jth host in kth FSU.

Disclosure

This is a substantially extended version of the paper presented at ICA3PP 2015 [3].

Competing Interests

The authors declare that they have no competing interests.

Acknowledgments

This work is partially supported by the National Natural Science Foundation of China under Grants nos. 61472181, 61100197, and 61202113; Jiangsu College Natural Science Foundation under Grant no. 14KJB520016; Jiangsu Natural Science Foundation under Grant no. BK20151392; and JSPS KAKENHI Grant no. 16K00117. And this work is also partially supported by Collaborative Innovation Center of Novel Software Technology and Industrialization.

References

[1] W. Forrest, "How to cut data centre carbon emissions?" 2008.

[2] A. Beloglazov, R. Buyya, Y. C. Lee et al., "A taxonomy and survey of energy-efficient data centers and cloud computing systems," *Advances in Computers*, vol. 82, no. 2, pp. 47–111, 2011.

[3] W. Huang, J. Shi, Z. Wang, and Z. Qian, "BiTEM: a two-tier energy efficient resource management framework for real-time tasks in clusters," in *Algorithms and Architectures for Parallel Processing*, G. Wang, A. Zomaya, G. M. Perez, and K. Li, Eds., vol. 9529 of *Lecture Notes in Computer Science*, pp. 494–508, Springer, Berlin, Germany, 2015.

[4] A. Verma, P. Ahuja, and A. Neogi, "pMapper: power and migration cost aware application placement in virtualized systems," in *Proceedings of the 9th ACM/IFIP/USENIX International Conference on Middleware (Middleware '08)*, pp. 243–264, Springer, Leuven, Belgium, December 2008.

[5] R. Raghavendra, P. Ranganathan, V. Talwar, Z. Wang, and X. Zhu, "No power struggles: coordinated multi-level power management for the data center," *ACM SIGARCH Computer Architecture News*, vol. 36, pp. 48–59, 2008.

[6] B. Guenter, N. Jain, and C. Williams, "Managing cost, performance, and reliability tradeoffs for energy-aware server provisioning," in *Proceedings of the 30th IEEE International Conference on Computer Communications (INFOCOM '11)*, pp. 1332–1340, Shanghai, China, April 2011.

[7] D. Kusic, J. O. Kephart, J. E. Hanson, N. Kandasamy, and G. Jiang, "Power and performance management of virtualized computing environments via lookahead control," *Cluster Computing*, vol. 12, no. 1, pp. 1–15, 2009.

[8] R. Buyya, A. Beloglazov, and J. Abawajy, "Energy-efficient management of data center resources for cloud computing: a vision, architectural elements, and open challenges," https://arxiv.org/abs/1006.0308.

[9] M. Cardosa, M. R. Korupolu, and A. Singh, "Shares and utilities based power consolidation in virtualized server environments," in *Proceedings of the IFIP/IEEE International Symposium on Integrated Network Management (IM '09)*, pp. 327–334, June 2009.

[10] Z. Cao and S. Dong, "An energy-aware heuristic framework for virtual machine consolidation in Cloud computing," *The Journal of Supercomputing*, vol. 69, no. 1, pp. 429–451, 2014.

[11] S. F. Piraghaj, A. V. Dastjerdi, R. N. Calheiros, and R. Buyya, "Efficient virtual machine sizing for hosting containers as a service (SERVICES 2015)," in *Proceedings of the IEEE World Congress on Services (SERVICES '15)*, pp. 31–38, New York, NY, USA, June-July 2015.

[12] Z. Zhou, Z. Hu, and K. Li, "Virtual machine placement algorithm for both energy-awareness and sla violation reduction in cloud data centers," *Scientific Programming*, vol. 2016, Article ID 5612039, 11 pages, 2016.

[13] G. Semeraro, D. H. Albonesi, S. G. Dropsho, G. Magklis, S. Dwarkadas, and M. L. Scott, "Dynamic frequency and voltage control for a multiple clock domain microarchitecture," in *Proceedings of the 35th Annual IEEE/ACM International Symposium on Microarchitecture (MICRO '02)*, pp. 356–367, IEEE, November 2002.

[14] C.-H. Hsu and W.-C. Feng, "A power-aware run-time system for high-performance computing," in *Proceedings of the ACM/IEEE Supercomputing Conference (SC '05)*, IEEE Computer Society, Seattle, Wash, USA, November 2005.

[15] J. P. Halimi, B. Pradelle, A. Guermouche et al., "Reactive DVFS control for multicore processors," in *Proceedings of the IEEE Green Computing and Communications (GreenCom '13)*, pp. 102–109, August 2013.

[16] M. Lim, V. W. Freeh, and D. K. Lowenthal, "Adaptive, transparent frequency and voltage scaling of communication phases in mpi programs," in *Proceedings of the ACM/IEEE Conference on Supercomputing (SC '06)*, p. 14, Tampa, Fla, USA, November 2006.

[17] D. Li, B. R. de Supinski, M. Schulz, D. S. Nikolopoulos, and K. W. Cameron, "Strategies for energy-efficient resource management of hybrid programming models," *IEEE Transactions on Parallel and Distributed Systems*, vol. 24, no. 1, pp. 144–157, 2013.

[18] L. Tan, Z. Chen, Z. Zong, D. Li, and R. Ge, "A2E: adaptively aggressive energy efficient DVFS scheduling for data intensive applications," in *Proceedings of the IEEE 32nd International Performance Computing and Communications Conference (IPCCC '13)*, pp. 1–10, IEEE, San Diego, Calif, USA, December 2013.

[19] L. Wang, G. Von Laszewski, J. Dayal, and F. Wang, "Towards energy aware scheduling for precedence constrained parallel tasks in a cluster with DVFS," in *Proceedings of the 10th IEEE/ACM International Symposium on Cluster, Cloud and Grid Computing (CCGrid '10)*, pp. 368–377, IEEE, Melbourne, Australia, May 2010.

[20] H. Kimura, M. Sato, Y. Hotta, T. Boku, and D. Takahashi, "Empirical study on reducing energy of parallel programs using slack reclamation by DVFS in a power-scalable high performance cluster," in *Proceedings of the IEEE International Conference on Cluster Computing (Cluster '06)*, pp. 1–10, September 2006.

[21] S. U. Khan and I. Ahmad, "A cooperative game theoretical technique for joint optimization of energy consumption and response time in computational grids," *IEEE Transactions on Parallel and Distributed Systems*, vol. 20, no. 3, pp. 346–360, 2009.

[22] M. Mezmaz, N. Melab, Y. Kessaci et al., "A parallel bi-objective hybrid metaheuristic for energy-aware scheduling for cloud

computing systems," *Journal of Parallel and Distributed Computing*, vol. 71, no. 11, pp. 1497–1508, 2011.

[23] M. A. Awan and S. M. Petters, "Energy-aware partitioning of tasks onto a heterogeneous multi-core platform," in *Proceedings of the IEEE 19th Real-Time and Embedded Technology and Applications Symposium (RTAS '13)*, pp. 205–214, Philadelphia, Pa, USA, April 2013.

[24] J.-J. Chen, A. Schranzhofer, and L. Thiele, "Energy minimization for periodic real-time tasks on heterogeneous processing units," in *Proceedings of the 23rd IEEE International Parallel and Distributed Processing Symposium (IPDPS '09)*, pp. 1–12, IEEE, Rome, Italy, May 2009.

[25] H.-R. Hsu, J.-J. Chen, and T.-W. Kuo, "Multiprocessor synthesis for periodic hard real-time tasks under a given energy constraint," in *Proceedings of the Conference on Design, Automation and Test in Europe (DATE '06)*, pp. 1061–1066, European Design and Automation Association, Munich, Germany, March 2006.

[26] W. Y. Lee, "Energy-saving DVFS scheduling of multiple periodic real-time tasks on multi-core processors," in *Proceedings of the 13th IEEE/ACM Symposium on Distributed Simulation and Real-Time Applications (DS-RT '09)*, pp. 216–223, IEEE Computer Society, October 2009.

[27] J. Luo and N. K. Jha, "Power-efficient scheduling for heterogeneous distributed real-time embedded systems," *IEEE Transactions on Computer-Aided Design of Integrated Circuits and Systems*, vol. 26, no. 6, pp. 1161–1170, 2007.

[28] M. Etinski, J. Corbalan, J. Labarta, and M. Valero, "Understanding the future of energy-performance trade-off via DVFS in HPC environments," *Journal of Parallel and Distributed Computing*, vol. 72, no. 4, pp. 579–590, 2012.

[29] L. Tan, Z. Chen, Z. Zong, R. Ge, and D. Li, "A2E: adaptively aggressive energy efficient DVFS scheduling for data intensive applications," in *Proceedings of the IEEE 32nd International Performance Computing and Communications Conference (IPCCC '13)*, pp. 1–10, San Diego, Calif, USA, December 2013.

[30] M. A. Blackburn, *Five Ways to Reduce Data Center Server Power Consumption*, Green Grid, 2008.

[31] E. N. (Mootaz) Elnozahy, M. Kistler, and R. Rajamony, "Energy-efficient server clusters," in *Power-Aware Computer Systems*, B. Falsafi and T. N. Vijaykumar, Eds., vol. 2325 of *Lecture Notes in Computer Science*, pp. 179–197, Springer, Berlin, Germany, 2003.

[32] X. Fan, W.-D. Weber, and L. A. Barroso, "Power provisioning for a warehouse-sized computer," in *Proceedings of the 34th Annual International Symposium on Computer Architecture (ISCA '07)*, pp. 13–23, ACM, June 2007.

[33] A. Gandhi, M. Harchol-Balter, R. Das, and C. Lefurgy, "Optimal power allocation in server farms," in *Proceedings of the ACM 11th International Joint Conference on Measurement and Modeling of Computer Systems (SIGMETRICS '09)*, vol. 37, pp. 157–168, Seattle, Wash, USA, June 2009.

[34] T. Mudge, "Power: a first-class architectural design constraint," *Computer*, vol. 34, no. 4, pp. 52–58, 2001.

[35] S. Kirkpatrick, C. D. Gelatt Jr., and M. P. Vecchi, "Optimization by simulated annealing," *Science*, vol. 220, no. 4598, pp. 671–680, 1983.

[36] J. Hromkovič, *Algorithmics for Hard Problems: Introduction to Combinatorial Optimization, Randomization, Approximation, and Heuristics*, Springer Science & Business Media, 2013.

[37] N. Metropolis, A. W. Rosenbluth, M. N. Rosenbluth, A. H. Teller, and E. Teller, "Equation of state calculations by fast computing machines," *The Journal of Chemical Physics*, vol. 21, no. 6, pp. 1087–1092, 1953.

[38] V. Pallipadi and A. Starikovskiy, "The ondemand governor," in *Proceedings of the Linux Symposium*, vol. 2, pp. 215–230, Ottawa, Canada, 2006.

5

The Study of Pallet Pooling Information Platform Based on Cloud Computing

Jia-bin Li [ID],[1,2] **Shi-wei He** [ID],[1] **and Wei-chuan Yin** [ID][1]

[1]*School of Traffic and Transportation, Beijing Jiaotong University, Beijing 100044, China*
[2]*School of Business Administration, Henan University of Engineering, Zhengzhou 451191, China*

Correspondence should be addressed to Shi-wei He; shwhe@bjtu.edu.cn

Academic Editor: Emiliano Tramontana

Effective implementation of pallet pooling system needs a strong information platform to support. Through the analysis of existing pallet pooling information platform (PPIP), the paper pointed out that the existing studies of PPIP are mainly based on traditional IT infrastructures and technologies which have software, hardware, resource utilization, and process restrictions. Because of the advantages of cloud computing technology like strong computing power, high flexibility, and low cost which meet the requirements of the PPIP well, this paper gave a PPIP architecture of two parts based on cloud computing: the users client and the cloud services. The cloud services include three layers, which are IaaS, PaaS, and SaaS. The method of how to deploy PPIP based on cloud computing is proposed finally.

1. Introduction

The pallet pooling system refers to the management system of renting, recycling, tracking, and maintaining of pallets by professional companies [1]. Zhang Xueyan [2] pointed out that an effective operation of pallet pooling system on the one hand depends on a good mode; on the other hand, it needs a strong information platform to support. Therefore, the construction of the PPIP is particularly important and it has been studied by some researchers [3–15]. For example, Based on RFID technologies Jinshou Song et al. [3]; Liu Ye et al. [4]; Li Xiao et al. [5]; Xu Qi et al. [6]; Liang Q et al. [7]; Murray. J [8]; Ding Z et al. [9]; Bottani E et al. [10]; Harris J S et al. [11]; Lin X Z [12]; Ilic A et al. [13]; Vitzthum S et al. [14]; Elia V et al. [15] analyzed the architecture, functions and business processes of the pallet pool information system. Based on grid technology, Ren J et al. [16] gave a seven tier architecture and five-tier security framework of a railway pallet pool information system. Based on SOA and RFID, Zhang X et al. [17] analyzed the Chinese pallet pool information system which consisted of a public information system and a set of terminal information systems. Based on cloud computing, Ren J et al. [18] proposed a PPIP which included four layers.

Daniluk D et al. [19] and Niharika G [20] described an approach and architecture based on cloud computing for logistics business, but they did not study the PPIP.

From the above, we know that most of the PPIP were based on the traditional information infrastructures and technologies. The PPIP based on traditional information infrastructures and technologies are vulnerable to the restrictions of hardware, software, information resource utilization, and business processes. Cloud computing is an effective way to build a dynamic information system infrastructure. But there are few studies to PPIP based on cloud computing. Although there is one cloud platform research in PPIP, it did not discuss it in detail. Therefore, this paper further studies the business model and the needs of PPIP based on cloud computing. The paper is structured as follows: The first section gives an introduction and literature review of PPIP. Section 2 presents the meaning of cloud computing architecture and its advantages. Section 3 gives a business model and needs analysis of the PPIP under cloud computing. Section 4 designs an architecture and deployment model of PPIP based on the cloud computing. Section 5 concludes the paper for further research.

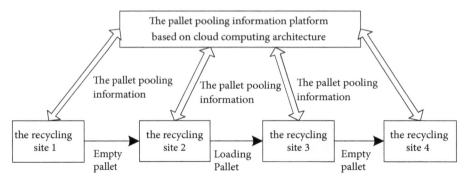

FIGURE 1: The business model of pallet pooling.

2. The Meaning of Cloud Computing Architecture and Its Advantages

The meaning of cloud computing can be interpreted from different perspectives. This article uses the official NIST definition [21]: cloud computing is a model for enabling ubiquitous, convenient, on-demand network access to a shared pool of configurable computing resources (e.g., networks, servers, storage, applications, and services) that can be rapidly provisioned and released with minimal management effort or service provider interaction. Cloud computing has the advantages of strong computing power, virtualization, high reliability, high versatility, high flexibility, on-demand services, low cost, and other advantages.

We can understand the meaning and its advantages of cloud computing architecture like this: cloud computing architecture looks like a power plant with centralized power supply architecture; the users do not need to buy their own power generation equipment; they use electricity based on their needs only by a wire which gets access to the grid. The same is to the cloud computing architecture; the users do not need to buy new information system hardware and related software; just with a network cable they can get access to the cloud services provided by service providers. This kind of architecture will greatly reduce the cost and time to build a variety of information systems.

3. The Business Model and Needs Analysis of PPIP under Cloud Computing

3.1. The Business Model of Pallet Pooling System under Cloud Computing Architecture. The business model of the pallet pooling system under cloud computing architecture is shown in Figure 1.

The system consists of a pallet pooling information platform based on cloud computing architecture and an extensible pallet recycling network. The PPIP is mainly composed of servers, communications, and other components which are built on the cloud for storage, transmission, and handling of pallet pooling information. Pallet recycling network includes all the enterprises like pallet suppliers, pallet renting, and recycling customers and other logistics enterprises belong to

the recycling network. The PPIP supports mobile phones, tablet PCs, laptops, car terminals, and other equipment as the system entrance.

Pallet renting and recycling customers complete the specific business through the portal entrance to the cloud, including the demand for pallet renting, pallet tracking, pallet recycling, and so on. The main work of the PPIP is to coordinate the management of the renting and recycling sites. Through the PPIP, it can set the relevant parameters of the whole pallet pooling system, such as the rental rate and deposit and so on. At the same time, the renting and recycling information on the leased outlets is used to calculate the distribution and flow of all the shared pallets which may improve the decision of inventory configuration and empty pallet dispatching.

3.2. Needs Analysis of PPIP under Cloud Computing Architecture. The PPIP is the core of the entire pallet pooling system. In order to promote the seamless integration of business flow, logistics, and capital flow among the information platform enterprises, pallet customers, and the pallet suppliers, the PPIP should use the information technologies such as RFID (Radio Frequency Identification), GPS (Global Positioning System), GIS (Geographic Information System), and EDI (Electronic Data Interchange) to collect, store, transmit, and process the information timely according to the requirements of the pallet pooling business model and process.

Other than providing pallet pooling suppliers and customers with on-line transaction support such as pallet recycling, pallet transportation and tracing, the charge counting and other business, the platform also provides big data analysis and other value-added services for all the users of the PPIP. Through the analysis of the business model and technical requirements of the PPIP, we could easily get the "cloud computing" characteristics of the PPIP as follows:

(a) The Demand for Hardware and Software Resources in the PPIP Is Flexible and Massive. With the increasing size of the pallet pooling system, there will be new enterprises to join in. Thus the PPIP needs to collect, store, process, and integrate massive information from production enterprises, logistics

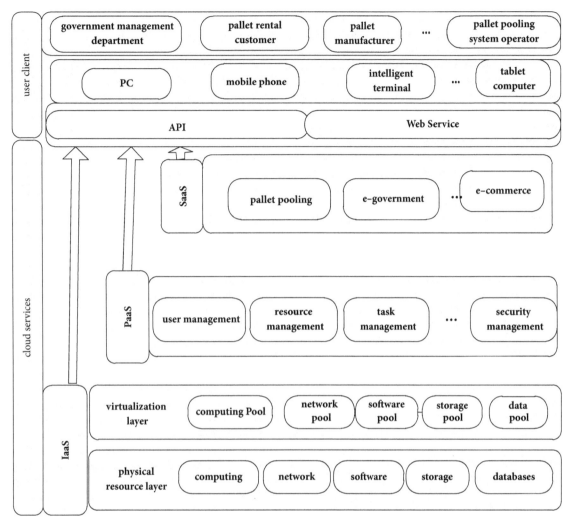

FIGURE 2: The PPIP architecture diagram under cloud computing.

enterprises, government departments, and other links which requires flexible and massive information system in real time.

(b) The Big Load Changes of the PPIP. The PPIP provides the pallet pooling suppliers and customers, logistics enterprises, and government departments with many logistics services. The demand for logistics services is subject to rises and falls with the level of production and consumption of goods which results in a large number or little of hardware and software resources requirements for the PPIP.

(c) The PPIP Based on Cloud Computing Is Easily Accepted by the Users. At present, most of small logistics enterprises, manufacturing enterprises, and retail enterprises have no mature logistics information systems because they could not spend a lot of money on purchasing and developing large and complex logistics management information systems; the PPIP under cloud computing architecture well met their information management requirements of business, which has the advantages of volume charging, low cost, rich interfaces, and easy sharing.

4. The Architecture and Deployment Model of PPIP Based on Cloud Computing

4.1. The Architecture of PPIP Based on Cloud Computing. Architecture refers to the logical structure which is used to represent and formalize the relationship between the various components. In this paper, it introduces a cloud computing architecture for constructing the information platform of the pallet pooling system borrowing from the literature. The information platform architecture based on cloud computing adopts hierarchical design which includes the following aspects: cloud infrastructure layer (IaaS), cloud platform layer (PaaS), cloud application layer (SaaS), and user client. See Figure 2 in detail.

(a) Cloud Infrastructure Layer (IaaS). This layer includes the physical resource layer and the resource pool layer (or virtualization layer) under the cloud computing architecture, which is primarily intended to provide hardware infrastructure as a service to the users. Physical resources include computing resources, network resources, storage resources, databases,

and software resources. The resource pool layer includes computing resource pool, storage resource pool, network resource pool, data resource pool, and software resource pool. Companies that offer an IaaS include Amazon, Microsoft, VMware, Rackspace, and Red Hat.

After the introduction of IaaS layer for the PPIP, all the related parties do not need to build their own hardware facilities. They all share a virtual equipment pool composed of multiple facilities and equipment allocated dynamically according to the actual needs. Then it can attain the goal of quickly building and decreasing fixed capital investment and equipment operating costs.

(b) Cloud Platform Layer (PaaS). The PaaS layer includes user management, resource management, task management, security management, and other modules. This layer provides information system development environment services to the users so they can develop and share their required applications with relevant users.

By using any PaaS service from Google App Engine, Microsoft Azure, Force.com, Heroku, Engine Yard, and so on, the users of PPIP can develop and deploy its pallet pooling information systems that realize the collection, storage, calculation, statistics analysis, sharing, and other functions. This layer also meets the big data and real time processing requirements of the pallet pooling system by use of distributed storing and computing technologies.

(c) Cloud Application Layer (SaaS). This layer is to provide services including pallet pooling, e-government, e-commerce, and other services through the Internet. The pallet pooling services include business applications such as the release of pallet renting and recycling demand information, pallet cargo tracking, pallet inventory management, and pallet pooling cost settlement. E-government includes the portal platform, document exchange, command coordination, single sign on, and certification authority interfaces and so on that distinguish it from the past ones that must be communicated through the traditional way. E-commerce mainly includes the on-line business marketing, on-line pallet rental, and other applications on the network.

In this mode, the service providers of PPIP deploy the pallet pooling application software on its own cloud servers. The users of PPIP do not need to purchase, build, and maintain the infrastructure or application software; they just pay for the actual use of appropriate application software according to the number and the length of time. The PPIP service providers are responsible for the full management, maintenance, and upgrading of the software, allowing users to use the platform at any time and anywhere with its latest version.

(d) The Pallet Pooling Client. The users of the PPIP under cloud computing architecture mainly include government management departments, pallet suppliers and customers, and pallet pooling system operators. All users can get access to the PPIP through the web service or API (APP by mobile) by using hardware like mobile phone, notebook computer, intelligent terminal, tablet computer, and so on.

It must be stated that the construction of the PPIP under cloud computing architecture may be established on a hierarchical basis based on different levels, or by integrating these parts into a whole, each of which performs its own different functions. This information system provides a fast, secure, inexpensive, and secure information service for the pallet pooling system.

4.2. The Deployment Model of PPIP Based on the Cloud Computing. There are four kinds of cloud computing for deployment, including public cloud, private cloud, hybrid cloud, and industry cloud. These four modes can be fit for different application requirements with different advantages and disadvantages. According to the business characteristics and requirements of the PPIP, it is obvious that the PPIP under the cloud computing architecture should adopt the hybrid cloud deployment mode, that is, the combination of private cloud and public cloud. The non-main applications use the public cloud, while for the key, confidentiality and core applications use the private cloud. This will balance the security and the cost between private cloud and public cloud.

5. Conclusion

This paper presents a PPIP based on the cloud computing architecture. Of course, this paper only put forward an application model and the basic framework of PPIP with cloud computing; there must be a gap for the real implementation. How to combine the practicality of the pallet pooling system with fully implementing the information platform under the framework of cloud computing remains to be further studied in detail.

Conflicts of Interest

The authors declare that there are no conflicts of interest regarding the publication of this paper.

Acknowledgments

The authors would like to thank Dr. Ming-kai BI who has helped them a lot to improve the English sentences and style of the paper.

References

[1] L. Tai-Ping, "Study on the pattern of overseas pallet circulation and its implication," *Logistics Sci-Tech*, vol. 6, pp. 73–77, 2008.

[2] X. Y. Zhang and J. W. Ren, "The conception model of pallet pool system," *China Market*, vol. 11, pp. 23–26, 2009.

[3] S. S. Jin, Q. X. Xiong, M. X. Jiang et al., "Study on chinese pallet pool Co.Ltd and its construction stratagem," *Industrial Engineering Journal*, vol. 11, no. 4, pp. 19–23, 2008.

[4] Y. Liu, "Study on the Solution Program for pallet pooling information platform," *Value Engineering*, vol. 31, no. 30, pp. 184-185, 2012.

[5] L. Xiao, S. Jin, and D. Z. Feng, "A pallet rental system based on RFID," *Journal of Zhejiang University of Technology*, vol. 6, pp. 666–669, 2011.

[6] X. U. Qi, "Collaborated optimal pricing strategy of pallets pooling supply chain system," *China Business & Market*, vol. 7, pp. 54–59, 2011.

[7] Q. Liang, Y. Liu, and Y. Wang, "Study on pallet pooling management system based on RFID and big data," *Logistics Technology*, vol. 8, pp. 406–408, 2014.

[8] J. Murray, "Pallet pool is key to swedish cargo handling efficiency," *The Journal of ICHCA*, vol. 3, pp. 27–29, 1969.

[9] Z. Ding and Q. Xu, "Research on the RFID-based pallet pool information system," *International Conference of Logistics Engineering and Management*, pp. 2551–2558, 2010.

[10] E. Bottani and A. Rizzi, "Economical assessment of the impact of RFID technology and EPC system on the fast-moving consumer goods supply chain," *International Journal of Production Economics*, vol. 112, no. 2, pp. 548–569, 2008.

[11] J. S. Harris and J. S. Worrell, "Pallet management system: a study of the Implementation of UID/RFID technology for tracking shipping materials within the department of defense distribution network," Defense Technical Information Center, 2008.

[12] X. Z. Lin, "Unified traceability information system of logistics pallet based on the Internet of Things," *Advanced Materials Research*, vol. 765–767, pp. 1181–1185, 2013.

[13] A. Ilic, J. W. P. Ng, P. Bowman, and T. Staake, "The value of RFID for RTI management," *Electronic Markets*, vol. 19, no. 2-3, pp. 125–135, 2009.

[14] S. Vitzthum and B. Konsynski, "CHEP, the net of things," *Communications of the Association for Information Systems*, vol. 22, 2008.

[15] V. Duraccio, V. Elia, and A. Forcina, "An activity based costing model for evaluating effectiveness of RFID technology in pallet reverse logistics system," in *Proceedings of the International Conference of Numerical Analysis & Applied Mathematics (Icnaam '15)*, AIP Publishing LLC, 2015.

[16] J. Ren, X. Zhang, J. Zhang, and P. Wang, "Design of a railway pallet pool information system on grid," *International Conference of Logistics Engineering and Management*, pp. 1252–1258, 2010.

[17] X. Zhang, J. Ren, and Y. Sui, "Operation model and information system of China pallet pool system," *International Conference of Logistics Engineering and Management*, pp. 2162–2168, 2010.

[18] J. Ren, "Design of a loose pallet pool based on cloud computing," *International Conference of Logistics Engineering and Management*, pp. 1111–1115, 2014.

[19] D. Daniluk and B. Holtkamp, "Logistics mall—a cloud platform for logistics," *Cloud Computing for Logistics*, pp. 13–27, 2015.

[20] G. Niharika and V. Ritu, "Cloud architecture for the logistics business," *Procedia Computer Science*, vol. 50, pp. 414–420, 2015.

[21] P. Mell, *The NIST Definition of Cloud Computing*, National Institute of Standards and Technology, 2011.

6

Data Sets Replicas Placements Strategy from Cost-Effective View in the Cloud

Xiuguo Wu

School of Management Science and Engineering, Shandong University of Finance and Economics, Jinan 250014, China

Correspondence should be addressed to Xiuguo Wu; xiuguosd@163.com

Academic Editor: Ligang He

Replication technology is commonly used to improve data availability and reduce data access latency in the cloud storage system by providing users with different replicas of the same service. Most current approaches largely focus on system performance improvement, neglecting management cost in deciding replicas number and their store places, which cause great financial burden for cloud users because the cost for replicas storage and consistency maintenance may lead to high overhead with the number of new replicas increased in a pay-as-you-go paradigm. In this paper, towards achieving the approximate minimum data sets management cost benchmark in a practical manner, we propose a replicas placements strategy from cost-effective view with the premise that system performance meets requirements. Firstly, we design data sets management cost models, including storage cost and transfer cost. Secondly, we use the access frequency and the average response time to decide which data set should be replicated. Then, the method of calculating replicas' number and their store places with minimum management cost is proposed based on location problem graph. Both the theoretical analysis and simulations have shown that the proposed strategy offers the benefits of lower management cost with fewer replicas.

1. Introduction

Today, several cloud providers offer storage as a service, such as Amazon S3 [1], Google Cloud Storage (GCS) [2], and Microsoft Azure [3]. All of these services provide storage in several data centers distributed around the world. Clients can store and retrieve data sets without buying and maintaining their own expensive IT (Information Technology) infrastructures. Ideally, CSPs (Cloud Service Providers) should be able to provide low-latency service to their clients by leveraging the distributed locations for storage offered by these services. However, today's Internet still cannot guarantee quality of services and potential congestions can result in prolonged delays. Replication technology has been commonly used to minimize the communication latency by bringing the copies of data sets close to the clients [4]. Moreover, they also provide data availability, increased fault tolerance, improved scalability, and reduced response time and bandwidth consumption. Amjad et al. [5] have presented various dynamic replication strategies.

Compared with the definitions of conventional computing paradigms such as cluster [6], grid [7], and peer-to-peer (p2p) [8], "economics" is a noticeable keyword in cloud computing which has been neglected in data sets replicas placements. "Economics" denotes that cloud computing adopts a pay-as-you-go model, where clients are charged for consuming cloud services such as computing, storage, and network services like conventional utilities in everyday life (e.g., water, electricity, gas, and telephony) [9]. However, most current replicas approaches largely focus on improving reliability and availability [10, 11] by providing users with different replicas of the same service, ignoring the management cost spending on replicas, which cause great financial burden (storage cost, transfer cost, etc.) not only for cloud users, but also for CSPs.

It is obvious that the client access latency can be reduced with the number of replicas increased. And every client demands to access its data set from a replica that is as close as possible in order to minimize its delay. However, there are at least two challenges while replicating all data sets to all data centers can ensure low-latency access [12]. First, the system can not offer unlimited storage resources, and that approach is costly and may be inefficient for the extra storage resource consumption. Second, the problem is more complicated when the data set may be updated, and the more the replicas are in the system, the higher the update cost will be. Thus, data set replicas need to be carefully placed to avoid unnecessary expense. And the replicas number and their store placements may have a profound impact on the optimal replicas distribution in a balance way from cost-effective view. The resulting tradeoff between the number of replicas and the data set delay maps precisely to the replicas placement problem.

In practice, CSPs supply a pool of resources, such as hardware (storage, network), development platforms, and service at the expense of cost. And data set storage and transfer costs are the two most important components in data management, which are caused by storage resource and bandwidth consumption, respectively. Also, with the number of new replicas increased, the transfer cost will be declined because the data set can transfer more effectively; but the storage cost is getting bigger because of new replicas' existence. That is to say, too many replicas in the cloud may lead to high storage cost, and the increased storage cost for replicas may be greater than the reduced transfer cost, if there is no suitable replicas placements strategy. Therefore, it is urgent to find a balance selectively to replicate the popular data or not.

Based on the analysis above, there are at least three important issues that must be solved in order to achieve the minimum-cost data set replicas placements scheme: (1) whether or not to create a replica in cloud computing environment; (2) how many data set replicas should be created in the cloud; (3) where the new replicas should be placed to meet the system task successful execution rate and bandwidth consumption requirements.

Therefore, in this paper, towards achieving the minimum-cost replicas distribution benchmark in a practical manner, we propose a replicas placements strategy model, including the way to identify the necessity of creating replica, and design an algorithm for replicas placements that can easily reduce the total cost in the cloud.

The main contributions of this paper include (1) proposing data sets management cost models, involving storage cost and transfer cost; (2) presenting a novel global data set replicas placements strategy from cost-effective view named MCRP, which is an approximate minimum-cost solution; (3) evaluating replicas placements algorithms using analysis and simulations.

The remainder of this paper is organized as follows: Section 2 presents related works in data set replicas placement and management cost. Then, in Section 3, data sets cost models are proposed, and a replicas scarce resource test algorithm is shown in Section 4. Section 5 describes the data sets replicas number and store places from cost-effective view based on Steiner Graph. Section 6 addresses the simulation environments, parameters setup, and performance evaluations of proposed replicas solutions. Finally, conclusions and future works are given in Section 7.

2. Related Works

We will present in this section the background related to data sets replicas placements and management cost models in the cloud.

2.1. Data Sets Placements Strategies. Data sets replication is considered to be an important technique used in cloud computing environment to speed up data access, reduce bandwidth consumption and user's waiting time, and increase data availability [13]. Data sets replicas placement is the problem of placing duplicate copies of data set in the most appropriate node in the cloud, which can be logically divided into two stages, namely, replication decision and replicas placements. The replication decision stage decides whether to create the replica. If the decision is not to replicate, the data set will be read remotely. The second stage is to select the best sites to store the new replicas. There are two types of replicas placements techniques: centralized and distributed. Distributed replicas placements can be further classified according to different implementation: free-scale topology [14, 15]; graph topology [16]; multitier architecture [17]; hierarchical architecture [18, 19]; peer-peer architecture [20]; tree architecture [21]; and so on. As a typical centralized replication placements technology, Andronikou et al. have proposed a dynamic QoS-aware data replication technique which is based on data importance in [22]. Kalpakis et al. considered the minimum cost of servicing read and write requests in a distributed system; however it is in a tree network [23].

Conclusions as a result, the above-mentioned replication technologies have not involved data set storage and transfer cost, which are the most important elements for the clients in deciding whether or not to use cloud storage system, especially for small business. Therefore, we will consider the data sets management cost as a basis for replicas placements in order to minimize the storage and transfer costs on the premise that system performance satisfies data set availability requirements in this paper.

2.2. Data Set Management Cost. In a pay-as-you-go paradigm, all the resources in the cloud carry certain costs, so the more the replicas the more we have to pay for the corresponding resources used. Some of them may often be reused while the others may not be. So, once we decide to create a replica, we need to evaluate its access frequency as well as management cost, especially when large data sets—or "big data"—are usually common in the cloud. In [23], toward practically achieving the minimum data set storage cost in the cloud, a runtime local-optimization based storage strategy has been developed. The strategy is based on the enhanced linear CTT-SP algorithm used for the minimum-cost benchmarking. Theoretical analysis and random simulations have shown its validity and reliability. Auction protocol is used by Bell et al. to select the best replica of a data file, where the total cost is computed as the sum of file transfer cost and estimated queuing time for all jobs in the queue [24].

Base on the analysis, it is very necessary to design the data sets replicas placements strategy from cost-effective view. And this research is very significant for business, especially for small businesses, which usually use big data on cloud computing platforms.

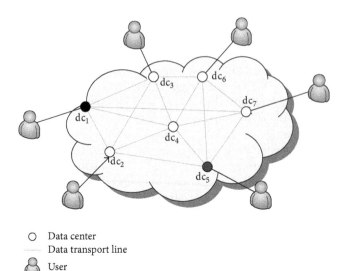

○ Data center
— Data transport line
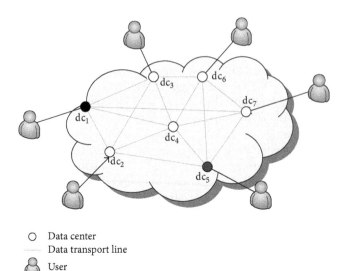 User

FIGURE 1: Architecture of cloud environment.

3. Data Sets Cost Models in the Cloud

In this section, we will first present some concepts in cloud environment; then we propose storage cost model and single transfer cost model, respectively. At last, we present data set management cost model in the cloud.

3.1. Some Concepts in the Cloud. In cloud storage system, there are some distributed data centers in cloud environment for data sets storage. And each data center has some properties, such as storage capacity, CPU speed, and network bandwidth, and read/write speed. Similarly, different configurations of data center lead to different quality of service (QoS).

Definition 1 (cloud computing environment, CCE). Cloud computing environment (CCE) can be regarded as a set of distributed data centers, written as $CCE = \bigcup_{i=1,2,\ldots,|DC|}\{dc_i\}$, where dc_i denotes the ith data center.

Figure 1 describes basic architecture of cloud computing environment constituted by seven data centers.

Definition 2 (data center, DC). In CCE, each data center dc_i can be described as a 5-tuple: $(dc_i, s_i, vs_i, sp_i, tp_i)$, where dc_i is the identifier of data center, which is a unique identification in CCE; s_i is the total space of data center dc_i, whose unit is TB; vs_i is the size of vacant space on data center, which means the extra storage capacity of dc_i; sp_i means the storage price of data, determined by the service provider; and tp_i is transfer cost ratio with each unit size data set.

Definition 3 (data set, d). Data set d_m in CCE can be described as a 3-tuple: (d_m, s, p), where d_m is the identifier of data set, and it is unique in the whole cloud environment; s is the size of data set; and p is its store place, $p \in DC$.

In the following section, we assume that the architecture of CCE and data set d_m are relatively fixed during a period of time for simplicity.

3.2. Data Sets Storage Cost Model. In a commercial cloud computing environment, service providers have their cost models to charge users. For example, Amazon cloud service's prices are as follows: $0.15 per gigabyte per month for the storage resource [1]. Storage cost depends on parameters such as the CSP's price policy, the size of the data set (original data set and inserted data set), and the storage time.

Definition 4 (storage cost, c_s). Data set d_m's storage cost is a function of its data size $d_m \cdot s$, storage time t, and its deployed data center dc_i's storage cost ratio sp_i, and can be represented as follows: $c_s = sp_i \times d_m \cdot s \times t$.

That is to say, the total storage cost is the CSP's storage cost ratio function multiplied by the size of the data set and its storage time, for example, using Amazon S3 for storage pricing and considering that 0.5 T (512 G) data set has been stored for 6 months. The storage cost is $0.15 * 512 * 6 = $460.8.

3.3. Data Sets Transfer Cost Model. In the cloud, the data sets transfers are absolutely necessary once a request arrives, in which process the transfer cost will be generated inevitably for the reason for network consumption. In this model, the input data sets transfers are free, whereas output transfer cost varies with respect to data set volume and the CSP's atomic transfer cost ratio function.

Definition 5 (transfer cost, c_t). Data set d_m's transfer cost is the product of its data sets transfer time t_t and data center dc_i's atomic transfer cost tp_i, which can be described as follows: $c_t = tp_i \times t_t$.

It is noted that the transfer time t_t depends heavily on the data set size and network bandwidth. And in practice, the bandwidth may fluctuate from time to time according to peak and off-peak data access time. In this paper, we simplify the problem and regard the bandwidth as a static value, ignoring the volatility over time. For example, for a 10 G data set, the single transfer cost is $0.12 * 10 = $1.2, if the transfer cost ratio is $0.12 per GB data set.

3.4. Data Sets Management Cost Model. In this paper, we facilitate a data set d_m's management cost during a period depending on several parameters: the size of the data sets $d_m \cdot s$, the time t, and the requests times n during t. And d_m's total management cost can be defined as follows.

Definition 6 (data set d_m's total management cost, tc). Data set d_m's total management cost during a period of t is the sum of its storage cost c_s and transfer cost c_t: $tc = c_s + n \times c_t = sp_i \times d_m \cdot s \times t + tp_i \times t_t \times n$, where n is the requested times.

Let us introduce a simple example: a 500 G data set is stored in the cloud for a month, and the storage cost is $0.1 per GB and per month. The transfer cost is $0.12 per GB data set, and the number of requests is 10. Then, storage cost is $50, and transfer cost is $600, for a total of $650 in a month.

> **Input**: data set d_m, ε_{af}, ε_{rt}, t;
> **Output**: if d_m is a replica scarce resource, return true; else return false;
> (01) count the data set d_m's requested access times n using logs files;
> (02) set $af_{d_m} = n/t$;
> (03) sum the data set d_m's response time rt_i using logs files;
> (04) set $art_{d_m} = (\sum_{k=1}^{i} rt_k)/n$;
> (05) set $rsr_{d_m} = art_{d_m}/d_m \cdot s$;
> (06) if $((af_{d_m} > \varepsilon_{af})$ and $(rsr_{d_m} > \varepsilon_{rt}))$
> (07)   return true;
> (08) else
> (09)   return false;
> (10) End.

ALGORITHM 1: Replica scarce resource testing.

4. Replicas Scarce Resource Model in the Cloud

In this section, we will present the replicas scarce resource model in order to determine whether or not to create a new replica in the cloud.

4.1. Replicas Scarce Resource. There are many data sets stored on the data center in the cloud environment. And it is not necessary to replicate the data set on all the data centers. It is intelligent to replicate the popular data sets with high user frequencies for reducing data set transfer delay. In this way, we will define replica scarce degree as a criterion of adding replicas.

Definition 7 (access frequency, af). For a data set d_m, its access frequency is the requested access times per unit of time and can be represented as follows: $af = \sum_{i=0}^{n} times_i/n$, where $times_i$ indicates the number of accesses to the replicas on data center dc_i of unit time interval and n is the total number of replicas.

If a data set d_m's access frequency is greater than a preset threshold ε_{af}, then data set d_m is hot data.

Definition 8 (response time, rt). Response time rt is the time that elapses when a service requests a data set until the user receives the complete data set.

It is obvious that average response time can be calculated starting from the initial time when the request is submitted till the final response if received with the image from the target node.

Definition 9 (average response time, art). Average response time art is the ratio of total response time and the requested times per unit of time and can be represented as follows: art = $(\sum_{k=1}^{m} rt_k)/m$, where m is the requested times during a period of time t.

Average response time (art) is a basic parameter to determine the replicas numbers and stored places for the reason that the awt can be reduced by placing replicas on data

centers. However, awt is not the only valid parameter to create replicas. The reason is the average response time depends on a number of factors, such as bandwidth and data set size al. And the bigger the data set size, the longer the average response time. In this way, we will present replica scarce resource by introducing data set size.

Definition 10 (replica scarce resource, rsr). A data set d_m is a replica scarce resource if the ratio of a data set d_m's average response time art_{d_m} and its size are less than a preset threshold ε_{rt}, which can be described as $art_{d_m}/d_m \cdot s > \varepsilon_{rt}$.

To sum up, it is necessary to create replicas for replica scarce resource. And there are two important factors to be considered before creating new replica: (1) longer average response time and (2) higher requests frequency.

For those data sets with low requested frequency, and those with high requested frequency but short response time, there is no need to place replicas from cost-effective view. Algorithm 1 describes whether it is necessary to create replicas for data set d_m.

Algorithm 1 presents the way to determine the possibility of creating replicas. And its time complexity is $O(n)$, for the reason that line (04) sums up all the response time n times.

4.2. Replica Placements from Cost-Effective View. Once the decision to create replicas has been made, the most urgent problem needed to solve is where to place it. In this subsection, we will present a replica placement algorithm from cost-effective view.

It is obvious that the replica's candidate store places are not unique, but a set of data centers. Then the most economic way is to select the data centers with lower storage cost and transfer cost to other data centers on the basis of shorter average response time. And Algorithm 2 presents the suitable stored places choosing schema by comparing the data set management cost during a period of time t.

In Algorithm 2, line (01) defines the total cost cc as a largest value, which will be modified immediately after the first cycle. And the function min() in line (10) and line (25) will return the smaller response time and transfer cost, respectively. Line (14) is mainly used to compare average

```
Input: data set dₘ, data centers set DC = {dc₀, dc₁, dc₂, ..., dcₙ}, dc₀ stores the
       primitive data set dₘ, testing time t; pre-set average response time εᵣₜ;
Output: data center dcₘ with lowest cost;
(01) set cc = MAX_COST; //Assuming the cost is largest
(02) set m = 0; //Initialize return data center index
(03) for each data center dcⱼ (except data center dc₀)
(04)   begin
(05)      //Assuming the replica stores on dcⱼ;
(06)      set rsⱼ = 0; //record total response time
(07)      set nⱼ = 0; //record access times;
(08)      for data center dcₖ (except dc₀ and dcⱼ)
(09)         begin
(10)            set rsⱼ = rsⱼ + nₖ × min(rs_{k_dc₀}, rs_{k_dcⱼ});
(11)            set nⱼ = nⱼ + nₖ;
(12)         end
(13)      set arsⱼ = rsⱼ/nⱼ;
(14) if (arsⱼ > εᵣₜ)
(15)    continue;
(16) else
(17)    begin
(18)      calculate the storage cost scⱼ using Definition 4;
(19)      set tc = 0; //transfer cost is initialized to zero
(20)      set nⱼ = 0;
(21)      for data center dcₖ (except dc₀ and dcⱼ)
(22)         begin
(23)            calculate transfer cost c_{tdcₖ-dcⱼ} using Definition 5;
(24)            calculate transfer cost c_{tdcₖ-dc₀} using Definition 5;
(25)            set tc = tc + nₖ × min(c_{tdcₖ-dcⱼ}, c_{tdcₖ-dc₀});
(26)            set nⱼ = nⱼ + nₖ;
(27)         end
(28)      if tc < cc
(29)         m = j;
(30)   end
(31) end
(32) return m.
```

ALGORITHM 2: Select replica's economic stored placements.

response time before and after a replica is stored on data center dc_j. And the process will automatically break and turn into next cycle once average response time is still greater than preset threshold ε_{rt}.

Here, we will analyze the time complexity. Suppose there are n data centers, and in line (08), the loop times for transfer cost are $(n-1)$, the same in line (21). So, the total time complexity is $O(n^2)$.

5. Data Sets Replicas Placements from Cost-Effective View

In the previous sections, we have tentatively placed one replica on a data center and obtained high system performance with lowest data sets management cost. However, replicas number and their storage places are still urgent problems to be solved from cost-effective view in practice. In this section, we will present an approximate minimum-cost replicas placements algorithm based on location problem (LP).

5.1. Minimum-Cost Replicas Placements Model. In order to formulate the minimum-cost replicas placements problem, we make the following assumptions: (1) The cloud computing environment is a customer-to-server system, in which the data sets themselves travel to the facilities to be served. On the other hand, the user requests the data set for further analysis, not a result by computing or querying from the data set. (2) Each data center represents a candidate replica location as well as a data set demand point, for the reason that client requests data via data center. (3) Only one replica may be located per data center. (4) The replicas service is uncapacitated; that is, they may serve an unlimited amount of data sets requests.

In its simplest form, the minimum-cost replicas placements problem is as follows: given a set of data centers, which represent demand points as well as candidate replicas placements, and a set of connections between each pair of data centers. Each connection has a transport cost per unit data set and each data center is associated with a charge for data set storage. Also, all demands must be routed over

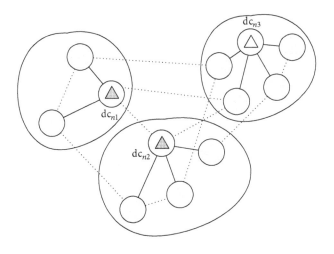

○ Data center

△ Data set

▲ Replica

FIGURE 2: Data set access domain with minimum management cost.

the connection to the nearest replica. The problem is to find the set of replicas placements that minimize the total management cost: the sum of data sets storage and transport cost.

Ideally, the optimal minimum-cost replicas placement is shown in Figure 2, where each replica is stored in a domain D, and the rest of the data centers retrieve data set from it. In this way, the transfer lines and the data centers constitute a tree.

Next, we model the minimum-cost replicas placements problem. Conventionally, a cloud environment is represented by a graph where two nodes have an edge if and only if two corresponding nodes can communicate with each other. In order to describe such a circumstance, we will transform them into a graph G. The transformation rules are as follows:

(1) Each data center dc_i is mapped to a node dc_i in the graph, and all nods constitute the node set V.

(2) Each connection line between two data centers should be classified according to the type of network and used for implementation: (i) lines in one domain from a node with a replica to others can be transformed into edges with weight 0, respectively; (ii) lines in one domain between nodes without replica can be transformed into edges, respectively, and their weight is minimum transfer cost between corresponding data centers; (iii) lines cross-domain can be transformed into edges between corresponding nodes, and its weight is the minimum transfer cost.

(3) The storage cost of each data center should be mapped to the first property of corresponding node.

(4) The product of access frequency and time of period t is mapped to second property of corresponding node.

In order to describe the nodes, we define a 3-tuple (dc_x, c_x, p_x) representing the identifier, storage cost, and transfer times, respectively.

In this way, we wish to find optimal locations at which we place replicas to serve a given set of n clients; we are also given a set of locations at which replicas may be stored, where store replica at data center incurs a cost of $f_1(v_i)$, and each client j must be assigned to one replica (or source data), thereby incurring a cost of c_{ij}, proportional to the distance between data centers dc_i and dc_j; the objective is to find a solution of minimum total cost.

The minimum-cost replicas placements problem is defined as follows.

Definition 11 (minimum-cost replicas placements, MCRP). Given a connected undirected and weighted graph $G = (V, E, w, f_1, f_2)$, (1) V is the set of nodes; (2) E is the set of edges; (3) w is a function $w : e(v_i, v_j) \rightarrow R^+$; (4) f_1 is a function: $v_i \rightarrow R^+$, $v_i \in V$, and $f_1(v_i)$ is a nonnegative real value; (5) f_2 is a function $V \rightarrow Z^+ : v_i \rightarrow Z^+$, and $f_2(v_i)$ is a nonnegative integer value associated with each node. The goal is to divide V into two subsets V_1 and V_2, and V_1 is nodes set with replicas, while V_2 is nodes set without replicas and any $v_i \in V_2$ need to request data set from ($v_j \in V_2$). The task is to construct a forest constituted by trees. Each subtree consists of a source node (with replica) and multiple destination nodes such that the sum of transfer cost and storage cost is minimized. That is, the value from each node v_i to its root multiplied by $f_2(v)$ is minimized, represented as

$$\text{Minimize} \left(\sum_{v_i \in V_1(T)} f_1(v_i) \right) + \sum_{v_i \in V_2(T)} \sum d(T, v_i) f_2(v_i). \tag{1}$$

Several aspects of this formulation are worth noting. First, we observe that if we set the transfer cost to the same, then the result is simple, which is an alternate formulation of the uncapacitated facility location problem (UFLP) in which link additions are disallowed. Thus, the UFLP is a special case of the UFLNDP in which link additions are disallowed. Since the UFLP is NP-hard (in the parlance of computational complexity) [25, 26], so is the more general MCRP. Therefore, we can conclude the following theorem.

Theorem 12. *MCRP is NP-hard.*

In the original problem, we need to decide d_m's replicas number and their places to put. Once we select a data center dc_k, then the sum of the rest of the data centers transfer cost and the storage cost must be minimal compared to selecting other data centers. In the same way, the question that how many replicas need to be placed in the cloud platform has turned into how to select a subset of nodes in graph G that can minimize the sum of nodes weight and edges weight.

Then, it can be regarded as a UFLP using mapping rules shown in Table 1.

Note that the storage cost for the node and cost of the edges should be expressed in comparable units; for example, the storage cost for each node can be expressed in dollars for

TABLE 1: Mapping rules from minimum-cost replica placements strategy to UFLP.

Index	Element in minimum-cost replica placements strategy	Mapping	Element in UFLP
(1)	The transfer cost ratio between data centers c_t	$\rightarrow$	$w(v_i, v_j)$
(2)	The storage cost of each data center c_s	$\rightarrow$	$f_1(v_i)$
(3)	The user requested access times	$\rightarrow$	$f_2(v_i)$
(4)	$\min\left(\text{Cost}_{\text{storage}}(dc_k) + \sum \text{Cost}_{\text{transfer}}\right)$	$\rightarrow$	$\min(\text{Cost}(T))$

```
Input: Graph G = (V, E, w, f₁, f₂) with edge-weighed and node-weighted;
Output: Graph G' = (V', E', w') with edge weighed;
(01) Initialize an edge-weighed graph G'', by setting V'' = V, and w'' = w;
(02) For each (vᵢ, vⱼ) ∈ E, do
(03)    Assign the weight of this edge as
(04)      w''(v''ᵢ, v''ⱼ) = w(vᵢ, vⱼ) + max(f₁(vᵢ) + f₂(vⱼ), f₂(vᵢ) + f₁(vⱼ), f₂(vᵢ) + f₂(vⱼ));
(05) EndFor
(06) Initialize an edge-weighted graph G' by setting V' = V'', and f'₁ = f''₁;
(07) For each vᵢ ∈ V', do
(08)    Assign the weight of edge from vᵢ to vⱼ
(09)      w''(v''ᵢ, v''ⱼ) = Dijkstra (vᵢ, vⱼ);
(10) Output G'.
```

ALGORITHM 3: Construct graph with edge weighted.

each replica, while the cost of each edge can be represented in dollars per request.

Theorem 13. *An optimal solution to the MCRP consists of p replicas and $|N|$-p connections, where N is the total number of data centers.*

This property quantifies our intuition about the tradeoff between constructing facilities and links; that is, as we build more facilities, fewer links are needed. The property also has implications in the identification of polynomial solvable cases, as has been discussed in [27].

In this way, the minimum-cost replicas placements problem is NP-hard. Therefore, no polynomial time algorithms of solving the problem are likely to exist for minimum-cost replica placements. Hence, it is of practical importance to obtain approximation methods whose costs are close to optimal.

5.2. Approximate Algorithm for Replicas Placements with Minimum Management Cost. In this subsection, we introduce an approximate algorithm for MCRP. The idea is first decomposing the transfer ratio to edge weight and then finding the candidate replicas placements data centers using graph G. Finally, the approximate solution for the graph G gives an approximate solution for the original problem.

5.2.1. Transformation from Edge and Node-Weighted Graph to Edge-Weighted Graph. First, we will construct a graph G and then move the user access frequency and storage cost to the edge as weight, constructing an edge-weighted graph. The basic idea can be summarized as follows: decomposing

the storage cost on adjacent edges according to degree of data centers. Algorithm 3 describes the setting of edge weight.

In Algorithm 3, function Dijkstra(v_i, v_j) returns a minimum transfer cost from v_i to v_j. And the time complexity of Dijkstra is $O(n^2)$; we know that the complexity of Algorithm 3 is $O(n^3)$ from line (07).

5.2.2. Approximate Algorithm for MCRP. Next, we will propose approximate minimum management cost replicas placement algorithms based on the graph G'. The basic idea is to obtain possible replicas placements according to the minimum spanning tree, as is shown in Algorithm 4.

In Algorithm 4, function $\deg(v_i)$ means the number of edges linked to node v_i. And Algorithm 4 requires the number of nodes greater than two; if not, the nodes with minimum storage cost are the better ones.

Here, we will analyze the time complexity of Algorithm 4. A simple implementation using an adjacency matrix graph representation and searching an array of weights to find the minimum weight edge to add requires $O(|V|^2)$ running time. Kruskal Algorithm is greedy algorithm that runs in polynomial time, whose time complexity is $O(n^2)$; n is the number of vertexes. In the other steps, such as in line (03), its time complexity is $O(n^2)$. So, the total time complexity of MCRP is $O(n^2)$. A detailed example will be shown in Section 6.2.

The data center that deployed the original data set is responsible for the data set and its replicas' management, including when to create replicas and where to place them. With the data set requests increased (e.g., the number of requests amounts to 5000 in a month), the data set replicas placements algorithm with minimum management cost data

Input: Graph $G' = (V', E', w', f_1', f_2')$ with edge-nodes weighted as (dc_i, c_i);
Output: The nodes set for replicas placements.
(01) Generate a minimum-cost spanning tree from G' using Kruskal Algorithm;
(02) v_i = node with maximum degree;
(03) While $\deg(v_i) \geq 2$ do
(04)   Begin
(05) v_i = node with maximum degree;
(06)   Print v_i;
(07)   For $v_j \in V$ and $i \neq j$ do
(08) If $e(v_i, v_j) \in E$
(09)   Begin
(10)   Delete $e(v_i, v_j)$;
(11)   If $\deg(v_j) = 0$ Delete v_j;
(12)   EndIF
(13)   Delete v_i;
(14) v_i = node with maximum degree;
(15)   EndWhile
(16) End.

ALGORITHM 4: Replicas placements with approximate minimum management cost.

center will start up, and the data set replicas will be transferred to other data centers according to the computation results. Also, a replicas distribution table including some important information such as original data set and its replicas' location will be placed, and its size, most recent update time, and so forth al, will send to each data center, in order to let the others know where the data sets are placed. In this model, a user that connected the data center accesses a data set as follows: First he/she tries to locate the data set replica locally. If the object replica is not present, he/she goes to check the data placement directory residing on each data center, which stored a data set replicas distribution structure. After that, the user's request goes to the nearest data placements center and then will transfer the data set to user via near data center.

6. Analysis and Evaluation

In this section, we first present the experimental setups and then discuss the tradeoff between storage cost and transfer cost. Next, we describe the whole procedures of MCRP approximate algorithm using an example step by step. At last, we compare the result among different circumstances to demonstrate how our replicas placements strategy works.

6.1. Experimental Setup. The experiments were conducted on a cloud computing simulation environment built on the computing facilitates at Network & Information Security Lab, Shandong University of Finance and Economics (SDUFE), China, which is constructed based on SwinDeW [28] and SwinDeW-G [29–31]. The cloud system contains 10 data centers (servers) and 50 high-end PCs (clients), where we install VMWare (http://www.vmware.com), so that it can offer unified computing and storage resources.

Figure 3 describes the simulation architecture model of cloud storage platform, and the prices of cloud services follow the well-known Amazon's cost model: (1) $0.15 per gigabyte

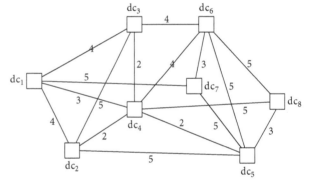

FIGURE 3: Architecture of cloud environment.

TABLE 2: Data sets access configurations.

Data centers	dc_1	dc_2	dc_3	dc_4	dc_5	dc_6	dc_7	dc_8
Users number m_i ($\times 100$)	1	0.6	0.8	1.1	0.6	0.7	0.9	1
Access frequency π ($\times 10$)	2	3	3	5	4	6	5	4

per month for storage; (2) $0.1 per gigabyte for data sets transfer process.

And in the analysis, we observe and study the running conditions for a period of one month. The usage frequency is according to Poisson distribution. Table 2 describes the data centers users' number m, access frequency π, and so forth.

6.2. Tradeoff between Storage and Transfer Costs. We define the cost of a solution in MCRP as the sum of storage cost and transfer cost. In order to compare the total costs with different replicas numbers, we have computed the storage and transfer costs, respectively. The result is shown in Figure 4. Every point on the black thick line in this diagram represents a value of sum cost.

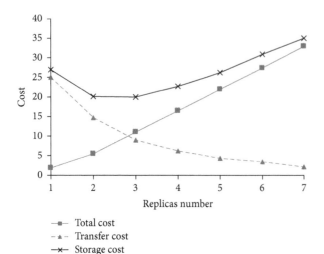

FIGURE 4: Tradeoff between storage and transfer costs.

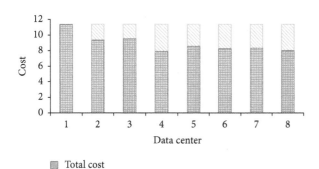

FIGURE 5: Reduced cost comparisons of data centers.

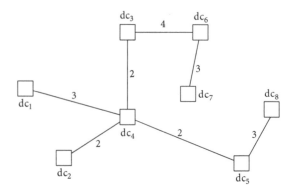

FIGURE 6: Minimum-cost spanning tree.

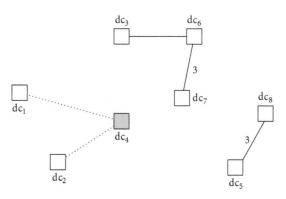

FIGURE 7: Result after first deletion.

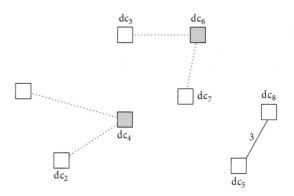

FIGURE 8: Result after second deletion.

From Figure 4, we can see that, without replica, the storage cost is less than transfer cost for the reason that many data sets are transported in the system. However, with replicas number increased, the storage cost is gradually getting bigger for the reason that more replicas need to be stored on data centers, while the transfer cost becomes smaller for the nearby replicas access. Furthermore, the total cost has a minimum value with three replicas, which means the optimal solution.

Similarly, Figure 5 describes the reduced cost with one replica. And the green part is the value that can be saved. Also, it is obvious that the cost will be reduced with the replicas added. Also, we can see that the data center dc_4 is the replica storage place with maximum saved cost.

6.3. Approximate Algorithm for MCRP.

In this section, we will analyze the MCRP algorithms proposed in Section 5.

First, we need to generate a minimum-cost spanning tree from Figure 3 using Kruskal Algorithm. And Figure 6 shows the result, including seven edges.

Then, we will select the node with maximum linked edges, for example, dc_4, and delete its adjacent edges. Also, if the degree of adjacent node is zero, then remove it at the same time, for example, nodes dc_1 and dc_2. Figure 7 shows the

result after first deletion. And in this step, dc_4 is the first selected replica store location.

It is obvious that there still exist nodes with degree greater than two, for example, dc_6, and then the node should be deleted and also its linked edges. In this way, dc_6 is the second selected replica store location. Figure 8 shows the result after second deletion.

In this case, the maximum degree of all nodes is only one, and then the node with small storage cost value is the suitable place to store replica, for the reason that they have the same transfer cost despite where the replica store place is. Figure 9 shows the result of replica store place, that is, a node set of $\{dc_4, dc_6, dc_8\}$.

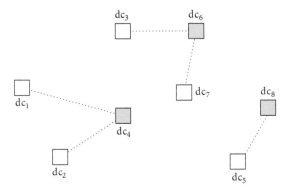

FIGURE 9: Result of replicas store places $\{dc_4, dc_6, dc_8\}$.

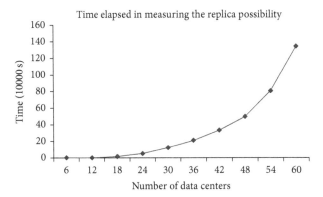

FIGURE 10: Elapsed time in measuring the replica possibility.

6.4. System Performance Comparisons of Replicas and No Replicas. The random simulations are conducted on randomly generated data sets of different sizes, generation times, and usage frequencies. In the simulations, we use a number of 50 data sets, each with a random size from 100 GB to 1 TB. And the usage frequency is also random from 1 to 10 times.

Simulation 1 (time complexity with one replica strategy). In the previous section, we have simulated the possibility of creating replicas in cloud platform. However, the algorithm used is exhaustive method, whose time complexity is very high. Figure 10 describes the elapsed time with increased number of nodes. From Figure 10, we can see that the time has a sharp increase. It is reasonable that we have to consider several data centers as the candidate place for replica.

Simulation 2 (comparisons of replicas numbers between MCRP and optimal strategy). Next, we evaluate the efficiency of MCRP strategy with the optimal solution in different number of usage frequencies. In the simulation, we assume that there is different number of data centers in cloud environment. And also data set usage frequency via each data center is random.

Figure 11 describes comparisons of the replicas numbers with different usage frequency, where we can see that the numbers beyond the optimal values are in tolerable limitations. Also, it is obvious that, with the increase of usage

frequency, the amount of replica numbers increased quickly. The reason is that too much of data access leads to a big burden for network transmission in current conditions, such as network latency and bandwidth.

Simulation 3 (comparison of total cost between MCRP, optimal strategy, "each data center with one replica (ARS)," and "only original data set with no replica (NRS)" strategies). MCRP is a minimum-cost replicas placements strategy that can meet the system requirements under the condition of minimum overall data set cost. In this simulation, we will put the emphasis on the reduced cost between MCRP.

Figure 12 describes comparisons of total cost among different replicas placements strategies, where we can see that the total cost of MCRP is greatly decreased compared to other two straightforward strategies NRS and ARS. However, the total cost of MCRP is higher than the optimal strategy though the time complexity is lower.

From the above experimental and simulation results, the following conclusions can be drawn: (1) the proposed data sets replicas placements strategy effectively reduces the cost of application data set; (2) the proposed data replica strategy reduces the number of replicas; also (3) the proposed data replica strategy can effectively achieve system load balance by placing the popular data files according to the cost and user access history.

7. Conclusions and Future Works

In this paper we have investigated a model that simultaneously optimizes replicas placements from cost-effective view in the cloud. This model has a number of important applications in replication technology. Also, our current research, including experiments and simulations, is based on Amazon cloud's cost model, which can be reused by replacing the corresponding cost ratio. The data sets replicas placements strategy proposed in this paper is generic and dynamic, which can be used in any data intensive applications with different price models of cloud service. As presented in Section 5 and demonstrated in Section 6, minimum-cost replica placements strategy is close to the optimal cost benchmark, though it may not achieve the minimum cost. Therefore, it has great significance in theory and application explained as follows:

(1) The strategy proposed in this paper mainly focused on only one data set d_m, not all the data sets in a dynamic cloud computing system, which is simple and clear in practice. In this way, the popular data sets with high user frequencies are of particular concern, for the reason that they are important factors determining the system performance. However, for those data sets with low access frequency, even never used since generated, we have no need to consider their replicas.

(2) Considering the dynamic nature, which is the main metric of the cloud computing system, such as cost of transfer and storage and the user access frequency, the minimum-cost replica strategy is still available and

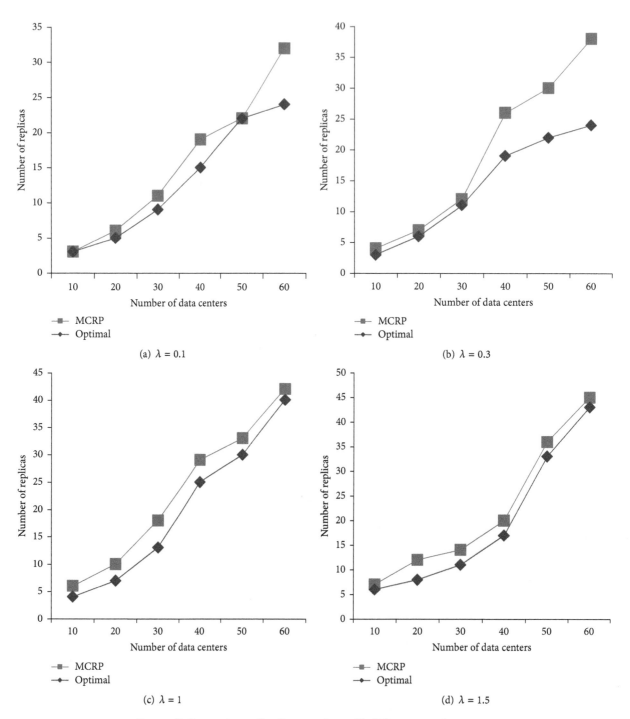

FIGURE 11: Comparisons of replicas numbers with different usage frequency.

effective, since we focus on a period of time T, not a time point t. In this way, the strategy is still applicable as long as we know the total cost in the past time.

(3) The replica deletion and maintenance strategies are also easy to obtain from the minimum-cost replica strategy. The basic idea is that when comparing the total cost with replica and the cost of no replica, then delete replicas once the cost with replicas is greater than no replica. On the other hand, we can update

the replicas stored places according to the minimum-replicas strategy at scheduled time intervals.

Furthermore, experimental results and analysis show that the proposed strategy in cloud environment is feasible, effective, and universal. Hence, we deem that it is highly practical as a replica strategy. However, this paper presents the first attempt to apply the technique to solve the problem as how to place data sets replicas in the most appropriate data centers in the cloud from the minimum-cost view. It must

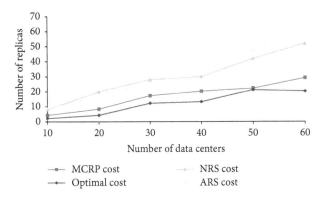

FIGURE 12: Comparisons of total cost among different strategies.

be kept in mind that these findings are the results of a preliminary study. To be more useful in practice, future works can be conducted from the following aspects:

(1) The current work in this paper has an assumption that the data set's usage frequencies are obtained from the system log files. Models of forecasting data set usage frequency can be further studied, with which our benchmarking approaches and replicas strategies can be adapted more widely to different types of applications.

(2) The replicas placements strategy should incorporate the data set generation, and deduplication technology, especially data content based deduplication technology, which is a strong and growing demand for business to be able to more cost-effectively manage big data while using cloud computing platforms.

Competing Interests

The author declares having no competing interests.

Acknowledgments

Some experiments in this paper were done on the cloud platform of SwinDeW-C in Swinburne University of Technology during Xiuguo WU's visiting period, which is sponsored by Shandong Provincial Education Department, China. Moreover, we want to show thanks to Doctor Dong Yuan and Professor Yun Yang, Swinburne University of Technology, Australia, for their valuable feedback on earlier drafts of this paper. In addition, this work presented in this paper is partly supported by Project of Shandong Province Higher Educational Science and Technology Program (no. J12LN33), China; the Doctor Foundation of Shandong University of Finance and Economics under Grant no. 2010034; and the Project of Jinan High-Tech Independent and Innovation (no. 201303015), China.

References

[1] Amazon S3, http://aws.amazon.com/s3.

[2] Google cloud storage, https://cloud.google.com/storage/.

[3] Windows Azure, https://www.azure.cn/.

[4] C.-H. Zuo, Z.-D. Lu, and R.-X. Li, "Load balancing in peer-to-peer systems using dynamic replication policy," *Journal of Chinese Computer Systems*, vol. 28, no. 11, pp. 2020–2024, 2007.

[5] T. Amjad, M. Sher, and A. Daud, "A survey of dynamic replication strategies for improving data availability in data grids," *Future Generation Computer Systems*, vol. 28, no. 2, pp. 337–349, 2012.

[6] A. Martínez, F. J. Alfaro, J. L. Sánchez, F. J. Quiles, and J. Duato, "A new cost-effective technique for QoS support in clusters," *IEEE Transactions on Parallel and Distributed Systems*, vol. 18, no. 12, pp. 1714–1726, 2007.

[7] I. Foster, Y. Zhao, I. Raicu, and S. Lu, "Cloud computing and grid computing 360-degree compared," in *Proceedings of the Grid Computing Environments Workshop (GCE '08)*, pp. 1–10, IEEE, Austin, Tex, USA, November 2008.

[8] Y. Yang, K. Liu, J. Chen et al., "Peer-to-peer based grid workflow runtime environment of SwinDeW-G," in *Proceedings of the IEEE International Conference on e-Science and Grid Computing*, pp. 51–58, Bangalore, India, December 2007.

[9] R. Buyya, C. S. Yeo, S. Venugopal, J. Broberg, and I. Brandic, "Cloud computing and emerging IT platforms: vision, hype, and reality for delivering computing as the 5th utility," *Future Generation Computer Systems*, vol. 25, no. 6, pp. 599–616, 2009.

[10] S. Bansal, S. Sharma, I. Trivedi et al., "Improved self fused check pointing replication for handling multiple faults in cloud computing," *International Journal on Computer Science & Engineering*, vol. 4, no. 6, pp. 1146–1152, 2012.

[11] I. Arrieta-Salinas, J. E. Armendáriz-Iñigo, and J. Navarro, "Classic replication techniques on the cloud," in *Proceedings of the 7th International Conference on Availability, Reliability and Security (ARES '12)*, pp. 268–273, IEEE, Prague, Czech Republic, August 2012.

[12] W. Lloyd, M. J. Freedman, M. Kaminsky et al., "Don't settle for eventual: scalable causal consistency for wide-area storage with COPS," in *Proceedings of the 23rd ACM Symposium on Operating Systems Principles*, pp. 401–416, ACM, Cascais, Portugal, October 2011.

[13] W. Hoschek, J. Jaen-Martinez, A. Samar et al., "Data management in an international data grid project," in *Grid Computing—GRID 2000: First IEEE/ACM International Workshop Bangalore, India, December 17, 2000 Proceedings*, vol. 1971 of *Lecture Notes in Computer Science*, pp. 77–90, Springer, Berlin, Germany, 2000.

[14] D.-W. Chen, S.-T. Zhou, X.-Y. Ren, and Q. Kong, "Method for replica creation in data grids based on complex networks," *The Journal of China Universities of Posts and Telecommunications*, vol. 17, no. 4, pp. 110–115, 2010.

[15] X.-Y. Ren, R.-C. Wang, and Q. Kong, "Using optorsim to efficiently simulate replica placement strategies," *The Journal of China Universities of Posts and Telecommunications*, vol. 17, no. 1, pp. 111–119, 2010.

[16] M. Tu, P. Li, I.-L. Yen, B. Thuraisingham, and L. Khan, "Secure data objects replication in data grid," *IEEE Transactions on Dependable and Secure Computing*, vol. 7, no. 1, pp. 50–64, 2010.

[17] K. Ranganathan and I. Foster, "Identifying dynamic replication strategies for a high-performance data grid," in *Grid Computing—GRID 2001*, C. A. Lee, Ed., vol. 2242 of *Lecture Notes in Computer Science*, pp. 75–86, Springer, Berlin, Germany, 2001.

[18] R.-S. Chang, J.-S. Chang, and S.-Y. Lin, "Job scheduling and data replication on data grids," *Future Generation Computer Systems*, vol. 23, no. 7, pp. 846–860, 2007.

[19] K. Sashi and A. S. Thanamani, "Dynamic replication in a data grid using a modified BHR region based algorithm," *Future Generation Computer Systems*, vol. 27, no. 2, pp. 202–210, 2011.

[20] K. Ranganathan, A. Iamnitchi, and I. Foster, "Improving data availability through dynamic model-driven replication in large peer-to-peer communities," in *Proceedings of the 2nd IEEE/ACM International Symposium on Cluster Computing and the Grid*, p. 376, IEEE, May 2002.

[21] R. M. Rahman, K. Barker, and R. Alhajj, "A predictive technique for replica selection in grid environment," in *Proceedings of the 7th IEEE International Symposium on Cluster Computing and the Grid (CCGRID '07)*, pp. 163–170, Rio de Janeiro, Brazil, May 2007.

[22] V. Andronikou, K. Mamouras, K. Tserpes, D. Kyriazis, and T. Varvarigou, "Dynamic QoS-aware data replication in grid environments based on data 'importance'," *Future Generation Computer Systems*, vol. 28, no. 3, pp. 544–553, 2012.

[23] K. Kalpakis, K. Dasgupta, and O. Wolfson, "Steiner-optimal data replication in tree networks with storage costs," in *Proceedings of the International Symposium on Database Engineering and Applications*, pp. 285–293, IEEE Computer Society, Grenoble, France, July 2001.

[24] W. H. Bell, D. G. Cameron, R. Carvajal-Schiaffino, A. P. Millar, K. Stockinger, and F. Zini, "Evaluation of an economy-based file replication strategy for a data grid," in *Proceedings of the 3rd IEEE/ACM International Symposium on Cluster Computing and the Grid (CCGrid '03)*, pp. 661–668, IEEE, May 2003.

[25] S. Melkote and M. S. Daskin, "An integrated model of facility location and transportation network design," *Transportation Research Part A: Policy and Practice*, vol. 35, no. 6, pp. 515–538, 2001.

[26] D. B. Shmoys, É. Tardos, and K. Aardal, "Approximation algorithms for facility location problems," in *Proceedings of the 29th Annual ACM Symposium on Theory of Computing (STOC '97)*, pp. 265–274, ACM, May 1997.

[27] S. Melkote and M. S. Daskin, "Capacitated facility location/network design problems," *European Journal of Operational Research*, vol. 129, no. 3, pp. 481–495, 2001.

[28] Y. Yang, K. Liu, J. Chen, X. Liu, D. Yuan, and H. Jin, "An algorithm in SwinDeW-C for scheduling transaction-intensive cost-constrained cloud workflows," in *Proceedings of the IEEE Fourth International Conference on eScience (eScience '08)*, pp. 374–375, IEEE, Indianapolis, Ind, USA, December 2008.

[29] J. Yan, Y. Yang, and G. K. Raikundalia, "SwinDeW-a p2p-based decentralized workflow management system," *IEEE Transactions on Systems, Man, and Cybernetics Part A: Systems and Humans*, vol. 36, no. 5, pp. 922–935, 2006.

[30] Y. Yang, K. Liu, J. Chen, J. Lignier, and H. Jin, "Peer-to-peer based grid workflow runtime environment of SwinDeW-G," in *Proceedings of the IEEE International Conference on e-Science and Grid Computin*, pp. 51–58, Bangalore, India, December 2007.

[31] D. Yuan, Y. Yang, X. Liu, and J. Chen, "A local-optimisation based strategy for cost-effective datasets storage of scientific applications in the cloud," in *Proceedings of the IEEE 4th International Conference on Cloud Computing (CLOUD '11)*, pp. 179–186, Washington, DC, USA, July 2011.

7

Task Classification Based Energy-Aware Consolidation in Clouds

HeeSeok Choi,[1] JongBeom Lim,[2] Heonchang Yu,[1] and EunYoung Lee[3]

[1]*Department of Computer Science and Engineering, Korea University, Seoul, Republic of Korea*
[2]*IT Convergence Education Center, Dongguk University, Seoul, Republic of Korea*
[3]*Department of Computer Science, Dongduk Women's University, Seoul, Republic of Korea*

Correspondence should be addressed to EunYoung Lee; elee@dongduk.ac.kr

Academic Editor: Zhihui Du

We consider a cloud data center, in which the service provider supplies virtual machines (VMs) on hosts or physical machines (PMs) to its subscribers for computation in an on-demand fashion. For the cloud data center, we propose a task consolidation algorithm based on task classification (i.e., computation-intensive and data-intensive) and resource utilization (e.g., CPU and RAM). Furthermore, we design a VM consolidation algorithm to balance task execution time and energy consumption without violating a predefined service level agreement (SLA). Unlike the existing research on VM consolidation or scheduling that applies none or single threshold schemes, we focus on a double threshold (upper and lower) scheme, which is used for VM consolidation. More specifically, when a host operates with resource utilization below the lower threshold, all the VMs on the host will be scheduled to be migrated to other hosts and then the host will be powered down, while when a host operates with resource utilization above the upper threshold, a VM will be migrated to avoid using 100% of resource utilization. Based on experimental performance evaluations with real-world traces, we prove that our task classification based energy-aware consolidation algorithm (TCEA) achieves a significant energy reduction without incurring predefined SLA violations.

1. Introduction

Nowadays, cloud computing has become an efficient paradigm of offering computational capabilities as a service based on a pay-as-you-go model [1] and many studies have been conducted in diverse cloud computing research areas, such as fault tolerance and quality of service (QoS) [2, 3]. Meanwhile, virtualization has been touted as a revolutionary technology to transform cloud data centers (e.g., Amazon's elastic compute cloud and Google's compute engine) [4]. By taking advantage of the virtualization technology, running cloud applications on virtual machines (VMs) has become an efficient solution of consolidating data centers because the utilization rate of data centers has been found to be low, typically ranging from 10 to 20 percent [5]. In other words, a single host (physical machine) can run multiple VMs simultaneously and VMs can be relocated dynamically by live migration operations, leading to high resource utilization. Another issue of data centers is high energy consumption, which results in substantial carbon dioxide emissions (about 2 percent of the global emissions). A typical data center consumes as much energy as 25,000 households do [6]. In this regard, an efficient energy consumption strategy in nonvirtualization environments (smart grids) has been carried out [7].

As the virtualization technology [8, 9] has become popular widely, organizations or companies began to build their own private cloud data centers using commodity hardware. In this regard, there exists a need for designing more efficient and effective VM consolidation techniques to reduce energy consumption in cloud data centers. The simplest way to achieve energy reduction in cloud computing environments is to minimize the number of physical machines (PMs) by allocating more VMs in a PM. However, this solution may lead to a high degree of service level agreement (SLA) violations when each VM requires the host's limited resources. Moreover, the relationship between CPU utilization and power consumption is not linear as shown in Figure 1. The power consumption of CPU increases more than linearly as utilization increases. More importantly, when the CPU utilization is above 90%, the power consumption jumps up quickly due to the architectural design and turbo boost

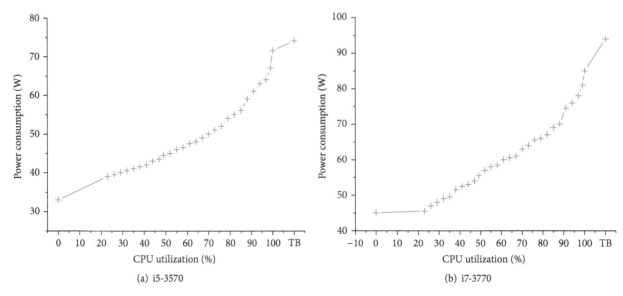

FIGURE 1: Energy consumption of i5 and i7 CPUs (TB indicates turbo boost).

feature. In other words, the performance to power ratio [10] exhibits sublinear growth, and therefore, just putting many VMs to a PM utilizing 100% of CPU is not always the best solution in terms of performance, energy consumption, and SLA violations. We take Intel i5 and i7 CPUs in our experiments, rather than server class CPUs in Figure 1, because, for small and medium sized companies, using commodity hardware like Intel i5 or i7 to build a private cloud is more affordable and accessible [11].

In this paper, we present a new VM and task consolidation mechanism in cloud computing environments. The proposed method is based on task classification, in which we divide cloud tasks into two categories: computation-intensive and data-intensive tasks. A computation-intensive task refers to a computation-bounded application program. Such applications devote most of their execution time to fulfill computational requirements as opposed to I/O and typically require small volumes of data, while a data-intensive task refers an I/O-bounded application with a need to process large volumes of data. Such applications devote most of their processing time to I/O, movement, and manipulation of data. The basic idea of our approach is twofold. One is that when we need to migrate cloud tasks due to a migration policy, we favor a computation-intensive task for migration rather than a data-intensive task since the migration time for computation-intensive tasks is shorter than that of data-intensive tasks. In order to migrate data-intensive tasks, it is necessary to move data for processing as well, and this transferring of data generates communication overheads. Then, we prefer the target VM with no computation-intensive tasks because data-intensive tasks consume less CPU resources, thereby providing a comfortable executing environment for the computation-intensive task. The other is to use a double threshold approach (i.e., upper threshold and lower threshold) for VM migrations and optimization. When a VM's utilization is either above the upper threshold or below the lower threshold, the VM is scheduled for migration. Our

double threshold approach is different from previous work in that no algorithm is proposed to use the upper and lower thresholds simultaneously in an effective way to the best of our knowledge. With an extensive measurement observation, we identified that there is much room for optimization by balancing performance and energy consumption.

Our work differs from traditional scheduling algorithms in the literature by designing and implementing a novel consolidation mechanism based on a task classification approach. We develop corresponding task scheduling and VM allocation algorithms for cloud tasks executed in virtualized data centers.

The major contributions of this paper are summarized as follows:

(i) We designed an energy-aware cloud data center consolidation mechanism based on task classification, while preserving performance and SLA guarantee.

(ii) We developed a cloud task scheduling and VM allocation algorithms that solve problems about when and how to migrate tasks and VMs in an energy efficient way.

(iii) We formulated a double threshold algorithm for further optimization to improve the performance to power ratio.

(iv) We undertook a comprehensive analysis and performance evaluation based on real-world workload traces.

The rest of this paper is organized as follows. Section 2 describes our research motivation and our intuition for consolidation in virtualized clouds. In Section 3, the task classification based energy-aware consolidation scheduling mechanism and the main principles behind it are presented. The experiments and performance analysis are given in Section 4. The related work in the literature is summarized in Section 5. Finally, Section 6 concludes the paper.

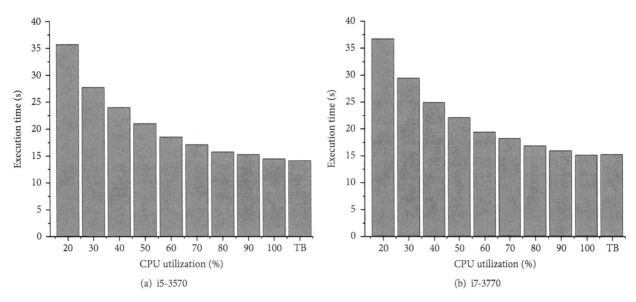

FIGURE 2: Energy consumption and execution time of matrix multiplication of i5 and i7 CPUs.

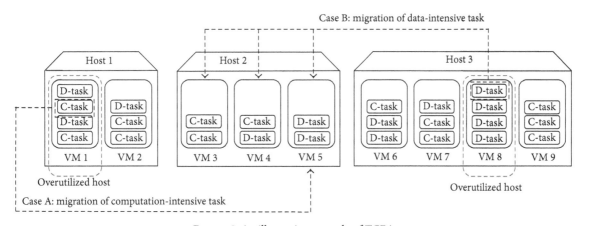

FIGURE 3: An illustrative example of TCEA.

2. Motivation and the Basic Idea

As the virtualization technology has been widely used, it is easily possible to construct a private cloud computing environment with open-source infrastructure as a service (IaaS) solutions and commodity hardware (e.g., desktop-level CPUs and peripherals). Figure 2 shows execution time of a matrix multiplication benchmark program and its performance to power ratio with CPU utilization for Intel i5-3570 and i7-3770 CPUs. With CPU utilization below 50%, the performance gain from the CPUs is noticeable as CPU utilization increases as the performance to power ratio indicates. However, when CPU utilization is above 50% the performance to power ratio grows sublinearly. This means that using high CPU utilization is not always an energy-efficient way to perform tasks. Even when we use a turbo boost feature, one of dynamic voltage and frequency scaling (DVFS) techniques, the performance gain of high frequency of CPU operations is not big considering the performance to power ratio.

Hence, we devise another approach using a threshold of CPU utilization so that a host that manages a couple of VMs does not exceed a predefined CPU utilization threshold. When a host exceeds the threshold, our consolidation algorithm determines to migrate one of the tasks or VMs on the host to another as depicted in Figure 3. Each task is categorized as C-task (computation-intensive task) or D-task (data-intensive task) and is assumed to use 25% of resources or utilization for a VM for simplicity in this example. Note that the task categorization mechanism of C-task and D-task is explained in the next section. Assuming that the threshold is 75% for a VM, tasks in VM 1 and VM 8 should be migrated to underutilized VMs. For Case A, in which there are C-tasks and D-tasks in a VM, our consolidation algorithm chooses a C-task to be migrated and preferentially selects a target VM with no C-tasks since migrating a C-task takes much shorter time compared to a D-task and migrating a D-task introduces a major I/O bottleneck in the host. For Case B, in which there are only D-tasks but C-tasks, we only consider underutilized

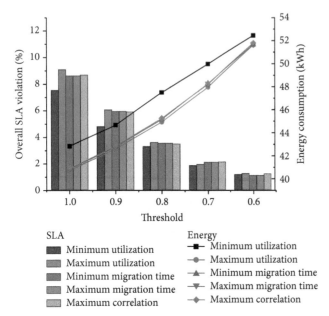

FIGURE 4: Energy consumption and SLA violations with threshold and migration policies.

VMs for target, disregarding the category of tasks running on the target VM. For task migration, there are many prevalent software and management technologies, such as openMosix, which is a Linux kernel extension that allows processes to migrate to other nodes seamlessly.

On the other hand, choosing a proper threshold value is an important factor that influences the overall performance and there is a tradeoff between the threshold value and SLA violation. Figure 4 shows the tradeoff with various migration policies. Obviously, lowering the threshold value leads to lower energy consumption, but it causes SLA violations, meaning a user's request for tasks cannot guarantee to be succeeded in preagreed metrics. In a condensed situation, where there is no host that can afford additional VMs and the ratio of PM to VM is low, it is more desirable to use a higher threshold value, whereas, in a sparse situation, where there are many free hosts available for additional VMs and the ratio of PM to VM is high, it allows having a lower threshold value but it is energy consuming and wastes resources. As far as the latter case is concerned, we use a double threshold approach to reduce energy consumption more, while incurring the overall SLA violation as little as possible. The resource types for a system are CPU, memory, storage, network, and so forth. Among them, CPU is the most dominant factor that influences energy consumption [12]. In this paper, we focus on CPU utilization for migration policies and leave integrating other types of resource into the migration policies as future work.

3. Task Classification Based Energy-Aware Consolidation Algorithm (TCEA)

As shown in Figure 5, we consider a typical cloud data center with a cloud portal. When a user submits a task to the

cloud portal, TCEA first performs a task classification process based on configurations of the task and historical logs. The task is categorized as either computation-intensive or data-intensive. Then, with this task classification information, we assign the task to an appropriate VM and consolidate VMs in the data center in an energy-aware way. After that, TCEA periodically checks hosts with a predefined threshold value so that unnecessary hosts are powered down after migrating their VM to others, while maintaining SLA. The detailed description of our proposed algorithms is given below.

(A) Double Threshold Scheme. Our consolidation algorithms are based on the double threshold scheme. In order to save energy consumption of a cloud data center, one may consider using the minimum number of hosts by utilizing CPU as much as possible for VMs. However, this approach is not an energy efficient solution because it disregards the performance to power ratio. Thus, TCEA uses the upper threshold to prevent heating CPUs up. On the other hand, when many of the hosts are easygoing as a whole, it is necessary to minimize active hosts to save superfluous energy consumption by consolidating VMs. For that purpose, we employ the lower threshold. With the lower threshold, TCEA periodically checks hosts and VMs whether it requires VM or task consolidation. For example, if a host operates with CPU utilization below the lower threshold, we migrate VMs on the host to other hosts as long as there are available hosts to accommodate the VMs without restricting VMs' liberty. With these in mind, it is important to choose proper values for the double threshold scheme, that is, the upper threshold and lower threshold, considering the tradeoff between performance and energy consumption. To determine the conditions of suitable threshold values, we conduct several experiments in Section 4.

(B) Task Classifier. Unlike previous work, we consider a task's characteristics in consolidating a cloud data center. Towards this end, we place a task classifier module to categorize tasks into computational-intensive or data-intensive tasks. When a user submits a task, it examines history log files to check whether it has been performed before. If so, TCEA uses the previous classification information without performing the task classification process. If not, it performs the task classification process as shown in Algorithm 1.

The criteria of classifying tasks in the task classifier function are based on the communication to computation ratio [13]. By examining the execution time and task transfer time of a task, it puts the task to the corresponding queue. In other words, when computation time is greater than task transfer time of a task, the task classifier makes the task resident in $taskQueue_{computation}$. Otherwise, the task is considered as data-intensive. The classification information of the task is also stored in the storage for future use.

(C) Task Assignment. The next step after performing the task classification process is to assign tasks to appropriate VMs. When assigning a task, TCEA first tries to find a host whose utilization is relatively low as shown in Algorithm 2. Then, it checks all the VMs in the host by counting the number

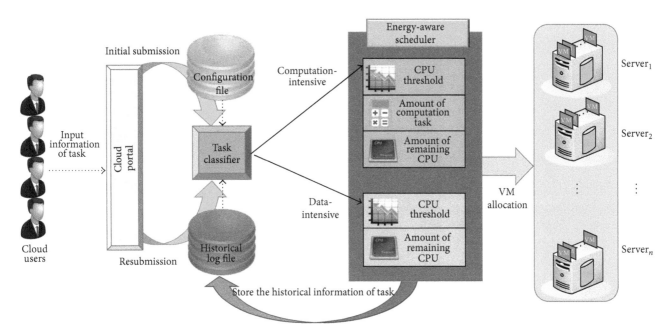

FIGURE 5: System architecture of TCEA.

of computation-intensive tasks. Out of the VMs, a VM that has the least number of computation-intensive tasks can be a candidate when the task is computation-intensive. After iterating this phase, the task assignment function selects a VM for the task.

When the type of a task is data-intensive, TCEA does not care about the types of tasks for finding target VMs. The only consideration is the number of tasks running in VMs. Thus, it finds a VM that runs the minimum number of tasks in order to balance the load. For optimization, the task assignment function migrates a task to another VM. At this stage, we favor computation-intensive tasks for migration because migrating data-intensive tasks is inefficient. In other words, migrating data-intensive tasks takes more time than migrating computation-intensive tasks since it is necessary to move the data of data-intensive tasks as well. When finding an overutilized host, TCEA prefers a VM that runs the largest number of computation-intensive tasks for migration. This is based on the fact that migrating a computation-intensive task is more efficient than migrating a data-intensive task with regard to the number of migrations and utilization shifting. Once a task is chosen for migration, the next step is to choose a target VM. There are two conditions for choosing a target VM. One is CPU utilization and the other is the number of computation-intensive tasks. Among VMs whose host's CPU utilization is low, a VM that runs the least number of computation-intensive tasks will be chosen for the target VM. Then, the task is scheduled to be migrated accordingly.

(D) Consolidation of VMs. For VM consolidation, it is essential to handle and manage VMs and hosts chosen by the double threshold scheme. Algorithm 3 shows the VM consolidation in TCEA in detail. When a host's utilization is above the upper threshold (i.e., overutilized hosts), TCEA

chooses a VM to be migrated considering the number of computation-intensive tasks. The more computation tasks a VM has, the more likely the VM is to be a source for migration. Once a source VM is selected, a target host selection phase is performed. Since a source VM will occupy a large portion of utilization, it is preferable to choose a target host whose utilization is relatively low. Therefore, the chosen target host may have fewer numbers of computation-intensive tasks than others. On the other hand, when managing underutilized hosts chosen by the lower threshold, all the VMs in the host will be migrated to hosts whose utilization is normal across the data center. The reason why TCEA chooses normally utilized hosts as migration targets is to exploit the performance to power ratio. Choosing a host of full utilization as a target will result in more energy consumption and consolidation management overheads. For example, when a host becomes overutilized and is chosen as a target host, TCEA will perform redundant load balancing operations.

(E) Task Classification Based Energy-Aware Consolidation Algorithm (TCEA). Algorithm 4 covers our overall consolidation and scheduling scheme. Note that the procedure of lines (1)–(6) is triggered upon receipt of a set of tasks and that of lines (7)–(18) is performed periodically. The task classifier function and the task assignment function are responsible for consolidation and management of tasks in TCEA. TCEA monitors VMs and hosts in the cloud data center for status updates. With the predefined values including the upper and lower thresholds, TCEA maintains $list_{upper}$, $list_{normal}$, and $list_{lower}$ of hosts. To balance performance and energy consumption, VMs in $list_{upper}$ and $list_{lower}$ will be migrated to $list_{normal}$. It is worth noting that choosing the proper values of the upper threshold, lower threshold, and the number of

(1) if $task_i$ has no historical log file
(2)   if VM execution time is greater than data movement time
(3) $taskQueue_{Computation} \leftarrow taskQueue_{Computation} \cup task_i$;
(4)   else
(5) $taskQueue_{Data} \leftarrow taskQueue_{Data} \cup task_i$;
(6)   end if
(7) else // The $task_i$ has historical log file
(8)   Retrieve information from the configuration file;
(9)   Classify data type using obtained information;
(10) end if

ALGORITHM 1: *Task_Classifier ( )*.

(1) if $task_i \in taskQueue_{Computation}$
(2)   for all $host_i \in list_{normal}, \forall i \in \{1, 2, \ldots, n\}$;
(3)   Find a $host_i$ with the lowest CPU utilization;
(4)   for all $vm_i \in host_i, \forall i \in \{1, 2, \ldots, n\}$;
(5)   Check the number of computation-intensive tasks;
(6)   Find a vm_i having the least number of computation-intensive tasks;
(7)   end for
(8)   end for
(9)   Assign $task_i$ to vm_i
(10) else if $task_i \in taskQueue_{Data}$
(11)   for all $host_i \in list_{normal}, \forall i \in \{1, 2, \ldots, n\}$;
(12)   Find a $host_i$ with the lowest CPU utilization;
(13)   for all vm_i $host_i, \forall i \in \{1, 2, \ldots, n\}$;
(14)   Check the number of tasks;
(15)   Find a vm_i having the least number of tasks;
(16)   end for
(17)   end for
(18)   Assign $task_i$ to vm_i;
(19) end if

ALGORITHM 2: *Assign_Task ( )*.

(1) // for over-utilized hosts $\in list_{upper}$
(2) Find a $host_i$ with the highest CPU utilization $\in list_{upper}$;
(3) for all $vm_i \in host_i, \forall i \in \{1, 2, \ldots, n\}$;
(4)   Check the number of computation-intensive tasks;
(5)   Find a vm_i having the largest number of computation-intensive tasks;
(6) end for
(7) for all $host_j \in list_{normal}$;
(8)   Check the number of computation-intensive tasks;
(9)   Find a $host_j$ having the least number of computation-intensive tasks;
(10) end for
(11) Migrate vm_i to $host_j$;
(12) // for under-utilized hosts $\in list_{lower}$
(13) for all $host_j \in list_{lower}, \forall j \in \{1, 2, \ldots, n\}$;
(14)   Find a $host_j$ with the lowest CPU utilization;
(15) end for
(16) Migrate all VMs $\in host_j$ to $host_k \in list_{normal}$;
(17) Switch off $host_j$;

ALGORITHM 3: *Consolidate_VM ( )*.

```
(1)   for all task_i, where task_i ∈ Task, ∀i ∈ {1, 2, ..., n};
(2)       Task_Classifier ( )
(3)       Assign_Task ( )
(4)   end for
(5)   Update the status of each task;
(6)   Store monitored status information;
(7)   for all host_i, where host_i ∈ Host, ∀i ∈ {1, 2, ..., n};
(8)       Monitor the status of host;
(9)       if CPU utilization is higher than threshold_upper
(10)          list_Upper ← list_Upper ∪ host_i;
(11)      else if CPU utilization is lower than threshold_lower
(12)          list_lower ← list_lower ∪ host_i;
(13)      else
(14)          list_normal ← list_normal ∪ host_i;
(15)      end if
(16)      Store monitored status information;
(17)  end for
(18)  Consolidate_VM ( )
```

ALGORITHM 4: Task classification based energy-aware consolidation algorithm.

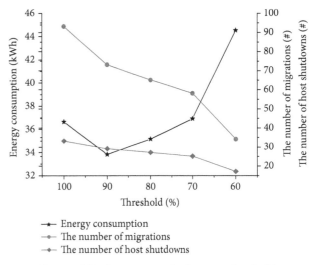

FIGURE 6: Performance results for upper threshold.

VMs to be migrated influences the performance of TCEA. In the next section, we validate TCEA for energy efficiency and performance with these parameters.

4. Performance Evaluation

In this section, we present experimental results that demonstrate the performance of TCEA for reducing energy consumption by managing VM consolidation while achieving SLA satisfaction. As input, we use real task traces (Intel Netbatch logs [14]) and artifact task logs for a fixed combination of computation-intensive tasks and data-intensive tasks. For experiments, we assume that there are 50 hosts and 100 VMs running in the cloud data center unless specified otherwise. A host is equipped with a quad-core CPU (i7-3770) with 4 GB of RAM and gigabit Ethernet. A user can specify the type of a VM such as the number of vCPU, RAM, and storage capacity. Otherwise, a default VM setting with 1 GB of RAM and 1 vCPU is used.

In this experiment, we analyze the runtime of TCEA with varying upper thresholds from 100% to 60%. We conduct this experiment for the real world datasets mentioned above. In Figure 6, x-axis denotes the upper threshold and y-axis represents the energy consumption, the number of VM migrations, and the number of host shutdowns. The number of VM migrations and the number of host shutdowns are constantly going down as the upper threshold decreases. With decreased upper threshold, the available hosts tend to remain alive because VMs should reside in hosts whose utilization is below the upper threshold, and therefore, the number of VM migrations is reduced as well. For energy consumption, 90% is optimal. This indicates that (1) although hosts with 100% of upper threshold maintain more VMs, 100% is not the best threshold due to the performance to power ratio, (2) even though the number of host shutdowns peaks with

100% of upper threshold, the energy reduction of using the lower threshold (90%) dominates that of the number of host shutdowns, and (3) the number of VM migrations decreases with lower upper threshold because the probability of finding satisfactory target VMs gets lower too. For the rest of experiments, we use 90% of upper threshold unless specified otherwise.

For a sparse situation, where there are many free hosts available for additional VMs and the ratio of PM to VM is high, we devise an optimization algorithm to migrate VMs from underutilized hosts to others and shutdown the hosts, thereby reducing energy consumption. To this end, we use a lower threshold such that VMs in a host below the lower threshold are scheduled to be migrated to other hosts, and then the host gets shutdown. Figure 7 shows energy consumption, the number of VM migrations, and the number of host shutdowns with varying lower thresholds (e.g., 0.8 of x-axis means that 20% of hosts are chosen by the lower threshold). Comparing with default (no task classification is performed), TCEA consumes 14.05% less energy on average. When the lower threshold is 50%, the difference between default and TCEA reaches a peak. With respect to energy consumption, the number of VM migrations, and the number of host shutdowns, we use 50% of lower threshold for the rest of experiments unless specified otherwise.

To verify the effectiveness of lower thresholds, we conduct another experiment showing energy consumption, the number of VM migrations, and the number of host shutdowns with VM ratios by increasing the number of VMs and hosts (1x means a default setting of 100 VMs and 50 hosts). Note that, in this experiment, 0.9 of VM ratio means that 10% of hosts whose utilization is below the lower threshold are scheduled to be powered down by migrating their VMs. As shown in Figure 8, around 50% of the VM ratio suits our purpose in terms of energy consumption, the number of VM migrations, the number of host shutdowns, and SLA violations. The ratio below 0.5 leads to SLA violations; therefore we do not use ratio lower than 0.5.

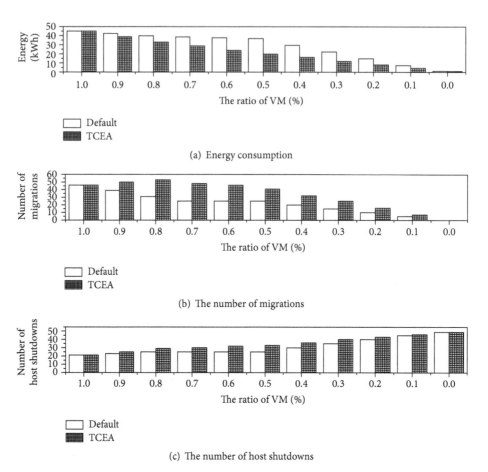

(a) Energy consumption

(b) The number of migrations

(c) The number of host shutdowns

FIGURE 7: Performance results for lower threshold.

To investigate the respective improvement brought by TCEA's double threshold scheme, we compare the performance of TCEA (double threshold) with the single threshold scheme and default (no threshold and no task classification) setting. In this experiment, we use real task trace logs and artifact task logs for a fixed combination of computation tasks and data-intensive tasks. In Figure 9, "Job" indicates real task traces, Job_c indicates only computation-intensive tasks, Job_d indicates only data-intensive tasks, and Job_cd indicates 50% of computation-intensive tasks and 50% of data-intensive tasks.

As shown in Figure 9, there is no difference for the results with the default setting (no threshold) in terms of energy consumption because a threshold scheme is not applicable. Nevertheless, we leave them for comparison. The double threshold scheme saves 47.6% of energy compared to the default setting. For the single threshold scheme, there is no big difference between 90% and 100% but there are more VM migration operations with 100% of upper threshold, which leads to overheads. Of job categories (Job, Job_c, Job_d, and Job_cd), Job_d shows a little performance impact with single threshold because it uses relatively less CPU utilization, and Job_cd has performance improvement when the single threshold is above 80%. The result for double threshold shows similar phenomenon when the single threshold is used. However, the double threshold scheme further reduces energy

consumption by 14.2% compared to the single threshold scheme.

An important requirement for achieving the optimal performance of virtualized cloud environments is to find the appropriate number of VMs per PM. In such an environment, the ratio of PM to VM affects the overall performance. To validate the effect of the ratio of PM to VM, we compare the threshold schemes (default, single, and double). The double scheme achieves the largest energy reduction, followed by the single scheme and by the default scheme as shown in Figure 10. The double threshold scheme saves energy consumption by 11.3% and 27.2% comparing with single and default, respectively. For the number of VM migrations, there are some points where the double threshold scheme exhibits more VM migrations than the single threshold scheme does, but it stabilizes when the ratio of PM to VM is 1:9 or more. In addition, the double threshold scheme always outperforms with respect to the number of host shutdowns.

To measure the scalability for the number of PMs and VMs, we increase the number of PMs and VMs from 1:2 up to 10:20 as shown in Figure 11. As expected, TCEA consumes less energy by 17.9% on average than the default scheme and outnumbers the default scheme in terms of the number of shutdowns. For VM consolidation, TCEA has a higher number of VM migrations. For task scalability, we compare energy consumption by increasing the task log size

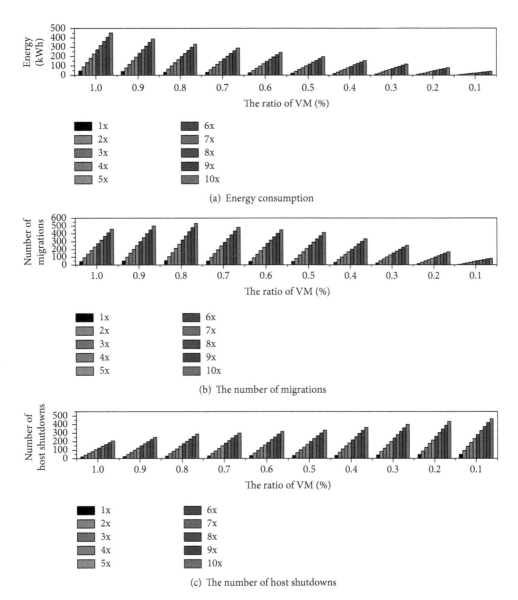

(a) Energy consumption

(b) The number of migrations

(c) The number of host shutdowns

FIGURE 8: Performance scalability for the number of nodes with lower threshold.

up to 10 times as depicted in Figure 12. Comparing with the default scheme, TCEA consumes less energy by 15.8% on average. Obviously, TCEA has more VM migration and host shutdown operations than the default scheme has for VM consolidation.

5. Related Work

We summarize the related work across three perspectives: resource allocation and scheduling in data centers and clouds, threshold-based schemes with different objectives, and energy savings in data centers. To balance energy consumption and VM utilization, the authors of [10] used a performance to power ratio. It schedules VM migration dynamically and consolidates servers in clouds. They compared their proposed algorithm with three different algorithms including the DVFS algorithm using real trace log files. The authors of [13] proposed a criterion to divide computation-intensive tasks and data-intensive tasks using a communication to computation ratio. The rationale of this task classification is to employ resource allocation methods based on tasks or workflows to improve performance.

In [15], they developed an energy-aware scheduling to reduce total processing time for VMs in a precedence-constrained condition, while maximizing PM's utilization considering communication costs. In [16], they proposed a prediction algorithm for finding overutilized servers and a best-fit algorithm for hosts and VMs. The results show that the algorithms reduce the number of migration operations, rebooting servers, and energy consumption, while achieving SLA guarantee. A separation mechanism of I/O tasks to perform computation-intensive tasks in a batch in virtualized servers to mitigate virtualization overheads is proposed in

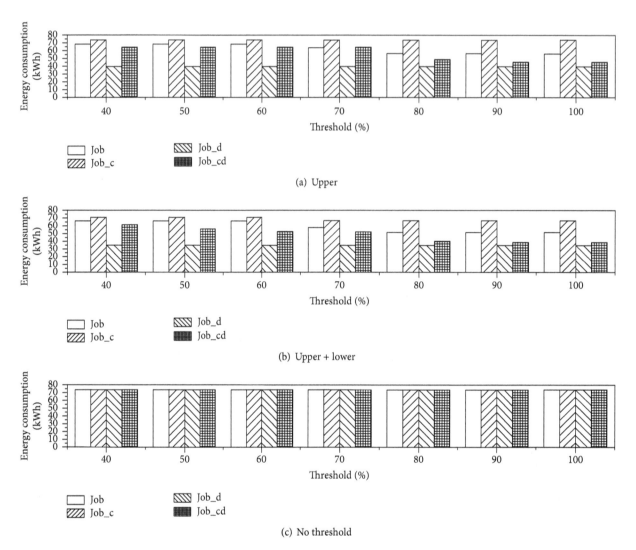

FIGURE 9: Performance comparison with task types and threshold schemes.

[17]. Because energy consumption and the frequency of SLA violations determine the quality of service [18], in this paper, we balance the tradeoff between energy consumption and SLA violations using the double threshold schemes based on tack classification and none of the abovementioned studies consider the energy saving objectives in the context of task classification.

For data-intensive workflows, where the majority of energy consumption accounts for storing and retrieving data, the authors of [19] consider not using DVFS. Instead, they installed and used an independent node to store data-intensive tasks. They endeavor to reduce energy consumption by minimizing data access and then performed evaluations by increasing the communication to computation ratio. The authors of [20] proposed a VM scheduling algorithm to reduce energy consumption with DVFS. By dynamically adjusting clock frequency and its corresponding voltage, it results in energy reduction in idle and computation stages. In [21], they proposed a scheduling algorithm based on priority and weight with DVFS. It increases servers' resource

utilization to reduce energy consumption of the servers. In [22], they used a threshold value to migrate a VM to another host. When a host's utilization is below the threshold value, all the VMs belonging to the host are scheduled to be migrated to other hosts to save idle power consumption. In addition, some VMs are scheduled to be migrated when the host's utilization exceeds a certain threshold value to avoid SLA violations. A service framework that allows monitoring energy consumption and provisioning of VMs to appropriate location in an energy-efficient way is designed in [23].

Various CPU consolidation techniques including DVFS, dynamic power shutdown (DPS), and core-level power gating (CPG) are introduced in [24]. The authors of [25] used a threshold value to migrate VMs and consider resource, temperature, and network conditions for optimization. They considered migration time to minimize the number of VMs that are in progress of migration simultaneously. The authors of [26] designed an energy-aware resource allocation heuristic for VMs' initial placement, VM selection policy for migration, and migration policy in virtualized cloud

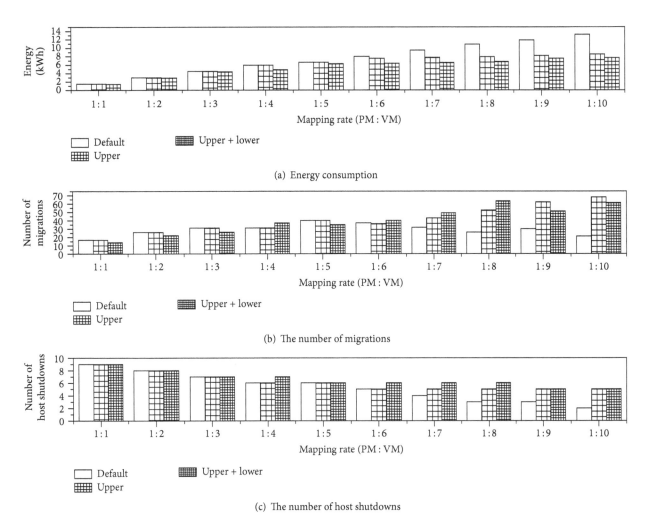

(a) Energy consumption

(b) The number of migrations

(c) The number of host shutdowns

FIGURE 10: Performance comparison with PM to VM ratio.

computing environments. The authors of [27] developed a resource allocation method at the cloud application level. In the application's perspective, it allocates virtual resources for the application with a threshold-based dynamic resource allocation algorithm to improve resource utilization. In [28], they developed a VM placement algorithm based on the evolutionary game theory. According to their experiments, when the loads of the data center are above 50%, the optimizations are unnecessary.

However, the design objective and the implementation methods of these cloud data center schedulers and consolidation algorithms are different from TCEA in terms of the following aspects. First, the target of these cloud data center schedulers is to enforce resource allocation strategy based on fairness or priorities when sharing the resources of large-scale cloud data centers among VMs, while TCEA is aimed at improving both energy consumption and the performance of tasks by dynamically migrating VMs in runtime. Second, we extend a single threshold scheme to further improve the overall performance and energy consumption by incorporating the double threshold scheme and task classification together. Finally, they cannot solve both the maximum utilization problem and the host shutdown problem in an efficient

way, while TCEA takes the performance to power ratio into consideration and employs the host shutdown mechanism by migrating VMs on underutilized hosts while maintaining SLA violations.

6. Conclusions

As green IT and its related technologies have received much attention recently, reducing the power consumption of cloud data centers is one of the critical issues to address, thereby reducing the carbon dioxide footprints. In this paper, we propose two consolidation mechanisms for a cloud data center. One is the task consolidation based on task classification (computation-intensive or data-intensive) and the other is the VM consolidation that uses a double threshold scheme (upper and lower). We optimize energy consumption in a virtualized data center not by maximizing resource utilization but by balancing resource utilization of hosts with migrating appropriate VMs. We prove that our task classification based energy-aware consolidation algorithm (TCEA) achieves significant energy reduction without incurring predefined SLA violations.

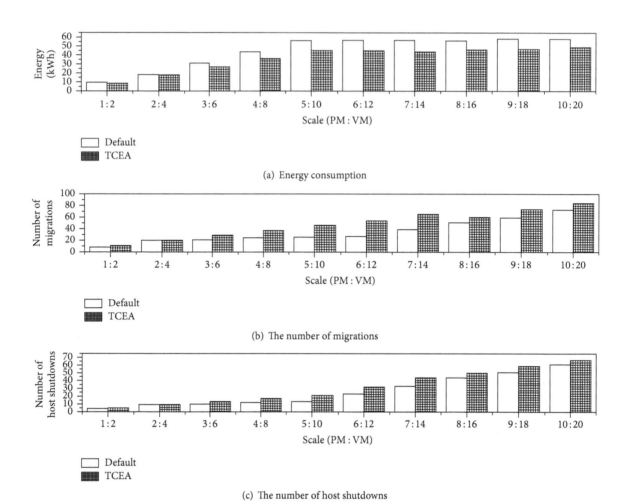

(a) Energy consumption

(b) The number of migrations

(c) The number of host shutdowns

FIGURE 11: Performance comparison with scalability.

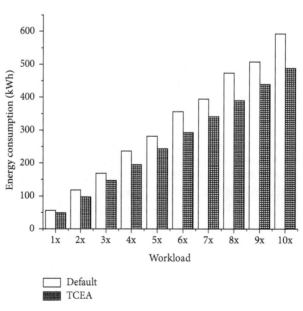

FIGURE 12: Scalability for the number of tasks.

Competing Interests

The authors declare that they have no competing interests.

Acknowledgments

This research was supported by Basic Science Research Program through the National Research Foundation of Korea (NRF) funded by the Ministry of Science, ICT & Future Planning (NRF-2015R1C1A2A01054813).

References

[1] W. Ai, K. Li, S. Lan et al., "On elasticity measurement in cloud computing," *Scientific Programming*, vol. 2016, Article ID 7519507, 13 pages, 2016.

[2] J. Lim, T. Suh, J. Gil, and H. Yu, "Scalable and leaderless Byzantine consensus in cloud computing environments," *Information Systems Frontiers*, vol. 16, no. 1, pp. 19–34, 2014.

[3] S. K. Choi, K. S. Chung, and H. Yu, "Fault tolerance and QoS scheduling using CAN in mobile social cloud computing," *Cluster Computing*, vol. 17, no. 3, pp. 911–926, 2014.

[4] M. Armbrust, A. Fox, R. Griffith et al., "A view of cloud computing," *Communications of the ACM*, vol. 53, no. 4, pp. 50–58, 2010.

[5] Y. Wen, X. Zhu, J. J. P. C. Rodrigues, and C. W. Chen, "Cloud mobile media: reflections and outlook," *IEEE Transactions on Multimedia*, vol. 16, no. 4, pp. 885–902, 2014.

[6] M. Dayarathna, Y. Wen, and R. Fan, "Data center energy consumption modeling: a survey," *IEEE Communications Surveys & Tutorials*, vol. 18, no. 1, pp. 732–794, 2015.

[7] N. Boumkheld, M. Ghogho, and M. E. Koutbi, "Energy consumption scheduling in a smart grid including uding renewable energy," *Journal of Information Processing Systems*, vol. 11, no. 1, pp. 116–124, 2015.

[8] P. Barham, B. Dragovic, K. Fraser et al., "Xen and the art of virtualization," *ACM SIGOPS Operating Systems Review*, vol. 37, no. 5, pp. 164–177, 2003.

[9] I. Habib, "Virtualization with KVM," *Linux Journal*, vol. 2008, no. 166, article 8, 2008.

[10] X. Ruan and H. Chen, "Performance-to-power ratio aware Virtual Machine (VM) allocation in energy-efficient clouds," in *Proceedings of the IEEE International Conference on Cluster Computing (CLUSTER '15)*, pp. 264–273, Chicago, Ill, USA, September 2015.

[11] D. Sood, H. Kour, and S. Kumar, "Survey of computing technologies: distributed, utility, cluster, grid and cloud computing," *Journal of Network Communications and Emerging Technologies*, vol. 6, no. 5, pp. 99–102, 2016.

[12] Y. Gao, H. Guan, Z. Qi, B. Wang, and L. Liu, "Quality of service aware power management for virtualized data centers," *Journal of Systems Architecture*, vol. 59, no. 4-5, pp. 245–259, 2013.

[13] W. Guo, W. Sun, W. Hu, and Y. Jin, "Resource allocation strategies for data-intensive workflow-based applications in optical grids," in *Proceedings of the 10th IEEE Singapore International Conference on Communications Systems (ICCS '06)*, pp. 1–5, IEEE, Singapore, November 2006.

[14] O. Shai, E. Shmueli, and D. G. Feitelson, "Heuristics for resource matching in Intel's compute farm," in *Job Scheduling Strategies for Parallel Processing*, vol. 8429, pp. 116–135, Springer, 2013.

[15] V. Ebrahimirad, M. Goudarzi, and A. Rajabi, "Energy-aware scheduling for precedence-constrained parallel virtual machines in virtualized data centers," *Journal of Grid Computing*, vol. 13, no. 2, pp. 233–253, 2015.

[16] J. Huang, K. Wu, and M. Moh, "Dynamic Virtual Machine migration algorithms using enhanced energy consumption model for green cloud data centers," in *Proceedings of the International Conference on High Performance Computing & Simulation (HPCS '14)*, pp. 902–910, Bologna, Italy, July 2014.

[17] P. Xiao, Z. Hu, D. Liu, X. Zhang, and X. Qu, "Energy-efficiency enhanced virtual machine scheduling policy for mixed workloads in cloud environments," *Computers & Electrical Engineering*, vol. 40, no. 5, pp. 1650–1665, 2014.

[18] A. Paya and D. C. Marinescu, "Energy-aware load balancing policies for the cloud ecosystem," in *Proceedings of the 28th IEEE International Parallel and Distributed Processing Symposium Workshops (IPDPSW '14)*, pp. 823–832, IEEE, Phoenix, Ariz, USA, May 2014.

[19] P. Xiao, Z.-G. Hu, and Y.-P. Zhang, "An energy-aware heuristic scheduling for data-intensive workflows in virtualized datacenters," *Journal of Computer Science and Technology*, vol. 28, no. 6, pp. 948–961, 2013.

[20] G. von Laszewski, L. Wang, A. J. Younge, and X. He, "Power-aware scheduling of virtual machines in DVFS-enabled clusters," in *Proceedings of the 2009 IEEE International Conference on Cluster Computing and Workshops (CLUSTER '09)*, pp. 1–10, IEEE, New Orleans, La, USA, September 2009.

[21] C.-M. Wu, R.-S. Chang, and H.-Y. Chan, "A green energy-efficient scheduling algorithm using the DVFS technique for cloud datacenters," *Future Generation Computer Systems*, vol. 37, pp. 141–147, 2014.

[22] L. Luo, W. Wu, W. Tsai, D. Di, and F. Zhang, "Simulation of power consumption of cloud data centers," *Simulation Modelling Practice and Theory*, vol. 39, pp. 152–171, 2013.

[23] G. Katsaros, J. Subirats, J. O. Fitó, J. Guitart, P. Gilet, and D. Espling, "A service framework for energy-aware monitoring and VM management in Clouds," *Future Generation Computer Systems*, vol. 29, no. 8, pp. 2077–2091, 2013.

[24] I. Hwang, T. Kam, and M. Pedram, "A study of the effectiveness of CPU consolidation in a virtualized multi-core server system," in *Proceedings of the ACM/IEEE International Symposium on Low Power Electronics and Design (ISLPED '12)*, pp. 339–344, Redondo Beach, Calif, USA, August 2012.

[25] K. Maurya and R. Sinha, "Energy conscious dynamic provisioning of virtual machines using adaptive migration thresholds in cloud data center," *International Journal of Computer Science and Mobil Computing*, vol. 2, no. 3, pp. 74–82, 2013.

[26] A. Beloglazov, J. Abawajy, and R. Buyya, "Energy-aware resource allocation heuristics for efficient management of data centers for Cloud computing," *Future Generation Computer Systems*, vol. 28, no. 5, pp. 755–768, 2012.

[27] W. Lin, J. Z. Wang, C. Liang, and D. Qi, "A threshold-based dynamic resource allocation scheme for cloud computing," *Procedia Engineering*, vol. 23, pp. 695–703, 2011.

[28] Z. Xiao, J. Jiang, Y. Zhu, Z. Ming, S. Zhong, and S. Cai, "A solution of dynamic VMs placement problem for energy consumption optimization based on evolutionary game theory," *Journal of Systems and Software*, vol. 101, pp. 260–272, 2015.

8

ANCS: Achieving QoS through Dynamic Allocation of Network Resources in Virtualized Clouds

Cheol-Ho Hong, Kyungwoon Lee, Hyunchan Park, and Chuck Yoo

Korea University, 145 Anam-ro, Seongbuk-gu, Seoul 02841, Republic of Korea

Correspondence should be addressed to Chuck Yoo; chuckyoo@os.korea.ac.kr

Academic Editor: Zhihui Du

To meet the various requirements of cloud computing users, research on guaranteeing Quality of Service (QoS) is gaining widespread attention in the field of cloud computing. However, as cloud computing platforms adopt virtualization as an enabling technology, it becomes challenging to distribute system resources to each user according to the diverse requirements. Although ample research has been conducted in order to meet QoS requirements, the proposed solutions lack simultaneous support for multiple policies, degrade the aggregated throughput of network resources, and incur CPU overhead. In this paper, we propose a new mechanism, called ANCS (*Advanced Network Credit Scheduler*), to guarantee QoS through dynamic allocation of network resources in virtualization. To meet the various network demands of cloud users, ANCS aims to concurrently provide multiple performance policies; these include weight-based proportional sharing, minimum bandwidth reservation, and maximum bandwidth limitation. In addition, ANCS develops an efficient work-conserving scheduling method for maximizing network resource utilization. Finally, ANCS can achieve low CPU overhead via its lightweight design, which is important for practical deployment.

1. Introduction

The use of cloud computing technology is rapidly increasing, because it can provide computing resources to remote users efficiently in terms of time and cost. By using cloud platforms, cloud users can run diverse applications without considering the arrangement of the hardware platforms. In addition, because of the agile and elastic traits of cloud computing, the amount of computing resources can be adjusted to reflect the requirements of each user. Therefore, cloud computing is rapidly being disseminated for general-purpose, network and database server, and high-performance computing applications [1].

System virtualization [2] is an enabling technology of cloud computing. A hypervisor or virtual machine monitor (VMM) provides cloud users an illusion of running their own operating system (OS) on a physical platform. Using a hypervisor in the basement of the software layer, cloud vendors can realize IaaS (Infrastructure as a Service), PaaS (Platform as a Service), and SaaS (Service as a Service), which are core services of cloud computing. Recent representative hypervisor titles for cloud computing include KVM [3], Xen [4], and VMware ESXi [5].

To satisfy the diverse requirements of cloud users, cloud computing providers have recently allowed users to select the Quality of Service (QoS) of each resource. As a result, users can specify the needs appropriate to their programs and pay fees according to the QoS level. However, it is challenging for cloud providers to support stable QoS for applications in each virtual machine (VM) because of interference between cloud users [6]. In such environments, users can experience unpredictable performance and performance degradation. Therefore, research on achieving performance isolation during resource sharing is gaining significant attention [6–10].

In particular, guaranteeing network performance is widely studied because network performance influences the Quality of Experience (QoE) that defines the satisfaction level of each user. Most previous research efforts [11–14] focused on methods to dynamically adjust network performance. However, the proposed methods have limitations in that (1) they can support only one type of policy among several viable ones and (2) they incur high CPU overhead by adopting feedback control, which frequently monitors the

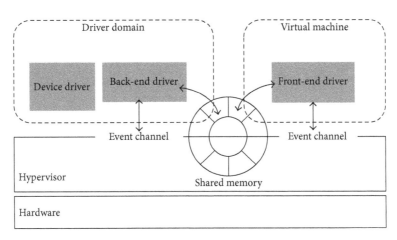

FIGURE 1: Xen I/O architecture.

actual usage of the network and compensates insufficient resources. Therefore, a new approach is required to meet the demands of the users while significantly reducing overhead.

In this paper, we propose ANCS (*Advanced Network Credit Scheduler*), which can dynamically provide network performance according to the requirements of each user of a virtualized system. Compared to solutions proposed in the previous research, ANCS can support several network performance control policies simultaneously; these include weight-based proportional sharing, minimum bandwidth guarantees, and maximum bandwidth guarantees. In addition, at all times ANCS provides a work-conserving scheme [15] that distributes the unused resources of any VM to other VMs, which maximizes total network utilization. Finally, ANCS incurs low CPU overhead through its lightweight design.

The main contributions of this paper related to previous studies are as follows:

(i) We deliver the details of ANCS that can satisfy diverse performance demands through multiple performance policies in virtualization. Each cloud computing tenant has different performance requirements. In order to satisfy the needs, ANCS provides three performance policies: weight-based proportional sharing, minimum bandwidth reservation, and maximum bandwidth limitation. We elaborate on how to guarantee desired performance according to each demand.

(ii) We develop an efficient work-conserving method for utilizing network resources. In a non-work-conserving method, when a VM cannot fully utilize an allocated resource, the unused amount is wasted, resulting in decreased overall network utilization. To maximize the utilization, ANCS develops an efficient work-conserving method to guarantee high utilization regardless of the resource usage of each VM.

(iii) We design ANCS to use minimal CPU resources when managing the network performance of VMs. We do not utilize packet inspection or packet queuing to reduce overhead in the QoS control.

The remainder of this paper is structured as follows: In Section 2, we explain the background of virtualization and the methods it uses to distribute network resources. Section 3 elaborates on the design of ANCS. Section 4 shows the performance evaluation results. Section 5 explains related work. Finally, we present our conclusions in Section 6.

2. Background and Motivation

We select Xen [4] for implementing ANCS because it is an open-source hypervisor and also supports a simple round robin scheduling method. We can regard this scheduling method as a baseline for our experiment and intend to improve the scheduling method in terms of supporting weight-based proportional sharing, minimum bandwidth reservation, and maximum bandwidth limitation.

2.1. System Virtualization and Xen. System virtualization allows several OSs to be consolidated on a single physical machine. At the bottom of the system software stacks, the hypervisor multiplexes all system resources, including processors, memory, and I/O devices; it exports the virtualized resources in the form of a VM. Therefore, each VM can provide a complete system environment (composed of virtual CPUs, virtual memory, and virtual devices) to each guest OS.

Xen [4] is an open-source hypervisor that adopts a paravirtualization technique to minimize virtualization cost. The paravirtualization technique enables communication between the hypervisor and a guest OS by providing a communication channel, which is referred to as a hypercall. Hypercalls are analogous to system calls between an OS and a user application. Hypercalls request Xen to execute sensitive instructions on behalf of the guest OS. They include processor state update operations such as memory management unit (MMU) updates and physical interrupt masking operations, which guest OSs cannot execute directly. To contain hypercalls, the source code of a guest OS must be modified to facilitate paravirtualization.

2.2. The I/O Model of Xen. To process I/O requests from guest OSs, Xen adopts the back-end driver in domain 0, which is a driver domain, and the front-end driver in the guest OS [16], as depicted in Figure 1. The back-end driver delivers

I/O requests using the shared memory from the front-end drivers to the actual device driver in domain 0. Afterward, the back-end driver conveys the responses to each front-end driver by notifying them via virtual interrupts. The front-end driver behaves as an actual device driver in the guest OS. It receives I/O requests from the guest OS and delivers them to the back-end driver. It also brings the processed result to the guest OS. For network devices, the front-end network driver creates virtual network interfaces called *vif*s. The virtual network interfaces behave as the actual network devices in the guest OS. In systems that have several VMs, the back-end network driver processes the requests of several virtual network interfaces in a round-robin manner without a proportional sharing policy. Therefore, each competing guest OS will have the same network performance, which cannot satisfy the different requirements.

3. Design of ANCS

In this section, we present the details of ANCS, an advanced network credit scheduler that dynamically allocates network resources to VMs for guaranteeing the network performance of VMs under various scenarios. First, we describe the design goals of ANCS that aim to guarantee QoS for network virtualization. Next, we elaborate on the coarse-grained algorithm of ANCS using its flow chart. Finally, we explain the fine-grained subalgorithms of ANCS for achieving diverse performance goals.

3.1. Design Goals. The goals of ANCS that aim to implement a network scheduler for guaranteeing QoS in virtualization are as follows.

(i) Multiple Performance Policies. ANCS aims to meet the network demands of each VM, which are described by multiple performance policies. Recent cloud computing users tend to run diverse network applications on their VMs. These applications have different performance demands, especially in terms of networks; minimum sustainable bandwidth is an example of such a requirement. In order to meet the various needs, ANCS provides the following three performance policies: weight-based proportional sharing, minimum bandwidth reservation, and maximum bandwidth limitation. ANCS aims to satisfy the desired performance of cloud users by allowing them to select an appropriate performance policy among the three policies, according to their demands.

(ii) High Network Resource Utilization. ANCS endeavors to efficiently utilize the total network resources of a system by applying a work-conserving method. In a non-work-conserving environment, when a VM receives network resources in proportion to its weight and does not consume its allocated amount, the unused network resources then become wasted, resulting in decreased total network utilization. In order to enhance resource management efficiency, ANCS adopts a work-conserving method, which yields unused network resources to other VMs that have pending network requests. This maximizes the resource utilization of the entire system regardless of the usage of each VM.

(iii) Low CPU Overhead. ANCS focuses on minimizing additional CPU overhead in achieving QoS for networks. Other research efforts that aimed to guarantee QoS failed to reduce CPU overhead, because of the complexity of the proposed algorithms [12, 14, 17]. These studies adopted either packet inspection or packet queuing for throttling the sending packet rate per network interface, and therefore this mechanism demands nonnegligible computation resources. Unfortunately, this causes total network performance to deteriorate. ANCS adopts a credit-based simple accounting algorithm that incurs only minimal overhead, which prevents performance degradation during the QoS control.

Although ANCS is implemented in the back-end driver of the Xen hypervisor, ANCS can be applied to other hypervisors that use a paravirtual model where the back-end and the front-end cooperate with each other to deal with network packets. In a paravirtual model, each hypervisor processes packets in a similar manner. For example, the back-end receives/sends packets from/to the front-end by using shared memory composed of descriptor rings. Also, after receiving and sending packets, the back-end delivers virtual interrupts to the front-end in order to notify that the packets have been processed. Because of this architectural similarity, we believe that ANCS can still satisfy the performance requirements in other hypervisors.

3.2. ANCS Algorithm. In basic terms, ANCS is based on the proportional share scheduling mechanism that allocates network resources to each virtual interface in proportion to its weight. Each virtual interface, called *vif*, is owned by its VM and behaves like an actual network interface within the VM. ANCS operates in the driver domain of the Xen hypervisor, particularly in the back-end driver that plays the role of the communication channel between the hardware device driver and VMs, as depicted in Figure 2. ANCS processes the network operation requests of VMs in a round-robin manner, checking whether a *vif* has sufficient resource allocation to possess the network resources. For this purpose, ANCS uses the credit concept [18, 19] to represent the amount of resource allocation. While network resources are being used, every *vif* consumes its credit according to the requested size; the credit value of a *vif* is recharged regularly in proportion to its weight. If the credit value that a *vif* has is less than the requested size, ANCS does not process its requests. The *vif* must then wait for the next credit value to be allocated. Therefore, the amount of credit a *vif* has determines the network bandwidth of the corresponding VM. The amount of credits allocated is calculated by the configured performance policy of each VM.

Figure 3 depicts an overall flow chart of the ANCS algorithm. In this section, we elaborate on the coarse-grained algorithm of ANCS using the flow chart. We introduce variables used in the ANCS algorithm and provide a general description of them. Then, we explain the fine-grained subalgorithms of ANCS. The detailed operations of ANCS will be described in Sections 3.3 and 3.4.

The accounting function of ANCS runs every 30 ms and allocates network resources to *vif*s on a physical machine in order. The value of 30 ms is selected to decrease the

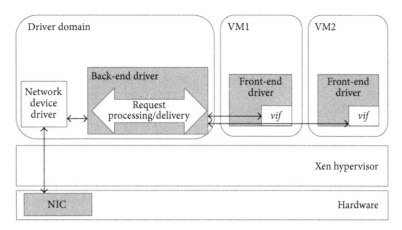

Figure 2: Virtualized system architecture with ANCS.

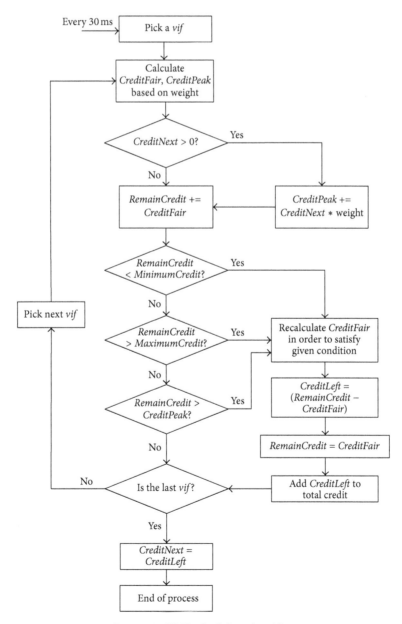

Figure 3: ANCS scheduling algorithm.

overhead of periodically running the accounting function. Please note that regardless of this period each virtual interface can execute if it has sufficient credit values to process its network packets. Therefore, the 30 ms period does not affect the network latency of each virtual interface. The following procedure is performed per *vif*.

First, the two variables required to obtain the fair share of each *vif* are calculated: *CreditFair* and *CreditPeak*. *CreditFair* is determined depending on the weight of a *vif*. *CreditFair* represents the fair share of network resources for a *vif* according to its weight. Then, *CreditPeak* is calculated. *CreditPeak* indicates the amount of available resources for a *vif* based on the assumption that the *vif* dominates the network resource when other *vif*s are idle. *CreditPeak* is used to maintain the total amount of credits in the system in order to distribute the proper amount of credits to each *vif*.

Second, the procedure to support work-conserving and various performance policies is performed. ANCS checks whether *CreditNext* is greater than zero. *CreditNext* is accumulated in the previous scheduling period when some *vif*s did not fully use their credit values. A positive *CreditNext* value indicates that there were unused credits in the previous scheduling period. This value is added to *CreditPeak* in order to distribute unused credits in the current scheduling period. We will explain this in more detail in Section 3.4. Then, for proportional sharing, ANCS adds *CreditFair* to *RemainCredit*, which is the current credit value of the *vif*. In order to support minimum bandwidth reservation and maximum bandwidth limitation, ANCS determines whether the credits allocated to the *vif* satisfy the configured performance policy, which will be explained in depth in Section 3.3.

Finally, if the current *vif* is the last *vif* in the system, the ANCS process for a single scheduling period is finished. If there are additional *vif*s to which credits can be allocated, ANCS selects the next *vif* and iterates the credit calculation. If a VM does not consume its allocated credits in the current period, ANCS adds the remaining credit value to *CreditNext* to give other VMs a chance to consume unused credits.

3.3. Multiple Performance Policies. For the diverse performance requirements of cloud computing users, ANCS provides multiple performance policies, including weight-based proportional sharing, minimum bandwidth reservation, and maximum bandwidth limitation. Weight-based proportional sharing is a base policy that proportionally differentiates the amount of allocated resources based on the weight of each VM. Minimum bandwidth reservation guarantees that the quantitative network performance of a VM is always greater than the configured value, *MinimumCredit*, as shown in Figure 3. When the amount of credits allocated to a *vif* becomes less than *MinimumCredit*, ANCS adjusts *CreditFair* to satisfy the minimum bandwidth; the *CreditFair* value of the *vif* is set to *MinimumCredit* in order to support minimum bandwidth. When supporting minimum bandwidth, the aggregated amounts of minimum bandwidth requests from all *vif*s should not exceed the total throughput of the physical device. By using the minimum bandwidth reservation, ANCS can prevent performance degradation of a specific VM and guarantee

sustainable minimum bandwidth. On the other hand, maximum bandwidth limitation prevents aggressive resource consumption by a specific VM. If the resources allocated to a *vif* exceed the *MaximumCredit* value, ANCS reclaims surplus resources from the *vif* for distribution to other VMs.

The administrator can apply an appropriate performance policy to each VM according to the performance demands of each user. The designated policy can be dynamically changed during runtime. In addition, multiple performance policies can be applied in a conjunctive form. For instance, when a user requires a specific boundary of network performance (e.g., larger than 200 Mbps and less than 500 Mbps), both the reservation and limitation requirements can be applied by specifying the minimum and maximum bandwidth values. Moreover, ANCS can satisfy the different performance demands of multiple applications in a single VM, because the designated performance policy is based on a *vif*, not a VM. Therefore, a VM with several *vif*s can establish various network performance requirements by assigning a different performance policy to each *vif*.

3.4. Support for Work-Conserving. ANCS supports work-conserving, in which a *vif* is idled when it does not have network requests or responses. Work-conserving is a crucial factor in cloud computing; it allows resources to be allocated efficiently and system utilization to be maximized. For work-conserving, ANCS modifies the amount of allocated credits according to fluctuations in network usage. When a VM does not fully use its credits, ANCS gives other VMs a chance to receive unused credits by distributing additional credits to them.

When a *vif* is idled for a certain amount of time, the *RemainCredit* value of the *vif* can exceed *CreditPeak*, which denotes the maximum credit value a *vif* can have. Then, the credits of this *vif* must be distributed to other *vif*s. For this purpose, *CreditLeft*, which is obtained by subtracting *CreditFair* from *RemainCredit*, is added to the total credit value. This increases the credits that can be allocated to the next *vif*s. If a *vif* exceeds its *CreditPeak*, ANCS resets the credit value of the *vif* to *CreditFair*, to give it a credit value according to its weight. By distributing idle resources to active VMs, ANCS can efficiently utilize network resources of the entire system.

4. Evaluation

For evaluation, we implement ANCS in the driver domain, domain 0, of the Xen hypervisor. The Linux version of domain 0 is 3.10.55, and the version of Xen is 4.2.1. The experiments are conducted on two identical physical servers, each of which has an Intel i7 Quad core 3770 CPU running at 3.5 GHz, 16 GB of RAM, and a Gigabit Ethernet card. One of them runs the Xen hypervisor with our modified driver domain, and the other one runs vanilla Linux 3.10.11 working as an evaluation machine. Because ANCS does not require any modification on guest OSs, we run unmodified vanilla Linux 3.2.1 for each VM. Iperf [20] benchmark is used to measure the network performance of each VM. In addition,

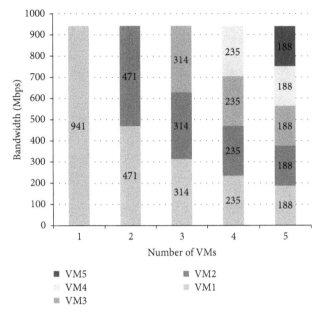

FIGURE 4: Bandwidth of VMs without ANCS.

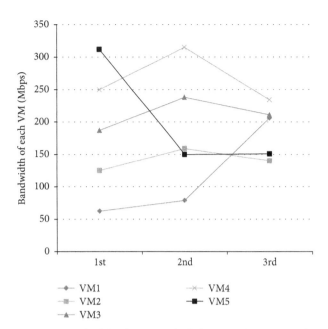

FIGURE 5: Bandwidth of VMs with different performance policy settings.

we use Xentop to measure the CPU utilization of the driver domain, which is described in Section 4.4.

4.1. Base Performance.

Before we show the evaluation results of ANCS, we produce the base performance for comparison. For this purpose, we measure the network performance of default VMs on the Xen hypervisor without ANCS. We ran Iperf while launching up to five VMs one by one. As depicted in Figure 4, the network performance of each VM on our system is always even. When there is only one VM, the VM (VM1) consumes all network resources, achieving 941 Mbps bandwidth. As the number of VMs increases, the system's network resources are equally shared among VMs. This occurs because the unmodified driver of the Xen hypervisor processes the requests of several virtual network interfaces in a round-robin manner with the same weight. Therefore, each guest OS has the same network performance.

4.2. Multiple Policies.

To demonstrate that ANCS guarantees the network performance of VMs under various scenarios, we change the performance policy during runtime and observe that the change is reflected properly in the system. When the system is started, we set the weights of five VMs for weight-based proportional sharing as {VM1 = 1/15, VM2 = 2/15, VM3 = 3/15, VM4 = 4/15, VM5 = 5/15}; thus, the ratio of the weights is 1 : 2 : 3 : 4 : 5. After measuring the performance of each VM, we additionally set the maximum bandwidth limitation policy to VM5. The bandwidth of VM5 is set to 150 Mbps while the weight-based proportional sharing is maintained. Finally, the minimum bandwidth reservation is set to VM1 with a value of 200 Mbps. Similarly, the previous configuration applied to other VMs is maintained.

The results of the experiment are shown in Figure 5. At the beginning of the experiment, ANCS allocates credits to *vif*s according to their weights. Therefore, the network performance of each VM is differentiated proportionally, as expected. When the maximum bandwidth limitation policy is applied to VM5 in the second phase, VM5 shows the bandwidth limited to 150 Mbps. As the credit value allocated to VM5 decreases compared to the first phase, the network performance of other VMs increases naturally. Moreover, the increment in the bandwidth of other VMs is proportional to their weights. During the last phase, the bandwidth of VM1 increases to 200 Mbps because of the reservation policy, while the bandwidth of VM5 is preserved as 150 Mbps, the same as it was in the second phase. Then, VM2, VM3, and VM4 receive less credit value compared to the second phase, and therefore their performance decreases.

Based on the above experiment, ANCS shows that it guarantees the network performance of VMs under various scenarios that combine the policies explained in Section 3.3. The scenarios include all three performance policies provided by ANCS. Our evaluation demonstrates that ANCS is capable of handling various performance requirements in cloud computing.

4.3. Support for Work-Conserving.

In cloud computing, efficient resource management is crucial for reducing maintenance costs. For better efficiency in resource management, ANCS maximizes resource utilization even if the number of VMs and their performance policies are changed. We evaluated the efficiency of ANCS in resource management by measuring aggregated bandwidth in different environments.

First, Figure 6 provides the bandwidth results of the VMs on a physical server. We configured only one policy (weight-based proportional sharing) on all VMs. In addition, we maintained the weight of each VM for weight-based proportional sharing as {VM1 = 1/15, VM2 = 2/15, VM3 = 1/5, VM4 = 4/15, VM5 = 1/3}, throughout the remaining experiments.

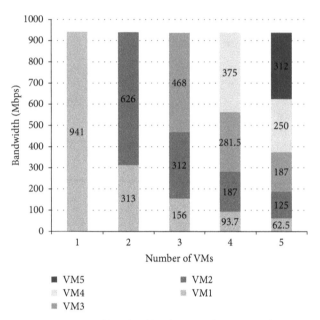

FIGURE 6: Aggregated bandwidth of VMs with ANCS (only weight-based proportional sharing is applied).

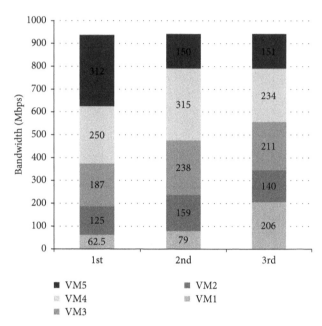

FIGURE 7: Aggregated bandwidth of VMs with ANCS.

We then launched the VMs sequentially (VM1 through VM5) and measured the network performance of each VM. Evaluation results show that the network performance of each VM is proportional to the weight. While the network performance of each VM changes according to the weight, the aggregated bandwidth maintains 940 Mbps. We find that ANCS fully supports work-conserving scheduling by achieving the maximum aggregated bandwidth, independent of the number of VMs on the physical server.

Next, Figure 7 shows the aggregated bandwidth in the three experiment scenarios described in Section 4.2. Through this experiment, we aimed to show that ANCS maximizes resource utilization even if the performance policy of each VM is changed. In the first phase, only weight-based proportional sharing is applied to all VMs. In the second phase, the maximum limitation policy is applied to VM5 while maintaining the weight-based proportional sharing of the other VMs. Finally, the minimum bandwidth reservation is set to VM1. In the final phase, all of the performance policies that ANCS provides are applied on the system: reservation to VM1 (200 Mbps), limitation to VM5 (150 Mbps), and weight-based proportional sharing to all VMs. As depicted in Figure 7, the aggregated bandwidth always achieves the maximum bandwidth, 940 Mbps, in all the experiment scenarios. It is clear that the work-conserving property of ANCS is not affected by the required performance policy of each VM, or by the number of VMs.

4.4. CPU Overhead. In cloud computing, it is important to decrease CPU overhead in terms of energy efficiency when applying a new policy to the system. To illustrate the CPU overhead caused by ANCS, we measured the CPU utilization in the driver domain while sequentially generating VMs one by one. Figure 8 shows the CPU utilization in

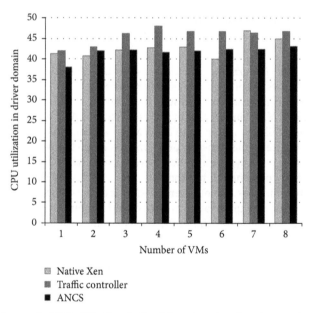

FIGURE 8: CPU utilization in the driver domain when the number of VMs is increased from one to eight.

three cases: Native Xen, Linux traffic controller, and ANCS. Both Native Xen and the traffic controller are based on the Xen hypervisor; they run unmodified Linux for driver domains. In the experiment with Native Xen, the network performance of each VM is equal because the default setting of Xen is fair sharing. For the traffic controller experiment, we utilize the Linux traffic controller in the driver domain to differentiate the network performance of VMs, similar to ANCS. The traffic controller does not support work-conserving and only provides network performance policies with fixed performance values; this is different from ANCS,

TABLE 1: Latency values in ms measured by a ping program when the number of VMs is increased from one to five.

	Number of VMs				
	1	2	3	4	5
Native Xen	0.30	0.34	0.25	0.30	0.32
Traffic controller	0.30	0.30	0.30	0.32	0.32
ANCS	0.24	0.28	0.23	0.23	0.34

TABLE 2: Latency values in ms measured by Netperf when the number of VMs is increased from one to five.

	Number of VMs				
	1	2	3	4	5
Native Xen	0.12	0.13	0.12	0.12	0.12
Traffic controller	0.12	0.12	0.12	0.13	0.13
ANCS	0.12	0.12	0.12	0.12	0.12

which dynamically adjusts the network performance of VMs. As depicted in Figure 8, the traffic controller demands nonnegligible computation resources as it adopts packet queuing for throttling the sending packet rate. As ANCS adopts a credit-based simple accounting algorithm that incurs only minimal overhead, ANCS shows low CPU utilization in the driver domain, which is comparable to the two different techniques.

4.5. Network Latency. In this section, we evaluate network latency in ANCS and compare the results with Native Xen and the Linux traffic controller in the same experiment setup described in Section 4.4. For the performance policy, we configure the weight of each VM as one to provide the same bandwidth to VMs, which prevents different resource allocation from affecting network latency. We use both a ping program and Netperf [21] with TCP_RR to quantify the latency of UDP and TCP pings, respectively. The ping program sends 64-byte UDP packets to a client whereas Netperf with TCP_RR sends 1-byte TCP packets to a client. For these experiments, we respectively execute both programs between a client and a VM for 60 seconds and take the average value, because network latency fluctuates on each measurement. Tables 1 and 2 show the latency values (in ms) of each method measured by the ping program and Netperf, respectively, when the number of VMs is increased from one to five. In both results, ANCS shows lower or similar latency compared to Native Xen and the traffic controller. As explained in Section 3.2, although the accounting function of ANCS runs every 30 ms, virtual interfaces with sufficient credit values can run at certain points regardless of this period. Therefore, the 30 ms period does not affect the network latency of each virtual interface.

5. Related Work

As cloud computing based on virtualization becomes prevalent and the requirements of each user are diversified, techniques for improving QoS are increasingly studied. In particular, network devices are considered to offer unstable QoS, because sharing of the devices involves another scheduling layer (such as the scheduler in the back-end driver).

vSuit [11] adopts a feedback controller in order to analyze variations in network performance and to react to such deviations by adjusting network resources to each guest OS. Using this mechanism, vSuit can offer maximum bandwidth reservation and limitation for each VM. Furthermore, CPU overhead is shown to be under 1%. However, this research does not support weight-based proportional sharing, and the experiments are performed in 100 Mbps environment.

DMVL [12] provides a technique to distribute the network bandwidth to each VM in a stable and fair manner. For this purpose, it separates the logical data path and the request I/O queue belonging to each VM. In addition, it records the allocated and consumed amounts of network bandwidth for each VM by using shared memory. This information is used to adjust the amount of network bandwidth allocated in the next iteration. The limitation of this research is that this technique incurs nonnegligible CPU overhead in domain 0, up to 7%.

PSD [13] differentiates the network performance of each VM based on each virtual network interface. It schedules each virtual interface by means of a leaky bucket controller and a time slot-based resource allocator, which distribute the resource in proportion to a different ratio. However, this approach cannot provide absolute bandwidth assignment.

The Linux traffic controller [14, 17] is a traditional approach to adjusting the network bandwidth of each network application. It classifies each packet according to its header information and configures different bandwidths according to each classification. In the paravirtualized Xen, the traffic controller in domain 0 can be used to perform network performance differentiation by classifying the packets based on the IP address of each VM. In this case, severe CPU utilization occurs (up to 12%) when the number of VMs increases, as shown in Figure 8.

Recently, Silo [22] proposes to consider both VM placement and end host pacing to guarantee message latency in cloud computing. In Silo, message latency between two VMs is determined by the capacity of network switches connecting two virtual machines. End host pacing controls the transmission rate in a server by utilizing hierarchical token bucket scheduling. Even though Silo guarantees quantitative network latency in cloud computing, it only covers communication between two specific VMs. When a VM starts new connection with another VM or migrates to a different server, Silo needs to recalculate guaranteed latency.

Cerebro [23] predicts bounds on the response time performance of web APIs exported by applications hosted in a PaaS cloud. However, Cerebro only predicts response time of cloud applications and does not involve network scheduling in the case of violation of predicted response time. Moreover, Cerebro incurs computational overheads since it adopts a static analysis to predict the response time.

As shown in Table 3, the solutions proposed to enhance network QoS either provide only a single policy or incur high CPU overhead through the use of high-frequency feedback controllers. ANCS can support various policies, including proportional sharing and minimum/maximum network bandwidth reservation. It also maximizes the total

TABLE 3: Comparison of virtual network scheduling methods.

	ANCS	vSuit	DMVL	PSD	Traffic controller	Silo	Cerebro
Work-conserving	o	o	o	x	o	x	x
Proportional sharing	o	x	o	o	o	x	x
Minimum and maximum reservation	o	o	x	x	x	o	x
CPU overhead	Low	Low	High	N/A	High	Low	High

network bandwidth by supporting work-conserving while reducing CPU overhead as much as possible.

6. Conclusion

In this paper we propose ANCS, which dynamically enhances network performance to meet the various requirements of users in cloud computing environments. Compared to solutions proposed in previous research efforts, ANCS can provide several network performance control policies, including weight-based proportional sharing, minimum bandwidth guarantees, and maximum bandwidth guarantees, while achieving low CPU overhead.

Competing Interests

The authors declare that they have no competing interests.

Acknowledgments

This work was supported by Institute for Information & Communications Technology Promotion (IITP) grant funded by the Korea Government (MSIP) (no. R0126-16-1066, (SW StarLab) Next Generation Cloud Infra-Software toward the Guarantee of Performance and Security SLA) and Grant no. B0126-16-1046 (Research of Network Virtualization Platform and Service for SDN 2.0 Realization). This work was also supported by Korea University Grant.

References

[1] R. Buyya, C. S. Yeo, S. Venugopal, J. Broberg, and I. Brandic, "Cloud computing and emerging IT platforms: vision, hype, and reality for delivering computing as the 5th utility," *Future Generation Computer Systems*, vol. 25, no. 6, pp. 599–616, 2009.

[2] J. Smith and R. Nair, *Virtual Machines: Versatile Platforms for Systems and Processes*, Elsevier, New York, NY, USA, 2005.

[3] I. Habib, "Virtualization with KVM," *Linux Journal*, vol. 2008, no. 166, article 8, 2008.

[4] P. Barham, B. Dragovic, K. Fraser et al., "Xen and the art of virtualization," *ACM SIGOPS Operating Systems Review*, vol. 37, no. 5, pp. 164–177, 2003.

[5] C. Chaubal, "The architecture of VMware ESXi," VMware White Paper, 2008.

[6] X. Pu, L. Liu, Y. Mei et al., "Who is your neighbor: net I/O performance interference in virtualized clouds," *IEEE Transactions on Services Computing*, vol. 6, no. 3, pp. 314–329, 2013.

[7] H. Park, S. Yoo, C.-H. Hong, and C. Yoo, "Storage SLA guarantee with novel SSD I/O scheduler in virtualized data centers," *IEEE Transactions on Parallel and Distributed Systems*, 2015.

[8] J. Hwang, C. Hong, and H. Suh, "Dynamic inbound rate adjustment scheme for virtualized cloud data centers," *IEICE Transactions on Information and Systems*, vol. E99.D, no. 3, pp. 760–762, 2016.

[9] N. Jain and J. Lakshmi, "PriDyn: enabling differentiated I/O services in cloud using dynamic priorities," *IEEE Transactions on Services Computing*, vol. 8, no. 2, pp. 212–224, 2015.

[10] V. Jalaparti, P. Bodik, I. Menache, S. Rao, K. Makarychev, and M. Caesar, "Network-aware scheduling for data-parallel jobs: plan when you can," in *Proceedings of the ACM Conference on Special Interest Group on Data Communication (SIGCOMM '15)*, pp. 407–420, ACM, 2015.

[11] F. Dan, W. Xiaojing, Z. Wei, T. Wei, and L. Jingning, "VSuit: QoS-oriented scheduler in network virtualization," in *Proceedings of the 26th IEEE International Conference on Advanced Information Networking and Applications Workshops (WAINA '12)*, pp. 423–428, Fukuoka, Japan, March 2012.

[12] H. Tan, L. Huang, Z. He, Y. Lu, and X. He, "DMVL: an I/O bandwidth dynamic allocation method for virtual networks," *Journal of Network and Computer Applications*, vol. 39, no. 1, pp. 104–116, 2014.

[13] S. Lee, H. Kim, J. Ahn, K. Sung, and J. Park, "Provisioning service differentiation for virtualized network devices," in *Proceedings of the the International Conference on Networking and Services (ICNS '11)*, pp. 152–156, 2011.

[14] W. Xiaojing, Y. Wei, W. Haowei, D. Linjie, and Z. Chi, "Evaluation of traffic control in virtual environment," in *Proceedings of the 11th International Symposium on Distributed Computing and Applications to Business, Engineering and Science (DCABES '12)*, pp. 332–335, Guilin, China, October 2012.

[15] L. Cherkasova, D. Gupta, and A. Vahdat, "Comparison of the three CPU schedulers in Xen," *ACM SIGMETRICS Performance Evaluation Review*, vol. 35, no. 2, pp. 42–51, 2007.

[16] K. Fraser, S. Hand, R. Neugebauer, I. Pratt, A. Warfield, and M. Williamson, "Safe hardware access with the Xen virtual machine monitor," in *Proceedings of the 1st Workshop on Operating System and Architectural Support for the on Demand IT Infrastructure (OASIS '04)*, pp. 3–7, October 2004.

[17] W. Almesberger, "Linux network traffic control-implementation overview," in *Proceedings of the 5th Annual Linux Expo LCA-CONF- 1999-012*, pp. 153–164, Raleigh, NC, USA, 1999.

[18] K. Mathew, P. Kulkarni, and V. Apte, "Network bandwidth configuration tool for Xen virtual machines," in *Proceedings of the 2nd International Conference on COMmunication Systems and NETworks (COMSNETS '10)*, pp. 1–2, IEEE, Bangalore, India, January 2010.

[19] C.-H. Hong, Y.-P. Kim, H. Park, and C. Yoo, "Synchronization support for parallel applications in virtualized clouds," *The Journal of Supercomputing*, 2015.

[20] A. Tirumala, F. Qin, J. Dugan, J. Ferguson, and K. Gibbs, "Iperf: The TCP/UDP bandwidth measurement tool," http://software.es.net/iperf/.

[21] R. Jones, *NetPerf: A Network Performance Benchmark*, Information Networks Division, Hewlett-Packard Company, 1996.

[22] K. Jang, J. Sherry, H. Ballani, and T. Moncaster, "Silo: predictable message latency in the cloud," in *Proceedings of the 2015 ACM Conference on Special Interest Group on Data Communication*, pp. 435–448, ACM, 2015.

[23] H. Jayathilaka, C. Krintz, and R. Wolski, "Response time service level agreements for cloud-hosted web applications," in *Proceedings of the 6th ACM Symposium on Cloud Computing*, pp. 315–328, ACM, Kohala Coast, Hawaii, August 2015.

9

Feedback-Based Resource Allocation in MapReduce-Based Systems

Bunjamin Memishi,[1] María S. Pérez,[1] and Gabriel Antoniu[2]

[1]*OEG, ETS de Ingenieros Informáticos, Universidad Politécnica de Madrid, Campus de Montegancedo, s/n Boadilla del Monte, 28660 Madrid, Spain*
[2]*Inria Rennes-Bretagne Atlantique Research Centre, Campus Universitaire de Beaulieu, Rennes, 35042 Brittany, France*

Correspondence should be addressed to Bunjamin Memishi; bmemishi@fi.upm.es

Academic Editor: Zhihui Du

Containers are considered an optimized fine-grain alternative to virtual machines in cloud-based systems. Some of the approaches which have adopted the use of containers are the MapReduce frameworks. This paper makes an analysis of the use of containers in MapReduce-based systems, concluding that the resource utilization of these systems in terms of containers is suboptimal. In order to solve this, the paper describes AdaptCont, a proposal for optimizing the containers allocation in MapReduce systems. AdaptCont is based on the foundations of feedback systems. Two different selection approaches, Dynamic AdaptCont and Pool AdaptCont, are defined. Whereas Dynamic AdaptCont calculates the exact amount of resources per each container, Pool AdaptCont chooses a predefined container from a pool of available configurations. AdaptCont is evaluated for a particular case, the application master container of Hadoop YARN. As we can see in the evaluation, AdaptCont behaves much better than the default resource allocation mechanism of Hadoop YARN.

1. Introduction

One of the most relevant features of cloud is virtualization. Many cloud infrastructures, such as Amazon EC2, offer virtual machines (VMs) to their clients with the aim of providing an isolated environment for running their processes. MapReduce systems [1] are also important cloud frameworks that can benefit from the power of virtualization. Nevertheless, VMs are extremely complex and heavyweight, since they are intended to emulate a complete computer system. This capability is not needed in MapReduce systems, since they only have to isolate the map and reduce processes, among other daemons. For this reason, containers, a much more lightweight virtualization abstraction, are more appropriate. Containers support the virtualization of a single application or process, and this is enough for MapReduce systems. Due to their nature, mainly by sharing a unique operating system kernel in a host, and being infrastructure independent, containers can start and

terminate faster, which makes the container virtualization very efficient.

A container represents a simple unit of a box-like packed collection (or encapsulation) of resources, placed on a single node of a cluster. Whereas it shares many similarities with a VM, it also differs in some essential aspects. First, the container can represent a subset of a VM; conceptually, the VM could also be subset of a large container, but the practice suggests that it is better to avoid this scenario. The virtualization level is another crucial difference. VMs are designed to emulate virtual hardware through a full operating system and its proper additional add-ons, at the expense of more overhead. On the other hand, containers can easily use and share the host operating system, because they are envisioned to run a single application or a single process. Similarities between a container and VM are strongly linked in the manner of how they use resources. As in any VM, the main resources of a container are the main memory (RAM) and the computing processing unit (CPU).

The data storage and the data bandwidth are left in a second place.

Due to the less overhead of containers, a considerable number of cloud solutions, not only MapReduce-based clouds, are using currently these abstractions as resource allocation facility. Indeed, many experts are seeing containers as a natural replacement for VMs in order to allocate resources efficiently, although they are far from providing all the features needed for virtualizing operating systems or kernels. However, the coexistence between both abstractions, containers and VMs, is not only a feasible future but indeed now a reality.

According to our analysis made in Hadoop YARN [2], its containers allocation is not efficient. The current form of resource allocation at container level in Hadoop YARN makes it impossible to enforce a higher level of cloud elasticity. Elasticity can be defined as the degree to which a cloud infrastructure is capable of adapting its capacity to different workloads over time [3]. Usually, the number of containers allocated is bigger than needed, decreasing the performance of the system. However, occasionally, containers do not have sufficient resources for addressing the request requirements. This could lead to unreliable situations, jeopardizing the correct working of the applications. For the sake of simplicity, we only consider the main computing resources, the main memory (RAM), and the computing processing unit (CPU).

We present a novel approach for optimizing the resource allocation at the container level in MapReduce systems. This approach, called *AdaptCont*, is based on feedback systems [4], due to its dynamism and adaptation capabilities. When a user submits a request, this framework is able to choose the amount of resources needed, depending on several parameters, such as the real-time request input, the number of requests, the number of users, and the dynamic constraints of the system infrastructure, such as the set of resources available. The dynamic reaction behind the framework is achieved thanks to the real-time input provided from each user input and the dynamic constraints of the system infrastructure. We define two different selection approaches: Dynamic Adapt-Cont and Pool AdaptCont. Whereas Dynamic AdaptCont calculates the exact amount of resources per each container, Pool AdaptCont chooses a predefined container from a pool of available configurations.

In order to validate our approach, we use AdaptCont for a particular case study on a particular MapReduce system, the Hadoop YARN. We have chosen the application master of Hadoop YARN instead of the YARN workers, because of the importance of this daemon and because it involves the most complex use of containers. The application master container is required in every application. Additionally, the master orchestrates its proper job, but its reliability can jeopardize the work of the job workers. On the other hand, a particular worker usually does not have impact on the reliability of the overall job, although it may contribute to the delay of the completion time. The experiments show that our approach brings about substantial benefits compared to the default mechanism of YARN, in terms of use of RAM and CPU. Our evaluation shows improvements in the use of these resources, which range from 15% to 75%.

In summary, this paper has the following main contributions:

(1) Definition of a general-purpose framework called AdaptCont, for the resource allocation at the container level in MapReduce systems.

(2) Instantiation of AdaptCont for a particular case study on Hadoop YARN, that is, the application master container.

(3) Evaluation of AdaptCont and comparison with the default behavior of Hadoop YARN.

The rest of the paper is organized as follows. In Section 2, we introduce AdaptCont as a general framework based on feedback systems for allocating container resources. We introduce a case study of the framework in Section 3. We evaluate AdaptCont in Section 4. In Section 5, we discuss the related work. Finally, we summarize the main contributions and outline the future work in Section 6.

2. AdaptCont Framework

According to [4], feedback systems refer to two or more dynamical systems, which are interconnected in such a way that each system affects the behavior of others. Feedback systems may be open or closed. Assuming a feedback system F, composed of two systems A and B, F is closed if their components form a cycle, with the output of system A being the input of system B and the output of system B the input of system A. On the contrary, F is open when the interconnection between systems B and A is broken.

Feedback systems are based on a basic principle: correcting actions should always be performed on the difference between the desired and the actual performance. Feedback allows us to (i) provide robustness to the systems, (ii) modify the dynamics of a system by means of these correcting actions, and (iii) provide a higher level of automation. When a feedback system is not properly designed, a well known drawback is the possibility of instability.

An example of a dynamic system that can benefit from the feedback theory nowadays is a production cloud [5]. In this scenario, users, applications, and infrastructure are clearly interconnected and the behaviors of any of these systems influence each other. Our approach, AdaptCont, is a feedback system, whose main goal is to optimize the resource allocation at the container level in clouds and specifically in MapReduce-based systems.

Before designing the feedback system, it is necessary to define the features of a cloud:

(i) A cloud has a limited set of nodes $n_1, n_2, \ldots, n_m$.

(ii) Each node n_i has a limited set of containers $c_i 1, c_i 2, \ldots, c_i l$.

(iii) The system can receive a limited set of job requests $j_1, j_2, \ldots, j_r$.

(iv) Every job request has its workload input. These jobs are part of applications.

(v) The same workload can be used as an input for different applications.

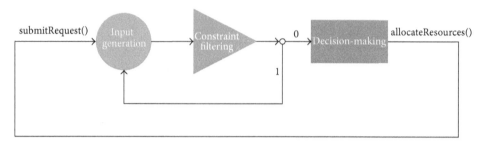

FIGURE 1: A generalized framework for self-adaptive containers, based on the feedback theory.

(vi) Applications could divide a large workload into small input partitions called *splits*, each split being a workload of a particular container.

(vii) Depending on the cluster size and scheduler limitations, simultaneous containers could run in single or multiple sequential groups called *waves*.

(viii) By default, all the containers should finish before the application submits the final output to the user.

(ix) Applications may introduce different job completion time, though under the same user, input, and allocated resources.

In a dynamic cloud, these parameters may change in real time. Detecting these changes is strongly dependent on the monitoring system, which should be particularly focused on the infrastructure [6].

At a generic level, we can follow a feedback-based approach based on three stages: input generation, constraint filtering, and decision-making. The general pattern is shown in Figure 1. This approach is closed. In real time, the input generation module could receive several constraints in sequence. After generating the initial parameters (by taking into account the initial constraints), an additional follow-up constraint may require another parameters calculation before being sent to the decision-making module. Consequently, the number of runs of the input generation module is proportional to the modifications (constraints) identified from the system.

2.1. Input Generation. The input generation module of AdaptCont collects or generates the required parameters for making decisions about efficient resource allocation. These parameters are as follows:

(i) The input workload size.

(ii) The input split size enforced by the application.

(iii) The total number of available containers per each user.

(iv) The wave size in which these containers may be run.

(v) The constraints introduced by users.

Some of these parameters are collected directly from the application. For instance, the input workload size comes in every job request. Other parameters are more complex to be generated. For instance, the number of waves w depends on the number of input splits n_s and the number of available containers per user n_c, being calculated as $w = n_s/n_c$.

2.2. Constraint Filtering. This stage is needed because clouds have a limited number of costly resources. Constraints may be imposed by the infrastructure, application, and/or users.

Infrastructure constraints are those constraints related to the limitation of the cloud provider, since not always the number of resources is enough for fulfilling the resource requests of all the applications and users.

Some constraints are enforced by applications. For instance, some applications require a certain type of sequential container. This is the case of MapReduce systems, where, by default, containers of the first phase (map) need to finish before the containers of the second phase (reduce) start [7, 8].

Finally, other constraints are defined by users. For instance, some users have a limited capability for buying resources.

2.3. Decision-Making. Based on the parameters coming from the previous modules, the decision-making module outputs the final resource allocation. In particular, this module decides the minimum recommended container memory c_{RAM} and CPU power c_{CPU} per every container. This decision depends on the particular problem addressed by these containers.

Once this module has decided these values for a specific application of a user, the rest of the process is automatic, since all the containers of an application are equal. This process has to be called for different applications or different users.

2.4. Predefined Containers. A possible improvement of AdaptCont is enabling the use of predefined containers with different configurations (e.g., small, medium, and large). This means that a cloud has a pool of static containers that can be used for different user request. In this way, it will not be necessary to trigger a new container, but a predefined one ready to be used. This reduces the overhead of the resource allocation process during the job submission. This feature should be part of the decision-making module.

How can the framework define this pool of containers? First, it should be able to identify the typical user requests in the system. These requests may be evaluated from (i) previous (stored) monitoring values or from (ii) other monitoring variables measured at the same time, according to [9].

What happens if the container does not have the exact configuration we need? In this case, the decision-making module establishes a threshold. If the difference between the required and existing configurations is below this threshold,

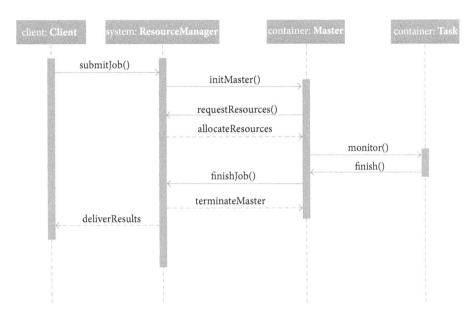

FIGURE 2: Job flow messages in Hadoop YARN: a sequence diagram.

the system uses the already existing container. Otherwise, the system triggers a new container.

3. AdaptCont Applied to YARN

We have chosen as a case of study the analysis of a relevant type of a container in a specific kind of cloud systems, that is, MapReduce-based clouds. Namely, the chosen container is the application master in the next-generation MapReduce system called YARN [2].

3.1. Background. YARN constitutes the new version of Apache Hadoop. This new implementation was built with the aim of solving some of the problems shown by the old Hadoop version. Basically, YARN is a resource management platform that, unlike the former Hadoop release, provides greater scalability and higher efficiency and enables different frameworks to efficiently share a cluster. YARN offers, among others, MapReduce capabilities.

The basic idea behind YARN is the separation between the two main operations of the classic Hadoop master, resource management and job scheduling/monitoring, into separate entities or daemons. The resource manager consists of two main components: the *scheduler* and the *application manager*. While the scheduler's duty is resource allocation, the application manager accepts job submissions and initiates the first job container for the application master. After this, the job is managed by the application master, which starts negotiating resources with the resource manager and collaborates with the node managers to run and monitor its tasks. Finally, it informs the resource manager that has been completed and releases its container. The resource manager delivers the results to the client. A simple sequence of these steps is given in Figure 2.

For each job submission, the application master configuration is static and does not change for different scenarios.

According to the state-of-the-art literature [10–14], most large-scale MapReduce clusters run small jobs. As we will show in Section 4, even the smallest resource configuration of the application master exceeds the requirements of these workloads. This implies a waste of resources, which could be alleviated if the configuration is adapted to the workload size and the infrastructure resources. Moreover, some big workloads could fail if the container size is not enough for managing them. At large-scale level, this would have a higher impact. Therefore, our goal is to choose an appropriate container for the application master.

3.2. Design. In order to optimize containers for the application master, we will follow the same pattern of the general framework, that is, AdaptCont.

The input generation module divides the workload input size into splits. The YARN scheduler provides containers to users, according to the number of available containers of the infrastructure each instant of time. As we mentioned above, the input generation module calculates the number of waves from the number of input splits and the number of available containers per user. Figure 3 shows how the application master manages these waves.

Many constraints can be raised from the scheduler. An example of this is the phase priority. It is well known that the map phase input is by default bigger than or equal to the reduce phase input [15]. This is one of the reasons why the number of mappers is higher than the number of reducers. Due to this, as a reasonable constraint, the constraint filtering module prioritizes the number of mappers with regard to the number of reducers.

Decision-making module considers mainly two parameters, total workload and wave sizes. Contrary to what it may seem at first sight, the type of application does not affect the resource allocation decision of our use case. Some applications could have more memory, CPU, or I/O

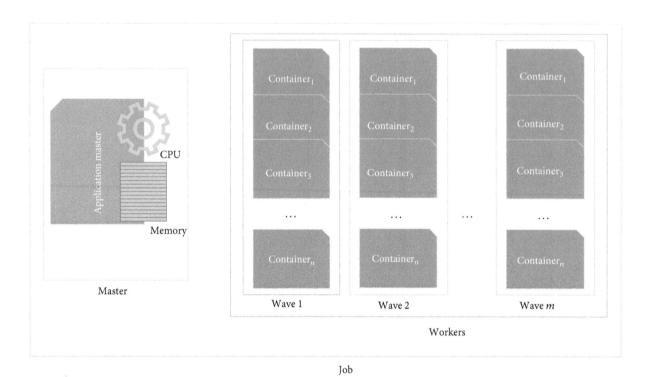

FIGURE 3: Workers containers monitored in waves by the application master container.

requirements, influencing the number and types of needed containers. However, this would only determine the size of the worker containers, and, in this case study, our scope is focused only on the master containers, which contribute largely to the reliability of the application executions.

Decision-making module uses two parameters: Ω and Ψ. The first parameter represents the minimum recommended memory size for an application master container that manages one unit wave, w_{unit}. Our goal is to calculate c_{RAM} from the value of Ω, with c_{RAM} being the recommended memory size for the application master. In the same way, we aim to calculate c_{CPU} as the recommended CPU power for the application master, from Ψ, which is the minimum recommended CPU power for an application master that manages w_{unit}.

To calculate the memory, if the actual wave w is bigger than what could be handled by Ω, that is, bigger than w_{unit}, then we declare a variable λ that measures this wave magnitude: $\lambda = w/w_{unit}$. Now, it is easy to find c_{RAM}:

$$c_{RAM} = \lambda * \Omega + Stdev, \quad Stdev \in \left[0; \frac{\Omega}{2}\right]. \quad (1)$$

Regarding the CPU power, the formula for c_{CPU} is

$$c_{CPU} = \lambda * \Psi + Stdev, \quad Stdev \in \left[0; \frac{\Psi}{2}\right]. \quad (2)$$

Figure 4 represents the AdaptCont modules, which are executed in the context of different YARN daemons. Whereas the input generation and the decision-making modules are part of the application manager, the constraint filtering module is part of the scheduler. The combination of both daemons forms the resource manager. The resource manager has a complete knowledge about each user through the application manager and the available resources through the scheduler daemon. When the application manager receives a user request, the resource manager is informed about the workload input. The scheduler informs the application manager of every important modification regarding the monitored cluster. According to this, the application manager reacts upon the user request, by optimizing the container for its application master.

4. Experimental Evaluation

We have performed a set of experiments to validate our approach and compare it with YARN. These experiments have been made by means of simulations. In order to make this evaluation, we have followed the methodology of Section 4.1. Results of the evaluation are described in Section 4.2. Finally, the discussion about these results is shown in Section 4.3.

4.1. Methodology. To evaluate AdaptCont, we have considered three different schedulers and three different application master configurations, as is shown in Table 1. Below we give details for all of them.

Scheduler. We have taken into account three important schedulers, already implemented in YARN:

(i) *FIFO Scheduler.* This was the first scheduling algorithm that was implemented for MapReduce. It works on the principle that the master has a queue of jobs, and it simply pulls the oldest job first.

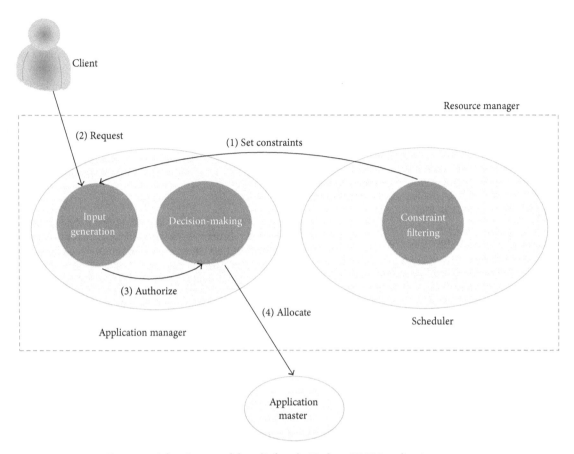

FIGURE 4: AdaptCont model applied to the Hadoop YARN application master.

TABLE 1: Methodology description, taking into account different schedulers and masters.

Scheduler	Master		
	YARN	Dynamic	Pool
FIFO	FIFO-YARN	FIFO-Dynamic	FIFO-Pool
Fair	Fair-YARN	Fair-Dynamic	Fair-Pool
Capacity	Capacity-YARN	Capacity-Dynamic	Capacity-Pool

FIFO: FIFO scheduler. Fair: Fair scheduler. Capacity: Capacity scheduler. YARN: YARN master. Dynamic: Dynamic master. Pool: Predefined containers-based master.

(ii) *Fair Scheduler*. It assigns the same amount of resources (containers) to all the workloads, so that on average every job gets an equal share of containers during its lifetime.

(iii) *Capacity Scheduler*. It gives different amount of resources (containers) to different workloads. The bigger the workload is, the more the resources are allocated to it.

Master. To compare YARN with AdaptCont, we use the following application master configurations:

(i) *YARN Application Master (YARN)*. This is the default implementation of the application master in YARN.

(ii) *Dynamic Master (Dynamic AdaptCont)*. This master container is adjusted in accordance with AdaptCont. Namely, it calculates the memory and CPU, according to the decision-making module and only after this does it initiate the master.

(iii) *Predefined Containers-Based Master (Pool Adapt-Cont)*. As defined in Section 2.4, the resource manager has a pool of master containers, which can be allocated depending on the workload size. This is an optional optimization of AdaptCont.

Workload. According to the job arrival time, we consider two additional sets of experiments:

(i) *Set-All*. In this scenario, all the jobs are already in the queue of the scheduler. We are going to combine this scenario with all the values of Table 1, since it is important to evaluate the approach under pressure, that is, when the load reaches high values.

(ii) *Set-Random*. This is a more realistic scenario, where jobs arrive at random times. Again, this scenario is evaluated in combination with all the values of Table 1, in order to simulate the behavior of a common MapReduce cluster.

An important parameter to take into account is the workload size. We introduce two additional scenarios:

(i) *Workload-Mixed.* In this case, the workload size will be variable, ranging from 500 MB to 105 GB, taking (1) 500 MB, (2) 3.5 GB, (3) 7 GB, (4) 15 GB, (5) 30 GB, (6) 45 GB, (7) 60 GB, (8) 75 GB, (9) 90 GB, and (10) 105 GB as workload size inputs. We have used these boundaries, because of the average workload sizes of important production clusters. For instance, around 90% of workload inputs in Facebook [12] are below 100 GB.

(ii) *Workload-Same.* In this case, every input (10 workloads) is the same: 10 GB. We have used this value, since, on average, the input workloads at Yahoo and Microsoft [12] are under 14 GB.

Therefore, we evaluate AdaptCont with the values of Table 1 and the 4 combinations from previous scenarios: *Set All-Workload Mix*, *Set All-Workload Same*, *Set Random-Workload Mix*, and *Set Random-Workload Same.*

Constraints. In MapReduce, the application master has to manage both map and reduce workers. The map phase input is always bigger than or equal to the reduce phase input [15]. This is one of the reasons why the number of mappers is bigger than the number of reducers. On the other hand, both phases are run sequentially. Thus, we can assume as constraint that the master container resources depend on the number of mappers and not on the number of reducers.

In order to simulate a realistic scenario, we have introduced in our experiments a partition failure that will impact around 10% of the cluster size. We assume that this failure appears in the fifth iteration (wave). This constraint forces AdaptCont to react in real time and adapt itself to a new execution environment, having to make decisions about future resource allocations.

Setup. In our experiments, 250 containers are used for worker tasks (mappers and reducers). This number of containers is sufficient to evaluate the approach, considering 25 containers per workload. We consider that every map and reduce container is the same and can execute a particular portion (split) of the workload. Each task runs on a container that has 1024 MB RAM and 1 virtual core. According to [16–18], a physical CPU core is capable of giving optimal performance of the container, if it simultaneously processes 2 containers at most. Therefore, we take 1 CPU core as equivalent to 2 virtual cores.

Our goal is to evaluate the resource utilization of the application masters, in terms of CPU and RAM. To get this, we consider an isolated set of resources oriented only to application masters. In this way, it will be easier to measure the impact of AdaptCont on saving resources.

4.2. Results. In this section, we compare the CPU and memory efficiency of YARN versus Dynamic AdaptCont and Pool AdaptCont. Before that, we analyze the wave behavior of the 10 workloads.

Wave Behavior. Figure 5 represents the resource allocation (maximum number of containers or wave sizes) for the combination we have mentioned before: *Set All-Workload Mix*, *Set All-Workload Same*, *Set Random-Workload Mix*, and *Set Random-Workload Same.*

Figure 5(a) shows different workload sizes with the same arrival time (already in the scheduler queue). The experiments demonstrate that a maximum wave is dependent on the workload size and the scheduler. Regarding the FIFO scheduler, since the queue order is formed by the smallest workload first, for these small workloads, the maximum wave is represented by the needed containers. For instance, the first workload needs only 8 containers. This number of containers is calculated dividing the workload size by the split size (64 MB). These 8 containers are provided by the infrastructure, and this is the case of the second workload (56 containers) and the third workload (112 containers). For the fourth workload, the infrastructure is not capable of providing the needed containers, which only has 74 containers in the first wave, that is, 250 − (8 + 56 + 112). The fourth workload needs 240 containers in total. Thus, the remaining containers (240 − 74 = 166) will be provided in the next wave.

In the second wave, since the first three workloads have finished, the scheduler will provide 166 containers to the fourth workload and the rest (250 − 166 = 84) to the fifth workload. This process is repeated until all the workloads are given the necessary containers and every job has terminated. As we can notice, the maximum wave for the latest workloads reaches higher amount of allocated containers, since the workload is bigger, and in most of the cases the scheduler is busy with a unique job. Although initially the infrastructure has 250 containers, from the fifth wave, there is a slight decrease (225), due to the partition failure (10% of the resources). This only affects the workloads not having finished before this wave (in this case, the fifth).

The main drawback of the FIFO scheduler is that it may delay the completion time of the smallest jobs, especially if they arrive late to the queue. In general, this scheduler is not fair in the resource allocation and depends exclusively on the arrival time.

Regarding the fair scheduler, this scheduler allocates the same number of containers to all the workloads and consequently to all the users, that is, 250/10 = 25. The partition failure forces the fair scheduler to decrease the number of containers to 22 (225/10) from the fifth wave.

With regard to the capacity scheduler, this scheduler takes advantage of available resources once some jobs have finished. At the beginning, it behaves like the fair scheduler. However, when some small jobs have terminated, the available resources can be reallocated to the rest of the workloads. This is the reason why the biggest workloads in the queue get a higher number of containers. As in the previous case, the partition failure also implies a slight decrease in the number of containers from the fifth wave.

Figure 5(b) represents the same mixed workloads but when they arrive randomly to the scheduler queue. Clearly, the main differences are noted in the FIFO scheduler, because the arrival time of the workloads is different and now one of the biggest workloads (9) appears in first place.

The other subplots of Figure 5 show the experimental results of the same workloads with an input of 10 GB. This

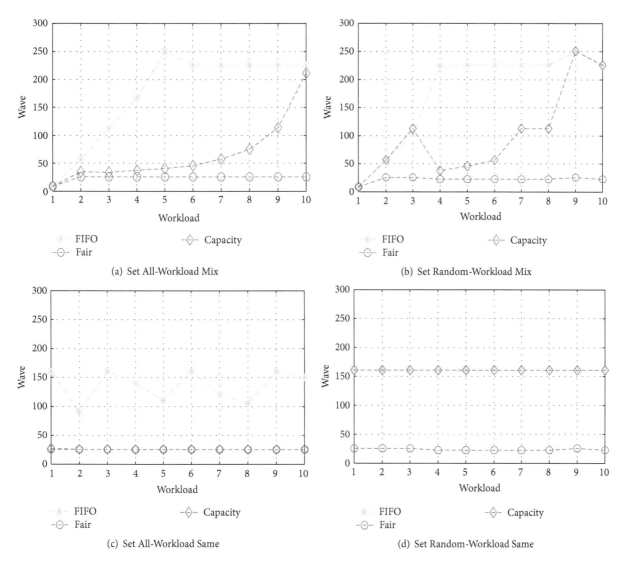

FIGURE 5: Wave behavior: wave size according to the scheduler and the workload type.

input requires a static number of containers (in this case, 160 containers).

In Figure 5(c), all the jobs have arrived to the queue. In this scenario, the FIFO allocation oscillates between the maximum wave of 160 containers and the smallest wave of 90 containers (250 − 160). This oscillation is caused by the allocation of resources to the previous workload, which does not leave enough resources for the next one, and then the cycle is repeated again.

In this case, the fair and capacity schedulers have the same behavior, since all the workloads are equal.

Figure 5(d) shows the number of containers for the same workload with random arrival. The difference of this scenario versus the scenario shown in Figure 5(c) is twofold:

(1) The arrival of these jobs is consecutive. In every wave, a job arrives. Due to this, the FIFO scheduler is forced to wait after each round for a new workload, even though at every round there are available resources

(250 − 160 = 90), not allocated to any job. Thus, the FIFO scheduler always allocates 160 containers in every wave.

(2) Whereas, in the previous scenario, the fair and capacity schedulers behave the same, in this case, the capacity scheduler acts similarly to the FIFO scheduler. This is because the capacity scheduler adapts its decisions to the number of available resources, which is enough in every moment for addressing the requirements of the jobs (160 containers). Thus, the capacity scheduler achieves a better completion time, compared to the fair scheduler.

According to this analysis, we can conclude that the wave behavior and size are decisive in the application master configuration.

Memory Usage. Figure 6 shows for the 4 scenarios the total memory used by the three approaches: YARN, Dynamic AdaptCont, and Pool AdaptCont.

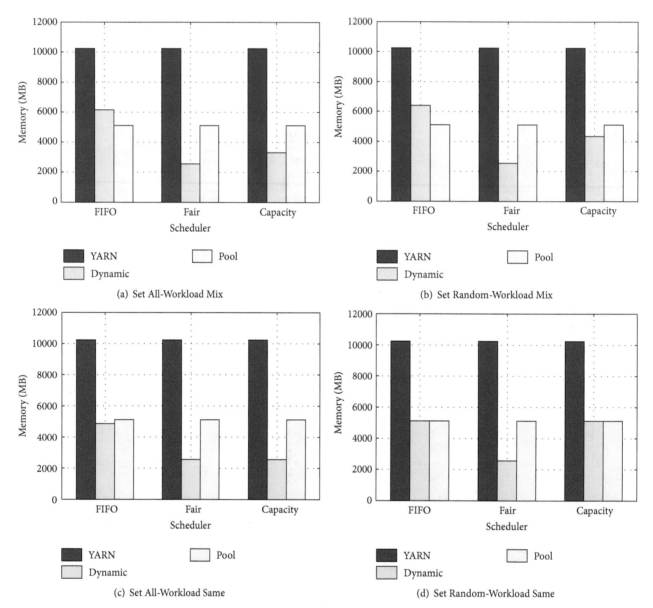

FIGURE 6: Memory usage and master type versus scheduler.

In the case of YARN, we have deployed the default configuration, choosing the minimum memory allocation for the application master (1024 MB).

The Dynamic AdaptCont-based application master memory is dependent on the waves size. If the wave size is under 100, the decision-making module allocates a minimum recommended memory of 256 MB. For each increase of 100 in the wave size, the memory is doubled. The reasons behind this are as follows:

(1) A normal Hadoop task does not need more than 200 MB [12], and this is even clearer in the case of the application master.

(2) As most of the jobs are small [12–14], consequently, the maximum number of mappers is also small and, therefore, the application master requires less memory.

(3) The minimum recommended memory by Hortonworks [17] is 256 MB.

The Pool AdaptCont-based application master works in a different way, constituting an alternative between the YARN master and the Dynamic master. This application master has three default configurations: *small*, *medium*, and *big*. The small master has 512 MB of memory, for all small jobs that need a maximum of 250 containers. The medium master has 1024 MB, as it is the default minimum YARN setting. In order to deal with big waves, the big configuration has 2048 MB.

As we can see in Figure 6, YARN is outperformed by both AdaptCont approaches. YARN always consumes 10 GB, not depending on the different use cases. For instance, in Figure 6(a), Dynamic AdaptCont has memory usage of 6144 MB versus 10 GB in YARN, achieving 40% memory improvement. In this case, Pool AdaptCont only uses 5120 MB, that is, 50% improvement compared to YARN. This difference between Dynamic AdaptCont and Pool AdaptCont for the FIFO scheduler is due to the way of providing memory in both approaches. If the workload needs 250 containers, Dynamic AdaptCont provides $256\lceil(250/100)\rceil$ MB, that is, $256 * 3 = 768$ MB. In the same scenario, Pool AdaptCont provides 512 MB, corresponding to the small size configuration.

In general, Dynamic AdaptCont is the best approach in terms of memory usage, except in the case of the FIFO scheduler, where the performance is close to and slightly worse than the performance of Pool AdaptCont. In the case of fair and capacity schedulers, Dynamic AdaptCont is the best alternative, achieving on average 75% and 67.5% improvement compared to YARN, versus 50% improvement provided by Pool AdaptCont.

CPU Usage. The CPU usage is another relevant parameter to take into account. In order to measure it, we have correlated memory and CPU, considering that we need higher CPU power to process a larger amount of data, stored in memory.

In YARN, you can assign a value ranging from 1 up to 32 of virtual cores for the application master. This is also the possible interval allocation for every other container. According to [16], 32 is the maximum value. In our experiments, we use the minimum value for the YARN master (1 virtual core for its container) per 1024 MB.

For the Dynamic AdaptCont, the decision-making module increases the number of virtual cores after two successive increments of 256 MB of memory. This decision is based on the abovementioned methodology, which states that a physical CPU core is capable of giving optimal performance of the container, if it simultaneously processes 2 containers at most [16–18]. To be conservative, we address the smallest container, that is, a container of 256 MB. For instance, if the memory usage is 768 MB, the chosen number of virtual cores is 2.

The same strategy is valid for the Pool AdaptCont, assuming 1 virtual core for small containers, 2 virtual cores for medium containers, and 3 virtual cores for large containers.

Due to this policy, the CPU does not change so abruptly as the memory for Dynamic and Pool AdaptCont. Thus, as is shown in Figure 7, both approaches behave similarly, except in the case of FIFO with Workload Mix. This was previously justified in the memory usage evaluation. As the CPU is proportional to the memory usage, the behavior of Dynamic AdaptCont with FIFO for Workload Mix is again repeated in the case of CPU.

In most of the cases, the improvement of both Dynamic and Pool AdaptCont against YARN reaches 50%.

4.3. Discussion. In this section, we discuss what combination of approaches and schedulers can be beneficial in common scenarios.

As a result of the experiments, we can conclude that YARN used by default is not appropriate for optimizing the use of MapReduce-based clouds, due to the waste of resources.

In the presence of heavy and known advanced workloads (this is the usual case of scientific workloads), according to our results, the best recommended strategy is to use Dynamic AdaptCont combined with FIFO scheduler.

However, if we have limited resources per user, a better choice could be Dynamic AdaptCont combined with fair scheduler. This scheduler allocates a small set of resources to every workload, improving the overall performance.

In a scenario where we have a mixture of large and small workloads, the choice should be Dynamic AdaptCont combined with capacity scheduler. This is due to the adaptability of this scheduler with regard to the input workload and available resources.

Finally, as shown in the experiments, if our focus is on CPU and not on memory, we can decide to use Pool AdaptCont (combined with any schedulers) instead of the dynamic approach.

5. Related Work

As far as we know, this paper is the first contribution that proposes a MapReduce optimization through container management. In particular, linked to our use case, it is the first contribution that aims to create reliable masters, by means of the allocation of sufficient resources to their containers.

There are many contributions on MapReduce whose goal is optimizing the framework from different viewpoints. An automatic optimization of the MapReduce programs has been proposed in [19]. In this work, authors provide out-of-the-box performance for MapReduce programs that need to be run using as input large datasets. In [20], an optimization system called Manimal was introduced, which analyzes MapReduce programs by applying appropriate data-aware optimizations. The benefit of this *best-effort* system is that it speeds up these programs in an autonomic way, without human intervention. In [21], a new classifications algorithm is introduced with the aim of improving the data locality of mappers and the task execution time. All these contributions differ from our contribution since they are only software-oriented optimizations for the MapReduce pipeline, and they do not take into account the resource allocation or the CPU and memory efficiency.

FlexSlot [22] is an approach that resizes map slots and changes the number of slots of Hadoop in order to accelerate the job execution. With the same aim, DynamicMR [23] tries to relax the slot allocation constraint between mappers and reducers. Unlike our approach, FlexSlot is only focused on the map stage and both FlexSlot and DynamicMR do not consider the containers as resource allocation facility.

In [24], authors introduce MRONLINE, which is able to configure relevant parameters of MapReduce online, by collecting previous statistics and predicting the task configuration in fine-grain level. Unlike MRONLINE, AdaptCont uses a feedback-control approach that also enables its application to single points of failure.

Cura [25] automatically creates an optimal cluster configuration for MapReduce jobs, by means of the framework profiling, reaching global resource optimization. In addition, Cura introduces a secure instant VM allocation to reduce

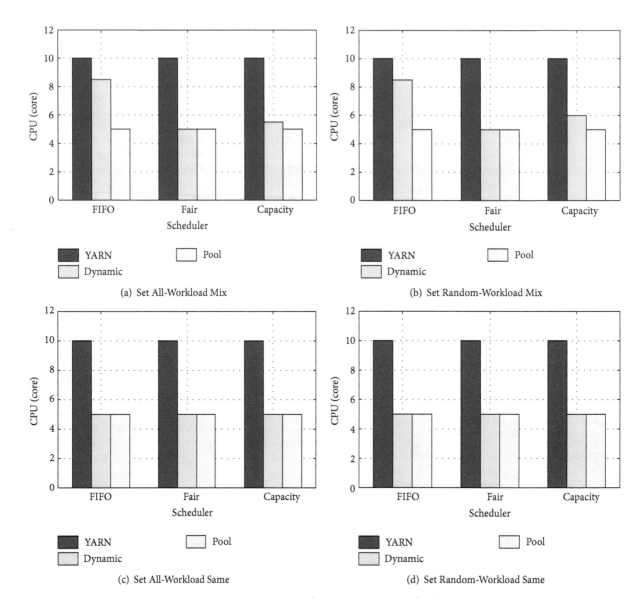

FIGURE 7: CPU usage and master type versus scheduler.

the response time for the short jobs. Finally, it applies other resource management techniques such as cost-aware resource provisioning, VM-aware scheduling, and online VM reconfiguration. Overall, these techniques lead to the enhancement of the response time and reduce the resource cost. This proposal differs from our work, because it is mostly concentrated in particular workloads excluding others. Furthermore, it is focused on VMs management and not on containers, as AdaptCont.

Other proposals aim to improve the reliability of the MapReduce framework, depending on the executional environment. The work proposed in [26] is a wider review that includes byzantine failures in Hadoop. The main properties upon which the UpRight library is based are safety and eventual liveliness. The contribution of this paper is to establish byzantine fault tolerance as a viable alternative to crash fault tolerance for at least some cluster services rather than any individual technique.

The work presented in [27] represents a byzantine fault-tolerant (BFT) MapReduce runtime system that tolerates faults that corrupt the results of computation of tasks, such as the cases of DRAM and CPU errors/faults. The BFT MapReduce follows the approach of executing each task more than once, but in particular circumstances. This implementation uses several mechanisms to minimize both the number of copies of tasks executed and the time needed to execute them. This approach has been adapted to multicloud environments in [28].

In [29], authors propose another solution for intentional failures called Accountable MapReduce. This proposal forces each machine in the cluster to be responsible for its behavior, by means of setting a group of auditors that perform an accountability test that checks the live nodes. This is done in real time, with the aim of detecting the malicious nodes.

In order to improve master reliability, [30] proposes to use a clone master. All the worker nodes should report their activity to this clone master. For unstable environments, some other works [31–33] introduce dedicated nodes for the main daemons, including the master daemon.

Unlike our approach, these contributions related to reliability do not deal with the resource utilization.

6. Conclusions

The classic Apache Hadoop (MapReduce 1.0) has evolved for a long time by means of the release of several versions. However, the scalability limitations of Hadoop have only been solved partially with Hadoop YARN (MapReduce 2.0). Nevertheless, YARN does not provide an optimum solution to resource allocation, specifically at container level, causing both performance degradation and unreliable scenarios.

This paper proposes AdaptCont, a novel optimization framework for resource allocation at the container level, based on feedback systems. This approach can use two different selection algorithms, Dynamic AdaptCont and Pool AdaptCont. On the one hand, Dynamic AdaptCont figures out the exact amount of resources per each container. On the other hand, Pool AdaptCont chooses a predefined container from a pool of available configurations. The experimental evaluation demonstrates that AdaptCont outperforms the default resource allocation mechanism of YARN in terms of RAM and CPU usage, by a range of improvement from 40% to 75% for memory usage and from 15% to 50% for CPU utilization.

As far as we know, this is the first approach to improve the resource utilization at container level in MapReduce systems. In particular, we have optimized the performance of the YARN application master. As future work, we will explore the adaptation of AdaptCont for other containers of MapReduce worker tasks and deploy AdaptCont on real distributed infrastructures. We also expect to explore AdaptCont for VMs, in particular for allocating raw VMs to different user requests. We believe that fine-tuning a VM can be optimized, driven by requirements coming from an intersection between performance, reliability, and energy efficiency.

Competing Interests

The authors declare that they have no competing interests.

Acknowledgments

The research leading to these results has received funding from the H2020 project Reference no. 642963 in the call H2020-MSCA-ITN-2014.

References

[1] J. Dean, S. Ghemawat, and Google Inc, "MapReduce: simplified data processing on large clusters," in *Proceedings of the 6th Conference on Symposium on Operating Systems Design & Implementation (OSDI '04)*, USENIX Association, San Francisco, Calif, USA, December 2004.

[2] V. K. Vavilapalli, A. C. Murthy, C. Douglas et al., "Apache hadoop YARN: yet another resource negotiator," in *Proceedings of the 4th Annual Symposium on Cloud Computing (SoCC '13)*, pp. 5:1–5:16, ACM, Santa Clara, Calif, USA, 2013.

[3] N. R. Herbst, S. Kounev, and R. Reussner, "Elasticity in cloud computing: what it is, and what it is not," in *Proceedings of the 10th International Conference on Autonomic Computing (ICAC '13)*, pp. 23–27, USENIX, San Jose, Calif, USA, 2013.

[4] K. J. Astrom and R. M. Murray, *Feedback Systems: An Introduction for Scientists and Engineers*, Princeton University Press, Princeton, NJ, USA, 2008.

[5] M. Armbrust, A. Fox, R. Griffith et al., "Above the clouds: a berkeley view of cloud computing," Tech. Rep., University of California, Berkeley, Calif, USA, 2009.

[6] J. Montes, A. Sánchez, B. Memishi, M. S. Pérez, and G. Antoniu, "GMonE: a complete approach to cloud monitoring," *Future Generation Computer Systems*, vol. 29, no. 8, pp. 2026–2040, 2013.

[7] A. Verma, B. Cho, N. Zea, I. Gupta, and R. H. Campbell, "Breaking the MapReduce stage barrier," *Cluster Computing*, vol. 16, no. 1, pp. 191–206, 2013.

[8] T.-C. Huang, K.-C. Chu, W.-T. Lee, and Y.-S. Ho, "Adaptive combiner for MapReduce on cloud computing," *Cluster Computing*, vol. 17, no. 4, pp. 1231–1252, 2014.

[9] F. Salfner, M. Lenk, and M. Malek, "A survey of online failure prediction methods," *ACM Computing Surveys*, vol. 42, no. 3, article 10, 2010.

[10] S. Y. Ko, I. Hoque, B. Cho, and I. Gupta, "Making cloud intermediate data fault-tolerant," in *Proceedings of the 1st ACM Symposium on Cloud Computing (SoCC '10)*, pp. 181–192, ACM, New York, NY, USA, June 2010.

[11] F. Dinu and T. S. Eugene Ng, "Understanding the effects and implications of compute node related failures in Hadoop," in *Proceedings of the 21st ACM Symposium on High-Performance Parallel and Distributed Computing (HPDC '12)*, pp. 187–197, Delft, The Netherlands, June 2012.

[12] R. Appuswamy, C. Gkantsidis, D. Narayanan, O. Hodson, and A. Rowstron, "Scale-up vs scale-out for hadoop: time to rethink?" in *Proceedings of the 4th Annual Symposium on Cloud Computing (SOCC '13)*, pp. 20.1–20.13, ACM, New York, NY, USA, 2013.

[13] G. Ananthanarayanan, A. Ghodsi, A. Wang et al., "PACMan: coordinated memory caching for parallel jobs," in *Proceedings of the 9th USENIX Conference on Networked Systems Design and Implementation (NSDI '12)*, p. 20, USENIX Association, Berkeley, Calif, USA, 2012.

[14] K. Elmeleegy, "Piranha: optimizing short jobs in hadoop," *Proceedings of the VLDB Endowment*, vol. 6, no. 11, pp. 985–996, August 2013.

[15] T. White, *Hadoop: The Definitive Guide: Storage and Analysis at Internet Scale*, O'Reilly, 3rd edition, 2012.

[16] Apache Software Foundation, *Apache Hadoop NextGen MapReduce (YARN)*, 2015, http://hadoop.apache.org/docs/current/hadoop-yarn/hadoop-yarn-site/YARN.html.

[17] Hortonworks, *Hortonworks Data Platform: Installing HDP Manually*, 2013.

[18] M. Zaharia, D. Borthakur, J. Sen Sarma, K. Elmeleegy, S. Shenker, and I. Stoica, "Delay scheduling: a simple technique for achieving locality and fairness in cluster scheduling," in *Proceedings of the 5th ACM EuroSys Conference on Computer Systems (EuroSys '10)*, pp. 265–278, ACM, Paris, France, April 2010.

[19] S. Babu, "Towards automatic optimization of MapReduce programs," in *Proceedings of the Proceedings of the 1st ACM Symposium on Cloud Computing*, pp. 137–142, ACM, New York, NY, USA, June 2010.

[20] E. Jahani, M. J. Cafarella, and C. Ré, "Automatic optimization for MapReduce programs," *Proceedings of the VLDB Endowment*, vol. 4, no. 6, pp. 385–396, 2011.

[21] Z. Tang, J. Zhou, K. Li, and R. Li, "A MapReduce task scheduling algorithm for deadline constraints," *Cluster Computing*, vol. 16, no. 4, pp. 651–662, 2013.

[22] Y. Guo, J. Rao, C. Jiang, and X. Zhou, "FlexSlot: moving hadoop into the cloud with flexible slot management," in *Proceedings of the International Conference for High Performance Computing, Networking, Storage and Analysis (SC '14)*, pp. 959–969, IEEE Press, New Orleans, La, USA, November 2014.

[23] S. Tang, B.-S. Lee, and B. He, "DynamicMR: a dynamic slot allocation optimization framework for mapreduce clusters," *IEEE Transactions on Cloud Computing*, vol. 2, no. 3, pp. 333–347, 2014.

[24] M. Li, L. Zeng, S. Meng et al., "MRONLINE: mapReduce online performance tuning," in *Proceedings of the ACM 23rd International Symposium on High-Performance Parallel and Distributed Computing (HPDC '14)*, pp. 165–176, New York, NY, USA, 2014.

[25] B. Palanisamy, A. Singh, L. Liu, and B. Langston, "Cura: a cost-optimized model for MapReduce in a cloud," in *Proceedings of the 27th IEEE International Parallel and Distributed Processing Symposium (IPDPS '13)*, pp. 1275–1286, IEEE, Boston, Mass, USA, May 2013.

[26] A. Clement, M. Kapritsos, M. Kapritsos et al., "Upright cluster services," in *Proceedings of the ACM SIGOPS 22nd Symposium on Operating Systems Principles (SOSP '09)*, pp. 277–290, New York, NY, USA, 2009.

[27] P. Costa, M. Pasin, A. Bessani, and M. Correia, "Byzantine fault-tolerant MapReduce: faults are not just crashes," in *Proceedings of the 3rd IEEE International Conference on Cloud Computing Technology and Science (CLOUDCOM '11)*, pp. 17–24, IEEE Computer Society, Washington, DC, USA, 2011.

[28] M. Correia, P. Costa, M. Pasin, A. Bessani, F. Ramos, and P. Verissimo, "On the feasibility of byzantine fault-tolerant mapreduce in clouds-of-clouds," in *Proceedings of the 31st Symposium on Reliable Distributed Systems (SRDS '12)*, pp. 448–453, IEEE, Irvine, Calif, USA, October 2012.

[29] Z. Xiao and Y. Xiao, "Achieving accountable MapReduce in cloud computing," *Future Generation Computer Systems*, vol. 30, no. 1, pp. 1–13, 2014.

[30] F. Wang, J. Qiu, J. Yang, B. Dong, X. Li, and Y. Li, "Hadoop high availability through metadata replication," in *Proceedings of the 1st International Workshop on Cloud Data Management (CloudDB '09)*, pp. 37–44, ACM, Hong Kong, November 2009.

[31] H. Lin, X. Ma, and W.-C. Feng, "Reliable MapReduce computing on opportunistic resources," *Cluster Computing*, vol. 15, no. 2, pp. 145–161, 2012.

[32] N. Chohan, C. Castillo, M. Spreitzer, M. Steinder, A. Tantawi, and C. Krintz, "See Spot Run: using spot instances for mapreduce workflows," in *Proceedings of the 2nd USENIX Conference on Hot Topics in Cloud Computing (HotCloud '10)*, p. 7, USENIX Association, Berkeley, Calif, USA, 2010.

[33] H. Liu, "Cutting mapReduce cost with spot market," in *Proceedings of the 3rd USENIX Conference on Hot Topics in Cloud Computing (HotCloud '11)*, p. 5, Berkeley, Calif, USA, 2011.

10

MultiCache: Multilayered Cache Implementation for I/O Virtualization

Jaechun No[1] and Sung-soon Park[2]

[1]College of Electronics and Information Engineering, Sejong University, 98 Gunja-dong, Gwangjin-gu, Seoul 143-747, Republic of Korea
[2]Department of Computer Engineering, Anyang University and Gluesys Co. LTD, Anyang 5-dong,
 Manan-gu 430-714, Republic of Korea

Correspondence should be addressed to Jaechun No; jano@sejong.edu

Academic Editor: Zhihui Du

As the virtual machine technology is becoming the essential component in the cloud environment, VDI is receiving explosive attentions from IT market due to its advantages of easier software management, greater data protection, and lower expenses. However, I/O overhead is the critical obstacle to achieve high system performance in VDI. Reducing I/O overhead in the virtualization environment is not an easy task, because it requires scrutinizing multiple software layers of guest-to-hypervisor and also hypervisor-to-host. In this paper, we propose multilayered cache implementation, called MultiCache, which combines the guest-level I/O optimization with the hypervisor-level I/O optimization. The main objective of the guest-level optimization is to mitigate the I/O latency between the back end, shared storage, and the guest VM by utilizing history logs of I/O activities in VM. On the other hand, the hypervisor-level I/O optimization was implemented to minimize the latency caused by the "passing I/O path to the host" and the "contenting physical I/O device among VMs" on the same host server. We executed the performance measurement of MultiCache using the postmark benchmark to verify its effectiveness.

1. Introduction

Recently, VDI (Virtual Desktop Infrastructure) is becoming an essential aspect of the cloud-based computing environment due to its advantages such as user customization, easy-to-maintain software, and location-transparent accesses [1–3]. VDI multiplexes hardware resources of the host among VMs, which can improve server resource utilization and density. Also, VDI is capable of isolating VMs on the same host platform, which can offer the performance isolation and the secure application execution in the guest. This is performed by using the hypervisor that is responsible for coordinating VM operations and for managing physical resources of the host server.

While VDI offers several benefits, such as the increased resource utilization and the private data protection, there exist problems that can deteriorate the system performance, including I/O virtualization overhead [4, 5]. Before I/O requests issued in VMs are completed in VDI, they should go through multiple software layers, such as the layer from

the back end, shared storage to the host server [6, 7], and the layers between guest operating system, hypervisor, and eventually host operating system.

Figure 1 shows the I/O virtualization path using KVM hypervisor and QEMU emulator. The application I/O requests are first handled by the guest kernel before being passed to the virtual, emulated device executing in the user space. After executing several modules including ones for the image format, those requests are entered to the host kernel by calling posix file system interface. The virtual disk is typically a regular file from the perspective view of the host file system. The files necessary for I/O requests can be stored either in the local disk attached to the host or in the shared storage connected by network.

As depicted in Figure 1, because the I/O virtualization path is organized with multiple software layers, optimizing I/O cost is very challenging, which requires scrutinizing various virtualization aspects. In this paper, we are interested in mitigating such an overhead by implementing the

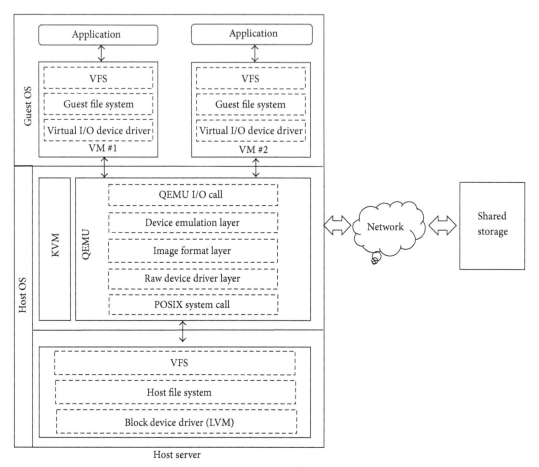

FIGURE 1: I/O virtualization path in KVM/QEMU.

appropriate cache mechanism in the guest and KVM using QEMU emulator [8–10].

Due to the thick software stack of VDI, implementing the virtualization cache method needs to take into account several layers with each I/O request passing through. For example, considering only the guest VM for the cache may not be enough to achieve the desirable I/O performance, because the latency occurring in the hypervisor, such as the context switching between the nonroot mode and the root mode, can substantially deteriorate application executions. Also, the OS dependency makes it difficult to port the guest-level cache method across VMs, especially in the case where VMs execute different guest operation systems.

In this paper, we propose the virtualization cache mechanism on top of KVM, called MultiCache (Multilevel virtualization Cache implementation), which combines VM's guest-level component with QEMU's hypervisor-level component. The main goal of the guest-level component of MultiCache is to alleviate the I/O overhead occurring in the file transmission between the back end, shared storage, and the guest. Also, caching on the guest level can give the better chance to retain the application-specific data. This is because while the guest needs to consider only the applications running on top of it, the hypervisor should control all the data necessary for VMs on the same host, which can cause the cache miss for the desired data due to the limited cache size or the swapping

activity. Finally, by tightly coupling with the light-weight resource monitoring module, the component can manage the effective cache size in the guest.

The hypervisor-level component of MultiCache attempts to reduce I/O latency by supplying the desired data in QEMU instead of accessing the physical device of the host. The other contribution of the hypervisor-level component is to provide fast responsiveness by reducing the application process block time before I/O completion. The hypervisor mainly uses the hypercall to transit process control from the guest operation system to the hypervisor itself. Because such a transition requires the mode switching between nonroot mode and root mode, the application process on the guest should remain blocked, lagging the I/O performance behind. The hypervisor-level component tries to optimize such an overhead by providing the necessary data in QEMU.

This paper is organized as follows. In Section 2, we discuss the related studies and, in Section 3, we describe the overall structure of MultiCache. In Section 4, we present the performance measurement and, in Section 5, we conclude with a summary.

2. Related Studies

Reducing I/O virtualization cost is the critical issue to accelerate I/O bandwidth of virtual machines. There have been several researches targeting I/O virtualization overhead. First of all, most VDI schemes use the back end and shared storage as a persistent data reservoir, such as DAS (host's direct attached storage), NAS (network-attached storage), or SAN (storage area network) [6, 11]. This storage is used to store read-only image templates or shared libraries and files for VMs. As the virtual machine has gained a widespread use in the cloud computing, managing the optimal cost for transferring the image contents and files between the storage and the host is becoming the essential research aspect. For example, Tang [6] proposed FVD (Fast Virtual Disk) consisting of VM image formats and the block device driver for QEMU. FVD enables supporting the instant VM creation and migration on the host by using copy-on-write, copy-on-read, and adaptive fetching.

As the technology of SSD (Solid State Disk) is rapidly growing, there have been several attempts to boost I/O bandwidth by adopting SSD in the virtualized environment [12–15]. For example, in vCacheShare [12], instead of proportionally allocating the flash cache space on the shared storage, vCacheShare uses the information about I/O accesses from VMs and trace processing data to extract reuse patterns in order to calculate the appropriate flash cache size. Mercury [13] is the client-server, write-through based flash cache method in the hypervisor. Byan et al. [13] argued that placing the flash cache either in the networked storage server or in VM may not be beneficial for speeding up I/O performance due to the network latency or VM migration [16, 17]. Also, utilizing flash cache with the write-back policy might not satisfy high I/O demand, because every write should still be written to the shared storage via a network hop for data consistency and availability.

S-CAVE [14] is a hypervisor-level flash cache to allocate the cache space among VMs. Similar to vCacheShare, S-CAVE monitors I/O activities of VMs at runtime and uses them to determine their cache space demand. Arteaga et al. [15] proposed a flash cache on the client-side storage system (VM host). They used dm-cache [18] block-level cache interface in their method and also argued that write-back policy is beneficial in the cloud environment. Razavi and Kielmann [19] tried to reduce the network overhead to be occurring during VM startup time, by placing VM cache either on the compute node or on the storage memory. They found that when the cloud environment supports a master image to be shared among multiple VMs, caching VM images on the compute node would efficiently reduce network traffics. Also, with the cloud environment, where many compute nodes simultaneously use multiple VMs, placing VM cache image to the storage memory can help reduce the disk queuing delay.

Besides between the shared storage and the host, the I/O latency taking place in the hypervisor should also be addressed to achieve the desirable system bandwidth in the virtualization environment. One of such overheads is VM exit. The I/O requests issued in VMs are asynchronously handled by the host while passing through the hypervisor and the emulator such as QEMU. Since VMs run on the nonroot mode and the hypervisor runs on the root mode, servicing I/O requests causes exiting VM first to go to the hypervisor, which incurs the context switching overhead. Also, the replies from the hypervisor to VMs adversely affect I/O performance. Since the application which issued those I/O requests remains blocked on VM, such a switching overhead can eventually slow down the application execution.

There are several researches on this issue. For example, SR-IOV [20, 21] was implemented to obtain the benefits of direct I/O on physical devices, by defining extensions to the PCIe specification. In SR-IOV, VDD running in the guest either is connected to VF executing on the shared sources for direct data movement or forwards the request to dom 0 where PF driver manages and coordinates the direct accesses to the shared resources for VFs. Yassour et al. [22] proposed a device assignment, where VM can access physical I/O resources directly, without passing through the host emulation software.

However, the direct device assignment cannot work for virtual resources such as virtual disk, losing the strength of virtualization flexibility. To overcome such a drawback, Har'El et al. [23] proposed a new form of paravirtual I/O, which tried to overcome the weakness of the existing paravirtual I/O scheme [4, 24, 25]. Their I/O scheme attempts to alleviate I/O overhead by providing the dedicated I/O core controlled by a single I/O thread. Instead of mixing I/O and guest workloads in the same core, using a dedicated I/O not only can assign more cycles to guests but also can improve overall system efficiency by reducing the context switching cost.

The other issue of the I/O virtualization overhead is that I/O requests should go through a thick I/O stack to complete. In the case of KVM using QEMU, the typical way of writing data in the guest is that, after passing the file system and device driver layer of the guest kernel, the data necessary for the write should be transferred to the emulated device driver in the hypervisor. Also, the data enters the host kernel that has the similar software structure to the guest kernel (assuming the guest and host run the same OS) and reaches the physical I/O device attached to the host. Appropriately placing cache is a way of reducing such traffics in the virtualization environment [26, 27].

Capo [27] uses local disks as a persistent cache. Shamma et al. insisted that the majority of requests on VMs are redundant and can be served by local disk. In order to justify their argument, they first traced a production VDI workload and found that caching below the individual VMs is effective to improve I/O performance. Capo was integrated with XenServer [28], by putting it into domain 0. Also, Gupta et al. [29] studied the page sharing and memory compression to save the memory consumption of VMs. Their difference engine method searches for the identical pages by using the hashing function. If pages have the same value, then it reclaims the pages and updates the virtual memory to point out the shared copy. Detecting the page sharing in their method goes further by eliminating the subpage sharing using page patching and by adapting in-core memory compression.

Ongaro et al. [30] studied the impact of Xen scheduling policy on I/O bandwidth with several applications showing the different performance characteristics. They found that

Xen's credit scheduler does not lower the response latency in the situation where several domains are concurrently performing I/O, even with BOOST state. One of the reasons is that the event channel driver always scans the pending vector from the beginning, instead of resuming from where it left. Also, they found the possibility of priority inversion of which delivering the highest-priority packet is postponed by preemption. Lu and Shen [31] traced the page miss ratio of VMs, by employing the hypervisor-level exclusive cache. They captured the pages evicted from VM memory into the hypervisor exclusive cache, while avoiding containing the same data in VM and exclusive cache. Jones et al. [32] also proposed a way of inferring promoting and evicting pages of buffer cache in the virtual memory. In order to correctly infer page cache activities, they observed some sensitive events causing control to be transferred to VMM, such as page faults, page table updates, and disk I/Os.

However, optimizing either in the guest or in the hypervisor might not be enough to produce the desirable performance because I/O path in the virtualization involves several software layers including the shared storage to guest and the guest to host. In this paper we attempted to target both layers by implementing the guest-level component and the hypervisor-level component.

3. MultiCache

3.1. System Structure. MultiCache was implemented to exploit I/O optimizations targeting multiple layers of I/O virtualization stack. Figure 2 represents an overall structure of MultiCache. As can be seen in the figure, MultiCache is divided into three components: guest-level component, hypervisor-level component, and resource monitoring component. The main goal of the guest-level component is to mitigate the I/O latency between the shared storage and the guest, by utilizing the history information of application I/O executions. Furthermore, by retaining the application-specific data in the guest, it can reduce I/O accesses to the physical device attached to the host. Finally, it tries to determine the effective cache size while taking into consideration VM and host resource usages in real time.

The guest-level component works at VM and consists of three tables, including hash table, history table and I/O map, to detect application's I/O activities and to retain the associated metadata representing the execution history logs. Those logs are used to predict the next I/O behaviour to preload the preferential files from the shared storage and also used to maintain recently referenced files in VM.

The hypervisor-level component was implemented in QEMU. The primary objective of this component is to minimize the I/O latency incurred in the virtual to hypervisor transition, by using the I/O access frequency measured in QEMU. Also, by intercepting I/O requests before they go to the host kernel, the component tries to reduce I/O contention among VMs. The first attribute of the component is the module interface interacting with QEMU I/O call while exchanging the associated I/O metadata with it, such as sector numbers requested. The main module of the component receives the I/O metadata from the interface and determines

the hit or miss, while communicating with the metadata repository that contains the history logs of hypervisor's I/O execution, such as I/O access frequency. The device driver of the component is responsible for managing the hypervisor cache memory.

The third component of MultiCache is the real-time resource monitoring component. The monitoring module works at the hypervisor independently of guest operating systems, collecting the resource usage information from all VMs and the host server. The monitoring information is used by both components of MultiCache to effectively perform I/O optimization schemes. There are two tables associated with the monitoring component: VM resource table for storing VM resource usages and host resource table for host resource usages.

3.2. Differences between Two Components of MultiCache. There are four differences between the guest-level component and the hypervisor-level component of MultiCache. First, the main goal of the guest-level component is to mitigate I/O overhead between the shared storage and the guest VM, by prefetching and retaining files that will likely be used in the near future. On the other hand, the hypervisor-level component is to minimize I/O overhead between the guest VM and the host, by cutting down I/O software stack inside QEMU.

Second, two components of MultiCache use the different I/O unit: files in the guest-level component and sectors in the hypervisor-level component. While the guest-level component uses files for I/O optimization, the hypervisor-level component uses sectors that have been divided from files in the guest kernel before arriving at QEMU I/O call.

Third, to mitigate I/O overhead, the guest-level component utilizes the usage count that indicates how many times files have been referenced after they were brought into the guest. By caching the files that have high usage counts, the component attempts to reduce the network and I/O overheads between the shared storage and the guest VM. Also, this information is used to reduce I/O accesses from the host. The hypervisor-level component utilizes the I/O access frequency that implies how often sectors have been accessed from the host. Instead of forwarding sectors having frequently been used to the host, the hypervisor-level component caches those sectors in memory to reduce application process block time and I/O contention on the host.

Finally, while the guest-level component reserves the cache memory in the guest VM, the hypervisor-level component reserves the cache memory in the hypervisor, which is managed independently of guest operation systems. Table 1 illustrates the brief description about the differences between two MultiCache components.

3.3. MultiCache Guest-Level Component. The guest-level component of MultiCache was implemented to optimize network and I/O overheads incurring in file transmissions between the shared storage and the guest VM. Furthermore, by monitoring and accumulating I/O history information,

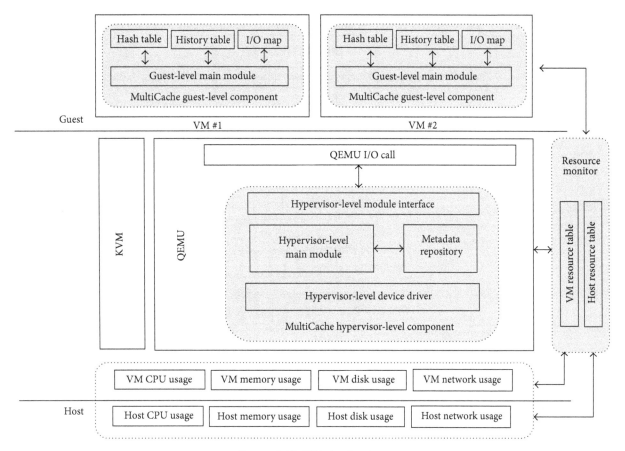

FIGURE 2: MultiCache structure.

TABLE 1: Difference between two MultiCache components.

	Guest-level component	Hypervisor-level component
Objective	To minimize the overhead between the shared storage and the guest VM	To minimize the overhead between the guest VM and the host
I/O unit	File	Sector
Optimization hint	File usage count	Sector I/O access frequency
Cache memory	Placed in the guest VM	Placed in the hypervisor
OS dependency	Yes	No

MultiCache enables providing better I/O responsiveness and data reliability.

To maintain the history information, MultiCache uses two kinds of tables: hash table and history table. The hash table is constructed with hash keys and is used to locate the associated history table containing the corresponding file metadata. There are λ history tables organized to solve the hash collision. One of the important file metadata in the history table is the usage count. Every time files are accessed for read and write operations, their associated usage count is increased by one to indicate the file access frequency. Also,

MultiCache uses two I/O maps to determine the number of files to prefetch it from and to replace it to the shared storage.

Figure 3 shows the structure of MultiCache guest-level component. First, with the file inode, the hash key to access the hash table is calculated. The associated hash table entry contains the current history table address and its entry number where the desired file metadata can be retrieved. If the new file is used for I/O, then the next empty place in the current history table is provided to store its metadata.

In order to maintain the appropriate cache memory size in the guest, only the files with each having the usage count no less than *USAGE_THRESHOLD* are stored in the cache and their file metadata is inserted into the read or write map, based on file read or write operations. Separately maintaining read and write maps offers two benefits. First, it enables cashing more files showing frequent read executions in order to support the better chance for the fast read responsiveness. Second, it can contribute to enhancing data reliability and availability by flushing out more dirty files at the replacement phase. Besides, the I/O map enables maintaining files in the guest according to their frequency and recentness to reduce I/O accesses to the host.

In Figure 3, sections A (cache window size) and C in the read and write maps, respectively, illustrate the files that should be maintained in the cache memory; sections B and D are the candidates to be replaced under the cache memory pressure. MultiCache can enhance the read responsiveness

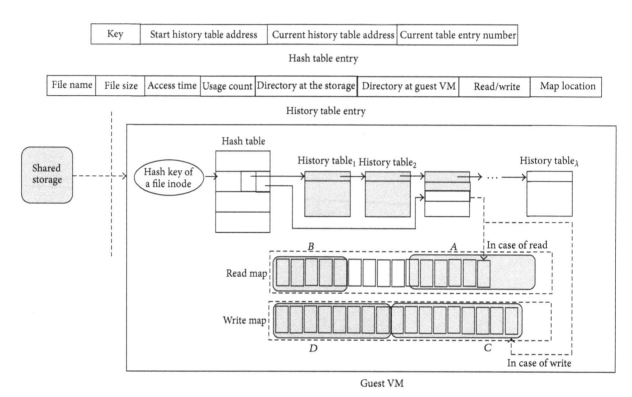

Key	Start history table address	Current history table address	Current table entry number

Hash table entry

File name	File size	Access time	Usage count	Directory at the storage	Directory at guest VM	Read/write	Map location

History table entry

FIGURE 3: MultiCache guest-level component.

by caching more files whose most recent I/O accesses are read operations. Such a process involves replacing less files mapped in section B. Similarly, MultiCache can replace more dirty files mapped to section D for data reliability and availability. Let M_g be the guest-level cache memory size and let *MEM_THRESHOLD* be the memory usage limitation over

which files designated at sections B and D must be flushed out to maintain the appropriate cache memory capacity. Finally, let f_a, f_b, g_c, and g_d be files whose metadata are mapped to sections A, B, C, and D, respectively. At each time epoch, MultiCache checks M_g by communicating with the resource monitor to see if the following condition is satisfied:

$$\frac{\left\{\sum_{f_a \in A} \text{size}\left(f_a\right) + \sum_{f_b \in B} \text{size}\left(f_b\right) + \sum_{g_c \in C} \text{size}\left(g_c\right) + \sum_{g_d \in D} \text{size}\left(g_d\right)\right\}}{M_g} \leq MEM\_THRESHOLD. \tag{1}$$

Algorithm 1 shows the steps involved in the guest-level component of MultiCache. Let i and k be the most recent positions of the read and write maps, respectively. Also, let f be the file for read and let g be the file for write.

In steps (1) and (2), MultiCache calculates the hash keys of f and g to access their file metadata from two tables. Also, the usage counts of two files are increased. In steps (4) to (17), if the usage count is larger than or equal to the threshold, then the metadata of f and g are inserted into the read and write maps, respectively, to store the associated data to MultiCache. In particular, if the last access of f was write, then the metadata is migrated from the write map to the read map, while erasing its history from the write map. The same procedure is applied for g to save its metadata to the write map. Steps (18) to (24) describe the procedure to maintain the appropriate cache size by taking into account condition (1). In the case that the condition is not satisfied, files mapped

to sections B and D are flushed out to eliminate the memory pressure.

3.4. MultiCache Hypervisor-Level Component. The hypervisor-level component was implemented to minimize the I/O overhead caused by the software stack between the guest VM and the host. Before completing I/O requests, there are several mode transitions taking place between nonroot mode and root mode, which incurs the application execution being blocked. Furthermore, because those requests require accessing the data from the physical device attached to the host, the optimization at the hypervisor needs a way of reducing I/O contention on the device during the service time.

MultiCache hypervisor-level component uses several tables, called the metadata repository, to maintain I/O-related metadata at the hypervisor. Figure 4 shows the tables

(1) calculate the hash keys of f and g to retrieve their file metadata from the hash and history tables;
(2) **if** (not found) **then** insert their metadata to the hash table and the history table **end if**
(3) increase the usage counts of f and g by one;
(4) **if** (the usage count of $f \geq USAGE\_THRESHOLD$) **then**
(5)   **if** ($f \in read\ map$ and its position in *read map* is a where $a < i$) **then**
(6) i++; move the metadata of f from ath position to ith position of *read map*;
(7)   **else if** ($f \in write\ map$) **then**
(8) i++; move the metadata of f to ith position of *read map*; delete it from *write map*;
(9)   **else** i++; insert the metadata of f to ith position of *read map* **end if**
(10) **end if**
(11) **if** (the usage count of $g \geq USAGE\_THRESHOLD$) **then**
(12)   **if** ($g \in write\ map$ and its position in *write map* is b where $b < k$) **then**
(13) k++; move the metadata of g from bth position to kth position of *write map*;
(14)   **else if** ($g \in read\ map$) **then**
(15) k++; move the metadata of g to kth position of *write map*; delete it from *read map*;
(16)   **else** k++; insert the metadata of g to kth position of *write map* **end if**
(17) **end if**
(18) **for each time epoch**
(19)   receive the current guest VM memory size from the resource monitor;
(20)   check the condition specified in (1);
(21)   **if** (the condition is not satisfied) **then**
(22)   flush out files depicted in the section B or D until memory pressure is eliminated;
(23)   **end if**
(24) **end for**

ALGORITHM 1: MultiCache guest-level component.

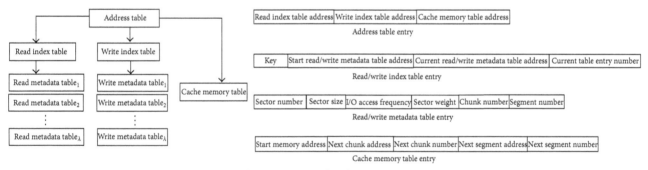

FIGURE 4: Metadata repository of the hypervisor-level component.

in the metadata repository. The address table stores the addresses of the read and write index tables containing the hash key and the start and current addresses of the read and write metadata tables. Similar to the history tables of the guest-level component, λ read metadata tables and λ write metadata tables are organized to target the collision problem. The read and write metadata tables contain the access information about the sectors transferred from QEMU I/O calls; the cache memory table maintains the next chunk and segment addresses of the hypervisor cache memory.

The hypervisor-level component uses I/O access frequencies of sectors to determine if those sectors should be retained in the cache memory. The I/O access frequency indicates how many times the associated sectors were used in I/O requests. There are two reasons for utilizing I/O access frequency. First, because the cache memory maintained in MultiCache is of a restricted size, a criterion is needed to filter sectors before storing them in the cache memory. In MultiCache, only those sectors that have been accessed no less than a threshold ($FREQ\_THRESHOLD$) are stored in the cache memory.

Second, besides optimizing the mode transition and I/O contention aforementioned, MultiCache gives an opportunity to prioritize I/O requests, according to the VM's different importance. In other words, I/O requests issued in the high-priority guest VM can be executed first, despite their access frequency. In MultiCache, the priority of VM is determined by the number of CPUs and the memory capacity with which the VM was configured: the more number of CPUs and the larger memory size it is assigned, the higher priority the guest is given.

Let S be a set of sectors consisting of I/O requests in a guest. Consider a host where N number of VMs are currently executing. Also, each VM(i) is configured with u_i number of CPUs and v_i memory capacity.

Definition 1. A sector sc $\in S$ issued from VM(i) is defined by four components: p_{sc}, w_{sc}, δ_{sc}, and m_{sc}:

(1)   apply the hash function to obtain a hash key using sc;
(2)   access the read index table with the hash key to retrieve the metadata of sc from the read metadata table;
(3)   **if** no metadata about sc is available in the read index table **then**
(4)   store it in the read index table and the current read metadata table;
(5)   update the read index table to point out the next entry of the current read metadata table;
(6)   **end if**
(7) p_{sc}++; $w_{sc} = p_{sc} \times$ the weight of guest VM;
(8)   **if** ($w_{sc} <$ FREQ_THRESHOLD) **then** $\delta_{sc} = 0$; exit to access sc from the host **end if**
(9)   **if** sc has not been mapped to the cache memory **then**
(10) $\delta_{sc} = 0$;
(11)   map sc to the cache, by retrieving the chunk and segment numbers from the cache memory table;
(12) **else**
(13) $\delta_{sc} = 1$;
(14)   access the cache memory with the chunk and segment numbers of sc retrieved;
(15) **end if**

ALGORITHM 2: MultiCache hypervisor-level component.

(1) p_{sc} is the I/O access frequency of sc.

(2) w_{sc} is the weight of sc satisfying $w_{sc} = p_{sc} \times (u_i / \sum_{k=1}^{N} u_k) \times (v_i / \sum_{k=1}^{N} v_k)$, where $(u_i / \sum_{k=1}^{N} u_k) \times (v_i / \sum_{k=1}^{N} v_k)$ is the weight of VM(i).

(3) δ_{sc} is the mapping function, indicating either cache hit ($\delta_{sc} = 1$) or miss ($\delta_{sc} = 0$).

(4) m_{sc} is the position of the cache memory, where sc is stored if $w_{sc} \geq$ FREQ_THRESHOLD.

Algorithm 2 represents the steps for reading sc at the hypervisor-level component of MultiCache.

Suppose that sc is one of the sectors consisting of a read request in the guest. MultiCache calculates a hash key to access the read index table containing the corresponding read metadata table address. After retrieving the associated metadata from the table, the I/O access frequency is multiplied by the VM weight to obtain the weight of sc. In the case where the weight of sc is less than FREQ_THRESHOLD, MultiCache passes sc to the host kernel to access it from the physical I/O device. Otherwise, from step (9) to step (15), MultiCache checks to see if sc has been stored in the cache memory. If not, sc is stored in the memory by using the chunk and segment numbers retrieved from the cache memory table. In the case where sc is found in the cache memory, it returns to the guest without going down to the host kernel. In the write operation, after updating the associated metadata to the write index table and the write metadata table, the sector is mapped to the cache table. If the associated metadata is available in the table, then the sector having been mapped in the cache memory is overwritten to update.

The cache memory handled by the hypervisor-level component is partitioned into chunks that consisted of a number of pages. In case of the write cache memory, the sectors stored in the chunk are transmitted to the host kernel, either after the chunk is filled with valid sectors or when the current checkpoint (currently every 30 seconds) for the chunk comes. Let M_h be the size of the cache memory; let C_i be the ith chunk; and let $|C_i|$ be the size of C_i. Also, let seg_k be the kth

segment of C_i whose size, $|seg_k|$, is the same as that of a sector. The chunk validity and segment validity are determined by the chunk map and the segment map, respectively.

Definition 2. The allocation status of C_i in the chunk map and the one of seg_k of C_i in the segment map are defined as follows:

For any chunk C_i, bit: $C[i] \rightarrow \{0, 1\}$, $1 \leq i \leq M_h/|C_i|$.

For any segment $seg_k \in C_i$, bit: $seg[i, k] \rightarrow \{0, 1\}$, $1 \leq k \leq |C_i|/|seg_k|$.

If bit($seg[i, k]$) = 1, then the segment contains a valid sector that should be transferred to the host. Otherwise, bit($seg[i, k]$) = 0. Also, bit($C[i]$) = 1 implies that all the segments consisting of C_i contain the valid sectors. Algorithm 3 shows the steps involved in the write process for the cache memory.

3.5. MultiCache Resource Monitor. The resource monitor calculates the resource statuses of guest VMs and host server at the hypervisor level because it should monitor the usage information independently of guest operating systems. Also, it is organized with the light-weight modules so that it rarely affects I/O bandwidth on VMs. During application executions, the monitor periodically notifies the resource usage information to the guest-level and hypervisor-level components to help them maintain the effective cache capacity for I/O improvement.

The resource monitor is composed of three modules: resource collection module, resource calculation module, and usage container. The resource collection module works on top of the server, while communicating with *proc* file system and *libvirt* to collect the resource status information such as CPU, memory, disk I/O, and network status. The resource calculation module calculates resource usages and, finally, the usage container stores the calculated information to offer it to both components of MultiCache.

Figure 5 represents the functions to be called in the resource monitor. To activate the monitor, the resource

(1) **for** each chunk C_i
(2)   **if** ($\text{bit}(C[i]) = 1$) **then** transfer C_i to the host; $\text{bit}(C[i]) = 0$ **end if**
(3) **end for**
(4) /* let sc be the current sector to be stored in the cache memory */
(5) /* let i and k be the chunk and segment numbers, respectively, selected from the cache memory table */
(6) store sc to seg_k of C_i; $\text{bit}(\text{seg}[i, k]) = 1$; update $\text{bit}(C[i])$ while reflecting $\text{bit}(\text{seg}[i, k])$ value;
(7) k++;
(8) **if** (($k < |C_i|/|\text{seg}_k|$) and $\text{bit}(\text{seg}[i, k]) = 0$) **then**
(9)   store i and k to the cache memory table as the next position in the cache memory; exit;
(10) **end if**
(11) /* find the next empty chunk in the cache memory */
(12) search for C_i such that ($i = (i + 1)\%(M_h/|C_i|)$ and $\text{bit}(C[i]) = 0$);
(13) store i and 0 to the cache memory table as the next position in the cache memory;

ALGORITHM 3: Cache memory management.

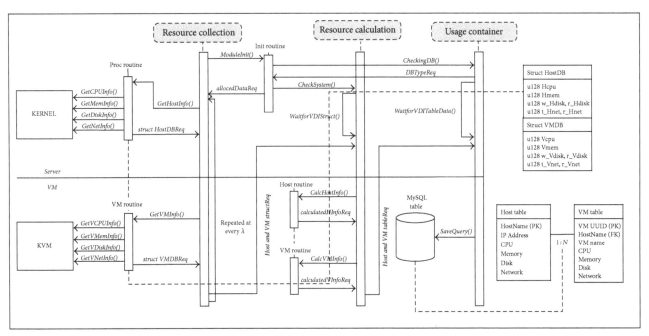

FIGURE 5: Resource monitor structure in MultiCache.

collection first initializes the functions to be called in the resource calculation and the usage container, by issuing *ModuleInit*( ). Also, it communicates with /*proc* and *libvirt* at every time period λ by calling *GetXXXInfo*( ) and accumulates the resource status information to store it to the usage container. The resource calculation module retrieves the status information, by calling *calcHostInfo* and *calcVMInfo*( ), and calculates the resource usages by applying the formulas described in Table 2. Finally, the results are stored in the usage container.

4. Performance Evaluation

4.1. Experimental Platform. We executed all experiments on a host server equipped with an AMD FX 8350 eight-core processors, 24 GB of memory, and 1 TB of Seagate Barracuda ST1000DM003 disk. Also, the other server having the same hardware specification as the host server is configured as the shared storage node. Two servers are connected with 1 Gbit of network. The operating system was Ubuntu release 14.04 with 3.13.0-24 generic kernel. We installed the virtual machine on top of the host server by using KVM hypervisor. Each VM was configured with two-core processors, 8 GB of memory, and 50 GB of virtual disk using virtIO. The operating system of each VM was CentOS release 6.5 with 2.6.32-431 kernel. We used postmark benchmark for the evaluation.

4.2. MultiCache Guest-Level Component Evaluation. We first evaluated the guest-level component of MultiCache. In order to analyze the accurate I/O performance pattern of the guest-level component, we used the original KVM/QEMU version that is not integrated with the MultiCache hypervisor-level component. Also, we modified postmark to connect between the host server and the shared storage node. As a result, when files are generated from postmark, the files already brought into the guest from the storage node are read from

TABLE 2: Formulas and data structures for calculating resource usages.

Resource usage formula	Resource monitor data structure

$\text{CPU\%} = 100 - \dfrac{100}{\text{total}} \times (\text{idle}_{\text{now}} - \text{idle}_t)$
 (i) Total: total CPU usage
 (ii) idle_{now}, idle_t: idle values at the moment and at t
	struct S_ProcCpuInfo {
	   _u128 user, nice, system, idle, iowait;
	   _u128 irq, softirq, steal, guest;
	 }

$\text{Memory usage} = 100 \times \dfrac{\text{total} - \text{free}}{\text{total}}$
 (i) Total, free: total and free memory sizes, respectively
	struct S_ProcMemInfo {
	   _u128 total, free;
	   _u128 buffers, cached;
	 }

$\text{Disk usage} = (\text{sectr}_{\text{now}} - \text{sectr}_t) \times 512$
 (i) $\text{sectr}_{\text{now}}$, sectr_t: sector usages up to now and at t, respectively
	struct S_ProcDiskInfo {
	   char disk_name[20];
	   _u128 r_compl, r_merge, r_sectr, r_milsc;
	   _u128 w_compl, w_merge;
	   _u128 w_sectr, w_milsc;
	   _u128 io_c_prc, io_milsc, io_w_milsc;
	 }

Network usage
 	
 $\text{PPS} = \text{packet}_{\text{now}} - \text{packet}_t$
 $\text{PacketSize} = \dfrac{(\text{byte}_{\text{now}} - \text{byte}_t) \times 8}{\text{PPS}} + 12 + 7 + 1$
 $\text{BPS} = \text{PPS} \times \text{PacketSize}$
 (i) PPS: number of packets transmitted per second
 (ii) BPS: network bandwidth in bit per second
	struct S_ProcNetInfo {
	   char net_name[20];
	   char net_hwaddr[20];
	   _u128 r_byte, r_pack, r_err, r_drop;
	   _u128 r_fifo, r_frm, r_cmp, r_mult;
	   _u128 t_byte, t_pack, t_err, t_drop;
	   _u128 t_fifo, t_col, t_cal, t_cmp;
	 }

MultiCache (*cached*) and the other files not residing in MultiCache are read from the storage through NFS (*not cached*).

Figure 6 shows I/O bandwidth while varying file sizes from 4 KB to 1 MB. x-axis represents the ratio of *not cached* to *cached*. For example, 90 : 10 implies that 90% of files to be needed during transactions are exchanged with the shared storage node. The number of transactions is 20000 and the ratio of read to write is 50 : 50. In the figure, as the percentage of files being accessed from MultiCache becomes high, better I/O bandwidth is achieved. Moreover, the effect of MultiCache is more apparent with large files. For example, with 20 : 80, where 80% of files are accessed from MultiCache, about 53% of I/O bandwidth improvement is observed with 1 MB of files as compared to that of 4 KB of files. The reason is that as more number of large files is accessed from MultiCache the network overhead to transfer data to VM becomes small, resulting in the bandwidth speedup.

In the evaluations, we observed that the effect of Multi-Cache is especially obvious with read operations, as shown in Figure 7. In order to see the impact of MultiCache in the mixed I/O operations, we varied the read and write percentages while increasing the number of transactions. In Figure 7, 80 : 20 means that 80% of transactions are read operations and 20% of transactions are writes. Also, we used 1 MB of file size. Figure 7 exhibits that better I/O throughput is generated with the large number of transactions and especially with the larger percentage of read operations. This is because write operations inevitably incur network and I/O overheads to store data to the shared storage and such burdens may lower the throughput.

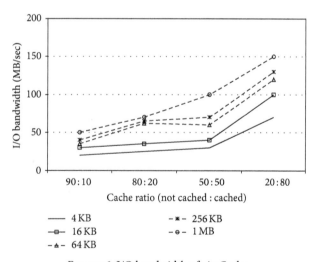

FIGURE 6: I/O bandwidth of virtCache.

However, I/O latency between the shared storage and the VM is not the only one that should be addressed to achieve the desirable performance. As mentioned, the I/O path from the guest to the host should also be scrutinized because there are multiple places causing the performance slowdown, such as I/O contention to physical devices and mode transition between the guest and the hypervisor. We will observe how the hypervisor-level component of MultiCache can achieve better bandwidth by overcoming such latencies.

4.3. I/O Bandwidth of Hypervisor-Level Component. We measured the I/O performance of the hypervisor-level component. In this experiment, there is no file transmission between

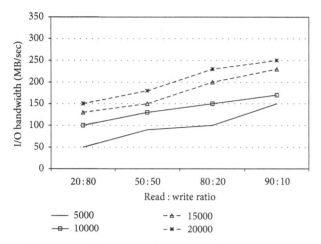

FIGURE 7: Performance evaluation based on I/O accesses.

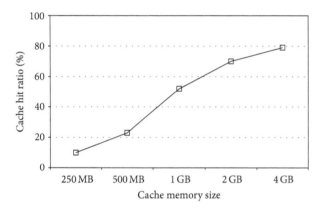

FIGURE 8: The effect of the cache memory.

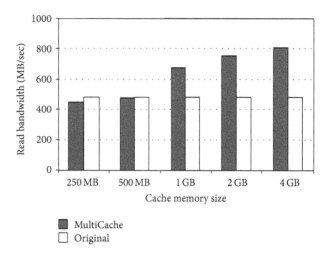

FIGURE 9: Read bandwidth based on the cache memory.

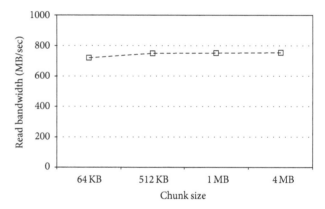

FIGURE 10: The effect of the chunk size on read.

the shared storage and the guest. In other words, all files for I/O were generated from the postmark benchmark running on the guest. The file sizes vary between 4 KB and 1 MB.

First of all, we observed the effect of the hypervisor cache memory in Figure 8, while changing the cache memory size from 250 MB to 4 GB. To warm the cache, we executed the modified postmark for 5 seconds and took the average value of each test case. Figure 8 shows the cache hit ratio obtained while changing the cache memory size. The figure shows that as the cache memory size becomes large, so does the hit ratio. For example, increasing the memory size from 250 MB to 4 GB shows the hit ratio improvement by up to 6.9x.

However, there is a subtle difference worthwhile to observe in the figure. While the hit ratio improves 126% from 500 MB to 1 GB, the hit ratio from 1 GB to 2 GB increases 34%. Extending the cache memory from 2 GB to 4 GB produces even the smaller percentage of hit ratio improvement. We guess that this is because the locality is shifted as time goes on. Also, the metadata stored in the metadata repository are replaced to the new ones due to the space restriction.

Figure 9 shows the I/O bandwidth obtained while varying the cache memory size from 250 MB to 4 GB. We can notice that Figure 9 depicts the similar performance pattern to that of Figure 8: the larger cache memory size is, the better

I/O bandwidth is. Also, while increasing the cache memory size from 500 MB to 1 GB shows about 43% of bandwidth speedup, the cache memory extension from 1 GB to 2 GB produces only 12% of performance improvement.

In Figure 9, we compared the I/O performance of Multi-Cache to that of the original KVM/QEMU. With the small cache memory size such as 250 MB, the I/O bandwidth of MultiCache is less than that of the original version because of the cache miss incurred by space restriction. However, the performance difference becomes large as the memory size of MultiCache increases. With 2 GB of cache memory size, MultiCache produces about 37% of I/O bandwidth improvement compared to that of the original version. We currently use 2 GB of cache memory size. The RAM size of the host is 24 GB; therefore we use only about 8% of the total size as the cache memory.

Figure 10 shows the read results while changing the chunk size from 64 KB to 4 MB in the cache memory. As can be seen in the figure, changing the chunk size does little affect I/O bandwidth in the read operation because no write occurred to the host.

Figure 11 shows the write bandwidths of MultiCache while comparing to those of the original KVM/QEMU. The original version supports three write modes: default, write-through,

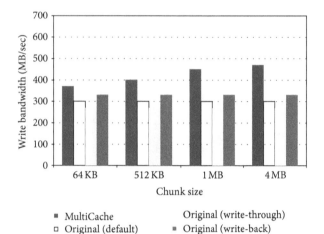

FIGURE 11: Write bandwidth based on the chunk size.

and write-back. In the case of using 1 MB of chunk size in MultiCache, it generates about 33% and 27% higher bandwidth than the default mode and the write-back mode of the original version, respectively. There are two reasons to explain such I/O bandwidth improvements. In the case of write-back mode of the original version, it buffers the data for I/O in the host kernel so that I/O requests issued in the guest should go through the guest kernel and QEMU before arriving at the host. Second, instead of flushing the data out to the physical device, the hypervisor-level component intercepts them in QEMU and collects in the cache memory in a big I/O unit. Such a method can contribute to accelerating I/O bandwidth, because, in Figure 11, we can notice that as the chunk size increases, the write performance also becomes large. However, based on the result with 4 MB of chunk size, increasing the size more than 1 MB might not produce significant performance speedup due to the write latency in the host.

5. Conclusion

We proposed a multilayered cache mechanism, called MultiCache, to optimize I/O virtualization overhead. The first layer of MultiCache is the guest-level component whose main goal is to optimize the I/O overhead between the back end, shared storage, and the guest. Also, caching the application-specific data in the guest can contribute to accelerating the performance speedup. In order to achieve this goal, the guest-level component uses the history logs of file usage metadata to preload preferential files from the shared storage and to maintain recently referenced files in the guest. The second layer of MultiCache is to minimize the I/O latency between the guest and the host, by utilizing the I/O access frequency in QEMU. Also, by intercepting I/O requests in QEMU before they are transferred to the host kernel, the component can mitigate I/O contention on the physical device attached to the host. In the component, we accumulated the I/O access information about application executions in the metadata repository and used it to retain data with high I/O access frequency in the cache memory. Both components of MultiCache were

integrated with the real-time resource monitoring module collecting the resource usage information of VMs and host at the hypervisor. The performance measurement with the postmark demonstrates that our approach is beneficial in achieving high I/O performance in the virtualization environment. As a future work, we will evaluate MultiCache with more real applications to prove its effectiveness in improving I/O performance.

Competing Interests

The authors declare that they have no competing interests.

Acknowledgments

This work was supported by the National Research Foundation of Korea (NRF) grant funded by the Korea government (MSIP) (NRF-2014R1A2A2A01002614).

References

[1] R. Spruijt, "VDI Smackdown," White Paper, v.1.4, 2012.

[2] J. Hwang and T. Wood, "Adaptive dynamic priority scheduling for virtual desktop infrastructures," in *Proceedings of the IEEE 20th International Workshop on Quality of Service (IWQoS '12)*, pp. 1–9, IEEE, Coimbra, Portugal, June 2012.

[3] D.-A. Dasilva, L. Liu, N. Bessis, and Y. Zhan, "Enabling green IT through building a virtual desktop infrastructure," in *Proceedings of the 8th International Conference on Semantics, Knowledge and Grids (SKG '12)*, pp. 32–38, Beijing, China, October 2012.

[4] J. Santos, Y. Turner, G. Janakiraman, and I. Pratt, "Bridging the Gap between Software and Hardware Techniques for I/O Virtualization," in *Proceedings of the USENIX Annual Technical Conference*, Boston, Mass, USA, 2008.

[5] Y. Dong, J. Dai, Z. Huang, H. Guan, K. Tian, and Y. Jiang, "Towards high-quality I/O virtualization," in *Proceedings of the Israeli Experimental Systems Conference (SYSTOR '09)*, article 12, May 2009.

[6] C. Tang, "FVD: a high-performance virtual machine image format for cloud," in *Proceedings of the USENIX Annual Technical Conference*, Portland, Ore, USA, June 2011.

[7] D. Le, H. Huang, and H. Wang, "Understanding performance implications of nested file systems in a virtualized environment," in *Proceedings of the 10th USENX Conference on File and Storage Technologies (FAST '12)*, San Jose, Calif, USA, February 2012.

[8] A. Kivity, Y. Kamay, D. Laor, U. Lublin, and A. Liguori, "KVM: the Linux virtual machine monitor," in *Proceedings of the Ottawa Linux Symposium (OLS '07)*, pp. 225–230, July 2007.

[9] R. Russell, "Virtio: towards a De-Facto standard for virtual I/O devices," *ACM SIGOPS Operating Systems Review*, vol. 42, no. 5, pp. 95–103, 2008.

[10] F. Bellard, "QEMU, a fast and portable dynamic translator," in *Proceedings of the Annual Conference on USENIX Annual Technical Conference*, Anaheim, Calif, USA, April 2005.

[11] V. Tarasov, D. Hidebrand, G. Kuenning, and E. Zadok, "Virtual machine workloads: the case for new benchmarks for NAS," in *Proceedings of the 11th USENIX Conference on File and Storage Technologies (FAST '13)*, pp. 307–320, Santa Clara, Calif, USA, 2013.

[12] F. Meng, L. Zhou, X. Ma, S. Uttamchandani, and D. Liu, "vCacheShare: automated server flash cache space management in a virtualization environment," in *Proceedings of the 2014 USENIX conference on USENIX Annual Technical Conference (USENIX ATC '14)*, pp. 133–144, Philadelphia, Pa, USA, June 2014. ·

[13] S. Byan, J. Lentini, A. Madan et al., "Mercury: host-side flash caching for the data center," in *Proceedings of the IEEE 28th Symposium on Mass Storage Systems and Technologies (MSST '12)*, pp. 1–12, IEEE, San Diego, Calif, USA, April 2012.

[14] T. Luo, S. Ma, R. Lee, X. Zhang, D. Liu, and L. Zhou, "S-CAVE: effective SSD caching to improve virtual machine storage performance," in *Proceedings of the 22nd International Conference on Parallel Architectures and Compilation Techniques (PACT '13)*, pp. 103–112, Edinburgh, UK, September 2013.

[15] D. Arteaga and M. Zhao, "Client-side flash caching for cloud systems," in *Proceedings of the 7th ACM International Systems and Storage Conference (SYSTOR '14)*, Haifa, Israel, June 2014.

[16] H. Jin, W. Gao, S. Wu, X. Shi, X. Wu, and F. Zhou, "Optimizing the live migration of virtual machine by CPU scheduling," *Journal of Network and Computer Applications*, vol. 34, no. 4, pp. 1088–1096, 2011.

[17] T. C. Ferreto, M. A. S. Netto, R. N. Calheiros, and C. A. F. De Rose, "Server consolidation with migration control for virtualized data centers," *Future Generation Computer Systems*, vol. 27, no. 8, pp. 1027–1034, 2011.

[18] dm-cache, http://visa.lab.asu.edu/dmcache.

[19] K. Razavi and T. Kielmann, "Scalable virtual machine deployment using VM image caches," in *Proceedings of the International Conference for High Performance Computing, Networking, Storage and Analysis (SC '13)*, Denver, Colo, USA, November 2013.

[20] S. Bhosale, A. Caldeira, B. Grabowski et al., *IBM Power Systems SR-IOV*, IBM Redpaper, IBM, 2014.

[21] Y. Dong, X. Yang, J. Li, G. Liao, K. Tian, and H. Guan, "High performance network virtualization with SR-IOV," *Journal of Parallel and Distributed Computing*, vol. 72, no. 11, pp. 1471–1480, 2012.

[22] B. Yassour, M. Ben-Yehuda, and O. Wasserman, "Direct device assignment for untrusted fully-virtualized virtual machines," Tech. Rep. H-0263, IBM Research, 2008.

[23] N. Har'El, A. Gordon, A. Landau, M. Ben-Yehuda, A. Traeger, and R. Ladelsky, "Efficient and scalable paravirtual I/O system," in *Proceedings of the USENIX Annual Technical Conference*, pp. 231–242, San Jose, Calif, USA, 2013.

[24] A. Menon, A. Cox, and W. Zwaenepoel, "Optimizing network virtualization in Xen," in *Proceedings of the USENIX Annual Technical Conference*, Boston, Mass, USA, 2006.

[25] P. Barham, B. Dragovic, K. Fraser et al., "Xen and the art of virtualization," *ACM SIGOPS Operating Systems Review*, vol. 37, no. 5, pp. 164–177, 2003.

[26] H. Kim, H. Jo, and J. Lee, "XHive: efficient cooperative caching for virtual machines," *IEEE Transactions on Computers*, vol. 60, no. 1, pp. 106–119, 2011.

[27] M. Shamma, D. Meyer, J. Wires, M. Ivanova, N. Hutchinson, and A. Warfield, "Capo: recapitulating storage for virtual desktops," in *Proceedings of the 9th USENIX Conference on File and Storage Technologies*, San Jose, Calif, USA, February 2011.

[28] C.-H. Hong, Y.-P. Kim, S. Yoo, C.-Y. Lee, and C. Yoo, "Cache-aware virtual machine scheduling on multi-core architecture," *IEICE Transactions on Information and Systems*, vol. E95-D, no. 10, pp. 2377–2392, 2012.

[29] D. Gupta, S. Lee, M. Vrable et al., "Difference engine: harnessing memory redundancy in virtual machines," *Communications of the ACM*, vol. 53, no. 10, pp. 85–93, 2010.

[30] D. Ongaro, A. L. Cox, and S. Rixner, "Scheduling I/O in virtual machine monitors," in *Proceedings of the 4th International Conference on Virtual Execution Environments (VEE '08)*, pp. 1–10, Seattle, Wash, USA, March 2008.

[31] P. Lu and K. Shen, "Virtual machine memory access tracing with hypervisor exclusive cache," in *Proceedings of the USENIX Annual Technical Conference*, Santa Clara, Calif, USA, June 2007.

[32] S. T. Jones, A. C. Arpaci-Dusseau, and R. H. Arpaci-Dusseau, "Geiger: monitoring the buffer cache in a virtual machine environment," *ACM SIGPLAN Notices*, vol. 40, no. 5, pp. 14–24, 2006.

11

Cloud for Distributed Data Analysis Based on the Actor Model

Ivan Kholod, Ilya Petukhov, and Andrey Shorov

Faculty of Computer Science and Technology, Saint Petersburg Electrotechnical University (LETI), Professora Popova Street 5, Saint Petersburg 197376, Russia

Correspondence should be addressed to Andrey Shorov; ashxz@mail.ru

Academic Editor: Fabrizio Messina

This paper describes the construction of a Cloud for Distributed Data Analysis (CDDA) based on the actor model. The design uses an approach to map the data mining algorithms on decomposed functional blocks, which are assigned to actors. Using actors allows users to move the computation closely towards the stored data. The process does not require loading data sets into the cloud and allows users to analyze confidential information locally. The results of experiments show that the efficiency of the proposed approach outperforms established solutions.

1. Introduction

Presently the terms "cloud computing," "Internet of Things," and "Big Data" have become quite popular. They refer to technologies for collecting, storing, and handling large volumes of data, with a variety of types and a high rate of generation (Big Data). Modern data warehouses provide storage for large amounts of different data. However, all these are worthless if it is not possible to apply analysis and obtain new knowledge from the data.

The technologies machine learning, data mining, and knowledge discovery are used for the aforementioned used tasks. They use complex mathematical methods and algorithms that need powerful computing resources to analyze vast amounts of data. Cloud and cluster technologies provide scalable resources for those tasks.

During the last year, solutions in this area developed from research to product level. The leaders in cloud services are Amazon, Microsoft, IBM, and Google. They all recently launched their public Clouds for Data Analysis (CDA). They provide services for different user requirements and solve different tasks. However, they suffer from a restricted set of analysis tasks and do not extend. Also all of them are paid services and allow only to analyze data that have been uploaded into the cloud. Therefore these services can hardly be used to analyze confidential information.

We suggest to build a Cloud for Distributed Data Analysis (CDDA) that uses the approach *decomposition of data mining algorithms into sets of functional blocks* [1, 2]. It allows us to extend cloud services with new algorithms and modifications of existing algorithms. The mapping of functional blocks on distributed environments (in particular on actor environments) allows us to distribute calculations among different clouds. Moving the data mining algorithm closely to the data removes the restriction and keeps the data in the cloud.

In contrast to existing approaches, CDDA has the following key characteristics:

(i) implementation of both SaaS and PaaS cloud computing service models;

(ii) extension list of data mining algorithms in the cloud by adding new or modifying their functional blocks;

(iii) processing of data sets stored outside the cloud;

(iv) ability to analyze confidential information;

(v) execution of distributed data analysis among several clouds.

The paper is organized as follows. Section 2 is a review of similar cloud-based systems. Section 3 contains the description of a general approach that allows the decomposition of an algorithm into blocks on actor-model systems. Section 4 describes the CDDA architecture. Section 5 discusses experiments and compares the performance of the developed prototype with similar solutions. Finally, Section 6 presents the main conclusions and future work directions.

2. Related Work

Nowadays, a series of cloud computing service platforms have been developed to provide data analysis services for the public sector.

The Chinese Mobile Institute was one of the first who began working in this field. In 2007 they started their research in cloud computing. Later, in 2009, a platform for cloud computing, BigCloud, has been officially announced: *Data Mining Big Cloud-Parallel Data Mining* (BC-PDM) [3]. It is a collection of tools for the parallel execution of algorithms.

BC-PDM is a SaaS platform based on Apache Hadoop. Users can upload data to a repository (hosted in the cloud) from different sources and apply a variety of applications for data management, data analysis, and business applications. Those include the analysis of the performance of parallel operating applications: ETL processing, social network analysis, analysis of texts (text mining), data analysis (data mining), and statistical analysis.

It includes about ten algorithms and cannot be extended by the user. This cloud is only used for research in the Chinese Mobile Institute. Therefore it is not available for public use.

Azure Machine Learning (Azure ML) [4] is a SaaS cloud-based predictive analytics service from Microsoft Inc. It has been launched in February 2015. Azure ML provides paid services, which allow users to execute the full cycle of data mining: data collection, preprocessing, defining features, choosing and applying an algorithm, evaluating a model, and publication. The service is for experienced users with knowledge in machine learning algorithms.

The analysis process is designed as a workflow. Each step of the workflow is a module, designed to execute a single subtask of the analysis (data reader, data transformation, an algorithm, or other). A module can be executed on a single cluster node. Thus, a number of modules can be executed in parallel if the workflow allows it.

Azure ML can import data from local files, online sources, and other cloud projects (experiments). The reader module allows us to load data from external sources on the Internet or other file storages.

The user can only apply the proprietary machine learning algorithms of Azure ML: classification (Boosted Decision Trees, Random Forests, Logistic Regression, SVM, Averaged Perceptron, and neural networks), regression (Linear Regression, Boosted Decision Trees, and neural networks), anomaly detection (SVM, PCA), and clustering (*K*-Means). Additional algorithms are available for purchase at the Machine Learning Marketplace.

In April 2015 Amazon has launched their *Amazon Machine Learning* service that allows users to train predictive models in the cloud [5]. This service provides all required stages of data analysis: data preparation, construction of a machine learning model, its settings, and eventually the prediction. The user can build and fine-tune predictive models using large amounts of data.

Special knowledge in the field of machine learning is not required. Amazon Machine Learning solves only classification and regression tasks. It supports three distinct types of tools: binary classification, multiclass classification, and regression. New algorithms and machine learning tasks cannot be implemented into the service.

It allows users to analyze data stored in others Amazon services (Amazon Simple Storage Service, Amazon Redshift, or Amazon Relational Database Service). To scale computations, the service uses Apache Hadoop.

Google made its *Cloud Machine Learning* platform [6], which is used by Google Photos, Translate, and Inbox, available to developers in March 2016. It is a managed platform that empowers users to build machine learning models. The platform provides pretrained models and helps to generate customized models. It allows users to apply neural network based machine learning methods, which are used by other Google services including Photos (image search), the Google app (voice search), Translate, and Inbox (Smart Reply).

The Google services will provide application programming interfaces (APIs) for automatic image recognition, speech recognition, language translation, and more. The cloud provides four basic machine learning services:

(i) Vision API enables developers to recognize the content of an image by encapsulating powerful machine learning models.

(ii) Speech API enables developers to convert audio to text by applying powerful neural network models.

(iii) Translate API provides a simple programmatic interface to translate arbitrary strings into any supported language.

(iv) Prediction API can help to analyze users' data to add applicable features (customers sentiment analysis, message routing decisions, churn analysis, and others) to a user's application.

All of these services are provided by REST API for client applications. Users can only analyze data stored in Google storage. Also user cannot add new machine learning algorithms.

In the beginning of 2016, IBM presented their analytic service—*Watson Analytics* [7]. It is a smart data discovery service, available on the IBM cloud. The service solves high-level analytic tasks. Users are able to deploy queries in natural language. Watson Analytics' three main areas are Explore, Predict, and Assemble:

(i) Explore allows users to create queries to data. Users can use existing templates or enter text based queries.

(ii) Predict allows predicting one or more variables based on other variables. Therefore classification and regressions methods are used.

(iii) Assemble allows users to create analytic reports, presentations, and data visualization.

Watson Analytics handles data sets that have been uploaded into the cloud in .csv or MS Excel (.xls) formats. Users can only use methods, provided by Watson Analytics.

There are also some data mining algorithm libraries for distributed environments. They can be used to create a CDA. The most famous are the following.

Data Mining Cloud Framework (DMCF) [8] is designed for developing and running distributed data analytics applications as a collection of services. The first implementation of the framework has been carried out on the Windows Azure cloud platform and has been evaluated through a set of data analysis applications executed on a Microsoft Cloud data center. The framework treats the data sets, data mining algorithms, and mining models as services, which can be combined through a visual interface to produce distributed workflows executed on a cloud platform. DMCF supports JavaScript for Clouds (JS4Cloud) as an additional and more flexible programming interface.

Apache Spark Machine Learning Library (MLlib) [9] is a scalable machine learning library for the Apache Spark platform. It consists of common learning algorithms and utilities, including classification, regression, clustering, collaborative filtering, dimensionality reduction, and lower-level optimization primitives and higher-level pipeline APIs. It has an own implementation of MapReduce, which uses memory for data storage (versus Apache Hadoop that uses disk storage). It allows us to increase the efficiency of the algorithm's performance. The user can extend the set of machine learning algorithms by own implementations. However, users must decompose their algorithms according to MapReduce and other Spark's specific functions. It strongly limits the abilities for parallelization of data mining algorithms.

Apache Mahout [10] is also a data mining library concerning the MapReduce paradigm. It can be executed on Apache Hadoop or Spark based platforms. It contains only a few data mining algorithms for distributed execution: collaborative filtering (User-Based, Item-Based, and Matrix Factorization with ALS), classification (Naive Bayes/Complementary Naive Bayes, Random Forests), clustering (*K*-Means, Fuzzy *K*-Means, Streaming *K*-Means, and Spectral Clustering), and dimensionality reduction (Stochastic SVD, PCA, and QR Decomposition). Users can extend the library by adding new data mining algorithms. The core libraries are highly optimized and also show good performance for nondistributed execution.

Weka4WS [11] is an extension of the famous open-source data mining library Weka (The Waikato Environment for Knowledge Analysis) [12]. The extension implements a framework to support the execution in WSRF [13] enabled grids. Weka4WS allows the distribution and execution of all its data mining algorithms on remote grid nodes. To enable remote invocation, the data mining algorithms provided by the Weka library are extended to a Web Service, which can be easily deployed on the available Grid nodes. Weka4WS can only handle a data set contained in a single storage node. This data set is then transferred to computing nodes to be mined. Unfortunately, this library is not supported now. The latest version is from July 2008.

Table 1 summarizes some features of the above-mentioned systems. They also show the following disadvantages:

(i) the fact that data sets must be stored inside a cloud, which does not allow users to analyze confidential information;

(ii) a restricted number of analysis tasks in public clouds and no full analysis tool chain in the frameworks;

(iii) using basically MapReduce paradigm (in particular the Apache Hadoop) for distributed analysis.

The MapReduce paradigm is adapted only for data processing functions, which are list homomorphisms [14]. Therefore, not all data mining algorithms can be decomposed into map and reduce functions.

We suggest the architecture of a cloud, based on the actor model, that allows users to execute data mining algorithms on a hybrid cloud (public and private cloud). The proposed cloud uses an approach to map an algorithm, decomposed into functional blocks, on a set of actors. Using actors allows users to move handling data sets towards the stored data. The process does not request uploading data sets into the cloud and allows users to analyze confidential information locally.

3. Mapping Data Mining Algorithms in Distributed Environments

3.1. Common Approach. According to [15], a data mining algorithm can be written as a sequence of functional blocks (based on functional language principles). Classical functions in functional languages are pure functions. A data mining algorithm can be written as a function (with two input arguments: data set d and mining model m) that can be decomposed into a number of nested functions:

$$\begin{aligned} \mathrm{dma}\,(d,m) &= f_n \circ f_{n-1} \circ \cdots \circ f_i \circ \cdots \circ f_1\,(d,m) \\ &= f_n\,(d, f_{n-1}\,(d,\ldots,f_i\,(d,\ldots,f_1\,(d,m),\ldots),\ldots)), \end{aligned} \quad (1)$$

where f_i is pure function of the type FB:: $D \to M \to M$, in which

(i) D is the input data set that is analyzed by function f_i and

(ii) M is the mining model that is built by function f_i.

We called this function functional block.

For example, we decomposed the *K*-Means algorithm into a set of functional blocks, ready for distributed execution. Therefore it can be represented as a chain of functional expressions:

$$K\text{-Means} = \mathrm{findClusters} \circ \mathrm{initClusters}, \quad (2)$$

in which

(i) *initClusters* creates a set of centroids in a random way;

(ii) *findClusters* finds centroids of clusters.

The *findClusters* block is the cycle which calls the next functional block while the cluster's centroids are changed:

(i) *distributeVectors* computes the distances between vectors (from data set D) and centroids of the clusters to distribute the vectors between the clusters;

(ii) *updateCentroids* updates centroids of clusters with new sets of vectors.

According to the Church-Rosser theorem [16] the reduction (execution) of such functional expressions (algorithm) can be done concurrently.

TABLE 1: The solutions for building data analysis cloud services.

Capabilities	BC-PDM	Azure ML	Amazon machine learning	Google Cloud machine learning	Watson Analytics	DMCF	Apache Spark MLlib	Apache Mahout	Weka 4 WS
Cloud service model	SaaS	SaaS	SaaS	SaaS	SaaS	SaaS	—	—	—
User interface	Web	Web	Web	API	Web	Web	—	—	Desktop
User's level	Developer	Knowledge ML algorithms	Analytic	Developer	Analytic/manager	Developer	Developer	Developer	Developer
API Interface	No	REST	REST	REST	REST	JS4Cloud	Yes	Yes	Yes
Scalable computing	Yes	For single modules	Yes	Yes	Yes	Yes	Yes	Yes	No
Data source location	Inside cloud	Inside cloud	Inside cloud	Inside cloud	Inside cloud	Inside cloud	Outside	Outside	Any
Distributed computing platform	Apache Hadoop	—	Apache Hadoop	Apache Hadoop	—	SOA	Apache Spark	Apache Hadoop	WSRF
Full analysis cycle	Yes	Yes	Yes	Yes	No	Yes	No	No	No
Included data mining algorithms	Classification, clustering, and association	Classification, anomaly detection, regression, and clustering	Classification, regression	Classification, regression	Classification, regression	Classification, regression, and clustering	Classification, regression, Clustering, dimensionality reduction, and feature extraction	Collaborative filtering, classification, clustering, and dimensionality reduction	Classification, association, regression, and clustering
Adding new algorithms	No	From Machine Learning Marketplace	No	No	No	Yes	Yes	Yes	Yes
Using	No	Paid	Paid	Paid	Paid	No	Open Source	Open Source	Open Source

3.2. The Function for Parallel Execution of a Data Mining Algorithm. One of the main advantages of building algorithms from functional blocks is the possibility of parallel execution. For this task we need to transform the sequential expression (1) into a form, in which the functional blocks will be invoked as arguments. For this the high-order *map* function can be used. It allows us to apply some functions to elements of lists. The function can be executed parallel for different elements. The *map* function returns the list of results. To reduce the list into a single result the high-order *fold* function can be used. Thus, the function for the transformation of sequential expressions into a parallel form can be presented as follows:

$$\text{parallel: } FB \longrightarrow D \longrightarrow M \longrightarrow ([M] \longrightarrow M) \longrightarrow (FB \longrightarrow [FB]) \longrightarrow (D \longrightarrow [D]) \longrightarrow (M \longrightarrow [M]) \longrightarrow (FB \longrightarrow D \longrightarrow M \longrightarrow H) \longrightarrow (H \longrightarrow M) \longrightarrow M,$$

$$\text{parallel}\,(f, d, m, join, distrF, distrD, distrM, start, get) = \text{fold}\,(join, m, get, (map\,(start, distrF\,(f), distrD\,(d, m), distrM\,(d, m)))), \tag{3}$$

in which

(i) f (1st argument of the parallel function) is a functional block that is executed concurrently;

(ii) distr$F$, distr$D$, and distr$M$ functions divide the the functional block f, the input data set d, and the mining model m into the lists:

$$\text{distr}F: (D \longrightarrow M \longrightarrow M) \longrightarrow [(D \longrightarrow M \longrightarrow M)]$$

$$\text{distr}D: D \longrightarrow [D] \tag{4}$$

$$\text{distr}M: M \longrightarrow [M];$$

(iii) *start* function applies each functional block f from the list $[F]$ to the elements of the lists $[D]$ and $[M]$ and returns a handler h for the parallel execution of the parallel functional block f:

$$\text{start: } FB \longrightarrow D \longrightarrow M \longrightarrow H; \tag{5}$$

(iv) *get* function reads the mining model from the handler h:

$$\text{get: } H \longrightarrow M; \tag{6}$$

(v) *join* function joins the mining models from the list $[M]$ and returns the merged mining model M:

$$\text{join: } [M] \longrightarrow M; \tag{7}$$

(vi) *map* function applies function *start* to elements of the lists $[F]$, $[D]$, and $[M]$:

$$\text{map: } (FB \longrightarrow D \longrightarrow M \longrightarrow H) \longrightarrow [FB] \longrightarrow [D] \longrightarrow [M] \longrightarrow [H]$$

$$\text{map}\,(start, \{f_0, f_1, \ldots, f_k\}, \{d_0, d_1, \ldots, d_k\}, \{m_0, m_1, \ldots, m_k\}) = \text{list}\,((start\,(f_0, d_0, m_0)), \ldots, (start\,(f_k, d_k, m_k))); \tag{8}$$

(vii) *fold* function reduces the list of mining models to a single result:

$$\text{fold: } ([M] \longrightarrow M) \longrightarrow M \longrightarrow (H \longrightarrow M) \longrightarrow [H] \longrightarrow M$$

$$\text{fold}\,(join, m, get, \{h_0, h_1, \ldots, h_k\}) \tag{9}$$

$$= join\,(m, get\,(h_0), get\,(h_1), \ldots, get\,(h_k)).$$

3.3. Mapping the Parallel Function on Actor Model. A list of handlers parsing between the *map* and *fold* functions is part of some distributed execution environments. In general, an execution environment can be represented as a set of handlers:

$$E = \{h_0, h_1, \ldots, h_j, \ldots, h_n\}, \tag{10}$$

in which

(i) h_0 is handler to execute sequential functional blocks of an algorithm;

(ii) h_1–h_n are handlers to execute parallel functional blocks in the distributed environment.

Each handler must implement the *start* and *get* functions to use them in the *parallel* function. The implementation of the *start* and *get* functions is specified by the execution environment which includes these handlers. Examples of these handlers are threads, actors, web services, and others.

The execution environment, which is implemented on the basis of the actor model [17, 18], uses actors as handlers. Actors interact with each other through the exchange of messages.

In order to send and receive a message, actors implement two functions:

(i) *send (msg, a)*: to send the message *msg* to the actor *a*;

(ii) *receive(a)*: to receive the message *msg* from the actor *a*.

One of the popular implementations of the actor model is the AKKA system, which uses the following actors to route messages:

(i) x is the inbox, which receives messages from actors, stores them in the memory, and sends them to other actors;

(ii) r is the router, which obtains messages from the inbox and distributes them among actors, depending on their type and load.

Thus, the actors environment can be written as

$$E = \left\{ r, x, a_0, a_1, a_2, \ldots, a_j, \ldots, a_n \right\}, \tag{11}$$

in which

(i) x is the inbox, which stores messages;

(ii) r is the router, which distributes messages among actors;

(iii) a_0 is the actor, which carries out the main algorithm sequence;

(iv) a_1–a_n are the actors, which carry out the parallel function of the algorithm.

The functions of the handlers *start* and *get* can be presented in the following way:

$$start\left(f, d, m \right) = send\left(\left\langle f, d, m \right\rangle, x \right);$$
$$get\left(x \right) = receive\left(x \right). \tag{12}$$

Thus, actors can execute functional blocks and therefore carry out a distributed implementation of the data mining algorithm.

The described approach was implemented as the data mining algorithm library DXelopes [19]. The library has adapters for the integration in different distributed environments. We used the actor model environment to create the prototype of a cloud for distributed data mining.

4. Architecture of the Cloud for Distributed Data Analysis

4.1. Levels of the Cloud for Distributed Data Analysis. The architecture of CDDA can be divided into several levels (Figure 1):

(i) Hardware;

(ii) virtual distributed environment;

(iii) analysis services.

The *hardware level* includes the pool of computers, storage, and networking resources, available in the cloud. We distinguish the following nodes:

(i) control nodes that run services to manage computation nodes and virtual networks between them;

(ii) computation nodes that run the hypervisor portion of computation, operating tenant virtual machines or instances;

(iii) storage nodes that contain the disks that provide space for tenant virtual machine instances.

The *virtual distributed environment level* provides controls for the virtual machines, the network connections between them, the disk spaces, and the user authorization. Therefore, we use a stack of cloud technologies: hypervisors, network managers, file storages, and so forth. The OpenStack software [20] integrates these technologies and allows us to control all the resources.

This level keeps previously prepared images of the virtual machines (VMs). Each VM has preinstalled software to execute the functional blocks of data mining algorithms: OS, AKKA, and DXelopes libraries (Figure 2). The VMs are united in a virtual network. Thus it forms the environment for distributed execution of a data mining algorithms. OpenStack balances VMs loads and provides optimal execution of the data mining algorithm in the cloud.

The *analysis services level* includes modules to work with the CDDA. They are installed on the control nodes and the VMs. The following units are deployed on the control nodes: Web interface, API CDDA, user control module, project control module, and analysis control module.

Each VM includes the following modules: analysis control module, data mining algorithms library, that is, DXelopes, ETL tools, and distributed system.

The user interface is implemented as a Web interface and users can do the full cycle of the analysis: data preprocessing, setting and execution of data mining algorithms, selecting and setting of the execution environment, estimation of the created mining model, and visualization and application of the created mining model.

The CDDA provides an API interface. It is REST API according to JSR 73 JDM API [21]. It allows developers to integrate other third-party systems with the CDDA.

Thus the users can manage work with the CDDA through the Web and the API interfaces with the help of the following modules:

(i) user control module provides the user authorization, verification of user permissions, and user registration;

(ii) project control module provides the user's projects management: creating, editing, and removing;

(iii) analysis control module provides the execution of full analysis cycle.

The data mining library DXelopes is the engine of the CDDA. It can be extended by

(i) data mining algorithms;

(ii) adapters for different ETL tools;

(iii) adapters for different execution environments.

The DXelopes library allows us to add algorithms as well as to construct new algorithms from existing functional blocks or the restructuring of the existing algorithms. The adapters for the ETL tools allow us to integrate the library within different systems, which implement data extraction, data transformation, and data loading. Thus, the integration of the DXelopes library and the ETL tools enables analysis of Big Data in the CDDA.

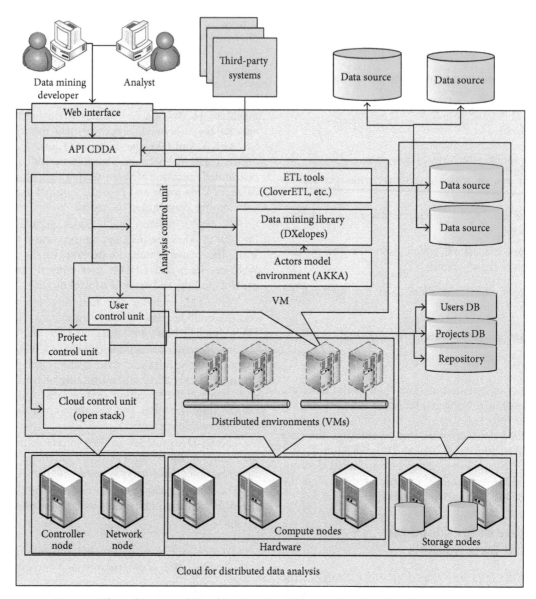

FIGURE 1: The architecture of Cloud for Distributed Data Analysis based on the actor model.

4.2. Using the Actor Model for the Cloud for Distributed Data Analysis. The adapters for the execution environment allow us to integrate the library within different distributed systems. So far the library has been integrated with the actor model environment (the actor model environment is presented by AKKA framework [22]). Thus, all data mining algorithms implemented in the library can be executed in these environments.

For each environment the CDDA contains sets of VMs with installed software (Figure 2):

(i) analysis control module;

(ii) DXelopes library;

(iii) configured actor system from the AKKA framework.

Such an approach to CDDA architecture allows us to transfer VMs to other clouds, hence distributing the analysis among them. This property is important when working with "private" clouds; the data of the latter must not be transferred to public clouds (e.g., CDDA). In order to fulfill this requirement using an image of a VM, which is stored in the CDDA repository, a VM must be designed with an installed actors environment and executed in a private cloud (Figure 3). A part of the data mining algorithm will be executed in this VM. This part will directly process data. The results of data processing will be sent to the CDDA as a knowledge model, which will actually not contain the data.

For example, concerning the *K*-Means algorithm, the actor with the *distributeVectors* functional block can handle all the vectors on the VM in a private cloud and then the actor with the *updateCentroids* functional block will recalculate the centroids of the clusters in the CDDA (Figure 3). The *distributeVectors* functional block receives the clusters centroids, determinates a vector belonging to the cluster, and sends

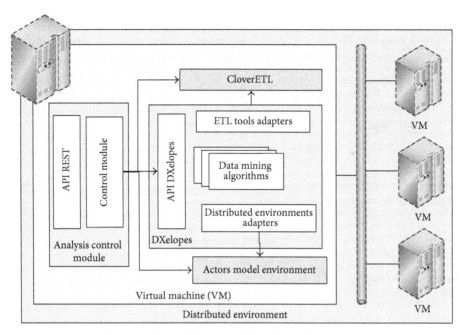

FIGURE 2: The configuration of the VM for data mining.

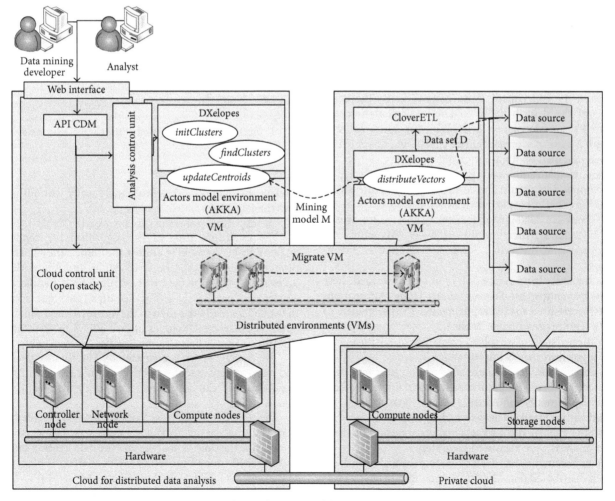

FIGURE 3: The configuration of the VM for data mining.

TABLE 2: Cloud computing infrastructure.

Characteristics	IBM FlexSystem X240	IBM FlexSystem P260	Huawei FusionServer RH2288 V3
CPU	Intel Xeon 2.9 GHz (2 CPU on 6 cores)	Power 7 3.3 GHz (2 CPU on 4 cores)	Intel® Xeon® E5-2600 (2 CPU on 4 cores)
RAM	128 GB	128 GB	128 GB
OS	3 win 2012/Hyper-V systems, 5 rhel/kvm systems	2 AIX/PowerVM systems	3 win 2012/ Hyper-V systems, 5 rhel/kvm systems
Performance	200 GFlops	400 GFlops	200 GFlops

TABLE 3: Experimental data sets.

Input data set	Number of rows	Number of attributes	Size of file (Kb)
Iris two-class data (ITCD)	100	4	2
Telescope data (TD)	19020	10	1 499
Breast cancer info (BCI)	102294	5	4 832
Movie ratings (MR)	227472	4	6 055
Flight on-time performance (FOTP) (raw)	504397	5	39 555
Flight delays data (FDD)	2719418	5	136 380

the accumulated distances of each vector for each cluster to the cloud. The *updateCentroids* functional block receives the accumulated distances, updates the centroids, and sends them to the VM in the private cloud. Thus the information is not transferred from the private cloud in the public the CDDA.

5. Experiments

A series of the experiments were done to verify the effectiveness of the described the CDDA implementation. We compared the performance of CDDA with Azure ML and the Spark MLlib's performance. The CDDA and Spark MLlib had been executed on high-performance servers, supporting hardware virtualization and providing high-performance cloud computing systems. The computing cluster infrastructure for the experiments is shown in Table 2.

We checked availability of distributed analysis for private and public clouds. Therefore we deployed VMs with actor environments into the second cloud based on Huawei Fusion-Server.

The data sets from Azure ML (you can download these data sets from https://studio.azureml.net/Home/Anonymous as Guest) were used for the experiments. The parameters of the data sets are presented in Table 3.

For these data sets we solved clustering task with the *K*-Means algorithm that is implemented in Azure ML, Spark MLlib, and CDDA. To compare acceleration for centralized systems we performed experiments for 1 and for 4 handlers

The experiments for Azure ML and Spark MLlib are executed with centralized data sets. Hence we loaded all data sets into the clouds. The data sets loading time and the time for data analysis were measured separately.

The experiments with CDDA were executed with local and with distributed data sets. In the second case all data sets were stored in the second cloud. We transferred the VM with the actor system (AKKA) into this cloud (see Figure 3). As

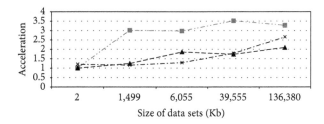

FIGURE 4: The acceleration of the parallel execution.

a result the data sets were processed locally without upload into the CDDA.

The experimental results are provided in Table 4.

The execution time of the algorithm for centralized analysis in all systems is almost the same. The CDDA is a little bit faster than Apache Spark MLlib and Azure ML. The acceleration (as time for 1 handler/time for 4 handlers) and efficiency of parallel algorithm execution (see Figures 4 and 5) in the CDDA are better than in the Azure ML and the Apache Spark because the DXelopes library allows to distribute the algorithm's blocks between the handlers more flexibly.

The Apache Spark is restricted by MapReduce paradigm and can parallely execute only the map and reduce functions. The Azure ML can only execute whole algorithms on single nodes.

The centralized analysis of local data sets is executed faster than the analysis of distributed data sets. However, if we summarize the time of analysis and the data loading time, the accumulated time of centralized data analysis is bigger than that in distributed data analysis (Figure 6).

This effect is achieved by reduction of data transferred within a network. In case of distributed data analysis,

TABLE 4: Experimental results (s).

Cloud	Action	ITCD	TD	MR	FOTP	FDD
—	Data set loading time	1	1	2	5	15
Azure ML	Local data centralized analysis (1 handler)	4	5	13	26	132
	Local data centralized analysis (4 handlers)	4	4	11	17	63
	Data set loading and centralized analysis	**5**	**7**	**20**	**43**	**83**
Spark MLlib	Local data centralized analysis (1 handler)	3	4	6	11	157
	Local data centralized analysis (4 handlers)	2	3	5	6	59
	Data set loading and centralized analysis	**3**	**6**	**10**	**16**	**76**
CDDA	Local data centralized analysis (1 handler)	0.4	1	9	12	121
	Local data centralized analysis (4 handlers)	0.5	1	3	4	37
	Data set loading and centralized analysis	**1.5**	**2.8**	**8**	**15**	**74**
CDDA	Distributed data analysis (4 handlers)	**1**	**2**	**4**	**6**	**41**

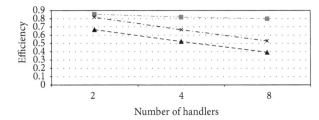

- CDDA
- Azure ML
- Spark MLlib

FIGURE 5: The efficiency of the parallel execution.

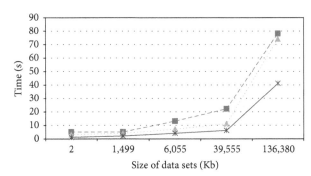

- Centralized data analysis with Azure ML
- Centralized data analysis with Spark MLlib
- Centralized data analysis with CDDA
- Distributed data analysis with CDDA

FIGURE 6: Comparison of the experimental results.

a mining model is transferred between the clouds instead of the data sets.

By increasing the amount of data being analyzed the difference between distributed and centralized analyses is increasing. This is due to the difference between the transfer time of the data and time to transfer the model. When a substantial increase in the size of data occurs the size of the model increases slightly. Therefore, the time to transfer the model also increases slightly.

6. Conclusion

The representation of a data mining algorithm as functional expression makes it possible to divide the algorithm into blocks. Such a splitting helps to map it to an actor environment. We implemented this approach as the DXelopes library. It contains different algorithms and allows us to add new algorithms. The library has adapters to support the integration within actor-model system—AKKA. It allowed us to create a prototype of the cloud for distributed data analysis.

The cloud uses clusters of VMs. Each VM contains the DXelopes library and an AKKA system. A user can deploy VMs in other clouds and execute distributed data analysis.

Thus the created CDDA has the following key characteristics, which distinguish it from other similar solutions:

(i) implementation of both SaaS and PaaS cloud computing service models;

(ii) extension list of data mining algorithms in the cloud by adding new functional blocks or modifying their functional blocks;

(iii) processing of data sets stored outside the cloud;

(iv) ability to analyze confidential information;

(v) execution of distributed data analysis among several clouds.

The last property allows us

(i) to increase data security and to do so without the storage of data in a public cloud;

(ii) to reduce network traffic due to the prevention of data transfer between the clouds;

(iii) to enhance the efficiency due to the "localization" of calculations.

Available solutions do not have the above-mentioned features and limit the advantages of cloud technologies and data analysis technologies integration significantly.

In the future we plan to extend the supported distributed platforms and ETL tools and develop a release version of the CDDA.

Competing Interests

The authors declare that there is no conflict of interests regarding the publication of this paper.

Acknowledgments

This work has been performed in Saint Petersburg Electrotechnical University (LETI) within the scope of the contract Board of Education of Russia and Science of the Russian Federation under the Contract no. 02.G25.31.0058 from 12.02.2013. The paper has been prepared within the scope of the state project "Organization of Scientific Research" of the main part of the state plan of the Board of Education of Russia, the project part of the state plan of the Board of Education of Russia (Task 2.136.2014/K) as well as supported by grant of RFBR 16-07-00625, supported by the Russian President's fellowship.

References

[1] I. Kholod, M. Kupriyanov, and A. Shorov, "Decomposition of data mining algorithms into unified functional blocks," *Mathematical Problems in Engineering*, vol. 2016, Article ID 8197349, 11 pages, 2016.

[2] I. Kholod and I. Petukhov, "Creation of data mining algorithms as functional expression for parallel and distributed execution," in *Parallel Computing Technologies*, V. Malyshkin, Ed., vol. 9251 of *Lecture Notes in Computer Science*, pp. 62–67, Springer, New York, NY, USA, 2015.

[3] L. Yu, J. Zheng, W. C. Shen et al., "BC-PDM: data mining, social network analysis and text mining system based on cloud computing," in *Proceedings of the 18th ACM SIGKDD International Conference on Knowledge Discovery and Data Mining (KDD '12)*, pp. 1496–1499, ACM, Beijing, China, August 2012.

[4] C. J. Gronlund, "Introduction to machine learning on Microsoft Azure," https://azure.microsoft.com/en-gb/documentation/articles/machine-learning-what-is-machine-learning/.

[5] J. Barr, "Amazon Machine Learning-Make Data-Driven Decisions at Scale," Amazon Machine Learning, 2016, https://aws.amazon.com/ru/blogs/aws/amazon-machine-learning-make-data-driven-decisions-at-scale/.

[6] Google Cloud Machine Learning at Scale, https://cloud.google.com/products/machine-learning/.

[7] A. Lally, J. M. Prager, M. C. McCord et al., "Question analysis: how Watson reads a clue," *IBM Journal of Research and Development*, vol. 56, no. 3-4, pp. 2:1–2:14, 2012.

[8] F. Marozzo, D. Talia, and P. Trunfio, "A workflow-oriented language for scalable data analytics," in *Proceedings of the 1st International Workshop on Sustainable Ultrascale Computing Systems (NESUS '14)*, Porto, Portugal, August 2014.

[9] X. Meng, J. Bradley, B. Yavuz et al., "MLlib: machine learning in apache spark," *Journal of Machine Learning Research*, vol. 17, pp. 1–7, 2016.

[10] G. Ingersoll, *Introducing Apache Mahout. Scalable, Commercial-friendly Machine Learning for Building Intelligent Applications*, IBM, 2009.

[11] D. Talia, P. Trunfio, and O. Verta, "The Weka4WS framework for distributed data mining in service-oriented Grids," *Concurrency Computation: Practice and Experience*, vol. 20, no. 16, pp. 1933–1951, 2008.

[12] M. Hall, E. Frank, G. Holmes, B. Pfahringer, P. Reutemann, and I. H. Witten, "The WEKA data mining software: an update," *ACM SIGKDD Explorations Newsletter*, vol. 11, no. 1, pp. 10–18, 2009.

[13] K. Czajkowski, D. Ferguson, I. Foster et al., "From open grid services infrastructure to ws-resource framework: refactoring & evolution," 2004.

[14] S. Gorlatch, "Extracting and implementing list homomorphisms in parallel program development," *Science of Computer Programming*, vol. 33, no. 1, pp. 1–27, 1999.

[15] I. Kholod and I. Petukhov, "Creation of data mining algorithms as functional expression for parallel and distributed execution," in *Parallel Computing Technologies*, pp. 62–67, Springer, 2015.

[16] A. Church and J. B. Rosser, "Some properties of conversion," *Transactions of the American Mathematical Society*, vol. 39, no. 3, pp. 472–482, 1936.

[17] C. Hewitt, P. Bishop, and R. Steiger, "A universal modular actor formalism for artificial intelligence," in *Proceedings of the 3rd International Joint Conference on Artificial Intelligence*, pp. 235–245, Morgan Kaufmann Publishers, Stanford, Calif, USA, August 1973.

[18] W. D. Clinger, *Foundations of Actor Semantics*, 1981.

[19] I. Kholod, "Framework for multi threads execution of data mining algorithms," in *Proceedings of the 2015 IEEE North West Russia Section Young Researchers in Electrical and Electronic Engineering Conference (ElConRusNW '15)*, pp. 82–88, IEEE, St. Petersburg, Russia, February 2015.

[20] K. Jackson, C. Bunch, and E. Sigler, *OpenStack Cloud Computing Cookbook*, Packt Publishing, 2015.

[21] JSR-000073 Data Mining API. (Maintenance Release), https://jcp.org/aboutJava/communityprocess/mrel/jsr073/index.html.

[22] D. Wyatt, *Akka Concurrency*, Artima Incorporation, 2013.

12

On Elasticity Measurement in Cloud Computing

Wei Ai,[1] **Kenli Li,**[1] **Shenglin Lan,**[1] **Fan Zhang,**[2] **Jing Mei,**[1] **Keqin Li,**[1,3] **and Rajkumar Buyya**[4]

[1]*College of Information Science and Engineering, Hunan University, Changsha, Hunan 410082, China*
[2]*IBM Massachusetts Lab, 550 King Street, Littleton, MA 01460, USA*
[3]*Department of Computer Science, State University of New York, New Paltz, NY 12561, USA*
[4]*Department of Computing and Information Systems, University of Melbourne, Melbourne, VIC 3010, Australia*

Correspondence should be addressed to Kenli Li; lkl@hnu.edu.cn

Academic Editor: Florin Pop

Elasticity is the foundation of cloud performance and can be considered as a great advantage and a key benefit of cloud computing. However, there is no clear, concise, and formal definition of elasticity measurement, and thus no effective approach to elasticity quantification has been developed so far. Existing work on elasticity lack of solid and technical way of defining elasticity measurement and definitions of elasticity metrics have not been accurate enough to capture the essence of elasticity measurement. In this paper, we present a new definition of elasticity measurement and propose a quantifying and measuring method using a continuous-time Markov chain (CTMC) model, which is easy to use for precise calculation of elasticity value of a cloud computing platform. Our numerical results demonstrate the basic parameters affecting elasticity as measured by the proposed measurement approach. Furthermore, our simulation and experimental results validate that the proposed measurement approach is not only correct but also robust and is effective in computing and comparing the elasticity of cloud platforms. Our research in this paper makes significant contribution to quantitative measurement of elasticity in cloud computing.

1. Introduction

(1) Motivation. As a subscription-oriented utility, cloud computing has gained growing attention in recent years in both research and industry and is widely considered as a promising way of managing and improving the utilization of data center resources and providing a wide range of computing services [1]. Virtualization is a key enabling technology of cloud computing [2]. System virtualization is able to provide abilities to access software and hardware resources from a virtual space and enables an execution platform to provide several concurrently usable and independent instances of virtual execution entities, often called virtual machines (VMs). A cloud computing platform relies on the virtualization technique to acquire more VMs to deal with workload surges or release VMs to avoid resource overprovisioning. Such a dynamic resource provision and management feature is called elasticity. For instance, when VMs do not use all the provided resources, they can be logically resized and be migrated from a group of active servers to other servers, while the idle servers can be switched to the low-power modes (sleep or hibernate) [3].

Elasticity is the degree to which a system is able to adapt to workload changes by provisioning and deprovisioning resources in an autonomic manner, such that at each point in time the available resources match the current demand as closely as possible [4]. By dynamically optimizing the total amount of acquired resources, elasticity is used for various purposes. From the perspective of service providers, elasticity ensures better use of computing resources and more energy savings [5] and allows multiple users to be served simultaneously. From a user's perspective, elasticity has been used to avoid inadequate provision of resources and degradation of system performance [6] and also achieve cost reduction [7]. Furthermore, elasticity can be used for other purposes, such as increasing the capacity of local resources [8, 9]. Hence, elasticity is the foundation of cloud performance and can be considered as a great advantage and a key benefit of cloud computing.

Elastic mechanisms have been explored recently by researchers from academia and commercial fields, and tremendous efforts have been invested to enable cloud systems to behave in an elastic manner. However, there is no common and precise formula to calculate the elasticity value. Existing definitions of elasticity in the current research literature are all vague concepts and fail to capture the essence of elastic resource provisioning. These formulas of elasticity are not suitable for quantifying and measuring elasticity. Moreover, there is no systematic approach that has been proposed to quantify elastic behavior. Only quantitative elasticity value can produce better comparison between different cloud platforms. Therefore, the measurement of cloud elasticity should be further investigated. As far as we know, the current reported works are ineffective to cover all aspects of cloud elasticity evaluation and measurement. Therefore, we are motivated to develop a comprehensive model and an analytical method to measure cloud elasticity.

(2) Our Contributions. In this paper, we propose a clear and concise definition to compute elasticity value. In order to do that, an elasticity computing model is established by using a continuous-time Markov chain (CTMC). The proposed computing model can quantify, measure, and compare the elasticity of cloud platforms.

The major contributions of this paper are summarized as follows.

(i) First, we propose a new definition of elasticity in the context of virtual machine provisioning and a precise computational formula of elasticity value.

(ii) Second, we develop a technique of quantifying and measuring elasticity by using a continuous-time Markov chain (CTMC) model. We investigate the elastic calculation model intensively and completely. The model is not only an analytical method, but also an easy way to calculate the elasticity value of a cloud platform quantitatively.

(iii) Third, we examine and evaluate our proposed method through numerical data, simulations, and experiments. The numerical data demonstrate the basic parameters which affect elasticity in our analytical model. The simulation results validate the correctness of the proposed method. The experimental results on a real cloud computing platform further show the robustness of our model and method in predicting and computing cloud elasticity.

The rest of the paper is organized as follows. Section 2 reviews the related work. Section 3 describes the definition of cloud elasticity. Section 4 develops the computing model of cloud elasticity. Sections 5, 6, and 7 present simulation and numerical and experimental results, respectively. Section 8 concludes this paper.

2. Related Work

2.1. Elasticity Definition and Measurement. There has been some work on elasticity measurement of cloud computing. In [4], elasticity is described as the degree to which a system is able to adapt to workload changes by provisioning and deprovisioning resources in an autonomic manner, such that at each point in time the available resources match the current demand as closely as possible. In [10], elasticity is defined as the ability of customers to quickly request, receive, and later release as many resources as needed. In [11], elasticity is measured as the ability of a cloud to map a single user's request to different resources. In [12], elasticity is defined as dynamic variation in the use of computer resources to meet a varying workload. In [13], an elastic cloud application or process has three elasticity dimensions, that is, cost, quality, and resources, enabling it to increase and decrease its cost, quality, or available resources, as to accommodate specific requirements. Recently, in [14], elasticity is defined by using the expression $1/(\theta \times \mu)$, where θ denotes the average time to switch from an underprovisioning state to an elevated state and μ denotes the offset between the actual scaling and the autoscaling. Existing definitions of elasticity fail to capture the essence when elastic resource provisioning is performed with virtual machines, and the formulas of elasticity are not suitable for quantifying elasticity. For example, μ in the above expression is difficult to obtain when resource of a cloud is increasing or decreasing. In contrast, the definition proposed in our work reflects the essence of elasticity, and the calculation formula focuses on how to measure the elasticity value effectively.

There are many approaches to predicting elasticity, anticipating the system load behavior, and deciding when and how to scale in/out resources by using heuristics and mathematical/analytical techniques. In [4], the authors established an elasticity metric aiming to capture the key elasticity characteristics. In [15], the authors proposed *execution platforms* and *reconfiguration points* to reflect the proposed elasticity definition. In [5, 7, 16–18], the authors adopted predictive techniques to scale resources automatically. Although these techniques perform well in elasticity prediction, further measurement of elasticity is not covered. In [4], the authors just outlined an elasticity benchmarking approach focusing on special requirements on workload design and implementation. In [15], the authors used thread pools as a kind of elastic resource of the Java virtual machine and presented preliminary results of running a novel elasticity benchmark which reveals the elastic behavior of the thread pool resource. These studies mainly present initial research. In most elasticity work, different elasticity benchmark programs are expected to execute on different systems over varying data sizes and reflect their potential elasticity, but they can only get a macroscopic view of elasticity analysis rather than the calculation of the elasticity value. In contrast, our work performs in-depth research focusing on the measurement of elasticity value.

2.2. Analytical Modeling. Continuous-time Markov chain (CTMC) models have been used for modeling various random phenomena occurring in queuing theory, genetics, demography, epidemiology, and competing populations [19]. CTMC has been applied in a lot of studies to adjust resource allocation in cloud computing. Khazaei et al. proposed an analytical performance model that addresses the complexity of cloud data centers by distinct stochastic submodels using

CTMC [20]. Ghosh et al. proposed a performance model that quantifies power performance trade-offs by interacting stochastic submodels approach using CTMC [21]. Pacheco-Sanchez et al. proposed an analytical performance model that predicts the performance of servers deployed in the cloud by using CTMC [22]. Ghosh et al. proposed a stochastic reward net that quantifies the resiliency of IaaS cloud by using CTMC [23, 24]. However, to the best of our knowledge, CTMC has never been applied in the research of cloud elasticity. Our work in this paper adopts a CTMC model for effective elasticity measurement.

3. Definition of Cloud Elasticity

In this section, we first present a detailed discussion of different states which characterize the elastic behavior of a system. Then, we formally define elasticity that is applied in cloud platforms.

3.1. Notations and Preliminaries. For clarity and convenience, Notations describes the correlated variables which are used in the following sections. To elaborate the essence of cloud elasticity, we give the various states that are used in our discussion. Let i denote the number of VMs in service and let j be the number of requests in the system.

(1) *Just-in-Need State.* A cloud platform is in a just-in-need state if $i < j \leq 3i$. T_j is defined as the accumulated time in all just-in-need states.

(2) *Overprovisioning State.* A cloud platform is in an overprovisioning state if $0 \leq j \leq i$. T_o is defined as the accumulated time in all overprovisioning states.

(3) *Underprovisioning State.* A cloud platform is in an underprovisioning state if $j > 3i$. T_u is defined as the accumulated time in all underprovisioning states.

Notice that constants 1 and 3 in this paper are only for illustration purpose and can be any other values, depending on how an elastic cloud platform is managed. Different cloud users and/or applications may prefer different bounds of the hypothetical just-in-need states. The length of the interval between the upper (e.g., $3i$) and lower (e.g., i) bounds controls the reprovisioning frequency. Narrowing down the interval leads to higher reprovision frequency for a fluctuating workload.

The just-in-need computing resource denotes a balanced state, in which the workload can be properly handled and quality of service (QoS) can be satisfactorily guaranteed. Computing resource overprovisioning, though QoS can be achieved, leads to extra but unnecessary cost to rent the cloud resources. Computing resource underprovisioning, on the other hand, delays the processing of workload and may be at the risk of breaking QoS commitment.

3.2. Elasticity Definition in Cloud Computing. In this section, we present our elasticity definition for a realistic cloud platform and present mathematical foundation for elasticity evaluation. The definition of elasticity is given from a computational point of view and we develop a calculation formula

for measuring elasticity value in virtualized clouds. Let T_m be the measuring time, which includes all the periods in the just-in-need, overprovisioning, and underprovisioning states; that is, $T_m = T_j + T_o + T_u$.

Definition 1. The elasticity E of a cloud perform is the percentage of time when the platform is in just-in-need states; that is, $E = T_j/T_m = 1 - T_o/T_m - T_u/T_m$.

Broadly defining, elasticity is the capability of delivering preconfigured and just-in-need virtual machines adaptively in a cloud platform upon the fluctuation of the computing resources required. Practically it is determined by the time needed from an underprovisioning or overprovisioning state to a balanced resource provisioning state. Definition 1 provides a mathematical definition which is easily and accurately measurable. Cloud platforms with high elasticity exhibit high adaptivity, implying that they switch from an overprovisioning or an underprovisioning state to a balanced state almost in real time. Other cloud platforms take longer time to adjust and reconfigure computing resources. Although it is recognized that high elasticity can also be achieved via physical host standby, we argue that, with virtualization-enabled computing resource provisioning, elasticity can be delivered in a much easier way due to the flexibility of service migration and image template generation.

Elasticity E reflects the degree to which a cloud platform changes upon the fluctuation of workloads and can be measured by the time of resource scaling by the quantity and types of virtual machine instances. We use the following equation to calculate its value:

$$E = 1 - \frac{(T_o + T_u)}{T_m} = 1 - \frac{T_o}{T_m} - \frac{T_u}{T_m}, \qquad (1)$$

where T_m denotes the total measuring time, in which T_o is the overprovisioning time which accumulates each single period of time that the cloud platform needs to switch from an overprovisioning state to a balanced state and T_u is the underprovisioning time which accumulates each single period of time that the cloud platform needs to switch from an underprovisioning state to a corresponding balanced state.

Let P_j, P_o, and P_u be the accumulated probabilities of just-in-need states, overprovisioning states, and underprovisioning states, respectively. If T_m is sufficiently long, we have $P_j = T_j/T_m$, $P_o = T_o/T_m$, and $P_u = T_u/T_m$. Therefore, we get

$$E = P_j = 1 - P_o - P_u. \qquad (2)$$

Equation (1) can be used when elasticity is measured by monitoring a real system. Equation (2) can be used when elasticity is calculated by using our CTMC model. If elasticity metrics are well defined, elasticity of cloud platforms could easily be captured, evaluated, and compared.

We would like to mention that the primary factors of elasticity, that is, the amount, frequency, and time of resource reprovisioning, are all summarized in T_o and T_u (i.e., P_o and P_u). Elasticity can be increased by changing these factors. For example, one can maintain a list of standby or underutilized compute nodes. These nodes are prepared for the upcoming

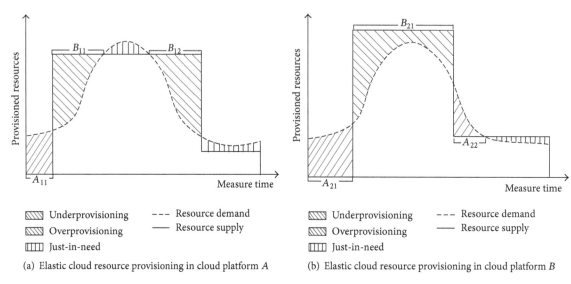

(a) Elastic cloud resource provisioning in cloud platform *A*

(b) Elastic cloud resource provisioning in cloud platform *B*

FIGURE 1: An example of elasticity metrics.

surge of workload, if there is any, to minimize the time needed to start these nodes. Such a hot standby strategy increases cloud elasticity by reducing T_u.

3.3. An Example.
In Figure 1, A_{11} = 3 hours, A_{21} = 5 hours, and A_{22} = 4 hours are the time spans in underprovisioning states, and B_{11} = 4 hours, B_{12} = 5 hours, and B_{21} = 10 hours are the time spans in overprovisioning states. The measuring time of cloud platform A is T_m^A = 24 hours and cloud platform B is T_m^B = 26 hours. So $T_u^A = A_{11}$ = 3 hours (i.e., underprovisioning time of cloud platform A), $T_o^A = B_{11} + B_{12}$ = 9 hours (i.e., overprovisioning time of cloud platform A), $T_u^B = A_{21} + A_{22}$ = 9 hours (i.e., underprovisioning time of cloud platform B), and $T_o^B = B_{21}$ = 10 hours (i.e., overprovisioning time of cloud platform B). According to (1), the elasticity value of cloud platform A is $E^A = 1 - T_o^A/T_m^A - T_u^A/T_m^A$ = 0.5, and the elasticity value of cloud platform B is $E^B = 1 - T_o^B/T_m^B - T_u^B/T_m^B$ = 0.27. As can be seen, a greater elasticity value would exhibit better elasticity.

3.4. Relevant Properties of Clouds.
In this section, we compare cloud elasticity with a few other relevant concepts, such as cloud resiliency, scalability, and efficiency.

Resiliency. Laprie [25] defined resiliency as the persistence of service delivery that can be trusted justifiably, when facing changes. Therefore, cloud resiliency implies (1) the extent to which a cloud system withstands the external workload variation and under which no computing resource reprovisioning is needed and (2) the ability to reprovision a cloud system in a timely manner. We think the latter implication defines the cloud elasticity while the former implication only exists in cloud resiliency. In our elasticity study, we will focus on the latter one.

Scalability. Elasticity is often confused with scalability in more ways than one. Scalability reflects the performance

speedup when cloud resources are reprovisioned. In other words, scalability characterizes how *well* in terms of performance a new compute cluster, either larger or smaller, handles a given workload. On the other hand, elasticity explains how *fast* in terms of the reprovisioning time the compute cluster can be ready to process the workload. Cloud scalability is impacted by quite a few factors such as the compute node type and count and workload type and count. For example, Hadoop MapReduce applications typically scale much better than other single-thread applications. It can be defined in terms of scaling number of threads, processes, nodes, and even data centers. Cloud elasticity, on the other hand, is only constrained by the capability that a cloud service provider offers. Other factors that are relevant to cloud elasticity include the type and count of standby machines, computing resources that need to be reprovisioned. Different from cloud scalability, cloud elasticity does not concern workload/application type and count at all.

Efficiency. Efficiency characterizes how cloud resource can be efficiently utilized as it scales up or down. This concept is derived from speedup, a term that defines a relative performance after computing resource has been reconfigured. Elasticity is closely related to efficiency of the clouds. Efficiency is defined as the percentage of maximum performance (speedup or utilization) achievable. High cloud elasticity results in higher efficiency. However, this implication is not always true, as efficiency can be influenced by other factors independent of the system elasticity mechanisms (e.g., different implementations of the same operation). Scalability is affected by cloud efficiency. Thus, efficiency may enhance elasticity, but not sufficiency. This is due to the fact that elasticity depends on the resource types, but efficiency is not limited by resource types. For instance, with a multitenant architecture, users may exceed their resources quota. They may compete for resources or interfere each other's job executions.

FIGURE 2: State-transition-rate diagram for a birth-death process.

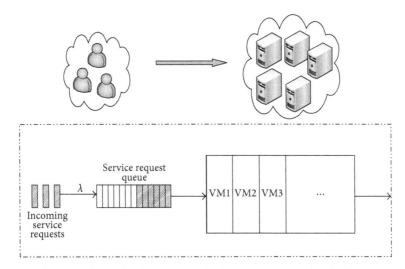

FIGURE 3: Modeling an elastic cloud computing platform as an extended $M/M/m$ queuing system.

4. Elasticity Analysis Using CTMC

In this paper, we implement the cloud elasticity computing model using CTMC.

4.1. A Queuing Model. This section mainly explains why the continuous-time Markov chain (CTMC) can be applied to compute cloud elasticity and the connection between them.

A continuous-time Markov chain is a continuous time, discrete-state Markov process. Many CTMC have transitions that only go to neighboring states, that is, either up one or down one; they are called birth-and-death processes. Motivated by population models, a transition up one is called a birth, while a transition down one is called a death. The birth rate in state i is denoted by λ_i, while the death rate in state i is denoted by μ_i. The state-transition-rate diagram for a birth-and-death process (with state space $\{0, 1, \ldots, n\}$) takes the simple linear form shown in Figure 2.

In many applications, it is natural to use birth-and-death processes. One of the queuing models is $M/M/m$ queue, which has m servers and unlimited waiting room. The main properties of a queuing system are as follows.

(1) Requests arrive in a Poisson process with parameter λ.

(2) The service times are exponential random variables with parameter μ.

So a queuing system is a birth-and-death process with Markov property.

A cloud computing service provider serves customers' service requests by using a multiserver system. An elastic cloud computing platform treated as a multiserver system

and modeled as an extended $M/M/m$ queuing system is shown in Figure 3. Assume that service requests arrive by following a Poisson process and task service times are independent and identically distributed random variables that follow an exponential distribution. When a running request finishes, the capacity used by the corresponding VM is released and becomes available for serving the next request. The request at the head of the queue is processed (i.e., first-come-first-served) on a running VM if there is capacity to run a scheduled request. Elastic resource provisioning cannot be done with physical machines, and only virtual machines can be reconfigured in real time. A cloud platform is able to adapt to variation in workload by starting up or shutting off VMs in an autonomic manner, avoiding overprovisioning or underprovisioning. If no enough running VMs are available (e.g., underprovisioning state), a new VM is started up and used for service. If there are excessive VMs (e.g., overprovisioning state), redundant VMs are shut off.

According to (1) and (2), the calculation of the elasticity value needs to count the accumulated time in all the overprovisioning and underprovisioning states. In real cloud platforms, it is possible to record the overprovisioning time and underprovisioning times. Furthermore and fortunately, the accumulated probability of both overprovisioning and underprovisioning states can be computed using our proposed CTMC model as discussed in the next section.

4.2. Elastic Cloud Platform Modeling. To model elastic cloud platforms, we make the following assumptions.

(i) All VMs are homogeneous with the same service capability and are added/removed one at a time.

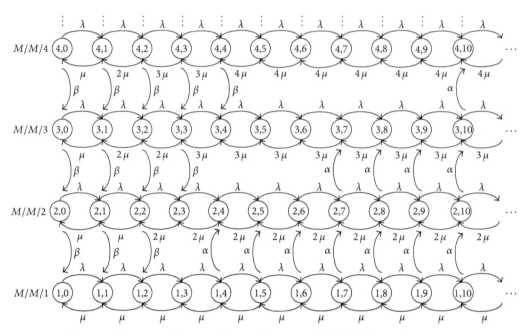

FIGURE 4: State-transition-rate diagram of our extended $M/M/m$ queuing system.

(ii) The user request arrivals are modeled as a Poisson process with rate λ.

(iii) The service time, the start-up time, and the shut-off time of each VM are governed by exponential distributions with rates μ, α, and β, respectively [26].

(iv) Let i denote the number of virtual machines that are currently in service, and let j denote the number of requests that are receiving service or in waiting.

(v) Let statev(i, j) denote the various states of a cloud platform when the virtual machine number is i and the request number is j. Let the hypothetical just-in-need state, overprovisioning state, and underprovisioning state be JIN, OP, and UP, respectively. We can set the equations of the relation between the virtual machine number and the request number as follows:

$$\text{statev}\,(i, j) = \begin{cases} \text{OP}, & \text{if } 0 \leq j \leq i; \\ \text{JIN}, & \text{if } i < j \leq 3i; \\ \text{UP}, & \text{if } j > 3i. \end{cases} \tag{3}$$

The hypothetical just-in-need state, overprovisioning state, and underprovisioning state are listed in Table 1.

Based on these assumptions, we build a two-dimensional continuous-time Markov chain (CTMC) for our extended $M/M/m$ queuing system shown in Figure 4, which is actually a mixture of $M/M/m$ systems for all $m = 1, 2, 3, \ldots$. The CTMC model records the number of VMs and the number of user requests received for service, which can eventually be employed to calculate the elastic value E.

Each state in the model, shown in Figure 4, is labeled as (i, j), where i ($i \in \{1, \ldots, m\}$) denotes the number of virtual machines that are currently processing requests and

TABLE 1: The relation between the virtual machine number and the request number.

VM number	Overprovisioning state	Just-in-need state	Underprovisioning state
1	$0 \leq j \leq 1$	$1 < j \leq 3$	$j > 3$
2	$0 \leq j \leq 2$	$2 < j \leq 6$	$j > 6$
3	$0 \leq j \leq 3$	$3 < j \leq 9$	$j > 9$
4	$0 \leq j \leq 4$	$4 < j \leq 12$	$j > 12$
$\vdots$	$\vdots$	$\vdots$	$\vdots$
i	$0 \leq j \leq i$	$i < j \leq 3i$	$j > 3i$
$\vdots$	$\vdots$	$\vdots$	$\vdots$

j ($j \in \{0, 1, \ldots, m\}$) denotes the number of requests that are receiving service. For the purpose of numerical calculation, we set the maximum number of VMs that can be deployed as m, which is sufficiently large to guarantee enough accuracy. Similarly, the maximum j is m. Let μ be the service rate of each VM. So the total service rate for each state is the product of number of running VMs and μ.

The state transition in an elastic cloud computing model can occur due to user request arrival, service completion, virtual machine start-up, or virtual machine shut-off. In state (i, j), according to Table 1, the state can be determined as "just-in-need," "underprovisioning," or "overprovisioning." Depending on the upcoming event, four possible transitions can occur.

Case 1. When a new request arrives, the system transits to state $(i, j + 1)$ with rate λ.

Case 2. When a requested service is completed, if the system examines the state as not "overprovisioning," the system moves back to state $(i, j - 1)$ with total service rate $i\mu$. If the system examines the state as "overprovisioning" and $i = j$, the system moves back to state $(i, j - 1)$ with total service rate $(j - 1)\mu$, because a server is shutting off and cannot perform any task at the moment. If the system examines the state as "overprovisioning" and $i \neq j$, the system moves back to state $(i, j - 1)$ with total service rate $j\mu$.

Case 3. The system examines the state as "underprovisioning" and transits to state $(i + 1, j)$ with rate α.

Case 4. The system examines the state as "overprovisioning" and transits to state $(i - 1, j)$ with rate β.

We use $P_{i,j}$ to denote the steady-state probability that the system stays in state (i, j), where $i \in \{1, \ldots, m\}$ and $j \in \{0, 1, \ldots, m\}$. We can now set the balance equations as follows:

$$\lambda P_{i,j} = K_2 \mu P_{i,j+1} + \beta P_{i+1,j},$$
$$\text{if } i = 1, \ j = 0;$$

$$(\lambda + K_1 \mu) P_{i,j} = \lambda P_{i,j-1} + K_2 \mu P_{i,j+1} + \beta P_{i+1,j},$$
$$\text{if } i = 1, \ 0 < j \leq i + 1;$$

$$(\lambda + K_1 \mu) P_{i,j} = \lambda P_{i,j-1} + K_2 \mu P_{i,j+1},$$
$$\text{if } i = 1, \ i + 1 < j \leq 3i;$$

$$(\lambda + K_1 \mu + \alpha) P_{i,j} = \lambda P_{i,j-1} + K_2 \mu P_{i,j+1},$$
$$\text{if } i = 1, \ 3i < j < m;$$

$$(K_1 \mu + \alpha) P_{i,j} = \lambda P_{i,j-1}, \quad \text{if } i = 1, \ j = m;$$

$$(\lambda + \beta) P_{i,j} = K_2 \mu P_{i,j+1} + \beta P_{i+1,j},$$
$$\text{if } 1 < i < m, \ j = 0;$$

$$(\lambda + K_1 \mu + \beta) P_{i,j} = \lambda P_{i,j-1} + K_2 \mu P_{i,j+1} + \beta P_{i+1,j},$$
$$\text{if } 1 < i < m, \ 0 < j \leq i;$$

$$(\lambda + K_1 \mu) P_{i,j} = \lambda P_{i,j-1} + K_2 \mu P_{i,j+1} + \beta P_{i+1,j},$$
$$\text{if } 1 < i < m, \ j = i + 1;$$

$$(\lambda + K_1 \mu) P_{i,j} = \lambda P_{i,j-1} + K_2 \mu P_{i,j+1},$$
$$\text{if } 1 < i \leq m, \ i + 1 < j \leq 3(i - 1);$$

$$(\lambda + K_1 \mu) P_{i,j} = \lambda P_{i,j-1} + K_2 \mu P_{i,j+1} + \alpha P_{i-1,j},$$
$$\text{if } 1 < i < m, \ 3(i - 1) < j \leq 3i;$$

$$(\lambda + K_1 \mu + \alpha) P_{i,j} = \lambda P_{i,j-1} + K_2 \mu P_{i,j+1} + \alpha P_{i-1,j},$$
$$\text{if } 1 < i < m, \ 3i < j < m;$$

$$(K_1 \mu + \alpha) P_{i,j} = \lambda P_{i,j-1} + \alpha P_{i-1,j},$$
$$\text{if } 1 < i < m, \ j = m;$$

$$(\lambda + \beta) P_{i,j} = K_2 \mu P_{i,j+1}, \quad \text{if } i = m, \ j = 0;$$

$$(\lambda + K_1 \mu + \beta) P_{i,j} = \lambda P_{i,j-1} + K_2 \mu P_{i,j+1},$$
$$\text{if } i = m, \ 0 < j \leq i + 1;$$

$$(\lambda + K_1 \mu) P_{i,j} = \lambda P_{i,j-1} + K_2 \mu P_{i,j+1} + \alpha P_{i-1,j},$$
$$\text{if } i = m, \ 3(i - 1) < j < m;$$

$$K_1 \mu P_{i,j} = \lambda P_{i,j-1} + \alpha P_{i-1,j},$$
$$\text{if } i = m, \ j = m,$$

$$\tag{4}$$

where

$$K_1 = j, \quad \text{if } i > j;$$
$$K_1 = j - 1, \quad \text{if } i = j, \ j \neq 1;$$
$$K_1 = 1, \quad \text{if } i = j, \ j = 1;$$
$$K_1 = i, \quad \text{if } i < j;$$
$$K_2 = j + 1, \quad \text{if } i > j + 1;$$
$$K_2 = j, \quad \text{if } i = j + 1, \ j + 1 \neq 1;$$
$$K_2 = 1, \quad \text{if } i = j + 1, \ j + 1 = 1;$$
$$K_2 = i, \quad \text{if } i < j + 1,$$

$$\tag{5}$$

$$\sum_{i=1}^{m} \sum_{j=0}^{m+1} P_{i,j} = 1.$$

In the above equations, λ, μ, α, and β are the request arrival rate (i.e., the interarrival times of service requests are independent and identically distributed exponential random variables with mean $1/\lambda$), the service rate (i.e., the average number of tasks that can be finished by a VM in one unit of time), the virtual machine start-up rate (i.e., a VM needs time $T = 1/\alpha$ to turn on), and the virtual machine shut-off rate (i.e., a VM needs time $T = 1/\beta$ to shut down), respectively. The balance equations link the probabilities of entering and leaving a state in equilibrium. The total number of equations is $m \times (m + 1) + 1$, but there are only $m \times (m + 1)$ variables: $P_{1,0}, P_{1,1}, \ldots, P_{m,m}$. Therefore, in order to derive $P_{i,j}$, we need to remove one of the equations to obtain the unique equilibrium solution. Unfortunately, the steady-state balance equations cannot be solved in a closed form; hence, we must resort to a numerical solution.

The input and output parameters of our CTMC model are summarized in the following.

Input. The request arrival rate is λ, the service rate is μ, the virtual machine start-up rate is α, and the virtual machine shut-off rate is β. (In addition, the definitions of "just-in-need," "underprovisioning," and "overprovisioning" states should also be included.)

Output

   (i) The accumulated underprovisioning state probability P_u of a cloud platform is as follows:

$$P_u = \sum_{i=1}^{m} \sum_{j=3i+1}^{m+1} P_{i,j}, \qquad (6)$$

where $P_{i,j}$ is the steady-state probability.

   (ii) The accumulated overprovisioning state probability P_o of a cloud platform is as follows:

$$P_o = \sum_{i=2}^{m} \sum_{j=0}^{i} P_{i,j}, \qquad (7)$$

where $P_{i,j}$ is the steady-state probability.

   (iii) The elasticity value E of a cloud platform is obtained by (2), (6), and (7).

5. Model Analysis

In this section, we present some numerical results obtained based on the proposed elastic cloud platform modeling, illustrating and quantifying the elasticity value under different load conditions and different system parameters. All the numerical data in this section are obtained by setting $m = 1{,}000$, that is, the maximum number of VMs that can be deployed, to guarantee sufficient numerical accuracy.

5.1. Varying the Arrival Rate. For the first scenario, we have considered a system with different service rates ($\mu = 100, 120, 140, 160,$ and 180 jobs/hour), while the arrival rate is a variable from $\lambda = 100$ to 400 jobs/hour in sixteen steps. In all cases, the virtual machine start-up rate and virtual machine shut-off rate are assigned values of $\alpha = 120$ VMs/hour and $\beta = 540$ VMs/hour.

   Figure 5 illustrates that the elasticity value is an increasing function of the arrival rate. As can been seen, it increases rather quickly when the arrival rate is up to 300 and smoothly when the arrival rate is higher. This behavior is due to the fact that increasing λ results in noticeable reduction of the probability of overprovisioning but slight change of the probability of underprovisioning. Furthermore, it is observed that the elasticity value decreases as the service rate increases, as described in the next section.

5.2. Varying the Service Rate. For the second scenario, we have considered a system with different arrival rates ($\lambda = 200, 220, 240, 260,$ and 280 jobs/hour), while the service rate is a variable from $\mu = 10$ to 290 jobs/hour in fifteen steps. In all cases, the virtual machine start-up rate and virtual machine shut-off rate are assigned values of $\alpha = 120$ VMs/hour and $\beta = 540$ VMs/hour.

   Figure 6 illustrates that the elasticity value is a decreasing function of the service rate. It shows that, for a fixed arrival rate, increasing service rate decreases the elasticity value sharply and almost linearly. This phenomenon is due to the fact that increasing μ results in noticeable increment of the

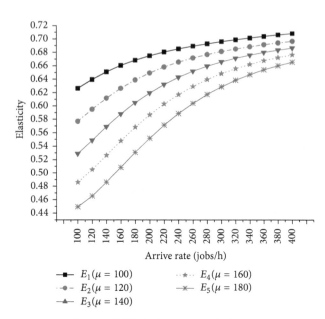

FIGURE 5: Elasticity versus arrival rate.

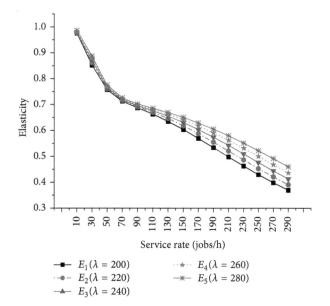

FIGURE 6: Elasticity versus service rate.

probability of overprovisioning, and change of the probability of underprovisioning does not affect the decreasing trend of the just-in-need probability. Figure 6 also confirms that the elasticity value is an increasing function of the arrival rate.

5.3. Varying the Virtual Machine Start-Up Rate. For the third scenario, Figure 7 shows numerical results for a fixed arrival rate, service rate, and virtual machine shut-off rate but different virtual machine start-up rates.

   First, we characterize the elasticity value by presenting the effect of different arrival rates ($\lambda = 200, 220, 240, 260,$ and 280 jobs/hour) and the virtual machine start-up rate is a variable from $\alpha = 120$ to 260 VMs/hour in fifteen steps. In all cases, other system parameters are set as follows. The service rate is

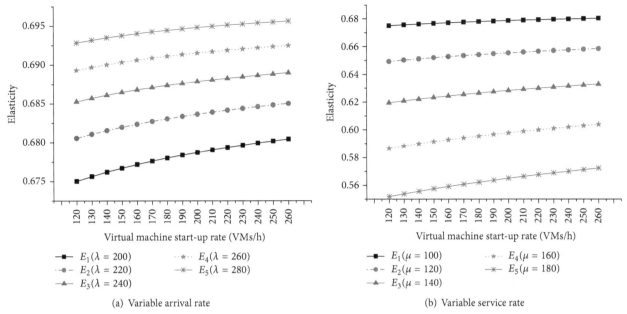

(a) Variable arrival rate

(b) Variable service rate

FIGURE 7: Elasticity versus virtual machine start-up rate.

$\mu = 100$ jobs/hour, and the virtual machine shut-off rate is $\beta = 540$ VMs/hour. As can be seen in Figure 7(a), it increases slightly when the virtual machine start-up rate increases. This is due to the fact that, for high virtual machine start-up rate, each virtual machine start-up time is shorter, meaning that less time is needed to switch from an underprovisioning state to a balanced state, so the probability of underprovisioning P_u is smaller, while the probability of overprovisioning P_o does not change too much, and the probability of just-in-need P_j is increasing.

Second, we also analyze the effects of different service rates ($\mu = 100, 120, 140, 160,$ and 180 jobs/hour), while the virtual machine start-up rate is a variable from $\alpha = 120$ to 260 VMs/hour in fifteen steps. In all cases, other system parameters are set as follows. The arrival rate is $\lambda = 200$ jobs/hour, and the virtual machine shut-off rate is $\beta = 540$ VMs/hour. It can be seen in Figure 7(b) that the elasticity value increases slightly with increasing virtual machine start-up rate.

The results allow us to conclude the increasing elasticity value at increasing virtual machine start-up rate for a fixed arrive rate, service rate, and virtual machine shut-off rate. In other words, increasing the virtual machine start-up rate will decrease the probability of underprovisioning and increase the just-in-need probability. These behaviors (see Figure 7) confirm that the elasticity value of a cloud platform has a relationship to its virtual machine start-up speed.

5.4. Varying the Virtual Machine Shut-Off Rate. For the fourth scenario, Figure 8 shows numerical results for a fixed arrival rate, service rate, and virtual machine start-up rate but different virtual machine shut-off rates.

We examine the effect of virtual machine shut-off rate on elasticity. For different arrival rates ($\lambda = 200, 220, 240, 260,$ and 280 jobs/hour), the virtual machine shut-off rate is a variable from $\beta = 540$ to 680 VMs/hour in fifteen steps. In all

cases, other system parameters are set as follows. The service rate is $\mu = 100$ jobs/hour, and the virtual machine start-up rate is $\alpha = 120$ VMs/hour. It can be seen from Figure 8(a) that the elasticity value increases slightly where the virtual machine shut-off rate is increased from 540 to 680 VMs/hour. This happens because the virtual machine shut-off time is shorter, and a platform becomes more responsive, resulting in diminishing overprovisioning time which is the accumulate time for the system to switch from an overprovisioning state to a balanced state. Furthermore, the probability of overprovisioning P_o is smaller, the probability of underprovisioning P_u shows slight change, and the probability of just-in-need P_j is increasing.

We also calculate the elasticity value under the different service rates ($\mu = 100, 120, 140, 160,$ and 180 jobs/hour), while the virtual machine shut-off rate is a variable from $\beta = 540$ to 680 VMs/hour in fifteen steps. The arrival rate is $\lambda = 200$ jobs/hour, and the virtual machine start-up rate is $\alpha = 120$ VMs/hour. In Figure 8(b), the elasticity value increases slightly by increasing the virtual machine shut-off rate. This is also because of the corresponding reduction in virtual machine shut-off time, guaranteeing shorter overprovisioning probability P_o.

Based on these results, we can conclude the increasing elasticity value at increasing virtual machine shut-off rate for a fixed arrive rate, service rate, and virtual machine start-up rate. In other words, increasing the virtual machine shut-off rate will decrease the probability of overprovisioning and increase the just-in-need probability. These behaviors of Figure 8 confirm that the elasticity value of a cloud platform has a relationship to its virtual machine shut-off speed.

6. Simulation Results

In this section, we present our elastic cloud simulation system called *Cloud Elasticity Value*. Its aim is to demonstrate

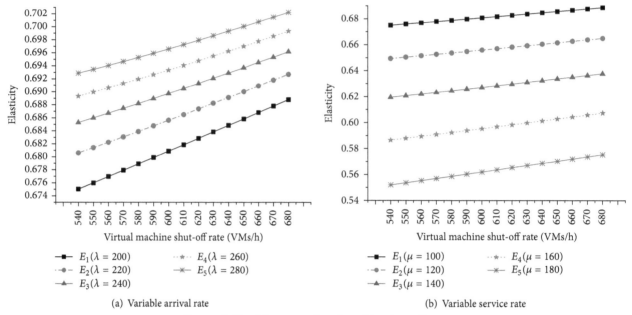

(a) Variable arrival rate

(b) Variable service rate

FIGURE 8: Elasticity versus virtual machine shut-off rate.

that our elasticity measurement is correct and effective in computing and comparing the elasticity value and to show cloud elasticity under different parameter settings.

6.1. Design of the Simulator. Our simulation uses the same code base for the elasticity measurement as the real implementation. The simulator is implemented in about 40,000 lines of C++ code. It runs in a Linux box over a rack-mount server with Intel®Core™2 Duo CPU and 4.00 GB of memory.

The simulator consists of four modules, that is, the task generator module, the virtual machine monitor module, the request monitor module, and the queue module. The task generator module produces simulation of Poisson distribution requests. The virtual machine monitor module is used for deciding whether to start up and shut off the virtual machines and recording the start-up and shut-off times. The request monitor module is used to count how many requests are being serviced in the system and to record the service times. Arrived service requests are first placed in a queue module and recorded their arrival times before they are processed by any virtual machine.

The main process of the simulator is listed as follows.

Step 1. The task generator module produces simulation of Poisson distribution requests. When the service requests arrive, they are placed in a queue module and recorded their arrival times.

Step 2. The virtual machine monitor module determines whether to start up or shut off the VMs and records the start-up and shut-off times.

Step 3. The request monitor module determines whether there is a request in the queue. If there is a request, it takes a request and assigns it to a running virtual machine and records the service time.

Step 4. After the simulation time is over, the simulator counts up the accumulated time in overprovisioning and underprovisioning states and returns the elasticity value using (1).

6.2. Simulation Results and Analysis. We have evaluated cloud elasticity values using two methods, that is, (1) the elasticity values in terms of the steady-state probabilities obtained for the given parameter and (2) the elasticity values in terms of our simulation system obtained for the same parameters. We compare our CTMC model solutions with the results produced by the simulation method.

We have considered the arrival rate characterized by $\lambda = 60$, 200, and 600 jobs/hour. The service rate values chosen are $\mu = 60$, 200, and 600 jobs/hour. In all cases, the virtual machine start-up rate is assigned the value of $\alpha = 300$ VMs/hour, while the virtual machine shut-off rate is $\beta = 540$ VMs/hour.

Table 2 shows the difference between the elasticity values obtained by the CTMC model and the simulator. From Table 2, we can see that the elasticity values between the two cases are very close, with the maximum relative difference only 0.8 percent. The agreement between the simulation and CTMC model results is excellent, which confirms the validity of our CTMC model. So we conclude that the proposed elasticity quantifying and measuring method using the continuous-time Markov chain (CTMC) model is correct and effective.

7. Experiments on Real Systems

7.1. Experiment Environment. We have conducted our experiments on LuCloud, a cloud computing environment located in Hunan University. On top of hardware and Ubuntu Linux 12.04 operating system, we install KVM virtualization

TABLE 2: Comparison of CTMC model results and simulation results.

| Arrival rate | Service rate | Start-up rate | Shut-off rate | Method | | Difference |
				CTMC model	Simulation	
60	60	300	540	0.705212	0.702837	0.3%
60	200	300	540	0.445756	0.475257	0.4%
60	600	300	540	0.635151	0.637240	0.3%
200	60	300	540	0.735167	0.739055	0.5%
200	200	300	540	0.543948	0.546414	0.5%
200	600	300	540	0.235727	0.234727	0.4%
600	60	300	540	0.827098	0.828784	0.2%
600	200	300	540	0.688974	0.684784	0.6%
600	600	300	540	0.435171	0.438784	0.8%

TABLE 3: Comparison of CTMC model results and experimental results with exponential service times.

| Arrival rate | Service rate | Start-up rate | Shut-off rate | Method | | Difference |
				CTMC model	Experiment	
60	60	120	540	0.701205	0.706082	0.6%
60	200	120	540	0.475480	0.479752	0.9%
60	600	120	540	0.631525	0.649275	3.0%
200	60	120	540	0.731117	0.739533	1.2%
200	200	120	540	0.516099	0.521308	1.0%
200	600	120	540	0.221065	0.269039	2.2%
600	60	120	540	0.817088	0.826455	1.1%
600	200	120	540	0.687533	0.681169	0.9%
600	600	120	540	0.409537	0.491034	0.9%

software which virtualizes the infrastructure and provides unified computing and storage resources. To create a cloud environment, we install CloudStack open-source cloud environment, which is composed of a cluster and responsible for global management, resource scheduling, task distribution, and interaction with users. The cluster is managed by a cloud manager (8 AMD Opteron Processor 4122 CPU, 8 GB memory, and 1 TB hard disk). We use our elasticity testing platform to achieve the allocation of resources, that is, virtual machine start-up and shut-off on LuCloud.

7.2. Experiment Process and Results. First, in order to validate the proposed model, Table 3 summarizes the comparison between the two approaches, that is, the CTMC model and the experiments on LuCloud. We have considered the arrival rate characterized by $\lambda = 60$, 200, and 600 jobs/hour. The service rate values chosen are $\mu = 60$, 200, and 600 jobs/hour. The virtual machine start-up rate is assigned the value of $\alpha = 120$ VMs/hour, and the virtual machine shut-off rate is assigned the value of $\beta = 540$ VMs/hour.

In Table 3, we can observe that the elasticity values of both approaches are very close, with the maximum relative difference only 3.0 percent. We conclude that the proposed CTMC model can be used to compute the elasticity of cloud platforms and can offer accurate results within reasonable difference.

Our second set of experiments focus on the robustness of our model and method, that is, its applicability when

the assumptions of our model are not satisfied. We have considered Gamma distributions for the service times. The Gamma(k, θ) distribution is defined in terms of a shape parameter k and a scale parameter θ [27]. We use the same parameter settings in Table 3, except that the exponential distributions of service times are replaced by Gamma distributions, that is, Gamma(0.0083, 2), Gamma(0.0025, 2), and Gamma(0.00083, 2), such that the service rates are still $\mu = 60$, 200, and 600 jobs/hour.

From Table 4, we can see that the elasticity values of the CTMC model and the experiments are very close, with the maximum relative difference only 3.3 percent. We observe that the experimental results with Gamma service times match very closely with those of the proposed CTMC model. So we conclude that the proposed model and method for quantifying and measuring elasticity using continuous-time Markov chain (CTMC) are not only correct and effective, but also robust and applicable to real cloud computing platforms.

8. Conclusion

In this paper, we have introduced a new definition of cloud elasticity. We have presented an analytical method suitable for evaluating the elasticity of cloud platforms, by using a continuous-time Markov chain (CTMC) model. Validation of the analytical results through extensive simulations has shown that our analytical model is sufficiently detailed to capture all realistic aspects of resource allocation process,

TABLE 4: Comparison of CTMC model results and experimental results with Gamma service times.

Arrival rate	Start-up rate	Shut-off rate	Service distribution	Method		Difference
				CTMC model	Experiment	
60	120	540	Gamma(0.0083, 2)	0.701205	0.716401	2.2%
60	120	540	Gamma(0.0025, 2)	0.475480	0.476752	0.3%
60	120	540	Gamma(0.00083, 2)	0.631525	0.612930	3.0%
200	120	540	Gamma(0.0083, 2)	0.731117	0.711420	2.7%
200	120	540	Gamma(0.0025, 2)	0.516099	0.522762	1.3%
200	120	540	Gamma(0.00083, 2)	0.221065	0.227146	2.8%
600	120	540	Gamma(0.0083, 2)	0.817088	0.835865	2.3%
600	120	540	Gamma(0.0025, 2)	0.687533	0.667146	3.0%
600	120	540	Gamma(0.00083, 2)	0.409537	0.395865	3.3%

that is, virtual machine start-up and virtual machine shut-off, while maintaining excellent accuracy between CTMC model results and simulation results. We have examined the effects of various parameters including request arrival rate, service time, virtual machine start-up rate, and virtual machine shut-off rate. Our experimental results further evidence that the proposed measurement approach can be used to compute cloud elasticity in real cloud platforms. Consequently, cloud providers and users can obtain quantitative, informative, and reliable estimation of elasticity, based on a few essential characterizations of a cloud computing platform.

Notations

E: The elasticity value
i: The number of VMs in service
j: The number of requests in the queue
T_j: The accumulated just-in-need time
T_o: The accumulated overprovisioning time
T_u: The accumulated underprovisioning time
T_m: The measuring time
P_j: The accumulated probability of just-in-need states
P_o: The accumulated probability of overprovisioning states
P_u: The accumulated probability of underprovisioning states
λ: The request arrival rate
μ: The request service rate
α: The virtual machine start-up rate
β: The virtual machine shut-off rate
(i, j): A state in our CTMC model
$P_{i,j}$: The steady-state probability of state (i, j)
N: The average number of requests in the queue
T: The average response time
M: The average number of VMs in service
CPR: The cost-performance ratio.

Competing Interests

The authors declare that they have no competing interests.

Acknowledgments

The research was partially funded by the Key Program of National Natural Science Foundation of China (Grants nos. 61133005 and 61432005) and the National Natural Science Foundation of China (Grants nos. 61370095 and 61472124).

References

[1] J. Cao, K. Li, and I. Stojmenovic, "Optimal power allocation and load distribution for multiple heterogeneous multicore server processors across clouds and data centers," *IEEE Transactions on Computers*, vol. 63, no. 1, pp. 45–58, 2014.

[2] M. Bourguiba, K. Haddadou, I. E. Korbi, and G. Pujolle, "Improving network I/O virtualization for cloud computing," *IEEE Transactions on Parallel and Distributed Systems*, vol. 25, no. 3, pp. 673–681, 2014.

[3] Cost-efficient consolidating service for Aliyun's cloud-scale computing, http://kylinx.com/papers/c4.pdf.

[4] N. R. Herbst, S. Kounev, and R. Reussner, "Elasticity in cloud computing: what it is, and what it is not," in *Proceedings of the 10th International Conference on Autonomic Computing (ICAC '13)*, pp. 23–27, San Jose, Calif, USA, June 2013.

[5] Z. Shen, S. Subbiah, X. Gu, and J. Wilkes, "CloudScale: elastic resource scaling for multi-tenant cloud systems," in *Proceedings of the 2nd ACM Symposium on Cloud Computing (SOCC '11)*, p. 5, ACM, Cascais, Portugal, October 2011.

[6] G. Galante and L. C. E. de Bona, "A survey on cloud computing elasticity," in *Proceedings of the IEEE/ACM 5th International Conference on Utility and Cloud Computing (UCC '12)*, pp. 263–270, Chicago, Ill, USA, November 2012.

[7] U. Sharma, P. Shenoy, S. Sahu, and A. Shaikh, "A cost-aware elasticity provisioning system for the cloud," in *Proceedings of the 31st International Conference on Distributed Computing Systems (ICDCS '11)*, pp. 559–570, IEEE, Minneapolis, Minn, USA, July 2011.

[8] R. N. Calheiros, C. Vecchiola, D. Karunamoorthy, and R. Buyya, "The Aneka platform and QoS-driven resource provisioning for elastic applications on hybrid clouds," *Future Generation Computer Systems*, vol. 28, no. 6, pp. 861–870, 2012.

[9] J. O. Fitó, Í. Goiri, and J. Guitart, "SLA-driven elastic cloud hosting provider," in *Proceedings of the 18th Euromicro Conference on Parallel, Distributed and Network-based Processing (PDP '10)*, pp. 111–118, IEEE, Pisa, Italy, February 2010.

[10] L. Badger, T. Grance, R. Patt-Corner, and J. Voas, *Draft Cloud Computing Synopsis and Recommendations*, vol. 800, NIST Special Publication, 2011.

[11] R. Cohen, *Defining Elastic Computing*, 2009, http://www.elasticvapor.com/2009/09/defining-elastic-computing.html.

[12] R. Buyya, J. Broberg, and A. M. Goscinski, *Cloud Computing: Principles and Paradigms*, vol. 87, John Wiley & Sons, New York, NY, USA, 2010.

[13] S. Dustdar, Y. Guo, B. Satzger, and H.-L. Truong, "Principles of elastic processes," *IEEE Internet Computing*, vol. 15, no. 5, pp. 66–71, 2011.

[14] K. Hwang, X. Bai, Y. Shi, M. Li, W. Chen, and Y. Wu, "Cloud performance modeling with benchmark evaluation of elastic scaling strategies," *IEEE Transactions on Parallel and Distributed Systems*, vol. 27, no. 1, pp. 130–143, 2016.

[15] M. Kuperberg, N. Herbst, J. von Kistowski, and R. Reussner, *Defining and Quantifying Elasticity of Resources in Cloud Computing and Scalable Platforms*, KIT, Fakultät für Informatik, 2011.

[16] W. Dawoud, I. Takouna, and C. Meinel, "Elastic VM for cloud resources provisioning optimization," in *Advances in Computing and Communications*, A. Abraham, J. L. Mauri, J. F. Buford, J. Suzuki, and S. M. Thampi, Eds., vol. 190 of *Communications in Computer and Information Science*, pp. 431–445, Springer, Berlin, Germany, 2011.

[17] N. Roy, A. Dubey, and A. Gokhale, "Efficient autoscaling in the cloud using predictive models for workload forecasting," in *Proceedings of the IEEE 4th International Conference on Cloud Computing (CLOUD '11)*, pp. 500–507, IEEE, Washington, DC, USA, July 2011.

[18] Z. Gong, X. Gu, and J. Wilkes, "Press: predictive elastic resource scaling for cloud systems," in *Proceedings of the International Conference on Network and Service Management (CNSM '10)*, pp. 9–16, IEEE, Ontario, Canada, October 2010.

[19] W. J. Anderson, *Continuous-Time Markov Chains*, Springer Series in Statistics: Probability and Its Applications, Springer, New York, NY, USA, 1991.

[20] H. Khazaei, J. Mišić, V. B. Mišić, and S. Rashwand, "Analysis of a pool management scheme for cloud computing centers," *IEEE Transactions on Parallel and Distributed Systems*, vol. 24, no. 5, pp. 849–861, 2013.

[21] R. Ghosh, V. K. Naik, and K. S. Trivedi, "Power-performance trade-offs in IaaS cloud: a scalable analytic approach," in *Proceedings of the IEEE/IFIP 41st International Conference on Dependable Systems and Networks Workshops (DSN-W '11)*, pp. 152–157, IEEE, Hong Kong, June 2011.

[22] S. Pacheco-Sanchez, G. Casale, B. Scotney, S. McClean, G. Parr, and S. Dawson, "Markovian workload characterization for QoS prediction in the cloud," in *Proceedings of the IEEE 4th International Conference on Cloud Computing (CLOUD '11)*, pp. 147–154, IEEE, Washington, Wash, USA, July 2011.

[23] R. Ghosh, F. Longo, V. K. Naikz, and K. S. Trivedi, "Quantifying resiliency of IaaS cloud," in *Proceedings of the 29th IEEE Symposium on Reliable Distributed Systems*, pp. 343–347, IEEE, New Delhi, India, November 2010.

[24] R. Ghosh, D. Kim, and K. S. Trivedi, "System resiliency quantification using non-state-space and state-space analytic models," *Reliability Engineering & System Safety*, vol. 116, pp. 109–125, 2013.

[25] J.-C. Laprie, "From dependability to resilience," in *Proceedings of the 38th IEEE/IFIP International Conference on Dependable Systems and Networks*, pp. G8–G9, Anchorage, Alaska, USA, June 2008.

[26] M. Mao and M. Humphrey, "A performance study on the VM startup time in the cloud," in *Proceedings of the IEEE 5th International Conference on Cloud Computing (CLOUD '12)*, pp. 423–430, IEEE, Honolulu, Hawaii, USA, June 2012.

[27] S. Ali, H. J. Siegel, M. Maheswaran, and D. Hensgen, "Task execution time modeling for heterogeneous computing systems," in *Proceedings of the IEEE 9th Heterogeneous Computing Workshop (HCW '00)*, pp. 185–199, Cancun, Mexico, 2000.

13

An Invocation Cost Optimization Method for Web Services in Cloud Environment

Lianyong Qi,[1] Jiguo Yu,[1] and Zhili Zhou[2]

[1]*School of Information Science and Engineering, Qufu Normal University, Rizhao 276826, China*
[2]*School of Computer and Software, Nanjing University of Information Science and Technology, Nanjing 210044, China*

Correspondence should be addressed to Lianyong Qi; lianyongqi@gmail.com

Academic Editor: Basilio B. Fraguela

The advent of cloud computing technology has enabled users to invoke various web services in a "pay-as-you-go" manner. However, due to the flexible pricing model of web services in cloud environment, a cloud user' service invocation cost may be influenced by many factors (e.g., service invocation time), which brings a great challenge for cloud users' cost-effective web service invocation. In view of this challenge, in this paper, we first investigate the multiple factors that influence the invocation cost of a cloud service, for example, user's job size, service invocation time, and service quality level; and afterwards, a novel Cloud Service Cost Optimization Method named *CS-COM* is put forward, by considering the above multiple impact factors. Finally, a set of experiments are designed, deployed, and tested to validate the feasibility of our proposal in terms of cost optimization. The experiment results show that our proposed *CS-COM* method outperforms other related methods.

1. Introduction

The advent of cloud computing technology has provided us with a light-weight resolution for building various complex business applications [1–3]. With the flexible provision of cloud computing infrastructure, a service user can invoke his/her interested web services in an "easy-to-access" and "pay-as-you-go" manner, which significantly benefits the users who request dynamic and variable computing resources [4–6].

However, the flexible pricing model in cloud environment brings users a challenging task to find the optimal service invocation cost [7], as the cost is often varied with many impact factors, such as user job size, service invocation time, and user's requested service quality [8]. For example, let us consider a video-on-demand scenario [9, 10] where a service $service_{VOD}$ can help users to enjoy movies located on remote servers. Then when $service_{VOD}$ is invoked by a user, the invocation cost often depends on many context factors, such as movie size, service invocation time, and movie display quality. Therefore, from the perspective of a cloud user, it becomes a necessity and a challenge to find the optimal service invocation time as well as the minimal service invocation cost, when he/she utilizes $service_{VOD}$ to enjoy his/her preferred movies.

In view of this challenge, in this paper, we first investigate and analyze the impact factors that influence the invocation cost of a cloud service; afterwards, a novel Cloud Service Cost Optimization Method, that is, *CS-COM*, is brought forth in this paper, by combining the above multiple impact factors.

The rest of paper is structured as follows. In Section 2, we first investigate the impact factors that influence the invocation cost of a cloud service. Afterwards, an optimization method for invocation cost of cloud services, that is, *CS-COM*, is put forward in Section 3, by considering the investigated multiple impact factors. A set of experiments are designed and deployed in Section 4, to validate the feasibility of our proposal in terms of cost optimization. Related works and further discussions are presented in Section 5. And finally, in Section 6, we conclude the paper and point out our future research directions.

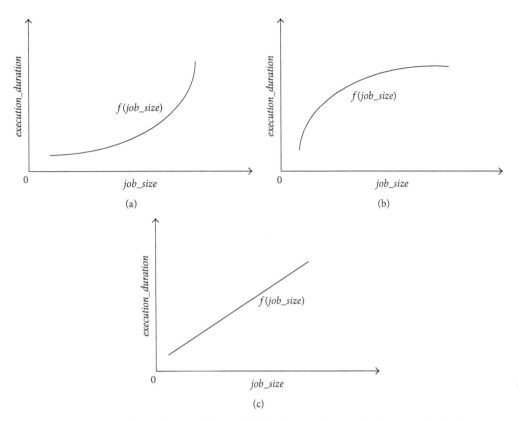

FIGURE 1: Positive correlation between *job size* of a cloud user and *execution duration* of a cloud service.

2. Impact Factor Analyses for Web Service Invocation Cost in Cloud

Due to the flexible pricing models in cloud environment, the invocation cost for a cloud service is often not static but varied with many impact factors. In this section, we will investigate these context factors. Concretely, the following three context factors play important roles in cloud service charging.

2.1. Job Size. Size of a cloud user' job (or task), whose units are KB, MB, GB, TB, PB, and so forth. Generally, for a job of a cloud user, a larger *job size* often leads to longer service execution duration. Let us consider the example of *service$_{VOD}$* introduced in Section 1. A 2 GB movie often takes more time cost (e.g., decoding time or transmission time) than a 1 GB movie does.

With the above observation, a conclusion could often be drawn that there is a positive correlation between a user's *job size* and a cloud service's *execution duration*. Here, we utilize formula (1) to depict the relationship between them. Then according to the above analyses, in (1), the first-order derivative $f'(job\_size) > 0$ often holds. Concretely, for simplicity, we utilize the three submodels in Figure 1 to depict the positive correlation between a cloud user's *job_size* and a cloud service's estimated *execution_duration*. As Figure 1 shows, a cloud service's estimated *execution_duration*s all increase with the growth of *job_size*. The major difference among these three submodels is as follows: *execution_duration* increases faster with the growth of *job_size* in Figure 1(a) (e.g., when

the cloud load is becoming heavier and heavier), while in contrast, *execution_duration* increases more slowly when *job_size* grows in Figure 1(b) (e.g., when the cloud load is becoming smaller and smaller); and in Figure 1(c), *execution_duration* increases linearly with the growth of *job_size* (e.g., when the cloud load stays approximately stable).

$$execution\_duration = f\left(job\_size\right). \qquad (1)$$

For a cloud service, larger *execution duration* often means higher service invocation cost. Therefore, there is an indirect positive correlation between *job size* of a cloud user and invocation cost of a cloud service. For example, a 2 GB movie may be charged more than a 1 GB movie when a user invokes *service$_{VOD}$*.

2.2. Service Invocation Time. It means the time point that a cloud service begins to execute. Generally, a cloud user would be charged more when he/she invokes a cloud service in busy hours (e.g., 08:00 am~18:00 pm of a day) or on busy days. In contrast, when the cloud service is not busy, a cloud user would be charged less. Let us take the *service$_{VOD}$* introduced in Section 1, for example. If a user invokes *service$_{VOD}$* service on free days (e.g., Monday~Thursday), a small fee would be charged (i.e., cost per hour *cph* is low in Figure 2), while on other busy days (e.g., Friday~Sunday), the invocation cost of *service$_{VOD}$* would rise significantly due to the heavy network load on weekends.

Here, we utilize the following pricing model in (2) to depict the relationship between a cloud service's *cph* and

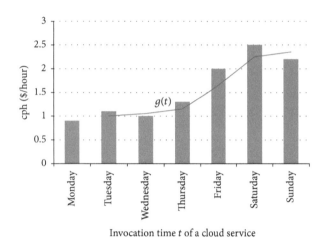

FIGURE 2: Cloud services' pricing model regarding invocation time t: an example.

invocation time point t. Generally, the time-aware pricing model of a cloud service is often provided by its service provider.

$$cph = g(t). \tag{2}$$

2.3. Service Quality Level. It means a cloud service's quality level that is requested by a cloud user. Generally, a cloud provider often publishes its cloud service with multiple quality levels so as to accommodate the various preferences of different cloud users [11]. Here, we utilize set $\{ql_1, \ldots, ql_n\}$ to denote a cloud service's n service quality levels that could be delivered to its cloud users (ql_1 denotes the lowest quality level, while ql_n denotes the highest quality level). Generally, the service invocation cost would be high if a cloud user requests a high service quality level. For example, let us consider the example of $service_{VOD}$ (introduced in Section 1) as well as its two service quality levels shown as follows. As 1080 P > 720 P holds, a user would be charged more if he/she selects *service-quality-level*-1 instead of *service-quality-level*-2, as *service-quality-level*-1 requires more transmission cost than *service-quality-level*-2 does:

service-quality-level-1: 1080 P (high video_quality)

service-quality-level-2: 720 P (middle video_quality)

3. Cost Optimization Method for Cloud Service Invocation

In Section 2, we have analyzed the three important impact factors that are related to the invocation cost of a cloud service, that is, *job size*, *service invocation time*, and *service quality level*. Next, we combine the above three impact factors together to develop a novel cost optimization method for cloud services, that is, *CS-COM*, so as to help cloud users to find the optimal service invocation time and the minimal service invocation cost. Concretely, our proposed *CS-COM* method consists of the following four steps.

TABLE 1: An example of parameters a and b in (4).

Parameter	ql_x			
	ql_1	ql_2	$\cdots$	ql_n
a	1	2		n
b	$1/n$	$2/n$		1

Step 1. Estimate a cloud service's *execution duration* based on a cloud user's *job size*.

In Section 2 (see Figure 1 and formula (1)), we have introduced three pricing submodels between a cloud user's *job_size* and a cloud service's estimated *execution_duration*. Therefore, given a cloud user's job size, we can estimate a cloud service's execution duration based on (1). Here, please note that formula (1) can be in the form of Figure 1(a) or Figure 1(b) or Figure 1(c), depending on the service provider's pricing strategy. Next, we utilize range $[t_0, t_0 + execution\_duration]$ to denote the running period of a cloud service, where t_0 is the time point that the cloud service starts to execute.

Step 2. According to the estimated service *execution_duration* (in Step 1) and the time-aware pricing model (in (2)), calculate the original service invocation cost P (without considering *service quality level*).

As introduced in Step 1, a cloud service starts to execute at $t = t_0$ and ends at $t = t_0 + execution\_duration$. Therefore, through the integral operation over cph in (2), we can obtain the original service invocation cost P (without considering *service quality level*). Concretely, P could be calculated by (3), where $cph = g(t)$ holds (see formula (2)).

$$P = \int_{t_0}^{t_0 + execution\_duration} cph \, dt$$
$$= \int_{t_0}^{t_0 + execution\_duration} g(t) \, dt. \tag{3}$$

Step 3. Calculate the comprehensive service invocation cost $P^{(x)}$ based on the requested *service quality level* ql_x and the original invocation cost P derived in Step 2.

In Step 2, we have derived the original invocation cost P of a cloud service without considering the service quality level. As analyzed previously in Section 2, service quality level often plays an important role in service charging. Therefore, in this step, original service invocation cost P is modified to be $P^{(x)}$ by considering the cloud user's requested service quality level ql_x where $ql_x \in \{ql_1, \ldots, ql_n\}$ holds (here, we assume that there are n quality levels for a cloud service; ql_1 and ql_n denote the lowest and highest service quality levels, resp.).

As analyzed in Section 2, a higher service quality level often leads to larger service invocation cost. In view of this intuitive observation, we utilize the simple linear formula in (4) to depict the correlation between $P^{(x)}$ and P. In (4), a and b are two parameters that are determined by the service quality level ql_x. A concrete example is presented in Table 1

```
┌─────────────────────────────────────────────────────────────────┐
│  Input: user: a cloud user                                        │
│         cs: a cloud service ready to be invoked by user           │
│         job_size: user's job (or task) size                       │
│         ql_x: service quality level of cs requested by user       │
│         f(job_size): execution_duration = f(job_size) in (1)      │
│         g(t): cph = g(t) in (2)                                    │
│  Output: t_{0(optimal)}: optimal service invocation start time of cs │
│          P^{(x)}_{(optimal)}: optimal invocation cost of cs by user │
│                                                                   │
│  (1)  Set variable t_0 // service invocation start time           │
│  (2)  Get models f(job_size) and g(t) from service provider       │
│  (3)  Get parameters a and b in (4) from service provider based on ql_x │
│  (4)  Estimate cs's execution_duration based on job_size and (1)  │
│  (5)  Calculate P based on t_0, execution_duration and (3)        │
│         // P: original service invocation cost of cs by user      │
│  (6)  Calculate P^{(x)} based on a, b, P and (4)                  │
│         // P^{(x)}: comprehensive invocation cost of cs by user   │
│  (7)  Set objective function: Minimize P^{(x)}                    │
│  (8)  Determine t_{0(optimal)} by combining (1)–(5)               │
│  (9)  Determine P^{(x)}_{(optimal)} based on (6)                  │
│  (10) Return t_{0(optimal)} to user                               │
│  (11) Return P^{(x)}_{(optimal)} to user                          │
└─────────────────────────────────────────────────────────────────┘
```

ALGORITHM 1: $CS\text{-}COM$ $(user, cs, job\_size, ql_x, f(job\_size), g(t))$.

to demonstrate the relationship between parameter values of (a, b) and service quality level ql_x. Generally, parameters a and b could be obtained from the cloud service provider.

$$P^{(x)} = h\left(ql_x, P\right) = a * P + b. \qquad (4)$$

Step 4. Optimize cost $P^{(x)}$ derived in Step 3.

Our final goal is to minimize the comprehensive service invocation cost $P^{(x)}$ derived in (4). Next, through combining (1)–(4) and objective function (i.e., Minimize $P^{(x)}$), we can obtain an optimal value for service invocation start time t_0, denoted by $t_{0(optimal)}$ in (5). And correspondingly, when $t_0 = t_{0(optimal)}$ holds, the optimal service invocation cost $P^{(x)}_{(optimal)}$ is achieved, which could be calculated by (6).

$$t_{0(optimal)} = \left\{ t_0 \mid P^{(x)} = \min\left\{P(x)\right\} \right\} \qquad (5)$$

$$P^{(x)}_{(optimal)} = a * \int_{t_{0(optimal)}}^{t_{0(optimal)} + execution\_duration} g(t)\, dt + b. \qquad (6)$$

With Steps 1–4 of our proposed $CS\text{-}COM$ method, we can determine the optimal service execution start time t_0 as well as the optimal (i.e., the lowest) service invocation cost $P^{(x)}_{(optimal)}$, by considering a cloud user's job size and requested service quality level ql_x. Next, more formally, the pseudocode of our proposed $CS\text{-}COM$ method is specified as Algorithm 1. Here, the functions $execution\_duration = f(job\_size)$ in (1), $cph = g(t)$ in (2), and parameters a and b are all regarded as known already, as they all depend on the pricing models of cloud service providers.

4. Experiments

In this section, a set of simulated experiments are designed and tested, to validate the feasibility of our proposed $CS\text{-}COM$ method in terms of cost optimization.

4.1. Experiment Settings. Next, we introduce the concrete parameters or environment settings adopted in the experiments.

4.1.1. Relationship between execution_duration and job_size (See Formula (1)). As work [12] indicates, a cloud service's *execution_duration* (without considering the data transfer between user client and cloud server) mainly depends on the CPU processing speed and user *job_size*. Due to the flexible resource provision in cloud environment, we can assume that the CPU processing speed stays approximately stable. In this situation, there is an approximately linear relationship between estimated *execution_duration* (unit: hour) of a cloud service and *job_size* (unit: GB) of a cloud user. So in the experiments, we utilize the linear function in (7) to model their relationship where k ($k > 0$) is a parameter. Here, we utilize the well-known cloud simulation tool *CloudSim* [13] developed by Melbourne University for generating the user job 1000 times randomly, through which the user *job_size* could be obtained.

$$execution\_duration = f(job\_size) = k * job\_size. \qquad (7)$$

4.1.2. Relationship between cph and t (See Formula (2)). Generally, a cloud service's pricing model, that is, *cph* (cost per hour), heavily depends on the service invocation time t [14]. In the experiments, we generate the random pricing models with the help of *CloudSim* (concretely, cloud services including pricing models in (1)–(4) are encapsulated in a service entity in *CloudSim* and registered in CloudInformationService component; our proposed cost optimization method *CS-COM* and other related methods are located in the component of Data Center Proxy so as to estimate the service invocation cost).

4.1.3. Relationship between Invocation Cost $P^{(x)}$ and Service Quality ql_x (See Formula (4) and Table 1). According to the experiment results observed by [14], there is an approximate linear relationship between service invocation cost $P^{(x)}$ and service quality ql_x (see formula (8)). In the experiments, we adopt this experienced data in (8) to approach formula (4) in our paper.

$$P^{(x)} = 2 * ql_x + 0.4. \tag{8}$$

Besides, we test and compare our *CS-COM* method with four related methods: *FCFS* (First Come First Serve) [15], *FL-FL* (cost evaluation based on historical records) [16], *Cost-plus* (considering service invocation cost and user benefit simultaneously) [17], and *CB* (considering time-depended pricing model only) [14].

The experiments were conducted on a HP laptop with 2.40 GHz processors and 4.0 GB RAM. The machine is running under Windows 7 and JAVA 1.5. Each experiment was carried out 10 times and the average results were adopted. Concretely, three experiment profiles are tested and compared.

4.2. Experiment Results

4.2.1. Profile 1: Invocation Cost Comparison with respect to Job Size. In this profile, we test and compare the service invocation costs of our proposed *CS-COM* method and other four methods. Here, in *CS-COM*, parameters $k = 2$, $a = 2$, and $b = 0.4$ hold (see (8)); parameter L in *FL-FL* is equal to 3; parameter *conversion* = 0.4 holds in *Cost-plus*. Cloud user's *job_size* is varied from 1 GB to 10 GB.

The experiment results are presented in Figure 3. As Figure 3 shows, the service invocation costs of five methods all increase with the growth of *job_size* approximately; this is because processing a larger job often takes more time cost and hence leads to a higher invocation cost. Moreover, the service invocation cost of *Cost-plus* method is high as it considers the user benefit as an optimization object, while more user benefit often means higher charging fees. Besides, the service invocation cost of *FCFS* method often fluctuates frequently as its service invocation time is randomly selected, while different service invocation time means varied service charging. The rest three experiment curves increase approximately in polynomial manners, where *FL-FL* method utilizes the past service invocation costs to estimate the future invocation cost and *CB* method considers the time-dependent pricing models of cloud services, while our proposed *CS-COM* method consider a cloud user's job size,

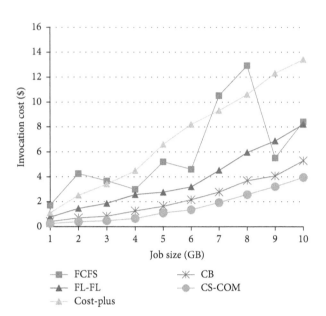

FIGURE 3: Invocation cost comparison of five methods with respect to job size.

service invocation time, and requested service quality level simultaneously. Therefore, *CS-COM* method outperforms the other four methods in terms of service invocation cost, which could also be observed from Figure 3.

4.2.2. Profile 2: Invocation Cost Comparison with respect to t. In this profile, we compare the service invocation costs of five methods with respect to the service invocation time. As the "*cph-t*" charging models (see formula (2)) randomly generated by *CloudSim* make it hard to observe the stable variation trend of invocation cost, in this profile, we choose a randomly generated but fixed "*cph-t*" charging model ($t \in$ [1:00 pm, 12:00 pm]) where [6:00 pm, 9:00 pm] is the busy hour. To observe the cost variation trend with invocation time t, we tune parameter *job_size* so that the user job could be finished within one hour. Other parameter settings are the same as in Profile 1.

The experiment results are shown in Figure 4. As Figure 4 indicates, the service invocation cost of *Cost-plus* is high as it considers both user benefit and service cost, while larger user benefit often means higher charging fees. The *FCFS* method achieves the approximate cost variation trend with the preset "*cph-t*" charging model as no cost optimization strategy is adopted in *FCFS*. In *FL-FL* method, sampling technique is recruited to approximately approach original "*cph-t*" charging model, which achieves the similar cost variation trend as in *FCFS*. The rest two methods, that is, *CB* and *CS-COM*, perform better than the previous three methods in terms of cost optimization, as the dynamic time-aware cost optimization strategy is considered in these two methods. Besides, as supposed in this profile, the execution duration of user job is one hour; therefore, at the last o'clock (i.e., 12:00 pm), time-aware cost optimization strategy does not work anymore and hence, the five cost variation curves converge.

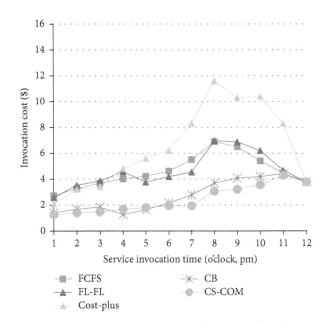

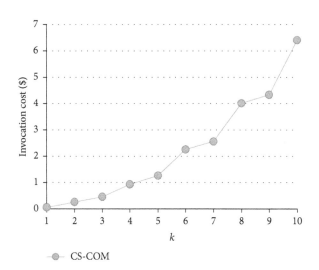

FIGURE 6: Service invocation cost of *CS-COM* with respect to *k*.

FIGURE 4: Invocation cost comparison of five methods with respect to service invocation time (1:00 pm~12:00 pm).

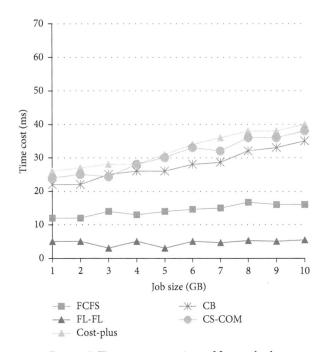

FIGURE 5: Time cost comparison of five methods.

4.2.3. Profile 3: Time Cost Comparison. In this profile, we test the time costs of five methods. Here, sampling technique is recruited to convert the continuous function $cph = g(t)$ in (2) into d discrete values with same intervals, so as to facilitate the further computation of service invocation cost. Concretely, $d = 100$ holds in this profile. Other parameter settings are the same as those in Profile 1.

The concrete experiment results are presented in Figure 5. As can be seen from Figure 5, *FL-FL* method achieves the least time cost as it only considers the past few historical

service invocation costs of a cloud service, without further complicated computation. The rest four time cost curves all increase approximately linearly with the growth of job size. The time cost of *FCFS* method is not very large as it only refers to an integral operation associated with $cph = g(t)$ and t. The execution efficiencies of rest three methods, that is, *Cost-plus*, *CB*, and *CS-COM*, are very close, as they all contain some extra computation processes associated with cloud users' job size; concretely, *Cost-plus* needs to calculate the benefit of a cloud user based on the service invocation cost (derived based on job size) and *CB* needs to optimize the service invocation cost based on the time-dependent pricing model (depends on job size), while our proposed *CS-COM* method employs job size to estimate the service execution duration. As Figure 5 shows, the time costs of all the five methods are not high (at "millisecond" level).

4.2.4. Profile 4: Service Invocation Cost of CS-COM with respect to k. As formula (7) indicates, k is an important parameter that bridges the estimated service *execution_duration* and a cloud user's *job_size* and consequently influences the finally derived optimal service invocation cost. In this profile, we test the relationship between k and the optimal service invocation cost in our proposed *CS-COM* method. Concretely, k is varied from 1 to 10, *job_size* is equal to 1 GB, and parameters $a = 2$ and $b = 0.4$ hold in (4).

The concrete experiment results are presented in Figure 6. As can be seen from Figure 6, the invocation cost of *CS-COM* method increases approximately in a polynomial manner with the growth of k, this is because k appears in the upper bound of t (i.e., $t_{0(optimal)} + execution\_duration = t_{0(optimal)} + f(job\_size)$) of invocation cost integration $\int_{t_{0(optimal)}}^{t_{0(optimal)}+execution\_duration} g(t)\, dt$ in (6), while $g(t)$ is often a polynomial function associated with t. So after the integral operation, the service invocation cost becomes a polynomial function associated with parameter k.

From the above three sets of experiment results, we can conclude that our proposed *CS-COM* method outperforms the rest four methods in terms of service invocation cost (concretely, compared to *FCFS*, *FL-FL*, *Cost-plus*, and *CB*, the cost reduction ratios of our proposal are 74.9%, 62.8%, 80.1%, and 35.1%, resp.). Besides, the time cost of our proposal is at the "ms" level, which is acceptable for most business applications. Finally, in our proposed *CS-COM* method, the derived optimal service invocation cost has a positive correlation with parameter k in formula (7), which approximately coincides with most existing cloud pricing models. Actually, for a cloud service, the value of parameter k could be published by its service provider in a flexible manner so as to maximize the economic gains.

5. Related Work and Further Discussions

5.1. Related Work and Comparison Analyses. Cloud computing technology, on one hand, facilitates cloud users' sharing and use of various computing resources by providing an "easy-to-access" and "pay-per-use" resource provision manner and, on the other hand, brings a great challenge to minimize or optimize cloud users' service invocation cost. Many researchers have investigated this hot research topic and brought forth their respective resolutions [12, 14–17].

In [12], the authors divided the invocation cost of a cloud service into three categories: data-storage cost, CPU processing cost, and data-transfer cost. In order to evaluate and predict a cloud user's service invocation cost, *FL-FL* method was put forward in [16] by considering the service's past invocation costs; however, *FL-FL* method fails to generate an accurate service invocation cost as the latter is often influenced by some other factors. Work [17] analyzed the relationship between service invocation cost and user benefits and finally introduced a cost-benefit-aware cloud service scheduling method *Cost-plus*. However, one final optimization goal was to maximize user profits, not to minimize the service invocation cost. In order to minimize the service invocation cost, *FCFS* method was put forward in [15]. *FCFS* adopted the "First Come First Serve" rule so as to reduce the waiting time of user job and optimize the service invocation cost. However, *FCFS* did not consider the dynamic and varied time-aware pricing model in cloud environment. In view of this, work [14] took the time-dependent pricing model of cloud services into consideration and brought forth an invocation cost optimization method *CB*. However, *CB* method only considered service invocation time when optimizing the invocation cost, while neglecting some other important factors, for example, user job size and user's requested service quality level.

In view of the above shortcomings, a novel service invocation cost optimization method named *CS-COM* is put forward in this paper, which considers the multiple factors that influence the invocation cost in cloud environment. Experiment results show that *CS-COM* outperforms other related methods in terms of cost optimization.

5.2. Further Discussions. In this paper, we put forward a cost optimization method for web services based on multiple

impact factors. Generally, the proposed multifactors-based optimization strategy can also be applied in other application domains with multiple factors, for example, performance optimization [18–23], feature analysis [24–29], quality evaluation [30–32], knowledge learning [33–37], and data mining [38–40]. However, several shortcomings are still present in our approach.

(1) Only three factors (i.e., *job size*, *service invocation time* and *service quality level*) are considered in our cost optimization method named *CS-COM*, which are not enough for real cloud service scheduling applications. Therefore, in the future, we will further improve our proposal by introducing more charging factors.

(2) Users' subjective preferences that play an important role in users' final service invocation decisions are not considered in our proposed *CS-COM* approach. In the future, we will refine our work by taking user preferences into consideration.

6. Conclusions

Cloud computing has provided an "easy-to-access" and "pay-per-use" resource delivery manner, to help users build their various complex business applications quickly and conveniently. However, due to the flexible pricing model of cloud services, a cloud service's invocation cost is often not fixed but varied, which brings a great challenge to optimize the service invocation cost when a cloud user requests a cloud service. In view of this challenge, we first analyze the multiple factors that may influence the invocation cost of a cloud service, for example, user job size, service invocation time, and service quality level. Afterwards, through considering the above multiple factors, a novel service invocation cost optimization method named *CS-COM* is put forward in this paper, to aid a cloud user to find the optimal service invocation start time as well as the lowest service invocation cost. Finally, through a set of simulated experiments deployed on *CloudSim* platform, we further demonstrate the feasibility and advantages of our proposed *CS-COM* method in terms of cost optimization.

In the future, we will further refine our proposed *CS-COM* method by introducing more charging factors, so as to make it more comprehensive and more applicable in real cloud service scheduling applications.

Conflicts of Interest

The authors declare that they have no conflicts of interest.

Acknowledgments

This paper is partially supported by Natural Science Foundation of China (no. 61402258, no. 61602253, no. 61373027, and no. 61672321) and Open Project of State Key Laboratory for Novel Software Technology (no. KFKT2016B22).

References

[1] K. Habak, M. Ammar, K. A. Harras, and E. Zegura, "Femto clouds: leveraging mobile devices to provide cloud service at the edge," in *Proceedings of the 8th IEEE International Conference on Cloud Computing (CLOUD '15)*, pp. 9–16, July 2015.

[2] Z. Xia, X. Wang, X. Sun, Q. Liu, and Q. Wang, "A secure and dynamic multi-keyword ranked search scheme over encrypted cloud data," *IEEE Transactions on Parallel and Distributed Systems*, vol. 27, no. 2, pp. 340–352, 2015.

[3] Z. Fu, X. Sun, Q. Liu, L. Zhou, and J. Shu, "Achieving efficient cloud search services: multi-keyword ranked search over encrypted cloud data supporting parallel computing," *IEICE Transactions on Communications*, vol. E98B, no. 1, pp. 190–200, 2015.

[4] Y. Kong, M. Zhang, and D. Ye, "A belief propagation-based method for task allocation in open and dynamic cloud environments," *Knowledge-Based Systems*, vol. 115, pp. 123–132, 2016.

[5] Z. Xia, X. Wang, L. Zhang, Z. Qin, X. Sun, and K. Ren, "A privacy-preserving and copy-deterrence content-based image retrieval scheme in cloud computing," *IEEE Transactions on Information Forensics and Security*, vol. 11, no. 11, pp. 2594–2608, 2016.

[6] L. Qi, W. Dou, and J. Chen, "Weighted principal component analysis-based service selection method for multimedia services in cloud," *Computing*, vol. 98, no. 1-2, pp. 195–214, 2016.

[7] D. M. Divakaran and M. Gurusamy, "Towards flexible guarantees in clouds: adaptive bandwidth allocation and pricing," *IEEE Transactions on Parallel and Distributed Systems*, vol. 26, no. 6, pp. 1754–1764, 2015.

[8] Z. Fu, K. Ren, J. Shu, X. Sun, and F. Huang, "Enabling personalized search over encrypted outsourced data with efficiency improvement," *IEEE Transactions on Parallel and Distributed Systems*, vol. 27, no. 9, pp. 2546–2559, 2016.

[9] Z. Pan, Y. Zhang, and S. Kwong, "Efficient motion and disparity estimation optimization for low complexity multiview video coding," *IEEE Transactions on Broadcasting*, vol. 61, no. 2, pp. 166–176, 2015.

[10] Z. Pan, J. Lei, Y. Zhang, X. Sun, and S. Kwong, "Fast motion estimation based on content property for low-complexity H.265/HEVC encoder," *IEEE Transactions on Broadcasting*, vol. 62, no. 3, pp. 675–684, 2016.

[11] A. K. Talukder and L. Zimmerman, "Cloud economics: principles, costs, and benefits," in *Cloud Computing*, pp. 343–360, Springer, London, UK, 2010.

[12] E. Deelman, G. Singh, M. Livny, B. Berriman, and J. Good, "The cost of doing science on the cloud: the montage example," in *Proceedings of the ACM/IEEE Conference on Supercomputing*, pp. 1–12, IEEE Press, November 2008.

[13] R. N. Calheiros, R. Ranjan, A. Beloglazov, C. A. F. de Rose, and R. Buyya, "CloudSim: a toolkit for modeling and simulation of cloud computing environments and evaluation of resource provisioning algorithms," *Software: Practice and Experience*, vol. 41, no. 1, pp. 23–50, 2011.

[14] C. Chawla and I. Chana, "Optimal time dependent pricing model for smart cloud with cost based scheduling," in *Proceedings of the 3rd International Symposium on Women in Computing and Informatics (WCI '15)*, pp. 522–526, August 2015.

[15] M. Li, D. Subhraveti, A. R. Butt, A. Khasymski, and P. Sarkar, "CAM: a topology aware minimum cost flow based resource manager for MapReduce applications in the cloud," in *Proceedings of the 21st ACM Symposium on High-Performance Parallel and Distributed Computing (HPDC '12)*, pp. 211–222, June 2012.

[16] Q. Liu, W. Cai, J. Shen, Z. Fu, X. Liu, and N. Linge, "A speculative approach to spatial-temporal efficiency with multi-objective optimization in a heterogeneous cloud environment," *Security and Communication Networks*, vol. 9, no. 17, pp. 4002–4012, 2016.

[17] W.-H. Choi and K.-S. Kang, "A Study on deciding optimal price of bioinformatics services," *Journal of the Korea Safety Management and Science*, vol. 18, no. 1, pp. 203–208, 2016.

[18] Z. Fu, X. Wu, C. Guan, X. Sun, and K. Ren, "Toward efficient multi-keyword fuzzy search over encrypted outsourced data with accuracy improvement," *IEEE Transactions on Information Forensics and Security*, vol. 11, no. 12, pp. 2706–2716, 2016.

[19] Z. Pan, P. Jin, J. Lei, Y. Zhang, X. Sun, and S. Kwong, "Fast reference frame selection based on content similarity for low complexity HEVC encoder," *Journal of Visual Communication and Image Representation*, vol. 40, part B, pp. 516–524, 2016.

[20] Y. Xue, J. Jiang, B. Zhao, and T. Ma, "A self-adaptive articial bee colony algorithm based on global best for global optimization," *Soft Computing*, 2017.

[21] Y. Zhang, X. Sun, and W. Baowei, "Efficient algorithm for k-barrier coverage based on integer linear programming," *China Communications*, vol. 13, no. 7, pp. 16–23, 2016.

[22] X. Chen, S. Chen, and Y. Wu, "Coverless information hiding method based on the Chinese character encoding," *Journal of Internet Technology*, vol. 18, no. 2, pp. 91–98, 2017.

[23] C. Yuan, Z. Xia, and X. Sun, "Coverless image steganography based on SIFT and BOF," *Journal of Internet Technology*, vol. 18, no. 2, pp. 209–216, 2017.

[24] Z. Xia, X. Wang, X. Sun, and B. Wang, "Steganalysis of least significant bit matching using multi-order differences," *Security and Communication Networks*, vol. 7, no. 8, pp. 1283–1291, 2014.

[25] J. Li, X. Li, B. Yang, and X. Sun, "Segmentation-based image copy-move forgery detection scheme," *IEEE Transactions on Information Forensics and Security*, vol. 10, no. 3, pp. 507–518, 2015.

[26] Z. Xia, X. Wang, X. Sun, Q. Liu, and N. Xiong, "Steganalysis of LSB matching using differences between nonadjacent pixels," *Multimedia Tools and Applications*, vol. 75, no. 4, pp. 1947–1962, 2016.

[27] J. Wang, T. Li, Y.-Q. Shi, S. Lian, and J. Ye, "Forensics feature analysis in quaternion wavelet domain for distinguishing photographic images and computer graphics," *Multimedia Tools and Applications*, 2016.

[28] Z. Zhou, C.-N. Yang, B. Chen, X. Sun, Q. Liu, and Q. M. Jonathan Wu, "Effective and efficient image copy detection with resistance to arbitrary rotation," *IEICE Transactions on Information and Systems*, vol. E99-D, no. 6, pp. 1531–1540, 2016.

[29] C. Yuan, X. Sun, and R. Lv, "Fingerprint liveness detection based on multi-scale LPQ and PCA," *China Communications*, vol. 13, no. 7, pp. 60–65, 2016.

[30] Y. Chen, C. Hao, W. Wu, and E. Wu, "Robust dense reconstruction by range merging based on confidence estimation," *Science China Information Sciences*, vol. 59, no. 9, Article ID 092103, pp. 1–11, 2016.

[31] Z. Zhou, Y. Wang, Q. M. J. Wu, C.-N. Yang, and X. Sun, "Effective and effcient global context verifcation for image copy detection," *IEEE Transactions on Information Forensics and Security*, vol. 12, no. 1, pp. 48–63, 2017.

[32] Z. Fu, F. Huang, X. Sun, A. V. Vasilakos, and C.-N. Yang, "Enabling semantic search based on conceptual graphs over encrypted outsourced data," *IEEE Transactions on Services Computing*, 2016.

[33] B. Gu and V. S. Sheng, "A robust regularization path algorithm for v-support vector classification," *IEEE Transactions on Neural Networks and Learning Systems*, vol. 28, no. 5, pp. 1241–1248, 2016.

[34] B. Gu, X. Sun, and V. S. Sheng, "Structural minimax probability machine," *IEEE Transactions on Neural Networks and Learning Systems*, 2016.

[35] B. Gu, V. S. Sheng, K. Y. Tay, W. Romano, and S. Li, "Incremental support vector learning for ordinal regression," *IEEE Transactions on Neural Networks and Learning Systems*, vol. 26, no. 7, pp. 1403–1416, 2015.

[36] B. Gu, V. S. Sheng, Z. Wang, D. Ho, S. Osman, and S. Li, "Incremental learning for v-support vector regression," *Neural Networks*, vol. 67, pp. 140–150, 2015.

[37] Q. Tian and S. Chen, "Cross-heterogeneous-database age estimation through correlation representation learning," *Neurocomputing*, vol. 238, pp. 286–295, 2017.

[38] Z. Qu, J. Keeney, S. Robitzsch, F. Zaman, and X. Wang, "Multilevel pattern mining architecture for automatic network monitoring in heterogeneous wireless communication networks," *China Communications*, vol. 13, no. 7, pp. 108–116, 2016.

[39] N. Zhang, J. Wang, and Y. Ma, "Mining Domain Knowledge on Service Goals From Textual Service Descriptions," *IEEE Transactions on Services Computing*, 2017.

[40] J. Wang, Z. Zhu, J. Liu, C. Wang, and Y. Xu, "An Approach of Role Updating in Context-Aware Role Mining," *International Journal of Web Services Research*, vol. 14, no. 2, pp. 24–44, 2017.

14

A Game-Theoretic Based Resource Allocation Strategy for Cloud Computing Services

Wang Yan,[1] Wang Jinkuan,[1] and Sun Jinghao[2]

[1]*College of Information Science and Engineering, Northeastern University, Shenyang, Liaoning 110819, China*
[2]*College of Computer and Communication Engineering, Northeastern University at Qinhuangdao, Qinhuangdao, Hebei 066004, China*

Correspondence should be addressed to Wang Yan; wangyan@mail.neuq.edu.cn

Academic Editor: Jun Zheng

We propose an economics-oriented cloud computing resources allocation strategy with the use of game theory. Then we develop a resource allocation algorithm named NCGRAA (noncooperative game resource allocation algorithm) to search the Nash equilibrium solution that makes the utility of various resource providers achieve optimum. We also propose an algorithm named BGRAA (bargaining game resource allocation algorithm) to further increase the overall revenue with the constraints of efficiency and fairness. Based on numerical results, we discuss the influence of NCGRAA and BGRAA for the utility of resource on the system performance. It shows that the choice of parameters of the two algorithms is significant in improving the system performance and converging to the Nash equilibrium and Nash bargaining.

1. Introduction

Cloud service is the commercial implementation of computing resources and essentially a producers-consumers model. From the perspective of economics, the service is as the valuable economic goods that providers produce and lease to consumers. Cloud users can purchase goods from the provider according to their own needs in global scope and in a certain paying mode.

Advancement in cloud resource allocation is urgently needed to satisfy service-specific QoS (Quality of Service) requirements. At the same time, system performance must be mathematically analyzed and numerically evaluated for design of the strategies. The generally accepted view is that typical cloud computing resource allocation strategies are mainly based on multistage resource pool of rent-borrow theory, the random integer programming optimal resource strategy, and economics resource strategy.

Our research on cloud computing resources provisioning strategy is based on the market economic model and the advantages of game theory in resource management. First, we establish a noncooperative resource provision model and a corresponding game algorithm. The aim of the algorithm is to provide resources strategy by solving equilibrium so that each utility function could achieve optimum to obtain a reasonable strategy. Meanwhile, in order to further increase the overall revenue, the strategy is proposed by taking the efficiency and fairness constraints in noncooperative bargaining game into account. The according algorithm achieves higher collective utility by solving bargaining problem. Finally, experiment verifies the effectiveness and superiority of the two algorithms.

In Section 2, we analyze the related work. In Section 3, we analyze the framework of cloud resources based on game theory and establish the market model of resources provided. In Section 4, we propose an algorithm named NCGRAA to solve the Nash equilibrium in order to obtain reasonable resource allocation strategy. In Section 5, we propose an algorithm named BGRAA to search the Nash bargaining solution in order to make higher utility of resources. In Section 6, based on simulation, we evaluate the performance of the two algorithms. Finally, concluding remarks are given in Section 7.

2. Related Work

Researchers [1, 2] used a random integer programming method to optimize resource allocation and introduced two ways which are in advance order and pay-as-you-go to provide users with resources. This strategy can provide dynamic resource allocation methods, considering the cost of various stages resources. However the uncertain resource prediction accuracy needs to be improved.

Then the cloud resource management model [2, 3] was designed based on SLA (Service Layer Agreement). Although the perspective of economics has been taken into account, this strategy is still lacking factors like the resources and the price dynamic. Literature [4] had studied the resource management system based on QoS.

In recent years, various resource management methods with different policies and principles were proposed in some literatures [5–14]. But most literatures were relevant to complex cloud based on applications consisting of multiple subtasks. Therefore collaboration between tasks should be considered. Meanwhile, existing algorithms were obviously too conservative without considering the communications among tasks. As we know, the dependent task scheduling problem is NP-hard [15–17]. Thus some heuristic algorithms were proposed for near-optimal solution [18, 19]. Simultaneously, numerous methods were proposed to solve the optimization problem with game theory [20, 21]. Moreover, game theory can be divided into noncooperative game theory and cooperation game theory [22]. Typical noncooperative game solution is the Nash equilibrium.

Based on the Nash equilibrium, numerous works were proposed. For instance, Kwok et al. [23] proposed a level game model under the environment of multiple administrative domains. It studied the selfish behavior of resource for the influence of user task execution. However, the research does not put the relationship between the resource providers into consideration. In literature [24], a distributed actively noncooperative abandon model was presented. The model reduced the task execution time considering the selfish and priority of resource allocation. Ghosh et al. [25] proposed a pricing strategy solving the Nash bargaining problem based on game theory. But the uniqueness of Nash equilibrium solution was not discussed.

Existing works generally consider the relationship between the user and resource provider, but the resource provider is neglected as rational body when the relationship between competition and cooperation on the result of final resources is provided. Researchers proposed resource management on the basis of the principle of market economics [26] and focused on how to improve the benefits of resource provider with the constraints of efficiency and fairness.

To the best of our knowledge, although the resource allocation strategies have been studied in previous works, allocation strategy aims at achieving the optimal allocation of resources that has been less proposed. Therefore, we focus on giving the dynamic change among supply-demand, resource load, and congestion by prices floating reflections and also focus on achieving the optimal resources allocation

by equilibrium theory. Thus we propose the supply strategy for cloud computing resources based on market economics model in this paper and two resources allocation algorithms for increasing both efficiency and fairness. Inspecting our experimental results, the proposed algorithms improve the resource allocation performance effectively. The experimental results indicate that the resources allocation problems that are solved by noncooperative theory could converge to the Nash equilibrium solution. The utility of the resource provider is optimal. While bargaining, noncooperative game analysis with Pareto improvements is made on the basis of satisfying the efficiency and fairness. Moreover, two algorithms are effective to improve the efficiency of resource allocation.

3. The Game Theory for Resource Allocation Strategy

As utility computing, cloud computing has a lot of economy features, including market features of computing resource, the scale of the cloud market economy, and the provider paid features of resources. One of the advantages of using economics principle to solve the cloud resource allocation is the market mechanism. The market mechanism is well known as that commodity prices floating reflections resource load, congestion, and the dynamic change of supply or demand condition. Therefor it can achieve the optimal allocation of resources with equilibrium theory. This dynamic coordination of resources allocation provides a mechanism that is suitable for dynamic characteristic of the cloud computing environment. Each participant in the market is in pursuit of maximizing individual interests. That makes the whole resource allocation gradually tend to optimum condition. It is one of the traditional resources allocation methods pursued but difficult to achieve.

Hence we analyze the situation above and give the architecture based on economics. The cloud architecture is shown in Figure 1. It has four parts: the users, resource consumers, resource market, and resource providers.

(1) Users. We mean the users who use cloud computing resources. Cloud users put forward their own requirements from their agent to the cloud market, including the required QoS description. And this requires many aspects to complete the task, such as CPU type, the number of the CPU, memory size, operating system, and its version number.

(2) Resource Consumers. Private cloud is as a resource consumer, even though it provides users with resources. When it cannot meet users' need, it still gets resources from the public cloud.

(3) Resource Market. Resource market is the core of this architecture module. It is the management for users, it calculates risk, and it is autonomous. The market is the interface for data center/cloud service providers and the user/agent, using some kind of negotiation mechanism to coordinate the two requirements. It mainly includes the following six kinds of mechanisms.

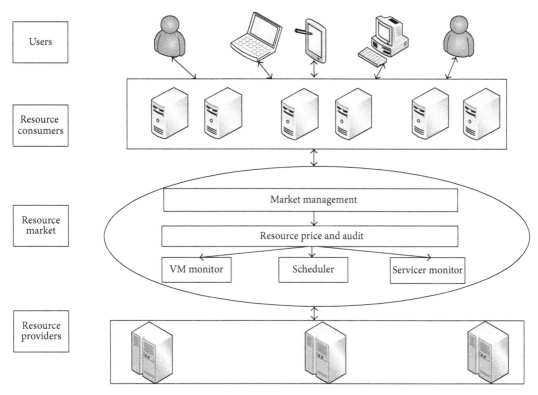

FIGURE 1: The cloud architecture based on economics.

Permission control mechanisms for service request: when a service request is submitted for the first time, the mechanism submits request for QoS explanation before determining whether to accept or reject the request. Pricing mechanism: pricing as a basic mechanism manages the resources allocation and demand of data center. Pricing mechanism decides the price of service request. Audit mechanism: audit mechanism records the actual use of the requested resources, in order to make the final cost that can be calculated and credited for the user. VM (Virtual Machine) monitoring mechanism: monitoring mechanism monitors VM available. Scheduler: it allots and executes the service requests. Monitoring system for service request: the service request monitoring mechanism monitors the implementation of the service request.

(4) Resource Providers. The public cloud is represented.

We build the system model with the $M/M/n/n+l$ queue. The model has some features: the model is a mixed queue model. Tasks arrive at the queue in accordance with the parameter λ of the Poisson flow and service time for each task obeys the negative exponential distribution with parameter μ. The order of the service is in accord with First Come First Served. Length of the queue is $n+l$ and l is the length of buffer. If task arrives at the system, when the queue has not been occupied, it enters the queue to wait for service or it waits in the buffer. Parameters of the model are shown in Parameters section.

(1) Response Time. It has proved that when the communication intensity $\rho < 1$, there is a stable equilibrium state in

system [12, 13]. Therefore, we consider the queue for $\rho < 1$. Probability π_k of queue length is k: $\pi_k = \lim_{t\to\infty} P\{N(t) = k\}$.

Typically, we measure response time with the percentage φ, which is in response to a predetermined percentage of the time. In the SLA (Service Layer Agreement), performance indicator of response time is described as follows:

$$\int_0^{\Delta T} f(t)\,dt \ge \varphi, \tag{1}$$

where the $f(x)$ is a random function and is also the probability density function. ΔT represents the period during which task uses the service.

Equation (1) represents the probability of response time; when the response time is less than the period ΔT, then the probability must be equal to or more than φ. For example, in $M/M/1$ queuing model, the probability density function of the response time is $f(t) = \mu(1 - \rho)e^{-\mu(1-\rho)t}$. Thus we can give the equation as follows:

$$\mu \ge \frac{-\ln(1-\varphi)}{\Delta T} + \lambda. \tag{2}$$

From (2), we know that, when the arrival rate λ is constant, the time period ΔT is unchanged. If we improve the probability of response time φ, service rate will increase. We must deploy more computing resources.

In $M/M/n/n+l$ queue model, system transition probability between states is as follows:

$$\pi_k = \begin{cases} \dfrac{(n\rho)^k}{k!}\pi_0, & 0 \leq k < n \\[2ex] \dfrac{n^n \rho^k}{n!}\pi_0, & n \leq k \leq n+l. \end{cases} \quad (3)$$

When $\sum_{i=1}^{n+l} \pi_i = 1$, we obtain π_0 as follows:

$$\pi_0 = \left(\sum_{k=0}^{n-1} \frac{(n\rho)^k}{k!} + \frac{(n\rho)^n \left(1 - \rho^{l+1}\right)}{n! \left(1 - \rho\right)} \right)^{-1}, \quad \rho < 1, \quad (4)$$

where π_0 means the probability that all hosts are idle and there is no task in system.

Response time is the sum of waiting time and service time. Waiting time can be calculated in the following manner method: When a task arrives, if the buffer queue is not full, the user can enter the queue to wait. q_i represents the steady probability that the number of tasks waiting for service is i. q_i is given as follows:

$$q_i = \frac{P\{N(t) = i\} P\{l \neq 0\}}{P\{l \neq 0\}} = \frac{\pi_i}{1 - \pi_{n+l}}, \quad (5)$$

$$i = 0, 1, \ldots, n + l - 1.$$

When the buffer queue is not full, hosts service the tasks immediately; then the probability distribution at this time is as follows:

$$W_a(t) = q_0 + q_1 + q_2 + \cdots + q_{n-1} = \sum_{i=1}^{n-1} \frac{\pi_i}{1 - \pi_{n+l}}. \quad (6)$$

When a task arrives at the buffer, if there are tasks already in the queue, the newly arriving task has to wait until its front tasks have been completed. Distribution of exit tasks stream for each host is following negative exponential distribution with parameter μ. When the number of the hosts is n, the system distribution for exit tasks stream is subject to negative exponential distribution with parameter $n\mu$. In these circumstances, we derive the Erlang distribution as follows:

$$W_a(t) = W_a(0) + \sum_{i=n}^{n+l-1} P\{0 < W_a \leq t\}$$

$$= W_a(0) + \sum_{i=n}^{n+l-1} q_i \int_0^t \frac{n\mu (n\mu x)^{i-n}}{(i-n)!} e^{-n\mu x} dx \quad (7)$$

$$= \sum_{i=1}^{n-1} \frac{\pi_i}{1 - \pi_{n+l}} + \sum_{i=n}^{n+l-1} q_i \int_0^t \frac{n\mu (n\mu x)^{i-n}}{(i-n)!} e^{-n\mu x} dx.$$

Response time is equal to the waiting time and the service time; consider the following:

$$W(t) = P\{W \leq t\} = \int_0^t P\{W_a \leq t - x\} \mu e^{-\mu t} dx$$

$$= \int_0^t W_a(t) \mu e^{-\mu t} dx. \quad (8)$$

By responding to the distribution function of time, the relationship between the percentage of the number of servers and QoS can be obtained. If the response time in the percentage of ΔT is φ, then $W \geq \varphi$; consider $T < 0.05$; it indicates that the response time is less than 0.05 seconds.

(2) The Average Queue Length. Depending on the desired definition, the average queue length in the buffer can be written as follows:

$$\overline{N_a} = \sum_{k=n}^{n+l} (k - n) \pi_k$$

$$= \frac{n^n \rho^{n+1} \pi_0}{n! \left(1 - \rho\right)^2} \left(1 - (l+1)\rho^l + l\rho^{l+1}\right), \quad \rho < 1. \quad (9)$$

The average queue length is equal to the queued requests waiting for service and the sum of the number of requests. The average queue length is as follows:

$$\overline{N} = \overline{N_a} + \overline{N_s} = \overline{N_a} + \rho\left(1 - \pi_{n+l}\right)$$

$$= \frac{n^n \rho^{n+1} \pi_0}{n! \left(1 - \rho\right)^2} \left(1 - (l+1)\rho^l + l\rho^{l+1}\right)$$

$$+ n\rho\left(1 - \frac{n^n \rho^{n+l} \pi_0}{n!}\right) \quad (10)$$

$$= \frac{n^n \rho^{n+1} \pi_0 \left(1 - (l+1)\rho^l + l\rho^{l+1}\right)}{n! \left(1 - \rho\right)^2}$$

$$+ n\rho\left(1 - \frac{n^n \rho^{n+l} \pi_0}{n!}\right).$$

According to queuing model proposed above, when all hosts in private cloud have been fully allocated, VM manager buys VMs resources. For this situation, we give the system benefits function as follows:

$$F\left(c, h'\right) = \delta N' - \left[\varepsilon W_a + c\left(h' - n\right) + En\right], \quad (11)$$

where c represents the price of buying VMs in the market. h' represents the number of hosts being demanded. δ and ε represent constant factors. N' represents the throughput of processing tasks. E represents the cost of energy of provided VMs in a private cloud.

The goal of this paper is to solve the provisioning strategy to ensure the best interests of resource providers in different relations, based on the assumption of considering the market as a whole.

Resource consumer demand F_c is a function of the price c. Demand function is as follows:

$$F_c = \arg\max F\left(c, h'\right). \quad (12)$$

For the resource requirements of a private cloud, the demand function is as follows:

$$F_d(c) = \sum_{k=0}^{I} h'_{d,k} \chi_{\Xi_{d,k}}(c) = \begin{cases} \sum_{k=0}^{I} h'_{d,k}, & c \in \Xi_{d,k} \\[2ex] 0, & \text{otherwise,} \end{cases} \quad (13)$$

where I indicates the total number of steps. $h'_{d,k}$ represents the number of VMs that buyer needs at the stage of step k. Ξ is the price range at step k. $\Xi_{d,k} = (\Phi_{d,k-1}, \Phi_{d,k}]$, where $\Phi_{d,k}$ is the right margin. d is the number of buyers. For $d \in [1, 2, \ldots, D]$, $\Xi_{d,0} = 0$, $\Xi_{d,1} = (0, \Phi_{d,1}]$. $\chi_{\Xi_{i,k}}$ is the index function of demand.

$$\chi_{\Xi}(c) = \begin{cases} 1, & c \in \Xi \\ 0, & \text{otherwise} \end{cases}$$

$$\Phi_i = \Phi_{\widehat{d}, \widehat{k}}$$

$$h' = \sum_{d=1}^{D} F_{(c,h')}(\Phi_i) \tag{14}$$

s.t. $\quad (\widehat{d}, \widehat{k}) = \arg \min_{\Phi_{i,k'} \in \mathbb{Q}_k} \Phi_{i,k'}$

$$Q_k = \{(\Phi_{i,k'}) \mid \Phi_{i,k'} > \Phi_{k-1}\}.$$

Therefore, the total consumer demand is

$$F(c) = \sum_{k=0}^{I} h'_k \chi_{\Xi_k}(c). \tag{15}$$

From the above analysis, we get the total demand price function. That is an inversion of the consumer demand function, given as follows:

$$F^{-1}(c') = \sum_{k=0}^{I} \Phi_{I-1} \chi_{\Xi_k}(c') = \begin{cases} \sum_{k=0}^{I} \Phi_{I-1}, & c' \in \Xi_k \\ 0, & \text{otherwise}, \end{cases} \tag{16}$$

where $\Phi_0 = 0$, $\Xi_k = (\Phi_{k-1}, \Phi_k]$, $\Xi_I = (\Phi_{I-1}, \infty]$, and $\chi_{\Xi}(c')$ is the index function of price:

$$\chi_{\Xi}(c') = \begin{cases} 1, & c' \in \Xi \\ 0, & \text{otherwise}. \end{cases} \tag{17}$$

4. Noncooperative Game Based NCGRAA

In the market, the situation that multiple cloud resource providers compete with each other may be noncooperative game model. Noncooperative game theory is perfectly rational in the context of the strategy with interdependence interaction theory. Particularly, noncooperative game theory focuses on solving the problem for rational stakeholders from multiple rows cooperative game resources, mutual influence, and effect arising from the analysis of the resources. The most excellent choice is a function that all other competitors selected. Nash equilibrium strategies seek to optimize the effectiveness of the time optimized configuration of resources.

We express resource providers providing VMs as space strategy. In cloud computing market, the behavior of all the resources providers can be represented as Cartesian product $S = S_1 \times S_2 \times \cdots \times S_o$, where S_o represents a resource provider o's strategy set.

Utility represents obtained satisfaction by providing a service or a resource rent and each resource provider's expected revenue is represented by the utility function, that is, $\{U_o\} = \{U_1, U_2, \ldots, U_O\}$, $o \in \{1, 2, \ldots, O\}$. s is the choice strategy of the resource providers in the game. If the game participant o is with the strategy s_o, $s_{o'}$ is the representation of selection strategy by all other resource providers except o and $s_{o'} = s - s_o$. Then the participant utility is expressed as $U_o(s)$.

In the cloud computing market, all the resource providers want to obtain the most optimal strategy according to price function. Considering the case of a single resource provider, the returns function is as follows:

$$u(s) = sF_{(c,h')}^{-1}(s) - F_c(s). \tag{18}$$

Among them, the right first term indicates the total income provided by the VMs. Introducing cost function can improve the system performance and it is defined as follows:

$$F_c(s) = sF_{uf} - F_f, \tag{19}$$

where F_{uf} is the variable costs of resource providers providing VMs and it includes the cost of the buffer. F_f is the fixed costs of resource providers providing VMs.

Strategic optimization can be formalized as

$$s^+ = \arg \max_s u(s). \tag{20}$$

According to (20), benefits of single resource provider are as follows:

$$u^+(s) = s^+ F_{(c,h')}^{-1}(s^+) - F_f - s^+ F_{uf}, \tag{21}$$

where price function is nonincreasing step function. The number of steps is finite and it can be solved by enumeration method.

For a cloud resource market with resource providers o, given other resource providers VMs, the strategy of VMs providing of resource provider o is optimal. For all resources providers, the following equation is given:

$$U_o(s_o^+, s_{o'}) \geq U_o(s_o, s_{o'}). \tag{22}$$

There is the following optimization problem solution:

$$s_o^+ \in \arg \max_{s_o \in S_o} U_o(s_o, s_{o'}). \tag{23}$$

Suppose resource providers provide alternatives with fixed costs and there is variable cost. Marginal cost is zero. The utility function is

$$U_o = sF_{(c,h')}^{-1}(s) - F_f^{(o)} - sF_{uf}^{(o)}, \tag{24}$$

where $F_f^{(o)}$ is fixed cost and $F_{uf}^{(o)}$ is variable cost.

In order to obtain Nash equilibrium strategy, we describe Nash equilibrium as follows: we find out the best solution for each player in game and then figure out strategy combination composed of the best strategy for each player.

Optimal response strategy means that the strategy is optimal among the given strategies of all other resource providers.

$$s_o^+ = \arg\max U_o\left(s_o, s_{o'}\right), \tag{25}$$

where $U_o(s_o, s_{o'}) = s_o F_{(c,h')}^{-1}(s_o + s_{o'}) - F_f^{(o)} - sF_{uf}^{(o)}$.

As the price function is nonincreasing step function, we obtain that

$$s_o^+ = h_{k^+}' - s_{o'}$$

$$j^+ = \underset{j \in \{1,2,\dots,j'\}}{\arg\max} \quad \left[\Phi_k\left(h_k' - s_{o'}\right) - F_f^{(o)} - \left(h_k' - s_{o'}\right)F_{uf}^{(o)}\right]$$

$$\text{s.t.} \quad j' = \underset{h_k' \in \mathbb{Z}}{\arg\min} h_k' \tag{26}$$

$$Z = \left\{\left(h_k'\right) \mid h_k' > s_{o'}\right\}.$$

Using the optimal response, Nash equilibrium is defined as

$$s_{o'}^+ = f\left(\overrightarrow{s_{o'}^+}\right)$$

$$\overrightarrow{s_{o'}^+} = \left[s_1^+, s_2^+, \dots, s_{o-1}^+, s_{o+1}^+, \dots, s_O^+\right]^T, \tag{27}$$

where $\overrightarrow{s_{o'}^+}$ represents the optimal response vector.

At this time, utility function with Nash equilibrium strategy of resource provider o represents the receipts of noncooperation market resulting as follows:

$$R_{\text{MR}}^+ = U_o\left(s_o^+, \overrightarrow{s_{o'}^+}\right). \tag{28}$$

Theorem 1. *If a task selects a VM which is not in the possible set of optional VMs, the task scheduling scheme is not a Nash equilibrium solution.*

Proof. The current task number is greater than or equal to the VMs set, so there is no task that can be chosen, except the set of VMs. The number of tasks is less than that of the VMs, assuming that a task i is scheduled to VM except the possible set. Then according to the possible set of VMs, besides i task, the number of rest tasks is assigned as $N - 1$. According to the principle of Nash, there must be at least one VM which may not be assigned, so, for this task, $U_i > U_{\text{oth}}$. U_i is the benefit for the reason that the task i is scheduled to the possible VM and U_{oth} is the benefit for the reason that the task i is scheduled to the VM not in the possible set.

Because Nash equilibrium is defined under the condition of invariable environment, the entire individual cannot achieve higher yields by changing its own strategy. The formula below is tenable:

$$\forall k, \quad f\left(s_1, \dots, s_i, \dots, s_n\right) \geq f\left(s_1, \dots, s_k, \dots, s_n\right), \tag{29}$$

where s_i is the strategy for the task i and $f(s_1, \dots, s_i, \dots, s_n)$ is the benefit at the strategy s_i.

It is at odds with the definition of Nash equilibrium solutions, so if task i selects the possible VMs, the task scheduling scheme is not Nash equilibrium solution of the scheduling problem. $\square$

Theorem 2. *In the noncooperative game with a finite number of players model, for $o \in \{1, 2, \dots, O\}$, sufficient conditions for the existence of Nash equilibrium are the following:*

(1) *Strategy space $\{S_o\}$ is a nonempty compact convex set in Euclidean space.*

(2) *Utility function $U_o(s)$ is continuous in $\{S_o\}$ and is quasi-concave function.*

Proof. As the number of VMs available is limited for each resource provider in terms of a single integer point set, its strategy space for real axis is clearly a nonempty compact convex set in Euclidean space. Because the number of VMs is an integer number and greater than zero, the price function is as the number of linearly decreasing functions at this time. The utility function is continuous in space strategy map.

$$\frac{\partial U_o\left(s_o, \overrightarrow{s_{o'}}\right)}{\partial s_o} = F_{(c,h')}^{-1}\left(s_o\right) + s\frac{\partial F_{(c,h')}^{-1}\left(s_o\right)}{\partial s_o}$$

$$- \frac{\partial F(s)}{\partial s_o} \tag{30}$$

$$\frac{\partial^2 U_o\left(s_o, \overrightarrow{s_{o'}}\right)}{\partial s_o^2} = 2\frac{\partial F_{(c,h')}^{-1}\left(s_o\right)}{\partial s_o} + \frac{\partial^2 F_{(c,h')}^{-1}\left(s_o\right)}{\partial s_o^2},$$

where the price function is a decreasing linear function and $\partial^2 U_o(s_o, \overrightarrow{s_{o'}})/\partial s_o^2 < 0$. Then $U_o(s)$ is concave in the strategy space.

By Theorem 2, it shows that there is Nash equilibrium strategy for cloud resources provided in a competitive market.

$$\frac{\partial U_o\left(s_o, \overrightarrow{s_{o'}}\right)}{\partial s_o} = 0 \Longrightarrow$$

$$s_o = \frac{-F_{(c,h')}^{-1}\left(s_o\right) + \partial F(s)/\partial s_o}{\partial F_{(c,h')}^{-1}\left(s_o\right)/\partial s_o}. \tag{31}$$

By the above formula, Nash equilibrium can be represented as a matrix form.

$$\mathbf{E}(\mathbf{s}) = \mathbf{C}\overline{\mathbf{s}} + \mathbf{Z}, \tag{32}$$

where $\mathbf{E}(\mathbf{s})$ represents a mapping from the space $\mathbf{R}^O$ to $\mathbf{R}^O$. $\mathbf{C}$ and $\mathbf{Z}$ are zero-order matrixes.

Nash equilibrium is to prove that the uniqueness of $\mathbf{E}(\mathbf{s})$ is a standard function that satisfies the following:

(1) Positive: $\mathbf{E}(\mathbf{s}) > 0$.

(2) Monotonic: if $x < y$, then $\mathbf{E}(x) \geq \mathbf{E}(y)$.

(3) Scalability: for any $\omega > 1$, there is $\omega\mathbf{E}(x) \geq \mathbf{E}(\omega x)$.

Since each cloud resource provider in the market obtains certain benefits through the VMs providing, namely, $\mathbf{E}(\mathbf{s}) > 0$, that meets (1). Proving the existence of the process, because the price is understood to be a linear decreasing function, we can see that the nature (2) is satisfied. For a linear function, a function of the nature (3) scalability is satisfied.

To sum up, $E(s)$ is a standard function and, for a standard function, fixed point is unique. Therefore, Nash equilibrium of NCGRAA algorithm is unique.

The process of algorithm of NCGRAA is as follows.

Step 1. When there is a set of a new request arriving, it makes this set of VMs have the maximum profit and minimum completion time of the VMs.

   (a) According to the system running state and the tasks users submit, compute the running time and make sure that each task has the profit of each VM.

   (b) Sort each task profit and find out each set for the task.

   (c) Summarize set.

Step 2. Find all possible task groups with the intersection and generate the corresponding conflict task group. Perform the noncooperative game analysis and then identify Nash equilibrium for all conflict task groups and generate for each conflict task group the Nash equilibrium solution. Generate Nash equilibrium solution set for all conflict task groups, the Nash equilibrium solution for task scheduling problem and optimal Nash equilibrium solution.

   (a) Analyze the task groups. After that, find out the tasks with intersection and generate the corresponding conflict task group.

   (b) For each conflict set, find out the Nash equilibrium solution and generate the Nash equilibrium solution set and the Nash equilibrium solution for the corresponding task scheduling problem.

   (c) According to the system revenue for Nash equilibrium solution to the current task scheduling problem and the overall completion time for task, find out the optimal Nash equilibrium solution for the current task scheduling problem.

Step 3. According to the task scheduling result with the optimal Nash equilibrium, each task is assigned to the selected VM. The allocation results are recorded in task scheduling log.

   (a) According to the task scheduling result with the optimal Nash equilibrium, determine the service VM and perform the task.

   (b) Record the task scheduling results in the log.

Step 4. Continue monitoring a user action, running the task scheduling algorithm for the next set of task scheduling requests. □

5. Bargaining Game Based BGRAA

Although NCGRAA makes resource provider optimal profit, it is not the biggest gain. If resource providers can mutually agree, it will have more collective gains. The kind of bargain in the market resource provider of income will be greater than or equal to the cooperative competition in the market returns.

In a negotiated market, resource providers improve their income by the way of negotiating. Market can benefit from the

bargaining game model. The resource providers can mutually agree to bargain to get the satisfaction, which has the two aspects, both efficiency and fairness of the VM provided on the basis of strategy. Efficiency requirements can contain Pareto efficiency and the overall revenue maximization. The solution is defined as Nash bargaining equilibrium of bargaining game.

5.1. Nash Bargaining Game Model for Resource Allocation

Definition 3. All the resource providers in the cloud computing market environment are defined as the game participants, expressed as RP_o, $o \in \{1, 2, \ldots, O\}$.

Definition 4. B is the set of VM bargaining problem, $F \in \mathbf{R}^O$ is the set space of resource provider, and Γ is the minimum expected value for earnings. $\Gamma = (R_{\mathrm{MR}}^{(1)*}, \ldots, R_{\mathrm{MR}}^{(o)*}, \ldots, R_{\mathrm{MR}}^{(O)*})$.

Definition 5. When $\{R_{\mathrm{bar}}^{(o)} \in \mathbf{F} \mid R_{\mathrm{bar}}^{(o)} \geq R_{\mathrm{MR}}^{(o)*}, \forall o\}$ is not empty bounded set, $(\mathbf{F}, \Gamma) \in \mathbf{B}$ is the bargaining game problem.

A bargaining solution is to put each bargaining problem $(\mathbf{F}, \Gamma) \in \mathbf{B}$ linked with a special result $R_{\mathrm{bar}}^* = \psi(\mathbf{F}, \Gamma)$ as a function, named $\psi : \mathbf{B} \to \mathbf{R}^O$.

Axiom 1. Feasibility of axioms: $R_{\mathrm{bar}}^* \in \mathbf{F}$.

Axiom 2. Individual rational axiom: $R_{\mathrm{bar}} \geq R_{\mathrm{NE}}^*$, $\forall o$.

Axiom 3. Pareto efficiency axiom: $R_{\mathrm{bar}} \geq R_{\mathrm{bar}}^* = \psi(\mathbf{F}, \Gamma) \Rightarrow R_{\mathrm{bar}} = R_{\mathrm{bar}}^* = \psi(\mathbf{F}, \Gamma)$.

Axiom 2 shows that in addition to the bargaining solution there is no other way for Pareto improvement. We can derive the following axiom.

Axiom 4. The invariance of the linear transformation axiom: $R_{\mathrm{bar}}^* \in \mathbf{F}$; for any linear transformation ϕ, there is $\phi(\psi(\mathbf{F}, \Gamma)) = \psi(\phi(\mathbf{F}), \phi(\Gamma))$.

Axiom 5. Independence of the axiom of choice: to any convex set $\mathbf{E}$ there is a subset $\mathbf{F}$, and it is given as follows:

$$R_{\mathrm{bar}}^* \in \mathbf{E} \subseteq \mathbf{F} \Longrightarrow$$
$$\psi(\mathbf{E}, \Gamma) = \psi(\mathbf{F}, \Gamma). \tag{33}$$

Axiom 6. Symmetry axiom: for any $(\mathbf{F}, \Gamma)$, there is $R_{\mathrm{MR}}^{(i)*} = R_{\mathrm{MR}}^{(j)*}$, $(R_{\mathrm{bar}}^{(i)}, R_{\mathrm{bar}}^{(j)}) \in \mathbf{F}$. It means that, for any $(R_{\mathrm{bar}}^{(i)}, R_{\mathrm{bar}}^{(j)}) \in \mathbf{F}$, $R_{\mathrm{bar}}^{(i)*} = R_{\mathrm{bar}}^{(j)*} \in \psi(\mathbf{F}, \Gamma)$ must satisfy $R_{\mathrm{bar}}^{(i)*} = R_{\mathrm{bar}}^{(j)*}$.

Nash bargaining solution: Nash bargaining solution refers as the Nash equilibrium solution that the participants gain their interests in a game, when they have many times of bargaining and gradually eliminating the Nash solution.

Introduction of Pareto evolutionary method is to obtain the optimal solution of BGRAA.

We give a multiobjective optimization problem and make a feasible solution set as the optimization goal. If there is a feasible solution, for each solution, it would be either the global optimal solution or the global extreme value point.

Evolving any two different individuals in population, if there is dominance, it must meet the following two conditions: there is at least one target and the subgoals are not bad.

Theorem 6. *Meeting axioms 1 to 6, the only solution of bargaining problem is the utility of vector that maximizes the product Nash bargaining solution. Namely, solutions meet the following constrained optimization problem:*

$$\psi(\mathbf{F}, \Gamma) \in \arg\max \prod_{o=1}^{O} \left(R_{bar}^{(o)*} - R_{MR}^{(o)*} \right)$$
$$s.t. \quad R_{bar}^{*} \in \mathbf{F} \tag{34}$$
$$R_{bar}^{(o)*} \geq R_{MR}^{(o)*}.$$

Considering the resource of resource provider $s^{\max}$ and the limitation of lowest income of resource provider in non-cooperative game, the optimization goal is to give the effective control to the resource provider and achieve the goal of utility optimization. The selection of the utility function U is given as follows:

$$U = \prod_{o=1}^{O} \left(R_{bar}^{(o)*} - R_{MR}^{(o)*} \right)$$
$$s.t. \quad R_{bar}^{*} \in \mathbf{F} \tag{35}$$
$$R_{bar}^{(o)*} \geq R_{MR}^{(o)*}$$
$$s_o \leq s^{\max}.$$

5.2. Solution for Bargaining Game Problem of BGRAA. The solution of (35) is needed to be divided into two kinds of solution as follows.

(a) Nash solution for bargaining for two people in the game is considered.

When $o = 2$, (35) can be represented as

$$\left(R_{bar}^{(i)*}, R_{bar}^{(j)*} \right) = \psi(\mathbf{F}, \Gamma)$$
$$= \arg\max \left(R_{bar}^{(i)} - R_{MR}^{(i)*} \right) \left(R_{bar}^{(j)} - R_{MR}^{(j)*} \right). \tag{36}$$

The resources provisioning algorithm when $o = 2$ is as follows:

Step 1. Initialize the parameters $s_i = s_i^{\text{init}}$, $s_j = s_j^{\text{init}}$.

Step 2. Select the increment step length I, where $s_i^{(k+1)} = s_i^{(k)} + I$, $s_j^{(k+1)} = s_j^{(k)} + I$, and calculate the Pareto optimal point between $[0, s_i^{\max}]$, $[0, s_j^{\max}]$.

Step 3. From $(R_{bar}^{(i)} - R_{MR}^{(i)*}) \times (R_{bar}^{(j)} - R_{MR}^{(j)*}) = C$, calculate the corresponding strategy s_i, s_j, and the earnings of resource providers in NBS.

IF s_i and s_j reach convergence **THEN**

> Return to Step 2.

ELSE

Record each convergence value. s_i and s_j are the optimal solution of the system.

Or calculate content conditions: $\pi = \arg\max((R_{\text{bar}}^{(i)} + R_{\text{bar}}^{(j)})/((s_i + s_j)|R_{\text{bar}}^{(i)} - R_{\text{bar}}^{(j)}|))$, then return s_i and s_j.

ENDIF

(b) Nash solution for bargaining when the number of people is o in the game.

By Hungary algorithm, the problem can be converted into $o = 2$ bargaining problems, so as to provide the optimal system resources. Bargaining algorithm is shown as follows.

Step 1. Obtain the parameters from the provider and demand ones in the cloud market environment.

Step 2.

IF the number of the resource provider is even number **THEN**

> Go to the Step 3.

ENDIF

IF the number of the resource provider is odd number **THEN**

> Give an provider with none resource.

ENDIF

Step 3. Using the Hungarian method to make the resource provider into two groups.

Step 4. Through bargaining algorithm, return to the two bargaining Nash standard solution, and compute s_i, s_j, $R_{\text{bar}}^{(i)}$, $R_{\text{bar}}^{(j)}$.

Step 5. Go to Steps 3 and 4, until the NBS cannot be effective, return the parameters: s_i, s_j, $R_{\text{bar}}^{(i)}$, $R_{\text{bar}}^{(j)}$.

6. Performance Evaluation

Considering three types of resources, the CPU, memory, and hard disk, we use Google Cluster Trace workload reference data source as the data center, including user information, task types, task number, the number of subtasks, the subtasks resource request parameters, and resource utilization. Local clusters are composed of four computers and each computer is configured to CPU Intel (R) Core (TM) 2 Duo E8200 2.66 GHz, 3 GB memory, and 160 GB hard drive. These nodes are interconnected by a 1 Gbps bandwidth switch. Amazon EC2 environment consists of 80 small instances, which are configured to Inter Xeon CPU E5430 2.66 GHz, 1.7 GB memory, and 146.77 GB hard drive.

First, we show the performance of the algorithm itself. Then, we compare the performance with HM (Hadoop

Mechanism) and GM (Google Management Mechanism) individually, in the aspect of fair distribution, average utility, and the system throughput. Finally, we compare the algorithms NCGRAA, BGRAA, and GEA (General Equilibrium Algorithm) at the average utility, system throughput, and fairness.

In simulation, considering the length of the buffer and the queue, when $n = 100$, $n = 200$, and $n = 400$, the diversification of average queue length in the system is shown in Figure 2.

In Figure 2, in $M/M/50/50 + l$ model, the average queue length curve with increasing buffer changes smoothly. In $M/M/100/100 + l$, then, the average queue length slowly increases. In $M/M/200/200 + l$, the change of the buffer size does not affect the average queue length. From Figure 2, we can provide a buffer to ease the pressure on scarce resources in the system, while it will not cause big losses. In terms of shared resources in cloud computing system, equitable distribution of resources is especially important. Thus, the establishment of a buffer can reduce the load on the system to some extent, and it improves the overall performance of the system.

Figure 3 shows the influence of different task arrival rate on resource consumer revenue.

Task arrival rate is defined as the number of tasks when tasks arrive per minute. For fixed task arrival rate, the revenue increases with an increasing number of VMs. The lesser the request of the number of VMs, the longer the waiting time and the higher the loss for users. Thus performance degradation speed is fast. As the request of the number of VMs increases, the price of resource consumers paying the provider will also increase. The change of revenue is from increase to decrease; at this situation, the optimal number of VMs can maximize resources consumer revenue.

We set different number of resource providers, to make a research on the influence between the different size of the market resources and the convergence property. We give the number of resource providers from 3 to 6. With these numbers of resources providers, Figures 4(a) and 4(b) show how the utility changes with the number of iterations at the NCGRAA algorithm.

In Figures 4(a) and 4(b), initially, the resource providers constantly adjust strategy, to seek the best Nash equilibrium solution for resources provided. Subsequently, utility tends to be steady, and the resources reach equilibrium. At the same time, the lesser the number of resource providers is, the faster the NCGRAA algorithm can converge. As the number of resource providers increases, more iteration is needed to achieve utility state of stability. The overall situation is that the strategy can get a good convergence.

The results above indicate the robustness and convergence of the NCGRAA algorithm. In convergence condition, the number of the VMs to provide is the focus problem in Nash equilibrium strategy for resource provider; therefore, the cooperation in the market resource provider can timely adjust the strategy to achieve Nash equilibrium.

The third set of experiments investigates the performance of several algorithms, including the average utility, system throughput, and fairness.

Figures 5(a) and 5(b) show the changes of utility with BGRAA algorithm under different size of the market, the initial parameters, and size of the market that is the same to NCGRAA algorithm's.

It can be seen in Figures 5(a) and 5(b) that, with the increase of number of resource providers, more iteration is needed to achieve Nash bargaining equilibrium strategies. Namely, the Nash bargaining solution is in the Pareto optimal set which makes the products of the utility maximize. When utility has reached the convergence, then Pareto optimal solution reaches the border part of the negotiation strategy sets. At this point, the corresponding negotiation strategies and the corresponding utility for all resource providers are fair.

Figure 6 shows the influence of the amount of resources consumers on the average utility of the resource provider. It can be seen in Figure 6, with the increase of number of consumers, that utility increases. This is due to the increase of resource request. In addition, for the same resource consumer number, the effectiveness of the algorithm BGRAA is always higher than or equal to the utility of NCGRAA algorithm. This is because in bargaining negotiation among resources providers can reduce the number of VMs but enhance the utility of resource prices. In the market competition, resource providers compete against each other for more VMs. The disadvantage of this issue is that the resource price is low. Then the overall effect cannot achieve the maximum, but it can achieve the optimal value. Each HM or GM adjusts resource prices, based on general equilibrium without considering the relationship between competition and cooperation. Thus the average utility of HM and GM is lower than the ones of NCGRAA and BGRAA.

Figure 7 shows the change of system throughput. It can be seen in Figure 7 that as the number of resource providers increases the number of tasks per unit time also increases. Therefore, the system throughput has increased continuously. The throughput of BGRAA algorithm is the biggest of these algorithms by reducing resource price offering more VMs. In NCGRAA algorithm, when the total utility increases at the same time, the throughput increases. Although the HM and GM without the game theory are effective, they are not suitable for the system with some market parameters.

Figure 8 shows the fairness of the comparison results. The fairness of the allocation of resources in the cloud computing is significantly important. In BGRAA algorithm, performance parameter π is related to fairness and the throughput. It can be seen from Figure 8, along with the increase of the number of resource providers, that the change trend of HM and GM is bigger than that of NCGRAA and BGRAA algorithms. HM and GM algorithms ignore the mutual relationship between resource providers and resource allocation. The NBS of BGRAA algorithm encourages devotion to their utility. In NCGRAA algorithm, the utility is optimal and fairness principle is stable.

As shown in Figure 9, it can be seen that with the increasing number of consumers utility increases, because of the number of requested resources. As can be seen from Figure 9, the effectiveness of the algorithm is always higher than or equal to the utility algorithms. This is

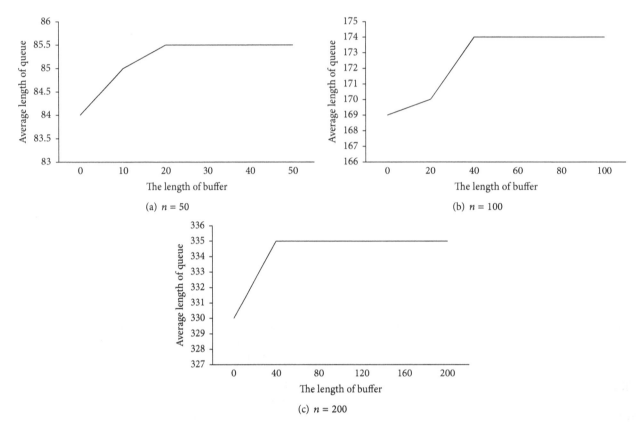

(a) $n = 50$

(b) $n = 100$

(c) $n = 200$

FIGURE 2: Influence of l on the average of length of queue.

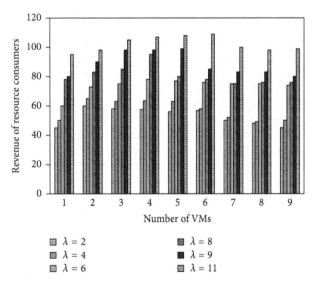

FIGURE 3: Influence between the number of VMs and revenue of resource consumers.

because in the negotiable market consultations between the resource providers can reduce the number of VMs and reach higher resource prices and utility. In noncooperative market competition, the resource providers provide more VMs competing for more market sharing. However, with lower resource prices, the overall effectiveness only achieves mutual optimum. GEA algorithm does not consider competition

and cooperation between providers of resources. And the resources are adjusted according to consumers' needs. That is bounded to affect the individual income.

Figure 10 shows the changes in system throughput; it can be seen that with the increased number of resource providers the number of tasks processed per unit of time also increases, so system throughput increases. NCGRAA by reducing resource prices provides more VMs and obtains the maximum throughput. On the contrary, the total utility increases with the loss of some throughput. GEA's throughput improvement curve is lower than the algorithms without considering cooperation competition between resources and users.

Figure 11 shows a fair comparison of the three algorithms. In the algorithm BGRAA, the parameter π is involved in fairness and throughput. As can be seen from the figure, as the number of resource providers increases, trends of NCGRAA and BGRAA are significantly greater than the GEA, which ignores the interaction between resource providers and lacks fairness. The welfare of bargaining between the two sides attaches great importance. It does not encourage the two sides to pursue their own utility while ignoring the other utilities.

7. Conclusion

The high efficiency and stable resources mechanism is needed for study of cloud computing resources management. Therefore, NCGRAA and BGRAA algorithms were proposed in

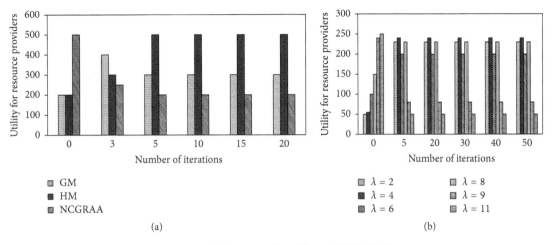

(a)   (b)

FIGURE 4: Influence on the utility with NCGRAA.

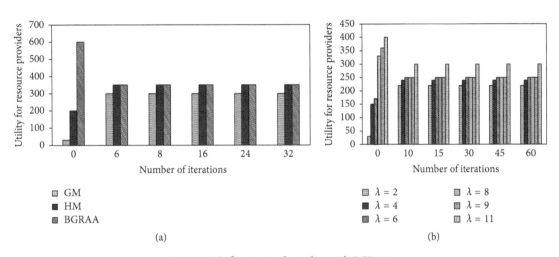

(a)   (b)

FIGURE 5: Influence on the utility with BGRAA.

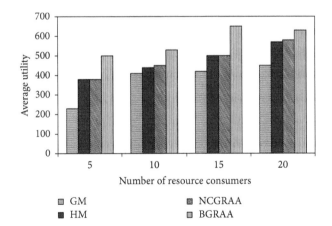

FIGURE 6: Influence of resource provider number on the system average utility.

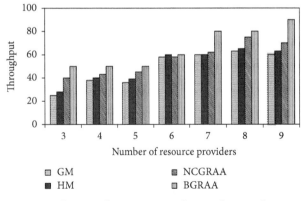

FIGURE 7: Influence of resource provider number on the system throughput.

this paper to solve this problem. The algorithms made competing resource allocation converge to the Nash equilibrium strategy. Meanwhile, algorithms bring resource competitors optimal benefits and improved collective benefits. Based on the numerical results of some key performance measures, we discussed the influence of NCGRAA and BGRAA algorithms. These algorithms not only ensured fair constraints,

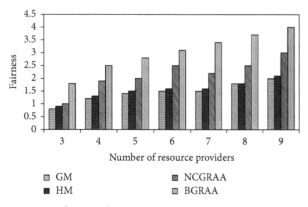

FIGURE 8: Influence of resource provider number on the fairness.

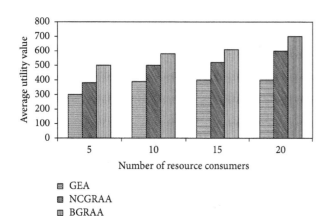

FIGURE 9: Comparison of average utility in different algorithms.

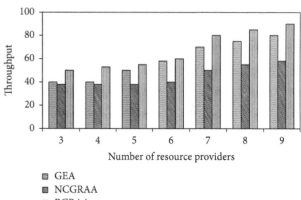

FIGURE 10: Comparison of throughput in different algorithms.

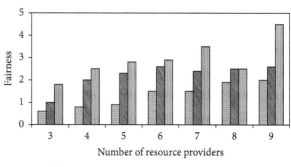

FIGURE 11: Comparison of fairness in different algorithms.

but also improved the efficiency of resource allocation. Meanwhile, it also shows that NCGRAA and BGRAA algorithms result in the slight increase of consumption.

In this work, we only focus on the resource allocation in the cloud computing. As a future work, we will extend the research by considering data transmission in other specific circumstances and security transaction in the negotiation process.

Parameters

λ: Arrival rate of task
l: Buffer length
π_k: Probability of the queue length being k
$N(t)$:   Queue length at time t
$\overline{N_a(t)}$:   Average queue length
N: Number of tasks
$W_a(t)$:   Waiting time
$W(t)$:   Response time.

Competing Interests

The authors declare that they have no competing interests.

Acknowledgments

This research was supported by the Natural Science Foundation of China (no. 61300194).

References

[1] J. Nim and A. Anandasivam, "SORMA-business cases for an open grid market: concept and implementation," in *Proceedings of the 5th International Workshop on Grid Economics and Business Models*, pp. 173–184, August 2003.

[2] A. J. Younge and Z. Wang, "Efficient resource management for cloud computing environments," in *Proceedings of the Green Computing International Conference*, pp. 357–364, August 2010.

[3] W. Yang, Z. Peng, L. Dong, Z. Hualiang, and Y. Haibin, "A performance modeling of decentralized cloud computing based on multiple $M/M/m/m+m$ queuing systems," *Acta Electronica Sinca*, vol. 42, no. 10, pp. 2055–2059, 2015.

[4] G. Ping and B. Ling-ling, "The resource management model for cloud computing based on electronics," in *Proceedings of the Electrical & Electronics Engineering (EEESYM '12)*, pp. 471–474, Kuala Lumpur, Malaysia, June 2012.

[5] R. J. Al-Ali, K. Amin, G. V. Laszewski et al., "Scheduling independent multiprocessor tasks," *Journal of Grid Computing*, vol. 2, no. 2, pp. 163–182, 2004.

[6] A. K. Amoura, E. Bampis, C. Kenyon, and Y. Manoussakis, "Scheduling independent multiprocessor tasks," *Algorithmica*, vol. 32, no. 2, pp. 247–261, 2002.

[7] S. Borst, O. Boxma, J. F. Groote, and S. Mauw, "Task allocation in a multi-server system," *Journal of Scheduling*, vol. 6, no. 5, pp. 423–436, 2003.

[8] R. Buyya, D. Abramson, J. Giddy, and H. Stockinger, "Economic models for resource management and scheduling in grid computing," *Concurrency and Computation: Practice and Experience*, vol. 14, no. 13–15, pp. 1507–1542, 2002.

[9] A. Doğan and F. Özgüner, "Scheduling independent tasks with QoS requirements in grid computing with time-varying resource prices," in *Proceedings of the 3rd International Workshop on Grid Computing, Baltimore, Md, USA, November 2002*, vol. 2536, pp. 58–69, Springer, 2002.

[10] M. A. Iverson, F. Özgüner, and L. Potter, "Statistical prediction of task execution times through analytic benchmarking for scheduling in a heterogeneous environment," *IEEE Transactions on Computers*, vol. 48, no. 12, pp. 1374–1379, 1999.

[11] L. Keqin, "Experimental performance evaluation of job scheduling and processor allocation algorithms for grid computing on metacomputers," in *Proceedings of the 18th International Parallel and Distributed Processing Symposium (IPDPS '04)*, pp. 170–177, Santa Fe, NM, USA, April 2004.

[12] K. Ranganathan, M. Ripeanu, A. Sarin, and I. Foster, "Incentive mechanisms for large collaborative resource sharing," in *Proceedings of the IEEE International Symposium on Cluster Computing and the Grid (CCGrid '04)*, pp. 1–8, IEEE, Chicago, Ill, USA, April 2004.

[13] R. Wolski, J. S. Plank, T. Bryan, and J. Brevik, "G-commerce: market formulations controlling resource allocation on the computational grid," in *Proceedings of the 15th International Parallel and Distributed Processing Symposium*, pp. 46–52, April 2000.

[14] J. K. Lenstra, D. B. Shmoys, and É. Tardos, "Approximation algorithms for scheduling unrelated parallel machines," *Mathematical Programming*, vol. 46, no. 1, pp. 259–271, 1990.

[15] G. Christodoulou, E. Koutsoupias, and A. Vidali, "A lower bound for scheduling mechanisms," *Algorithmica*, vol. 55, no. 4, pp. 729–740, 2009.

[16] C. Askarian, "A survey for load balancing in mobile WiMAX networks," *Advanced Computing*, vol. 3, no. 2, pp. 119–137, 2012.

[17] D. Gkantsidis, O. Vytiniotis, D. Hodson, F. Narayanan Dinu, and A. Rowstron, "Rhea: automatic filtering for unstructured cloud storage," in *Proceedings of the 10th USENIX Symposium on Networked Systems Design and Implementation (NSDI '13)*, vol. 106, no. 40, pp. 343–355, Lombard, Ill, USA, 2013.

[18] Y. Dongmei and L. Chenghua, "Optimized collaborative filtering recommendation based on users' interest degree and feature," *Application Research of Computers*, vol. 29, no. 2, pp. 497–500, 2012.

[19] H. Guodong, Z. Yige, and Z. Fan, "A dynamic replica placement approach based on cognition," *Computer Applications and Soft*, vol. 30, no. 1, pp. 83–87, 2013.

[20] L. Wang, J. Luo, J. Shen, and F. Dong, "Cost and time aware ant colony algorithm for data replica in alpha magnetic spectrometer experiment," in *Proceedings of the IEEE International Congress on Big Data (BigData Congress '13)*, pp. 247–254, Santa Clara, Calif, USA, June 2013.

[21] D. Yuan, Y. Yang, X. Liu et al., "A highly practical approach toward achieving minimum data sets storage cost in the cloud," *IEEE Transactions on Parallel and Distributed Systems*, vol. 24, no. 6, pp. 1234–1244, 2013.

[22] Dong and M. Wang, *Game Theory*, National Development and Reform Commission, Beijing, China, 2nd edition, 2008.

[23] Y.-K. Kwok, K. Hwang, and S. Song, "Selfish grids: game-theoretic modeling and NAS/PSA benchmark evaluation," *IEEE Transactions on Parallel and Distributed Systems*, vol. 18, no. 5, pp. 621–636, 2007.

[24] A. H. Elghirani, R. Subrata, and A. Y. Zomaya, "A proactive non-cooperative game-theoretic framework for data replication in data grids," in *Proceedings of the IEEE International Symposium on Cluster Computing and the Grid*, pp. 433–440, May 2008.

[25] P. Ghosh, N. Roy, S. K. Das, and K. Basu, "A pricing strategy for job allocation in mobile grids using a non-cooperative bargaining theory framework," *Journal of Parallel and Distributed Computing*, vol. 65, no. 11, pp. 1366–1383, 2005.

[26] C.-L. Li, D. Liao, L. Xiong, and Y.-J. Huang, "A service selection algorithm based on quantified QoE evaluation," *Acta Electronica Sinica*, vol. 43, no. 11, pp. 2145–2150, 2015.

15

Multiobjective Level-Wise Scientific Workflow Optimization in IaaS Public Cloud Environment

Phyo Thandar Thant,[1] Courtney Powell,[2] Martin Schlueter,[2] and Masaharu Munetomo[2]

[1]*Graduate School of Information Science and Technology, Hokkaido University, Sapporo, Japan*
[2]*Information Initiative Center, Hokkaido University, Sapporo, Japan*

Correspondence should be addressed to Phyo Thandar Thant; phyothandarthant@ist.hokudai.ac.jp

Academic Editor: Emiliano Tramontana

Cloud computing in the field of scientific applications such as scientific big data processing and big data analytics has become popular because of its service oriented model that provides a pool of abstracted, virtualized, dynamically scalable computing resources and services on demand over the Internet. However, resource selection to make the right choice of instances for a certain application of interest is a challenging problem for researchers. In addition, providing services with optimal performance at the lowest financial resource deployment cost based on users' resource selection is quite challenging for cloud service providers. Consequently, it is necessary to develop an optimization system that can provide benefits to both users and service providers. In this paper, we conduct scientific workflow optimization on three perspectives: makespan minimization, virtual machine deployment cost minimization, and virtual machine failure minimization in the cloud infrastructure in a level-wise manner. Further, balanced task assignment to the virtual machine instances at each level of the workflow is also considered. Finally, system efficiency verification is conducted through evaluation of the results with different multiobjective optimization algorithms such as SPEA2 and NSGA-II.

1. Introduction

Scientific experiments in fields such as bioinformatics, astronomy, elementary particle physics, and life science require the storing and processing of big data. The adoption of cloud computing to process these scientific data has increased recently as cloud enables data correlations, pattern mining, data predictions, and data analytics in a cost-efficient manner. Cloud provides resources such as networks, storage, applications, and servers can be allocated from a shared resource pool with minimal management or interaction [1]. In general, cloud computing provides Infrastructure as a Service (IaaS), Platform as a Service (PaaS), and Software as a Service (SaaS) in a pay-per-use model. Of these services, IaaS is the most frequently utilized as it provides customers with an elastic facility to provision or release virtual machines (VMs) in the cloud infrastructure [2]. The elastic nature of cloud facilitates changing of resource quantities and characteristics to vary at runtime, thus dynamically scaling up when there is a greater need for additional resources and scaling down when the demand is low [3]. As a result of its elastic resource provisioning mechanism, the cloud is widely used in several areas including large-scale scientific applications. With improved service support and cloud bursting technologies, users do not need to provision their resources for the worst-case scenarios. In the context of cloud computing, an application's execution cost means the monetary cost of renting resources from the cloud service provider. Addressing the issues of minimizing the resource usage with the best performance is an important research area in an IaaS cloud.

Scientific applications consist of thousands of tasks requiring heavy computation and data transfer. Workflow tasks also have certain dependencies during execution. Modeling of these scientific applications is necessary for effective processing. The most widely used representation model is in the form of directed acyclic graph (DAG) in which the structure of the workflow indicates the order of execution of tasks. Our optimization framework deals with scientific workflow in the form of DAG during optimization experimentations. In addition, it is assumed that the monetary cost for workflow execution in the cloud is based on the amount of resources used, that is, task execution cost correlated to the total number of CPU cycles for all tasks. By using cloud infrastructure, customers can also reduce the processing cost of workflow applications with the aid of the cloud's pay-per-use model. Moreover, a task that shares the same time interval with a previous task hosted in the same instance might not produce extra cost, reducing the overall workflow execution cost.

Khajemohammadi et al. [4] proposed a leveled fast workflow scheduling strategy that minimizes cost and time in a grid environment. However, in that approach, resource utilization is only possible within predefined set of service resources, which is irrelevant because of the dynamicity and elasticity of the cloud. Moreover, a service only processes one task at a time within a level. Our approach differs from the previous work in several aspects: (1) instead of a predefined set of service resources, randomized search on the number of VMs and various machine instance types is conducted during execution to benefit from cloud elasticity and monetary facility, (2) more than one task can share a single virtual machine instance for better resource utilization, (3) balanced task assignment is conducted to balance the load in each machine instance as well as reducing the wait time to proceed to the next level of tasks, and (4) minimizing failure of machine instances to improve the reliability during workflow execution is considered. In that way, the system searches for the Pareto-optimal solutions that exhibit the best performance with minimized failure at the lowest financial cost.

Our optimization idea is based on the widely used scientific workflows from the Pegasus project [5], which have control and dependencies. The experimental results obtained comprise a series of optimized VMs with optimized machine instance type for each level of the workflow with their respective makespan time, cost, and minimized machine instance failure. The current version of this paper is an extension of the previous studies [6] in the following aspects. First, we include another objective function which is machine instance failure minimization function, during optimization. Second, we extend our cloud system model from only four machine instance types of academic private cloud to 25 machine instance types of public cloud. The system implementation now conducts optimization on three minimization objectives (makespan, cost, and failures) with 25 virtual machine instance types from AWS. Third, we perform experiments and analysis on three real-world workflows using SPEA2 and NSGA-II algorithms to show the system effectiveness on three objective functions.

The remainder of this paper is organized as follows. Section 2 presents the theoretical background associated with scientific workflows, SPEA2 and NSGA-II. Section 3 outlines the proposed system, the objective functions used, and the proposed workflow execution optimization algorithm. Section 4 discusses the performance evaluation conducted. Section 5 presents related work. Finally, Section 6 concludes and outlines intended future work.

2. Background

This section presents the relevant theoretical background associated with the paper. First, scientific workflows and their features are discussed. Then, the multiobjective evolutionary algorithms SPEA2 [7] and NSGA-II [8] are presented.

2.1. Scientific Workflows. Scientific workflows are essential to facilitate and automate the processing of high-volume scientific data in large distributed computing structure such as grid [9]. These workflows describe the set of tasks needed to carry out computational experiments and provide scientists with the ability to expose, share, and reuse their work. The goals of these workflows are (i) to save human cycles by enabling scientists to focus on domain-specific aspects of their work, rather than dealing with complex data management and software issues, and (ii) to save machine cycles by optimizing workflow execution on available resources [10]. Scientific workflows are created with a corresponding workflow editor that usually provides a repository with predefined workflow activities.

In general, a scientific workflow is modeled as a directed acyclic graph (DAG). A DAG workflow, W, is defined as $W = (T, D)$, where $T = \{T_0, T_1, \ldots, T_n\}$ is a set of tasks and $D = \{(T_i, T_j) \mid T_i, T_j \in T\}$ is a set of data or control dependencies [7]. Each task has its respective execution time, task name, input data size, and resulting output data size. For a DAG with multiple entries and exits, it is necessary to add a pseudo T_{entry} and or a pseudo T_{exit} with no control and dependencies. In this study, we assumed that all DAG workflows have only one T_{entry} and one T_{exit}, and optimization is considered for the actual processing steps inside the workflow. A DAG is represented in either XML or JSON format and parsing is required to get the necessary information for further processing. A simple DAG is illustrated in Figure 1 with respective task labels.

2.2. Multiobjective Evolutionary Algorithms (MOEAs). Multiobjective evolutionary algorithms (MOEAs) have been proposed for finding multiple Pareto-optimal solutions in one single simulation run. MOEAs are an effective way to find the Pareto-optimal solutions among conflicting objectives. They produce nondominated solutions with respect to minimization or maximization of objectives for user satisfaction.

2.2.1. Improved Strength Pareto Evolutionary Algorithm (SPEA2). SPEA2 [7] is an improved version of the original Strength Pareto Evolutionary Algorithm (SPEA) by means of an improved fitness assignment scheme, nearest neighbor density estimation technique, and new truncation method.

The algorithm starts with a population and an archive (external set). Then it performs iterations for the evolution process. During the update operation in the evolution process, filling up with the dominated individuals or truncating individuals if necessary to fit in the fixed-size archive occurs. Unlike SPEA, SPEA2 only considers members of the archive to participate in the mating selection process.

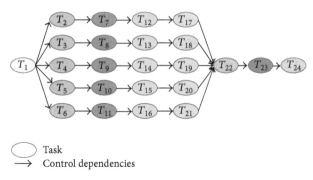

○ Task
→ Control dependencies

FIGURE 1: An example DAG workflow.

The objective of the algorithm is to locate and maintain a front of nondominated solutions, ideally a set of Pareto-optimal solutions. This is achieved by using an evolutionary process (with surrogate procedures for genetic recombination and mutation) to explore the search space and a selection process that uses a combination of the degree to which a candidate solution is dominated (strength) and an estimation of the density of the Pareto front as an assigned fitness. An archive of the nondominated set is maintained separate from the population of candidate solutions used in the evolutionary process, providing a form of elitism.

2.2.2. Nondominated Sorting Genetic Algorithm (NSGA-II). In 1995, nondominated sorting genetic algorithm (NSGA) [11], which improved computational complexity via a nonelitism approach and a sharing parameter, was developed. In 2002, Deb et al. developed NSGA-II [8], an improved version of NSGA which rectifies the problems found in NSGA. NSGA-II is a popular multiobjective optimization algorithm that is widely used in several application domains. The main features of NSGA-II are low computational complexity, parameter-less diversity preservation, and an elitism approach. The major components of NSGA-II include fast nondominated sorting and crowding distance assignment.

Fast Nondominated Sorting. Elitism is introduced in NSGA-II by storing all nondominated solutions discovered, starting with the initial population [12]. Elitism enhances the convergence properties towards the Pareto-optimal set. Sorting the individuals in the population according to the level of nondomination, each solution must be compared with every other solution to determine if it is dominated. Firstly, two entities are calculated for each solution: (1) n_p, the number of solutions that dominate solution p, and (2) S_p, a set of solutions that solution p dominates. All solutions that have $n_p = 0$, that is, nondominated solutions, are identified and placed in a current front list as first nondominated front list. Then, the algorithm repeatedly finds the second front, third front, and so on until all fronts are identified or the specified population size is reached.

Crowding Distance Algorithm. After completing nondominated sorting, crowding distance is assigned. In this process,

all the individuals in the population are assigned a crowding distance value and individual selection is conducted based on rank and crowding distance. Crowding distance comparison compares the individuals within the same front and distance calculation is conducted. In other words, crowding distance involves finding the Euclidean distance between each individual in a front based on their m objectives in an m-dimensional hyperspace. The individuals in the boundary are always selected because they have infinite distance assignment [13].

The solutions found in NSGA-II are said to be Pareto-optimal if they are not dominated by any other solutions in the solution space. Further, the set of all feasible nondominated solutions in the solution space is referred to as the Pareto-optimal set, and for a given Pareto-optimal set the corresponding objective function values in the objective space are called the Pareto front. The goal of multiobjective optimization is to identify the solutions in the Pareto-optimal set. In this proposed optimization system, we use NSGA-II because it is one of the most popular optimization approaches in several domains. Figure 2 depicts the process flow of NSGA-II optimization.

3. Proposed Workflow Optimization Framework

Search-based workflow optimization on makespan, machine instance failure, and virtual machine deployment cost in cloud computing environment is applied in our system with SPEA2 and NSGA-II. The details of our system are given in the ensuing sections.

3.1. System Overview. Figure 3 shows the architecture of our proposed multiobjective workflow optimization system. The operation of the system is as follows. First, workflow input in the form of a DAX (a DAG in XML representation) is given to the system for optimization and the system parses the necessary information at each level of tasks in the workflow DAG. Then, the system performs makespan minimization, virtual machine deployment cost minimization, and machine instance failure minimization based on the specific machine instance type throughout the search space.

3.2. Level-Wise Optimization. Level-wise workflow optimization is conducted in order not to violate the dependencies of workflow tasks in scientific workflow executions in the cloud. The system objective functions and balanced task assignment in the proposed cloud system model are described in the following sections in detail.

3.2.1. Objective Functions. The optimization problem involves resource optimization for workflow execution on the cloud infrastructure that gives the optimized makespan, cost, and VM instance failures. The specified parameters include the number of VM instances and the type of machine instances at each workflow level. The number of machine instances is encoded as integer values where each value specifies the number of VM instances for the specific workflow level. Further, the types of VM instances are also encoded as integer, where

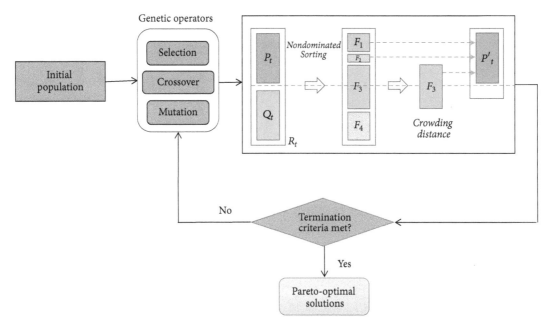

FIGURE 2: Process flow of NSGA-II optimization.

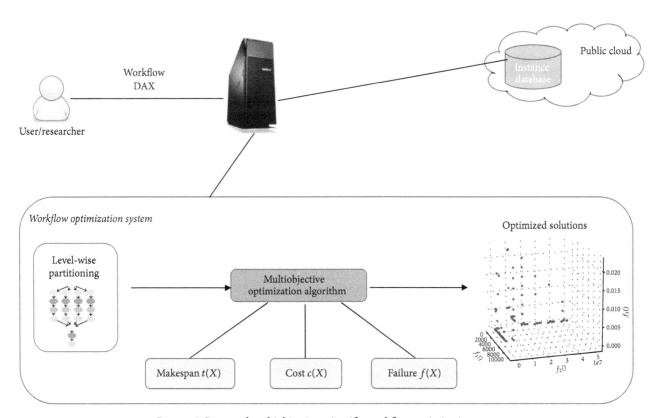

FIGURE 3: Proposed multiobjective scientific workflow optimization system.

each integer value specifies one of the machine instance types described in Table 2. Then, the functions that relate workflow makespan, cost, and VM instance failures for fitness evaluations are defined. The objective functions utilized in the proposed system are geared towards minimizing the overall makespan for workflow execution, machine instance deployment cost, and instance failure during workflow execution. They are expressed as follows:

$$\min t\,(X)\,, \min c\,(X)\,, \min f\,(X)\,, \tag{1}$$

TABLE 1: Machine instance CPU performance.

Number	Instance type	CPU type	PassMark CPU Mark	Speedup over m3 CPU performance (%)
(1)	m3	Intel Xeon E5-2670 v2	14975	—
(2)	m4	Intel Xeon E5-2686 v4	17795	18
(3)	c3	Intel Xeon E5-2680 v2	16341	9
(4)	c4	Intel Xeon E5-2666 v3	24877	66
(5)	r3	Intel Xeon E5-2670 v2	14975	—

where $X = [x_1, x_2, \ldots, x_l, \ldots, x_m]$ is the number of VMs and types of VMs in each level of the DAG; $t(X)$ is total workflow execution time; $c(X)$ is total workflow machine instance deployment cost; $f(X)$ is total workflow machine instance failure probability.

In scientific workflow applications, execution dependencies among tasks are important. Thus, level-wise execution resource selection is conducted in our proposed system. First, we optimize the makespan and the number of VMs at each execution level. Then, following optimization at all levels in the workflow, an optimized execution plan is identified for the overall workflow.

Moreover, the deployment cost differs per machine instance type used and the number of machine instances used during workflow optimization. According to the machine instance type, the runtime of each task in the workflow is also different. For the failure minimization case, the system uses the availability factor of the virtual machine instances provided by Amazon Web Services (AWS). No user-defined constraints are considered at this time and automatic makespan, failure, and resource usage cost optimization are performed by the system. The three objective functions for level-wise makespan cost, instance deployment cost, and virtual machine instance failure are calculated as follows:

(1) Level-wise makespan cost:

$$t(X) = \sum_{k=1}^{L} \sum_{j=1}^{\lceil |T_k|/x_k \rceil} \max_{l=1+(j-1)x_k}^{x_k \times j} T_k(l), \qquad (2)$$

where $|T_k|$ is total number of tasks in level k; x_k is number of machine instances in level k; $T_k(l)$ is execution time of the task in position l in the cluster task set with respect to the instance type; L is total number of levels in DAG.

(2) Level-wise virtual machine deployment cost:

$$c(X) = \sum_{k=1}^{L} \left(\sum_{j=1}^{\lceil |T_k|/x_k \rceil} \left(\sum_{l=1+(j-1)x_k}^{x_k \times j} T_k(l) \times P\left(x_j^k\right) \right) \right), \qquad (3)$$

where $P(x_j^k)$ is price of the jth virtual machine at kth workflow level.

(3) Level-wise virtual machine failure probability:

$$f(X) = \frac{\sum_{k=1}^{L} \left(\prod_{j=1}^{x_k} P_j^{\text{fail}} \right)}{L}, \qquad (4)$$

where P_j^{fail} is failure probability of the jth virtual machine.

3.2.2. *Cloud System Model.* In our study, the cloud is modeled as a set of virtual machine instances, $\text{Ins} = \{\text{ins}_1, \text{ins}_2, \ldots, \text{ins}_j\}$. Each instance, ins_j, can be one of 25 machine instance types and instance costs are calculated based on instance prices for Tokyo region in AWS pricing [14]. Table 2 shows the instance pricing used in our resource usage calculation. The performance difference of different machine instance types is specified based on the CPU used as well as the number of CPU cores in each machine instance. We refer to the CPU performance of various instances from the PassMark benchmark [15]. Instance type m3 is assumed to be the lowest performance machine instance with the lowest price. The CPU performance differences of m4, c3, c4, and r3 instance types with respect to m3 machine instance type are assumed to be as listed in Table 1.

The performance speed up of each machine instance group is specified based on the number of CPU cores used in each machine instance. In addition, we also assume that all virtual machine instances share data from the same data center. Thus, data communication and data transfer costs are constant.

3.2.3. *Balanced Task Assignment.* Level-wise balanced task assignment to the VMs is conducted in scientific workflow execution because the fine-grained tasks in each workflow must be processed in their dependency order. The objective of balanced task assignment is to reduce the waiting time to continue to the next level during workflow execution and to balance the loads in each machine instance at each workflow level allowing resource sharing facility. For those purposes, balanced clustering of tasks at each level is considered before execution in their respective virtual machine. Figure 4 shows the task clustering for balanced task assignment process. There are two stages for balanced clustering: (1) task sorting and (2) balanced clustering. In task sorting, all the tasks in each level are sorted according to their runtime. Then, the task cluster size decision for each task group in the sorted task list is conducted according to the following equation:

If (number of virtual machines for ith level $= n$), $\text{NC} = n$ ($1 \leq n \leq p$)

$$C_{\text{size}_j} = \frac{T_i}{\text{NC}} + s_k, \quad j = 1, \ldots, \text{NC}, \ k = 1, \ldots, n, \qquad (5)$$

where

TABLE 2: Machine instance pricing.

Number	Instance type	CPU (number of cores)	Memory (GB)	Price per second ($)
(1)	m3.medium	1	3.75	0.00002667
(2)	m3.large	2	7.5	0.00005361
(3)	m3.xlarge	4	15	0.00010694
(4)	m3.2xlarge	8	30	0.00021389
(5)	m4.large	2	8	0.00004833
(6)	m4.xlarge	4	16	0.00009667
(7)	m4.2xlarge	8	32	0.00019306
(8)	m4.4xlarge	16	64	0.00038639
(9)	m4.10xlarge	40	160	0.00096583
(10)	m4.16xlarge	64	256	0.00154528
(11)	c3.large	2	3.75	0.00003556
(12)	c3.xlarge	4	7.5	0.00007083
(13)	c3.2xlarge	8	15	0.00014194
(14)	c3.4xlarge	16	30	0.00028361
(15)	c3.8xlarge	32	60	0.00056750
(16)	c4.large	1	3.75	0.00003694
(17)	c4.xlarge	4	7.5	0.00007361
(18)	c4.2xlarge	8	15	0.00014750
(19)	c4.4xlarge	16	30	0.00029472
(20)	c4.8xlarge	36	60	0.00058944
(21)	r3.large	2	15	0.00005556
(22)	r3.xlarge	4	30.5	0.00011083
(23)	r3.2xlarge	8	61	0.00022167
(24)	r3.4xlarge	16	122	0.00044333
(25)	r3.8xlarge	32	244	0.00088667

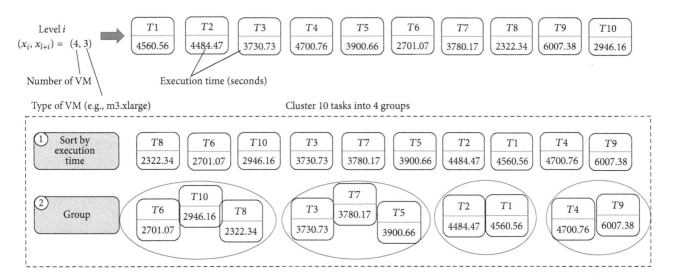

FIGURE 4: Level-wise balanced task assignment.

Input: Workflow DAG.
Output: Task Objects, Search Space (SP), total number of levels (L).
Step 1. Parse the workflow DAG
Step 2. Label tasks
Step 3. Assign workflow tasks to objects
Step 4. Retrieve maximum workflow level for chromosome length determination in optimization
Step 5. Retrieve maximum parallelization degree for search space determination

---

ALGORITHM 1: Preprocessing.

Input: Task Objects, Search Space (SP), total number of levels (L), N: Population size, G: number of generations, O: number of objectives, MP: mutation probability, CP: crossover probability.
Output: Pareto optimal solutions, W_{opt}.
Processing
Step 1. Generate random initial population, P_0 and empty archive $\overline{P_0} = \Phi$, $t = 0$.
    (1.1) Randomly generate integer chromosome C_i ($i = 1, 2, \ldots, N$) for P_0, $\overline{P_0}$.
      (truncate if necessary)
    (1.2) Calculate the fitness of each random chromosome
    (1.3) Copy all non-dominated individuals in P_t and $\overline{P_t}$ to $\overline{P_t + 1}$
Step 2. Evolve population ($t, P_t, \overline{P_t}, \overline{P_t + 1}$).
    (2.1) Select parents using tournament selection, $\overline{P_t + 1}$
    (2.2) Perform two-point dynamic crossover operation on parents with probability CP to produce offspring population.
    (2.3) Perform mutation operation with probability MP on random points applied to offspring
    (2.4) Calculate fitness of new offspring population and update population
    (2.5) Use non-dominated sorting to divide into several non-domination levels $F_1, F_2, \ldots, F_l$.
    (2.6) Update $\overline{P_t + 1}$
Step 3. Repeat Step 2 until termination condition is met.
Step 4. Output the list of optimal solutions at Pareto front, W_{opt}.

ALGORITHM 2: Workflow optimization using SPEA2.

$$s_k = \begin{cases} 0, & \text{if } T_i \% \text{ NC} = 0 \\ 1, & \text{if } 0 < T_i \% \text{ NC} < \text{NC} \end{cases} \qquad T_i = \text{total number of tasks in } i\text{th level, NC} = \text{number of task clusters.} \tag{6}$$

3.2.4. Virtual Machine Instance Failure.

In general, a cloud uses a large number of commodity servers; thus, the possibility of failure exists. Failures of cloud based resources may lead to failures of application processing. Consequently, these failures can have a significant impact on the performance of the workflow execution. Thus, it is necessary to minimize the possibility of failures in the system. Workflow task clustering sometimes may result in a higher failure rate if more than one task is assigned to a single machine instance [3]. In this proposed system, we calculated the failure of each virtual machine instance based on AWS availability with certain additional weighted value. First, the original failure probability of a virtual machine instance is assumed to be $p_f = 0.02337$. We assume that the more tasks in the virtual machine, the higher the weight of failure of that virtual machine. Weight values are calculated based on the number of tasks in the level and the original failure probability value. Each machine instance failure probability P_j^{fail} is calculated as follows:

$$P_j^{fail} = p_f + w_j,$$

$$w_j = \left(N_{tj} - 1\right)\left(\frac{p_f}{T_k}\right), \tag{7}$$

where N_{tj} is total number of tasks in the jth virtual machine.

3.3. Multiobjective Workflow Optimization Algorithm.

This section presents the SPEA2 and NSGA-II based optimization algorithms, which are the major component of the proposed system. The system uses NSGA-II because it outperforms other contemporary MOEAs, such as PAES [16] and SPEA [17], in terms of finding a diverse set of solutions and in converging near the true Pareto-optimal set [8]. SPEA2 is used to compare the Pareto-optimal solutions obtained from NSGA-II optimization. Algorithm 1 describes the preprocessing steps necessary for parsing the workflow tasks in DAG format to task objects. The workflow optimization algorithms using SPEA2 and NSGA-II are described in Algorithms 2 and 3, respectively.

Input: Task Objects, Search Space (SP), total number of levels (L), N: Population size, G: number of generations, O: number of objectives, MP: mutation probability, CP: crossover probability.
Output: Pareto optimal solutions, W_{opt}.
Processing
Step 1. Generate random initial population, IP.
      (1.1) Randomly generate integer chromosome C_i ($i = 1, 2, \ldots, N$).
      (1.2) Calculate the fitness of each random chromosome
      (1.3) Rank population P according to non-domination
Step 2. Evolve population (N, P, G).
      (2.1) Select parents using tournament selection, (P_1, P_2).
      (2.2) Perform two-point dynamic crossover operation on parents (P_1, P_2) with probability CP to produce
            offspring population.
      (2.3) Perform mutation operation with probability MP on random points applied to offspring
      (2.4) Calculate fitness of new offspring population and update population
      (2.5) Use non-dominated sorting to divide $P \leftarrow P \cup \{x^C\}$ into several non-domination levels $F_1, F_2, \ldots, F_l$.
      (2.6) Calculate Crowding Distance of all solutions
      (2.7) Identify the worst solution $x' \in F_l$ and set $\leftarrow P' \setminus \{x'\}$.
Step 3. Repeat Step 2 until termination condition is met.
Step 4. Output the list of optimal solutions at Pareto front, W_{opt}.

ALGORITHM 3: Workflow optimization using NSGA-II.

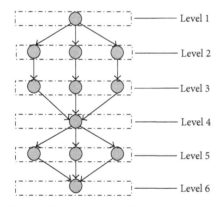

FIGURE 5: Level-wise workflow partitioning.

3.4. System Implementation.

Scientific workflows support and automate the execution of error-prone, repetitive tasks in scientific applications. It combines activities and computations to solve scientific problems. Task partitioning is important during workflow execution because it can affect the performance of the application. Three approaches to workflow partitioning before executing are reported in the literature: (1) horizontal workflow partitioning, (2) vertical workflow partitioning, and (3) arbitrary workflow partitioning.

In our proposed system, we use level-wise workflow partitioning which is a horizontal partitioning approach. We chose level-wise partitioning of structured scientific workflows because these workflows consist of different numbers of tasks with different resource requirements at each level of the workflow. The level-wise approach enables elastic provisioning of resources and load balancing at each workflow level. Level-wise partitioning of a simple DAG workflow is illustrated in Figure 5.

3.4.1. DAX Parsing. In the parsing stage, task information specified in the directed acyclic graph is retrieved. In this system, necessary information such as total number of levels in the workflow, task name and their relevant execution time, and the maximum parallelization degree for the input workflow to perform automatic optimization are retrieved. Subsequent chromosome length determination depends on the total number of levels in the workflow. Moreover, task labelling is also conducted at each level of the workflow to facilitate level-wise optimization of workflow tasks within the optimization process during workflow parsing.

3.4.2. Multiobjective Optimization. Following parsing and task labelling of the workflow, the system begins the multiobjective optimization process. First, random initial chromosome parameter lists comprising the number of VMs and the type of VMs suitable for each level of the workflow are generated to initiate the process. Next, fitness calculations are performed for the three objective functions. Genetic operators such as selection, crossover, and mutation are then chosen to be used during evolution. Then, the evolution process proceeds until the specified termination criterion is met. At this point, the Pareto front solutions from the evolution process are retrieved and the optimized number of VMs with optimized instance type at the Pareto front for optimal makespan and optimal deployment cost with the least failure for each workflow level are recommended for processing the scientific workflow applications in the cloud.

3.4.3. Chromosome Representation. The chromosome of the proposed system includes genes which represent the number of VMs and the type of VMs used for each level of the workflow. The system uses a fixed-length integer-encoding scheme, one of the most common representations of chromosomes in genetic algorithms (GA). The genes in the

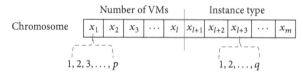

Encoding scheme: fixed length integer sequence

FIGURE 6: Chromosome structure for optimization during workflow execution.

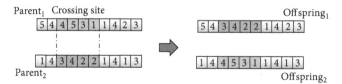

FIGURE 7: Crossover operation.

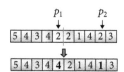

FIGURE 8: Mutation operation.

chromosomes are in the form of $\{1, p\}$ and $\{1, q\}$ with each gene representing the number of VMs for each level of workflow execution for parallelization, while p signifies the maximum number of concurrent tasks allowable in that workflow level, and q signifies the total possible number of instance types provided by the academic cloud system. A single gene represents one level and the chromosome length depends on the maximum number of levels in the workflow. The chromosome length, $2L$, where L is the highest level of the workflow DAG, varies according to the input workflow structure. Specifically, the chromosome length for a simple workflow in Figure 5 is $(2L = 12)$, where $L = 6$ and the gene value ranges are $(1, p) = (1, 3)$ and $(1, q) = (1, 25)$, respectively. An example chromosome for the optimization process is illustrated in Figure 6.

3.4.4. Genetic Operators. The genes in the chromosomes represent number of VMs and type of VMs at each workflow level and the proposed workflow optimization processes the execution of tasks in a level-wise manner to preserve the dependencies between tasks. During optimization, the genetic operators are used to guide the multiobjective optimization algorithm towards optimal solutions to a given problem. Three main operators, selection, crossover, and mutation, collaborate for successful processing.

(1) Selection. The select operation gives us a straightforward way of choosing offspring for the next generation. Tournament selection is used in this system as it reduces the computational cost associated with selection. In tournament selection, random T (user-defined tournament selection size) individuals from the population are chosen, their fitness values are compared, and the fittest is used in the recombination

process. The higher the T value, the higher the selection pressure in tournament selection.

(2) Crossover. The crossover operation takes two parent strings called $parent_1$ and $parent_2$ and generates two offspring, $offspring_1$ and $offspring_2$. The decision of whether to perform a crossover operation on the current pair of parent chromosomes is made according to the specified crossover probability (CP). If the random probability is less than CP, a crossing site is selected and partial exchange occurs between the two parents to produce the offspring. If the probability is greater than CP, the crossing site will be the entire chromosome length, which has no effect because of the crossover operator. Two-point crossover is applied in the proposed system, as illustrated in Figure 7.

(3) Mutation. Mutation is important because it allows the evolutionary process to explore new potential solutions to the problem. To avoid inbreeding in a small population problem, mutation is applied with small probability (MP) after the crossover operation. The selected MP should be reasonable because if it is too high or too low, a good solution will not be found during evolution. Random two-point mutation is used during evolution of the proposed system, as illustrated in Figure 8.

4. Performance Evaluation

This section outlines the experimental environment and presents the experimental results obtained for various scientific workflow applications. The simulation experiments were conducted on an Intel core i7 Dell PC with 16 GB RAM with Pegasus workflow dataset. The system implementation was

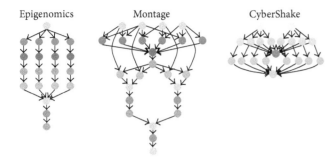

Epigenomics   Montage   CyberShake

FIGURE 9: Structure of the experimental scientific workflows.

TABLE 3: Experimental workflows.

Number	Workflow application	Number of task nodes (input size)			
(1)	Epigenomics	24	46	100	997
(2)	Montage	25	50	100	1000
(3)	CyberShake	30	50	100	1000

conducted using the Python programming language and the well-known DEAP framework [18].

4.1. Experimental Scientific Workflow Applications.

To demonstrate the proposed offline workflow optimization system, the experiments were conducted using three scientific workflow DAG applications (Epigenomics, Montage, and CyberShake) from Pegasus [5, 19], with various input data sizes. Epigenomics is a CPU-bound bioinformatics workflow with eight levels of workflow tasks. Montage is a collection of programs that combines multiple shots of astronomical images to generate a custom mosaic image [20]. CyberShake is a seismology workflow application that is used by the Southern California Earthquake Center to characterize earthquake hazards in a region [3]. The structures of the applications are illustrated in Figure 9. Table 3 shows the scientific workflows used for system evaluation along with their respective input data sizes.

4.2. Experimental Analysis.

Figures 10–13 show cost-makespan tradeoff solutions identified by the proposed system using NSGA-II and SPEA2. The experiments were conducted with a population size of 100 evolving over 500 generations with crossover probability 0.7 and mutation probability of 0.0625, 0.055, and 0.125—in accordance with the number of levels in the given workflow. The experimental results indicate that the system reduced the makespan effectively with acceptable cost tradeoff. The effectiveness of the system is reflected more in the larger data size workflows, in which makespan is significantly improved with only a small increase in deployment cost. For failure minimization objective, the system gives only some significant effectiveness in smaller input data size workflows compared with other two objective functions.

Figure 10 shows cost-makespan tradeoff solutions for three workflows with four input data size after 500 generations. Although the optimization was conducted on three objective functions, the distribution of the solutions is presented in two dimensions (2D) as 2D provides better clarity for comparison than 3D. In the figures, it is clear that makespan and deployment cost functions are strongly correlated with a negative slope. That is, the higher the makespan, the lower the deployment cost, and vice versa. As our objective functions are minimizing functions, we would like to choose the optimal solution which is as close to the X-Y origin as possible. The values in the figures also illustrate a gentle slope in small input data size that becomes steeper with increased data size. For the Montage case, there are gaps in the Pareto front; the reason will be determined in future studies. The scatter plots in Figure 11 illustrate the cost-failure tradeoff solutions. The values in the figures highlight that the two functions are not strongly correlated. Nevertheless, there is a weak correlation between these two functions except Montage 1000 task nodes and CyberShake 1000 task nodes. In those extra-size input workflows, all Pareto front solutions recommend to use similar instance type but with different number of machine instances at each workflow level. Moreover, the failure probability values of all solutions are very similar with only small differences in the 7th position of the fractional result values. This can affect the cost-failure tradeoff solutions of Montage 1000 and CyberShake 1000 to be a linear function with no correlation. For these reasons, the best optimal solution for the three objective functions should be selected based on the makespan, cost, and failure, respectively. In our evaluation, we identified two extreme points and one mid-point (the one closest to the origin) to be makespan best, time best, and mid-point solution to find out the system effectiveness. We found out that the system improves by 5.6, 10 times for makespan, cost for Epigenomics case with failure of 0.00559256, 1.5, 4.5 times improvement with failure of 0.0149133 for Montage, and 9, 9 times improvement with failure of 0.008948 for CyberShake, respectively. Figures 12 and 13 show the experimental results using SPEA2 algorithm and the results are quite similar for all three workflows.

For the evaluation of the evolutionary algorithms, several quality indicators such as convergence, diversity, inverse generational distance (IGD), and hypervolume exist. Among these indicators, convergence and diversity values of the optimal solutions obtained from the Pareto fronts over five independent test runs for 500 generations were used to calculate the average values and standard deviations listed in Table 4. These quality indicator calculations were conducted according to the DEAP framework, the smaller the convergence and diversity values the better. Convergence is a measure of the distance between the obtained nondominated front and the true Pareto-optimal front. Convergence metric, γ, is calculated by computing the minimum Euclidean distance of each obtained solution from the chosen solutions on the Pareto-optimal front and then averaging those distances [13]. The metric is calculated as below:

$$\text{Convergence, } \gamma = \frac{\sum_{i=1}^{N} |d_i|}{N}, \quad (8)$$

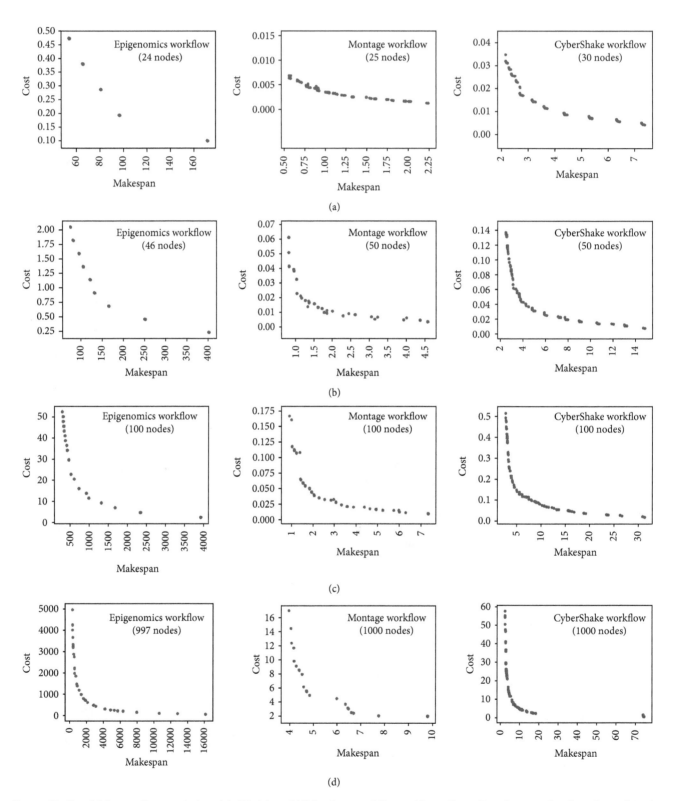

FIGURE 10: Cost_Makespan Pareto solutions (a), (b), (c), and (d) for three workflows with small, medium, large, and ex-large input data size using NSGA-II.

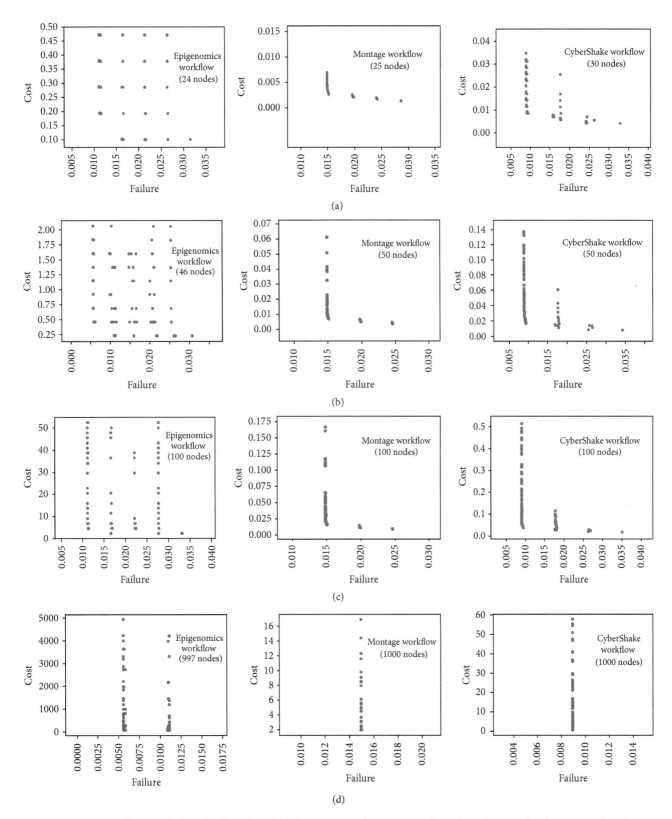

FIGURE 11: Cost_Failure Pareto solutions (a), (b), (c), and (d) for three workflows with small, medium, large, and ex-large input data size using NSGA-II.

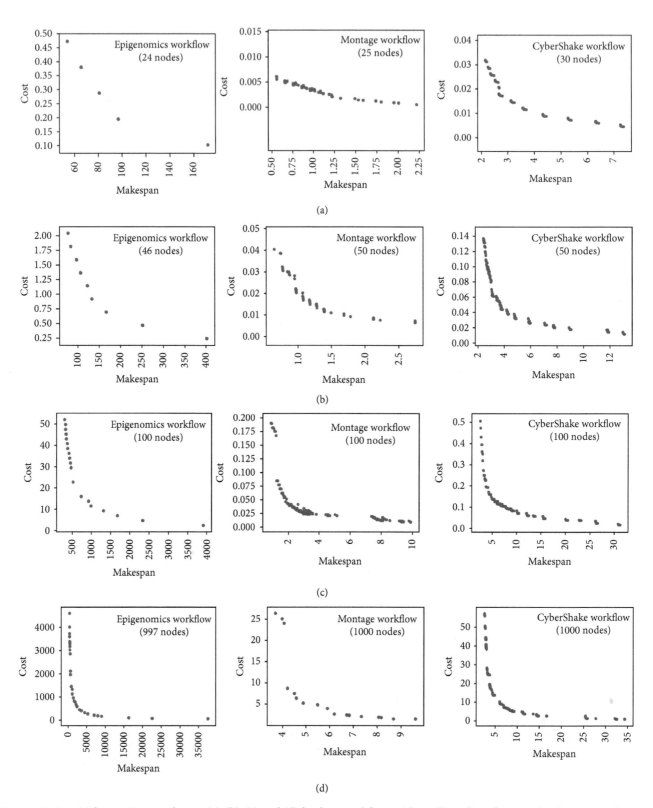

FIGURE 12: Cost-Makespan Pareto solutions (a), (b), (c), and (d) for three workflows with small, medium, large, and ex-large input data size using SPEA2.

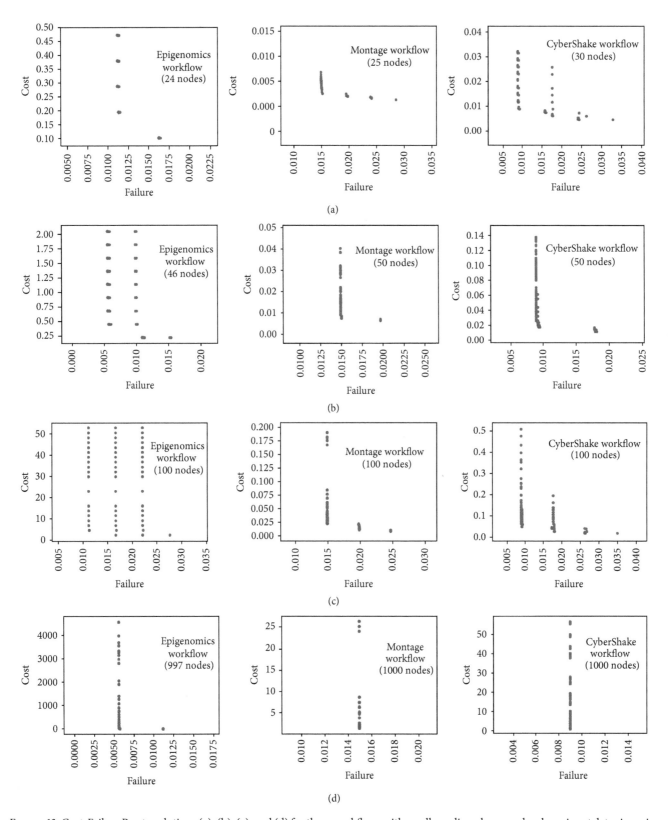

FIGURE 13: Cost_Failure Pareto solutions (a), (b), (c), and (d) for three workflows with small, medium, large, and ex-large input data size using SPEA2.

TABLE 4: Convergence, diversity, and execution time for SPEA2 and NSGA–II.

Workflow	Algorithm	Avg. Conv. ($\pm\sigma$)	Avg. Div. ($\pm\sigma$)	Avg. Exec. (sec) ($\pm\sigma$)
Epigenomics_24	SPEA2	0.0240 ($\pm$0.0011)	1.8554 ($\pm$0.0367)	406.5189 ($\pm$14.9)
	NSGA-II	0.0294 ($\pm$0.0177)	1.7936 ($\pm$0.0992)	74.5451 ($\pm$6.5)
Montage_25	SPEA2	0.0060 ($\pm$0.0039)	1.0104 ($\pm$0.4130)	372.7346 ($\pm$26.9)
	NSGA-II	0.0059 ($\pm$0.0005)	1.2770 ($\pm$0.1713)	68.5270 ($\pm$16.2)
CyberShake_30	SPEA2	0.0094 ($\pm$0.0012)	1.3485 ($\pm$0.0019)	414.6732 ($\pm$11.0)
	NSGA-II	0.0079 ($\pm$0.0012)	1.4026 ($\pm$0.0642)	53.9493 ($\pm$1.8)
Epigenomics_46	SPEA2	0.1661 ($\pm$0.2064)	1.7670 ($\pm$0.0390)	431.8035 ($\pm$30.5)
	NSGA-II	0.1118 ($\pm$0.0857)	1.7152 ($\pm$0.0918)	71.5525 ($\pm$5.5)
Montage_50	SPEA2	0.0033 ($\pm$0.0040)	1.4672 ($\pm$0.1394)	366.6482 ($\pm$21.9)
	NSGA-II	0.0100 ($\pm$0.0031)	1.2758 ($\pm$0.1414)	63.8932 ($\pm$4.6)
CyberShake_50	SPEA2	0.0209 ($\pm$0.0077)	1.3629 ($\pm$0.1168)	415.7871 ($\pm$17.6)
	NSGA-II	0.0224 ($\pm$0.0060)	1.3372 ($\pm$0.9048)	56.6219 ($\pm$3.5)
Epigenomics_100	SPEA2	0.1005 ($\pm$0.0518)	1.7229 ($\pm$0.0079)	388.3032 ($\pm$13.0)
	NSGA-II	0.1423 ($\pm$0.1108)	1.7188 ($\pm$0.0004)	74.4787 ($\pm$6.3)
Montage_100	SPEA2	0.0178 ($\pm$0.0140)	1.1626 ($\pm$0.2073)	375.2320 ($\pm$13.3)
	NSGA-II	0.0178 ($\pm$0.0055)	1.2122 ($\pm$0.1533)	71.6682 ($\pm$10.1)
CyberShake_100	SPEA2	0.0731 ($\pm$0.0116)	1.0607 ($\pm$0.0361)	388.4410 ($\pm$10.4)
	NSGA-II	0.0721 ($\pm$0.0240)	1.2178 ($\pm$0.0665)	60.2484 ($\pm$5.0)
Epigenomics_997	SPEA2	2.3735 ($\pm$1.7707)	1.5694 ($\pm$0.0521)	545.0587 ($\pm$16.3)
	NSGA-II	12.652 ($\pm$6.5924)	1.5404 ($\pm$0.0777)	225.4969 ($\pm$15.7)
Montage_1000	SPEA2	0.0027 ($\pm$0.0044)	1.5974 ($\pm$0.1057)	546.3927 ($\pm$27.2)
	NSGA-II	0.0573 ($\pm$0.0188)	1.6398 ($\pm$0.1235)	216.1495 ($\pm$4.0)
CyberShake_1000	SPEA2	0.2783 ($\pm$0.0532)	1.1775 ($\pm$0.1606)	522.4185 ($\pm$18.7)
	NSGA-II	0.3458 ($\pm$0.1087)	1.3284 ($\pm$0.0589)	170.0315 ($\pm$3.7)

where d_i is Euclidean distance between the obtained solutions and the nearest member of the best nondominated front.

Diversity is a measure of the sufficiency of the obtained nondominated solutions to represent the range of the Pareto-optimal front [19]. The equation for diversity calculation is described in [8] as follows:

$$\text{Diversity}, \Delta = \frac{d_f + d_l + \sum_{i=1}^{N-1}\left|d_i - \overline{d}\right|}{d_f + d_l + (N-1)\,\overline{d}}, \quad (9)$$

where d_f, d_l are Euclidean distances between the extreme solutions and the boundary solutions; d_i is a solution on the best nondominated front d_i, $i = 1, 2, 3, \ldots, (N-1)$; $\overline{d}$ is the average of all distances d_i.

The current research work focuses on optimization of scientific workflow executions in the cloud through multiobjective evolutionary algorithms such as SPEA2 and NSGA-II. According to the experimental results, the ability to identify the Pareto-optimal solutions of SPEA2 and NSGA-II is virtually the same. In some cases, SPEA2 gives better convergence and diversity values than NSGA-II. However, a longer execution time is required by SPEA2 which is very important for the search process during workflow optimization. In multiobjective evolutionary algorithms such as SPEA2 and NSGA-II, the most important parts of the algorithms are in fitness assignment based on Pareto-domination: domination counts, nondominated sorting, and identification of the nondominated solutions. These processes can be done within $O(MN^2)$, where M is the number of objectives and N is the population size in both SPEA2 and NSGA-II. The time complexities of SPEA2 and NSGA-II are beyond the scope of this paper, but interested readers can refer to Jessen [21] for further details on the time complexities of multiobjective evolutionary algorithms.

5. Related Work and Discussion

The use of cloud in scientific experiments is a popular alternative because transferring large volumes of data to processing nodes is impractical in this era of continuously increasing big data. However, the right virtual machine instance selection for a specific application is a challenging problem for the cloud users. Thus, optimization system approaches that easily facilitate optimized cloud resource selection are actively being researched. Thus, various single-objective and multiobjective optimization strategies have been proposed.

The proposed single-objective optimization strategies primarily focused on developing effective scheduling strategies to reduce makespan. For example, Tanaka and Tatebe [20] proposed a data-aware scheduling strategy that reduces makespan by minimizing data movement between cluster nodes was presented. However, their strategy can only operate with homogeneous resources during workflow execution and is not suitable for use in cloud environments. Chen and Deelman [1] proposed a workflow scheduling strategy that uses horizontal or vertical task clustering techniques to reduce the schedule overhead during workflow execution. Yan et al. [22] proposed a novel probability evaluation-based scheduling algorithm to address the problem of workflow deadline guarantee. They showed that their approach is effective in terms of adaptability and predictability under deadline constraints, but improvements in deadline distribution are still necessary. Kaur and Mehta [23] proposed workflow scheduling in clouds using augmented shuffled frog leaping algorithm (ASFLA). They improved the original shuffled frog leaping algorithm (SFLA) to speed up the overall execution time of the workflow. Experiments conducted showed significant reduction in overall workflow execution time, but resource usage cost was not accounted for in the system.

Poola et al. [24] presented a resource scheduling algorithm for workflow execution on heterogeneous cloud resources along with makespan and cost minimization. However, the robustness and effectiveness of their proposed system depend on an increased budget. Zhu et al. [2] proposed a multiobjective workflow scheduling approach for cloud infrastructure. In their proposed approach, they enhance the evolution process of their optimization by introducing two novel crossover and mutation operators. They conducted experiments based on actual pricing and resource parameters on Amazon EC2 but did not consider task dependencies during workflow executions and simply assumed that all tasks can be executed in parallel. Zhang et al. [25] proposed biobjective workflow optimization on energy consumption and reliability in heterogeneous computing systems.

Single-objective and multiobjective workflow execution optimization has been conducted on cluster, grid, and cloud infrastructure in recent years. Single-objective optimization approaches are focused on minimizing the workflow makespan through scheduling [20, 22, 23] and task clustering approach [1]. However, single-objective optimization is not sufficient for data intensive workflows. Our proposed method is focused on multiobjective workflow execution optimization in the cloud infrastructure. Although similar work [23, 24] has been carried out on cloud infrastructure, the approaches employed have limitations in terms of resource elasticity and task dependencies. Moreover, previous studies do not cover important issues associated with VM instances such as VM failure probability. Our proposed approach addresses these issues as follows:

(1) Randomized search-based resource selection to better fit resource usage

(2) Level-wise task processing approach for task dependencies and resource elasticity

(3) Balanced task clustering for better load balancing and resource sharing

(4) Optimized workflow execution on three objectives (including cloud SLA related objectives)

In this way, the proposed system helps with the selection of the right resources through multiobjective optimization during workflow executions that benefits both stakeholders (users and cloud service providers).

6. Conclusion and Future Work

Machine instance resource selection for scientific workflow applications with the best performance, the cheapest deployment cost, and minimum failure probability is still challenging in the cloud. Without proper resource selection, it may lead to user dissatisfaction (owing to high costs and unreliable result data) which can affect the service providers' business. In this study, we addressed this problem by modeling the workflow optimization problem as a three-objective optimization problem using SPEA2 and NSGA-II in the cloud. During workflow optimization, a fixed-length integer chromosome was used to represent a random number of VMs that can be deployed in each level of the workflow. The optimization process was conducted based on the random initial chromosome population and the respective fitness values of the chromosomes calculated. Our experimental results obtained on three real-world workflows available from the ongoing Pegasus research project [5] show that the proposed system reduces makespan with an acceptable cost tradeoff and instance failure. The results also indicated that the two objective functions (makespan and instance cost) are strongly related to each other, whereas failure minimization objective values are weakly related to or have no relation with the other two functions in some cases. Moreover, we found out that c4.xlarge machine instance type was a dominant instance type during optimization according to our model. In future work, we plan to include result comparisons with other multiobjective optimization algorithms such as NSGA-III and MOEA/D. In addition, many-objective optimization with makespan and budget constraints during workflow execution will be considered.

Conflicts of Interest

The authors declare that they have no conflicts of interest.

Acknowledgments

This work was supported by CREST, Japan Science and Technology Agency (Grant no. JPMJCR1501), and Nitobe School, Hokkaido University.

References

[1] W. Chen and E. Deelman, "WorkflowSim: A toolkit for simulating scientific workflows in distributed environments," in *Proceedings of the 2012 IEEE 8th International Conference on E-Science, e-Science 2012*, USA, October 2012.

[2] Z. Zhu, G. Zhang, M. Li, and X. Liu, "Evolutionary multi-objective workflow scheduling in cloud," *IEEE Transactions on Parallel and Distributed Systems*, vol. 27, no. 5, pp. 1344–1357, 2016.

[3] D. A. Prathibha, B. Latha, and G. Sumathi, "Efficient scheduling of workflow in cloud enviornment using billing model aware task clustering," *Journal of Theoretical and Applied Information Technology*, vol. 65, no. 3, pp. 595–605, 2014.

[4] H. Khajemohammadi, A. Fanian, and T. A. Gulliver, "Efficient Workflow Scheduling for Grid Computing Using a Leveled Multi-objective Genetic Algorithm," *Journal of Grid Computing*, vol. 12, no. 4, pp. 637–663, 2014.

[5] Pegasus Workflow Generator. http://confluence.pegasus.isi.edu/display/pegasus/WorkflowGenerator, 2016.

[6] P. T. Thant, C. Powell, M. Schlueter, and M. Munetomo, "A level-wise load balanced scientific workflow execution optimization using NSGA-II," in *Proceedings of the 2017 17th IEEE/ACM International Symposium on Cluster, Cloud and Grid Computing (CCGRID)*, pp. 882–889, Madrid, Spain, 2017.

[7] E. Zitzler, M. Laumanns, and L. Thiele, SPEA2: Improving the strength Pareto evolutionary algorithm for multiobjective optimization. Evolutionary Methods for Design Optimization and Control with Applications to Industrial Problems, 2001.

[8] K. Deb, A. Pratap, S. Agarwal, and T. Meyarivan, "A fast and elitist multiobjective genetic algorithm: NSGA-II," *IEEE Transactions on Evolutionary Computation*, vol. 6, no. 2, pp. 182–197, 2002.

[9] G. Scherp, *A Framework for Model Driven Scientific Workflow Engineering [Dissertation, thesis]*, Kiel Computer Science Series, University of Oldenburg, Germany, 2013.

[10] B. Ludashcer, M. Weske, T. McPhillips, and S. Bowers, "Scientific Workflows: Business as Usual?" in *Proceedings of the 7th International Conference on Business Process Management, BPM 2009*, pp. 31–47, Springer, 2009.

[11] N. Srinivas and K. Deb, "Multiobjective function optimization using nondominated sorting genetic algorithms," *Evolutionary Computation*, vol. 2, no. 3, pp. 221–248, 1995.

[12] C. Chitra, *Performance Comparison of Multi-objective Evolutionary Algorithms for QoS Routing Problems in Computer Networks [Dissertation, thesis]*, 2011.

[13] S. Kushwaha, *Multiobjective optimization of cluster measures in Microarray Cancer data using Genetic Algorithm Based Fuzzy Clustering [Dissertation, thesis]*, National Institute of Technology Rourkela, India, 2013.

[14] Amazon Service, Cloud. https://aws.amazon.com/ec2/instance-types/, 2017.

[15] PassMark Benchmark, CPU. https://www.umed.pl/zp/pliki/11412.pdf, 2017.

[16] J. Knowles and D. Corne, "The pareto archived evolution strategy: a new baseline algorithm for Pareto multiobjective optimisation," in *Proceedings of the Congress on Evolutionary Computation (CEC '99)*, vol. 1, pp. 98–105, July 1999.

[17] E. Zitzler, "Evolutionary algorithms for multiobjective Optimization: Methods and applications Doctoral dissertation ETH 13398," in *Swiss Federal Institute of Technology (ETH)*, Zurich, Switzerland, 1999.

[18] F.-M. De Rainville, F.-A. Fortin, M.-A. Gardner, M. Parizeau, and C. Gagné, "DEAP: A Python framework for Evolutionary Algorithms," in *Proceedings of the 14th International Conference on Genetic and Evolutionary Computation, GECCO'12*, pp. 85–92, USA, July 2012.

[19] S. Bharathi, A. Chervenak, E. Deelman, G. Mehta, M. Su, and K. Vahi, "Characterization of scientific workflows," in *Proceedings of the 3rd Workshop on Workflows in Support of Large-Scale Science (WORKS '08)*, 10, 1 pages, IEEE, November 2008.

[20] M. Tanaka and O. Tatebe, "Workflow scheduling to minimize data movement using multi-constraint graph partitioning," in *Proceedings of the 12th IEEE/ACM International Symposium on Cluster, Cloud and Grid Computing, CCGrid 2012*, pp. 65–72, Canada, May 2012.

[21] M. T. Jensen, "Reducing the Run-Time Complexity of Multiobjective EAs: The NSGA-II and Other Algorithms," *IEEE Transactions on Evolutionary Computation*, vol. 7, no. 5, pp. 503–515, 2003.

[22] C. Yan, H. Luo, Z. Hu, X. Li, and Y. Zhang, "Deadline guarantee enhanced scheduling of scientific workflow applications in grid," *Journal of Computers (Finland)*, vol. 8, no. 4, pp. 842–850, 2013.

[23] P. Kaur and S. Mehta, "Resource provisioning and work flow scheduling in clouds using augmented Shuffled Frog Leaping Algorithm," *Journal of Parallel and Distributed Computing*, vol. 101, pp. 41–50, 2017.

[24] D. Poola, S. K. Garg, R. Buyya, Y. Yang, and K. Ramamohanarao, "Robust scheduling of scientific workflows with deadline and budget constraints in clouds," in *Proceedings of the 28th IEEE International Conference on Advanced Information Networking and Applications, IEEE AINA 2014*, pp. 858–865, Canada, May 2014.

[25] L. Zhang, K. Li, C. Li, and K. Li, "Bi-objective workflow scheduling of the energy consumption and reliability in heterogeneous computing systems," *Information Sciences*, 2015.

16

MHDFS: A Memory-Based Hadoop Framework for Large Data Storage

Aibo Song,[1] **Maoxian Zhao,**[2] **Yingying Xue,**[1] **and Junzhou Luo**[1]

[1]*School of Computer Science and Engineering, Southeast University, Nanjing 211189, China*
[2]*College of Mathematics and Systems Science, Shandong University of Science and Technology, Qingdao 266590, China*

Correspondence should be addressed to Aibo Song; absong@seu.edu.cn

Academic Editor: Laurence T. Yang

Hadoop distributed file system (HDFS) is undoubtedly the most popular framework for storing and processing large amount of data on clusters of machines. Although a plethora of practices have been proposed for improving the processing efficiency and resource utilization, traditional HDFS still suffers from the overhead of disk-based low throughput and I/O rate. In this paper, we attempt to address this problem by developing a memory-based Hadoop framework called MHDFS. Firstly, a strategy for allocating and configuring reasonable memory resources for MHDFS is designed and RAMFS is utilized to develop the framework. Then, we propose a new method to handle the data replacement to disk when memory resource is excessively occupied. An algorithm for estimating and updating the replacement is designed based on the metrics of file heat. Finally, substantial experiments are conducted which demonstrate the effectiveness of MHDFS and its advantage against conventional HDFS.

1. Introduction

Recent years have seen an astounding growth of enterprises having urgent requirements to collect, store, and analyze enormous data for analyzing important information. These requirements continuously step over a wide spectrum of application domains, ranging from e-business and search engine to social networking [1, 2].

With the significant increment of data consumption in various applications, from the level of GB to PB, there is an urgent need for such platforms with superior ability to store and process this exploding information. As the most used commercial computing model based on the Internet, cloud computing is currently employed as the primary solution and can provide reliable, scalable, and flexible computing abilities as well as theoretically unlimited storage resources [3]. With necessary components available, such as networks, computational nodes, and storage media, large-scale distributed clouding platforms can be conveniently and quickly built for various data-intensive applications.

Conventional could computing systems mainly rely on distributed disk storages and employ the management subsystems to integrate enormous machines and build the effective computing platform. Typical cloud computing platforms include Apache Hadoop [4], Microsoft Azure [5], and Google MapReduce [6, 7], among which the open-source Hadoop system gains particular interests in practice. Generally, these platforms all provide high throughput in data access and data storing for clients by effectively managing distributed computer resources, which are proved to be appropriate to store and process large amount of data in real-world applications.

However, as the evolvement of modern computer hardware, the capacity of various memory media is continuously increasing, with the decline of their prices. Considering this situation, researchers and engineers have focused their effort on the employment and management of memory resources to step across the bottleneck of I/O rate in conventional distributed cloud computing systems.

Current memory-based distributed file systems are mostly designed for the real-time applications, including HANA [8] and Spark [9, 10] as the typical representatives. Their goal is to speed up the process of data writing and reading from different perspectives. HANA is the platform developed by SAP Inc. and is widely used in fast data processing by employing a specifically designed framework of memory-based distributed storing. Even though HANA platform is widely adopted, it is mainly designed to handle the structured data instead of semistructured data. Since there are quite a number of applications based on semistructured or even unstructured data, HANA is not suitable for them. Meanwhile, HANA is usually memory-intensive due to its high occupation of memory space. Spark is a recently involved cloud computing system based on memory that employs the basic concept of resilient distributed datasets (RDD) to effectively manage the data transformation and storage. Spark is a fast and general-purpose cluster computing system which provides high-level APIs and an optimized engine that supports general job executions. It is highly dependent on the third-party component Mesos [11], whose authority is to manage and isolate various memory resources. This causes the unreliability and absence of customization for Spark. Additionally, Spark is based on its self-developed data model called RDD (resilient distributed datasets) that differs significantly from the conventional HDFS data model. Thus, the problem of compatibility is also the crucial part for its limited employment on existing applications. Developers have to design their data structures and architectures from scratch.

Based on the above analysis, this paper mainly focuses on improving the current infrastructure of HDFS. We extended the storage media of HDFS from solely disk-based to memory-based, with disk storage as addition, and designed a proper strategy to preferentially store data into the memory. Meanwhile, we proposed an algorithm of memory data replacement for handling the overload of limited memory space and effectively increase the average I/O rate as well as overall throughput of the system.

The main difference of our MHDFS framework compared to Spark and HANA includes two aspects. Firstly, we developed the framework based on native Hadoop, which provides consistent APIs and data structures. So existing applications based on Hadoop can conveniently migrate to MHDFS with little changes. Secondly, we designed the memory data replacement module as the secondary storage. So MHDFS can automatically handle the situation when memory space is nearly occupied.

The remainder of this paper is organized as follows. Section 2 presents a brief description of our proposed MHDFS system and demonstrates the key architecture. Section 3 gives the strategies of allocating and deploying distributed memory resources. Section 4 introduces fault tolerance design based on memory data replacement. Then, in Section 5, experiments on different size of data are conducted to evaluate the effectiveness of our proposed model. Finally, we present related studies in Section 6 and conclude our work in Section 7.

2. Architecture

Based on the previous analysis, we now present MHDFS, a memory-based Hadoop framework for large data storage. MHDFS is an incremental system of the native HDFS. Other than the normal modules, it includes two other modules, the memory resource deployment module and the memory data replacement module. The architecture of MHDFS is shown in Figure 1. In MHDFS, name node accepts clients' requests and forwards them to assigned data nodes for specific writing or reading jobs. Data nodes are based on both memory and disk spaces, where memory space is selected as the preferred storing media against disk through the help of memory resource deployment module. Meanwhile, for handling the problem of limited memory space, memory data replacement module is involved as the middleware and swaps files into disk when necessary. And it is proved to be useful to the robustness of the whole system.

2.1. Memory Resource Deployment Module. This module is designed for configuring and allocating available memory space for deploying MHDFS. Based on the analysis on the historical physical memory usage of each data node, we estimate the size of available memory space, that is, the remaining memory space not occupied by ordinary executions of a machine. Then, the estimated memory space will be mapped to a file path and used for deploying MHDFS. Data will be preferentially written into the memory space instead of the conventional HDFS disk blocks.

2.2. Memory Data Replacement Module. This module is designed for swapping data between memory and disk when RAM space is occupied by executing jobs. In this module, a reasonable upper bound is set to start the data replacement process. In addition, a submodel based on file accessed heat is proposed to find the best swapping data block. Intuitively, the file heat is related to the access frequency of a file; that is, files being accessed frequently during recent period will generally have higher heats. Details will be presented in Section 3. In this submodel, heat of each file will be evaluated and files in the memory will be ranked according to their heat. Then, files with low heat will be swapped out to the local disk so as to ensure the available memory space for subsequent job executions.

3. Strategy of Memory Resource Deployment

3.1. Allocation of Memory Resources. In order to allocate available memory resources for deploying HDFS, we utilized the records of physical memory on each data node and estimate the reasonable memory spaces. The key strategy is stated as follows.

We denote the total memory capacity of each data node as M_T, which is related to the configuration of the physical machine. To calculate the available memory space for deploying MHDFS, we monitor the usage information of data node within a time duration of ΔT and record the maximal RAM usage as M_h. Since the memory usage is fluctuating continuously with enormous job executions, we give a relax to the local computing usage and set the maximal usage as $\delta \times M_h$. The value of δ is determined by the running status of different clusters, but generally we could set it as 120% to satisfy the local job executing requirements. Finally,

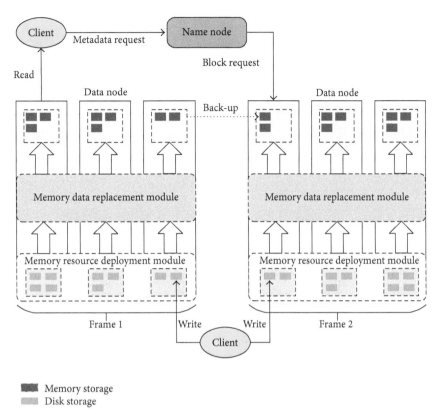

FIGURE 1: The architecture of MHDFS.

the remaining memory space is allocated as the resources for MHDFS, which is called the maximum available memory storage space (M_a):

$$M_a = M_T - M_h * 120\%. \tag{1}$$

If the calculated M_a is less than or equal to zero, the historical maximal memory usage on the node is convinced to exceed 83.3%, which further indicates the heavy load of physical memory. In this case, due to the lack of enough available memory spaces, this data node is decided to be unsuitable for allocating memory resources for MHDFS. Intuitively, when the total size of written data exceeds M_a, MHDFS will prevent subsequent data writing into the memory of this node.

Since HDFS requires the storage paths mapping to specific directories, we have to map the available memory space to a file path. For the sake of convenience, *Ramfs* is used as the developing tool [12]. It is a RAM-based file system integrated into the Linux kernel and works at the layer of virtual file system (VFS).

According to the maximal available memory space M_a proposed above, we use *Ramfs* to mount the memory space to a predefined file path, so that data could be written into the memory accordingly. *Ramfs* takes the advantage of dynamically allocating and utilizing memory resources. To be more specific, if the amount of written data is less then M_a, say M_d ($M_d < M_a$), *Ramfs* only occupies the memory space of size M_d while the remaining are still preserved for ordinary job executions. With the size of written data increasing continuously, *Ramfs* enlarges the total occupied

memory space to meet system requirements. The size of the remaining memory space could be marked as

$$M_p = M_T - M_d, \tag{2}$$

where M_T is the total memory space of the data node and M_d is the actual used memory space by MHDFS.

Ramfs ensures M_p always being positive along with the process of data reading and writing, which improves the effectiveness of memory utilization of the physical machine. And the mechanism of dynamically allocating memory resources further reduces its inferior effect to the capability of local job executions. Practically, we can set parameters in *hdfs-site.xml* file and configure the file path mapped from memory to another storage path of data block.

3.2. Management of Memory Resource. Conventionally, data is usually stored in the unit called data block in HDFS. Traditional data storing process in HDFS could be summarized as the following steps: (1) client requests for writing data, (2) name node takes charge of assigning data nodes for writing and recording the information of assigned nodes, and (3) specific data nodes store the writing data to its self-decided file paths.

The data storage structure of the data node could be demonstrated as in Figure 2. Each FSVolume represents a data storage path and the FSVolumeSet manages all FSVolumes which is configured in the directory of ${dfs.data.dir}$. Generally, there is more than one data storage path ${dfs.data.dir}$ on each data node; HDFS employs

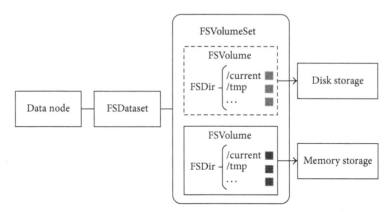

FIGURE 2: The data storage structure of MHDFS.

the strategy of round robin to select different paths so that data at each path could be balanced. The general idea of round-robin path selection is to use variable *curVolume* to record current selected storage path increasing it by one after a block of data is written each time. Then *curVolume* points to the next storage path in the volumes array. When each data block is written, storage path is changed and finally, after *curVolume* reaches the end of volumes array, it will be redirected to the head.

To ensure data written into the memory preferentially, we rewrite the policy of selecting storage path in HDFS. We assign different file paths with different priorities, sort them ordered by priority, and then store the file paths into the *volumes* array of the data node. Considering Figure 2, for example, with the memory-based storage path in array volumes[0] and the disk-based storage path in array volumes[1], we check the paths in the array from start when data is written. MHDFS will continuously check the paths subsequently until a satisfied one is found out.

4. Strategy of Memory Data Replacement

4.1. File Replacement Threshold Setting. Obviously, memory resource of physical machines is limited compared with disk spaces. When the remaining memory space of the data node is below a specific threshold, the process of replacing data stored in memory into disk will be triggered. In MHDFS, we design a strategy of threshold measuring and replacement trigger.

The threshold setting is specific to the user and application, whereas it is usually acceptable to set as the 10% of the maximal available storage space of the data node, which means when there is less than 10% of maximal available space remaining, MHDFS should start the process of replacement.

Based on the assumption that the maximum available memory on a data node DN is M_a and the already used memory space on DN is M_u, the trigger condition could be set that the remaining memory space is less than 10% of M_a. The data replacement trigger threshold on the DN node is denoted as T_{start}, and its formula could be wrote as follows:

$$T_{\text{start}} = (M_a - M_u) - 10\% * M_a. \tag{3}$$

After the writing operation has finished on DN, the detection of the threshold T_{start} will be conducted.

Replacing process is constantly conducted with low heat file swapped out from the memory until (4) is satisfied, which indicates that the available memory space on DN is sufficient again:

$$T_{\text{stop\_s}} \leq \frac{M_a - M_u}{M_a}. \tag{4}$$

Generally, the threshold for stopping the replacement process is very specific to different applications and configurations of clusters, which is decided by the user himself. In this paper, according to the environment of our experimenting cluster, the default stopping threshold is set as $T_{\text{stop\_s}} = 40\%$; that is, when the available memory on DN exceeds $40\% * M_a$ after the involvement of memory data replacement, the replacement process will be suspended and data will be still kept retaining in memory to ensure the efficiency of subsequent data accesses.

4.2. Measurement of File Heat. In order to make the file replacement effective, a strategy has to be proposed to identify the files to be replaced. Intuitively, if a file is accessed frequently by the applications, it is more preferable to retain in memory, while the less frequently visited files could be swapped into the disk to save memory space.

A frequency-based heat parameter is proposed in MHDFS to handle the problem stated above. The heat parameter will be stored in the metainformation of each file in the memory, which records the access frequency and access volume. Basically, there are three rules:

(1) Files with more frequent access have higher heat.

(2) Files with larger amount of data access have higher heat.

(3) Files with shorter survival time have higher heat.

We designed the heat metric based on the theory of time series which can evaluate the accessing status of each file. The frequency of the file being accessed is recorded within time interval. The heat is updated after the file is accessed. The

---

Input:
    Operation: Type of Operate of Write and Read
    RDatNum: Number of byte of requesting to access the file, or Number off byte of writing into file
    ⟨*Fseq, Heat, Life, AccessT, InVisitT*⟩: File List, Current Heat, Life Time, Access Time, Access Interval
Output: Result: Result of Update
(1) **Function** UpdateHeatDegree
(2)   Seq = Fseq;
(3)   //Get current time;
(4)   Time = getTime();
(5)   **if** (operation == read) **then**
(6)   factor = (Time − AccessT)/InvisitT + (Time − AccessT);
(7)   New_heat = (factor * RDatNum + (1 − factor) * heat)/(Time − Life);
(8)   InvisitT = Time − AccessT;
(9)   AccessT = Time;
(10)   Heat = New_Heat;
(11)   **return** Success, ⟨Fseq, Heat, Life, AccessT, InVisitT⟩
(12)   **end if**
(13)   **if** (operation == write) **then**
(14)   AccessT = Time;
(15)   InvisitT = Time − AccessT;
(16)   **if** (operation == create) **then**
(17)   Fseq = new Fseq();
(18)   New_heat = 0;
(19)   Life = Time;
(20)   Heat = New_heat;
(21)   **return** Success, ⟨Fseq, Heat, Life, AccessT, InVisitT⟩
(22)   **end if**
(23)   **if** (operation == add) **then**
(24)   **return** Success, ⟨Fseq, Heat, Life, AccessT, ReSetT⟩
(25)   **end if**
(26)   **end if**
(27)   **if** (operation == delete) **then**
(28)   delete(Fseq);
(29)   **return** null
(30)   **end if**
(31)   **return** Fail, ⟨Fseq, Heat, Life, AccessT, ReSetT⟩
(32) **End**

ALGORITHM 1: Memory file heat update.

shorter the interval is, the greater impact the access has, and vice versa.

We denote $H_i(f)$ as the head of the file on data nodes in the memory storage and propose the following equation:

$$H_0(f) = 0$$

$$H_i(f) = \frac{\beta * S_i + (1 - \beta) * H_{i-1}(f)}{T_i}, \tag{5}$$

where $\beta = \Delta t_i / (\Delta t_i + \Delta t_{i-1})$.

Apparently, the equation is consistent with the above three principles. When a file is accessed frequently, $H_{i-1}(f)$ gives more weight to $H_i(f)$, and if bytes of accessed data S_i are large or file survival time T_i is small, $H_i(f)$ will also generate a larger result. β is an adjustment factor based on the time series, which mainly works for adjusting the relationship between the current heat and historical heat.

A larger adjustment factor results in a greater impact of data accessed amount to the file heat, while a smaller one gives more weight to the historical heat value.

4.3. File Heat Update. As can be seen from Section 4.2, file heat updating process is specific to different data operations. In this paper, we categorize various data operations into three groups: (1) writing operation, including creating and adding, (2) reading operation, and (3) deleting operation. Considering the three kinds of operations, the updating strategy is demonstrated as pseudocodes in Algorithm 1.

The updating of file heat information includes adding, updating, and deleting. Initially, the heat of a file is zero which clearly means that newly created file with no reading access never has a positive heat. And if a file has never been read since creation, the associated heat value will remain unchanged. This indicates that reading operation is closely related to the increase of file heat which is confirmed to our common sense. The updating process can be summarized as follows.

(1) For reading operations, accessed data size and accessing time will be recorded, and our algorithm will update the file heat as well as the access interval parameter according to (5).

(2) For writing operations, we consider them as two cases: (a) creating operation: a file sequence number and file feat are initialized, with both creating time and access time as current system time and access interval as zero; (b) adding operation: adding time is recorded and access interval is updated, without updating the file heat. This is consistent with the above analysis that only reading operations can directly impact the altering of file heat.

(3) For deleting operations, file heat record will be deleted based on the defined file sequence number.

4.4. File Replacement. Based on the measurements of threshold setting and file heat updating strategy stated above, we designed the module of memory file replacement. The process can be summarized in Figure 3.

For the sake of simplicity, we set the starting threshold of replacement as 10% of total available memory space and the stopping threshold as 40% of total available memory space. The process could be summarized as the following steps:

(1) Check the remaining memory, and if remaining memory space is less than 10% of M_a, replacement process shall be started.

(2) Sort all files in memory by their file heats in descending order.

(3) Generally, each file may contain a number of data blocks. Replacement process starts from the data block with the longest survival time until all the data blocks are moved out.

(4) When all data blocks in a file have been replaced into the disk, the corresponding file heat is deleted and replacement process carries on to replace the data block in the file with secondary lowest file heat.

(5) Suspend replacement process when the remaining space reaches 40% of M_a again.

5. Experiment

In order to showcase the performance of our proposed MHDFS model, we did comparison experiments on stimulated datasets. Reading and writing performance is evaluated on different size of data, say, 2 GB and 8 GB. *Ramfs* is utilized as the developing tool for the mapping of memory space.

5.1. Experimental Setup. Experimental cluster is set up with nine nodes: one for the Hadoop name node and resource manager, and the others for the data nodes and data managers. Each node is a physical machine with dual 3.2 GHz

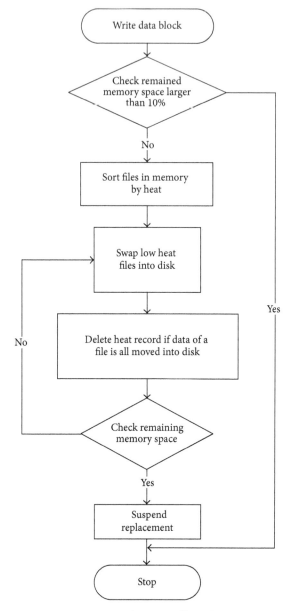

FIGURE 3: Process of memory file replacement.

Xeon EM64 CPU, 4 GB MEM, and 80 GB HDD, connected via Gigabit Ethernet. We use Red Hat Enterprise Linux Server Release 6.2 as the host operating system and the version of Hadoop distribution is 2.6.0.

For conducting the experiments, we map the memory of name node to the file storage path using *Ramfs* and configure two file paths (one for the disk storage and the other for the memory storage) in the Hadoop configuration file. After recompilation, HDFS can identify both the file paths and dynamically assign priority to them.

5.2. Performance Comparison on Single-Node Cluster

5.2.1. I/O Test with Small Datasets (Less Than 2 GB). Data reading and writing operations are conducted on MHDFS

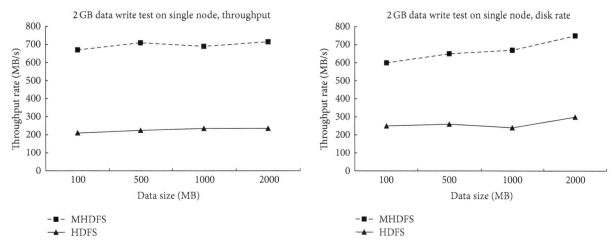

FIGURE 4: HDFS/MHDFS 2 GB data write test on single-node cluster.

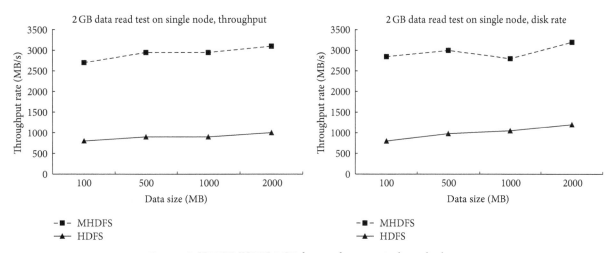

FIGURE 5: HDFS/MHDFS 2 GB data read test on single-node cluster.

and HDFS based on a single-node cluster and performance is recorded to evaluate the effectiveness of our proposed model. Data size increases continuously from 500 MB to 2 GB. The evaluating results are shown in Figures 4 and 5.

Generally, the throughput and average disk write rate of both models increase with the increment of data size. The throughput of HDFS is floating around 300 MB/s, whereas MHDFS reaches up to 700–800 MB/s, almost three times faster than HDFS. The result shows that MHDFS can significantly improve the performance of writing data compared with conventional HDFS.

Considering the reading performance shown in Figure 5, the throughput of HDFS is floating around 900 MB/s, while MHDFS is up to 3000 MB/s, which is also three times of HDFS. Internally, MHDFS is able to respond to data reading requests in time, since the data read by MHDFS is preferentially stored in memory, rather than disk. Besides, the relatively good performance of HDFS is highly related to the use of SSD, which further indicates the significant improvement of MHDFS against HDFS in various conditions.

5.2.2. I/O Test with Large Datasets (from 2 GB to 8 GB). In this subsection, we evaluate our proposed MHDFS model with larger size of datasets. Intuitively, when the written data exceeds a certain size, memory space is occupied, and subsequent writing will be directed to file paths in the disk.

Figure 6 shows the results of performance evaluation with data size varying from 2 GB to 8 GB. Generally, after the data size reaches over 2 GB, the throughout and average I/O rate both have declined due to the lack of memory space. In detail, the value of throughput and average I/O rate of writing and reading have declined from 800 Mps to 600 Mps and 3000 Mps to 2000 Mps, respectively. Even though both MHDFS and HDFS get declined performance with data increases, MHDFS still achieves higher results against HDFS. This is consistent with our expectation and can be explained as follows. When memory space is insufficient, data replacement operation will be started and data can only be stored into disk during the replacing period. This may lead to the declined performance of MHDFS for a while. After the complete of replacement, data is still written into the available

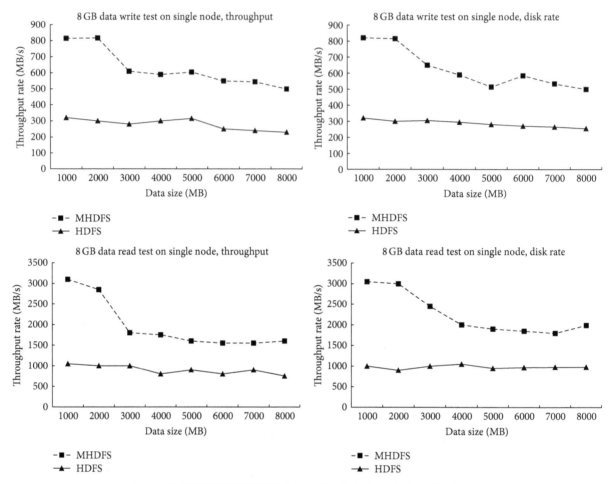

FIGURE 6: HDFS/MHDFS 8 GB data read/write test on single-node cluster.

memory space and reaches a relatively stable performance with subsequent writing requests.

5.3. Performance Comparison on Multinode Cluster.
For comparing the performance of MHDFS and conventional HDFS in real-world distributed environment, we conducted experiments on the multinode cluster. We configure different memory resources for MHDFS on each node to test the triggering and swapping strategy. The configuration is shown in Table 1.

Generally, nine nodes are selected for the experiment: one for master node and the others for data nodes. The total memory allocated for MHDFS is 10100 MB, where master node is allocated 2 GB for ensuring the execution of the whole cluster. Memory allocation on each data node is according to the historical maximal memory usage individually. We use the Linux command *top* to periodically monitor the ordinary memory usage of each machine and estimate the maximal one. And for testing the effectiveness of our memory data replacement strategy, the experiment data size is designed to exceed the available total memory space.

5.3.1. I/O Test with Small Datasets (Less Than 10 GB).
We evaluate the performance of MHDFS and HDFS on small

TABLE 1: Memory storage resources on each node.

Node	Historical maximal memory usage	Allocated memory size (MB)
Master	/	2000
N1	59.7%	1250
N2	62.6%	1000
N3	65.0%	900
N4	61.9%	1050
N5	68.1%	750
N6	58.9%	1200
N7	62.7%	1000
N8	64.1%	950

datasets, say, less than 10 GB, when memory space for the whole cluster is not fully occupied. In this case, MHDFS will not trigger the process of data swapping and disk storing. The amount of data is increasing from 1 GB to 10 GB, every 2 GB as the step. The results are shown in Figures 7 and 8.

As can be seen from Figure 7, the writing throughput and average writing rate of MHDFS are 45 Mbps and 50 Mbps, respectively, which only has a slight improvement over HDFS

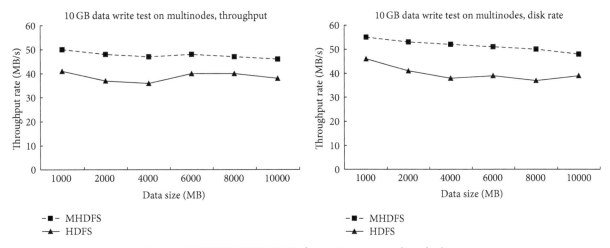

FIGURE 7: HDFS/MHDFS 10 GB data write test on multinode cluster.

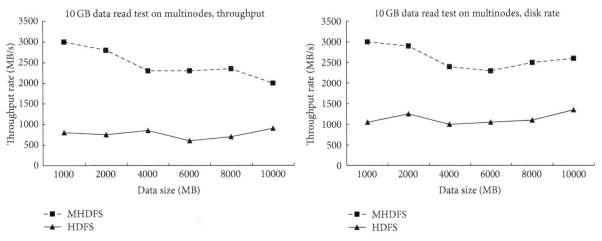

FIGURE 8: HDFS/MHDFS 10 GB data read test on multinode cluster.

compared with results in single-node environment. This is due to the fact that writing data into the cluster requires simultaneously copy writing; that is, for each writing, three copies of the data should be stored in different nodes. With 100 Mbps as the bandwidth of each node, the crucial cost of writing is actually the network overhead which cannot be improved by MHDFS. In fact, MHDFS is designed to leverage the memory space for handling disk writing overhead and thus can provide little help to other factors like network transferring.

Figure 8 presents the results of reading test. The reading throughput and average reading rate of MHDFS reaches 2600 Mbps and 2650 Mbps, respectively, which outperforms two and half times compared to HDFS. Undoubtedly, this is consistent with our theory that when reading data from cluster, data as well as its copies are mostly stored in memory and this provides very fast reading operations. Interestingly, however, with the increase of data size, the reading performance gets a few declines. This is because, for the single-node environment, all data can be read from memory while, for multinode clusters, some data must be transferred via network from other data nodes. The additional cost of

network transfer leads to the slightly decline when large amount of data is requested.

5.3.2. I/O Test with Large Datasets (from 10 GB to 25 GB). In this subsection, we evaluate our proposed MHDFS model with larger size of datasets in the environment of multinodes cluster. In this situation, MHDFS will employ the strategy of data replacement. Figures 9 and 10 demonstrate the writing and reading results.

From Figure 9, it is clear that when writing data exceeds 10 GB, that is, the allocated memory space for MHDFS, the writing performance declines due to the involvement of data replacement, even if it still outperforms HDFS with 5% to 15%.

Remarkably, different with the cases in single-node cluster, the adjective impact of data replacement is much slighter due to the fact that, in single-node situation, memory space is totally prohibited for writing when data replacement is conducted, while, for multinode cluster, replacing on one node will not affect another node's writing process; that is, data replacement seldom occurs on all nodes in the whole cluster.

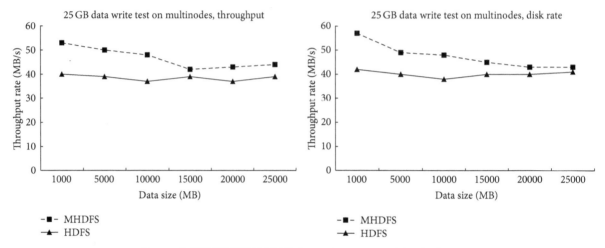

FIGURE 9: HDFS/MHDFS 25 GB data write test on multinode cluster.

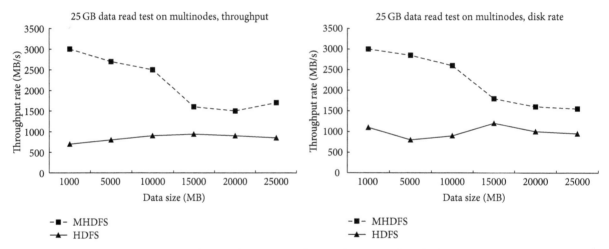

FIGURE 10: HDFS/MHDFS 25 GB data read test on multinode cluster.

The reading test result is undoubtedly consistent with other evaluations according to Figure 10, and, due to the factor of data locality, reading performance in multinode cluster declines faster than that in single-node situation. In detail, for single-node clusters, data is only read from local machine while, for multinode clusters, data shall occasionally be obtained from other machines via network.

5.4. A Real Case Benchmark. In this section, we benchmark our MHDFS framework compared with native HDFS based on the word-count case, that is, to evaluate the average performance when processing real-world applications. We evaluate the total executing time of the word-count cases as MapReduce jobs under different input sizes, and both the single-node and multinode clusters are examined (for the single-node case, we only use the name node as a stand-alone cluster). Figures 11 and 12 present the results of MHDFS and HDFS on various data sizes, respectively.

It is obvious that, on both single-node and multinode clusters, MHDFS achieves significant performance against traditional HDFS. This proves the improvement of our memory-based Hadoop framework that can accelerate the

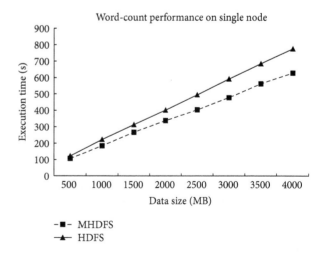

FIGURE 11: HDFS/MHDFS word-count test on single-node cluster.

execution of MapReduce jobs with the advantage of storing the input data and intermediate results into the memory space. Generally, the MapReduce process of word count can

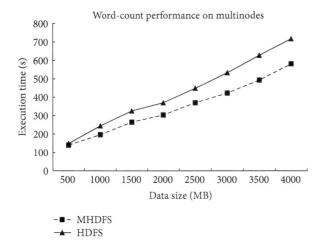

FIGURE 12: HDFS/MHDFS word-count test on multinode cluster.

generate double the sizes of its input; thus, for smaller size of input, MHDFS is quite close to HDFS, while, for larger size of input, MHDFS can notably benefit from the memory-based intermediate data storage.

The result on multinode cluster also indicates the overall better performance of MHDFS with the increasing of data size from 500 MB to 4 GB. Interestingly, due to the inferior capacities of data nodes, both MHDFS performance and HDFS performance are worse than that on single-node cluster from 500 MB to 1.5 GB. Since data processing is dispatched to various machines in a multinode cluster, the capability of machine is the major factor for smaller size of data, whereas, for larger size of data, it is the ability of parallel processing that counts, and thus HDFS and MHDFS achieve better performance than single-node situation, between which MHDFS costs less executing time owing to the employment of memory space.

6. Related Work

Despite its popularity and enormous applications, Hadoop has been the object of severe criticism, mainly due to its disk-based storage model [13]. The input and output data is required to be stored into the disk. Meanwhile, the inner mechanism for fault tolerance in Hadoop requires the intermediate results to be flushed into the hardware disk, which undoubtedly deteriorates the overall performance of processing large amount of data. In the literature, the existing improvement for Hadoop framework can be concluded as two categories: one aims at developing a wholly in-memory system that stores all the intermediate results into the memory, while the other focuses on employing a number of optimizations to make each usage of data more efficient [14, 15].

Spark [9, 10] and HANA [8] are typical examples belonging to the first category. They are totally in-memory systems that utilize the high throughput of memory media. Spark is a fast and general-purpose cluster computing system which provides high-level APIs and an optimized engine that supports general job executions. Resilient distributed datasets (RDD) are the key component for Spark to effectively manage the data transformation and storage in memory. HANA is the platform developed by SAP Inc. and is widely used in fast data processing by employing a specifically designed framework of memory-based distributed storing. The main shortcoming is that they are built upon another model completely different from native Hadoop which makes business migration inconvenient for companies. Meanwhile, the absence of disk utilization, to some extent, causes the systems' intensive dependence on limited memory spaces and lack of robust and fault tolerance. However, for those Hadoop-enhanced systems, these problems do not exist.

The second category, however, handles the problem from a different perspective. Hu et al. [15] analyzed the multiple-job parallelization problem and proposed the multiple-job optimization scheduler to improve the hardware utilization by paralleling different kinds of jobs. Condie et al. [16] added pipelined job interconnections to reduce the communication cost and lower the reading overhead from disk hardware. Since these researches mostly focus on designing probable scheduling strategies or intermediate result storing strategies, it is not necessary to enumerate them all, and although they can improve the performance to some extent, these works do not touch upon the idea of deploying Hadoop based on memory spaces.

Our research is distinct from the existing literatures mainly in the following aspects. First, we build MHDFS solely upon native Hadoop system without any modification to the crucial interfaces. This makes MHDFS compatible with currently existing systems and applications and makes migration much easier. Second, we design the strategy of memory data replacement to handle the situation when memory is fully occupied. Disk storages are still effectively utilized to improve the overall performance of our system.

7. Conclusion

As the basic foundation of Hadoop ecosystem, disk-dependent HDFS has been widely employed in various applications. Considering its shortcomings, mainly in low performance of the disk-based storage, we designed and implemented a memory-based Hadoop distributed file system named MHDFS. We proposed the framework of allocating reasonable memory space for our model and employed *Ramfs* tool to develop the system. Besides, the strategy of memory data replacement is studied for handling the insufficiency of memory space. Experiment results on different size of data indicate the effectiveness of our model. Our future study will focus on the further improvement of our proposed model and study the performance in more complicated situations.

Competing Interests

The authors declare that they have no competing interests.

Acknowledgments

This work is supported by the National Natural Science Foundation of China under Grants nos. 61370207, 61572128, and 61320106007, China National High Technology Research and Development Program (2013AA013503), SGCC Science and Technology Program "Research on the Key Technologies of the Distributed Data Management in the Dispatching and Control System Platform of Physical Distribution and Logical Integration," Collaborative Innovation Center of Wireless Communications Technology, Collaborative Innovation Center of Novel Software Technology and Industrialization, Jiangsu Provincial Key Laboratory of Network and Information Security (BM2003201), and Key Laboratory of Computer Network and Information Integration of Ministry of Education of China under Grant no. 93K-9.

References

[1] J. Dean and S. Ghemawat, *MapReduce: Simplified Data Processing on Large Clusters*, OSDI, San Francisco, Calif, USA, 2004.

[2] D. Howe, M. Costanzo, P. Fey et al., "Big data: the future of biocuration," *Nature*, vol. 455, no. 7209, pp. 47–50, 2008.

[3] L. Youseff, M. Butrico, and D. Da Silva, "Toward a unified ontology of cloud computing," in *Proceedings of the IEEE Grid Computing Environments Workshop (GCE '08)*, pp. 1–10, Austin, Tex, USA, November 2008.

[4] Apache Hadoop [EB/OL], http://hadoop.apache.org.

[5] M. Isard, M. Budiu, Y. Yu, A. Birrell, and D. Fetterly, "Dryad: distributed data-parallel programs from sequential building blocks," in *Proceedings of the 2nd ACM SIGOPS/EuroSys European Conference on Computer Systems (EuroSys '07)*, pp. 59–72, Lisbon, Portugal, March 2007.

[6] J. Dean and S. Ghemawat, "MapReduce: simplified data processing on large clusters," *Communications of the ACM*, vol. 51, no. 1, pp. 107–113, 2008.

[7] J. Dean and S. Ghemawat, "MapReduce: a flexible data processing tool," *Communications of the ACM*, vol. 53, no. 1, pp. 72–77, 2010.

[8] SAP, HANA[EB/OL], http://www.saphana.com/.

[9] SPARK, [EB/OL], http://www.sparkada.com/.

[10] M. Zaharia, M. Chowdhury, M. J. Franklin, S. Shenker, and I. Stoica, "Spark: cluster computing with working sets," in *Proceedings of the 2nd USENIX Conference on Hot Topics in Cloud Computing (HotCloud '10)*, USENIX Association, 2010.

[11] B. Hindman, A. Konwinski, M. Zaharia et al., "Mesos: a platform for fine-grained resource sharing in the data center," in *Proceedings of the 8th USENIX Conference on Networked Systems Design and Implementation*, Boston, Mass, USA, April 2011.

[12] M. Zhao and R. J. Figueiredo, "Experimental study of virtual machine migration in support of reservation of cluster resources," in *Proceedings of the 2nd International Workshop on Virtualization Technology in Distributed Computing (VTDC '07)*, ACM, November 2007.

[13] C. Doulkeridis and K. Nørvåg, "A survey of large-scale analytical query processing in MapReduce," *The VLDB Journal*, vol. 23, no. 3, pp. 355–380, 2014.

[14] A. Shinnar, D. Cunningham, V. Saraswat, and B. Herta, "M3R: increased performance for in-memory Hadoop jobs," *Proceedings of the VLDB Endowment*, vol. 5, no. 12, pp. 1736–1747, 2012.

[15] W. Hu, C. Tian, X. Liu et al., "Multiple-job optimization in mapreduce for heterogeneous workloads," in *Proceedings of the 6th International Conference on Semantics Knowledge and Grid (SKG '10)*, pp. 135–140, IEEE, Beijing, China, November 2010.

[16] T. Condie, N. Conway, P. Alvaro, J. M. Hellerstein, K. Elmeleegy, and R. Sears, "MapReduce online," in *Proceedings of the 7th USENIX Symposium on Networked Systems Design and Implementation (NSDI '10)*, vol. 10, p. 20, 2010.

17

Adaptive Cost-Based Task Scheduling in Cloud Environment

Mohammed A. S. Mosleh,[1] **G. Radhamani,**[1]
Mohamed A. G. Hazber,[2] **and Syed Hamid Hasan**[3]

[1]*School of IT & Science, Dr. GR Damodaran College of Science, Coimbatore, India*
[2]*International School of Software Engineering, Wuhan University, Wuhan, China*
[3]*Information Systems Department, King Abdulaziz University, Jeddah, Saudi Arabia*

Correspondence should be addressed to Mohammed A. S. Mosleh; mohammed.mosleh@grd.edu.in

Academic Editor: Frank De Boer

Task execution in cloud computing requires obtaining stored data from remote data centers. Though this storage process reduces the memory constraints of the user's computer, the time deadline is a serious concern. In this paper, Adaptive Cost-based Task Scheduling (ACTS) is proposed to provide data access to the virtual machines (VMs) within the deadline without increasing the cost. ACTS considers the data access completion time for selecting the cost effective path to access the data. To allocate data access paths, the data access completion time is computed by considering the mean and variance of the network service time and the arrival rate of network input/output requests. Then the task priority is assigned to the removed tasks based data access time. Finally, the cost of data paths are analyzed and allocated based on the task priority. Minimum cost path is allocated to the low priority tasks and fast access path are allocated to high priority tasks as to meet the time deadline. Thus efficient task scheduling can be achieved by using ACTS. The experimental results conducted in terms of execution time, computation cost, communication cost, bandwidth, and CPU utilization prove that the proposed algorithm provides better performance than the state-of-the-art methods.

1. Introduction

Cloud computing is a promising technology that provides efficient services to the customers in a distant virtual platform on a pay-per-use model. The definition for cloud computing given by NIST [1] is as follows: cloud computing is a model for enabling ubiquitous, convenient, on-demand network access to shared computing resources which can be provisioned and provided with minimal interaction. Cloud computing provides different types of services such as infrastructure, software, and platform to the requested users with a specific price for the services. Cloud services use the internet and the central remote servers to maintain the data and applications. Cloud computing allows consumers and businesses to use applications without installation and access their personal files at any computer with internet access. This approach improves the computing processes such as data storage and processing. Cloud is deployed in different models: public cloud, private clouds, hybrid cloud, community cloud, and distributed cloud are some examples.

Service oriented architecture is the basic principle of the cloud computing which considers everything on the cloud as a service [2]. Infrastructure-as-a-service (IaaS) is the service of providing the physical machines (PM) or virtual machines (VM) to the user for processing resources, data partitioning, scaling, security, and backup processes. Platform-as-a-service (PaaS) provides the vendors with the platforms for development of applications including databases, web servers, and developmental tools. Software-as-a-service (SaaS) provides services for the e-mails, virtual desktops, communication processes, and gaming applications. The services are normally paid services whose price is fixed by the service providers based on the usage level of the customers. The price of the cloud services is very less compared to the other installed services.

In cloud computing, the tasks are performed in the physical machines (PMs) or the VMs as per the task requirements. The data required for the execution of the tasks and services are stored at multiple distant storage locations called the data centers which are also used with specific cost [3]. When the tasks are performed in the processing machines, the required data are requested and obtained from the data centers. The data from the data centers has to reach the VM within the particular time which is always the access completion time. The problem with this process is that the data is accessed through certain paths which are bound by the computation and storage costs. So it is possible that either one of the two situations arises: in order to obtain the data in time, the cost has to be sacrificed or, in order to reduce the cost, the delay in data access has to be accepted. This problem reduces the overall scheduling performance.

In order to overcome the data access problem, an adaptive cost-based task scheduling (ACTS) is proposed in this paper so that the data is obtained at the required time without delay and through affordable cost paths. The proposed approach estimates the completion time for accessing the data [13] that are required by the VM machines during the particular task executions. Then the cost of each possible path is estimated by the sum of computation, communication, and storage costs [14] of the path. Using the completion time for data access the priority of the tasks is assigned. The paths with high cost but with quick data access are assigned to tasks with high priority and the paths with low cost are assigned to the low priority tasks. Thus the data paths can be adaptively selected to reduce the overall cost and effectively deliver the data at the required time.

The remainder of the paper is summarized as follows: Section 2 explains the related researches briefly and presents the analysis of scheduling schemes. Section 3 presents the methodologies utilized in the paper. Section 4 provides the experimental results and their discussions. Section 5 concludes the research.

2. Related Works

A cloud scheduler is a cloud-enable distributed resource manager. It manages virtual machines on clouds to create an environment for job execution. The FIFO scheduler in Hadoop MapReduce, fair scheduler in Facebook, and capacity scheduler in Yahoo are typical examples that serve the cloud systems with efficient and equitable resource management, but none of these schedulers satisfies QoS (quality of service) constraints. Therefore, they are not applicable to soft real-time needed applications and services, which are becoming more and more important and necessary in the hybrid cloud environment. The main objective of this section is not to propose methodologies to overcome all of the current issues in cloud task scheduling but to study and analyze some of the current methodologies and focus on finding their drawbacks.

Sahni and Vidyarthi [4] presented a cost-effective deadline constraint dynamic scheduling algorithm for the scientific workflows. The workflow scheduling algorithms in the grid and clusters are efficient but could not be utilized effectively in the cloud environment because of the on-demand resource provisioning and pay-as-you-go pricing model. Hence the scheduling using a dynamic cost-effective deadline-constrained heuristic algorithm has been utilized to exploit the features of cloud by considering the virtual

machine performance variability and instance acquisition delay to determine the time scheduling. The problem with the approach is that VM failures may adversely affect the overall workflow execution time.

Tsai et al. [5] proposed hyper-heuristic scheduling algorithm (HHSA) for providing effective cloud scheduling solutions. The diversity detection and improvement detection operators are utilized in this approach to dynamically determine the better low-level heuristic for the effective scheduling. HHSA can reduce the makespan of task scheduling and improves the overall scheduling performance. The drawback is that the approach has high overhead of connection which reduces the importance of scheduling and thus reduces the overall performance.

Zhu et al. [6] proposed an agent-based dynamic scheduling algorithm named ANGEL for effective scheduling of tasks in the virtualized clouds. In this approach, a bidirectional announcement-bidding mechanism and the collaborative process are performed to improve the scheduling performance. To further improve the scheduling, elasticity is considered to dynamically add VMs. The calculation rules are generated to improve the bidding process that in turn reduces the delay. The problem with this approach is that it reduces the performance as it does not consider the communication and dispatching times.

Zhu et al. [7] presented an evolutionary multiobjective (EMO) workflow scheduling approach to reduce the workflow scheduling problem such as cost and makespan. Due to the specific properties of the workflow scheduling problem, the existing genetic operations, such as binary encoding, real-valued encoding, and the corresponding variation operators are based on them in the EMO. The problem is that the approach does not consider monetary costs and time overheads of both communication and storage.

Zhang et al. [8] proposed a fine-grained scheduling approach called phase and resource information-aware scheduler for MapReduce (PRISM) for scheduling in the MapReduce model. MapReduce has been utilized for its efficiency in reducing the running time of the data-intensive jobs but most of the MapReduce schedulers are designed on the basis of task-level solutions that provide suboptimal job performance. Moreover, the task-level schedulers face difficulties in reducing the job execution time. Hence the PRISM was developed which divides tasks into phases. Each phase with a constant resource usage profile performs scheduling at the phase level. Thus the overall job execution time can be reduced significantly but the problem of meeting job deadlines in the phase level scheduling is a serious concern that requires specified attention.

Zhu et al. [9] presented real-time task oriented energy aware (EA) scheduling called EARH for the virtualized clouds. The proposed approach is based on rolling-horizon (RH) optimization and the procedures are developed for creation, migration, and cancellation of VMs to dynamically adjust the scale of cloud to achieve real time deadlines and reduce energy. The EARH approach has the drawback of the number of cycles assigned to the VMs that cannot be updated dynamically.

TABLE 1: Drawbacks of scheduling schemes in literature.

Author	Scheduling scheme	Drawbacks
Sahni and Vidyarthi [4]	Cost-effective deadline constraint dynamic scheduling algorithm	VM failures increase the workload of other VMs and affect the execution time
Tsai et al. [5]	Hyper-heuristic scheduling algorithm	High overhead of connection
Zhu et al. [6]	Agent-based scheduling algorithm in virtualized clouds (ANGEL)	Nonconsideration of communication and dispatching time reducing performance
Zhu et al. [7]	Evolutionary multiobjective (EMO) workflow scheduling	Nonconsideration of monetary costs and time overhead does not improve performance
Zhang et al. [8]	Phase and resource information-aware scheduler for MapReduce (PRISM)	Deadlines are not specified
Zhu et al. [9]	Energy aware rolling-horizon (EARH) optimization based scheduling	Lack of updation in number of VM cycles
Maguluri and Srikant [10]	Throughput-optimal scheduling & load-balancing algorithm	Utilizing queue lengths in weights is based on assumption
Zuo et al. [11]	Self-adaptive learning particle swarm optimization- (SLPSO-) based scheduling	Lack of priority to deadline constraint tasks results in task failures
Su et al. [12]	Cost efficient task scheduling	Does not consider the completion time and cost (computation cost and communication cost)

Maguluri and Srikant [10] suggested a scheduling method for job scheduling with unknown duration in the cloud environment. The job sizes are assumed to be unknown not only at arrival, but also at the beginning of service. Hence the throughput-optimal scheduling and load-balancing algorithm for a cloud data center is introduced, when the job sizes are unknown. This algorithm is based on using queue lengths for weights in max-weight schedule instead of the workload.

Zuo et al. [11] presented self-adaptive learning particle swarm optimization- (SLPSO-) based scheduling approach for deadline constraint task scheduling in hybrid IaaS clouds. The approach solves the problem of meeting the peak demand for preserving the quality-of-service constraints by using the PSO optimization technique. The approach provides better scheduling of the tasks with maximizing the profit of IaaS provider while guaranteeing QoS. The problem with this approach is the lack of priority determination which results in failure of deadline tasks.

Scheduling tasks in a cloud computing environment is a challenging process. In [12] Su et al. presented a cost efficient task scheduling method that can be utilized for processing large size programs. But the performance of the approach is not sufficient as it did not consider the completion time and cost for scheduling.

From the literature it is found that the major issues in the above described methods are high cost consumption especially for communication and computation of data from cloud data centers. The inability to meet up the deadlines, due to the inappropriate data path allocation while task scheduling, is another area of concern. The analysis of various scheduling schemes is listed as below.

2.1. Analysis of Scheduling Schemes. Generally, the efficient task scheduling concepts of the clusters and the grid are not effective in the cloud environment. The main reason is that in cloud computing the resource provision is on-demand and the resources are provided on the basis of pay-per-use. Hence the scheduling approach has to make use of the features of the cloud in order to efficiently schedule the tasks without time delay. While processing a task in a VM, the data are needed to be obtained from the distant data centers located at multiple locations. As the tasks are deadline constraint, the data are needed to be obtained within the particular time using effective scheduling approaches. However, the solution for scheduling deadline constraint tasks in the cloud leads to a new problem in the form of cost. The computation and the storage resources are the basic resources in the cloud environment that forms the cost models.

Table 1 shows the various scheduling schemes described in literature and their drawbacks.

The high cost problems can be reduced by effectively selecting the minimum cost paths based on availability of the data paths. The problem is that not all the tasks take the same execution time which means some tasks require data quicker than the other tasks. But when using only the minimum cost path, the data would have to wait in queue or might be lost due to queue overflow. So the cost paths are needed to be selected adaptively for deadline constraint tasks. These two problems are the major focus of this research.

3. Adaptive Cost-Based Task Scheduling

The proposed adaptive cost-based task scheduling (ACTS) is discussed in this section. The scheduling of the tasks to the VMs can be performed effectively using the proposed scheduling method. This work takes inspiration from the work of Su et al. In their work, cost efficient task scheduling is used which considers the overall execution time and total monetary costs for scheduling. Though the execution time and monetary cost are considered this scheme cannot be considered as efficient due to the reason that these two factors are collaborative factors. The execution time is the time for task completion. This means the execution time includes the time from which the tasks are assigned to a VM until the output of the tasks is obtained. However, the time consumed for each process in task execution varies and not all of them can be minimized. In this sense, the time taken for obtaining the data from the data centers for task execution is considerably higher than all other process in task execution. Similarly, the monetary cost is the combined cost of resources for computation, communication, storage, data transfer, and so forth; in these processes, the costs for computation and communication are normally higher than other costs. But Su et al. considered only the combined factors for scheduling. Hence in the proposed ACTS we focused on specifically considering the individual processes as factors for scheduling. The major factors are *data access completion time, computation cost,* and *communication cost.*

The data that are required to be processed in the VM or the PM are stored in the distant data centers. These data are needed to be fetched to the processing VMs from the data centers through the cost-effective paths. The data access of each VM follows an independent Poisson distribution associated with the average rate of the arrival rate of the network I/O requests. The data access to the driver domain (PM) is processed on the basis of providing the access to the first come users while the other users wait in the queue. The service time of a data access in the driver domain is represented in an arbitrary distribution.

The data access completion time is considered to be the determination point in the selection of the data paths. The completion time for the data access is calculated by utilizing the parameters of the network input/output requests in the physical machines. The mean of the service time network I/O requests in the PMs is given by μ and the variance of the service time network I/O requests in the PMs is given by σ. The arrival rate of the network I/O requests to the PMs is given by λ. Then the completion time t of a data access can be estimated using the formula

$$t = \frac{2\mu - \lambda + \lambda\mu^2\sigma^2}{2\mu^2 - 2\lambda\mu}. \tag{1}$$

The arrival rate of the network I/O requests to the PMs can be calculated by

$$\lambda = \sum \lambda^{(e)} \cdot r^{(e)} + \sum \lambda^{(n)} \cdot r^{(n)}, \tag{2}$$

where $r^{(e)}$ and $r^{(n)}$ are the ratio of the CPU time allocated to the existing and new VMs. $\lambda^{(e)}$ and $\lambda^{(n)}$ are the arrival rate of the network I/O requests of the existing and new VMs to the PMs.

The tasks are performed in the virtual machine (VM) which obtains the data from cloud centers through the data access paths. Each data access path contains resources for processing the requests and accessing the data and also requires storage resources for storing the accessed data. Each of the resources carries certain costs for utilizing the resources. The computation cost includes the cost of resources for execution of the I/O requests for the data access and the cost for reaccessing the same data again.

It also includes the cost for regenerating the datasets. The communication cost is the total cost of the resources utilized for the processing of the I/O requests. It can be expressed as the product of the data set size and the network traffic price.

The cost of the possible data access paths is analyzed in order to determine the minimum cost path. The cost of each path can be estimated by

$$\text{Cost} = \text{Computation cost} + \text{Communication cost}. \tag{3}$$

The computation cost and communication cost are vital in the determination of the cost-effective paths as these resources handle the I/O requests of the VMs. When the VM executes a task, for accessing the data from the data centers, the VM sends request for the access. The data centers receive the I/O requests and then provide access for the data.

The proposed ACTS considers both the cost and the completion time of data access for efficiently scheduling the tasks. ACTS assigns priority to the tasks based on the completion time. Time T is chosen as a fixed time and the completion time is compared with T to determine the priority. The low priority tasks are those that have more completion time and hence the path is selected as minimum cost path to reduce the overall cost. The reason for this approach to low priority tasks is because these tasks can be executed in a normal time without much urgency. Similarly, the high priority tasks are those that require data within the less completion time and hence the paths that provide quicker data access are selected without waiting for the minimum cost path. This may increase the cost but the main aim is to obtain the requested data within the time and hence the small variation in the overall cost can be negligible. After the execution of the tasks, the CPU utilization and the bandwidth utilization are estimated.

Figure 1 shows the proposed ACTS procedure. This work focuses on scheduling the tasks to the VMs with minimum cost paths to reduce the complexity in the data accessing from the cloud data center. The tasks are allocated to the under-loaded VMs based on the normal load conditions. The tasks allocated to VMs access the data from the distant cloud data centers. The cost that recurred for I/O processing is computed and the completion time for data access is estimated. Then the CPU utilization and bandwidth utilization are calculated and updated for successive task executions.

For example, let us consider V tasks of simple mathematical programs with flexible properties of bandwidth, random access memory (RAM), and million instructions per second (mips). These parameters of the cloud tasks are user defined and can be flexibly chosen. Moreover, the simulations are made in the real-time simulation environment (CloudSim) which provides user friendly behavior. The tasks are nonpreemptive dependent tasks.

The VMs are initiated from the cloud environment with existing VMs denoted as E and the newly initiated VMs are placed under N. This is because when there is large load, the new VMs are introduced. The tasks execute the simple mathematical programs with the length differing based on the initiated codes. The addition program of $(a + b)$ is executed once for a task with 4 bits while it is repeated to achieve the prescribed length in the chosen tasks.

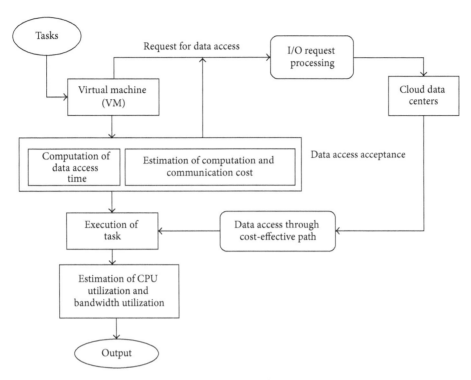

FIGURE 1: Adaptive cost-based task scheduling.

Now let us take task v with m resources available. Initially the tasks are checked for possible execution. All the VMs are running in parallel and are unrelated and each VM runs on its own resources. There is no sharing of its own resources by other VMs. We schedule nonpreemptive dependent tasks to the VMs. For each task v, the arrival rate λ_j and $T(v_i, m_j)$ are calculated. Then the costs C_{comp} and $C_{\text{communication}}$ are computed for each data path d using (2), (7), and (9). The computation cost in equation (7) is estimated as the sum of all costs incurred for running a task v on a VM m of a provider p (8) while the communication cost (9) is the product of cost for data required and the inbound network traffic prices. Based on the completion time, the tasks priority is assigned. Then based on $T(v_i, m_j)$ and cost, the paths are sorted. Then the paths are allocated to each task and then the underloaded VMs are loaded with the tasks which access the data from the cloud data center at the deadline time. Then the CPU utilization (11) and bandwidth utilization (12) are calculated for determining the efficiency of the system. This scheduling procedure is sorted in the following algorithm.

Algorithm 1 (adaptive cost-based task scheduling).

Input: number of tasks, VMs

Output: task scheduling

Begin

Deploy the set of physical machines.

E = set of existing VMs present in the cloud computing system.

N = set of new VMs to be created.

Set of tasks $V = \{v_1, v_2, \ldots, v_i\}$.

Set of resources $M = \{m_1, m_2, \ldots, m_n\}$.

For each task v_i,

Arrival rate λ_j to PM$_j$ using (1)

$$\lambda_j = \sum_{i \in E} \lambda_i^{(e)} \cdot r_i^{(e)} + \sum_{i \in N} \lambda_i^{(n)} \cdot r_i^{(n)}, \tag{4}$$

//where $r_i^{(e)}$ and $r_i^{(n)}$ are the ratio of the CPU time allocated to the existing and new VMs. $\lambda_i^{(e)}$ and $\lambda_i^{(n)}$ are the arrival rate of the network I/O requests of the existing and new VMs to the PMs. Compute completion time of data access $T(v_i, m_j)$ using (2)

$$T(v_i, m_j) = \frac{2\mu_j - \lambda_j + \lambda_j \mu_j^2 \sigma_j^2}{2\mu_j^2 - 2\lambda_j \mu_j}, \tag{5}$$

//where μ_j is the mean service time of network I/O requests in m_j, σ_j is the variance of the service time distribution, and λ_j is the arrival rate of network I/O requests to m_j

End for

Compute cost of each possible data path d using (3)

Cost = Computation cost + Communication cost,

$$C_d = C_{\text{comp}} + C_{\text{communication}}. \tag{6}$$

Computation cost

$$C_{\text{comp}} = \sum_{v_i}^{V} \min_{m_j}^{M} \left(C_{\text{task}} \left(v_i, p, m_j \right) \right), \qquad (7)$$

where the cost of running a task v_i on provider p with VM m_j is defined as

$$C_{\text{task}} \left(v_i, p, m_j \right) = \begin{cases} \text{RT}_{v_i}^{m_j,p} \cdot C_{m_j}^p, & \text{RT}_{v_i}^{m_j,p} \leq \text{DL}_a \\ \infty, & \text{RT}_{v_i}^{m_j,p} > \text{DL}_a \\ \infty, & m_j \notin M, \end{cases} \qquad (8)$$

//where set of tasks is given by V and p is the service provider. DL_a is the time to deadline of v_i. $RT_{v_i}^{m_j,p}$ is the runtime of a task v_i. $C_{m_j}^p$ is the cost of running an VM on p for one time unit.

Communication cost can be computed as

$$C_{\text{communication}} = D_a \cdot \text{NW}_p^{\text{in}}, \qquad (9)$$

//where D_a is the GB required for task v_i and NW_p^{in} is the inbound network traffic prices per GB of the provider p.

Select minimum cost path $C_{d\min}$.

Assign priority to tasks v_i.

If (Priority of v_i = low && $T(v_i, m_j) \geq T$)

$$\text{Data path} = C_{d\min}. \qquad (10)$$

Else if (Priority of v_i = high && $T(v_i, m_j) < T$)

    // T is a fixed time with which the data access completion time of the tasks is compared to determine the priority;

    analyze data paths C_d which satisfies the time to deadline DL_a for tasks v_i;

    data path = $C_{dt}[C_{dt} \neq C_{d\min}]$;

    // path has faster data access to satisfy time to deadline even without minimum cost

End if

Assign tasks to VMs.

Estimation of CPU utilization

$$\overline{\text{CPU}} = \frac{\text{cl}_{\text{MIPS}} \cdot \text{CPU}_{\text{MIPS}}}{1000 \cdot \text{cl}_{\text{ms}}}, \qquad (11)$$

// where CPU is the CPU utilization; cl_{MIPS} is the calculated cloudlet's MIPS length; CPU_{MIPS} is the MIPS ration of the CPU; cl_{ms} is the cloudlet's duration in milliseconds when executed on a CPU with a MIPS rating of CPU_{MIPS}

Estimation of bandwidth utilization

$$\text{BW}_u = \frac{\tau_v \times 100}{\text{BW}_v \times \psi_v}, \qquad (12)$$

// where BW_u is the bandwidth utilization; BW_v is the allotted bandwidth quota; τ_v is the amount of data transferred during the life of VM; ψ_v is the duration which is the VM lifetime and it is equal to the VM release time to the VM creation time.

Update VM characteristics for next iteration.

End.

3.1. Description. The tasks V, the number of VMs, and VM resources m are initialized.. The set of existing VMs E and the set of newly created VMs N are assigned. For each task, the data access completion time is calculated as $T(v_i, m_j)$. Similarly the computation cost and communication cost are also calculated in order to estimate the cost of each data path. Using the completion time and computation cost, and communication cost of each path, the scheduling is performed. The tasks are assigned priorities based on the completion time. The high priority tasks which have less completion time are allocated fast data access paths C_{dt} that satisfy the time to deadline without prioritizing the cost. But for the low priority tasks which have high completion time the minimum cost paths $C_{d\min}$ are allocated. Then the tasks are executed and the utilization of CPU and bandwidth are calculated.

4. Experimental Results

The experiments are conducted to evaluate the performance of the proposed adaptive cost-based task scheduling and the results are tabulated. The cost efficient task scheduling is presented in [12] utilized in this work for performance comparison without considering the cost and completion time of the data access and compared with the proposed ACTS considering the cost and data access completion time. The experiments are carried out using the CloudSim [15] tool. The classes of the CloudSim simulator have been extended (overridden) to utilize the newly written algorithm. The simulator CloudSim opens the possibility of evaluating the hypothesis prior to software development in an environment which can reproduce tests. Specifically, in case of cloud computing where the access to the infrastructure incurs payments in real currency, a simulation-based approach allows cloud customers to test their services in repeatable and controllable environment. Additionally it allows tuning the performance bottlenecks before the deployment on real clouds. The efficiency of the approaches is compared in terms of computation cost, communication cost, execution time, CPU utilization, and bandwidth.

The numbers of tasks and VMs considered are flexible to user requirements which mean the user provides memory, mips, and bandwidth values which are randomly utilized in the VM. The appropriate determination of the characteristics of the VM and the tasks is highly recommended for obtaining

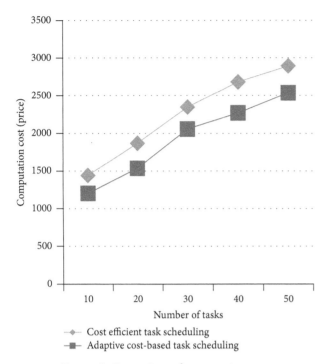

FIGURE 2: Comparison of computation cost.

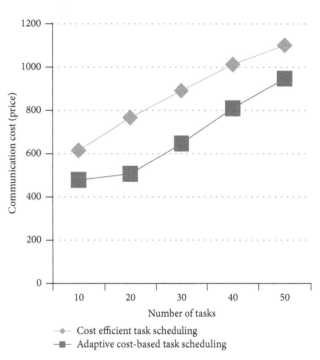

FIGURE 3: Comparison of communication cost.

desired performance evaluation results. The VM characteristics are as follows: ram (256, 312, 712, and 856) bytes; mips (330, 370, and 400); bandwidth (700, 750, 800, and 900) bits per second (bps). Likewise, the *I/O intensive tasks* are taken as follows: length (4, 8, 11, 5, 3, 9, and 10); memory (256, 312, 378, 280, 436, 553, and 375) bytes. An I/O intensive task performs the function of reading the input/output data and writes them onto the files. These values are user provided values and suppose if the number of VMs is 10 then the combination of ram, mips, and bandwidth is chosen randomly. For example, in case of the ram for 10 VMs, the one possible set of values would be 256, 312, 712, 856, 256, 312, 712, 856, 256, and 312, respectively.

4.1. Computation Cost. Computation cost is the cost that is required for utilizing the resources for computation of the I/O requests for the data access. It can be computed using (7).

Figure 2 shows the comparison of the existing cost efficient task scheduling without considering the completion time and the cost with the proposed adaptive cost-based task scheduling (ACTS) with considering the completion time and the cost in terms of the computation cost. In the *x*-axis, the number of tasks is taken while along the *y*-axis the computation cost (price) is taken. When the number of tasks is 50, the cost efficient task scheduling has computation cost of 2890 but the proposed ACTS has 2534.8. Thus the proposed ACTS provides better scheduling with minimal computation cost.

4.2. Communication Cost. Communication cost is the cost that is required for utilizing the resources for I/O requests and responses between the data center and the VM for the data access. It can be calculated using (9).

Figure 3 shows the comparison of the existing cost efficient task scheduling without considering the completion time and the cost with the proposed adaptive cost-based task scheduling (ACTS) with considering the completion time and the cost in terms of the communication cost. In the *x*-axis, the tasks are taken while along the *y*-axis the communication cost (price) is taken. When the number of tasks is 50, the existing cost efficient task scheduling has communication cost of 1100 but the proposed adaptive cost-based task scheduling has 946.6. This shows that the proposed ACTS consumes less cost than the existing scheme.

4.3. Execution Time. The execution time is the time required to process a task in a VM. The execution time is estimated as the product of number of cycles for executing per instruction, time per cycle, and the number of instructions.

Figure 4 shows the comparison of the existing cost efficient task scheduling without considering the completion time and the cost with the proposed Adaptive cost-based task scheduling (ACTS) with considering the completion time and the cost in terms of the execution time. In the *x*-axis, the tasks are taken while along the *y*-axis the execution time in milliseconds (ms) is taken. When the number of tasks is 50, the existing cost efficient task scheduling has execution time of 4.978 ms but the proposed ACTS has 2.56 ms. This shows that the proposed ACTS reduces the time taken for the overall process.

4.4. CPU Utilization. CPU utilization refers to the usage of processing resources or the amount of work handled by a CPU. CPU utilization varies depending on the amount and type of managed computing tasks. It is estimated using (11).

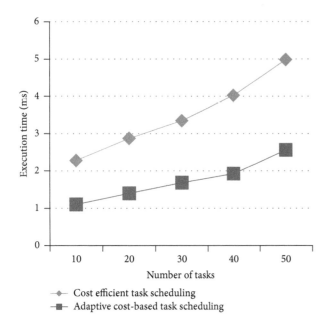

FIGURE 4: Comparison of execution time.

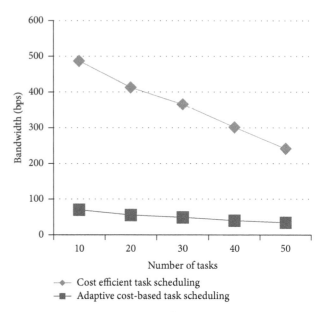

FIGURE 6: Comparison of bandwidth utilization.

Figure 6 shows the comparison of the existing cost efficient task scheduling with the proposed Adaptive cost-based task scheduling (ACTS) in terms of the bandwidth. In the x-axis, the number of tasks is taken while along the y-axis the bandwidth in bps is taken. When the number of tasks is 50, the existing cost efficient task scheduling has bandwidth of 240.98 bps but the proposed ACTS has 34.123 bps.

Thus from the experimental results it is clear that the proposed Adaptive cost-based task scheduling (ACTS) which considers the completion time and computation cost and communication cost is efficient compared to the existing cost efficient task scheduling.

5. Conclusion

Scheduling tasks in cloud computing with reduced delay and effective cost management are a challenging task. Hence in this paper, adaptive cost-based task scheduling (ACTS) is proposed considering the data access completion time and the cost for data access. By considering these two factors, the data can be fetched from the data centers effectively and the scheduling performance can be improved. The approach focuses on providing data access for executing each task with maintained costs. Experimental results also show that the proposed adaptive cost-based task scheduling provides better performance in terms of execution time, computation cost, communication cost, and bandwidth and CPU utilization when compared with existing cost-efficient task scheduling approach.

In this paper, the task scheduling is performed for the already determined task demands and it is quite challenging to schedule tasks with undetermined demands. This could be performed by utilizing efficient resource provisioning techniques in the future. The cost for regeneration of datasets is not computed in ACTS but it is not efficient for exception cases which should be considered in the future researches.

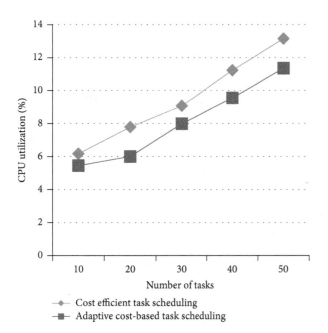

FIGURE 5: Comparison of CPU utilization.

Figure 5 shows the comparison of the existing cost efficient task scheduling with the proposed adaptive cost-based task scheduling (ACTS) in terms of the CPU utilization. In the x-axis, the number of tasks is taken while along the y-axis the CPU utilization in % is taken. When the number of tasks is 50, the existing cost efficient task scheduling has CPU utilization of 13.14% but the proposed ACTS has 11.345%. This shows that the proposed ACTS has less CPU utilization.

4.5. Bandwidth Utilization. Bandwidth is the amount of data that can be transmitted in a fixed amount of time. It is given in bits per second (bps). It is estimated using (12).

Moreover, the load-balancing problems are also needed to be resolved for providing efficient cloud computing services which would be our future scope of research.

Competing Interests

The authors declare that there is no conflict of interests regarding the publication of this paper.

References

[1] P. Mell and T. Grance, "The NIST definition of cloud computing," *National Institute of Standards and Technology*, vol. 53, no. 6, p. 50, 2009.

[2] Q. Zhang, L. Cheng, and R. Boutaba, "Cloud computing: state-of-the-art and research challenges," *Journal of Internet Services and Applications*, vol. 1, no. 1, pp. 7–18, 2010.

[3] K. Nanath and R. Pillai, "A model for cost-benefit analysis of cloud computing," *Journal of International Technology and Information Management*, vol. 22, no. 3, article 6, 2013.

[4] J. Sahni and D. Vidyarthi, "A cost-effective deadline-constrained dynamic scheduling algorithm for scientific workflows in a cloud environment," *IEEE Transactions on Cloud Computing*, 2015.

[5] C. W. Tsai, W. C. Huang, M. H. Chiang, M. C. Chiang, and C. S. Yang, "A hyper-heuristic scheduling algorithm for cloud," *IEEE Transactions on Cloud Computing*, vol. 2, no. 2, pp. 236–250, 2014.

[6] X. Zhu, C. Chen, L. T. Yang, and Y. Xiang, "ANGEL: agent-based scheduling for real-time tasks in virtualized clouds," *IEEE Transactions on Computers*, vol. 64, no. 12, pp. 3389–3403, 2015.

[7] Z. Zhu, G. Zhang, M. Li, and X. Liu, "Evolutionary multi-objective workflow scheduling in cloud," *IEEE Transactions on Parallel and Distributed Systems*, vol. 27, no. 5, pp. 1344–1357, 2016.

[8] Q. Zhang, M. F. Zhani, Y. Yang, R. Boutaba, and B. Wong, "PRISM: fine-grained resource-aware scheduling for MapReduce," *IEEE Transactions on Cloud Computing*, vol. 3, no. 2, pp. 182–194, 2015.

[9] X. Zhu, L. T. Yang, H. Chen, J. Wang, S. Yin, and X. Liu, "Real-time tasks oriented energy-aware scheduling in virtualized clouds," *IEEE Transactions on Cloud Computing*, vol. 2, no. 2, pp. 168–180, 2014.

[10] S. T. Maguluri and R. Srikant, "Scheduling jobs with unknown duration in clouds," *IEEE/ACM Transactions on Networking*, vol. 22, no. 6, pp. 1938–1951, 2014.

[11] X. Zuo, G. Zhang, and W. Tan, "Self-adaptive learning pso-based deadline constrained task scheduling for hybrid iaas cloud," *IEEE Transactions on Automation Science and Engineering*, vol. 11, no. 2, pp. 564–573, 2014.

[12] S. Su, J. Li, Q. Huang, X. Huang, K. Shuang, and J. Wang, "Cost-efficient task scheduling for executing large programs in the cloud," *Parallel Computing*, vol. 39, no. 4-5, pp. 177–188, 2013.

[13] J.-W. Lin, C.-H. Chen, and C.-Y. Lin, "Integrating QoS awareness with virtualization in cloud computing systems for delay-sensitive applications," *Future Generation Computer Systems*, vol. 37, pp. 478–487, 2014.

[14] D. Yuan, Y. Yang, X. Liu et al., "A highly practical approach toward achieving minimum data sets storage cost in the cloud," *IEEE Transactions on Parallel and Distributed Systems*, vol. 24, no. 6, pp. 1234–1244, 2013.

[15] R. N. Calheiros, R. Ranjan, A. Beloglazov, C. A. F. De Rose, and R. Buyya, "CloudSim: a toolkit for modeling and simulation of cloud computing environments and evaluation of resource provisioning algorithms," *Software—Practice and Experience*, vol. 41, no. 1, pp. 23–50, 2011.

18

Energy-Aware VM Initial Placement Strategy Based on BPSO in Cloud Computing

Xiong Fu[ID],[1] Qing Zhao,[1] Junchang Wang,[1] Lin Zhang[ID],[1] and Lei Qiao[2]

[1]*School of Computer Science and Technology, Nanjing University of Posts and Telecommunications, Nanjing 210023, China*
[2]*Beijing Institute of Control Engineering, Beijing 100190, China*

Correspondence should be addressed to Xiong Fu; fux@njupt.edu.cn

Academic Editor: Emiliano Tramontana

In recent years, high energy consumption has gradually become a prominent problem in a data center. With the advent of cloud computing, computing and storage resources are bringing greater challenges to energy consumption. Virtual machine (VM) initial placement plays an important role in affecting the size of energy consumption. In this paper, we use binary particle swarm optimization (BPSO) algorithm to design a VM placement strategy for low energy consumption measured by proposed energy efficiency fitness, and this strategy needs multiple iterations and updates for VM placement. Finally, the strategy proposed in this paper is compared with other four strategies through simulation experiments. The results show that our strategy for VM placement has better performance in reducing energy consumption than the other four strategies, and it can use less active hosts than others.

1. Introduction

As a new commercial calculation model, cloud computing is the evolution of distributed computing, parallel computing, and grid computing. With the advent of the era of big data, data has become a strategic resource of information society, and cloud computing can be more economical, effective, and efficient for mining data value, which has a revolutionary impact on human economic and social development. However, problems of high energy consumption have been given more and more attentions by enterprises and experts when the scale of data centers is constantly expanding. The increasing scale of data center mainly causes two kinds of serious energy problems. On the one hand, increasing physical servers can bring about more energy consumption; on the other hand, if a server loads few virtual machines or has few demands for resources, it will result in low utilization of server's resources, which will cause a huge waste of electric power. At present, rapid development of virtualization technology provides a new solution for power consumption in a data center. In particular, when cloud computing becomes a main developing direction in the future, due to its own server consolidation, online migration,

isolation, high availability, flexible deployment, low administrative overhead, and other advantages, there is more space for the development of virtualization. Cloud computing uses mature virtualization technology, which makes resources it uses required in the form of virtual machines and then allocates servers' part resources to them to perform corresponding tasks, so resource-scheduling process can be converted into the search process of virtual machines [1]. Because data centers in cloud computing have begun to widely use virtualization technology, exploring a VM placement strategy for low energy consumption in a cloud data center provides a new research direction for improving energy efficiency in a data center. VM initial placement according to the optimal goal can be used to reduce energy consumption and reduce the number of active servers after the completion of cloud computing platform in a certain degree, and it has a positive effect on the operation and subsequent optimization for VM consolidation of the cloud computing platform.

In this paper, we use binary particle swarm optimization (BPSO) to implement VM initial placement with comprehensive consideration of CPU and disk, then we use model of energy efficiency fitness to adjust each particle's velocity and displacement within the scope of certain iterations, update each particle's VM placement according to consideration of the globally optimal displacement and locally optimal displacement, and finally we can get a best VM placement which has the minimum energy consumption.

The rest of this paper is organized as follows: Section 2 discusses related work of VM placement. Section 3 discusses proposed model of energy efficiency fitness. Section 4 discusses VM placement strategy based on BPSO. Section 5 contains details of our algorithm. Section 6 is experiments. At last, Section 7 is the summary of this paper.

2. Related Work

With the rapid development of cloud computing, data centers also expand, as well as the energy consumption caused by data centers, which results in high operation costs. Therefore, reducing energy consumption of data centers is a problem that needs to be solved urgently. The energy consumption in a data center has a close relationship with utilization of resources; thus we should improve the utilization of resources to reduce energy consumption in order to reduce operation cost of data centers. At present, the most effective method to achieve the goal is to use virtualization technology, which can make better use of server resources.

Improving utilization of resources by using virtualization technology is mainly divided into two types: initial placement [2, 3] and dynamic VM consolidation [4, 5]. A lot of research on VM placement has been done by domestic and overseas scholars. Many studies have modeled VM placement as packing problems [6, 7]. The purpose of optimization of VM placement is to use the least amount of physical resources to meet demands of all virtual machines, which can improve efficiency and reduce energy consumption. Many works consider load condition or resource competition in terms of servers of CPU, memory, disk, network bandwidth, and so on. Because various factors should be considered to obtain the optimal solution of multiple dimensions, VM placement has been proved to be an NP-hard problem. The most basic method of VM placement is to use heuristic algorithms, such as best fit algorithm and first fit algorithm. Beloglazov and Buyya [8] have put forward MBFD (modified best fit decrease) algorithm which is used to consolidate virtual machines; the main idea of this literature is reallocating virtual machines which need to be migrated to servers to minimize the energy consumption. These simple methods fall into locally optimal solution because of less thought, resulting in extra waste of resources and increasing SLA violation, which has an effect on QoS as well. Therefore, we need to improve or replace heuristic algorithm.

Chen et al. [5] have described VM placement as a stochastic optimization problem. However, this approach is too simple, which only considers CPU and does not consider other resources. Li et al. [9] have proposed heuristic binary search algorithm, which places virtual machines in a few number of servers as far as possible to reduce energy consumption of the whole data center, and virtual machines of the same tenant are placed in the same server that can

reduce the network consumption. The practicality of this algorithm is not good because only one resource type is considered.

Some scholars adopt intelligent algorithm to solve the problem of VM placement. Xu and Fortes [10] have used genetic algorithm to solve the problem of VM placement, but this method does not consider the overhead of VM migration, so it does not have good practicability. Li et al. [11] have proposed a strategy for VM placement that is based on multiobjective genetic algorithm; however the strategy cannot be applied to solve the problem of power consumption. In addition, it does not combine resource control and energy consumption. Farahnakian et al. [12] have used ant colony algorithm for VM consolidation, which can ensure the relatively better original performance and reduce energy consumption at the same time, but this algorithm is too complex, and the speed of its convergence is slow; therefore it is difficult to be implemented.

In recent years, particle swarm optimization (PSO) algorithm has drawn more and more attention from the researchers, because it is similar to genetic algorithm in terms of function, and it has many other advantages: quicker convergence, less parameters, easier operation. In addition, BPSO can be applied to solve the problem of VM placement. In this article, we present an energy-aware strategy for VM initial placement based on BPSO. We first design a multiresource model of energy efficiency fitness and then use BPSO to place virtual machines based on this model. After comparing BPSO with some heuristic algorithms and GA through experiments, we obtained the experimental results, which show that our proposed VM placement strategy not only effectively reduces energy consumption of servers, but also reduces the number of active physical machines as well as the proportion of SLA violation in a certain extent.

3. Energy Efficiency Fitness Model

3.1. Fitting Distance. Every cloud data center will hold the pool of servers, where there are a large number of physical machines. And each physical machine can load virtual machines of different numbers and different specifications; task requests from users and applications are sent by virtual machines. In a data center, utilization of resources such as CPU, disk, memory, bandwidth has an important implication to servers. Because user requests and the sizes of applications are different, their consumption of different types of resources varies, some requests need to consume more CPU resources, and some tasks need more disk utilization, while others consume more bandwidth. In this article, we consider two types of resources: CPU and disk.

Current CPU utilization in a server can be achieved by calculating the sum of CPU utilization in virtual machines running on the server. Similarly, utilization of disk in a server can be achieved by calculating the sum of used disk in virtual machines running on the server. The utilization of CPU and disk affects the energy consumption. Srikantaiah et al. [13] have studied the relationship between energy consumption and utilization of resources. In the literature, results of many experiment shows that, when CPU utilization rate of a server reaches 70% and disk utilization rate reaches 50% at the same time, servers can not only get the minimum value of energy consumption, but also ensure a good performance. Therefore, in this literature, 70% and 50% can be seen as the optimal point for CPU utilization rate and disk utilization rate, respectively, in a server. Two values in the optimal point here are different from that considered separately, so we need to combine two parameters together when solving the problem of VM placement.

Next, we set up a fitness model. We put forward fitness distance Fit_k (k denotes k servers) to analyze the fitness of servers quantitatively; fitness distance can be gotten from Euclidean distance of resource utilization between current server and the optimal point. The function is shown as follows:

$$Fit_k = \begin{cases} \sqrt{\sum_{n=1}^{N} (S_{kn} - Sbest_n)^2} & \text{others} \\ 0 & S_{kn} = 0, \ n = 1, 2, \end{cases} \quad (1)$$

where S_{kn} is nth resource utilization rate in server k, $Sbest_n$ represents optimal utilization of nth resource, and n is the number of resource types; since CPU and disk are considered here, n is 2. Fit_k is the fitness distance of server k, it is a quantitative representation of energy efficiency fitness. When a server is placed with a running VM, Fit_k is the Euclidean distance of resource utilization from the optimal point in server k. When a server is an idle server, which means no VM is deployed on this server and its fitness distance is 0, then energy efficiency fitness of the whole data center is shown as follows:

$$Fit = \sum_k Fit_k. \quad (2)$$

It represents the sum of Euclidean distance in each server. Because the model refers to optimal point [13] and this adaptive point has confirmed its high energy efficiency through many experiments, it is of great value to VM placement by using BPSO. And due to the availability of resource parameters, the model is of high practicability.

3.2. Problem Formulation. Since the value of energy efficiency fitness in a whole data center is closely related to VM deployment in servers, to obtain the lowest value of energy efficiency fitness, a strategy for VM placement is proposed to make CPU utilization rate and disk utilization rate of each server with one or more virtual machines run closer to optimal point to a great extent; then we can achieve best energy efficiency in the whole data center. The following is problem formulation.

Suppose that a data center has N virtual machines that need to be deployed on M servers ($k \in K, i \in I$, where K is the set of servers and I is the set of virtual machines), and virtual machines in each server need enough resources to keep a stable state. S_i^n denotes nth resource demand of VM i, and S_k^n denotes the capacity of resource n in server k. And resources of each server are limited; to guarantee resource utilization of

each server in a proper range and ensure that the efficiency of each server is not too bad, we define a set of high and low threshold values of resource utilization: U_n^{high} represents the maximum utilization of resource n in a server that hosted one or more virtual machines; on the contrary, U_n^{low} represents the minimum utilization. The two thresholds play a decisive role in VM placement. Once the value of resource utilization is no longer within these two thresholds, virtual machines need to be migrated. Then we define two binary variables: X_{ik} represents the existence of VM i in server k, and 1 denotes that VM i is placed on server k; Y_k decides server k is idle or not, and if the value is 0, that means server k is in the idle state and needs to be adjusted to obtain a state of low energy consumption. The goal of this article is to obtain the minimum energy efficiency fitness; the formula is as follows:

$$\begin{aligned} Min \quad Fit &= \sum_{k=1}^{M} Fit_k \\ &= \sum_{k=1}^{M} \sqrt{\sum_{n=1}^{2} \left(\frac{\sum_{i=1}^{N} X_{ik} S_i^n}{S_k^n} - Sbest_n \right)^2} \end{aligned} \quad (3)$$

and constraints are as follows:

$$\sum_{i=1}^{N} X_{ik} = 1 \quad \forall i \in I$$

$$U_n^{low} \cdot S_k^n \leq \sum_{i=1}^{N} X_{ik} \cdot S_i^n \leq U_n^{high} \cdot S_k^n \quad \forall k \in K \quad (4)$$

$$X_{ik}, Y_k \in \{0, 1\} \quad \forall i \in I, \ \forall j \in J$$

$$n = 1, 2,$$

where $Sbest_n$ is the optimal point mentioned in the previous section.

4. Energy-Aware VM Initial Placement Strategy Based on BPSO

4.1. Introduction to BPSO. PSO is an intelligent optimization algorithm which was proposed originally by Eberhart and Kennedy according to the laws of some animals' food-searching [14, 15]. Subsequently, Zhang et al. improved this algorithm, added a dynamic weight to prevent too fast convergence which could lead to locally optimal solution, and then added the exploration of the PSO algorithm [16]. Compared to ant colony algorithm [12, 17, 18], genetic algorithm [7, 19, 20], and many other intelligent algorithm, PSO algorithm has fewer parameters, faster convergence, simpler code, easier operation, and so on, so it is of high practicability.

Standard PSO algorithm is only suitable for solving problems of continuous space; however, the problem of VM placement is a discrete optimization problem, so this algorithm cannot be directly applied to it. Improvement of PSO algorithm is necessary, and this improvement can be applied to solve optimization problems in the discrete space.

Then Kennedy and Eberhart designed corresponding binary version of PSO (BPSO) in 1997 [21], which is used to solve optimization problems in discrete space.

BPSO is similar to the original PSO; the difference is that its particles are composed of binary code. Each particle represents two variables: velocity and displacement. Each particle also stores the two values after each round of iteration: its own locally optimal location (L_i) and globally optimal location of the whole particle swarm (G). The two values are used to provide the basis of changes for the particle's velocity; the formula is as follows:

$$V_{id}(t+1) = \omega \cdot V_{id}(t) + c_1 \cdot r_d() \cdot (L_{id} - X_{id}(t)) + c_2 \\ \cdot r_d() \cdot (G_d - X_{id}(t)). \tag{5}$$

ω is a dynamic weight, which is used to adjust the speed of convergence. And c_1 and c_2 represent learning factors, which can be called acceleration constants as well, both of which are usually set to 2; $r_d()$ is a random number, its value is in the range of $[0,1]$. L_{id} and G_d are, respectively, locally optimal and globally optimal locations of server d in particle i. In order to guarantee the probability that the value of each bit in displacement is only 1 or 0, the sigmoid function is adopted:

$$S(V_{id}(t+1)) = \frac{1}{1 + \exp(-V_{id}(t+1))}. \tag{6}$$

Particles change their value by

$$X_{id}(t+1) = \begin{cases} 1 & \text{if } r_d() \leq S(V_{id}(t+1)) \\ 0 & \text{otherwise.} \end{cases} \tag{7}$$

4.2. VM Initial Placement Based on BPSO. Since BPSO is suitable to solve discrete optimization problems and has advantages over other algorithms, we use it to solve the problem of VM initial placement. In order to better use BPSO, we need to describe the structure of parameters and operation instructions, which can make the strategy of VM initial placement clearer. BPSO has not been used to solve the problem of the energy consumption in cloud data centers by now, so an improved BPSO algorithm is proposed in this article to deal with the problem of high energy consumption, which is a totally new idea.

4.2.1. Parameters Used by BPSO

① *Particle Displacement.* We define a particle swarm that has L particles; X_i^w is the displacement of particle w ($1 \leq w \leq L$), and i is the number of iterations. X_i^w is a N-bit vector:

$$X_i^w = (X_{i1}^w, X_{i2}^w, \ldots, X_{iL}^w). \tag{8}$$

Each bit corresponds to the status value of representative server; if one has a value of 1, it means corresponding server is in working status, and there is at least one VM in it; if the value is zero, the corresponding server does not have VMs and is in a state of low energy consumption.

② *Particle Velocity.* It is the same as particle displacement; V_i^w is the velocity of particle w. It is also a N-bit vector:

$$V_i^w = (V_{i1}^w, V_{i2}^w, \ldots, V_{iL}^w). \tag{9}$$

It decides whether the corresponding server of each bit needs to migrate VM or not. The initial state of each bit is 0.

③ *Locally Optimal Displacement and Globally Optimal Displacement.* We use Lb^w to define locally optimal displacement of particle w, which can get the best energy efficiency in particle w after iterations, and globally optimal displacement (Gb), which represents the best displacement of all particles that can lead to the best energy efficiency fitness so far. These two parameters play a critical role in changes of particle velocity; in other words, they determine the next step of VM deployment in particles through their locally and globally optimal displacement.

④ *Inertia Weight.* In particle swarm, if there is no inertia weight, the speed of convergence in BPSO will be greatly reduced, so inertia weight in BPSO plays a key role in searching results. However, too fast convergence will easily lead to locally optimal solution rather than globally optimal solution. And in different conditions, appropriate adjustment of inertia weight is extremely important. The start of BPSO carries out a global search ability, where a large inertia weight is needed to quickly find all solutions whose energy efficiency fitness is better than others. After the global search, BPSO should decrease the value of inertia weight and converts from global search to local search, which can get globally optimal solution in these good solutions, so dynamic inertia weight is necessary to improve the search ability of BPSO algorithm. The change rule of inertia weight is shown in

$$\omega = \omega_{\min} \cdot \exp\left[-\left(\frac{i}{\text{num}}\right)^p + 1\right]^r. \tag{10}$$

$\omega_{\min}$ is the lowest limit of inertia weight, i is the number of iterations, num is the total number of iterations, p is weight coefficient of changes, and r is the upper limit of weight adjustment. Overall, inertia weight gradually decreases by the increasing number of iterations, and, if needed, we can control the degree of urgency.

⑤ *Addition Operation and Subtraction Operation.* Since original formula of BPSO algorithm is a one-dimension formula, we need to define some mathematical operations. Addition operation is used to add those variables in the same dimension; similarly, subtraction operation is the subtraction of variables in corresponding dimension. For example, $(1, 0, 2, 1) + (2, 1, 0, 0) = (3, 1, 2, 1)$.

⑥ *Function Mapping.* Particle displacement needs a corresponding change according to particle velocity. Original BPSO is unlikely to converge to globally optimal particle, because if it converges to globally optimal particle, its velocity is zero, which will increase the possibility of changes in the corresponding bit; then the search will have more randomness and lack of direction. And original mapping does not conform to the problem of VM placement, because if particle velocity can lead to VM migration, it does not necessarily result in changes of particle displacement. For example, server A hosts VM$\{1, 2, 3\}$, and server B hosts VM$\{4\}$; then the value of the status in server A and B is $(1, 1)$. If VM3 is migrated from server A to B, then server A hosts VM$\{1, 2\}$ when server B hosts VM$\{3, 4\}$; the status still keeps unchanged. We have to improve the sigmoid function.

The following are improvements:

$$
V'_{id}(t+1)
$$
$$
= \begin{cases} 1 - \dfrac{2}{1 + \exp\left(-V_{id}(t+1)\right)} & V_{id}(t+1) \leq 0 \\[3mm] \dfrac{2}{1 + \exp\left(-V_{id}(t+1)\right)} - 1 & V_{id}(t+1) > 0. \end{cases} \quad (11)
$$

$V'_{id}(t+1)$ is the probability that $X'_{id}(t+1)$ is 1, and then we use $X'_{id}(t+1)$ to change particle velocity. If $V'_{id}(t+1)$ is less than 0,

$$
X'(t+1) = \begin{cases} 0 & r_d() \leq V'_{id}(t+1) \\ X'_{id}(t) & \text{others.} \end{cases} \quad (12)
$$

Otherwise,

$$
X'_{id}(t+1) = \begin{cases} 1 & r_d() \leq V'_{id}(t+1) \\ X'_{id}(t) & \text{others.} \end{cases} \quad (13)
$$

$X'_{id}(t+1)$ is the transition of $X_{id}(t+1)$. Next is multiplication operation.

⑦ *Multiplication Operation.* Multiplication operation updates particle displacement and denotes multiplication operation, and the formula is

$$
X(t+1) = X(t) \times X'(t+1). \quad (14)
$$

Both $X'_{id}(t+1)$ and $X_{id}(t)$ can only be assigned two values: 0 and 1. When the value of $X'_{id}(t+1)$ is 1, we do not need to change the displacement of corresponding bit. On the contrary, if the value is 0, we need to observe the value of corresponding bit, namely, $X_{id}(t)$; if the value is 1, we need VM migrations; otherwise, the server can be used as a destination server, and virtual machines can be migrated to this server.

4.2.2. Updating VM Deployment. Based on the above, we can calculate particle velocity of each generation and determine the adjustment of particle displacement. When the transition of particle displacement takes 1, it means that there is no change in corresponding bit of particle displacement; on the contrary, if some bit of the transition is zero, corresponding bit of particle displacement needs to be adjusted, according to VM reallocation.

In this article, we use an updating strategy based on FFD (first fit decreasing), which can update VM displacement.

In order to get a better updating strategy, we need to adjust the server whose value of displacement is 0, and we get a new collection about the adjusted server, which has a two-dimension parameter.

We need to normalize these two parameters. We list all of virtual machines in $\overline{X}$ and form the collection VM$_p\{$VM$_{1p}, \ldots,$ VM$_{np}\}$. And each VM in VM$_p$ has a normalized performance; its formula is

$$
M_{ip}
$$
$$
= \sqrt{\left(\frac{\text{CPU}_{ip} - \text{CPU}_p^{\min}}{\text{CPU}_p^{\max} - \text{CPU}_p^{\min}}\right)^2 + \left(\frac{\text{DISK}_{ip} - \text{DISK}_p^{\min}}{\text{DISK}_p^{\max} - \text{DISK}_p^{\min}}\right)^2}. \quad (15)
$$

$\text{CPU}_p^{\max}$ is the maximum CPU in VM$_p$, and $\text{CPU}_p^{\min}$ is the minimum. Similarly, $\text{DISK}_p^{\max}$ is the maximum disk of VMs in VM$_p$, and $\text{DISK}_p^{\min}$ is the minimum.

According to this formula, we can receive a collection of normalized performance VM$_p$, then sort the element decreasingly, and, finally, leverage the normalized performance to reallocate VMs in VM$_p$ based on BFD; then we will get new VM placement in VM$_p$. However, to prevent local optimum, we just use new VM placement in a certain probability.

We calculate two values of energy efficiency fitness according to formula (3), two values (Fit $\overline{X}$ and Fit $\overline{\overline{X}}$) denote the fitness of original VM placement and new VM placement in VM$_p$, respectively. The probability of using new VM placement in VM$_p$ is as follows:

$$
p = \frac{1/\text{Fit}\,\overline{\overline{X}}}{\left(1/\text{Fit}\,\overline{X}\right) + \left(1/\text{Fit}\,\overline{\overline{X}}\right)} = \frac{\text{Fit}\,\overline{X}}{\text{Fit}\,\overline{X} + \text{Fit}\,\overline{\overline{X}}}. \quad (16)
$$

5. Algorithm

Data Structure

(1) *PS[pnumber]*: it represents the total number of the particle swarms.

(2) *Iter*: it represents the number of iterations in BPSO.

(3) *ServerList*: it is a list of servers and stores the information of each server, such as id, CPU and disk, the velocity and displacement, the transitions value, and the collection of virtual machines.

(4) *VMList*: it stores all information of virtual machines, such as the label and demands for CPU and disk.

(5) *Lbest[pnumber]*: it deposits optimal placement of each particle that obtains minimum energy efficiency fitness.

(6) *Lvalue[pnumber]*: it is the minimum energy efficiency fitness of current particle during the current iteration.

(7) *Gbest*: it is the optimal placement of the particle swarm that obtains minimum energy efficiency fitness.

```
Input: VMList, pnumber, Iter, ServerList
Output: Gbest
(1)  Gvalue = ∞; Gbest = null;
(2)  for i in pnumber
(3)      ServerList = RandomVMPlacement(VMList);
(4)      PS[i] = ServerList;
(5)      Lbest[i] = ServerList;
(6)      Lvalue[i] = Fitness(ServerList);
(7)      if (Gvalue > Lvalue[i]) then
(8)          Gbest = Lbest[i];
(9)          Gvalue = Lvalue[i];
(10)     end if
(11) end for
(12) while Iter > 0
(13)     for i in pnumber
(14)         Lbest[i] = BPSO(ServerList, Lbest[i], Gbest);
(15)         Lvalue[i] = Fitness(ServerList);
(16)         if (Gvalue > Lvalue[i])
(17)             Gbest = Lbest[i];
(18)             Gvalue = Lvalue[i];
(19)         end if
(20)     end for
(21)     Iter = Iter − 1;
(22) end while
(23) return Gbest;
```

ALGORITHM 1: VM initial placement based on BPSO.

```
Input: VMList Output: ServerList
(1)  for vm in VMList
(2)      for server in ServerList
(3)          if (server has enough resources to hold vm) then
(4)              if (server.isEmpty()) then
(5)                  server.setDisplacement(1);
(6)              end if
(7)              server.add(vm);
(8)              break;
(9)          end if
(10)     end for
(11) end for
(12) for server in ServerList
(13)     server.setVelocity(0);
(14) end for
(15) return ServerList;
```

ALGORITHM 2: Random VM placement.

(8) *Gvalue*: it is the minimum energy efficiency fitness of the particle swarm during the current iteration.

The pseudocode for our proposed strategy is presented in Algorithm 1. Algorithm 1 describes the overall process of initial VM placement. First is the generation of *pnumber* particles, which are *pnumber* server lists based on given size of the particle swarm. Each server list has the same servers, but their deployment of virtual machines is not identical because of randomness. Then according to *pnumber* kinds of VM placement, we determine the globally optimal placement and locally optimal placement which can get the least value of energy efficiency fitness. These complete the preparation for the implementation of BPSO (lines 3–11).

Next, in the case of finite iterations, we need to use BPSO algorithm for each particle, which can update its optimal VM placement and globally optimal placement of the whole particle swarm (lines 12–22). After the iterations, the globally optimal VM placement of the particle swarm is the VM placement we want to get (line 23).

Algorithm 2 is the algorithm of random VM placement. Each virtual machine randomly selects a server; if the server has sufficient resources to accommodate a virtual machine, then it will be placed in a server. When the server does not host other VMs before placing this virtual machine, then its displacement is set to 1 (the initial value is 0), to indicate that the server has one or more virtual machines. If current server does not have enough resources for this virtual machine, the algorithm will continue to look for the next server, until finding the right server.

Algorithm 3 is the operation of updating each particle during the iterations in BPSO. First get particle velocity and particle displacement for corresponding arithmetic operations. It updates the velocity and displacement of each server (each bit of particle velocity and particle displacement represents the velocity and particle of a server, respectively; initial value of each server's velocity is 0), and then it changes corresponding transition value according to updated velocity (lines 3–6). Transition value determines whether the deployment of current server needs to change or not (lines 7–15). All servers whose transition value is 0 join a new list, which need to redeploy the placement of virtual machines and calculate the energy efficiency fitness of servers in this list. Based on the normalized parameter, the algorithm uses BFD to redeploy VMs in this list and calculates its fitness. Comparing to the fitness before redeployment, if the value of this new fitness is smaller, then it updates *ServerList* in the probability gotten from formula (16).

6. Experiment Evaluation

6.1. Experimental Setup. In order to assess the advantages and disadvantages of proposed strategy, we carry out various simulated tests to test performance. The results of performance are compared with those of other heuristic algorithms, which can objectively show how good or bad our proposed strategy is based on BPSO. In addition to these heuristic algorithms, we use the idea of GA algorithm in articles [10, 11] and design the experiments to compare it with our proposed algorithm. In this paper, all experiments are conducted on the same computer, whose processor is AMD A6-3400-m APU with Radeon HD Graphics, memory is 6 G, and operating system is Windows 7 Professional SP1, and simulation experiments are conducted using the platform of eclipse, whose version is Mars.1 Release (4.5.1). In order to ensure the practicability of the algorithm, the configuration of servers in the experiment refers to the configuration of servers on the market.

```
Input: ServerList, Lbest[i], Gbest
Output: Lbest[i], Gbest
(1) for server in ServerList
(2)    X = server.getDisplacement();
(3)    V = server.getVelocity();
(4)    Lx = Lbest[i].getServer(server.getId()).getDisplacement;
(5)    Gx = Gbest.getServer(server.getId()).getDisplacement;
(6)    V = ω · V + c₁ · rd(Lx − X) + c₂ · rd() · (Gx − X);
(7)       if (V ≤ 0) then
(8)    V' = 1 − 2 / (1 + exp(−V))
(9)       else
(10)   V' = 2 / (1 + exp(−V)) − 1
(11)      end if
(12)   X' = server.getTransition();
(13)      if (V' < 0 and r_d() ≤ V') then X' = 0
(14)      else if (V' > 0 and r_d() ≤ V') then X' = 1
(15)      end if
(16)      if (X' = 0) then
(17)         RedeployServerList.add(server);
(18)      end if
(19) end for
(20) OrginalMigrationServerList = RedeployServerList;
(21) RedeployServerList.sortByBFD();
(22) if (Fitness(OrginalMigrationServerList)>Fitness(RedeployServerList)) then
(23)    update the information of servers in RedeployServerList
(24)    update the VMList in ServerList according to RedeployServerList in the probability gotten from formula (16);
(25)    update Lbest[i], Gbest according to changed ServerList;
(26) end if
(27) return Lbest[i], Gbest;
```

Lines (6), (8), (10), (13), (14), (16) as equations:

(6) $V = \omega \cdot V + c_1 \cdot rd(Lx - X) + c_2 \cdot rd() \cdot (Gx - X);$

(8) $V' = 1 - \dfrac{2}{1 + \exp(-V)}$

(10) $V' = \dfrac{2}{1 + \exp(-V)} - 1$

(13) if $(V' < 0$ and $r_d() \le V')$ then $X' = 0$

(14) else if $(V' > 0$ and $r_d() \le V')$ then $X' = 1$

(16) if $(X' = 0)$ then

ALGORITHM 3: BPSO.

At the start of experiments, VMs are assigned resources of different orders of magnitude according to the demands. In order to ensure that servers have enough resources to hold virtual machines, we decide that the numbers of servers and VMs are the same in each experiment.

The following is the analysis of experimental results.

① *Energy Efficiency Fitness.* First, we compare our proposed strategy to other four algorithms based on energy efficiency fitness. Figure 1 shows the energy efficiency fitness of five methods under the conditions that different numbers of servers and virtual machines are deployed. In this experiment, the population of BPSO is 50, and the number of iterations is 100. In order to eliminate the interference of other factors in the experiment, upper and lower thresholds are consistent.

The result from Figure 1 concludes that the proposed strategy based on BPSO can get the smallest energy efficiency fitness in all scales of servers and VMs, and compared to the other four algorithms, its control of energy efficiency fitness is very obvious, mainly because BPSO has an adjustment of globally optimal solution and locally optimal solution in each iteration, which can ensure less energy consumption. While three heuristic algorithms are simple greedy algorithms, which lack such adjustment, they can easily lead to larger

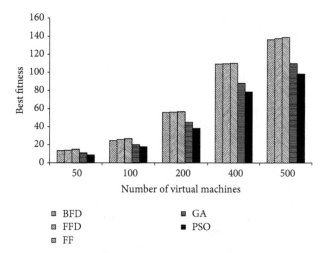

FIGURE 1: Energy efficiency fitness.

energy efficiency fitness and more energy consumption; GA can get lower values as well than the other three heuristic algorithms; however, there is a high probability that the results it get may be a locally optimal solution, so its values of best fitness are higher than that gotten by our proposed algorithm.

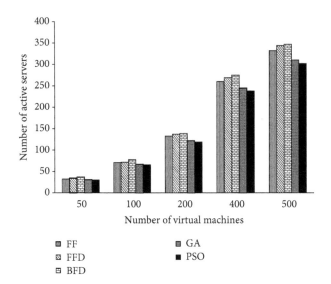

FIGURE 2: Number of active servers.

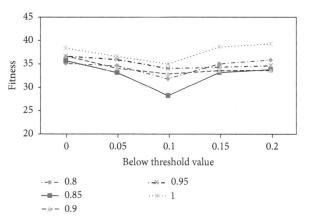

FIGURE 3: High and low threshold of CPU and disk.

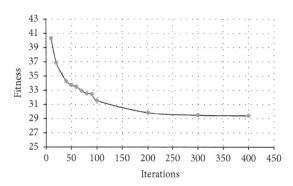

FIGURE 4: Iterations.

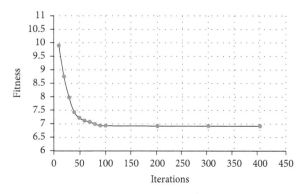

FIGURE 5: Iterations (50 virtual machines).

② *Number of Active Servers.* In addition to energy consumption, the number of active servers is also an important performance metric. We keep the parameters the same as what was set in the previous experiments and then compare numbers of active servers after initial VM placement based on five algorithms, respectively. Figure 2 is the result of experiments.

BPSO used in experiments has 100 populations and 100 iterations. And other parameters are consistent. Evidently compared to the other four algorithms, our proposed strategy based on BPSO can produce relatively fewer active servers, because our proposed strategy reallocates VM placement of abnormal servers by using BFD during iterations, which also ensures that the number of active servers cannot be too large; this also shows that proposed strategy can take advantages of other algorithms to improve superiority by itself; this also shows that proposed strategy outperforms the other algorithms.

③ *Parameter Setting.* According to BPSO algorithm introduced in this paper, some parameters need to be assigned suitable values. Next, we test the influence of BPSO caused by these parameters.

(A) High and Low Threshold of CPU and Disk. High and low threshold of CPU and disk may affect the status of VM placement; then we change them to observe changes of servers' energy efficiency fitness in this experiment, where the iterations are 200 and the number of VMs is 200. Figure 3 is the result of changes. We conclude from the figure that changes of energy efficiency fitness caused by two thresholds are not very evident; however there is a trend that when the high threshold is 0.85 and the low threshold is 0.1, we get the smallest value. And when the low threshold of CPU and disk is 0.1, values of energy efficiency fitness are smaller than those in other conditions.

(B) Iterations. Next we do a research on energy consumption influenced by iterations. According to the previous experimental results, 0.85 and 0.1 are set as the high and low thresholds of CPU and disk, respectively, and the number of generated virtual machines is 200, and the number of population is 50. Figure 4 shows that with the increase of iterations, the value of energy efficiency fitness is becoming more stable, and when the number of iterations is more than 200, the energy efficiency fitness is almost consistent.

The trend of changes of the fitness will not be affected when the number of VMs is changed. Figures 5 and 6 are the trends of energy efficiency fitness when a data center has 50 and 100 VMs, respectively.

Of course, changing the size of populations will not affect the trend of changes of fitness either. Figures 7 and 8

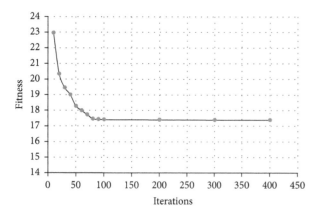

FIGURE 6: Iterations (100 virtual machines).

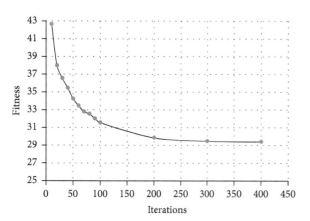

FIGURE 7: Iterations (30 populations).

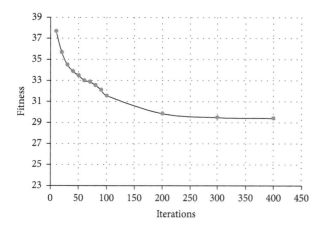

FIGURE 8: Iterations (100 populations).

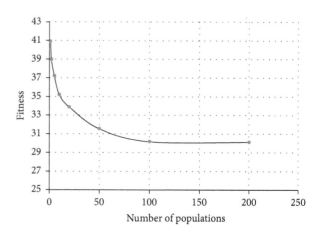

FIGURE 9: Number of populations.

energy efficiency fitness brought by different numbers of populations. The figure shows that energy efficiency fitness is in balance when the number of populations is more than 100.

To sum up, our proposed strategy based on BPSO is not only better than the other three heuristic algorithms (FF, FFD, BFD) and GA in terms of energy consumption gotten through value of energy efficiency fitness, but also better in other performances such as the number of active servers. In addition, this article finds through experiments that parameters in BPSO can affect the size of energy consumption, so we can adjust the various parameters to achieve optimal status of our proposed strategy.

7. Conclusion

With the rapid development of cloud computing, the demands of data centers are increasing. Larger scale of the cloud data center brings about enormous energy consumption, which cannot be ignored. Therefore, solving or alleviating energy problem becomes the urgency. VM initial placement is an important part of solution to reduce energy consumption. In this paper, we design energy-aware VM initial placement based on BPSO, which can obtain optimal VM placement that has a minimum energy consumption according to the adjustment of locally optimal placement and globally optimal placement. Through simulations and results, we can prove good performance of our proposed strategy based on BPSO. In addition, the influences of the performance caused by relevant parameters in BPSO are also discussed. In future work, we need to consider the best collocation of different parameters in detail and do further research about details of our proposed strategy based on BPSO.

Conflicts of Interest

The authors declare that there are no conflicts of interest regarding the publication of this paper.

are the trends of energy efficiency fitness when the size of populations is 30 and 100, respectively. With the increase of populations, the range of energy efficiency fitness is getting smaller.

(C) The Number of Populations. The number of populations is also an important parameter that influences energy consumption. If the size of populations is too small, it will affect the performance of BPSO, the convergence, and the value of energy efficiency fitness. Figure 9 is the result of

Acknowledgments

This work is sponsored by Primary Research & Development Plan (Social Development) of Jiangsu Province (BE2017743) and National Science Foundation of China (no. 61602264).

References

[1] M. Stillwell, D. Schanzenbach, F. Vivien, and H. Casanova, "Resource allocation algorithms for virtualized service hosting platforms," *Journal of Parallel and Distributed Computing*, vol. 70, no. 9, pp. 962–974, 2010.

[2] M. Cardosa, A. Singh, H. Pucha, and A. Chandra, "Exploiting spatio-temporal tradeoffs for energy-aware MapReduce in the cloud," *IEEE Transactions on Computers*, vol. 61, no. 12, pp. 1737–1751, 2012.

[3] C. C. T. Mark, D. Niyato, and T. Chen-Khong, "Evolutionary optimal virtual machine placement and demand forecaster for cloud computing," in *Proceedings of the 25th IEEE International Conference on Advanced Information Networking and Applications, AINA 2011*, pp. 348–355, Singapore, March 2011.

[4] T. Cerling, J. Buller, C. Enstall, and R. Ruiz, *Mastering Microsoft® Virtualization*, Wiley Publishing, Inc., Indianapolis, IN, USA, 2009.

[5] M. Chen, H. Zhang, Y. Y. Su, X. Wang, G. Jiang, and K. Yoshihira, "Effective VM sizing in virtualized data centers," in *Proceedings of the 12th IFIP/IEEE International Symposium on Integrated Network Management*, pp. 594–601, Dublin, Ireland, May 2011.

[6] B. Moores, "Autonomic virtual machine placement in the data center[C]//," in *Proceedings of the IEEE 33rd International Conference on Distributed Computing Systems Workshops*, pp. 220–225, 2013.

[7] H. Nakada, T. Hirofuchi, H. Ogawa, and S. Itoh, "Toward virtual machine packing optimization based on genetic algorithm," *Lecture Notes in Computer Science (including subseries Lecture Notes in Artificial Intelligence and Lecture Notes in Bioinformatics): Preface*, vol. 5518, no. 2, pp. 651–654, 2009.

[8] A. Beloglazov and R. Buyya, "Adaptive threshold-based approach for energy-efficient consolidation of virtual machines in cloud data centers," in *Proceedings of the ACM 8th International Workshop on Middleware for Grids, Clouds and e-Science (MGC '10)*, pp. 1–6, Bangalore, India, December 2010.

[9] X. Li, J. Wu, S. Tang, and S. Lu, "Let's stay together: Towards traffic aware virtual machine placement in data centers," in *Proceedings of the 33rd IEEE Conference on Computer Communications, IEEE INFOCOM 2014*, pp. 1842–1850, can, May 2014.

[10] J. Xu and J. A. B. Fortes, "Multi-Objective Virtual Machine Placement in Virtualized Data Center Environments," in *Ieee/acm International Conference on Green Computing and Communications & 2010 Ieee/acm International Conference on Cyber, Physical and Social Computing*, pp. 179–188, IEEE, Hangzhou, China, December 2010.

[11] Q. Li, Q. Hao, L. Xiao, and Z. Li, "Adaptive management and multi-objective optimization for virtual machine placement in cloud computing," *Chinese Journal of Computers*, vol. 34, no. 12, pp. 2253–2264, 2011.

[12] F. Farahnakian, A. Ashraf, T. Pahikkala et al., "Using Ant Colony System to Consolidate VMs for Green Cloud Computing," *IEEE Transactions on Services Computing*, vol. 8, no. 2, pp. 187–198, 2015.

[13] S. Srikantaiah, A. Kansal, and F. Zhao, "Energy aware consolidation for cloud computing[C]//," in *Proceedings of the Conference on Power Aware Computing and Systems*, pp. 10-10, 2008.

[14] R. C. Eberhart and J. Kennedy, "A new optimizer using particle swarm theory," in *Proceedings of the 6th International Symposium on Micromachine and Human Science*, pp. 39–43, IEEE, Nagoya, Japan, October 1995.

[15] J. Kennedy and R. Eberhart, "Particle swarm optimizatio," in *Proceedings of the IEEE International Conference on Neural Networks*, pp. 1942–1948, IEEE, Perth, Australia, December 1995.

[16] X. Zhang, Y. Du, Z. Qin, G. Qin, and J. Lu, "A Modified Particle Swarm Optimizer," in *Advances in Natural Computation*, vol. 3612 of *Lecture Notes in Computer Science*, pp. 592–601, Springer, Berlin, Germany, 2005.

[17] W. Qinghong U, J. Zhang H, and U. Xin He X, *AN ANT COLONY ALGORITHM WITH MUTATION FEATURES[J]. Journal of Computer Research*, 1999.

[18] P.-Y. Yin and J.-Y. Wang, "Ant colony optimization for the nonlinear resource allocation proble," *Applied Mathematics and Computation*, vol. 174, no. 2, pp. 1438–1453, 2006.

[19] H. Wang, D. Lin, and M.-Q. Li, "A competitive genetic algorithm for resource-constrained project scheduling problem," in *Proceedings of the International Conference on Machine Learning and Cybernetics, ICMLC 2005*, vol. 5, pp. 2945–2949, August 2005.

[20] S. Jang H, T. Kim Y, and J. Kim K, "The Study of Genetic Algorithm-based Task Scheduling for Cloud Computing[J]," in *Proceedings of the International Journal of Control Automation*, pp. 157–162, 2012.

[21] J. Kennedy and R. C. Eberhart, "A discrete binary version of the particle swarm algorithm," vol. 5, pp. 4104–4108, 1997.

19

A Randomization Approach for Stochastic Workflow Scheduling in Clouds

Wei Zheng, Chen Wang, and Dongzhan Zhang

Department of Computer Science, School of Information Science and Engineering, Xiamen University, Xiamen 361005, China

Correspondence should be addressed to Dongzhan Zhang; zdz@xmu.edu.cn

Academic Editor: Laurence T. Yang

In cloud systems consisting of heterogeneous distributed resources, scheduling plays a key role to obtain good performance when complex applications are run. However, there is unavoidable error in predicting individual task execution times and data transmission times. When this error is being not negligible, deterministic scheduling approaches (i.e., scheduling based on accurate time prediction) may suffer. In this paper, we assume the error in time predictions is modelled in stochastic manner, and a novel randomization approach making use of the properties of random variables is proposed to improve deterministic scheduling. The randomization approach is applied to a classic deterministic scheduling heuristic, but its applicability is not limited to this one heuristic. Evaluation results obtained from extensive simulation show that the randomized scheduling approach can significantly outperform its static counterpart and the extra overhead introduced is not only controllable but also acceptable.

1. Introduction

Workflows have been widely used in various domains to depict complex computational application with multiple indivisible tasks and the data dependencies between tasks [1]. These workflows are normally derived from scientific problems in the fields of mathematics, astronomy, and so forth, for example, Montage [2]. As the massive requirements of calculation and communication became overwhelming in these disciplines, clusters and grids, as evolutionary forms of distributed computing, have been used to run workflow applications since the end of the 20th century [3, 4]. Recently, with more flexible and scalable capacity on computation and storage and less hardware/software installation expense, it has been gaining increasing popularity of using cloud computing infrastructure to run workflows [5–9].

The assignment of workflow tasks to computing resources, which is called *workflow scheduling*, is one of the key effects on the execution performance of the workflow in distributed computing environments like clouds. In general form of scheduling problems, a workflow is frequently represented by a Directed Acyclic Graph (DAG), where the nodes symbolize the tasks and the arcs with direction symbolize the data dependencies between tasks. The two terms "node" and "arc" will be interchangeably used in the rest of this paper. The most commonly focused objective of DAG scheduling is the minimization of the makespan (namely, overall execution time) of the workflow. Generally a DAG scheduling problem has been proven to be NP-Hard [10]. For getting closer favourable solution to this problem with acceptable time and space complexity, many researches have been carried out, and many heuristics have been proposed and published in the literature [11, 12].

Nevertheless, for majority of the existing DAG scheduling heuristics, the targeted DAG is modelled deterministically [13]. This means that the heuristics assumptions to the problem of inputs like task execution times and intertask communication times are deterministic and precisely defined before. Clearly, the real-world workflow execution is much more complex than the above assumption because it is not possible to obtain accurate forecast of calculation and communication. Intuitively, the modelling of task computation times and communication times as random variables might be more realistic; it is also reasonabe to assume that the expected random variables and the variance can be predicted. In contrast to their deterministic counterparts, the DAG scheduling problems modelled in stochastic fashion are called *stochastic scheduling* [14]. A big number of heuristics have been proposed for deterministic scheduling, but a small number for stochastic. There have been a plethora of studies showing deterministic DAG scheduling heuristics can hardly work well for their stochastic counterpart problems. This motivates the research on somehow adapting the existing deterministic DAG scheduling heuristics into the stochastic context and making improvement in terms of minimizing makespan, which is also the main focus of this paper.

In this paper, we consider the problem of scheduling a workflow onto a set of heterogeneous resources based on stochastic modelling of task execution times and task communication times with the objective of minimizing the makespan. For such a problem, a novel randomization scheduling approach is proposed. The proposed approach is applied to a classic deterministic scheduling heuristic and evaluated via extensive simulation experiments and the results exhibit a significant improvement of workflow execution performance with an acceptable extra overhead.

The rest of the paper is structured as follows. Related work is discussed in Section 2. The stochastic DAG scheduling problem and relevant definitions are presented in Section 3. The proposed randomization scheduling approach with an illustrative example is described in Section 4. The evaluation results are provided and discussed in Section 5. Finally, a conclusion is provided in Section 6.

2. Related Work

The past few decades witnessed a large number of efforts on developing various deterministic DAG scheduling heuristics, including HEFT [11], HBMCT [16], CPOP [11], GDL (DLS) [17], WBA [18], ILS [19], GA [20], SA [21], Triplet [22], TDS [23], STDS [24], and LDBS [25]. For an extensive list and classification of these heuristics we refer to [15, 26]. These heuristics differentiate with our work at the fact that they are based on deterministic scheduling model other than our stochastic model. Apparently, even when task execution times and data transmission times are modelled by some sort of random distribution, one can still apply one of the aforementioned deterministic scheduling heuristics by using the means of the random variables as inputs. However, as will be demonstrated later in this paper, this idea does not lead to a preferable schedule in most cases. Therefore, we derive a randomization approach by taking advantage of properties of random task execution times and data transmission times (as opposed to constant values). Although our approach can work with any deterministic heuristic in stochastic scheduling problems, we choose using the commonly cited and well-known deterministic heuristic: HEFT [11].

HEFT [11] is a deterministic list scheduling heuristic which aims to minimize the makespan of DAG applications on a bounded number of heterogeneous resources. The heuristic consists of two phases. In the first phase, the heuristic computes numeric ranks for all tasks based on their execution time predictions and data dependencies and then prioritizes tasks in a list. In the second phase, by the prioritized order, each task is allocated in turn to the resource which is estimated to minimize finished time of the task. It is worth mentioning that HEFT allows a task to be inserted into the existing task queue of a resource as long as the task dependency is not violated.

It has been widely recognized that due to the inaccuracy in time prediction deterministic scheduling heuristic relying on constant input may result in bad decision [27]. Over the recent years, some works have been carried out to evaluate the performance of deterministic DAG scheduling heuristics with stochastic model, such as [26, 28]. However, the main focus of these works is not on proposing an efficient scheduling heuristic for the stochastic DAG scheduling problem. One of recently popular ideas of addressing stochastic DAG scheduling problems is adapting the existing deterministic heuristics by changing their ranking function and/or the way of comparing task attributes. Examples can be found in [29–31]. Nevertheless, these heuristics still make scheduling decision in a deterministic manner. In contrast, our heuristic is randomized.

In our previous study [15], a Monte-Carlo based approach has been applied to the stochastic DAG scheduling problem to acquire a schedule which can outperform schedules generated by other comparable means. In essence, this approach relies on a significant amount of random searches on the solution space as well as an extensive evaluation for picking up the result schedule. As a result, a result schedule with a reasonable performance requires a considerable overhead. This paper is an extension to our previous work [32]. In this paper, we only do local search around a well-crafted schedule and the cost of evaluation of the searching results is trivial. That is to say, the overhead of the heuristic proposed in this paper is much less than the Monte-Carlo based approach, while a significant improvement on makespan can still be achieved.

3. Problem Description

3.1. Application Model. In this paper, a workflow application is represented by a Directed Acyclic Graph (DAG) $G = \{V, E\}$, where V denotes a set of interdependent tasks, each of which is represented by v_i, that is, $V = \{v_i \mid i = 1, 2, \ldots, n\}$, and E denotes a set of directed arcs, each of which represents data dependency between two tasks, that is, $E = \{e_{j,k}\}$. For instance, $e_{j,k} = v_j \rightarrow v_k$ means the input of task v_k depends on the output of task v_j. In this case, v_k is a child of v_j and v_j is a parent of v_k; moreover, v_k cannot start to run before receiving all necessary data from its parents. The node without parents is called entry node, and the node without children exit node. For the sake of standardization we assume that every DAG here has only one single entry node and one single exit node. For illustration, Figure 1 presents an example of DAG with 10 nodes.

3.2. Platform Model. We assume that the underlying computing platform comprises a fixed number of heterogeneous resources and uses $R = \{r_1, r_2, \ldots, r_m\}$ to denote the set of resources. A task v can be executed at any resource p; however a resource cannot execute more than one task at a time. In addition, no temporal interruption is allowed

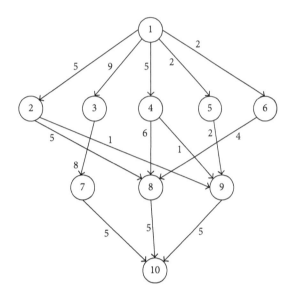

FIGURE 1: A DAG example.

during this execution. There is a dedicated dual-direction communication link between every pair of resources. This means that the tasks allocated onto different resources can transmit data to each other with no contention. For any random variable RV, we use $\mu(\text{RV})$ and $\sigma(\text{RV})$ to represent the expectation and the standard deviation of RV. Given that $\text{ET}_{i,p}$ represents the random variable modelling the execution time of task v_i on resource r_p and $\text{CT}_{i,j,p,q}$ the time for transmitting data from v_i located on r_p to v_j located on r_q, we assume that for each i and p ($1 \leq i \leq n$, $1 \leq p \leq m$) $\mu(\text{ET}_{i,p})$ and $\sigma(\text{ET}_{i,p})$ are known. We also assume the data amount transmitted on each edge (denoted by $\delta_{i,j}$), and the average time needed for transmitting one unit of data from one resource to another (denoted by $\gamma_{p,q}$) is known, so

$$\mu\left(\text{CT}_{i,j,p,q}\right) = \delta_{i,j} \cdot \gamma_{p,q}, \tag{1}$$

as well as $\sigma(\text{CT}_{i,j,p,q})$, is known. For illustration, Tables 1(a) and 1(b) show the stochastic model of task execution times and communication times of the DAG depicted in Figure 1. Table 2 shows an example of possible outcome of the stochastic model presented in Tables 1(a) and 1(b).

We use $\text{ST}_{j,q}$ to denote the start time of task v_j on resource r_q and $\text{FT}_{j,q}$ the finish time. In addition, we let pre(j) and suc(j) stand for the set of parents and children of v_j, respectively, and alloc(j) symbolize the resource where v_j is allocated. Obviously, we have

$$\text{FT}_{j,q} = \text{ST}_{j,q} + \text{ET}_{j,q}. \tag{2}$$

In addition,

$$\text{ST}_{j,q}$$

$$= \max\left\{\text{FT}_{i,p} + \text{CT}_{i,j,p,q} \mid i \in \text{pre}\,(j),\ p = \text{alloc}\,(i)\right\}. \tag{3}$$

TABLE 1: Stochastic model of the DAG example shown in Figure 1.

(a) Stochastic model of execution times

	Resource 1		Resource 2		Resource 3	
	Exp. val.	Std. dev.	Exp. val.	Std. dev.	Exp. val.	Std. dev.
Task 1	24.00	4.00	2.00	0.33	7.00	1.17
Task 2	36.00	6.00	32.00	5.33	49.00	8.17
Task 3	42.00	7.00	49.00	8.17	12.00	2.00
Task 4	12.00	2.00	8.00	1.33	56.00	9.33
Task 5	81.00	13.50	20.00	3.33	16.00	2.67
Task 6	9.00	1.50	30.00	5.00	24.00	4.00
Task 7	48.00	8.00	4.00	0.67	8.00	1.33
Task 8	64.00	10.67	18.00	3.00	42.00	7.00
Task 9	36.00	6.00	16.00	2.67	1.00	0.17
Task 10	54.00	9.00	28.00	4.67	63.00	10.50

(b) Stochastic model of communication times

	Resource 1		Resource 2		Resource 3	
	Exp. val.	Std. dev.	Exp. val.	Std. dev.	Exp. val.	Std. dev.
Resource 1	0.00	0	2.00	0.33	8.00	1.33
Resource 2	2.00	0.33	0.00	0.00	4.00	0.67
Resource 3	8.00	1.33	4.00	0.67	0.00	0.00

TABLE 2: A sampling of the stochastic model shown in Table 1.

(a) A sampling of stochastic task execution times

	Resource 1	Resource 2	Resource 3
Task 1	13.45	2.05	6.75
Task 2	33.44	22.64	45.42
Task 3	25.05	51.33	11.61
Task 4	14.82	8.85	47.48
Task 5	88.77	22.64	15.39
Task 6	6.59	25.23	26.17
Task 7	35.47	4.05	9.08
Task 8	54.31	22.29	50.60
Task 9	33.52	19.80	1.28
Task 10	56.57	28.59	77.36

(b) A sampling of stochastic task communication times

	Resource 1	Resource 2	Resource 3
Resource 1	0.00	2.58	8.46
Resource 2	2.58	0.00	5.58
Resource 3	8.46	5.58	0.00

3.3. *Problem Definition.* The main objective of this paper is to minimize the overall execution time of a DAG application. Given that the start time of entry node is always time 0, based on the definitions and assumptions presented above, the problem to be addressed in this paper is to generate a schedule S, which specifies the mapping of tasks and resources, as well as the execution order of tasks on each resource, so that the random variable $\text{FT}_{\text{exit\_node, alloc(exit\_node)}}$ can be minimized.

Input: DAG G on a set of resources R with stochastic model
Output: A schedule specifying task mapping and execution order
  (1)   Create a candidate schedule list $\mathscr{L}$, which is initially empty.
  (2)   Run a deterministic heuristic DH to generate the schedule entirely based on all mean values of task execution
       times and communication times, and put the schedule into $\mathscr{L}$.
  (3)   **while** the termination condition of the producing phase is not met **repeat**
  (4)   Run the randomized heuristic RH and push the result schedule into $\mathscr{L}$.
  (5)   **endwhile**
  (6)   Compute the expected makespan based on mean values of all stochastic inputs for each schedule in $\mathscr{L}$.
  (7)   **Return** the schedule with the minimum expected makespan as the result schedule.

ALGORITHM 1: The outline of the randomization scheduling approach.

4. Method

In this section, we firstly present the basic idea of the proposed randomization approach and then describe the details of the randomized HEFT heuristic (RHEFT), which is derived from the combination of our randomization approach and the classic HEFT heuristic. Furthermore, an enhanced version of RHEFT (named, ERHEFT) is proposed.

4.1. Basic Idea. Among different categories of deterministic DAG scheduling heuristics, list scheduling seems receiving most research attention, because this kind of heuristics can usually obtain a reasonably good schedule result without too much overhead. As mentioned in Section 1, deterministic DAG scheduling heuristics receive constant time prediction as inputs. List scheduling heuristics firstly sort all workflow tasks in terms of a rank, which is computed based on the time prediction and associated with each task, and then allocate the sorted tasks one after another onto a specific resource. The resource where a task is allocated is normally decided by which resource can minimize a certain time-related attribute (e.g., estimated finish time of the current task) that can be calculated based on the time prediction and is distinctive on different resources. By doing so, list scheduling aims at a good trade-off between optimization and algorithm complexity. However, there is no guarantee that the resource allocation made is the best possible decision for minimizing makespan.

The issue is more complicated in the case of stochastic scheduling model. It will be more doubtable whether the scheduling decision made by deterministic list scheduling results will be favourable for minimizing the makespan, because the time prediction based on which decision is made is unreliable.

Assuming the time prediction can be modelled by probability distribution, our hypothesis is that it is almost impossible to develop a static algorithm which can always obtain an optimal schedule. Therefore, we consider generating a set of various schedules based on the random prediction and pick up that one which has the best chance to win. As the time prediction is modelled randomly, when comparing two time-related variables, for example, task finish times of different tasks, there is no certain result. To decide which task finished earlier, we need to roll a dice. Apparently, by

randomly deciding the comparison result of task finish times, which is important factors for making scheduling decision, we will generate various scheduling results. We regard all these schedules as candidates and the one which has the smallest expectation of makespan as the final output of our approach.

The outline of our randomization scheduling approach is presented in Algorithm 1, where DH denotes a given deterministic DAG scheduling heuristic and RH means a randomized scheduling heuristic.

4.2. The Randomized HEFT Heuristic (RHEFT). Among existing list scheduling heuristics, the most well-known and commonly cited one is heterogeneous-earliest-finish-time (HEFT) heuristic [11]. We thereby choose to apply the aforementioned randomization approach to HEFT and propose a novel approach named RHEFT which is based on a randomized HEFT. Namely, we let DH be HEFT and RH the randomized HEFT.

The details of the randomized HEFT heuristic are presented in Algorithm 2. Similar to HEFT, the randomized HEFT has two phases. In the first phase (Algorithm 2, lines: 1-2), the upward ranking of each node (denoted by Urank) is computed as follows:

$$\text{Urank}(v_i) = \overline{\text{ET}_i} + \max_{v_j \in \text{suc}(i)} \left\{ \overline{\text{CT}_{i,j}} + \text{Urank}(v_j) \right\}, \quad (4)$$

where

$$\overline{\text{ET}_i} = \frac{\sum_{p=1}^{m} \mu\left(\text{ET}_{i,p}\right)}{m},$$

$$\overline{\text{CT}_{i,j}} = \frac{\sum_{p=1}^{m} \sum_{q=1}^{m} \mu\left(\text{CT}_{i,j,p,q}\right)}{m \cdot m}. \quad (5)$$

Especially for exit node, we have $\text{Urank}(v_{\text{exit\_node}}) = \overline{\text{ET}}_{\text{exit\_node}}$.

In the second phase of the randomized HEFT (Algorithm 2, lines: 3–9), it is needed to compute for each node on each resource the earliest estimate start time (denoted by

(1)   Compute Urank (as defined in (4)) for all tasks.
(2)   Sort all tasks in a list $\mathcal{L}$ in the non-descending order of Urank.
(3)   **for** $k := 1$ to n **do** (where n is the number of tasks)
(4)   Select the kth task v^* from the list $\mathcal{L}$.
(5)   **for** each resource $r_p \in R$ **do**
(6)   Compute the mean value and variance of estimated finish time of v^* on r_p (as defined in (7)).
(7)   **endfor**
(8)   Decide the winner resource of estimated finish time (r^*) for v^* according to the *random comparison policy*.
(9)   Allocate v^* to r^*.
(10)   **endfor**

ALGORITHM 2: The randomized HEFT heuristic.

EST) and the earliest estimate finish time (denoted by EFT), which are defined as follows:

$$\text{EST}_{j,q} = \max\left\{\text{AVT}_q, \max_{v_i \in \text{pre}(j)}\left\{\text{EFT}_{i,p} + \text{CT}_{i,j,p,q}\right\}\right\}, \quad (6)$$

$$\text{EFT}_{j,q} = \text{EST}_{j,q} + \text{ET}_{j,q}, \quad (7)$$

where AVT_q is the earliest available time of resource r_q to allocate v_j, taking into account the current load of r_q and the estimate execution time of v_j on r_q (i.e., $\omega(\text{ET}_{j,q})$). In addition, $r_p = \text{alloc}(i)$. Apparently, at this moment, v_i has already been allocated. Particularly, for the entry node, $\text{EST}_{\text{entry\_node},q} = 0$ for every r_q. The main difference between the randomized HEFT and its initial version is the random comparison policy mentioned in line 8. For each task, we use this comparison policy to compare the estimated finish times (i.e., EFT) of different resources, which are random variables in our stochastic model, as the estimated finish time is determined by summing up the task execution times and the communication times along the critical path. Let CP denote the critical path, ND the set of nodes, and ED the set of edges along with CP; then we have the earliest finish time as below:

$$\text{EFT} = \sum_{i \in \text{ND}} \text{ET}_i + \sum_{j \in \text{ED}} \text{CT}_j. \quad (8)$$

For ease of analysis, we assume all task execution times and communication times follow normal distribution. Then we have

$$\mu(\text{EFT}) = \sum_{i \in \text{ND}} \mu(\text{ET}_i) + \sum_{j \in \text{ED}} \mu(\text{CT}_j),$$

$$\sigma(\text{EFT})^2 = \sum_{i \in \text{ND}} \left(\sigma(\text{ET}_i)^2\right) + \sum_{j \in \text{ED}} \left(\sigma(\text{CT}_i)^2\right). \quad (9)$$

Say there are two random variables EFT and EFT$'$ to compare and determine which is larger. We let $\text{DV} = \text{EFT} - \text{EFT}'$. Then we have

$$\mu(\text{DV}) = \mu(\text{EFT}) - \mu(\text{EFT}'),$$

$$\sigma(\text{DV})^2 = \sigma(\text{EFT})^2 + \sigma(\text{EFT}')^2. \quad (10)$$

Apparently, the value of DV corresponds to the comparison result of EFT and EFT$'$. The key idea of our random comparison policy is to make a random draw of DV value, if the outcome is less than zero, EFT $<$ EFT$'$; otherwise, EFT $\geq$ EFT$'$. However, to implement a precise random draw of DV is not easy. Therefore, we use $\mu(\text{DV})$ and $\sigma(\text{DV})$ for approximation. In detail, without losing generality, we assume $\mu(\text{DV}) > 0$, and if $2 \times \sigma(\text{DV}) > \mu(\text{DV})$,

$$P(\text{DV} < 0) = \frac{2 \times \sigma(\text{DV}) - \mu(\text{DV})}{4 \times \sigma(\text{DV})}; \quad (11)$$

else $P(\text{DV} < 0) = 0$. One can easily get $P(\text{DV} \geq 0) = 1 - P(\text{DV} < 0)$. That is to say, the comparison result between EFT and EFT$'$ is a 0-1 random variable. With probability of $P(\text{DV} < 0)$, the outcome is EFT $<$ EFT$'$; with probability of $P(\text{DV} \geq 0)$, EFT $\geq$ EFT$'$. By this random comparison policy, the deterministic HEFT is randomized. Note that as described in Algorithm 1 (lines 3–5), RHEFT requires running the randomized HEFT for a certain number of times to generate candidate schedules.

For illustration purpose, we run HEFT and RHEFT to the DAG example modelled by Figure 1 and Table 1 and obtain scheduling results, respectively. For RHEFT, the scheduling result is picked up from 10 candidates. In order to present these scheduling results, we assume the values shown in Table 2 are the real task execution times and data transmission times. Then the scheduling details can be depicted by Figure 2. In this case, RHEFT obtains a makespan of 117.17, which makes a significant improvement (19.8%) to HEFT with a makespan of 146.15.

4.3. Further Investigation on RHEFT. Although the illustrative example shows that RHEFT can significantly outperform HEFT on minimizing makespan, there are still two open issues regarding with the configuration of RHEFT which are worthy of further investigation:

(i) In RHEFT, how many candidate schedules should we generate to gain substantial improvement on makespan without paying too much overhead?

(ii) How often and to what extent can RHEFT improve the makespan obtained by HEFT over various DAG examples?

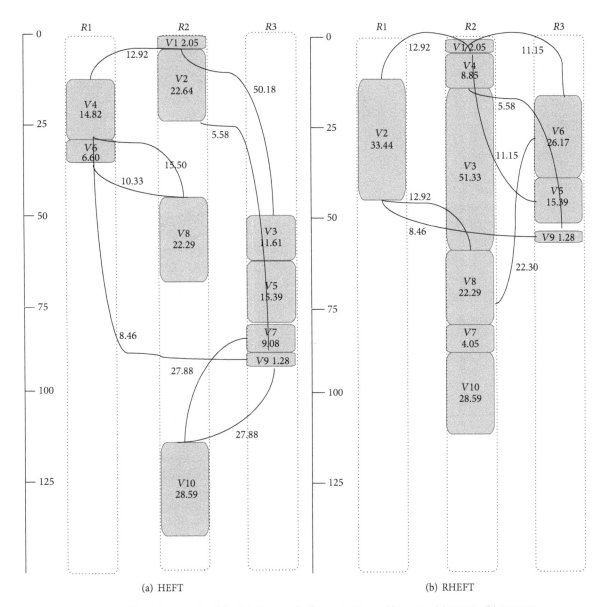

FIGURE 2: Scheduling result of the DAG example shown in Figure 1 by using (a) HEFT; (b) RHEFT.

We examine these two issues by evaluation in the rest of this subsection.

4.3.1. Evaluation Setting. We built a simulated computing system and a stochastic DAG generator, which allow various parameter settings. We use two types of DAGs: Montage [2] and LIGO [33] as shown in Figure 3, which are derived from real-world applications and have distinctive structures and sizes. We consider the number of resources used to be 3 and 8. All random variables used in our stochastic model are assumed to follow normal distribution. For the execution time of each task on each resource, we randomly select its expected value from the range of $[1, 100]$ and its standard deviation value as $1/6$ of its expected value. Similar setting is applied to the communication time between tasks on different resources. We specify a parameter named

communication-computation-ratio (CCR), which means the ratio between the average communication cost and the computation one, and adjust the value of communication times to meet the specified CCR value. We randomly specify the CCR value from $[0.5, 1.5]$ in our experiments.

4.3.2. How Many Candidate Schedules Are Needed? One can easily imagine that the more times RHEFT runs the randomized HEFT heuristic, the more likely a better candidate schedule may be obtained, and on the other hand the more time cost is needed to be paid. In order to examine how many times RHEFT should repeat running the randomized scheduling procedure, we specify four DAG instances and observe the expected makespan RHEFT can gain for these DAGs as the number of repetition grows. Figure 4 shows the observation results.

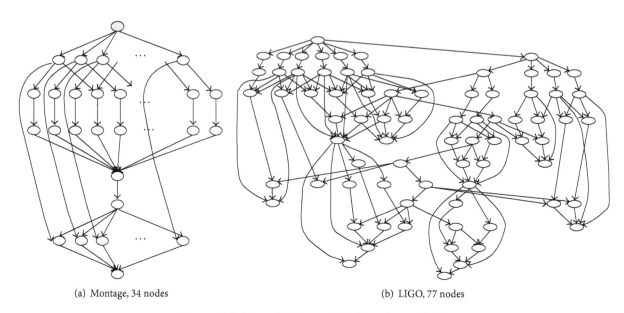

(a) Montage, 34 nodes   (b) LIGO, 77 nodes

FIGURE 3: DAG applications used in the evaluation [15].

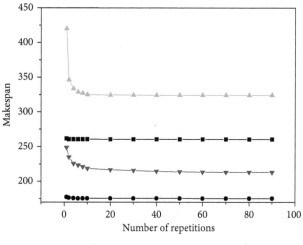

FIGURE 4: Change of expected makespan as the number of candidates generated by RHEFT increases.

4.3.3. Improvement Rate on Makespan. Next, we observe to what extent can a RHEFT schedule improve a HEFT schedule on the expected makespan. Again, we consider the DAG type to be Montage with 34 nodes and LIGO with 77 nodes and the number of resources to be 3 and 8. Then for each combination of the DAG type and the number of resources, we generate 100 instances of the stochastic model. For each instance, we collect the expected makespans obtained by RHEFT and HEFT, respectively. For comparison, we define the metric "improvement rate," which is the ratio between the reduced expected makespan and the expected makespan of HEFT. Figure 5 shows the results of improvement rate. In general, RHEFT obtains significant improvement on the expected makespan (above 20%) in the case where LIGO is used. Nevertheless, when Montage is used, RHEFT obtains a similar result in the majority of cases of the 100 instances. It can also be seen that the advantage of RHEFT over HEFT may be weakened as the number of resources increases. Anyway, with every setting of DAG type and resource number, there is always a chance that RHEFT can reduce the expected makespan more than 20%.

4.4. The Enhanced RHEFT Heuristic. By making random decision in the resource allocation phase of HEFT, we derive a novel scheduling approach RHEFT which significantly outperforms HEFT on minimizing makespan. This encourages us to extend RHEFT by making random decision when prioritizing the tasks in the listing phase.

The extension is fairly straightforward. In the first phase of the randomized HEFT (Algorithm 2, lines: 1-2), instead of defining task rank by the constant value Urank (as defined in (4)), we consider it as a random variable Rrank. The definition of Rrank is somehow correlated with Urank.

In the diagram shown in Figure 4, RHEFT with zero repetition actually boils down to HEFT. As we can see from the curves denoting "Montage on 3 resources" and "LIGO on 8 resources," the expected makespan of RHEFT reduces rapidly as the number of repetitions grows. After the number of repetitions reaches 10, no significant improvement can be observed on the expected makespan. This observation indicates that RHEFT is promising, as it can generate a candidate schedule which is fairly better than HEFT's with only few more repetitions.

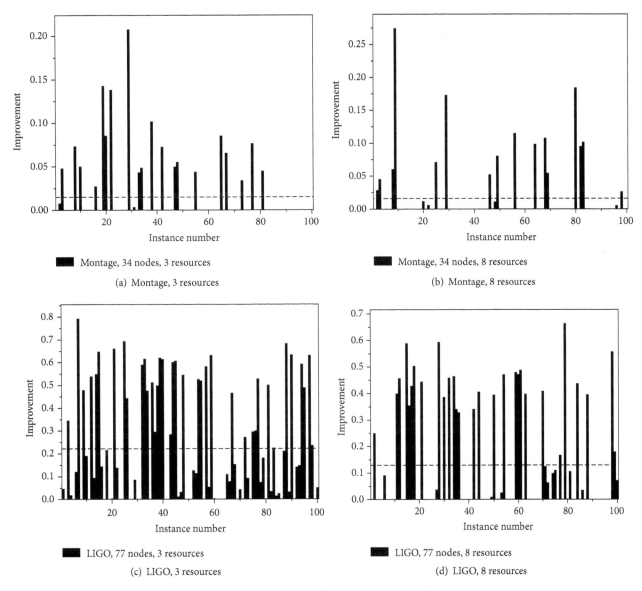

FIGURE 5: Makespan improvement of RHEFT over HEFT over 100 instances.

Recall that by (4), for task v_i, Urank(v_i) is calculated by accumulating the time costs associated with the nodes and edges along the critical path from v_i to the exit node. Let Ph_i denote this critical path for v_i, N_i the set of nodes, and E_i the set of edges along with Ph_i; then we have the definition of Rrank(v_i) as below:

$$\text{Rrank}(v_i) = \sum_{i \in N_i} \text{MET}_i + \sum_{j \in E_i} \text{MCT}_j, \qquad (12)$$

where

$$\text{MET}_i = \frac{\sum_{p=1}^{m} \text{ET}_{i,p}}{m},$$

$$\text{MCT}_j = \frac{\sum_{p=1}^{m} \sum_{q=1}^{m} \text{CT}_{j,p,q}}{m \cdot m}. \qquad (13)$$

Especially for exit node, we have Rrank($v_{\text{exit\_node}}$) = $\text{MET}_{\text{exit\_node}}$.

When prioritizing tasks in the listing phase, we need to compare the rank of v_i with v_j. The comparison procedure, which is named *randomized prioritizing procedure*, is carried out as follows:

(1) We firstly examine if there is any task dependency between v_i and v_j.

(2) If v_i is an ancestor of v_j, v_i should be given higher priority and placed before v_j in the list.

(3) If there is no dependency between v_i and v_j, random variables Rrank(v_i) and Rrank(v_j) will be compared by the random comparison policy as described in Section 4 to determine which one has the higher priority.

(1)   Compute Rrank (as defined in (12)) for all tasks.
(2)   Sort all tasks in a list $\mathcal{L}$ in the non-descending order of Rrank according to the *randomized prioritizing procedure*.
(3)   **for** $k := 1$ to n **do** (where n is the number of tasks)
(4)   Select the kth task v^* from the list $\mathcal{L}$.
(5)   **for** each resource $r_p \in R$ **do**
(6)   Compute the mean value and variance of estimated finish time of v^* on r_p (as defined in (7)).
(7)   **endfor**
(8)   Decide the winner resource of estimated finish time (r^*) for v^* according to the *random comparison policy*.
(9)   Allocate v^* to r^*.
(10)   **endfor**

ALGORITHM 3: The enhanced randomized HEFT heuristic.

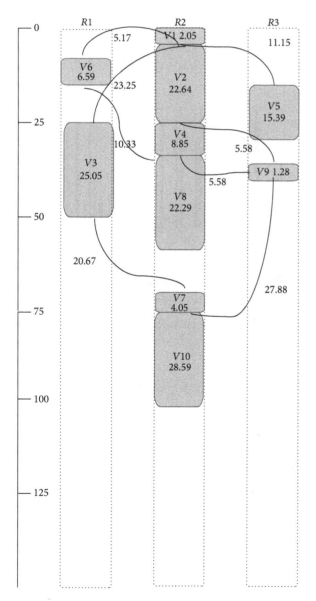

FIGURE 6: Scheduling result of the DAG example shown in Figure 1 by using ERHEFT.

We apply the above procedure to the listing phase of RHEFT and then derive the enhanced RHEFT heuristic, namely, ERHEFT. The details of the enhanced randomized HEFT heuristic are provided in Algorithm 3.

Apparently, when ERHEFT generates candidate schedules, the prioritized task list may be different from that of RHEFT. This makes it possible for ERHEFT to generate more candidate schedules than RHEFT can do. As a result, a schedule with better makespan may be obtained. For illustration, Figure 6 shows the scheduling result by applying ERHEFT to the DAG example modelled by Figure 1 and Table 1. This schedule has a makespan of 103.67 which is better than the schedule acquired by RHEFT as shown in Figure 2(b).

Similar to the way by which we investigate in Section 4.3.2, we observe how the expected makespan of ERHEFT changes as the number of repetitions used increases. Here, the same evaluation setting as specified in Section 4.3.2 is used and the result is shown in Figure 7. This result indicates that 200 may be the appropriate number of repetitions that should be used by ERHEFT.

5. Evaluation

In order to compare the performance of HEFT, RHEFT, and ERHEFT in stochastic scheduling model, we adopt the evaluation setting as mentioned in Section 4.3.1 and evaluate the expected makespan and the time cost of the competitors with different configurations of evaluation parameters. The machine we used to carry out the evaluation has the following hardware configuration: CPU Intel I3-4130 3.40 GHz, 4 G DDR3 memory, and 500 G hard disk. We used Java (JDK 1.7) to implement all heuristics and the simulation.

First, we evaluate the average makespan that HEFT, RHEFT, and ERHEFT can obtain with stochastic model. For each experiment, we firstly specify the DAG type and the number of resources we are going to use. Then we generate the expected value and variance for stochastically modelling

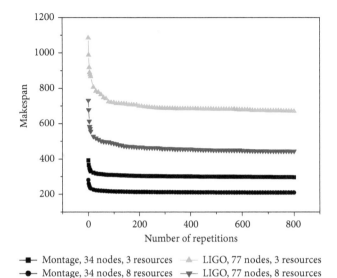

FIGURE 7: Change of expected makespan as the number of candidates generated by ERHEFT increases.

each task execution time and then generate communication times with specified CCR value, which as a whole is called a stochastic model of the given DAG and resources. For each combination of a DAG and a set of resources, we generate 100 stochastic models. And for each stochastic model, we run HEFT, RHEFT, and ERHEFT and obtain their schedules, respectively. Each time we take a sample for the stochastic model (as shown in Table 2, including all execution times and communication times), we can view them as runtime information gathered after the DAG application completes and use them to evaluate the performance of each schedule. To be fair, we take 100 samples from each stochastic model. So the result for each compared heuristic on a given DAG and given resources is averaged over 10000 experiments (100 stochastic models, each of which has 100 samples) in total. For comparison, we use the metric of "speedup" which is defined as the ratio between the average sequential execution time of all tasks and the makespan obtained by a heuristic.

In order to compare the heuristic competitors in different scenario, we consider the number of resources to be 3, 6, and 8 and collect the average speedup results for CCR being equal to 0.1, 1, and 10, respectively. The collected results are shown in Figure 8.

One can easily see that in all combination of evaluation parameter settings ERHEFT has better average speedup than RHEFT, while RHEFT has better average speedup than HEFT. The improvement on average speedup of ERHEFT over HEFT can be up to around 20% in the case where Montage is executed on 3 resources and CCR = 0.1 is used. It is interesting to see that the effectiveness of ERHEFT and RHEFT is closely related to CCR. When CCR is high, ERHEFT and RHEFT usually achieve more significant

improvement on average speedup over HEFT. This indicates our randomization approach may work better with workflow applications which are data intensive. However, when CCR turns to be as low as 0.1, the difference in the average speedup obtained by HEFT, RHEFT, and ERHEFT seems trivial. From a different perspective, this may also imply that HEFT works especially well with computation intensive applications and thus leave little space for further improving its makespan.

In addition, we measure the time cost needed by HEFT, RHEFT, and ERHEFT with different sizes of Montage DAG and different numbers of resources. We use the ratio of the time cost of RHEFT (ERHEFT) over that of HEFT as the metric and the measurement result is shown in Figure 9. From the diagram we can see that in most of the cases the ratio of RHEFT over HEFT is within the range of 5 to 15. Moreover, there is no rapid ascending trend as the DAG size or the number of resources, which represents the scale of the scheduling problem, grows. This indicates that the time complexity of RHEFT is close to HEFT. Because HEFT usually needs very little time to compute a schedule, the additional overhead introduced by a certain number of loops of running HEFT and extra computation of random variables, which results in 5 to 15 times of the time cost of HEFT, is acceptable. The radio of ERHEFT over HEFT exhibits a curve similar to RHEFT over HEFT. Even though the radio of ERHEFT over HEFT reaches the range of 100 to 500, as the time cost for a single execution of HEFT is tiny, the overall time cost for ERHEFT is still acceptable. For instance, in our empirical results, for DAG with 234 nodes ERHEFT runs for 3.2 seconds while for 12 resources ERHEFT runs for only 1.9 seconds. Moreover, by adjusting the number of loops used in the RHEFT approach, we can flexibly get a good trade-off between the scheduling performance and the heuristic overhead.

6. Conclusion

In this paper, we explore into the problem of scheduling workflow tasks onto a set of heterogeneous cloud resources with stochastic model of task execution and communication. We attempt to extend deterministic DAG scheduling heuristic, to gain better average makespan. As a progress, a randomization scheduling approach is proposed. We apply the randomization approach to the classic deterministic heuristic HEFT and two versions of novel randomized heuristic: RHEFT and ERHEFT, are produced. We evaluate and compare the performance of HEFT, RHEFT, and ERHEFT with extensive simulation experiments where two real-world workflow applications are used. The experimental results suggest that RHEFT and ERHEFT are both promising for stochastic workflow scheduling, as RHEFT and ERHEFT not only significantly reduce the average makespan in most cases of experimental setting, but also exhibit reasonable scalability. Our future work may consider more stochastic model other than normal distribution and/or randomizing other deterministic DAG scheduling heuristics.

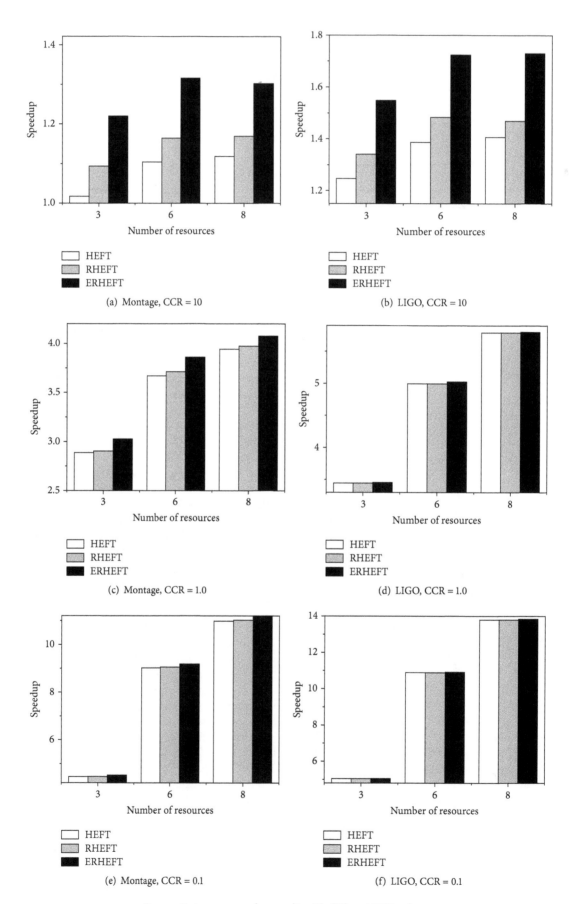

FIGURE 8: Average speedup results with different CCR values.

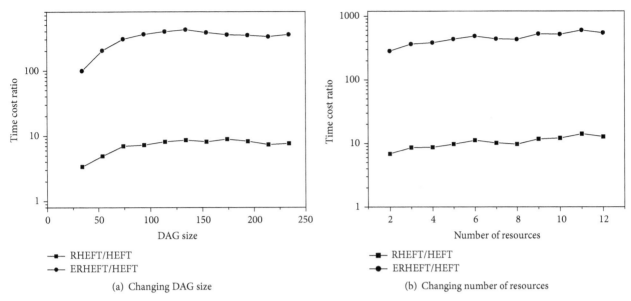

(a) Changing DAG size

(b) Changing number of resources

FIGURE 9: Time cost ratio of RHEFT and ERHEFT over HEFT.

Competing Interests

The authors declare that there is no conflict of interests regarding the publication of this paper.

Acknowledgments

The work is supported by National Natural Science Foundation of China (NSFC, Grant no. 61202361).

References

[1] E. Deelman, D. Gannon, M. Shields, and I. Taylor, "Workflows and e-science: an overview of workflow system features and capabilities," *Future Generation Computer Systems*, vol. 25, no. 5, pp. 528–540, 2009.

[2] G. B. Berriman, J. C. Good, A. C. Laity et al., "A grid enabled image mosaic service for the national virtual observatory," in *Proceedings of the Conference Series of Astronomical Data Analysis Software and Systems XIII (ADASS XIII)*, pp. 593–596, 2004.

[3] I. J. Taylor, E. Deelman, D. B. Gannon, and M. Shields, *Workflows for E-Science: Scientific Workflows for Grids*, Springer, New York, NY, USA, 2007.

[4] H. Casanova, F. Dufossé, Y. Robert, and F. Vivien, "Scheduling parallel iterative applications on volatile resources," in *Proceedings of the IEEE International Parallel & Distributed Processing Symposium (IPDPS '11)*, pp. 1012–1023, IEEE, Anchorage, Alaska, USA, May 2011.

[5] S. Yeo and H. S. Lee, "Using mathematical modeling in provisioning a heterogeneous cloud computing environment," *IEEE Computer*, vol. 44, no. 8, pp. 55–62, 2011.

[6] G. Juve and E. Deelman, "Scientific workflows and clouds," *ACM Crossroads*, vol. 16, no. 3, pp. 14–18, 2010.

[7] G. Juve, E. Deelman, G. B. Berriman, B. P. Berman, and P. Maechling, "An evaluation of the cost and performance of scientific workflows on Amazon EC2," *Journal of Grid Computing*, vol. 10, no. 1, pp. 5–21, 2012.

[8] J. Li, D. Li, Y. Ye, and X. Lu, "Efficient multi-tenant virtual machine allocation in cloud data centers," *Tsinghua Science and Technology*, vol. 20, no. 1, pp. 81–89, 2015.

[9] C. Cheng, J. Li, and Y. Wang, "An energy-saving task scheduling strategy based on vacation queuing theory in cloud computing," *Tsinghua Science and Technology*, vol. 20, no. 1, pp. 28–39, 2015.

[10] M. R. Garey and D. S. Johnson, *Computer and Intractability: A Guide to the Theory of NP-Completeness*, W. H. Freeman, 1979.

[11] H. Topcuoglu, S. Hariri, and M.-Y. Wu, "Performance-effective and low-complexity task scheduling for heterogeneous computing," *IEEE Transactions on Parallel and Distributed Systems*, vol. 13, no. 3, pp. 260–274, 2002.

[12] R. Sakellariou and H. Zhao, "A hybrid heuristic for DAG scheduling on heterogeneous systems," in *Proceedings of the 18th International Parallel and Distributed Processing Symposium (IPDPS '04)*, IEEE Computer Society, Santa Fe, NM, USA, April 2004.

[13] R. L. Graham, E. L. Lawler, J. K. Lenstra, and A. H. Rinnooy Kan, "Optimization and approximation in deterministic sequencing and scheduling: a survey," *Annals of Discrete Mathematics*, vol. 5, pp. 287–326, 1979.

[14] M. L. Pinedo, *Overview of Stochastic Scheduling Problems*, Springer, Berlin, Germany, 2011.

[15] W. Zheng and R. Sakellariou, "Stochastic DAG scheduling using a Monte Carlo approach," *Journal of Parallel and Distributed Computing*, vol. 73, no. 12, pp. 1673–1689, 2013.

[16] R. Sakellariou and H. Zhao, "A hybrid heuristic for DAG scheduling on heterogeneous systems," in *Proceedings of the 13th Heterogeneous Computing Workshop*, pp. 111–124, 2004.

[17] G. C. Sih and E. A. Lee, "A compile-time scheduling heuristic for interconnection-constrained heterogeneous processor architectures," *IEEE Transactions on Parallel and Distributed Systems*, vol. 4, no. 2, pp. 175–187, 1993.

[18] J. Blythe, S. Jain, E. Deelman et al., "Task scheduling strategies for workflow-based applications in grids," in *Proceedings of the IEEE International Symposium on Cluster Computing and the Grid (CCGrid '05)*, vol. 2, pp. 759–767, May 2005.

[19] G. Q. Liu, K. L. Poh, and M. Xie, "Iterative list scheduling for heterogeneous computing," *Journal of Parallel and Distributed Computing*, vol. 65, no. 5, pp. 654–664, 2005.

[20] L. Wang, H. J. Siegel, V. P. Roychowdhury, and A. A. MacIejewski, "Task matching and scheduling in heterogeneous computing environments using a genetic-algorithm-based approach," *Journal of Parallel and Distributed Computing*, vol. 47, no. 1, pp. 8–22, 1997.

[21] M. Coli and P. Palazzari, "Real time pipelined system design through simulated annealing," *Journal of Systems Architecture*, vol. 42, no. 6-7, pp. 465–475, 1996.

[22] B. Cirou and E. Jeannot, "Triplet: a clustering scheduling algorithm for heterogeneous systems," in *Proceedings of the International Conference on Parallel Processing Workshops*, pp. 231–236, Valencia, Spain, 2001.

[23] S. Ranaweera and D. P. Agrawal, "A task duplication based scheduling algorithm for heterogeneous systems," in *Proceedings of the 14th International Parallel and Distributed Processing Symposium*, pp. 445–450, Cancun, Mexico, May 2000.

[24] S. Ranaweera and D. P. Agrawal, "A scalable task duplication based scheduling algorithm for heterogeneous systems," in *Proceedings of the International Conference on Parallel Processing*, pp. 383–390, Toronto, Canada, 2000.

[25] A. Dogan and R. Ozguner, "LDBS: a duplication based scheduling algorithm for heterogeneous computing systems," in *Proceedings of the International Conference on Parallel Processing (ICPP '02)*, pp. 352–359, IEEE, 2002.

[26] L. Canon, E. Jeannot, R. Sakellariou, and W. Zheng, "Comparative evaluation of the robustness of DAG scheduling heuristics," in *Grid Computing: Achievements and Prospects*, S. Gorlatch, P. Fragopoulou, and T. Priol, Eds., pp. 73–84, Springer, Berlin, Germany, 2008.

[27] S. A. Jarvis, L. He, D. P. Spooner, and G. R. Nudd, "The impact of predictive inaccuracies on execution scheduling," *Performance Evaluation*, vol. 60, no. 1–4, pp. 127–139, 2005.

[28] M. M. López, E. Heymann, and M. A. Senar, "Analysis of dynamic heuristics for workflow scheduling on grid systems," in *Proceedings of the 5th International Symposium on Parallel and Distributed Computing*, pp. 199–207, IEEE, Timisoara, Romania, July 2006.

[29] A. Kamthe and S.-Y. Lee, "A stochastic approach to estimating earliest start times of nodes for scheduling DAGs on heterogeneous distributed computing systems," in *Proceedings of the 19th IEEE International Parallel and Distributed Processing Symposium (IPDPS '05)*, p. 121b, Denver, Colo, USA, April 2005.

[30] X. Tang, K. Li, G. Liao, K. Fang, and F. Wu, "A stochastic scheduling algorithm for precedence constrained tasks on grid," *Future Generation Computer Systems*, vol. 27, no. 8, pp. 1083–1091, 2011.

[31] K. Li, X. Tang, B. Veeravalli, and K. Li, "Scheduling precedence constrained stochastic tasks on heterogeneous cluster systems," *IEEE Transactions on Computers*, vol. 64, no. 1, pp. 191–204, 2015.

[32] W. Zheng, B. Emmanuel, and C. Wang, "A randomized heuristic for stochastic workflow scheduling on heterogeneous systems," in *Proceedings of the 3rd International Conference on Advanced Cloud and Big Data (CBD '15)*, pp. 88–95, Yangzhou, China, October 2015.

[33] E. Deelman, C. Kesselman, G. Mehta et al., "GriPhyN and LIGO, building a virtual data Grid for gravitational wave scientists," in *Proceedings of the 11th IEEE International Symposium on High Performance Distributed Computing (HPDC '02)*, pp. 225–234, IEEE, 2002.

20

Dynamic Scalable Stochastic Petri Net: A Novel Model for Designing and Analysis of Resource Scheduling in Cloud Computing

Hua He,[1] **Shanchen Pang,**[2] **and Zenghua Zhao**[1]

[1]*School of Computer Science and Technology, Tianjin University, Tianjin 300072, China*
[2]*College of Computer and Communication Engineering, China University of Petroleum, Qingdao 266580, China*

Correspondence should be addressed to Shanchen Pang; shanchenpang@sohu.com

Academic Editor: Fabrizio Messina

Performance evaluation of cloud computing systems studies the relationships among system configuration, system load, and performance indicators. However, such evaluation is not feasible by dint of measurement methods or simulation methods, due to the properties of cloud computing, such as large scale, diversity, and dynamics. To overcome those challenges, we present a novel Dynamic Scalable Stochastic Petri Net (DSSPN) to model and analyze the performance of cloud computing systems. DSSPN can not only clearly depict system dynamic behaviors in an intuitive and efficient way but also easily discover performance deficiencies and bottlenecks of systems. In this study, we further elaborate some properties of DSSPN. In addition, we improve fair scheduling taking into consideration job diversity and resource heterogeneity. To validate the improved algorithm and the applicability of DSSPN, we conduct extensive experiments through Stochastic Petri Net Package (SPNP). The performance results show that the improved algorithm is better than fair scheduling in some key performance indicators, such as average throughput, response time, and average completion time.

1. Introduction

Cloud computing provides shared configurable resources to users as services with pay-as-you-go scheme [1]. These services that consisted of set of components may be offered by different providers [2]. To meet the needs of customers, cloud service providers have to ensure that their profit and return on investment are not rapidly decreased due to increased costs, while maintaining a desirable level of the quality of service (QoS) of consumers, such as execution time, delay time, and budget restrictions [2–4]. To address this problem, most researches of cloud computing have focused on performance improvement and satisfaction of the QoS requirements and developed some efficient solutions. But for now, little work has been done about finding a convenient method of modeling, analyzing, and evaluating the performance of scheduling algorithms or systems in cloud environment

without spending too much time on comparison and analysis [5, 6].

Performance evaluation is important to cloud computing development. It is primarily aimed at selecting schemes that meet the requirements of consumers, finding out performance defects, predicting performance of the designed systems in future, and discovering better ways to achieve optimal resource allocation. In other words, performance evaluation is important in selecting, improving, and designing systems or scheduling algorithms in cloud computing environment [7]. The methods of performance evaluation are approximately divided into three types: measurement method, simulation method, and model method. However, measurement and simulation methods are only applicable to existing and running systems and might be time consuming. In addition, the two methods are incapable of finding out performance bottlenecks and analyzing large-scale and complicated cloud computing systems. In this study, we only focus on the model method.

Model method is a kind of analysis method of performance evaluation by studying and describing the relationships among performance, system, and load based on mathematical theories. To facilitate mathematical descriptions and calculation, it usually requires simplification of the system model and making some rational assumptions about the status of the system. Compared to the other two methods, model method is based on a mature theoretical foundation and can clearly describe the relationship among all factors with a lower cost.

Stochastic Petri Net (SPN) is a powerful tool of model method and can be applied to graphic modeling and mathematical analysis of many systems and areas, such as computer science, communication network, and multiprocessor system [8–13]. It can not only easily describe the properties of systems that have concurrency and synchronization characteristics but also clearly depict dynamic behaviors of systems in an intuitive and efficient way. In this way, it is easy to discover performance deficiencies and bottlenecks by using SPN in analysis.

However, SPN is still not entirely suitable for modeling and performance evaluation of cloud computing systems: (i) cloud computing offers scalable infrastructures to consumers on demand by utilizing the virtualization technology. SPN is not capable of adjusting models dynamically when the infrastructure changes [13]. (ii) Different workloads submitted by users, which are simultaneously running on cloud clusters, might have different QoS requirements, such as response time, execution time, and data traffic [14]. However, SPN is incapable of representing the diversity of cloud computing. (iii) The configurable shared resources in cloud computing are usually heterogeneous and geographically distributed, so using SPN to build up models will increase the computational complexity and result in state explosion. Because of the problems mentioned above, SPN does not adequately model and analyze the performance of cloud computing in many situations.

To overcome those challenges, we propose a novel extended form of SPN, which is called Dynamic Scalable Stochastic Petri Net (DSSPN), to conveniently model and analyze the performance of cloud computing systems. In order to support dynamic changes in cloud computing, three kinds of functions are introduced to enhance the dynamics of arcs, transitions, and places in DSSPN. In addition, many cloud service patterns under the same state can be compressed into a simple one by using DSSPN. Therefore, cloud computing systems can be easily modeled and analyzed by using DSSPN without changing the original graph structure. Consumers can easily evaluate performances only by setting the three functions of the DSSPN model without spending too much time on programming. According to the feature of SPN, system decomposition and model compression can be applied to reduce the complexity of the state space in DSSPN models.

The main contributions of this paper include (1) proposing Dynamic Scalable Stochastic Petri Net (DSSPN) and then further demonstrating firing rules and some properties of DSSPN; (2) presenting classified fair scheduling (CFS) taking into consideration job diversity and resource heterogeneity, which can improve throughput and response time; (3) validating the proposed approach and algorithm, where we conduct and evaluate DSSPN models of fair scheduling and CFS algorithms by using Stochastic Petri Net Package (SPNP) [15, 16] analysis and simulation.

The remainder of the paper is organized as follows. Section 2 describes the related works of this study. Section 3 specifies the novel analytical model called DSSPN and elaborates its dynamics as well as some other properties. In Section 4, we construct a DSSPN model of resource scheduling of fair scheduler and propose the classified fair scheduling (CFS) algorithm taking into consideration the workload and resources diversity. In addition, in order to alleviate the problem of state explosion, we adopt the multiuser multiserver model [17] and analyze some parameters by using equivalent Markov model to refine our original models in Section 4. Section 5 demonstrates the experimental parameters setup and evaluates the system performance of the two scheduling algorithms by using SPNP. Finally, conclusions and future works are given in Section 6.

2. Related Works

Performance evaluation mainly focuses on relationships among system configuration, system load, and performance indicators and has drawn much research attention recently. Due to the complexity of the problem, most studies adopt measurement and simulation methods to quantitatively analyze system performance [18].

By using some measuring devices or measuring programs, measurement and simulation methods can directly obtain the performance indicators of systems or closely related quantities and then work out performance indexes by the corresponding calculation. Ostermann et al. analyze the performance of the Amazon EC2 platform based on measurement at the background of scientific computing [19]. In addition, performance comparisons were made among EC2 and other platforms by using long-term traces of experimental data in some indicators, such as resource acquisition, release overheads, and system workload. Calheiros et al. propose extensible simulation toolkit CloudSim, which can model, simulate, and evaluate the performance of both cloud computing systems and application provisioning environments [20]. CloudSim supports single and internetworked cloud scenarios and is used by several organizations to investigate cloud resource allocation and energy efficiency management of data center resources. Bautista et al. present a performance measurement framework (PMF) for cloud computing systems with integration software quality concepts from ISO 25010 [21]. The PMF defines the requirements, data types, and evaluation criteria to measure "cluster behavior" performance. Mei et al. study performance measurement of network I/O applications in virtualized cloud [22]. This measurement is based on performance impact of coexisting applications in a virtualized cloud, such as throughput and resource sharing effectiveness. In addition, the measurement can quantify the performance gains and losses and reveal the importance of optimizing for application deployment.

Measurement and simulation methods are the most direct and basic ones on performance evaluation, which the model method partly depends on. However, the two methods are only applicable to existing and running systems, and there are a lot of insufficiencies and abuses in evaluating the performance of cloud systems which are under dynamic environments and involve lots of parameters, such as time consuming, low degree of simulation, and quantitative difficulty. In addition, measurement and simulation methods are also incapable of finding out performance bottlenecks. Therefore, how to provide powerful mathematic tool, intuitional description method of models, effective analysis method, and available analysis software is the urgent problem for performance evaluation of cloud systems, which is just the core of analysis technology based on SPN. However, there have been few studies on the application of SPN in cloud computing.

Cao et al. construct stochastic evaluation model based on Queuing Petri Net for "Chinese Cloud" of State Key Laboratory of High-End Server & Storage Technology [23]. They still present three kinds of cloud system architectures, distributed architecture, centralized architecture, and hybrid architecture, and then model the three architectures based on Queuing Petri Net. These models describe the relationships among network, CPU, I/O, and request queue. Finally, system throughputs of the three architectures are compared in different task types and workloads with QPME tool [24].

Targeting the dynamic feature of cloud computing, Fan et al. propose a systematic method to describe the reliability, running time, and failure processing of resource scheduling [25]. In this study, resources scheduling process is abstracted as metaobject by using a reflection mechanism, and Petri Net is introduced to model its components, such as base layer, metalayer, and metaobject protocol. In addition, they present an adaptive resource scheduling strategy described by Computation Tree Logic (CTL) [26], which can realize dynamic reoptimization and distribution of system resources at runtime. Finally, Petri Net and its state space are used to verify the correctness and effectiveness of the proposed algorithm.

In order to evaluate the performance of the Hadoop system, Ruiz et al. introduce Prioritised-Timed Coloured Petri Net (PTCPN) [27] to formally construct its stochastic model of MapReduce paradigm [28]. Tradeoffs are made between processing time and resource cost according to some performance evaluation parameters. In addition, state space and CPNTools [29] auxiliary software will execute the quantitative analysis of the system performance and the accuracy verification of the models.

It is concluded that the above-mentioned methods of performance evaluation of cloud computing can well describe and model the various properties of cloud computing, but there are difficulties in comparative analysis. To overcome these challenges, we present a novel Dynamic Scalable Stochastic Petri Net (DSSPN) to better depict the important properties of cloud systems. Compared to other SPNs, DSSPN has the following advantages: (1) intuitive graphical representation and model easy to understand; (2) no requirements for strong mathematical background; (3) capability of flexibly depicting characteristics of cloud systems, such as the relationship between network topology and other components; and (4) automatically deriving the steady-state probability of state transitions by using auxiliary software, such as SPNP and SHLPNA.

3. Dynamic Scalable Stochastic Petri Net

Cloud computing is a service-oriented computing model, with the characteristics of large scale, complexity, resource heterogeneity, requirement of QoS diversity, and scalability. Those characteristics make the resource scheduling of cloud computing too complicated to be modeled and analyzed by the traditional Stochastic Petri Net. To overcome the problem, a novel Dynamic Scalable Stochastic Petri Net (DSSPN) is proposed in this study. DSSPN is generated from SPN [9, 30] and Stochastic Reward Net (SRN) [31]. In later sections, we will further introduce the feasibility and applicability in both modeling and performance evaluation of cloud computing systems. To easily understand the definition of DSSPN, we firstly present some notations. Let us suppose that S is a set and e is a number. $|S|$ denotes the number of elements in S. $\widehat{S}$ represents the power set of S. $[e]$ indicates the maximal integer that is not larger than e. $\mathbb{N}$ stands for the set of natural numbers, that is, $\mathbb{N} = \{0, 1, 2, \ldots\}$, while $\mathbb{N}^+$ means the set of positive integers, that is, $\mathbb{N}^+ = \{1, 2, \ldots\}$. Let $M : P \rightarrow \mathbb{N}$ denote a marking of DSSPN. $R(M)$ represents the set of reachable marking of the marking M. For all $x \in P \cup T$, $^\bullet x = \{y \mid (y, x) \in P \cup T\}$ indicates the preset of x, while $x^\bullet = \{y \mid (x, y) \in P \cup T\}$ means the postset of x. Φ is an empty set, and ε represents an empty element.

3.1. Definitions of DSSPN

Definition 1. A Dynamic Scalable Stochastic Petri Net is a 12-tuple $(P, T, F, K, W, \lambda, \text{TS}, G, E, f, g, M^0)$, where

(1) $P = \{p_1, p_2, \ldots, p_n\}$ is a finite set of places, $n = |P|$;

(2) $T = \{T_I \cup T_T\}$ is a finite set of transitions, $T_I = \{t_{I1}, t_{I2}, \ldots, t_{Im}\}$ is a set of immediate transitions, and $T_T = \{t_{T1}, t_{T2}, \ldots, t_{Tl}\}$ is a set of timed transitions; $m = |T_I|$, $l = |T_T|$; note that $T_I \cap T_T = \Phi$;

(3) $P \cup T \neq \Phi$, and $P \cap T = \Phi$;

(4) $F \subseteq (P \times T) \cup (T \times P)$ is a set of arcs;

(5) $K : P \rightarrow \mathbb{N}^+ \cup \{\infty\}$ is a capacity function where $K(p)$ denotes the capacity of the place p; let $K(p) = k_1$ and $T_1 = {}^\bullet p$; if $M(p) = k_1$, for all $t \in T_1$, t cannot be enabled;

(6) let $\Pr(M(\widehat{P}))$ denote an expression of predicate logic related to the marking of the set $\widehat{P}$; $\widehat{P}$ means a subset of P;

(7) $W : F \rightarrow \mathbb{N} \cup \{\varepsilon\} \cup \{H\} \cup \{\Pr(M(\widehat{P}) \rightarrow \mathbb{N})\}$ is a weighted function; $W(p, t)$ and $W(t, p)$ denote the weight of the arc(p, t) and (t, p), respectively. It may be a natural integer, or a function depending on the marking of

the set $\widehat{P}$; if $W(x, y) = \varepsilon$, it can be viewed as the weight of $(x, y) = 1$; assume P_1 is a subset of P, and N_1 is a positive integer; if $W(x, y) = \text{Pr}(M(P_1)) \rightarrow N_1$, it means when $\text{Pr}(M(P_1)) = $ true, the weight of (x, y) is N_1;

(8) $H : M(\widehat{P}) \rightarrow \mathbb{R}^+ \cup \{0\}$ is a function which indicates the mapping from the marking of $\widehat{P}$ to a positive integer; let $P_1 \subseteq P$ and $Z = \{M(p) \mid p \in P_1\}$; then $H(Z) \in \mathbb{N}$;

(9) $\lambda = \{\lambda_1, \lambda_2, \ldots, \lambda_l\} * (1 \vee H)$ is a finite set of average transition enabling rates, where $l = |T_T|$;

(10) $\text{TS} = \{\text{TS}_1, \text{TS}_2, \ldots, \text{TS}_{n1}\}$ is a finite set of types, where $n1 = |\text{TS}|$;

(11) $G : P \rightarrow \text{TS}$ is a function denoting the type assigned to place p;

(12) $E : P \rightarrow \{\text{Pr}(M(\widehat{P})) \rightarrow \mathbb{N}\} \cup \{H * \mathbb{N}\} \cup \mathbb{N}$ is a function indicating the values of types; if $G(p) = \text{TS}_i$, then $E(\text{TS}_i)$ stands for the value of tokens with type TS_i in place p; note that $E(\text{TS}_i)$ may be time-variant; it generally denotes the value of current period of time when a process is executed;

(13) $f : T \rightarrow \{\text{Pr}(M(\widehat{P}))\} \cup \{\varepsilon\}$ is a function of enabling predicate, where $f(t)$ represents the enabling predicate of transition t. When $f(t) = \varepsilon$, it means that the enabling condition of transition t is the same as in SPN;

(14) $g : (T \rightarrow \{\varepsilon \cup \mathbb{R}^+ \cup H\}) \cup (P \rightarrow \mathbb{N}^+)$ is a function of random switch, where $g(t)$ denotes the enabling priority of transition t, while $g(p)$ means the priority of place p; if there is a transition without a random switch, that is, $g(t) = \varepsilon$, it represents that its enabling priority is 1 and $g(p) = \varepsilon$ has the same meaning of place p;

(15) $M_0 : P \rightarrow \mathbb{N}$ is the initial marking which models the initial status of a system and satisfies: for all $p \in P$, $M_0(p) \leq K(p)$.

As described above, DSSPN is a novel extended form of SPN. The major differences lie in that the weight of an arc (or the transition enabling rate) not only is a constant but also is a function depending on the marking of a subset of P. The weights of arcs and the transition enabling rates can be defined by customers. In addition, these values may actually change during the whole process. These features will increase the dynamic flexibility of SPN and allow the modeling process to automatically adjust.

Definition 2. The transition firing rule of DSSPN is elaborated as follows.

(1) For all $t \in T$, if $\forall p \in P$,

$$M(p) \geq W(p, t), \quad \text{if } (p \in {}^\bullet t) \wedge \{\text{true}, \varepsilon\}$$

$$M(p) + W(t, p) \geq W(p, t),$$

$$\text{if } (p \in t^\bullet - {}^\bullet t) \wedge (f(t) \in \{\text{true}, \varepsilon\})$$

$$M(p) + W(t, p) - W(p, t) \leq K(p),$$

$$\text{if } (p \in t^\bullet \cap {}^\bullet t) \wedge (f(t) \in \{\text{true}, \varepsilon\})$$

$$M(p), \quad \text{otherwise.}$$

(1)

It is said that transition t with the marking M is enabled, which is denoted as $M[t\rangle$.

(2) If $M[t\rangle$ and $g(t) = \max\{g(s) \mid s$ belongs to P and satisfies (1)$\}$, then transition t can fire. After t fired, a new subsequent marking M' is generated from M, which is denoted as $M[t\rangle M'$ or $M \xrightarrow{t} M'$. For all $p \in P$,

$$M'(p)$$

$$= \begin{cases} M(p) - W(p, t), & \text{if } (p \in {}^\bullet t) \wedge \{\text{true}, \varepsilon\} \\ M(p) + W(t, p), & \text{if } (p \in t^\bullet - {}^\bullet t) \\ M(p) + W(t, p) - W(p, t), & \text{if } (p \in t^\bullet \cap {}^\bullet t) \\ M(p), & \text{otherwise.} \end{cases}$$

(2)

In the marking M, there may be multiple transitions being enabled simultaneously. In this case, a transition is randomly chosen out from the set T' to be fired, where $T' = \{s \mid g(s) = \max\{g(t), t \in T''\}\}$, and $T'' = \{t \mid M[t\rangle, t \in T\}$.

In order to formalize the dynamics of DSSPN, incidence matrix is introduced to depict its structure and behaviors.

Definition 3. The structure of a DSSPN can be expressed by using a matrix (called the incidence matrix of DSSPN) with n rows and m columns, where $n = |P|$ and $m = |T|$:

$$A = \left[a_{ij}^+ - a_{ij}^-\right]_{n \times m}.$$

(3)

For $1 \leq i \leq n, 1 \leq j \leq m$,

$$a_{ij}^+$$

$$= \begin{cases} W(t_j, p_i), & \text{if } ((t_j, p_i) \in F) \wedge (W(t_j, p_i) \neq \varepsilon) \\ 1, & \text{if } ((t_j, p_i) \in F) \wedge (W(t_j, p_i) = \varepsilon) \\ 0, & \text{otherwise} \end{cases}$$

(4)

$$a_{ij}^-$$

$$= \begin{cases} W(p_i, t_j), & \text{if } (p_i, (t_j)) \in F) \wedge (W(p_i, t_j) \neq \varepsilon) \\ 1, & \text{if } ((p_i, t_j) \in F) \wedge (p_i, W(t_j) = \varepsilon) \\ 0, & \text{otherwise.} \end{cases}$$

Because $W(t_j, p_i)$ or $W(p_i, t_j)$ can be a constant or a function depending on the marking of a subset of P, we firstly divide the set of transitions into two subsets: T_c and T_v. Consider

$$T_c = \{t \mid \forall p \in {}^\bullet t \cup t^\bullet, M(p) \text{ is related to } a_{ij}\}$$

$$T_v = T - T_c.$$

(5)

That is, if any transition in T_c fired, the incidence matrix will be unchanged in current marking. Otherwise, a new marking will be generated and the value(s) of some element(s) will change. Suppose σ is a firing sequence of transitions. σ is firstly divided into two subsequences according to (6), σ_c and σ_v, where σ_c (or σ_v) only includes transitions in T_c (or T_v), and the orders of these transitions in σ_c and σ_v are the same as that in σ. Suppose C (an m-dimensional column vector) only counts the firing number of the transitions included in σ_c, and $\sigma = t_1 t_2 \cdots t_k$. Consider $M \xrightarrow{\sigma_c} M_1 \xrightarrow{t_1} M_2 \cdots M_k \xrightarrow{t_k} M_{k+1}$; then a fundamental equation [30] is obtained. The markings in the sequence change as follows:

$$
\begin{aligned}
M_1 &= M + A \cdot C \\
M_{j+1} &= M_j + A_{*j},
\end{aligned}
\tag{6}
$$

where $1 \le j \le k$. A_{*j} denotes the jth column vector of A. Note that if $t \in T_v$, the values of these elements in incidence matrix A, which are related to $\{M(p) \mid p \in t^\bullet \cup {}^\bullet t\}$, should be updated after t fired.

3.2. Properties of DSSPN. The major motivation to model systems or processes by DSSPN is the simplicity and dynamic expressions in representing systems with multiple users and dynamic environments. In some situations, there may be redundant transitions in DSSPN models. In order to precisely and concisely describe systems, we offer the following theorems.

Theorem 4. *If there are some transitions with the same meaning in a DSSPN model, these transitions can be merged into one so that each transition is unique in a DSSPN model; that is, transition redundancy can be eliminated.*

Proof. Assume transitions t_2 and t_2' have the same meaning. The preset and postset of t_2 are ${}^\bullet t_2$ and $t_2^\bullet$, respectively. Meanwhile the preset and postset of t_2' are ${}^\bullet t_2'$ and $t_2'^\bullet$. Their enabling predicates and random switches are $f(t_2)$, $f(t_2')$, $g(t_2)$, and $g(t_2')$, respectively. Let us suppose t_1 is a forerunner transition of t_2 and t_1' is a forerunner transition of t_2'. The two transitions can be merged as follows:

(a) Transitions t_2 and t_2' are merged into one transition t.

(b) The preset of t is ${}^\bullet t = {}^\bullet t_2 \cup {}^\bullet t_2'$. For all p, $s \in {}^\bullet t \cup t^\bullet$, $p \ne s$; if their types and values are the same, that is, $G(p) = G(s)$ and $E(p) = E(s)$, then places p and s will be merged into one place, denoted by p'. Moreover, the type and the corresponding value remain the same.

(c) The enabling predicate is $f(t) = f(t_2) \vee f(t_2')$, and the random switch is $g(t) = g(t_2) \wedge g(t_2')$.

(d) Assume p and s will be merged; if $p \in {}^\bullet t_2$ and $s \in {}^\bullet t_2'$ or $p \in t_2^\bullet$ and $s \in t_2'^\bullet$, the weights of arcs relating to merged transition t and place p' are set as follows:

$$
W(p', t) = \begin{cases} f(t_2) \longrightarrow W(p, t_2) \\ f(t_2') \longrightarrow W(s, t_2') \end{cases}
$$

$$
\text{or } W(t, p') = \begin{cases} f(t_2) \longrightarrow W(t_2, p) \\ f(t_2') \longrightarrow W(t_2', s). \end{cases}
\tag{7}
$$

Figure 1 shows an example to merge transitions t_2 and t_3 with the same meaning. For places p_2, p_3, p_4, and p_5, assume $G(p_2) = G(p_3)$, $E(p_2) = E(p_3)$, $G(p_4) = G(p_5)$, and $E(p_4) = E(p_5)$. Note that the weights of some arcs relating to merged transitions and places will be changed, where

$$
w_1' = \begin{cases} f(t_2) \longrightarrow w_1 \\ f(t_3) \longrightarrow w_2 \end{cases}
$$

$$
w_2' = \begin{cases} f(t_2) \longrightarrow w_3 \\ f(t_3) \longrightarrow w_4 \end{cases}
\tag{8}
$$

$$
w_3' = \begin{cases} f(t_3) \longrightarrow w_5 \\ 0. \end{cases}
$$

As illustrated in Theorem 4, a DSSPN model can eliminate redundant transitions. In DSSPN, each service or activity only corresponds to one transition that models a dynamic process or a system including multiple customers on a more convenient way. □

Theorem 5. *A DSSPN can be transformed into a simple net [17], such that, for all $x, y \in P \cup T$, the preset of x is equal to that of y while the postset of x is equal to that of y only if x equals y; that is,*

$$
({}^\bullet x = {}^\bullet y) \wedge (x^\bullet = y^\bullet) \longrightarrow x = y, \quad \forall x, y \in P \cup T.
\tag{9}
$$

Proof. First, we consider the case of two places with the same preset and postset, as shown in Figure 2. If $G(p) = G(s)$ and $E(p) = E(s)$, we can easily transform it into a simple net just as illustrated in Theorem 4. Otherwise, we insert two new immediate transitions and two new places into the original model. Then the original net transforms into a simple one. Two things to note here are the settings of new arcs and places, that is, $W(p_1, d_1) = W(d_1, p_3) = W(p_3, t_2) = W(p_1, t_2)$ and $W(p_2, d_2) = W(d_2, p_4) = W(p_4, t_2) = W(p_1, t_2)$, while the settings of p_3 and p_4 are the same as those of p_1 and p_2. Similarly, the case of two transitions with the same preset and postset can be proven, just as shown in Figure 3. □

4. System Model Based on DSSPN

Nowadays, numerous cloud computing platforms are commercially available, such as Eucalyptus, Hadoop, and Amazon EC2 [31–33]. In this study, we take a typical cloud system by adopting fair scheduling algorithm as an example to construct a DSSPN model. Figure 4 illustrates the basic working process of tasks on a cloud platform in the light of the characteristics of a typical cloud system architecture. In the cloud system, jobs submitted by different customers may have different QoS requirements on computing time, memory

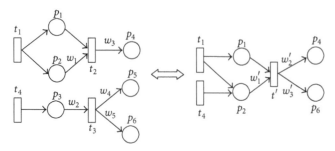

FIGURE 1: Equivalent transformation of merging two transitions with the same meaning.

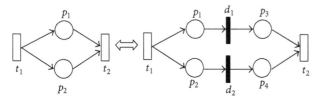

FIGURE 2: Equivalent transformation of two places with the same preset and postset.

space, data traffic, response time, and so forth. That is, a typical cloud platform can be viewed as a multiuser multitask system involving multiple data sets with different types of processing jobs at the same time [32]. In a cloud platform, tasks are the basic processing units in the executive process. Dispatchers firstly select tasks according to a certain rule from the waiting queues and then assign them to appropriate resources adopting some scheduling policies. However, the properties of cloud computing, such as large scale, dynamics, heterogeneity, and diversity, present a range of challenges for performance evaluation of cloud systems and cloud optimization problem [34]. In order to verify the applicability and feasibility of DSSPN, we will model and analyze the performance of a typical cloud system based on DSSPN in this section.

4.1. Modeling Abstract.
Without loss of generality, let us make the following assumptions for a typical cloud system:

(1) There are n clients, denoted by c_i. Client i submits jobs into a waiting queue (i.e., pool i) with a capacity of b_i.

(2) The minimum share of pool i is denoted by ms_i.

(3) In fair scheduling, the set of priorities of each pool is {VERY_HIGH, HIGH, NORMAL, LOW, VERY_LOW}. In order to facilitate the analysis, the set of priorities are set to $\{5, 4, 3, 2, 1\}$.

(4) The arrival process of tasks, submitted by client i, obeys the Poisson distribution with rate of λ_i. When the number of tasks submitted by client i exceeds b_i, the job submission is rejected.

(5) In each waiting queue, the scheduling discipline is First Come First Served (FCFS).

(6) There are m servers (denoted by s_i), each of which has r_i virtual machines (VMs) shared by n clients.

(7) The service rate of each VM on s_j is μ_j with exponent distribution. In addition, the service rates are generally independent of each other. Note that the sum of ms_i is equal to or smaller than the total number of resources; that is, $\sum_{i=1}^{n} \leq \sum_{j=1}^{m} r_j$.

4.2. DSSPN Model of Fair Scheduling.
Based on DSSPN, we model a typical cloud system adopting fair scheduling as a multiserver multiqueue system with n clients and m servers. The DSSPN model and involved notations are shown in Figure 5 and Notations. In order to simplify the description of the DSSPN model, we would not show the shared structures of servers.

All the places and transitions included in Figure 5 are described as follows ($1 \leq i \leq n, 1 \leq j \leq m$):

(1) c_i: a timed transition denotes client i submitting tasks with the firing rate of λ_i. The enabling predicate f_i of c_i is

$$f_i(M) : M(p_i) \leq b_i, \quad 1 \leq i \leq n. \tag{10}$$

That is, client i can submit tasks when the number of tasks is smaller than its capacity.

(2) p_i: a place indicates the pool storing these tasks submitted by client i, and $K(p_i) = b_i$. In addition, $G(p_i) = \text{MS}$, $E(p_i) = \text{ms}_i$, and $g(p_i) = \text{pl}_i$, where ms_i means the guaranteed minimum share of pool i, pl_i represents the priority of pool i, and $\text{pl}_i \in \{5, 4, 3, 2, 1\}$ (just as elaborated in previous section).

(3) R_j: a place stands for the status of server j; for simplicity, it is not shown in Figure 5. $M(R_j)$ is the number of idle VMs of server j. $K(R_j) = r_j$, which means the total number of VMs on server j.

(4) d_{ij}: an immediate transition indicates the execution of some scheduling or decision. The scheduling or decision is expressed by the enabling predicate f_{ij} and random switch g_{ij} associated with d_{ij}:

$$f_{ij} = \Bigg(\big((\text{AR}_i < E(p_i)) \vee (\text{dem}_i \geq E(p_i)) \big)$$
$$\wedge \left(\sum_{j=1}^{m} M(q_{ij}) = 0 \right) \wedge (|\text{SIDS}(M)| > 0) \Bigg)$$
$$\vee \big((\text{dem}_i \geq E(p_i))$$
$$\wedge (\text{for } \forall h \neq i, \ E(p_h) \leq E(p_i))$$
$$\wedge (|\text{SIDS}(M)| > 0) \big) \tag{11}$$

$$g_{ij} = \begin{cases} 5 \times \dfrac{1}{|\text{UDLMS}(M)|}, & \text{if } i \in \text{UDLMS}(M) \\[2mm] 4 \times \dfrac{1}{|\text{UDGMS}(M)|}, & \text{if } i \in \text{UDGMS}(M) \\[2mm] 3 \times \dfrac{1}{|\text{ULMS}(M)|}, & \text{if } i \in \text{DLMS}(M) \\[2mm] 2 \times \dfrac{1}{|\text{MMS}(M)|}, & \text{if } i \in \text{MMS}(M) \\[2mm] 0, & \text{otherwise.} \end{cases}$$

In this scheme, the highest priority is firstly given to the unallocated pools whose demand is smaller than its

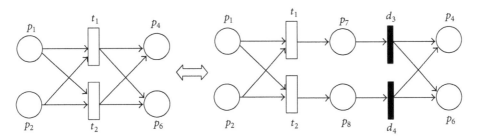

FIGURE 3: Equivalent transformation of two transitions with the same preset and postset.

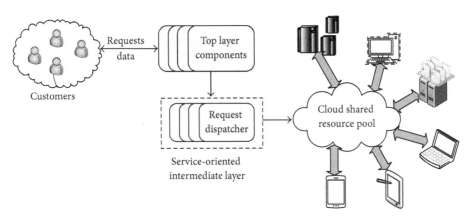

FIGURE 4: Basic working process of tasks on a cloud platform.

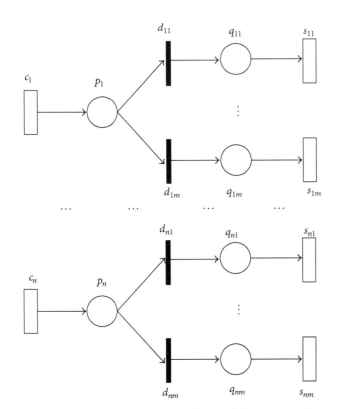

FIGURE 5: The refined DSSPN model of a typical cloud system adopting fair scheduling.

minimum share. Secondly, a higher priority is assigned to the unallocated pools whose demands are equal to or greater than its minimum share. Then, a normal priority is given to allocated pools included in DLMS(M). Finally, if there are any unallocated VMs, these idle resources will be assigned to the pools included in MMS(M).

(5) q_{ij}: a place indicates the queue receiving tasks with the capacity of r_{ij}; that is, $K(q_{ij}) = r_{ij}$.

(6) s_{ij}: a timed transition stands for a VM on server j with the firing rate of μ_{ij}. The server j is shared by VM s_{ij}, where $1 \le i \le n$ and $1 \le j \le m$.

4.3. DSSPN Model of Classified Fair Scheduling. Although fair scheduling can share a cluster among different users as fair as possible, it does not make good use of resources without considering various workload types or resource diversity. Various types of workload with different requirements of resources consequently launch different kinds of tasks, usually including CPU intensive tasks and I/O intensive tasks. Hence, it is beneficial for improving hardware utilization to distinguish types of tasks and resources. For example, the processing time of a CPU intensive task in resources with stronger computing power would be shorter than that in other resources. Let d_{ik} denote the demand with type of k, and R_k represent the total number of VMs with type of k. Because of limited space, we only illustrate the improved part in classified fair scheduling (CFS) algorithm, shown in Algorithm 1. The remaining part

(1) Initialize the classification of all available resources;
(2) Initialize the classification of tasks when they are submitted to pools;
(3) **for** each pool i whose demand $\leq$ its minimum share **do**
(3)   **for** each type k **do**
(4)   **if** $d_{ik} \leq R_k$ **then**
(5)   allocate the d_{ik} resources with type of k;
(6) $R_k - = d_{ik}$;
(6)   **else**
(7)   allocate the R_k resources with the type of k;
(8) $d_{ik} - = R_k$;
(9)   allocate d_{ik} resources with other types, while satisfying $R_j \geq d_{ik}, j \in \{1, 2, \ldots, l\}$;
(10)   **end if**
(11)   **end for**
(12) **end for**
(13) **for** (each pool i whose demand $>$ its minimum share) $\wedge$ (remaining idle unallocated VMs) **do**
(14)   add the similar process as described above in light of the assigning decision of each pool;
(15) **end for**

ALGORITHM 1: The improved part of fair scheduling in CFS.

of CFS is similar to that of fair scheduling presented by Zaharia et al. [35].

The descriptions of places and transitions in Figure 6 are similar to that in Figure 5. We will not reiterate them here. In order to facilitate understanding, we only emphasize the meaning of the subscripts for places and transitions. The subscript i denotes client i, the subscript k represents tasks with type k, and the subscript j describes server j. There are some differences on the values of some notations between Figures 5 and 6. The enabling rate of c_{ik} is λ_{ik}, and $K(q_{ikj}) = b_{ikj}$, where $\sum_{i=1}^{n} \sum_{k=1}^{l} b_{ikj} = b_j$. The enabling rate of s_{ikj} is μ_{ikj}, where $\sum_{i=1}^{n} \sum_{k=1}^{l} \mu_{ikj} = \mu_j$. In addition, the servers are classified; that is, $g(p_{ikj}) \in \{1, 2, \ldots, l\}$. The differences on the values between Figures 5 and 6 are described as follows:

$$AR_i = \sum_{k=1}^{l} \sum_{j=1}^{m} M\left(q_{ikj}\right) \times \mathbb{Z}$$

$$\text{dem}_i = \sum_{k=1}^{l} M\left(p_{ik}\right) + AR_i \qquad (12)$$

$$SIDS\left(M\right) = \left\{ h \mid \sum_{i=1}^{n} \sum_{k=1}^{l} M\left(q_{ikh}\right) \leq b_h \right\}.$$

Let y_{ikj} denote the service rate of s_{ikj} provided for the tasks in queue q_{ikj}:

$$y_{ikj} = \begin{cases} pl \times \mu_{ikj}, & \text{if } g\left(p_{ikj}\right) = k \\ pl' \times \mu_{ikj}, & \text{otherwise.} \end{cases} \qquad (13)$$

Note that $pl > pl'$. The scheme would ensure tasks whose types are the same as that of servers served at a higher priority.

The major difference between fair scheduling (FS) and CFS is that tasks and resources diversity are taken into

account. Without loss of generality, assume tasks and resources can be divided into l categories. The refined DSSPN model of CFS is shown in Figure 6. Note that Algorithm 1 only describes the improved part of FS [35], that is, the decision procedure to allocate resources with various types to different kinds of tasks.

4.4. Analysis and Solution of DSSPN Models.

Although the problem of state explosion is improved to some extent in DSSPN compared to other forms of Petri Nets, it is still difficult to analyze the performance of large-scale cloud systems. Model refinement techniques elaborated by Lin [17] can develop compact models and expose the independence as well as the interdependent relations between submodels of an original model. Model refinement can lay a foundation for the decomposition and analysis of models. Consequently, the refinement of models has become a necessary step of the model design. The refinement methods have been applied to the performance evaluation of high speed network and shared resources systems [17, 36].

4.4.1. Equivalent Refinement Model and Markov Model.

In this section, we will make further use of enabling predicates and random switches of transitions to refine the model proposed above. Figure 7 shows the equivalent model for models in Figures 5 and 6, while Figure 8 describes the equivalent Markov model of Figure 7.

Comparing Figure 7 with Figures 5 and 6, it can be found that the refined model is easier to understand and significantly reduces the state space by deleting any unnecessary vanishing states. In addition, refined model greatly decreases the complexity in performance evaluation because of structural similarities of submodels.

In Figure 7, immediate transitions and place p_i (or p_{ik}) and related arcs are removed from Figure 5 (or Figure 6), where $1 \leq i \leq n$ and $1 \leq k \leq l$. The enabling predicates

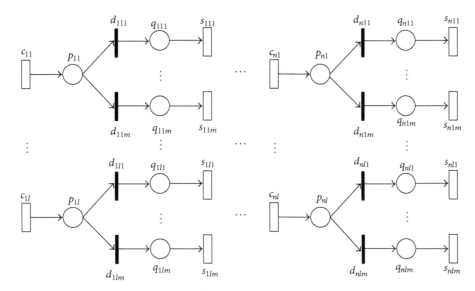

FIGURE 6: The refined DSSPN model of a typical cloud system adopting CFS algorithm.

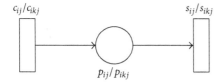

FIGURE 7: The refined DSSPN model of Figures 5 and 6.

and random switches associated with d_{ij} and c_{ij} (or d_{ikj} and c_{ikj}) have changed, while others are remaining the same. The random switch of transition c_{ij} is defined as follows:

$$g_{ij}(M) : \lambda_i \times g_{ij}(M). \tag{14}$$

The enabling switch of transition c_{ikj} is

$$g_{ikj}(M) : \lambda_{ik} \times g_{ikj}(M). \tag{15}$$

4.4.2. Parameters Analysis. In order to obtain the steady-state probabilities of all states, a state transition matrix can be constructed based on the state transition rate and Markov chain illustrated in Figure 8. Then, the performance parameters of the modeled cloud system can be discussed. Let $P[M]$ denote the steady-state probability of M.

The throughput of transition t is denoted as T_t:

$$T_t = \sum_{M \in H} P(M) \times \lambda_t, \tag{16}$$

where H is a set of all markings under which transition t is enabled with the enabling rate of λ_t in marking M.

The average number of tokens in place p is denoted as N_p:

$$N_p = \sum j \times P[M(p) = j]. \tag{17}$$

The throughput is a crucial indicator of the system performance. Let T_{ij} (or T_{ikj}) indicate the throughput of

subsystem A_{ij} (or A_{ikj}). According to the illustration in [16], the throughput of the model can be calculated as follows:

$$T = \sum_{i=1}^{n} \sum_{j=1}^{m} T_{sij} \tag{18}$$

$$\text{or } T = \sum_{i=1}^{n} \sum_{k=1}^{l} \sum_{j=1}^{m} T_{sikj}.$$

Another important indicator is response time. R_{ij} (or R_{ikj}), R_i, and R denote the response time of subsystem A_{ij} (or A_{ikj}), client i, and the system, respectively:

$$R_{ij} = \frac{D_{qij}}{T_{sij}}$$

$$R_i = \sum_{j=1}^{m} \left(T_{sij} \times R_{ij} \setminus \sum_{h=1}^{m} T_{sih} \right)$$

$$R = \sum_{i=1}^{n} \left(R_i \times \sum_{h=1}^{m} \frac{T_{sih}}{T} \right)$$

$$R_{ikj} = \frac{D_{qikj}}{T_{sikj}} \tag{19}$$

$$R_{ik} = \sum_{j=1}^{m} \left(T_{sikj} \times R_{ikj} \setminus \sum_{h=1}^{m} T_{sikh} \right)$$

$$R_i = \sum_{k=1}^{l} \left(T_{sik} \times R_{ik} \setminus \sum_{h=1}^{l} T_{sih} \right)$$

$$R = \sum_{i=1}^{n} \left(R_i \times \sum_{h=1}^{l} \frac{T_{sih}}{T} \right).$$

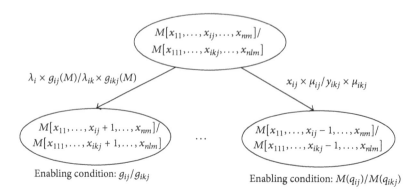

FIGURE 8: The equivalent Markov model of Figure 7.

The average rejection rate of tasks in the cloud system with FS at time t is expressed by AER(t):

$$\text{AER}(t) = \frac{\sum_{i=1}^{n} \left(\sum_{j=1}^{m} P\left(M\left(p_{ij} \right) \right) > b_i \right)}{n \times t}. \tag{20}$$

The average rejection rate of tasks in the cloud system with CFS at time t is expressed by $\text{AER}'(t)$:

$$\text{AER}'(t) = \frac{\sum_{i=1}^{n} \left(\sum_{k=1}^{l} \sum_{j=1}^{m} P\left(M\left(p_{ikj} \right) \right) > b_i \right)}{n \times t}. \tag{21}$$

The average idle rate of servers in the cloud system with FS at time t is expressed by AUR(t):

$$\text{AUR}(t)$$
$$= \frac{\sum_{j=1}^{m} \left(\sum_{i=1}^{n} \sum_{y=0}^{t} \left(1 - P\left(\text{enabled}\left(s_{ij}(y) \right) \right) \right) \right)}{m \times t}, \tag{22}$$

where $P(\text{enabled}(s_{ij}(y)))$ means the probability that transition $s_{ij}(y)$ can fire at time y.

The average idle rate of servers in the cloud system with CFS at time t is expressed by $\text{AUR}'(t)$:

$$\text{AUR}'(t)$$
$$= \frac{\sum_{j=1}^{m} \left(\sum_{i=1}^{n} \sum_{k=1}^{l} \sum_{y=0}^{t} \left(1 - P\left(\text{enabled}\left(s_{ikj}(y) \right) \right) \right) \right)}{m \times t}, \tag{23}$$

where $P(\text{enabled}(s_{ikj}(y)))$ means the probability that transition $s_{ikj}(y)$ can fire at time y.

In a multiuser multiserver cloud system, the performance parameters include the state changes of waiting queues and the service rates of shared servers. The improvement of throughput and the decrease of response time can be realized by furthest parallelizing the operations of n servers. In other words, load balance should be maintained.

5. Case Study and Evaluation

In this section, we provide a case to study the performance of the DSSPN model based on steady-state probabilities. To verify the applicability and feasibility of DSSPN, we

TABLE 1: Number of states and fired transitions.

	1 machine	2 machines	3 machines	4 machines
Reachable states	283	569	1088	1594
Fired transitions	923	1977	3928	5842

only study some performance indicators of FS and CFS by means of the above method. In addition, Stochastic Petri Net Package (SPNP) is applied to automatically derive the analytic solution of performance for the DSSPN model. This is beneficial in modeling and evaluating the performance of cloud systems, because the number of states might reach thousands even only including few machines, shown in Table 1.Table 2 describes the parameter settings in the simulation.

The simulation was conducted to the cloud system consisting of 3 servers, 2 customers, and 2 categories. That is, there are 4 waiting queues in FS, while 8 waiting queues are existing in CFS. Assume $g(s1) = 1$ and $g(s2) = 2$. The task submitted by each client can be classified into 2 groups. In the simulation scenario, there are 4 VMs that can be running on server 1 simultaneously, while 5 VMs are running on server 2.

As shown in Figure 9, when the configuration parameters are identical, the values of system average throughput in steady state of CFS are significantly greater than that of fair scheduling. Figure 10 describes the average delay, which is depicted by average response time in DSSPN models, in steady state of CFS and FS. Apparently, the average delay of CFS is prominently smaller than that of fair scheduling. That is, CFS is a powerful way to decrease waiting time for users. As can be seen from Figure 9, the difference of average throughput between CFS and FS can reach 14.8 when $\lambda_1 = 6/\text{sec}$, while the maximal difference of average delay between CFS and FS is 5.75 sec when $\lambda_1 = 6/\text{sec}$.

Figure 11 illustrates that average completion time of CFS is significantly better than that of FS. The simulation results present that the novel scheme (CFS) can efficiently increase the average system throughput and thus can improve utilization of resources. This means that it can realize economic benefits in the commercial cloud services.

Moreover, Figures 9, 10, and 11 also show that the performance of CFS is generally better than that of fair scheduling

TABLE 2: Parameter settings in simulation.

Algorithm	λ_2/λ_1	ms_1	ms_2	b_{1j}	b_{2j}	b_{1kj}	b_{2kj}	μ_{1j}	μ_{2j}	μ_{1kj}	μ_{2kj}	pl	pl$'$	b
FS	2/3	3	4	10	8			3	2					30
CFS	2/3	3	4			10	8			3	2	2	1	30

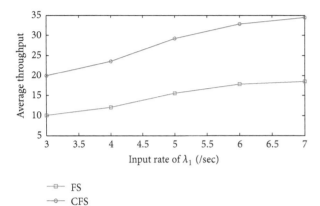

FIGURE 9: Average throughput when $\lambda_1 = \{3, 4, 5, 6, 7\}$.

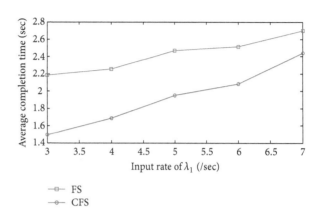

FIGURE 11: Average completion time when $\lambda_1 = \{3, 4, 5, 6, 7\}$.

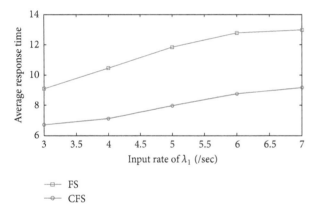

FIGURE 10: Average response time when $\lambda_1 = \{3, 4, 5, 6, 7\}$.

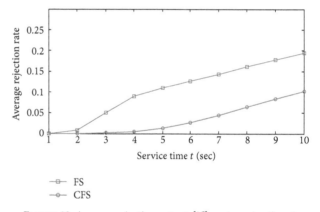

FIGURE 12: Average rejection rate at different service time t.

across all circumstances, especially at heavy load. However, queues cannot be simulated efficiently, because these schemes are only based on the current state of queues but ignore the dynamics of task in the queues. The simulation results are different by setting different input rates due to incapability of predicting the future state of the waiting queues.

Figure 12 shows how the average rejection rate of the cloud system changes as service time goes on. When the task request in one waiting pool is up to 30, the system will reject new requests submitted by the corresponding user. When $1 \leq t \leq 10$, the average rejection rate of FS is higher than that of CFS. The differences between FS and CFS in the average rejection rate are up to 40.08% at service time of 5 seconds. In addition, Figure 12 also illustrates that, along with the operation of the cloud system, the average reject rate increases with the accumulation of backlogs in waiting queues.

Figure 13 illustrates how the scheduling strategies affect the average resource utilization of the system. When $0 \leq t \leq 10$, the average idle rate of servers in FS is lower than that

in CFS. The maximal differences between FS and CFS in the average idle rate of servers at different service times are 4%. It means that there is potential to achieve higher utilization rate with CFS algorithm by increasing the system throughput.

6. Conclusion

In this paper, we propose the definition of DSSPN that can easily describe the multiple clients systems based on cloud services, such as a typical cloud platform. The major motivation to model systems or processes by DSSPN is its simplicity and dynamic expressions to represent systems with multiple users and dynamic environments. Moreover, we further elaborate dynamic property of DSSPN and analyze some properties of DSSPN. In the following section, for some shortcomings of fair scheduling, the classified fair scheduling (CFS) algorithm is proposed taking into consideration jobs and resources diversity.

In the real world, a typical cloud system is shared by multiple applications including production applications, batch

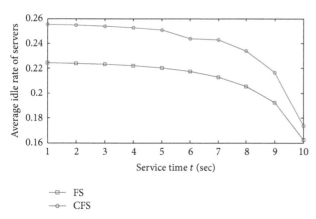

FIGURE 13: Average idle rate of servers at different service time t.

jobs, and interactive jobs. Meanwhile, different applications have different requirements on hardware resources and QoS parameters. Therefore, we adopt the multiuser multiserver model to analyze the performance analysis and design DSSPN models for FS and CFS. In order to avoid the state space explosion, the analysis techniques and model refinement techniques are applied to performance evaluation of their DSSPN models. Finally, SPNP is used to obtain some key indicators of QoS; that is, system average throughput, response time, and average completion time are compared between the two schemes. Just as shown from Figures 9–11, the performance of CFS is generally better than that of fair scheduling across all circumstances, especially at heavy load.

The following topics are of high interest for future work:

(1) Other quality metrics, such as energy consumption and cost, should be analyzed.

(2) The proposed model is without considering local task migrations among servers in the same data center.

(3) The theoretical derivations between simulation results and actual cloud systems will be studied.

Notations

Involved Notations and Equations in Figure 5

AR_i: The VMs allocated to pool i; $AR_i = \sum_{j=1}^{m} M(q_{ij})$

sms: The smallest minimum share among some pools; $sms = \min\{E(p_h), h \in DGMS(M)\}$

dem_i: The demand of pool i; $dem_i = M(p_i) + AR_i$

sdem: The smallest demand among some pools; $sdem = \min\{dem_h, \ h \in DGMS(M)\}$

def_i: The deficit between dem_i and ms_i; $def_i = E(p_i) - AR_i$

SIDS: The set of all servers that has idle slot waiting to be assigned; $SIDS(M) = \{h \mid \sum_{i=1}^{n} M(q_{ih}) \leq b_h\}$

DLMS: The set of all pools whose demand is less than its minimum share; $DLMS(M) = \{h \mid dem_h < E(p_i), \ 1 \leq h \leq n\}$

UDLMS: The set of all unallocated pools whose demand is less than its minimum share; $UDLMS(M) = \{i \mid \sum_{i=1}^{m} M(p_{ij}), \ i \in DLMS(M)\}$

DGMS: The set of all pools whose demand is equal to or larger than its minimum share; $DGMS(M) = \{h \mid dem_h \geq E(p_i), \ 1 \leq h \leq n\}$

UDGMS: The set of all pools in DGMS without any allocated resources at the current status; $UDGMS(M) = \{i \mid \sum_{j=1}^{m} M(q_{ij}) = 0, \ i \in DGMS(M)\}$

MMS: The set of pools with the smallest minimum share in DGMS; $MMS(M) = \{h \mid E(p_i) = sms, h \in DGMS\}$.

Competing Interests

The authors declare that they have no competing interests.

Acknowledgments

This work was partially supported by the National Natural Science Foundation of China (nos. 61172063, 61272093, and 61572523) and special fund project for work method innovation of Ministry of Science and Technology of China (no. 2015IM010300).

References

[1] P. Mell and T. Grance, *The NIST Definition of Cloud Computing*, Recommendations of the National Institute Standards and Technology-Special Publication 800-145, NIST, Washington, DC, USA, http://nvlpubs.nist.gov/nistpubs/Legacy/SP/nistspecialpublication800.

[2] S. Singh and I. Chana, "QRSF: QoS-aware resource scheduling framework in cloud computing," *Journal of Supercomputing*, vol. 71, no. 1, pp. 241–292, 2014.

[3] J. Baliga, R. W. A. Ayre, K. Hinton, and R. S. Tucker, "Green cloud computing: balancing energy in processing, storage and transport," *Proceedings of the IEEE*, vol. 99, no. 1, pp. 149–167, 2011.

[4] B. P. Rimal, A. Jukan, D. Katsaros, and Y. Goeleven, "Architectural requirements for cloud computing systems: an enterprise cloud approach," *Journal of Grid Computing*, vol. 9, no. 1, pp. 3–26, 2011.

[5] A. L. Bardsiri and S. M. Hashemi, "A review of workflow scheduling in cloud computing environment," *International Journal of Computer Science and Management Research*, vol. 1, no. 3, pp. 348–351, 2012.

[6] Y. Chawla and M. Bhonsle, "A study on scheduling methods in cloud computing," *International Journal of Emerging Trends and Technology in Computer Science*, vol. 1, no. 3, pp. 12–17, 2012.

[7] L. Chuang, *Stochastic Petri Net and System Performance Evaluation*, Tsinghua University Press, Beijing, China, 2005.

[8] M. K. Molloy, "Discrete time stochastic Petri nets," *IEEE Transactions on Software Engineering*, vol. 11, no. 4, pp. 417–423, 1985.

[9] M. A. Marsan, G. Balbo, G. Conte, S. Donatelli, and G. Franceschinis, "Modelling with generalized stochastic petri nets," *ACM SIGMETRICS Performance Evaluation Review*, vol. 26, no. 2, p. 2, 1998.

[10] W. M. P. van der Aalst, "The application of Petri nets to workflow management," *Journal of Circuits, Systems and Computers*, vol. 8, no. 1, pp. 21–66, 1998.

[11] K. Jensen, *Coloured Petri Nets: Basic Concepts, Analysis Methods and Practical Use*, Springer, New York, NY, USA, 2013.

[12] K. Jensen and G. Rozenberg, *High-Level Petri Nets: Theory and Application*, Springer Science and Business Media, Berlin, Germany, 2012.

[13] N. Ferry, A. Rossini, F. Chauvel, B. Morin, and A. Solberg, "Towards model-driven provisioning, deployment, monitoring, and adaptation of multi-cloud systems," in *Proceedings of the IEEE 6th International Conference on Cloud Computing (CLOUD '13)*, pp. 887–894, IEEE, Santa Clara, Calif, USA, June 2013.

[14] B. P. Rimal, E. Choi, and I. Lumb, "A taxonomy and survey of cloud computing systems," in *Proceedings of the 5th International Joint Conference on INC, IMS and IDC*, pp. 44–51, Seoul, Republic of Korea, August 2009.

[15] M. Llorens and J. Oliver, "Marked-controlled reconfigurable workflow nets," in *Proceedings of the 8th International Symposium on Symbolic and Numeric Algorithms for Scientific Computing (SYNASC '06)*, pp. 407–413, Timisoara, Romania, September 2006.

[16] L. Lei, C. Lin, J. Cai, and X. Shen, "Performance analysis of wireless opportunistic schedulers using stochastic Petri nets," *IEEE Transactions on Wireless Communications*, vol. 8, no. 4, pp. 2076–2087, 2009.

[17] C. Lin, "On refinement of model structure for stochastic Petri Nets," *Journal of Software*, vol. 1, p. 017, 2000.

[18] Y. Xia, M. Zhou, X. Luo, S. Pang, and Q. Zhu, "Stochastic modeling and performance analysis of migration-enabled and error-prone clouds," *IEEE Transactions on Industrial Informatics*, vol. 11, no. 2, pp. 495–504, 2015.

[19] S. Ostermann, A. Iosup, N. Yigitbasi, R. Prodan, T. Fahringer, and D. Epema, "A performance analysis of EC2 cloud computing services for scientific computing," in *Cloud Computing*, D. R. Avresky, M. Diaz, A. Bode, B. Ciciani, and E. Dekel, Eds., vol. 34 of *Lecture Notes of the Institute for Computer Sciences, Social-Informatics and Telecommunications Engineering*, pp. 115–131, Springer, Berlin, Germany, 2010.

[20] R. N. Calheiros, R. Ranjan, A. Beloglazov, C. A. F. De Rose, and R. Buyya, "CloudSim: a toolkit for modeling and simulation of cloud computing environments and evaluation of resource provisioning algorithms," *Software: Practice and Experience*, vol. 41, no. 1, pp. 23–50, 2011.

[21] L. Bautista, A. Abran, and A. April, "Design of a performance measurement framework for cloud computing," *Journal of Software Engineering and Applications*, vol. 5, no. 2, pp. 69–75, 2012.

[22] Y. Mei, L. Liu, X. Pu, and S. Sivathanu, "Performance measurements and analysis of network I/O applications in virtualized cloud," in *Proceedings of the IEEE 3rd International Conference on Cloud Computing*, pp. 59–66, Miami, Fla, USA, July 2010.

[23] Y. Cao, H. Lu, X. Shi, and P. Duan, "Evaluation model of the cloud systems based on Queuing Petri net," in *Algorithms and Architectures for Parallel Processing*, pp. 413–423, Springer International, Cham, Switzerland, 2015.

[24] S. Kounev and C. Dutz, "QPME: a performance modeling tool based on queueing Petri Nets," *ACM SIGMETRICS Performance Evaluation Review*, vol. 36, no. 4, pp. 46–51, 2009.

[25] G. Fan, H. Yu, and L. Chen, "A formal aspect-oriented method for modeling and analyzing adaptive resource scheduling in cloud computing," *IEEE Transactions on Network and Service Management*, vol. 13, no. 2, pp. 281–294, 2016.

[26] M. Reynolds, "An axiomatization of full computation tree logic," *The Journal of Symbolic Logic*, vol. 66, no. 3, pp. 1011–1057, 2001.

[27] K. Jensen and L. M. Kristensen, *Colored Petri Nets: Modelling and Validation of Concurrent Systems*, Springer, 2009.

[28] M. C. Ruiz, J. Calleja, and D. Cazorla, "Petri nets formalization of map/reduce paradigm to optimise the performance-cost tradeo," in *Proceedings of the IEEE Trustcom/BigDataSE/ISPA*, vol. 3, pp. 92–99, 2015.

[29] A. V. Ratzer, L. Wells, H. M. Lassen et al., "CPN tools for editing, simulating, and analysing coloured Petri nets," in *Applications and Theory of Petri Nets 2003*, pp. 450–462, Springer, 2003.

[30] C. Lin and D. C. Marinescu, "Stochastic high-level Petri nets and applications," in *High-Level Petri Nets*, pp. 459–469, Springer, Berlin, Germany, 1991.

[31] D. Nurmi, R. Wolski, C. Grzegorczyk et al., "The eucalyptus open-source cloud-computing system," in *Proceedings of the 9th IEEE/ACM International Symposium on Cluster Computing and the Grid (CCGRID '09)*, pp. 124–131, Shanghai, China, May 2009.

[32] T. White, *Hadoop: The Definitive Guide*, O'Reilly Media, 2012.

[33] J. Peng, X. Zhang, Z. Lei, B. Zhang, W. Zhang, and Q. Li, "Comparison of several cloud computing platforms," in *Proceedings of the 2nd International Symposium on Information Science and Engineering*, pp. 23–27, IEEE, Shanghai, China, December 2009.

[34] J. Xu, J. Tang, K. Kwiat, W. Zhang, and G. Xue, "Enhancing survivability in virtualized data centers: a service-aware approach," *IEEE Journal on Selected Areas in Communications*, vol. 31, no. 12, pp. 2610–2619, 2013.

[35] M. Zaharia, D. Borthakur, J. S. Sarma et al., "Job scheduling for multiuser mapreduce clusters," Tech. Rep. UCB/EECS-2009-55, EECS Department, University of California, Berkeley, Calif, USA, 2009.

[36] C. Lin, "A model of systems with shared resources and analysis of approximate performance," *Chinese Journal of Computers*, vol. 20, pp. 865–871, 1997.

Permissions

List of Contributors

Maciej Malawski and Kamil Figiela
Department of Computer Science, AGH University of Science and Technology, Aleja Mickiewicza 30, 30-059 Kraków, Poland

Marian Bubak
Department of Computer Science, AGH University of Science and Technology, Aleja Mickiewicza 30, 30-059 Krak´ow, Poland
ACC CYFRONET AGH, Ulica Nawojki 11, 30-950 Krak´ow, Poland

Ewa Deelman
USC Information Sciences Institute, 4676 AdmiraltyWay, Marina del Rey, CA 90292, USA

Jarek Nabrzyski
Center for Research Computing, University of Notre Dame, Notre Dame, IN 46556, USA

Yao Lu
School of Computer Science and Telecommunication Engineering Jiangsu University, Jiangsu, China

Lu Liu
School of Computer Science and Telecommunication Engineering Jiangsu University, Jiangsu, China
Department of Computing and Mathematics, University of Derby, Derby, UK

Yan Wu
School of Computer Science and Telecommunication Engineering Jiangsu University, Jiangsu, China
Department of Computer Science, Boise State University, Boise, USA

John Panneerselvam
Department of Computing and Mathematics, University of Derby, Derby, UK

Amany AlShawi
King Abdulaziz City for Science and Technology, Riyadh 11442, Saudi Arabia

Wei Huang
School of Computer Engineering, Nanjing Institute of Technology, Nanjing 211167, China

Zhen Wang and Zhuzhong Qian
State Key Lab. for Novel Software Technology, Nanjing University, Nanjing 210023, China

Mianxiong Dong
Department of Information and Electronic Engineering, Muroran Institute of Technology, Muroran 050-8585, Japan

Shi-wei He and Wei-chuan Yin
School of Traffic and Transportation, Beijing Jiaotong University, Beijing 100044, China

Jia-bin Li
School of Traffic and Transportation, Beijing Jiaotong University, Beijing 100044, China
School of Business Administration, Henan University of Engineering, Zhengzhou 451191, China

Xiuguo Wu
School of Management Science and Engineering, Shandong University of Finance and Economics, Jinan 250014, China

HeeSeok Choi and Heonchang Yu
Department of Computer Science and Engineering, Korea University, Seoul, Republic of Korea

JongBeom Lim
IT Convergence Education Center, Dongguk University, Seoul, Republic of Korea

EunYoung Lee
Department of Computer Science, DongdukWomen's University, Seoul, Republic of Korea

Cheol-Ho Hong, Kyungwoon Lee, Hyunchan Park, and Chuck Yoo
Korea University, 145 Anam-ro, Seongbuk-gu, Seoul 02841, Republic of Korea

Bunjamin Memishi and María S. Pérez
OEG, ETS de Ingenieros Inform´aticos, Universidad Polit´ecnica de Madrid, Campus de Montegancedo, s/n Boadilla del Monte, 28660 Madrid, Spain

Gabriel Antoniu
Inria Rennes-Bretagne Atlantique Research Centre, Campus Universitaire de Beaulieu, Rennes, 35042 Brittany, France

Jaechun No
College of Electronics and Information Engineering, Sejong University, 98 Gunja-dong, Gwangjin-gu, Seoul 143-747, Republic of Korea

Sung-soon Park
Department of Computer Engineering, Anyang University and Gluesys Co. LTD, Anyang 5-dong, Manan-gu 430-714, Republic of Korea

Ivan Kholod Ilya Petukhov and Andrey Shorov
Faculty of Computer Science and Technology, Saint Petersburg Electrotechnical University (LETI), Professora Popova Street 5, Saint Petersburg 197376, Russia

Wei Ai, Kenli Li, Shenglin Lan and Jing Mei
College of Information Science and Engineering, Hunan University, Changsha, Hunan 410082, China

Keqin Li
College of Information Science and Engineering, Hunan University, Changsha, Hunan 410082, China
Department of Computer Science, State University of New York, New Paltz, NY 12561, USA

Fan Zhang
IBM Massachusetts Lab, 550 King Street, Littleton, MA 01460, USA

Rajkumar Buyya
Department of Computing and Information Systems, University of Melbourne, Melbourne, VIC 3010, Australia

Lianyong Qi and Jiguo Yu
School of Information Science and Engineering, Qufu Normal University, Rizhao 276826, China

Zhili Zhou
School of Computer and Software, Nanjing University of Information Science and Technology, Nanjing 210044, China

Wang Yan and Wang Jinkuan
College of Information Science and Engineering, Northeastern University, Shenyang, Liaoning 110819, China

Sun Jinghao
College of Computer and Communication Engineering, Northeastern University at Qinhuangdao, Qinhuangdao, Hebei 066004, China

Phyo Thandar Thant
Graduate School of Information Science and Technology, HokkaidoUniversity, Sapporo, Japan

Courtney Powell, Martin Schlueter, and Masaharu Munetomo
Information Initiative Center, Hokkaido University, Sapporo, Japan

Aibo Song, Yingying Xue and Junzhou Luo
School of Computer Science and Engineering, Southeast University, Nanjing 211189, China

Maoxian Zhao
College of Mathematics and Systems Science, Shandong University of Science and Technology, Qingdao 266590, China

Mohammed A. S. Mosleh and G. Radhamani
School of IT & Science, Dr. GR Damodaran College of Science, Coimbatore, India

Mohamed A. G. Hazber
International School of Software Engineering,Wuhan University,Wuhan, China

Syed Hamid Hasan
Information Systems Department, King Abdulaziz University, Jeddah, Saudi Arabia

Xiong Fu, Qing Zhao, Junchang Wang and Lin Zhang
School of Computer Science and Technology, Nanjing University of Posts and Telecommunications, Nanjing 210023, China

Lei Qiao
Beijing Institute of Control Engineering, Beijing 100190, China

Wei Zheng, ChenWang and Dongzhan Zhang
Department of Computer Science, School of Information Science and Engineering, Xiamen University, Xiamen 361005, China

Hua He and Zenghua Zhao
School of Computer Science and Technology, Tianjin University, Tianjin 300072, China

Shanchen Pang
College of Computer and Communication Engineering, China University of Petroleum, Qingdao 266580, China

Index

Printed in the USA
CPSIA information can be obtained
at www.ICGtesting.com
JSHW051432221024
72173JS00006B/1449